THE SECOND WORLD WAR

A WORLD IN FLAMES

THE SECOND WORLD WAR

A WORLD IN FLAMES

Foreword by **Sir Max Hastings**

First published in Great Britain in 2004 by Osprey Publishing,
Elms Court, Chapel Way, Botley, Oxford OX2 9LP, UK
Email: info@ospreypublishing.com

Previously published as Essential Histories 18: *The Second World
War (1) The Pacific*, Essential Histories 35: *The Second World War
(2) Europe 1939–1943*, Essential Histories 30: *The Second World
War (3) The war at sea*, Essential Histories 48: *The Second World
War (4) The Mediterranean 1940–1945*, Essential Histories 24:
The Second World War (5) The Eastern Front 1941–1945, Essential
Histories 32: *The Second World War (6) Northwest Europe
1944–1945*

ISBN 1 84176 830 8

Editor: Alexander Stilwell
Design: Ken Vail Graphic Design, Cambridge, UK
Cartography by The Map Studio
Index by Alan Thatcher
Picture research by Image Select International
Origination by Grasmere Digital Imaging, Leeds, UK
Printed and bound in China by L. Rex Printing Company Ltd.

04 05 06 07 08   10 9 8 7 6 5 4 3 2 1

For a complete list of titles available from Osprey Publishing
please contact:

Osprey Direct UK, PO Box 140,
Wellingborough, Northants, NN8 2FA, UK.
Email: info@ospreydirect.co.uk

Osprey Direct USA, c/o MBI Publishing,
PO Box 1, 729 Prospect Ave,
Osceola, WI 54020, USA.
Email: info@ospreydirectusa.com

www.ospreypublishing.com

Contents

Part IV: The Pacific

Part V: The Eastern Front 1941–1945

Part VI: Northwest Europe 1944–1945

Foreword
by Sir Max Hastings

The Second World War was the greatest conflict in human history, and today must rank as its most exhaustively studied event. Hundreds of millions of individuals who lived through the period, whether in Nanking or Nuremburg, Leningrad or Luzon, endured a length and depth of suffering mercifully unknown to our generation, even among peoples who live in troubled regions of the world. Thus, personal memoirs of the war retain an enduring fascination, whether they tell the stories of soldiers or Holocaust survivors, maquisards or Chindits, bomber pilots or housewives.

Beyond personal memoirs, of course, there are vast collective issues. Some of the finest minds of the past half century have explored the phenomenon of Nazi Germany. None has yet produced a wholly satisfactory explanation of how a civilized, educated people could place itself in thrall to a coterie of uncultured gangsters, and under its tutelage embark upon institutionlised murder on a vast scale.

Too much modern research, especially in the United States, focuses upon the Holocaust in isolation. The Nazis singled out Jewish people for extinction, but they also carried out mass killings among all manner of other peoples, notably in Eastern Europe. Modern German research, for instance, highlights the fact that operational planning for the 1941 invasion of the Soviet Union, in which the German General Staff was fully complicit, scheduled millions of Ukrainians and Russians for starvation before the first shot of the campaign was fired. Their deaths were indispensable, to allow the grain and raw materials which supported them to be shipped to Germany.

Insofar as any struggle in history has been waged between good and evil, the Western Allies could claim the right to represent virtue, in their campaign to liberate Europe. However, the issue is hugely complicated by the participation of the Soviet Union in the Grand Alliance. In 1941, Stalin's regime had been responsible for the deaths of many more innocents than the Nazis. This fact caused moral confusion to thoughtful British and American people at the time, and continues to do so today.

Militarily, the struggle between the armies of Germany and the Soviet Union dominated the war. Some 29 million Soviet citizens died between 1941 and 1945. The Red Army was responsible for about 80 per cent of all casualties inflicted upon the German nation. By contrast, the peoples of the United States, Britain and France lost less than a million dead in Europe. Though the Allied bomber offensive against Germany played a significant part in weakening Hitler's empire, and killed some 600,000 Germans, mostly civilians, Allied land forces fought in north-west Europe only for the last 11 months of the war. Their campaign never absorbed much more than one-third of the number of German troops committed on the Eastern Front. The dominant Soviet role in destroying the Nazis gravely handicapped the Anglo-Americans in resisting Stalinist imperialism in eastern Europe in 1945. Soviet participation among the judges at the postwar Nuremburg trials was ironic. While it did not in the least diminish the guilt of the Germans indicted, all those concerned knew that a host of Stalin's minions could readily have been convicted on the same charges.

By far the bloodiest theatre in Asia's war was China. A large part of the Japanese Army was committed there until August 1945. Battlefield collisions between Chinese and Japanese forces were spasmodic and militarily unsophisticated. America's insistence that Chinese leader Chiang Kai-shek should be treated as a partner in the councils of the Grand Alliance was a political gesture, unsupported by any substantial Chinese military contribution to Allied victory. However, the Japanese occupiers killed untold millions of Chinese civilians by murder and starvation.

America's campaign against Japan was overwhelmingly naval, and dominated by air power. For more than three years, the United States conducted a painful struggle to translate its armed might westwards across the huge expanses of the Pacific, through a series of amphibious landings on remote islands, and fleet actions against the Japanese navy of a kind unknown in the European theatre. Japan's surrender was finally precipitated by the dropping of two atomic weapons, an American act which inaugurated a frightening new age, and continues to provoke bitter controversy. It is useful to recall that earlier American air attacks on Japanese cities had killed far more people with conventional incendiary weapons than the nuclear devices unleashed upon Hiroshima and Nagasaki.

Some historians have argued that the outcome of the Second World War was inevitable, given the vastly superior economic power of the Grand Alliance, measured against that of the Axis. Yet this begs the question. Only Britain and France entered the war in 1939, to honour guarantees to Poland. For some years during and after the conflict, the British flattered themselves that they had somehow defeated Hitler in 1940. It is undoubtedly true that the Battle of Britain averted a cross-Channel invasion, which Hitler would have undertaken, had he perceived the opportunity for a quick, easy victory. This the Royal Air Force denied him.

But thereafter, Germany's legions moved eastwards not because the British had vanquished them, or could ever have hoped to do so, but because Hitler's principal ambitions were always directed towards the Soviet Union, the key to his grand design for the Nazi empire. If Hitler had not chosen to invade Russia, it is perfectly possible that he could have invaded and defeated Britain in 1941.

John Keegan has justly remarked that Winston Churchill, by recognising that death was preferable to compromise with the absolute evil of Nazism, 'set the moral agenda of the Second World War'. Yet for all his magnificent defiance in 1940, Churchill always knew privately that Britain possessed no rational hope of beating Germany unless the United States entered the war. It is most unlikely that this would have happened, but for the crowning mercy of Pearl Harbor in December 1941. If Hitler had first disposed of Britain, while striving to avoid a showdown with the United States, he might later have achieved a successful conquest of the Soviet Union, and won the war.

As it was, mercifully, Hitler's ignorance of the economic might of the Soviet Union, together with his contempt for the United States, caused him to commit one act of madness after another, and to precipitate his own eventual downfall. It is striking that most of the Germans who eventually turned against their own leader did so not as a matter of principle, because they perceived his actions as evil, but because – like his early favourite Field Marshal Erwin Rommel – they became dismayed to realise that he was leading them to defeat.

No single historian, however talented, can hope to master in a lifetime the political, military and human complexities of a world war. Most of us become, in varying degrees, specialists in certain aspects of the conflict, at the expense of others. This is why the most convincing global histories of the period distil the labours of a range of authors. However, in studying any one theatre or experience, it is essential to recognise the wider context in which events unfolded.

Participants at the time understandably focused on what happened to them. To an American infantryman in the Bulge, amid the snowbound terrors of the German offensive in December 1944, it would have seemed grotesque to observe that most of Hitler's Wehrmacht was still deployed against the Red Army, and that the panzer assault represented Nazi Germany's last gasp. The GI in his foxhole could only see the Tiger tank threatening his own survival.

Likewise, what could it have availed a British prisoner dying in pitiless Japanese captivity on the Burma railway in 1945 to know that, once Germany was beaten, his own salvation must come, because Japan's collapse would become inevitable? Each man and woman who lived through the Second World War could comprehend only his or her own experiences, fears and frail hopes.

However, to us, 60 years later, a privileged window is opened: with the aid of all the research and wisdom that have accumulated across the globe since 1945, we can explore this vast human tragedy as an entity. We can attempt, however inadequately, to assess a place for what happened in North Africa or Sumatra, in Madagascar or the Crimea, in a grand tapestry of history.

An American academic acquaintance remarked to me two years ago that seven out of ten titles in the *New York Times* non-fiction bestseller list that week related to events between 1939 and 1945. Will the world's fascination with the period ever diminish? We should hope not. First, there are inexhaustible lessons to be learned from it – military, political and moral. Second, we should pray fervently that no future event in the history of the world will supplant the Second World War as the supreme catastrophe to befall mankind in his experience thus far.

Introduction

At 11.00 am on 11 November 1918, the First World War came to an end. The combined forces of Great Britain, France, Italy, and the USA had defeated the armies of Germany, Austria-Hungary, and Turkey. This war cost the lives of around 7 million combatants and a further 7 million civilians, although exact totals are difficult to ascertain. During the four years between 1914 and 1918, the 'Great War,' as it was being referred to even during the fighting, redefined the parameters of the experience of war.

The First World War was the first true 'industrial' war, where the nineteenth-century advances in technology and modes of production were harnessed to an insatiable war machine – with terrifying results. The impact of new and more efficient killing methods, backed by virtually the whole social, political, and economic infrastructure of the warring nations, produced a war of destruction unparalleled in human history. The cost of victory was such that in terms of casualty figures alone there was little to choose between winner and loser. At all levels of society – politicians, generals, ordinary soldiers, and the civilian population – there was a belief and a hope that this was the 'war to end all wars' and that in this fashion the tremendous sacrifice would not have been in vain.

Of course, tragically, the Great War did not prove to be the end of war. Instead, in many ways the Great War typified the future of war and not its past. The manner in which the war was fought, with an emphasis on the full utilization of all available resources and the involvement of the whole populace, pointed the way forward and offered a glimpse of how wars might be fought in years to come.

To those who witnessed the Armistice in 1918, the possibility of another major European conflict within their lifetime must have seemed an unimaginable horror, yet that was precisely what was to happen. Despite the shock of the Great War, of the endless lists of dead and wounded published daily in newspapers across Britain, Germany, and France, despite the widespread revulsion at war itself that the Great War engendered, Europe had barely 20 years of peace to enjoy. In 1939 Europe was plunged again into a major conflagration, and this time the cost, incredibly, would be even higher than 1914–18 in lives, in property, and, significantly, in morality.

As with the First World War, the Second World War began in Europe as a result of the actions of an aggressive Germany. Where the Second World War differed markedly from its predecessor, however, was in why the war was fought. The Second World War was not fought for material aggrandizement or for power-political advantage, although these factors had a considerable bearing on the course of the war. Fundamentally, the Second World War was fought because of political ideas – ideologies.

Political extremism in post-First World War Germany brought to power Adolf Hitler, a man convinced of his own infallibility and almost divine calling to lead Germany to victory in a race war that would establish the Germans in their rightful position of preeminence in a new global order. Hitler intended to lead the German people in a war of conquest in which the inherent superiority of the German race would be demonstrated and Germany's racial and ideological competitors would be destroyed, leaving Germany at the helm of a unified Europe. This ideological dimension underpinned the reasons for the fighting and also exercised an enormous bearing on how the fighting was conducted.

Up to August 1939, Adolf Hitler's Germany had achieved many of her initial, territorial, ambitions through a combination of threat and belligerent diplomacy. In August 1939, Hitler felt sufficiently confident to abandon diplomacy as his principal weapon and instead to use military force to overwhelm Germany's eastern neighbor, Poland. Hitler's invasion of Poland was the event that precipitated the Second World War. Britain and France were committed to Poland's independence and had pledged to come to her aid in the event of a German attack. The British and French governments issued an ultimatum to Germany, demanding her withdrawal. Hitler dismissed this threat, believing that the French and British were unlikely to do anything to stop the German invasion. When Germany failed to respond to the ultimatum, Britain and France were brought into another war and the Second World War was born.

However, unlike the attritional struggle and stalemate of the First World War, the Second World War was fought to quite a different tempo, initially at least. In the first nine months of the Second World War, Germany's military triumphs were nothing less than astonishing. She invaded and conquered Poland in little over a month, aided by an expedient alliance with the Soviet Union, which enthusiastically helped Germany to dismember and divide Poland. During the course of this opening campaign, Britain and France did nothing to come to Poland's aid.

The German invasion of Poland was followed by an attack on Norway and then, when Hitler's forces were fully prepared, on the combined British and French forces in the west. In a brilliant, if fortuitous campaign, the French and their Belgian, Dutch, and British allies (the British in the form of a large army dispatched to the Continent) were defeated in barely six weeks. By June 1940 all continental Europe, from Moscow to Madrid, had succumbed to Germany, was allied to her, or was neutral. Hitler's Germany had achieved in a little over nine months what Imperial Germany, the Germany of Kaiser Wilhelm, had failed to do over the course of four years.

After the fall of France and the loss of much of the British army's heavy equipment

during the fighting and the hasty evacuation from Dunkirk, Britain faced a desperate battle to maintain her freedom against what appeared to be an irresistible tide of German success. During what became known as the 'Battle of Britain,' a struggle in effect for air superiority, Germany suffered her first major setback of the war. Tenacious Royal Air Force (RAF) fighter pilots, mainly British but with many Australians, Americans, Canadians, New Zealanders, Poles, Czechs, and others among them, denied the Germans the freedom of the skies that they needed to launch their projected invasion of the British Isles.

Unable to implement Operation Sea Lion, the code name for the invasion of Britain, Hitler instead began planning for what he considered to be the main prize: the Soviet Union. Before this, however, Hitler's forces also occupied Greece and Yugoslavia and became active in North Africa in support of Italian forces. On 22 June 1941, Hitler's armed forces turned eastwards, attacking the Soviet Union in Operation Barbarossa and widening the war dramatically. On 12 July, Britain and the Soviet Union signed a mutual assistance agreement to fight their common enemy together. On 11 December 1941, following the surprise Japanese attack on the American Pacific fleet at Pearl Harbor, Germany also declared war on the USA, widening the war still further and, in doing so, increasing the odds considerably on conclusive German victory.

The war at sea

The Second World War at sea was a more genuinely global conflict than either the war on land or that in the air. Most of the world's navies were engaged and the conflict raged across every ocean and major sea. The struggles in the Atlantic, Mediterranean, Indian, and Pacific oceans were complemented by lesser-known battles in the Arctic, Baltic, Black, and Red Seas. Although the latter were geographically smaller and more confined, they were of no less interest and significance, for each aided in the overall aim of the combatants: supremacy on the land.

The sheer scale of the conflict can never be underestimated. The war was immense, not only in terms of geography, but also in terms of naval strengths, manpower, and industrial output. Far more than any before, this was a war not just of naval skill and tactics, but of economics and technology. Yet most navies found themselves unprepared for war, and were forced to develop and expand at a frightening rate, some more successfully than others. Some, such as the Royal Canadian Navy and the Soviet Navy, expanded from next to nothing to become huge fighting forces by the end of the conflict, whilst the established navies, particularly the American and British, grew to unprecedented proportions, with millions of personnel in naval uniforms and thousands of vessels to control.

Navies found themselves forced to make unexpected changes to their preconceived strategies. Technology, numbers, and naval platforms all underwent a revolution. The battleship was, for most navies in the 1920s and 1930s, the centerpiece of naval thinking. It was replaced by the submarine and the aircraft carrier at the heart of fleet tactics. The submarines' stealth and the carriers' firepower and range undermined the romance of the floating fortresses. There were still those who held onto the image of the great gray battleships dueling each other to the death, and they were not to be disappointed. But these were the dying moments of past technical glories. The Second World War belonged to a new and different naval age.

Yet navies did have to remember one role from the days before the steel battleship. Initially shunned by most in the interwar period, amphibious operations grew in significance as the war progressed, to the point of even deciding the war in western Europe, the Mediterranean, and the Pacific. Without the huge Allied amphibious capability, millions would have remained enslaved by Axis occupation.

The war was not all about sailors and ships, and soldiers storming the beaches. This was also a war of the civilian, of industry, and

supply. With 70 percent of the world's surface covered in water and all of the warring countries dependent on materials from overseas, it was only natural that the seas would be a vital supply route and thus the war's biggest battleground. Caught up in this were the various merchant navies and their seamen. Civilian mariners now wore two caps. They were legitimate targets as never before for the enemy, but they were also heroes for a country's survival. Thus they struggled and suffered at the hands of mines, torpedoes, gunfire, and bombs, with loss rates higher than most naval forces during the war. Three merchant campaigns in particular proved vital: the Battle of the Atlantic for the Allied convoys; the Mediterranean for the British submarines; and the Pacific for the American submariners. Success in these campaigns enabled victory on land.

The Mediterranean 1940–45

Confrontation in the Mediterranean region between the Western Allies and the Axis powers began seven months before Hitler occupied the Rhineland and ended only after his suicide in a Berlin bunker in May 1945. The repercussions of this epic struggle continued for many years, however, and still maintain the world's attention.

The road to war in Europe took an irrevocable turn when Mussolini invaded Ethiopia in October 1935. For the first time the old world powers and the international authority of the League of Nations succumbed to the aggressive ambition of the dictators and their fascist regimes. Mussolini was determined to redress the sense of national impotence that ensued from the settlement of the First World War, in which many Italians believed that Italy failed to receive the rewards due to a victor, by building a new Roman empire in the Mediterranean and assuming the status of a first-rate power from a position of strength.

Although the sun was setting on her empire, Britain retained a vital interest in the Mediterranean. The Suez Canal, which

Anthony Eden called the "windpipe" of the empire, cut about 5,600 km (3,500 miles) or almost one-third off the passage to the East. Through this vital artery flowed her commerce, her administrators and her military and, with a growing dependence on Middle-Eastern oil, the waterway gained a new significance. With naval bases at the colonial outposts of Gibraltar, Malta and Alexandria, Britain dominated the Mediterranean region, the strategic importance of which was immeasurable.

Tension in the region remained high as both sides used the Spanish Civil War as an effective dress rehearsal to prepare their armed forces. Moreover, this prelude also encouraged the natural coalescence of the Italian and German regimes into a fascist bloc, although each retained their own ambitions. Together France and Britain dominated the Mediterranean region and when war erupted in September 1939 Italy was in such a poor state of military preparation, despite 20 years of boasts to the contrary by Mussolini, that it was forced to remain neutral. The fall of France and the imminent collapse of Britain, however, presented an opportunity that Mussolini believed would enable him to reap the glory and spoils of victory without the need to fight, and war came to the Mediterranean in June 1940.

But the apparent lull was deceptive as the British used the time to strengthen their forces in the region and immediately took steps to show emphatically that not only was Britain not defeated but also she and the Commonwealth were determined to take the fight to the Axis. Unable to confront Germany directly on land, the Mediterranean was the only theater in which British armies could engage any of the Axis forces. Moreover, they had the advantage of fighting the weaker of the Axis Allies, Italy, whose forces were equipped with obsolescent equipment, and against the soft underbelly of Europe there were more strategic opportunities to take the war to continental Europe.

Although the Mediterranean campaign began much as a colonial war, its strategic dimensions rapidly expanded. Germany became embroiled to protect the southern flank of the invasion of Russia and to support its ailing ally. But while an African adventure was not foremost in Hitler's strategic aims the Axis commanders in the Mediterranean recognized that if they were successful in Egypt, ultimately Germany could win the war.

The Mediterranean theater stretched from the Atlantic coast of Africa to Persia, today known as Iran, and the border with India, and from the Alps to Equatorial Africa. For the first three years, fighting predominantly took place along a stretch of land between the Mediterranean Sea and the Sahara desert in Egypt and Libya, involving the legendary *Deutsches Afrika Korps*, commanded by General Rommel, and the British Eighth Army. The hot, dry and dusty conditions were completely unlike anything experienced in Europe and the vast, open spaces enabled a series of highly fluid armored battles that were more akin to naval operations.

The campaign was also peculiar because logistics were especially significant, since there were no local resources and every item the troops and their vehicles required had to be shipped from a base depot: Tripoli for the Axis and the Nile delta for the British. As one side advanced its own supply line became progressively overextended and less able to maintain the army, while the enemy retreated on its own base and supply became easier. Furthermore, marshes near El Agheila in the west and the Qattara depression near El Alamein in the east formed bottlenecks that were easily defended and could not be outflanked. An advancing army became weakest, therefore, just as the retreating army became strongest, which resulted in a series of advances and retreats back and forth across the same stretch of desert that became known as "the Benghazi Handicap." The inhospitable conditions and the almost complete absence of civilians, German SS and secret police lead to a conflict that, while savage, was still fought with honor and chivalry, rare characteristics in a war that was noted more for its brutality and inhumanity.

The war at sea centered on the small British island of Malta. Situated just 96 km (60 miles) from Sicily and amid the Axis shipping lanes to Africa it commanded a vital strategic position. The Italian Navy and the Royal Navy avoided a major fleet encounter but fought an intensive and costly "battle of the convoys," as the Italians struggled to maintain Axis troops in Africa and the British desperately kept Malta supplied, despite the most severe air assault of the war.

When America entered the war President Roosevelt resolved that US forces would be committed to the Mediterranean while preparations were made for the invasion of northern Europe. The British–US alliance was forged in the Mediterranean theater as great armadas were amassed for invasions of north Africa, Sicily and Italy. Although troops were withdrawn for the D-Day invasion of France, a dogged war of attrition continued in Italy until the end of the war.

The number of troops who fought in the Mediterranean was minuscule compared to the eastern front, but for the Western Allies it was the principal arena for active operations. It was also a war of innovation and the application of new military capabilities, including aircraft-carriers, large-scale airborne operations and midget submarines. The Allies also developed experience in coordinating air, ground and naval forces and in amphibious assaults that would prove invaluable later in the war in northern Europe and the Pacific.

The military conclusion to the war did not bring peace to the region, however. Partisan and irregular nationalist forces had been active during the war and a communist uprising occurred in the political vacuum that followed the German evacuation from Greece and Yugoslavia, while independence movements in Palestine, Algeria and Egypt fought against the British and French colonial control. The Mediterranean war completely reshaped the region and created political problems in the Balkans and the Middle East that remain unresolved even today.

The Pacific

The Pacific War, the most significant event in the modern history of the Asia-Pacific region, was both a part of the Second World War and a distinct entity within it. Of the Axis powers – Japan, Germany and Italy – Japan played the overwhelmingly major role in the Pacific: Germany and Italy were barely involved. By contrast, all the principal Allies – the United States, Britain, China, Australia, and the Netherlands – were deeply engaged, and the Soviet Union joined the war near its end. At the highest level, the Allies saw the Second World War as one conflict, in which the Pacific was just one theater. But although the Allied strategic planners had to juggle resources between theaters, the story of the Pacific War can be told separately, with the war against Germany appearing only as noises off-stage.

The Pacific War began on 7 and 8 December 1941 when Japan attacked Pearl Harbor, Malaya, and the Philippines, thereby initiating a war against the USA and Britain. Japan claimed that after the USA applied crippling economic sanctions in July 1941 it had no alternative. But the war owes its origins to Japanese expansionism and militarism over a period of half a century before 1941. Japan had been at war with China since 1937, when it invaded central China, and earlier, in 1931 and 1932, Japan had seized the Chinese territory of Manchuria. While one can argue about when the war began, however, there can be no doubt about its conclusion. It ended in August 1945 when US aircraft dropped atomic bombs on Hiroshima and Nagasaki, and Japan formally surrendered in Tokyo Bay on 2 September 1945.

The war was fought over a large part of the earth's surface. Land operations stretched from the fog-bound Aleutian Islands in the northern Pacific Ocean to the steaming tropical jungles of the Solomon Islands in the South Pacific. To the east, Japanese forces seized lonely Wake Island in the mid-Pacific; to the west, they fought in the jungle hills bordering India and Burma. Naval operations were more widespread, reaching east to Hawaii, south to Sydney Harbour and west to Madagascar, off the African coast.

It was a war of daring strategic maneuvers, generally in a maritime environment. These included Japan's astonishing advances during the first six months, the key struggles around the perimeter of the so-called Greater East Asia Co-prosperity Sphere and the Allied counteroffensives. It was a war of great naval battles, such as those in the Coral Sea, at Midway, at Leyte, and in the Philippine Sea. It was also a war of grim jungle battles, such as in Guadalcanal, New Guinea, and Burma. There were bold and bloody amphibious landings, large-scale land operations (in Burma and the Philippines), savage guerrilla wars, clandestine operations, fearsome bombing attacks, and a bitter submarine campaign.

The Pacific War saw the application of new military capabilities and technologies, such as aircraft carriers, ship-borne air power, submarines, amphibious warfare, and signals intelligence. Finally, atomic bombs were used for the first time. The war was fought by some famous military commanders – Generals Douglas MacArthur, William Slim, and Yamashita Tomoyuki, and Admirals Chester Nimitz, William Halsey, and Yamamoto Isoruku.

It was an unusual war in that, although Japan initiated it, it never had a chance of winning. The Japanese strategy was to seize south-east Asia and hope that the Allies would grow weary and allow them to keep at least some of their gains. After the 'infamy' of Pearl Harbor, however, the USA was never going to rest until Japan was crushed, and inevitably Japan was overpowered by American industrial might.

Although Japan was crushed, it did achieve some of its aims. Its successes splintered the invincibility of European colonial power, leading eventually to independence for the former European and American colonies: Indo-China, Burma, Malaya, Indonesia, and the Philippines. It also contributed to independence for India. Japan had hoped to find easy pickings in a weak and divided China; instead, China became unified under communist rule, except for the Nationalist bastion in the former Japanese colony of Taiwan. Japan lost its other colony in Korea, which became two separate but warring nations. And remarkably, Japan rose from the ashes to become an economic powerhouse.

Japan waged a pitiless war, including the massacre at Nanking, the brutal treatment and enslavement of prisoners of war, and the enforced recruitment of euphemistically called 'comfort women'. This left a legacy of bitterness across the whole region, but especially in China and Korea. For those whose lives were wrecked by the war, it was little consolation to learn that Japan also treated its own civilians and servicemen cruelly. As usual, the burden of war fell heaviest on the ordinary people, with millions of deaths in Japan, China, India, and south-east Asia.

The Pacific War therefore completely reshaped political entities in Asia and changed national attitudes. Although more than half a century has passed since the end of the war, an understanding of it is still crucial if one is to appreciate the problems faced by the dynamic area now known as the Asia-Pacific.

The Eastern Front 1941–1945

After the Bolsheviks seized power in Russia in November 1917, Lenin expected revolutions to sweep Europe. Several occurred, but all were suppressed, and to retain power the Bolsheviks had to win a long and savage civil war, during which foreign powers intervened, Ukraine tried to gain independence, and Finland, Estonia, Latvia, Lithuania, and Georgia succeeded in doing so. Poland, previously partitioned between Germany, Austria-Hungary, and Russia, also became independent, in the process seizing territory in Belorussia and Ukraine. Russia's Far East provinces did not rejoin Russia until 1922, and Russian invasion ended Georgia's independence in that year. The Soviet Union, established on 1 January 1923, was internationally isolated as the world's only 'socialist' state apart from its Outer Mongolian puppet. Most governments saw it as a pariah: conservatives because it constantly invited their subjects to revolt, socialists because its one-party dictatorship was alien to western Europe's and Scandinavia's democratic socialist traditions.

Russia therefore had to coexist with a hostile world, concluding peace treaties with its independent former provinces in 1920, and a trade agreement with Britain in 1921, then startling the world by signing in 1922 the Rapallo Treaty with Europe's other pariah, Germany. That treaty clandestinely helped Germany's rebirth as a military power. The Versailles Treaty of 1919 had limited its armed forces to 100,000, and banned conscription, military aircraft, tanks, and submarines. The Reichswehr's head, General von Seekt, saw cultivating relations with the nascent Red Army as a way to circumvent the restrictions.

The Rapallo Treaty gave Russia diplomatic recognition by Germany and the prospect of aid in restoring its ravaged economy, while Germany gained a food and raw materials supplier, and reduced dependence on its victorious enemies' goodwill. A secret agreement between the Reichswehr and the Red Army gave Germany facilities on Russian territory for testing, and training personnel to operate, weapons banned by Versailles, particularly tanks and aircraft. In return, Russia received substantial annual payments and access to information on designing, testing and using weapons. Three secret centers were established: a flying school at Lipetsk, a tank school at Kazan, and a chemical warfare establishment near Volsk. To preserve secrecy, Germans attended only in small numbers, were temporarily recorded as having left the Reichswehr, traveled on false passports, did not wear uniform, and were forbidden after return to say where they had been or for what purpose. Russian officers were sent to Germany, where they undertook courses, attended maneuvers and war games, and were shown much of Germany's military industry, and they observed similar restrictions.

The schools were small. Lipetsk graduated only 120–130 pilots during its existence. But they worked intensively on tactics for interceptors, ground attack aircraft, and day bombers, and several of them became Second World War 'aces'. The tank school accepted only 12 pupils per course, but they studied and tested the theories of armored mobile warfare advanced by Liddell Hart, Fuller, and Martel in Britain, and de Gaulle in France. German officers who went to Russia included future field marshals Brauchitsch, Keitel, Manstein, and Model, and several future generals, including the arch-proponent of mobile warfare, Heinz Guderian. The chemical warfare school conducted research into poison gases, anti-gas equipment, and antidotes.

Stalin abruptly ended this cooperation after Hitler came to power in 1933. Both armies by then had learnt much about each other, but the Germans benefited more, because in 1937–38 Stalin savagely purged the senior military. Most of those who had been to Germany were accused of spying for Stalin's exiled rival, Trotsky, or for Germany, Poland, and/or Japan, or plotting to lose a war and restore capitalism, and nearly all were shot. Their knowledge of the German army died with them, to be painfully relearned on Second World War battlefields. Only in 1956, three years after Stalin's death, were the charges denounced as false; he had been protecting not the country but his own power, and that of his incompetent Defense Minister, Kliment Voroshilov.

Northwest Europe 1944–1945

The Northwest Europe campaign was the decisive military operation conducted by the Western Allies in the European theater during the Second World War.

The Northwest Europe campaign witnessed the return to western Europe of American, British, and Commonwealth forces, as well as contingents drawn from the European countries occupied by Nazi Germany. In the D-Day landings on 6 June 1944, the Western Allies fought their way ashore in the face of strong enemy resistance and established a bridgehead in Normandy. Allied forces repulsed all German efforts to overrun the bridgehead, then assumed the offensive and captured the port of Cherbourg, crucial for the long-term viability of the lodgment, by the end of June. Thereafter, in a series of bitter battles, the Allies first captured the key cities of Caen and St Lô.

In late July, after many weeks of grim attritional warfare, the Americans finally broke out of the Normandy bridgehead. Aided by supporting landings on the French Mediterranean coast in mid-August, the Allies swept through France, pushed into Belgium and in early September captured the key port of Antwerp. But during 8–12 September the German defense regained coherence in northern Belgium and in front of Germany's western frontier. It took hard, brutal attritional battles to advance to the German West Wall defenses amid autumn mud and rain. While the Allies achieved several local penetrations of the West Wall, nowhere were they able to punch through the full depth of the German fortifications and achieve operational success.

During mid-December a major German counteroffensive in the Ardennes drove the Americans back in the thinly held Schnee Eifel, but fell far short of its overambitious goal of recapturing Antwerp and thus splitting the Allied front. The Germans followed up this partial success with an even less successful offensive in Alsace; and both offensives simply dissipated Germany's meager reserves of troops, weaponry, and supplies. Hard-fought Allied attacks finally broke through the West Wall during the late winter and drove the Germans back to the Rhine on a broad front.

With the arrival of spring, the Allies launched their final offensives that shattered the German defenses along the River Rhine, and advanced through western Germany into central Germany to meet advancing Soviet forces on the Elbe at Torgau on 25 April 1945. By this stage German resistance had disintegrated, and Western Allied forces swept through southwestern Germany and into Austria, while also advancing to the Elbe River on a broad front. Hitler committed suicide in Berlin on 30 April and Germany capitulated unconditionally on 8 May 1945, bringing to a close the Second World War in Europe.

Undoubtedly, without the Northwest Europe campaign the Second World War in Europe would have gone on much longer and thus the misery suffered by those languishing under harsh German occupation would have been the greater. Moreover, the postwar 'Iron Curtain' dividing capitalist and Communist blocs would have been moved much further west. For, in the long run, the Soviet Union – which bore the brunt of the fighting in the European theater – would have ground Germany into defeat. The Allied invasion of France, therefore, certainly speeded the demise of Hitler's Reich, which thus endured for only 12 – rather than 1,000 – years. Despite the Anglo-American command disputes that accompanied the campaign, this multinational effort also helped to reinforce the idea of a 'special relationship' between the USA and Great Britain, that, some would say, continues to this day.

Chronology

1931–32 Japan establishes puppet state of Manchukuo

1933 **25 March** Japan leaves League of Nations

1934 **19 December** Japan refuses to be bound by Washington Naval Treaties

1935 **April** United States Neutrality Act
18 June Anglo-German Naval Pact
3 October Italy invades Ethiopia

1936 **15 January** Japan leaves London Naval Conference
25 March Great Britain, United States and France sign London Naval Treaty
25 October Rome-Berlin Axis signed
5 November Japan signs Anti-Comintern Pact with Germany

1937 **7 July** Beginning of general attack by Japanese forces on China (China Incident)
13 August Fighting begins between Japanese and Chinese troops at Shanghai

1938 **12 March** German army marches into Austria
13 March Austria is incorporated into the greater German Reich
28 March Adolf Hitler encourages the German minority in Czechoslovakia to agitate for the break-up of the state
11 August Czechs open negotiations with the Germans after Britain and France apply pressure on them to do so

12 August Germans begin to mobilize
4 September Sudeten Germans reject offers of autonomy for the Sudetenland
7 September The French begin to mobilize
12 September Hitler demands that the Czechs concede to German claims on the Sudetenland
15 September British Prime Minister Chamberlain visits Hitler at his mountain retreat at Berchtesgaden, where Hitler affirms his determination to annex the Sudetenland completely
18 September Britain and France agree to try to persuade the Czechs to concede territory in which there are more than 50 per cent Germans
22 September Chamberlain meets Hitler at Godesberg, where Hitler demands the immediate German occupation of the Sudetenland
29 September After negotiations, Chamberlain, Mussolini, Daladier and Hitler agree to transfer the Sudetenland to Germany while guaranteeing Czechoslovakia's existing borders
30 September Hitler and Chamberlain sign the 'peace in our time' document
1 October Germans begin their occupation of the Sudetenland
5 October Czech premier, Benes, resigns

1939 **15 March** German troops occupy Prague
28 March Hitler denounces the 1934 non-aggression pact with Poland

16 April Soviet Union proposes a defensive alliance with France and Britain, but this offer is rejected

27 April Britain introduces conscription; Hitler abnegates the 1935 Anglo-German naval treaty

22 May Hitler and Mussolini sign the 'Pact of Steel'

2 July Japanese forces in Manchukuo cross into Outer Mongolia (Nomonhan Incident)

11 August Belated Anglo-French overtures to Soviet Union

23 August Soviet Union and Germany unveil a non-aggression treaty, the Molotov-Ribbentrop Pact, which contains a secret clause concerning the dismemberment of Poland

25 August Britain and Poland sign a mutual assistance pact

28 August Poles reject negotiations with Germans

31 August Royal Navy mobilizes for war

1 September Germans invade Poland

2 September Britain and France issue Germany with ultimatums over Poland

3 September Britain and France declare war on Germany

4 September RAF commences anti-German shipping strikes

16 September ceasefire with Soviet forces in Manchukuo

17 September Soviet Union invades eastern Poland

30 September Soviet Union and Germany partition Poland; BEF arrives in France

14 October HMS *Royal Oak* sunk by U-47 whilst at anchor in Scapa Flow

13 December Battle of the River Plate

17 December *Graf Spee* scuttles herself outside Montevideo harbour

1940 **February** Great Britain breaks German Enigma Code

9 April Germany invades Denmark and Norway

14 April British forces land in Norway

2 May British forces evacuated from Norway

10 May Chamberlain resigns; Churchill takes over as Prime Minister; Germany invades France and the Low Countries

26 May–4 June Operation Dynamo: withdrawal of Allied troops from Dunkirk

28 May Belgium surrenders

4–9 June Allies evacuate Norway

10 June Italy declares war on Britain and France and attacks Malta

22 June France signs Armistice with Germany

June–September Battle of Britain

3–5 July British naval Force H neutralizes French naval force at Mers-el-Kebir

17 July Burma Road closed for three months

24 July Japanese troops land in southern Indo-China

2 August Operation Hurry: first Royal Navy 'ferry flight' of aircraft to Malta

3 September British—United States lend-lease agreement for 50 US 'Four Stacker' destroyers in return for use of British bases

23–26 September French fleet in Dakar attacked by Royal Navy and Free French forces

27 September Tripartite Pact between Germany, Italy and Japan

28 October Italy invades Greece

11–12 November 21 Swordfish aircraft from HMS *Illustrious* disable half the Italian fleet at Taranto

7 December Operation Compass: Western Desert Force launch a five-day raid

1941 **19 January** British capture Kassala in Sudan and invade Eritrea

6 February Battle of Beda Fomm: Western Desert Force captures Benghazi

12 February Rommel and *Deutsches Afrika Korps* arrive in Tripoli

28 March Naval battle of Cape Matapan

2 April Rommel attacks Cyrenaica

6 April Operation Marita: German invasion of Greece and Yugoslavia

13 April *Deutsches Afrika Korps* besieges Tobruk

1 May British evacuation of Greece completed

5 May Emperor Haile Selassie returns to Addis Ababa

15 May Operation Brevity: Western Desert Force attacks Sollum and Fort Capuzzo

19 May Duke of Aosta signs Italian surrender: end of Abyssinian campaign

May Operation Merkur: German airborne invasion of Crete

6 June Operation Explorer: British invasion of Syria

15 June Operation Battleaxe: Western Desert Force attempt to relieve Tobruk

22 June Operation Barbarossa, the German invasion of the Soviet Union, begins; Italy and Romania declare war on Soviet Union

24 June Germans take Vilnius, capital of Lithuania

26-27 June Finland and Hungary declare war on the Soviet Union

1 July Riga, capital of Latvia, is taken

26 July American government freezes Japanese assets in the USA; General MacArthur appointed to command US army in Far East

27 July Japanese troops start occupying French Indo-China

13 August Siege of Odessa begins

28 August Tallinn, capital of Estonia, is taken

10 September Smolensk battle ends with Soviet retreat; Zhukov takes command at Leningrad

19 September Germans take Kiev; siege of Leningrad begins; Germans launch Moscow offensive, Operation Typhoon

22 September Japan granted bases in Indo-China

27 September Tripartite Pact between Germany, Italy and Japan

17 October General Tojo becomes Prime Minister of Japan

18 October Germans enter Crimea

25 October Germans take Kharkov; Soviets retreat to Sevastopol

30 October Siege of Sevastopol (until 4 July 1942) begins

15 November German Moscow offensive resumes

17 November Soviet counteroffensive in south begins

18 November Operation Crusader: Eighth Army offensive to clear Axis forces from Africa

20 November Germans take Rostov-on-Don

23 November Germans reach a point less than 19 miles (31km) from Moscow

29 November Soviets retake Rostov-on-Don

5 December Soviet Moscow offensive begins; continues till 20 April

7–8 December Japanese attack Malaya, Pearl Harbor, and the Philippines

8 December Siege of Tobruk raised

10 December *Prince of Wales* and *Repulse* sunk; main Japanese landing in the Philippines

13 December Naval encounter off Cape Bon

14 December Japanese start invasion of Burma

17 December First battle of Sirte

17 December Japanese land in British Borneo

19 December Hitler dismisses 19 generals and appoints himself Army Commander-in-Chief

19 December battleships HMS *Queen Elizabeth* and HMS *Valiant* sunk by Italian frogmen at Alexandria

24 December Wake Island captured by Japanese

26 December Surrender of Hong Kong

1942 **7 January** Battle of Moscow ends after advances of 60–150 miles (100–240km)
8 January Soviet general offensive begins; continues until 20 April
21 January Rommel launches counter-offensive
23 January Japanese forces attack Rabaul
30 January Japanese forces attack Ambon
31 January Defending forces in Malaya withdraw to Singapore Island
3 February Germans encircle Soviet 33rd Army at Yukhnov
6 February German IX Army encircles 29th Army near Rzhev
15 February Singapore Island surrenders
19 February Japanese bomb Darwin
19–20 February Japanese forces land on Timor
27 February Naval battle of Java Sea
28 February Japanese forces land in Java
8 March Japanese troops enter Rangoon; Japanese land in New Guinea
17 March MacArthur appointed to command South-West Pacific Area
22 March Second battle of Sirte
5 April Japanese carrier-borne aircraft attack Colombo
7 April American forces on Bataan surrender
16 April George Cross awarded to people of Malta
17 April Soviet 33rd Army destroyed
18 April Doolittle raid on Tokyo
20 April End of Soviet general offensive; Germans pushed back up to 200 miles (320km) from Moscow
5-8 May Battle of the Coral Sea
6 May American forces in Corregidor surrender
12 May Soviet Southwest Front attacks toward Kharkov
26 May Anglo-Soviet treaty on greater cooperation in war against Germany; Operation Venezia: *Panzerarmee Afrika* attacks Gazala line

29 May Battle of Kharkov ends; Soviet losses 230,000
31 May Attack on Sydney Harbour
4–6 June Battle of Midway Island
6 June Japanese land in Aleutian Islands
June *Panzerarmee Afrika* captures Tobruk
1–26 July First battle of El Alamein
8 July Army Group South begins advance along River Don
12 July Stalingrad Front formed
21 July Japanese land at Gona area, Papua
25 July Battle for Caucasus begins
28 July Stalin's Order 227, 'Not One Step Back'
7 August Americans land in Solomons
8-9 August Naval battle of Savo Island
11-13 August Pedestal convoy fortifies Malta; aircraft carrier HMS *Eagle* sunk
14 August Raid on Dieppe fails
23 August German VI Army reaches Volga north of Stalingrad
25-26 August Japanese land at Milne Bay
31 August–7 September Battle of Alam Halfa
12 September Germans reach centre of Stalingrad
17 September Japanese drive over Owen Stanley Range halted at Imita Ridge Guadalcanal
11 November Last German offensive in Stalingrad fails
19 November Southwest and Don Fronts launch Stalingrad counteroffensive's north pincer
20 November Stalingrad Front launches south pincer
23 November Pincers meet at Kalach, encircling 20 German and two Romanian divisions
12 December German Stalingrad relief attempt begins
30 December German Stalingrad relief force repulsed; Middle Don

campaign ends; Italian VIII, Romanian III and Hungarian II Armies defeated; Army Groups Don and A threatened in rear

1943 January Churchill and Roosevelt demand 'unconditional surrender' of Nazi Germany

8 January Germans in Stalingrad reject surrender terms

10 January Reduction of Stalingrad 'pocket' begins

January Organized Japanese resistance in Papua ends

28 January Eighth Army captures Tripoli

30 January South 'pocket' at Stalingrad surrenders; Field Marshal Paulus captured

2 February All remaining forces in Stalingrad surrender

7 February Last Japanese withdraw from Guadalcanal

13 February First Chindit operation into Burma

14–22 February Battle of Kasserine Pass

16 February Manstein launches Kharkov counteroffensive

2–4 March Battle of the Bismarck Sea

15 March Manstein retakes Kharkov; Soviets retreat 60–90 miles (96–145 km)

18 April Death of Admiral Yamamoto

8 May American forces land on Attu in Aleutian Islands

13 May Last Axis troops in Tunisia surrender: end of North African campaign

30 June Americans land on New Georgia

5 July Army Group Center begins 'Citadel'

10 July Operation Husky: Allied invasion of Sicily

12 July Germans lose Prokhorovka

13 July Hitler abandons 'Citadel' and orders several divisions to west; Bryansk, Central and West Fronts begin Operation Kutuzov, joined on the 17th by South and Southwest Fronts, on the 18th by Steppe, and on the 22nd by Volkhov and Leningrad Fronts.

25 July Fascist Grand Council overthrows and arrests Mussolini

1 August Japanese declare Burma independent

17 August Allies capture Messina: last Axis troops in Sicily surrender

18 August Operation Kutuzov ends after advances of up to 95 miles (155km)

3 September Operation Baytown: Eighth Army lands in Italy

4 September Australians land near Lae, New Guinea

9 September Operation Avalanche: Allied invasion of Salerno

11 September Italian fleet surrenders in Malta

16 September Australian divisions enter Lae

21 September Royal Navy midget submarines attack the *Tirpitz* in Norwegian fjord

1 October Fifth Army captures Naples

2 October Western and Kalinin Fronts end offensive after advancing 125–160 miles (200–260km) and beginning reconquest of Belorussia

7 October Mountbatten takes command of South-East Asia Command

12 October Fifth Army launches offensive across the river Volturno

14 October Japanese declare independence of the Philippines

1 November American troops land on Bougainville, northern Solomons

6 November Kiev taken

20 November American forces invade Makin and Tarawa on Gilberts

28 November Teheran Conference of Allied leaders opens; ends on 1 December

15 December Americans land on New Britain

24 December Offensive by 2nd Belorussian and all four Ukrainian Fronts begins

26 December *Scharnhorst* sunk off North Cape by British force led by battleship HMS *Duke of York*

1944

3 January Fifth Army launches offensive against Gustav Line, around Monte Cassino

9 January Allied forces overrun Maungdaw on Arakan front in Burma

22 January Operation Shingle: Fifth Army amphibious landing at Anzio

27 January Siege of Leningrad ended

28 January About 70,000 Germans encircled at Korsun-Shevechenkovsky

31 January Americans invade Marshall Islands

15 February New Zealand forces invade Green Island

29 February Americans invade Admiralty Islands

1 March Leningrad offensive ends; Germans forced back over 130 miles (210km)

2 March Second Chindit operation launched into Burma

15 March Japanese Imphal offensive from Burma begins

28 March 2nd Ukrainian Front crosses River Prut into Romania

3 April Aircraft from HMS *Furious* and *Victorious* and four CVEs attack the *Tirpitz*

22 April Americans land at Hollandia and Aitape

24 April Australians enter Madang

9 May 4th Ukrainian Front takes Sevastopol

18 May Polish troops capture Monastery Hill at Cassino

26 May Americans land on Biak Island

4 June Fifth Army captures Rome

5 June Start of Japanese withdrawal from Kohima

6 June D-Day landings

7 June British capture Bayeux

14 June Germans begin V1 rocket offensive on London

15 June Americans invade Saipan in the Marianas; American strategic air offensive against Japan begins from China

17 June Americans break out across Cotentin peninsula

19–20 June Battle of the Philippine Sea

19–30 June Battle for Cherbourg

23 June Main Soviet 'Bagration' offensive begins

26–27 June Montgomery launches Operation Epsom

28 June–2 July German counteroffensive by II SS Panzer Corps

2 July Americans land on Noemfoor

3 July Minsk liberated, about 100,000 Germans encircled

7 July Controversial Caen raid by Allied heavy bombers

8 July Anglo-Canadian Charnwood offensive begins

13 July 3rd Belorussian Front forces take Vilnius, capital of Lithuania

18 July General Tojo falls from power as Japanese Prime Minister; Anglo-Canadian Goodwood offensive begins

21 July Americans invade Guam

25 July American Cobra offensive

28 July 1st Belorussian Front reaches Vistula and nears Warsaw; British Bluecoat offensive

30 July Japanese begin withdrawal from Myitkyina, Burma

4 August Eighth Army captures Florence

6–8 August German Luttich counteroffensive on Avranches

8 August Canadian Operation Totalize launched

7 August 4th Ukrainian Front enters Czechoslovakia

13 August Eisenhower halts Patton's advance towards Falaise

14 August Canadians initiate Operation Tractable

15 August Operation Dragoon: Allied invasion of southern France

18 August Patton resumes his advance from Alencon towards Falaise

19 August Falaise pocket sealed; II SS Panzer Corps launches relief operation

20–22 August Partial German break-out from the Falaise pocket

21–31 August German strategic withdrawal behind the Seine

24 August Aircraft from HMS *Furious* and *Indefatigable* and two CVEs attack the *Tirpitz*

31 August 2nd Ukrainian Front enters Bucharest

1 September Eisenhower assumes position of Land Forces Commander from Montgomery; German V2 rocket offensive begins early September

4 September Antwerp captured

4–26 September German retreat behind the Scheldt estuary

5–30 September Subjugation of the Channel ports of Le Havre, Boulogne and Calais

13 September Battle for Aachen begins

15 September Americans land in Palau Islands (Peleliu) and on Morotai in the Halmaheras

15 September Soviet troops enter Sofia; Finland declares war on Germany

17–26 September Allied Operation Market Garden

26 September Leningrad Front forces capture Tallinn, occupies all mainland Estonia, reaches Baltic coast, and isolates Army Group North

2–16 October Canadian advance on South Beveland

4 October Operation Manna: British intervention in Greece to prevent communist coup

6 October Canadian Operation Switchback begins

10 October US Third Fleet attacks Okinawa

20 October Americans land on Leyte; Red Army captures Belgrade; Tito's partisans capture Dubrovnik

21 October Fall of Aachen – Siegfried Line penetrated

22 October Karelian Front enters Norway and liberates Kirkenes

23–26 October Naval battle of Leyte Gulf

27 October 3rd Belorussian Front enters East Prussia

29 October Karelian Front halts and hands over to Norwegian Resistance

1–7 November Canadian Operation Infatuate captures Walcheren

4 November Greece liberated

8–22 November Patton's Third US Army captures Metz

9 November 3rd Ukrainian Front seizes bridgehead over Danube

12 November RAF Lancasters armed with 12,000lb 'Tallboy' bombs sink the *Tirpitz*

13–23 November 6th US Army Group captures Strasbourg and advances to Upper Rhine

November Superfortresses attack Japan from bases in the Marianas

4 December Athens placed under martial law

16–22 December German counteroffensive in the Ardennes makes progress

18–26 December Battle for Bastogne rages

23 December Allied counterattacks in Ardennes begin

26 December 2nd and 3rd Ukrainian Fronts encircle Budapest

31 December Soviets enter western suburbs of Budapest

1945 **3 January** Allies occupy Akyab in Burma

9 January American forces land on Luzon

17 January 1st Belorussian Front takes Warsaw

22 January Burma Road reopened

8 February Anglo-Canadian Veritable offensive clears Reichswald Forest

13 February Budapest taken

19 February American forces land on Iwo Jima

23 February American Grenade offensive across the Roer

7 March American forces capture Rhine bridge intact at Remagen

8–10 March German Army Group H withdraws behind the Rhine

9 March Japanese seize control in French Indo-China

9–10 March First fire-bomb attack on Tokyo

10 March American forces land on Mindanao

20 March British capture Mandalay

22 March Americans cross the Rhine at Oppenheim

23 March Montgomery launches Operation Plunder - an assault across the Rhine at Wesel

28 March Second British Army breaks out from the Wesel bridgehead

30 March 3rd Ukrainian Front enters Austria

1 April American forces land on Okinawa; German Army Group B encircled in the Ruhr pocket

2 April 3rd Ukrainian Front on southern approaches to Vienna

6 April Tito's partisans capture Sarajevo

8 April British establish bridgeheads across the River Weser

13 April Vienna taken

14 April Fifth and Eighth Armies attack in Po Valley

16 April 1st and 2nd Belorussian and 1st Ukrainian Fronts open Berlin battle

17 April Resistance in the Ruhr pocket ceases

19 April Allies capture Nuremberg

24 April 1st Belorussian and 1st Ukrainian Fronts meet in Berlin suburbs

30 April Death of Hitler – Donitz becomes new head of state

1 May Australians invade Tarakan

2 May Berlin garrison surrenders; German forces in Italy surrender: formal end to war in Mediterranean

3 May British troops capture Rangoon; 2nd Belorussian Front

meets British, 1st Belorussian Front meets Americans, along Elbe; German forces in Bavaria and western Austria surrender to Americans

4 May American forces cross Brenner Pass and link up in northern Italy

6 May Fifth Army enters Austria from Italy

7 May German High Command representatives sign unconditional surrender at Eisenhower's HQ in Reims; Stalin insists on a signing in Berlin

8 May Surrender ceremony in Berlin (Karlshorst)

9 May Army Group North surrenders in Kurland

11 May Germans in Prague surrender

June Crimean Tatars forcibly deported for alleged collaboration with the Germans

10 June Australians land at Brunei Bay

1 July Australians land at Balikpapan

17 July Potsdam Conference of Allied leaders begins

26 July Potsdam Declaration by USA, Britain and China demands Japan surrender unconditionally; Stalin endorses demand

7 August Atomic bomb dropped on Hiroshima

9 August Atomic bomb dropped on Nagasaki; Soviet troops invade Manchukuo

10 August Japan accepts Potsdam Declaration and offers surrender provided Emperor retained

14 August Emperor Hirohito announces Japanese forces' unconditional surrender

15 August VJ-Day; all offensive action against Japan comes to an end

17 August Sukarno announces Indonesia independence

19 August Yamada unconditionally surrenders Kwantung Army

2 September Japanese sign instrument of surrender in Tokyo Bay

Hitler's accession to power in January 1933 marked a turning point in German
foreign policy, especially relations with other foreign powers. (IWM HU 63418)

Part I
Europe 1939–1943

Europe steers toward war

1. The Maginot Line was a series of fortifications designed as a physical barrier between France and Germany.
2. Hitler remilitarizes the Rhineland, March 1936.
3. Austria annexed by Germany, March 1938.
4. Germany acquires significant portions of Czechoslovakia as a result of the infamous 'Munich' agreement.
5. Germany invades Poland early September 1939.
6. The Soviet Union annexes parts of Eastern Europe as a result of the 1939 Nazi–Soviet Non-Aggression Pact.
7. Germany's brilliant military campaign through the Ardennes forest led to the fall of France in 1940.
8. On 22 June 1941, Hitler launched Operation Barbarossa, the invasion of the Soviet Union.

SWEDEN

ESTONIA

LATVIA

LITHUANIA

DENMARK

SOVIET UNION

Danzig EAST PRUSSIA

BRITAIN

THE NETHERLANDS

London

Berlin

Warsaw

1941

GERMANY

POLAND

BELGIUM

1940

1936

1938

1939

RHINELAND

LUXEMBOURG

Prague

Paris

CZECHOSLOVAKIA

Maginot Line

1938

Vienna

FRANCE

Budapest   ROMANIA

SWITZERLAND

AUSTRIA   HUNGARY

German expansion

0   200 miles

Soviet expansion   ITALY

0   250 km

The gathering storm

There are many considerations that made the outbreak of the Second World War possible. What made the war inevitable was one man: Adolf Hitler. Once Hitler had achieved power in Germany, war was certain to come. The combination of circumstances that allowed a man like Hitler to seize power, maintain it, and then take the opportunities presented to him on the international stage, however, were less inevitable and far more complicated.

Hitler made skillful use of the political and economic turmoil of post-First World War Germany. He also capitalized on the underlying sentiment in the army and among more right-wing elements of German society, that Germany's defeat in the First World War was attributable to a 'stab in the back' by socialists and communists at home, rather than to a conclusive military defeat, which of course is what had actually happened. Hitler was able to focus these feelings more strongly courtesy of the provisions of the Treaty of Versailles, which ended the war. This constant reminder of Germany's national humiliation was a useful tool for Hitler's broader aims.

Hitler's vehicle to power was the Nazi Party, 'Nazi' being an abbreviation of *Nationalsozialistische*. Hitler brought his personal dynamism to this rather directionless party and with it his own ideas. In particular, he brought a 'virulent strain of extreme ethnic nationalism' and the belief that war was the means by which the most racially pure and dynamic people could affirm their position as the rulers of a global empire. Mere revisions of the map were inconsequential in Hitler's larger scheme of things. His ultimate goals lay in the east, where a war of annihilation was to be waged against the Soviet Union.

The Soviet Union was the incarnation of many evils as far as Hitler was concerned. His eventual war in the east was designed to destroy the 'Judeo-Bolshevik' conspiracy that

The signing of the Treaty of Versailles, signed by the Allied and Associated Powers and Germany, on 28 June 1918. (Ann Ronan Picture Library)

he saw emanating from Moscow, and to remove the Slavic population, considered by Nazi ideology as *Untermenschen* or subhumans. The territory obtained would be effectively colonized by people of Germanic stock, enlarging and ensuring the survival of the Third Reich. It was this element that distinguished 'Hitler's war' from previous wars and Hitler's Germany from the Germany of the Kaisers. Germany, however, was no stranger to conflict.

A united Germany

The nation state of Germany is a comparatively new phenomenon. Only in 1871 did a united Germany come into existence. In 1866 the German state of Prussia decisively defeated Austria in the Seven Weeks' War and in doing so assured Prussian dominance of the collection of German-speaking states in central and eastern Europe. Following Prussia's further success against France, in the Franco-Prussian War of 1870, a united Germany was proclaimed on 18 January 1871, in the Hall of Mirrors at the Palace of Versailles, just outside Paris. Prussia was the largest German state and also the most advanced economically and militarily. The Prussian

capital, Berlin, became the capital of this new European power and the Prussian king, at this point Wilhelm I, became the first Emperor or *Kaiser* of a united Germany.

The ambitions of the new state grew considerably with the accession to the throne of Imperial Germany of Kaiser Wilhelm II in 1888. Wilhelm's foreign policy was an aggressive one. He sacked his Chancellor, Bismarck, the man whose political maneuvering had largely created the united Germany, and determined on building Germany up into a world, rather than just a European power. Wilhelm's reckless desire to acquire colonial possessions met with little success in the years prior to 1914, but his determination to build a navy to rival the British one inevitably brought him into conflict with Britain.

Wilhelm, himself a grandson of Queen Victoria, allowed and encouraged a belief that Germany must provide for herself in an increasingly competitive world. In 1914 the opportunity came for Germany to throw herself against France, her nearest continental rival. When Archduke Franz Ferdinand, the heir to the throne of Austria-Hungary, was assassinated, Germany grasped her chance enthusiastically. The rival power

Bismarck in the Hall of Mirrors, Versailles. (AKG Berlin)

blocs, complicated alliance systems, and powder keg diplomatic atmosphere ensured that there was no repetition of the comparatively short wars of the mid- to late nineteenth century. The First World War, the Great War, had begun.

Military defeat and the Weimar Republic

After four years of appalling slaughter, Germany was defeated decisively in 1918. Kaiser Wilhelm abdicated just days before the Armistice was signed and a left-wing government took over the country. This new government was obliged to sign what the Germans, at least, perceived to be an unfair diktat masquerading as a peace settlement. The Treaty of Versailles that formally brought the war to an end was a controversial settlement. The treaty laid the blame for starting the war squarely upon German, saddled her with enormous reparations payments, and also took away large areas of Germany territory, in many cases creating new states.

All of these considerations would have a bearing on the outbreak of the Second World War, although in all probability the failure to implement the treaty adequately was as serious a factor as its provisions. Of particular significance also was the fact that the government that signed the humiliating treaty found itself being blamed for doing so, when in reality it had little choice. The Social Democrats were also blamed for the German capitulation – many right-wingers and particularly the army considered that the German people had not been defeated, but rather had been 'stabbed in the back' by the government. This myth gained widespread credence in Germany during the interwar years.

In the early years after the war, Germany suffered along with most of the continent and political extremism was rife. The new German republic was established in the small town of Weimar, later to become famous for its proximity to the Buchenwald concentration camp. Hence this period of German history, the first ever of genuine German democracy, is known as the Weimar Republic. Weimar was chosen in preference to Berlin as the site of the new government because of Berlin's associations with Prussian militarism. Berlin was also a less than safe place.

The Weimar government was assailed from both sides of the political spectrum. Extremists fought in many large German cities and occasional attempts were made by left and right to overthrow the government; the insurrection led by Wolfgang Kapp (known as the 'Kapp Putsch') was one of the most serious. The constitutional system that underpinned the Weimar government also complicated matters. The system was so representative of political opinion that it produced only minority governments or fragile coalitions that had little opportunity to achieve anything. Meanwhile, international tensions rose when Germany suspended her reparations payments, as a result of which the French, eager to draw every pfennig from the Germans, occupied the Ruhr region in 1923. These international concerns were exacerbated by soaring inflation, with the German mark being traded at 10,000 million to the pound.

Hitler's rise to power

Amidst all this social, economic, and political turbulence, one radical among many was making a name for himself. Adolf Hitler, an Austrian by birth, had served in the German army throughout the First World War. In 1923 Hitler, who had become leader of the fledgling Nazi Party (then the German Workers' Party, *Deutsche Arbeiter Partei*) by virtue of his personal dynamism and skills of oratory, organized his first clumsy attempt to seize power. However, the Munich Putsch, on 9 November 1923, was a failure and earned him five years in Landsberg prison.

Despite the sentence, Hitler served only nine months in rather plush conditions. The authorities, many of whom had some

The freikorps (above) were dissolved in 1921 and many members later went on to join Hitler's SA. (US National Archives)

sympathy for Hitler's position, were persuaded to release him early, after Hitler temporarily resigned the leadership of the Nazi Party and agreed to refrain from addressing public meetings on political issues. However, Hitler neatly circumvented these restrictions by moving his meetings into the private homes of his wealthier supporters.

While Hitler was in jail, dictating his memoirs and thoughts, later to be published as *Mein Kampf*, the situation in Germany improved considerably. A new scheme, the Dawes Plan, was accepted to reschedule Germany's repayments, which now reflected more closely Germany's ability to pay. It also allowed Germany to borrow substantially, mainly from the USA, and fueled a brief flurry of credit-induced economic prosperity. Germany later ratified a more comprehensive restructuring of the payments in the Young Plan, which improved her economic situation.

Similarly, the efforts of a new Chancellor, Gustav Stresemann, led to Germany entering the League of Nations in 1926 and signing the Treaty of Locarno with Britain and France, which helped to thaw the international situation. This treaty confirmed the existing borders of the participating states of western Europe. The prevailing feeling of reconciliation appeared to usher in a more constructive period of international relations. Importantly, however, Locarno failed to guarantee the frontiers of Germany in the east, suggesting to many in Germany that the western powers would not be as concerned if Germany were to attempt to reclaim lost territory there.

However, the improvements in Germany's position by 1929 were undone totally by an unforeseen event that would have tremendous ramifications for the world at large. On 29 October 1929 came the Wall Street crash. The immediate effect was that all the American loans that had been artificially buoying up the world economy were recalled. The effects on the global economy were dramatic enough, but Germany, whose tenuous economic recovery had been fueled by extensive borrowing from the USA, was among the hardest hit. This new round of economic hardship gave Hitler another opportunity to make political capital, and he seized it with both hands.

Political violence on the streets of German cities characterized the years between 1929

and 1933 as Nazi fought communist and Germany's economy labored under the pressures of worldwide recession and reparations. It was Hitler and the Nazis who promised a brighter future for Germany, and on 29 January 1933, the President of the German Republic, Paul von Beneckendorff und Hindenburg, appointed Adolf Hitler as Chancellor of Germany. In the elections of the following March, the Nazi Party received 44 percent of all votes cast. Even in the overly representational system of the Weimar Republic, this was still sufficient to give the Nazis 288 out of the 647 seats in the Reichstag. Hitler made ample use of his position, passing various 'Enabling Laws' to make him effectively a legal dictator.

Once Hitler took power, he began immediately to destroy the old structures of society and rebuild them in the mode of National Socialism. All political parties other than the Nazi Party were banned. Progressively, Jews were excluded from

Chaos in the streets during the Wall Street crash. (Topham Picturepoint)

society and publicly shunned, culminating in the anti-Jewish pogrom of *Kristallnacht* in 1938 when Jewish property was vandalized. Concentration camps were also opened for 'undesirables' where hard work was the order of the day – the extermination role of these camps was as yet in the future. Hitler attempted to get Germans back to work with an ambitious program of public works, the planning and construction of the *Autobahnen* being the most famous.

Hitler was not above removing anyone who stood in his way. On 'the night of the long knives' he ordered the deaths of his old comrade and supporter Ernest Röhm, head of the Sturmabteilung (SA), and several hundred senior SA men. The SA was a large group of paramilitaries who had provided some of Hitler's earlier supporters. These men were a private army for the Nazi Party

Germany and Central Europe after the Treaty of Versailles

ESTONIA

LATVIA

DENMARK

NORTH SEA

LITHUANIA

SCHLESWIG-
HOLSTEIN

EAST
PRUSSIA

Polish
corridor

GREAT
BRITAIN

POLAND

Elbe

☐ Berlin

London ☐

HOLLAND

GERMANY

BELGIUM

Rhine

①

CZECHOSLOVAKIA

RHINELAND

④

LUXEMBOURG

②

Paris ☐

SAARLAND

③

HUNGARY

FRANCE

Rhône

AUSTRIA

SWITZERLAND

1. Rhineland demilitarized.
2. Saarland under League of Nations
    administration until 1935.
3. Alsace-Lorraine returned to France.
4. Upper Silesia ceded to Poland after plebiscite.

YUGOSLAVIA

ITALY

M E D I T E R R A N E A N   S E A

N

☐ Germany in 1918
▨ Land lost by Germany as a result
   of the Treaty of Versailles in 1919

0   200 miles

0   250 km

and kept order at political meetings as well as engaging in physical battles with communists and other opponents. Increasingly, however, Hitler doubted the loyalty of Röhm, and the activities of the SA alienated the army, whose support Hitler needed. In the wake of the SA emerged the Schutzstaffel (SS), under Heinrich Himmler. In removing the army's potential rivals, the SA, Hitler hoped to get the army more firmly on his side. Hitler also made the army swear a personal oath of allegiance to him as the 'Führer of the German Reich and people and Commander-in-Chief of the armed forces.'

At this time, Hitler began to revise the Treaty of Versailles. The treaty affected Germany in a number of ways. First, she lost in the region of one-eighth of her territory and one-tenth of her population: the provinces of Alsace and Lorraine, seized by Prussia as spoils of the 1870 war, were returned to France; Eupen-Malmedy was given to Belgium, and Schleswig-Holstein to Denmark. The most serious territorial losses were in the east, where Germany lost a large area of West Prussia to the recreated state of Poland. This left East Prussia cut off from Germany and accessible, by land, only across Polish territory – known as the 'Polish Corridor.' The city at the head of this corridor, Danzig, was to be a free city under the auspices of the League of Nations. Germany also lost territory to the new state of Czechoslovakia, created out of the ruins of the Austro-Hungarian Empire.

Importantly, these territorial losses in the east did not include a transfer of their German-speaking populations, who largely remained in situ and ripe for use as political pawns in the future. At the end of the Second World War, when Germany was once again dismembered, the Allies did not make the same mistake again and expelled millions of Germans to ensure that they would not become troublesome and vocal minorities in the future. Under the Treaty of Versailles, Germany was also forbidden to unite with Austria, the Rhineland was to be demilitarized in perpetuity, and all Germany's colonies were handed over to the Allies.

Germany's military capabilities were drastically reduced; she was to have no major navy or air force and only 100,000 men in the army. Germany was also required to pay a huge indemnity, £6,600 million. Perhaps the most controversial provision of the treaty was Article 231, the so-called war guilt clause, in which Imperial Germany, and Germany alone, was blamed for starting the war.

Much has been written about how the Treaty of Versailles played a role in the outbreak of the Second World War. Despite what turned out to be Marshal Foch's accurate prediction, that 'this [the treaty] is not a peace but an armistice for 20 years,' the treaty itself did not *cause* the Second World War. It certainly failed to prevent another war, but then the treaty was never enforced as it was originally meant to be. Nevertheless, the Treaty of Versailles provided Adolf Hitler with a useful vehicle for inciting German hatred. The inequities represented by the treaty, in particular the losses of land that in many cases had been German for hundreds of years, were a daily reminder that Germany had lost the war. Although the provisions of the treaty itself did not lead directly to war, the fact of the treaty was enormously useful for Hitler's purposes.

Hitler did not take long before he began to repudiate various elements of the treaty. In March 1935 he reintroduced conscription into Germany, announced that the peacetime army would be raised to 500,000 men, and also brazenly announced the existence of an army air arm, the Luftwaffe. All were in direct contravention of the treaty, yet none drew firm responses from the Allies, Britain and France. Hitler also signed a naval agreement with Britain allowing the new German navy a proportion of the tonnage of the Royal Navy.

In 1936 Hitler chanced his arm still further by reoccupying the demilitarized Rhineland. France was concerned by this resurgence of German confidence, but was unwilling to act without firm support from Britain. Many historians have interpreted this failure to act against Hitler at this early stage as disastrous. Certainly Hitler gained

German troops reenter the Rhineland on 7 March 1936.
(AKG Berlin)

strength from his inital successes, becoming
convinced that the British and French were
too weak to stop him. Indeed, during the
reoccupation of the Rhineland, German
troops were instructed to retreat if the
French merely looked as though they would
offer some resistance. On 14 October 1933,
Germany withdrew from the League of
Nations. In 1936 she sent men, aircraft, and
naval vessels to fight in the Spanish Civil
War, providing the new armed forces with a
real proving ground for their tactics and
equipment.

Responses to Hitler

There are several reasons why little was done
to stop Hitler at this early juncture. First,
although Hitler was considered something
of an extremist, he was not yet the
megalomaniac the world now knows him to
be. Although much of what was to follow
was mentioned in *Mein Kampf*, few outside
Germany had bothered to read this long and
dull work. Paradoxically, Hitler was also
considered a positive development by many.
His dynamic leadership appeared to bring
badly needed order and stability to
Germany. David Lloyd-George, the wartime
British Prime Minister, spoke of Hitler's

achievements in getting the unemployed back to work and famously visited Hitler in Germany, being greeted by him as 'the man who won the war.' Lloyd-George was neither the first nor the last senior politician to be hoodwinked by Hitler.

The new Germany was also considered to be a valuable bulwark against the threat of communism from the east and Hitler's authoritarian regime was seen as a small price to pay for such reassurance. This fear of communism was a significant force in interwar Europe and it prevented any meaningful development of an alliance between the western allies and the Soviet Union until Hitler had shown his hand completely.

Importantly, there were many on the Allied side who believed the Treaty of Versailles to be a mistake, neither harsh enough to punish nor lenient enough to conciliate. The treaty was greeted with less enthusiasm than might have been expected in some quarters. The eminent British economist John Maynard Keynes resigned from his position with the British team responsible for negotiating the treaty amid disagreements over what form it would eventually take. Keynes's criticism found form in his book *The Economic Consequences of the Peace*, and this began the subtle changing of opinion, at the highest levels at least, in Britain. Such feelings help explain why there was widespread antipathy toward enforcing such a treaty.

There were other factors that militated against a more unitary front towards the growing threat of Nazi aggression in Europe. There was still memory of the horrendous legacy of the First World War. The generation of politicians in office in the 1930s had served in the trenches and knew firsthand the cost of such a war. These sentiments had a profound echo in the public at large with the League of Nations Peace Ballot and the famous Oxford Union debate (when undergraduates debated and

passed the motion 'this house will not fight again for King and Country') all contributing to an air of pacifism. The belief that Hitler was at worst an ambiguous figure combined with an overwhelming reluctance to fight another war led to a profound inertia and perhaps an unwillingness to recognize the threat even when it became overt.

Underscoring the political vacillation and popular mood was a concrete economic reason for avoiding a costly conflict. The Wall Street crash and the consequent Great Depression had left most industrialized economies significantly weaker. The financial muscle required to prosecute another war was simply unavailable through the early to mid-1930s. Ironically, even though Nazi Germany and Roosevelt's America introduced programs (such as the New Deal in the USA) to stimulate the economy, it was rearmament that finally got men back to work.

Portrait of J. M. Keynes, the famous British economist. (Topham Picturepoint)

The road to war

The Second World War was fought between Britain, France, the USA, Poland, the Soviet Union and assorted smaller countries on one side, and Germany, Italy, Romania, and Hungary on the other. Matters are slightly complicated by the fact that the Soviet Union was allied to Germany from August 1939 until June 1941 when Germany attacked her. We will look here at Germany, France, Britain, and Poland, and make smaller mention of the other participants.

Germany

The German armed forces at the outbreak of the war were perhaps the best prepared for the ensuing conflict, although Germany did not possess the largest army in 1939. The Germans had worked out how best to utilize the various new technological developments in weaponry and harnessed them effectively to traditional German tactics as well as originating new tactical ideas.

In the aftermath of the First World War, the German military faced a sobering reappraisal of their position. Despite the many variations of the 'stab in the back' idea, that Germany had lost the war not because of military defeat but instead by the actions of left-wing elements at home, the German armed forces had been decisively defeated by 1918. Senior German officers were only too aware of where their shortcomings lay and set about addressing them.

The German armed forces responded to defeat with a thorough examination of the reasons that underpinned it, and set about providing practical military solutions to their problems. However, just as Germany had suffered extensive territorial loss as a result of the Treaty of Versailles, so too did she suffer considerable readjustment of the manning

and equipment levels of her armed forces. In November 1918, at the time of the Armistice, the Imperial German army could field in the region of 4 million men. After the Versailles settlement she was restricted to a formation that numbered only 100,000 troops, of whom 4,000 were officers. While this number was comparatively small, the men of the '100,000' Army would provide the nucleus of the enlarged army and their intensive training and proficiency would prove to be invaluable.

As well as these limitations on manpower, the German army was prohibited from possessing or developing tanks and the German air force was abolished altogether. The German navy, much of which had been scuttled at Scapa Flow as it was due to be handed over to the British, was confined to a few larger surface vessels from the pre-*Dreadnought* era, but was forbidden to have U-boats at all. These apparent disadvantages were overcome in a number of ways.

Under the enthusiastic and skillful leadership of Colonel-General Hans von Seeckt, many of the arrangements agreed upon at Versailles were sidestepped or negated. First, the German military spent a great deal of time *thinking* about the way in which their forces might be employed to face a larger enemy and also about why they had failed to win a victory between 1914 and 1918. While the Germans were denied access to new equipment, they considered how they might employ such equipment in the likely event of restrictions on Germany being lifted.

The Germans also went to considerable lengths to circumvent the restrictions on equipment. In 1922 a bilateral agreement was forged between Germany and Bolshevik Russia, the two pariah states of Europe, to cooperate on military matters. The Germans gained training areas away from the prying eyes of the Allies, while the Soviet Union

Hans von Seeckt (right). (AKG Berlin)

received technical aid. The training of pilots was also carried out clandestinely, with many pilots learning the principles of flight through the new glider clubs that grew during the 1920s and 1930s. When Hitler came to power in January 1933, he brought with him a resolve and an ideology to make Germany a great power once again. His accession brought a new commitment to rearmament and a determination to reassert Germany's international position.

When the new German army was unleashed on the Poles in 1939, and especially against the Anglo-French forces in 1940, it exhibited a flexible technique of command and control that proved the difference between the German soldiers and their opponents. This idea had its roots in the partially successful German spring offensive of 1918 and stressed the idea of *Aufragstaktic* or mission command. This focused on the need for all officers and NCOs to take decisions to achieve the goal of their mission, and encouraged initiative and freedom of action on the ground rather than waiting for orders from on high. This flexibility was aided by the development of wireless communications and the fact that all German tanks were equipped with radios.

In 1932 a Germany army captain named Bechtolsheim gave a lecture on German principles of war to the United States Artillery School. He stressed the following ideas:

The German Army has of course its principles as to what is to be done in war, but – please mark this well – no stereotyped rules as to how it is to be done. We believe that movement is the first element of war and only by mobile warfare can any decisive results be obtained … to do always what the enemy does not expect and to constantly [sic] change both the means and the methods and to do the most improbable things whenever the situation permits; it means to be free of all set rules and preconceived ideas. We believe that no leader who thinks or acts by stereotyped rules can ever do anything great, because he is bound by such rules. War is not normal. It cannot therefore be won by rules which apply in peacetime.

These ideas found their most effective expression in the employment of tanks and supporting arms acting in concert, and they were aided by the ideas of General Heinz Guderian, often called the 'father of the Panzers' (tanks). The sum total of German ideas of mission command and new technology would prove devastating in the early years of the Second World War and would introduce a new word to the military lexicon, *Blitzkrieg*.

Great Britain

At the end of the First World War, it was the British army that appeared to lead the world in terms of effective war fighting. The British skill in utilizing the all-arms concept (the interaction of artillery, tanks, infantry, and air power) had been very apparent at the end of 1918. By 1939, however, this effective lead had been lost. The reasons why this state of affairs developed are several.

Britain, like most of the major combatants in the First World War, was 'war weary.' In the late 1920s a rash of books was published detailing the experiences of British troops in the war. Almost all written by officers, these books played a significant role in defining or redefining the popular British perceptions of that conflict. Works such as Siegfried Sassoon's *Memoirs of a Fox Hunting Man*, Edmund Blunden's *Undertones of War*, and Robert Graves' *Goodbye to All That* (to name but three) meshed well with a general sense that the war was a tragedy, and rather eclipsed and replaced other modes of remembrance. Certainly at this time there were few books that celebrated the war as an unambiguous victory. In tandem with this literary response there came a wider, popular revulsion against war in the more general sense, underscored by the Peace Ballot. With this mood in the country and little money generally, it is hardly surprising that defense budgets were slashed.

In tandem with widespread anti-war sentiment, Britain also found herself in a precarious economic position. Having

Siegfried Sassoon was one of the many poets and writers who took part in the First World War, and whose experiences colored their writings. (Topham Picturepoint)

entered the war as the global economy's principal creditor – the one to whom the most money was owed – she finished it as one of the largest debtor states. The cost of the war had been enormous, absorbing British reserves and also bringing about the loss of many of Britain's overseas markets when production of consumer goods was switched to war materials. At the end of the war, British producers found that many of their prewar markets had been taken over by other countries, notably the USA. Indeed, it was the USA that emerged as the economic victor after 1918. Having capitalized on the absence of traditional European competition for trade and markets between 1914 and 1918, she also lent large amounts to the other Allied participants.

British strategy in the event of another war initially focused upon facing the imagined threat of air attack. The idea that 'the bomber will always get through' informed British defense thinking from 1934. To this end, priority was given to building up the Royal Air Force (RAF) and establishing the new 'radar' system to cover the British coast. The Royal Navy, although no longer the unchallenged master of the seas, was still a formidable force. The British army was the only fully mobile army in 1939 and the British Expeditionary Force (BEF) that was dispatched to France in 1939 was still a useful formation at 160,000 men. The interwar debate about the role of the tank in the British army had largely been resolved by 1939. The resolution had come in favor of those who believed that the tank should be the essential element of any formation, but acting alone, not as a component of a cohesive all-arms grouping.

France

In the interwar years, a great deal of security, real or imagined, was derived from the very existence of the French army. In March 1933, two months after Adolf Hitler became Chancellor of Germany, Winston Churchill made one of his customary and oft-quoted exclamations, declaring: 'thank god for the French army!' To such as Churchill, still a lone voice in the political wilderness in 1933, the French army was a significant bulwark against future German aggression. Few in Britain, however, agreed with him. Indeed there were many who saw the posturing of France with regard to Germany as the real threat to European stability and not Germany herself.

In many ways, France's experience of the First World War was quite different from that of her British allies, and it certainly exercised a far greater influence on her subsequent military organization, doctrine, and tactics. While the British army fought in several different theaters and pioneered the employment of tanks and the adoption of all-arms techniques of fighting toward the end of the war, with great success, the French successes between 1914 and 1918 were grounded in determinedly holding a defensive line. This static mentality found both its most eloquent expression and a source of national grandeur in the heroic fighting at Verdun, where the French army had endured horrific casualties yet had prevailed. Despite French offensive success and their own positive experiences of all-arms conflict toward the end of the First World War, French losses had been so significant between 1914 and 1918 that few Frenchmen would willingly go to war in the future.

The idea of the defense had a special poignancy for the French, as their losses in the First World War were taken on French soil and in defense of *La République*. It was no wonder, then, that future defensive arrangements should seek to learn from French successes and

also to build on them to such an extent that the devastation of 1914–18 would not be repeated. The result was the creation of the enormous and costly Maginot Line, a vast system of interconnected fortresses, linked underground via railways, comprising barracks and hospitals, ammunition stores, and fuel and ventilation systems that would allow the forts to continue to function – and fight – even if surrounded by the enemy. At 7 billion French francs, the final cost of the line was far more than the original estimate.

The cost of construction and also the ongoing cost of maintenance inevitably meant that the funding available for other areas of the French armed forces was reduced greatly. Despite these considerations, however, there were few in France who would dispute the necessity of such an arrangement. Marshal Pétain summed up the French national faith in such defenses, referring to them as 'lavish

The Maginot Line, constructed at massive cost, was the cornerstone of French defensive strategy. (Ann Ronan Picture Library)

with steel, stingy with blood,' and after the horrors of the trenches, few disagreed.

There was a weakness in the whole arrangement, in that the line did not extend the length of the Franco-Belgian frontier – the obvious route for an invading army – and in fact stretched only from Strasbourg as far as Montmédy. The reasons for this were partly practical and partly economic as well as a reluctance to exclude Belgium from an alliance with France. If Belgium were left out of the Maginot Line, in all likelihood she would once again revert to her previous neutrality – she had been neutral in 1914 – and thereby provide a conduit for German aggression. In the event, Belgium opted for neutrality anyway, effectively scuppering French plans to move into prepared positions on Belgian soil. Similarly, the Maginot Line did not cover the area opposite the Ardennes, a densely wooded forest area, as it was considered to be 'impenetrable' to modern armored columns.

The sum total of these many considerations – a misplaced optimism in the strength of the Maginot Line, worries about the political position of Belgium, financial concerns, and an unwillingness to conceive that offensive, maneuver-type operations might hold the upper hand in a future war – all led to the development of what would be termed the 'Maginot mentality.' This amounted to a belief in the superiority of the defensive arrangement of the Maginot Line and an unwillingness to believe or acknowledge that warfare might have moved on.

The Maginot Line was also tremendously important for the Germans. Almost unwittingly, it had imposed upon the French a strategic straitjacket. There was little chance that, having shackled herself so firmly (and expensively) to the defensive, France was likely to go onto the attack. In 1935 the French Minister of War, in a speech to the French Chamber of Deputies, asserted: 'How can we still believe in the offensive when we have spent thousands of millions to establish a fortified barrier? Would we be mad enough to advance beyond this barrier upon goodness knows what adventure!'

Not only had the French national mentality become inextricably wedded to the defensive – a mindset both created and reinforced by the Maginot Line – but there were also other practical considerations. The Maginot Line had been the product of tremendous investment in defense budgets and manpower. With the Maginot Line receiving so much of the available moneys for defense, it severely restricted other areas of defense spending. Even had the French army not been so deficient in the means to adopt offensive operations, the means to fund new equipment to that end was absent. The knowledge of this would obviously aid Adolf Hitler, who was reasonably secure that, whatever action he might take in the east, it was highly unlikely that France would threaten seriously the western border of the Reich.

The French army in the 1930s suffered from a number of problems, many of them reflected in French life more widely. French troops were underpaid and undervalued, and the army was riven by many of the social and political divisions of the country at large. The French army continued to rely on telephone communication rather than radio. Similarly, the French failed to take on board the new potential of tanks. The French army of 1918 did not manage to enact the all-arms battle with any degree of conviction, generally reducing its tanks to the role of infantry support vehicles that were the means to the end of an infantry breakthrough. This was despite developing some excellent vehicles toward the end of the war. The French all-arms battle generally geared the speed of the other elements down to that of the slowest component, the infantry, rather than seeking to motorize the infantry and allow them to maintain the speed of the armored elements. Despite the protestations of a few French officers during the interwar period, notably those of Charles de Gaulle, French doctrine remained stubbornly behind the times.

Belgium

The small Belgian army had played as active a role as it could during the First World War and in the aftermath made serious efforts to preserve its security. The Belgians signed defensive agreements with both Britain and France and endeavored to maintain a large standing army, courtesy of conscription. However, by 1926 this commitment to a reasonably strong standing army had largely been abandoned and a reliance on the inevitability of British and French support in the event of war informed Belgium's defense posture. The advent of Hitler in 1933 prompted a renewal of Belgian military spending and by the time of the Anglo-French declaration of war, the Belgian army stood at nearly 600,000 men. The Belgian army, despite a number of modern and effective weapons, planned to fight a defensive war in the event of her neutrality, reaffirmed with the Anglo-French declaration of war on Germany being breached.

Poland

The Poles were to have the dubious distinction of being Hitler's first military victims. The performance of the Polish army in the early battles of the Second World War has attracted considerable attention, if only for the apparent futility of its desperate efforts to repel the German invaders. The history of the Polish army is an interesting one. Poland, as an independent political entity, had effectively been off the map for the 123 years before 1918. Successive 'partitions' of Poland between Prussia, Imperial Russia, and the Austro-Hungarian Empire came to an end in 1918 when Poland was restored by the Treaty of Versailles, at the territorial expense of those same states.

Large numbers of Poles fought in the First World War, serving, ironically, in the armies of Germany, Russia, and also Austria-Hungry. It was the formations of Polish Legions raised by the Austro-Hungarians that were to have the largest and most disproportionate impact on the new army of independent Poland. A fledgling Polish army was soon established in the new Poland under the command of Jozef Pilsudski, the former commander of the Polish Legions in the Austrian army. Despite the unpromising origins of this essentially disparate, 'rag-tag' grouping, the Polish army was to score a notable success. The Poles were bolstered by a number of additional Polish formations, most notably the 'Haller' army, a formation of 25,000 Polish-American volunteers.

In the aftermath of the First World War and with the large empires of east and

Polish cavalry. (Topham Picturepoint)

Polish tankettes. (Steve Zaloga)

central Europe collapsing, there followed a general free-for-all as many states struggled to seize territory and incorporate ethnic kin within the boundaries of the new states. The Poles, emboldened by a number of local victories against the new masters of Russia, the Bolsheviks, joined with Ukrainian nationalist forces to invade the Ukraine and fight the Red Army. After the Poles enjoyed initial successes, the Red Army forced them all the way back to the gates of Warsaw. Then Pilsudski achieved an enormous reversal of Polish fortunes and defeated the Red Army so decisively that the Bolsheviks were obliged to conclude a humiliating peace settlement, something that rankled through the 1920s and 1930s and certainly contributed to Stalin's willingness to dismember the country in 1939.

Poland's strategic position was unpromising. Sandwiched between two powerful enemies, the Soviet Union to the east and Germany to the west, the nightmare scenario for Poland was, of course, a two-front war. Poland's strategic predicament was the source of considerable concern to Polish planners. In 1921 they managed to secure a defensive alliance with France. This obliged the French to assist the Poles in the event of Germany entering into a conflict that was already in progress between the Poles and Russia. If this criterion were fulfilled, France would attack Germany. This treaty had obvious benefits for the French, whose diplomatic maneuvering in the interwar years was directed toward containing and restricting

Germany. The Poles also secured a treaty with the Romanians that promised help against Russia rather than Germany.

The Treaty of Locarno, signed in 1925 between Britain, France and Weimar Germany, appeared to be a source of future trouble for Poland, guaranteeing as it did the frontiers of *western* Europe. The obvious problem lay in the fact that Germany, with her western borders secure from her most vehement enemy, France, might take the opportunity to redress some of her many territorial grievances in the east. In a masterstroke of diplomatic collusion, Hitler agreed a nonaggression pact between Germany and Poland.

Despite the judgement of history on the Polish army in the war with Germany, that it was fighting a thoroughly modern opponent with nineteenth-century tactics and equipment, the Polish army was in fact wedded to a doctrine of maneuver. These tactics were born of the successes and experiences of the fast-moving Russo-Polish War, but unfortunately while the ideas were modern, the means by which they were to be realized were most definitely from a bygone era. While the German ideas of maneuver utilized tanks, armored infantry, and self-propelled artillery, the Poles still placed their faith in cavalry and infantry marching on foot. The resulting clash could have only one winner.

'I have determined on a solution by force'

The Second World War began, effectively, with the German invasion of Poland. This event, in itself, might have been a comparatively local incident. What was required to turn it into a wider European war and a world war was the participation of Britain and France, which had both pledged to come to Poland's aid in the event of overt German aggression. The reasons why the British and French found themselves in this position may be traced to several years previously.

German territorial ambitions

Hitler intended to restore German power and prestige in Europe. To do so he first believed that it was necessary to secure the restitution of the territory and people that Germany had been obliged to give up under the terms of the Versailles settlement in 1919. Once all Germans had been incorporated into a Germany that itself encompassed traditional German territory, Hitler then had more ambitious plans. He intended that Germany should dominate Europe and conceived of such a situation in distinctly Darwinian terms. The Aryan Germans would demonstrate their superiority over races, such as the Slavs of eastern Europe, through war in a 'survival of the fittest' contest.

Hitler believed that a people must either expand or die and the area of expansion for the German superstate was to be in the east. The Slavic inhabitants of eastern Europe were to be reduced to a slave race, living openly to serve their German masters. The land conquered in the east would be colonized by Germans and would provide sufficient space for expansion (*Lebensraum*), something not available in Germany herself. Some peoples, the Jews and the gypsies for example, were not considered fit enough even to serve the Germans and were to be eliminated. Writing in *Mein Kampf*, Hitler made the following declaration:

The foreign policy of a nation state must assure the existence on this planet of a race ... by creating a healthy, life-giving and natural balance between the present and future numbers of the Volk [people] on the one hand and, on the other, the quantity and quality of its territory.

With the reoccupation of the Rhineland in 1936, it was obvious that Hitler was intent on addressing Germany's territorial grievances. Hitler ordered the army into the Rhineland against the better judgement of his generals, and the German success there persuaded him of both his own infallibility in such matters and the weakness and indifference of his likely opponents, Britain and France.

Anschluss

Union with Austria was another important step for Hitler. Although forbidden by the Treaty of Versailles, it also ran counter to the ideas of self-determination enshrined in the treaty itself, as many Germans living in Austria did not want to be incorporated into Germany. Hitler, however, was extremely keen to bring the Germans in Austria within the greater Reich, not only for racial reasons, but also because Austria was the land of his birth.

In 1934 the Austrian Nazi Party had been banned by the then Austrian Chancellor, Dollfuss. Later that year, the Austrian Nazis attempted a coup d'état, but Hitler was persuaded not to intervene when Mussolini threatened to intervene on Dollfuss's behalf.

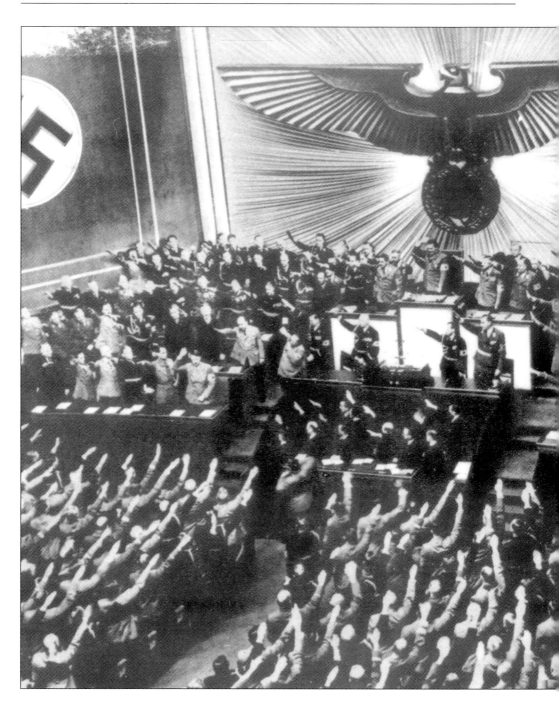

News of the *Anschluss* reaches the Reichstag. (Topham Picturepoint)

Four years later, following an improvement in Italian–German relations, with the announcement of the Rome–Berlin Axis and the more formal Anti-Comintern Pact, the Austrian Nazis began agitating again. At this juncture the Austrian Chancellor promised a plebiscite on Austria's future. Hitler was not confident that Austrians would vote to join Germany and this possibility forced his hand. Threatened with a German invasion, the government of Austria capitulated. In

For many in the outside world, the enforced separation of the ethnically similar Austrians and Germans was artificial and inappropriate. When Germany and Austria were united in what became known as the *Anschluss*, many observers dismissed Hitler's aggression on these grounds. But if they believed that this success would assuage rather than fuel his ambitions, they were certainly wrong.

The Sudetenland

Hitler's next concern was the future of the large numbers of Germans in Czechoslovakia, almost all of whom, unlike the Austrians, wished to be incorporated into Germany. The wholly artificial Czechoslovakian state had been constituted out of the former Austro-Hungarian Empire and German territory, and contained around 3 million ethnic Germans, living in that area of Czechoslovakia called the Sudetenland.

Since 1933, elements of the German minority in Czechoslovakia had been agitating for political autonomy from their ostensible parent nation, Czechoslovakia. They were led by a Nazi sympathizer, Konrad Henlein. There was some sympathy for the demands of the Sudeten Germans: after all, the right of self-determination had been enshrined in the Treaty of Versailles and what this minority wished for was, ostensibly, little different. At the 1938 Nazi Party rally in Nuremberg, Hitler made the following announcement, clearly demonstrating his ambitions over the future of the Sudeten Germans:

I believe that I shall serve peace best if I leave no doubt upon this point. I have not put forward the demand that Germany may oppress three and a half million Frenchmen or that, for instance, three and a half million of the English should be given up to us for oppression; my demand is that the oppression of three and a half million Germans in Czechoslovakia shall cease and that its place shall be taken by the

February 1938 the Austrian Chancellor, Schuschnigg, resigned and was replaced by the Nazi Seyss-Inquart, who invited in German troops. On 13 March he officially decreed Austria out of existence and Adolf Hitler became the Chancellor of a Greater Germany.

A poster advertising the plebiscite in the Sudetenland. (AKG Berlin)

free right of self-determination. We should be sorry if, through this, our relations to the other European states should be troubled or suffer damage. But in that case the fault would not lie with us.

While the British Prime Minister, Neville Chamberlain, appeared genuinely to believe in Hitler's sincerity, the truth was that the British and French were ill prepared for war. When Hitler moved German troops to the Czech border in early September, there appeared to be every likelihood that Germany would invade. However, Hitler was reasonably sure that he could obtain what he wanted through diplomacy and that the British and French were unwilling to fight for Czechoslovakia.

The British and French faced a number of problems with regard to aiding Czechoslovakia. The Czechs alone were insufficiently strong to resist the Germans in the event of war, and their most likely supporters, the Soviet Union, could only send aid by crossing Polish and Romanian territory,

Prelude to war: the Sudetenland, the Polish Corridor and Gleiwitz

1. German re-occupation of the Rhineland, May 1936.
2. Plebiscite in the Saarland, March 1935.
3. German occupation of Austria, March 1938.
4. Sudetenland given to Germany by Munich Agreement, September 1938.

something that the Poles and Romanians were unlikely to permit. In addition, the British and French were also uneasy about the prospect of Russian interference in Czechoslovakia. Although France and Czechoslovakia had a defensive agreement, there was consequently little will to fight, and even if there had been, Britain and France were too weak militarily to do so. The British and French therefore counseled the Czech leader Benes to agree to Hitler's demands and surrender the Sudetenland, even though this would entail the loss of the strategically most significant portion of Czechoslovakia and all her vital frontier fortifications, making any further German incursion a simple matter.

At a meeting on 15 September between Chamberlain and Hitler, at Hitler's mountain retreat of Berchtesgaden, Hitler revealed his intention to annex the Sudetenland under the principle of self-determination. After several days of escalating tension, during which time the Royal Navy prepared for war and France also began to mobilize, an agreement was reached to meet at Munich on 29 September. On 27 September, Chamberlain made this well-known comment:

How horrible, fantastic, incredible it is that we should be digging trenches and trying on gas masks here because of a quarrel in a far-away country between people of whom we know nothing. It seems still more impossible that a quarrel which has already been settled in principle should be the subject of war.

The Munich Conference, incredibly, did not feature a Czech representative, but instead Britain, France, Italy, and Germany met to decide the future of Czechoslovakia. Hitler signed an agreement promising that once the Sudetenland was transferred to Germany, the remaining Czech frontiers would be respected. After this Chamberlain flew back to England, landing at Croydon airport, and waved his famous piece of paper, signed by Hitler, which Chamberlain said guaranteed 'peace in our time.' On 15 March 1939, German troops entered the Czech capital, Prague, and occupied the Czech provinces of Bohemia and Moravia.

The Munich Conference. Left to right: Neville Chamberlain, Daladier, Adolf Hitler, Benito Mussolini, Count Gano (Ann Ronan Picture Library)

Chamberlain at Croydon after the Munich conference.
(Topham Picturepoint)

The Munich Conference of September 1938 has become shorthand for weakness in the face of obvious aggression and synonymous with the term 'appeasement.' Appeasement is an oft-heard term, but in this context it was the means by which the British and French in particular sought to pacify Hitler by agreeing to as many of his demands as possible in the hope of assuaging his ambition and, fundamentally, avoiding war. In fact the Munich Conference marked the end of appeasement and both Chamberlain and the French Prime Minister, Edouard Daladier, knew that rearmament must continue at a pace, as Hitler had only been temporarily satiated.

Poland

The final act that escalated local disputes into a major European and ultimately a world war was the German invasion of Poland. Following Hitler's move against the rump state of Czechoslovakia, the British government offered a military guarantee to Poland, intending to demonstrate to Hitler that a repetition of Munich would not be countenanced. This was also a recognition of the popular mood in Britain, where a measure of conscription was also introduced. Britain offered similar guarantees to both Romania and Greece, thereby reversing the longstanding pledge of previous British governments not to tie Britain into another continental commitment.

Hitler wanted Poland as the first major step toward obtaining *Lebensraum* in the east. The pretext was an obvious one: Germany proper was separated from her easternmost province, East Prussia, by a strip of Polish territory. It was not difficult to accuse the Poles of interfering with German access to East Prussia. Similarly, in the free city of Danzig, local Nazis went about the familiar business of creating trouble and demanding that the city be incorporated into the Reich. Hitler then had ample pretext to begin putting pressure on the Polish government to cede territory to Germany, in

the same fashion as the Czechs had been obliged to do.

The strategic position changed dramatically in August with the surprise announcement of the Molotov–Ribbentrop Pact between Germany and the Soviet Union. This expedient alliance brought together the two countries that would be deadly foes in only a couple of years. Stalin realized this and sought to delay the German assault on his country as long as possible. He also rationalized that a deeper border with Germany would have benefits for the Soviets, and readily agreed to help Germany attack Poland on the understanding that the Soviets would gain half of Polish territory. This accommodation gave Hitler the confidence to risk war, secure in the knowledge that the Soviet Union would not attack even if Britain and France did. Britain made it very clear to Germany that she would come to Poland's aid if need be. Hitler, however, was committed.

In defiance of British and French warnings, Adolf Hitler ordered his forces to invade. In OKW Directive No. 1, issued by Hitler on the last day of August 1939, he asserted the following: 'Having exhausted all political possibilities of rectifying the intolerable situation on Germany's eastern frontier by peaceful means, I have decided to solve the problem by force.'

The event needed to turn this action into a major European conflict occurred at 11.15 am on 3 September 1939. At 9.00 am, just over three hours previously, the British Prime Minister had issued Germany with an ultimatum, demanding that unless Britain heard by 11.00 am that Germany was prepared to withdraw her troops from Poland then a state of war would exist between Great Britain and Germany. At 11.15 am Neville Chamberlain made his immortal speech informing the British people that 'no such undertaking has been received and that, consequently, this country is at war with Germany.' Britain's ally, France, issued a similar ultimatum at noon on 3 September. When the deadline for the Germans' reply to that ultimatum came and

The Supreme Commander of the Armed Forces

OKW/Wfa Nr 170/39g. K. Chiefs. Li   Berlin
MOST SECRET   31st August 1939

Senior Commanders only   8 copies
By hand of Officer only   COPY No....

Directive No. 1 for the Conduct of War

1. Now that the political possibilities of disposing by peaceful means of a situation on the Eastern Frontier which is intolerable for Germany has been exhausted, I have determined on a solution by force.

2 The attack on Poland is to be carried out in accordance with the preparation made for 'Fall Weiss', with the alterations which result, where the Army is concerned, from the fact that it has in the meantime almost completed its dispositions. Allotment of tasks and the operational targets remain unchanged. The date of attack – 1 September, 1939. Time of attack – 4.45 [inserted in red pencil]. This timing also applies to operations at Gydnia, the bay of Danzig and the Dirschau bridge.

3. In the West it is important that the responsibility of the opening of hostilities should rest unequivocally with England and France. Minor frontier violations will be dealt with locally for the time being. The neutrality of Holland, Belgium, Luxemburg, Switzerland, which we have assured, is to be strictly observed. The Western frontier will not be crossed by land without my explicit orders. This also applies to all acts of war at sea. Defensive measures by the Luftwaffe are to be restricted to repulsing firmly any enemy air attacks on the frontiers of the Reich. Care must be taken to respect the frontiers of neutral countries as far as possible, when countering single aircraft or small units. Only when large numbers of British or French bombers are employed against German territory across neutral territory, will the Air Force be allowed to fly counterattacks over the same neutral soil. It is especially important to keep the IKW informed of every infringement of neutral territory by our Western enemies.

4. Should England and France open hostilities against Germany then it will be the duty of the Armed Forces operating in the West, while conserving their strength as much as possible, to maintain conditions for the successful conclusion of operations against Poland. The order to commence offensive operations is reserved absolutely to me.

The Army will hold the West Wall and should take steps to secure it from being outflanked in the north, by any violation of Belgian or Dutch borders by the Western powers. Should the French invade Luxembourg, permission is given to blow the frontier bridges.

The Navy will operate against merchant shipping, with England as the focal point. Certain zones may be declared danger areas in order to increase the effectiveness of such measures. The OKM will report on these areas and will submit the text of a public declaration in this matter, which is to be drawn up in collaboration with the Foreign Office and submitted to me for approval via the OKW. The Baltic Sea is to be secured against enemy incursions. OKM will decide if it is necessary to mine the entrances to the Baltic for this purpose.

The Air Force is primarily to prevent French or English air forces attacking German land forces or German territory. In operations against England it is the task of the Luftwaffe to harrass England's important trade at sea, her armaments industry and the transport of troops to France. Any favourable opportunity to attack enemy naval concentrations, especially battleships and aircraft carriers, must be taken. Any decision to attack London rests with me. Attacks against the English home land should be prepared, bearing in mind that partial success with insufficient forces is to be avoided at all costs.

signed: **ADOLF HITLER**

(translated from the original in Part II of the Nuremberg Documents)

Directive No. 1 for the conduct of war, reproduced from *The Fall of France*, by G. Fortey and John Duncan (Tunbridge Wells, 1990).

went, at 5.00 pm that day, France too was once again at war with Germany.

The American journalist William Shirer, who wrote regular dispatches from Germany during the early years of the Second World War, had this to say about the reaction of the German people to the announcement that Germany would now face a war against the British and the French:

In 1914, I believe, the excitement in Berlin on the first day of the world war was tremendous. Today, no excitement, no hurrahs, no cheering, no throwing of flowers, no war fever, no war hysteria. There is not even any hate for the British and French – despite Hitler's various proclamations to the people, the Party, the East Army, the West Army, accusing the 'English warmongers and capitalistic Jews' of starting this war. When I passed the French and British embassies this afternoon, the sidewalk in front of each of them was deserted. A lone schupo [short for Schutzspolizei *or policeman] paced up and down before each.*

Whatever the average German might have felt about the war, there was now no way back.

Hitler strikes

The invasion of Poland

The invasion of Poland was the first strike in a total war. Hitler's new army was now to be tested on the field of combat against the large and well-trained armed forces of the Polish state – the same nation that had famously stopped the Red Army before Warsaw in 1920. As it turned out, however, the poignant and tragic imagery of Polish cavalry fighting against, and hopelessly outclassed by, German armor would prove to be one of the most significant and defining images of the war. The years of training and exercises that the German army had engaged in since 1919 were now to be put into practice with devastating effect.

German troops cross the border into Poland. (Ann Ronan Picture Library)

Despite Hitler's ambition and confidence, the Germans went through an elaborate charade in order to convince the world that Germany was provoked. Men from the *Sicherheitsdienst* or SD department of the SS, under the overall direction of Reinhard Heydrich, planned an operation to precipitate the war that Hitler wanted. This operation, code-named Hindenburg, involved three simultaneous raids: the first was on the radio station at Gleiwitz, the second on the small customs post at Hochlinden, and the third on an isolated gamekeeper's hut at Pitschen. The raids were to be conducted by men dressed in Polish uniforms, and at Gleiwitz the plan was that the attack would be heard live on radio – with the attackers' voices, speaking in Polish and declaiming Germany, being broadcast live over the air to maximize their impact.

Reinhard Heydrich, 1904–42 was chief of the SS and the
originator of the Final Solution plan. (Topham Picturepoint)

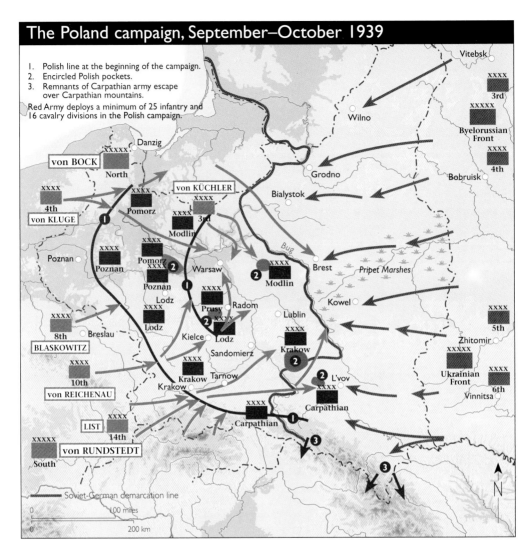

The Poland campaign, September–October 1939

1. Polish line at the beginning of the campaign.
2. Encircled Polish pockets.
3. Remnants of Carpathian army escape over Carpathian mountains.

Red Army deploys a minimum of 25 infantry and 16 cavalry divisions in the Polish campaign.

Soviet-German demarcation line

After a number of false starts and poor organization bordering on the farcical, the attacks took place. Four condemned men from the Sauchsenhausen concentration camp and a single German (a local Polish sympathizer) were murdered to provide evidence for the Polish incursions – the corpses, dressed in Polish uniforms, were photographed to complete the provocation. Despite the planning, the radio attack failed to be broadcast because of the poor strength of the transmitter. Hitler was nevertheless able to announce to the Reichstag on 1 September that 'Polish troops of the regular army have been firing on our territory during the night [of 31 August/1 September].

Since 05.45 we have been returning that fire.' The Second World War was up and running.

The German attack on Poland began on 1 September. The position was greatly aided by Hitler's successful 'annexation' of Czechoslovakia, as Poland was now situated uncomfortably between the twin prongs of German-held territory. To the east, Stalin's Red Army bided its time before, on 17 September, acting in accordance with the secret clauses of the Molotov–Ribbentrop Pact and also invading Poland. The Poles, caught between the forces of Nazi Germany and the Soviet Union, did not manage to maintain resistance for long.

The German plan for the invasion of Poland was termed *Fall Weiss* or 'Case White' and essentially aimed to defeat the Polish army by encircling and destroying Polish army formations. The Germans planned to do this at the tactical level, but also at the strategic level, with German sights focused upon Warsaw, the Polish capital. The Poles were outnumbered both in terms of modern tanks and also in terms of tactics. The Germans mobilized 50 divisions for the Polish campaign, including six Panzer divisions, four motorized divisions, and three mountain divisions. These sizable forces represented the bulk of the available German army, leaving only 11 divisions in the west, where the French army was 10 times that number.

The Germans deployed their armored formations in such a manner as to maximize the attributes of their Panzer troops, rapidly outflanking the slower-moving Poles and creating the conditions for the *Kesselschlachten*, or 'cauldron battles,' that the Germans were so keen to fight. These involved the rapid penetration of the enemy's defenses via the weakest spot, followed by the encirclement of the enemy. The enemy was therefore compelled either to stand and fight, suffering artillery and air bombardment, or to attempt a breakout, in which case it would be forced to relinquish the advantage conveyed by its prepared defensive positions.

The Germans made good progress across ground baked hard by the long, hot summer of 1939 and were aided also by their overwhelming air superiority, established within the opening three days by the vastly more impressive Luftwaffe. In a pattern that would be dreadfully familiar over the ensuing years, German aircraft struck at the Polish air force on the ground, effectively removing it from the equation. German aircraft flew hundreds of sorties in support of troops on the ground, operating essentially as an aerial dimension to the German army. While the Poles were acutely aware of the likelihood of the German military action and had reasonably good intelligence as to the growing concentrations of German forces, they were still taken by surprise when the attack actually happened. The Germans were able to seize the initiative and held it for the duration of what proved to be a depressingly short campaign.

Army Group North, comprising the 4th Army under Kluge and the 3rd Army under Kuchler, struck the first blow in the campaign. The two-army formation in East Prussia and Pomerania quickly overran the Polish Corridor and the free city of Danzig. Further to the south, Army Group South under the command of von Rundstedt had three army-sized formations, 8th Army (Blaskowitz), 10th Army (Reichenau), and 14th Army (List), which drove westwards into the heart of Poland. The Poles rallied briefly around the city of Poznan and succeeded in driving the Germans back, but this offered

German cavalry column in twos, possibly members of the 1st Cavalry Division. (IWM RML225)

only a brief respite and these Polish troops were eventually overrun. The Germans, courtesy of two encirclements (the second being required when the Poles withdrew faster than anticipated) were in a position by 16 September to have surrounded the bulk of Polish forces in western Poland. They were able to snap shut the pincers of their encircling operation at will.

By 16 September the German forces had the Polish capital, Warsaw, surrounded, and they proceeded to bombard the city from the air and the ground. Warsaw eventually surrendered on 27 September with around 40,000 civilian casualties. The Russian invasion of Poland on 17 September was the deathblow for Poland. Predictably, it met little or no resistance as the Poles were both taken completely by surprise and totally immersed in the fighting against German forces in the east of their country. The Polish General Staff had no plans for fighting a war on two fronts, east and west, simultaneously. In fact, the Poles had considered that it was impossible to wage a two-front war.

The timing of the Soviet assault was also of considerable surprise to Germany. Hitler had been attempting to persuade Stalin to enter the war against Poland for some time, reasoning that the western powers then might refrain from intervening at all (i.e. not declare war on Germany) or, if not, might declare war on the Soviet Union as well. Stalin, predictably, had his own agenda with regard to the hapless Polish state. Soviet forces refrained from entering the fighting in Poland while the Red Army organized and re-equipped.

When the Red Army finally crossed the border, it did so under the weak pretence that it was responding to alleged border violations and that the intervention was aimed purely at 'the protection of the Ukrainians and Belorussians, with full preservation of neutrality in the present conflict.' Stalin also asserted that, with no *effective* Polish government now in existence, the 'Soviet government is no longer bound by the provisions and demands of the Soviet–Polish non-aggression treaty,' and was therefore at liberty to enter the war against

its former ally. While the Soviets received little in the way of significant resistance from the Poles, they did engage in minor skirmishes with German troops whom they met on their advance. It took some time before the position was established and the German and Soviet formations respected the boundary line, which followed the course of the River Bug, along which the two unlikely allies had agreed to divide Poland.

On 19 September the Polish government left Warsaw and eventually established a government in exile. This government, under Wladyslaw Sikorski, finally settled in London after the fall of France. Besides the Polish leaders, many Polish servicemen also escaped, with some 90,000 making their way to France and Britain.

What were the key reasons for the rapid collapse of Poland? There are several. First, Poland's strategic situation was poor: with the conclusion of the Molotov–Ribbentrop Pact on 23 August 1939, Poland was effectively surrounded. The addition of the Soviet Union to the side of Germany compounded the territorial adjustments that had been wrought with Germany's successful dismemberment of Czechoslovakia. The surprise that characterized the German assault also prevented the Poles from doing a better defensive job. This, in combination with the new weaponry employed with such devastating effect by the Wehrmacht, left the Poles struggling to match the Germans, and with the invasion from the east by the Soviet Union, any hope of continuing the fight was effectively removed. Nevertheless, the Poles, for all the ultimate futility of their efforts, did manage to inflict significant casualties on the Germans. They destroyed in the region of 200 German tanks, about 10 percent of the total number deployed, and also killed 13,000 German soldiers, wounding a further 30,000.

The 'phoney war'

While Poland was fighting for her survival in the east, in the west her two allies, Britain and France, did nothing. Given that France and Britain had declared war on Germany because of the attack on Poland, and France and Britain were committed guarantors of Polish independence, this inaction seems strangely at odds. The British had successfully dispatched the British Expeditionary Force (BEF), numbering 140,000 men, to France by 30 September 1940, but even then no offensive action was contemplated.

Prior to this, on 7 September, elements of the French Fourth and Seventh Armies had advanced into Germany in the vicinity of Saarbrucken. This initial incursion reached no more than about 5 miles (8km) along a 16-mile (26km) front. German military formations in the area withdrew behind the Seigfried Line. At this point, the bulk of the German army was still in Poland and the *Daily Mail* in Britain ran a headline that claimed 'French Army pouring over the German border.' However, the French advance went no further, and following the Polish surrender, the French forces withdrew.

'It was only a token invasion. We did not wish to fight on their territory and we did not ask for this war,' a senior French officer was alleged to have said. Certainly, it was a fortuitous development for the Germans, who were surprised that the western allies did not make more of the strategic opportunity before them. After the war, the German Field Marshal, Keitel, commented that 'we were astonished to find only minor skirmishes undertaken between the Siegfried and the Maginot Lines. We did not understand why France did not seize this unique opportunity and this confirmed us in the idea that the Western Powers did not desire war against us.'

This period between the Anglo-French declaration of war and the fall of France is known as the 'phoney war' because of the very inaction of both sides. The Germans were honing their plans for the assault on the Allies in the west, and the Allies too were busying themselves with organizing their counter-effort. The BEF dug what was known as the 'Gort' Line (after General The

Viscount Gort, the commanding officer of the BEF) and civilians back in Britain also dug air-raid trenches and prepared for the air war that most thought would come.

The Russo-Finnish War

Elsewhere in Europe, more bitter fighting began with the outbreak of the Russo–Finnish War. This conflict has rarely received the coverage it perhaps deserves, peripheral as it was to the larger picture. Nonetheless, some important lessons were learnt from it. The war is known more commonly as the 'Winter War' and ran from 30 November until 13 March 1940, during which time Stalin's ill-advised thrust into his near neighbor's territory resulted in a bloody nose for the Red Army.

The Red Army, in November 1939, was a far cry from the powerful and well-organized force that would eventually defeat Hitler's Germany. In fact, in the Winter War against Finland, the Soviets proved remarkably inept. Their difficulties against the Finns, in combination with the purges of the 1930s, probably persuaded Hitler that the Red Army was not likely to prove a formidable opponent in the future. Certainly the Germans were to underestimate the courage and tenacity of the ordinary Soviet soldier when they eventually invaded the Soviet Union in June 1941.

In October 1939, flush from the success of the limited campaign in Poland, Stalin issued an ultimatum to the Finnish government demanding a redrawing of the Russo-Finnish border north of Leningrad, in the Karelian peninsula. The Finns, who had only won independence from Russian dominance in 1917, declined and a short, bitter war ensued. The Finns outfought their numerically superior opponents, using hit-and-run tactics and making the best use of the terrain and climate to thwart Soviet intentions. By January 1940, however, the Soviet attack had been stabilized and the Red Army began to employ its strengths in a more effective fashion.

A scene from the Russo-Finnish War. (Topham Picturepoint)

The Finns eventually sued for peace in March 1940 and were obliged to concede the territorial demands originally required of them in October 1939. The Finns suffered roughly 25,000 casualties, but the Red Army came off far worse. Around 200,000 Red Army soldiers were lost in Finland, many through exposure. The Red Army, however, had learnt some valuable lessons for the future.

Hostilities resumed between the Finns and the Soviet Union during what became known as the 'Continuation War' of 1941–44 when the Finns formally allied themselves to Germany. The Finnish leader, Mannerheim, skillfully detached himself from the Germans when their defeat became evident. Although his terms for peace with the Soviet Union meant a permanent acknowledgment of the border situation of spring 1940, Mannerheim's actions did at least ensure that his country did not fall under the sway of the Soviet Union, as did so many other states at the war's end.

The Norway campaign

While the western allies were content to bide their time in France, in Norway they at last took the offensive. The Allied campaign in Norway was to prove a fascinating mix of strategic ineptitude coupled with extraordinary individual heroism. The German economy was reliant on over 10 million tons of iron ore each year being imported from Sweden. The route of this vital component was overland from Sweden to Norway and thence from the Norwegian port of Narvik to Germany. If the Allies could

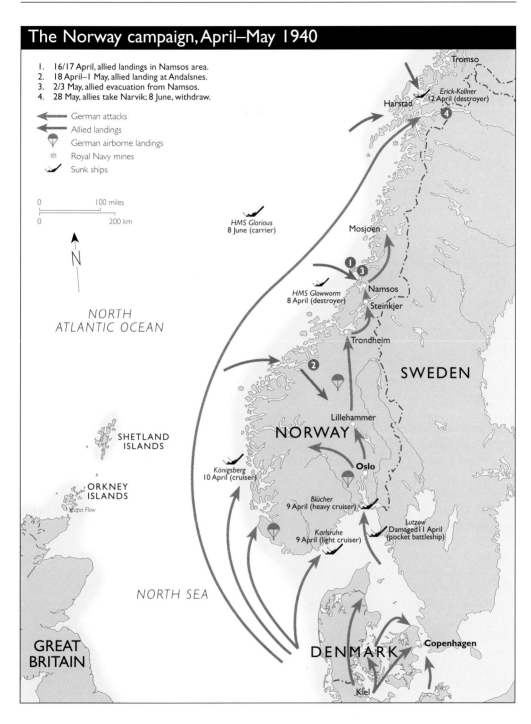

The Norway campaign, April–May 1940

1. 16/17 April, allied landings in Namsos area.
2. 18 April–1 May, allied landing at Andalsnes.
3. 2/3 May, allied evacuation from Namsos.
4. 28 May, allies take Narvik; 8 June, withdraw.

← German attacks
← Allied landings
⚑ German airborne landings
⬚ Royal Navy mines
↘ Sunk ships

0   100 miles
0   200 km

N

Tromso

Erick-Kollner
12 April (destroyer)

Harstad

HMS Glorious
8 June (carrier)

Mosjoen

NORTH
ATLANTIC OCEAN

HMS Glowworm
8 April (destroyer)

Namsos

Steinkjer

Trondheim

SWEDEN

SHETLAND
ISLANDS

Lillehammer

NORWAY

ORKNEY
ISLANDS

Scapa Flow

Königsberg
10 April (cruiser)

Oslo

Blücher
9 April (heavy cruiser)

Lutzow
Damaged 11 April
(pocket battleship)

Karlsruhe
9 April (light cruiser)

NORTH SEA

GREAT
BRITAIN

DENMARK

Copenhagen

Kiel

prevent the regular flow of ore, they would inflict a crucial blow against Germany's war effort. There was also some discussion of providing aid to the Finns in their struggle against the Soviets, and the easiest route to do this would be across Norway.

The Germans too were concerned at this vulnerability and resolved to take Norway, which would also provide bases for German surface vessels and submarines. First, however, German forces struck at Denmark. The Danes were ill prepared for a war against

German troops at the Polar circle in Norway. (AKG Berlin).

their powerful neighbor and the Danish government ordered that no resistance should be put up against the invading Germans. Denmark formally surrendered on the same day as the German invasion, 9 April 1940.

The Norwegians, however, were determined to put up a fight. Joining them were 12,000 British and French troops, originally earmarked to join the Finns in their battle against the Soviets. The Finnish capitulation meant that these Allied forces could endeavor to engage the Germans in Norway. Prompt action by the Germans meant that their invasion force landed first, at Oslo, Bergen, Stavanger, and Kristiansand. Fierce Norwegian resistance gave the Allies time and an Allied force landed in the vicinity of Trondheim, from where it engaged German forces heading north from Oslo. Despite success by the Royal Navy

against the German Navy, bad planning and confusion blighted the whole operation. After six weeks of fighting, the Allied troops were outfought and eventually evacuated on 8 June. The Norwegian government escaped to Britain and the Germans installed a puppet government under the Norwegian Vidkun Quisling.

France and the Low Countries

Having dealt with the Poles and secured Germany's eastern borders from the threat of attack by the Soviet Union, courtesy of the Molotov–Ribbentrop Pact, Hitler was finally able to deal with France. What was to happen now would astonish the world and turn traditional ideas of strategy and tactics on their head. To gain some idea of what the German armed forces managed to achieve in their invasion of France and the Low Countries, it is useful to draw a parallel with the First World War. Between 1914 and 1918 the armed forces of Imperial Germany had striven to defeat the combined forces of Britain and France. In four years they failed to achieve this aim and in doing so also suffered over 2 million dead as well as experiencing a revolution that swept away the Kaiser and all remnants of the overseas empire that he had tried so hard to establish. Now, in the spring of 1940, Adolf Hitler's new Germany would deal the western allies a crippling blow and achieve in five weeks, and for the loss of only 13,000 killed, what the armies of the Kaiser had not achieved in four years.

The eventual German plan of attack was arrived at only by much discussion and the intervention of fate as well as by judgement. The initial German plan was an uninspired repetition of the German advance of August 1914 and was based upon an invasion of Belgium. This operation, essentially a rerun of the Schlieffen Plan, was known as Case Yellow or *Fall Gelb*. The plan was a cautious one and reflected in part the concerns that many senior German officers had over the latent potential of the French army. Case Yellow would see German forces making a frontal assault on the Allied positions in Belgium and the Low Countries and a smaller, diversionary thrust of German forces through the densely wooded and seemingly impenetrable Ardennes region. The Allied response to this probable thrust was the Dyle Plan, which had the best French units and the BEF advancing into Belgium and Holland, thereby avoiding fighting in northern France as well as meeting the German advance.

This plan was not to last for long as the principal means of German advance. Hitler was not keen on the plan, believing that the potential for the German forces to stall and then become bogged down was too great. Hitler's vacillation over the plan was hastened by the crash landing, on 9 January, of a Luftwaffe aircraft with a German paratroops officer on board near Mechelen, in Belgium. In his possession was a copy of Case Yellow, the officer in question having been on his way to a conference in Cologne from his base in Münster. Although efforts were made to destroy the plans, enough remained of the documents to make it all too obvious that the Germans intended to strike at France, once again, through Belgium.

Once aware of the German intentions, the Allies changed the original Dyle Plan using a modification, known as the Breda variant, which called for the Allies to advance to the line of the Dyle River and also commit the bulk of their reserves. However, the capture of the German plans did nothing more than reinforce in the minds of the Allied generals, and the French Commander-in-Chief General Maurice Gamelin in particular, that their original assumptions about the likely German approach were correct.

The German response to the capture of the details of Case Yellow was also interesting. Hitler, as we have seen, was less than enthusiastic about the original idea and had some notions of his own about how to proceed. Simultaneously, and independently, General Erich von Manstein had been working on how to improve Case Yellow. The new plan, sometimes called the Manstein Plan, called for an audacious switch of effort, with the original, diversionary, thrust through the Ardennes now to be the main point of attack.

While the Ardennes was considered by most, the western allies included, to be 'impassable,' this was not the case. The Ardennes region did not have wide roads and was heavily wooded, with many streams and rivers. Despite this, it was passable, albeit slowly and with some difficulty. However, moving a formation the size that the Manstein plan envisaged through the narrow roads would be a tremendous gamble and would require a sophisticated deception plan and coordinated air support to ensure that the passage was neither discovered nor interdicted.

The Manstein Plan required Army Group A to effect a passage through the Ardennes, cross the River Meuse, and break out into the ideal tank country beyond. The formation

The original German plan for the invasion of France and the revised version

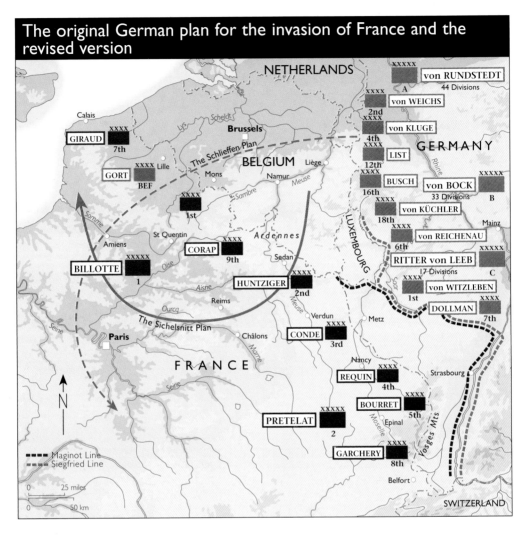

that was to have shouldered the original burden of the main thrust, Army Group B, was now to attack the Low Countries. Army Group B was to defeat the Dutch and Belgian forces while ensuring that the large numbers of quality British and French troops were 'fixed' to prevent them from acting against the main German effort. German aircraft were also tasked with ensuring that the Allies were kept well away from the Ardennes. The role of Army Group B in the north was crucial and likened to that of 'the matador's cloak,' a target tempting enough to persuade the Allied bull to engage it. Army Group C, further south, was to carry out a deception plan opposite the Maginot Line so as to confuse matters still further.

In March 1940, Hitler approved this plan, with additional embellishments from General Franz Halder. The role of Army Group B, the deception formation, has traditionally been given scant attention amidst the dynamic and audacious activities of the other German formations. However, the Germans themselves set a great deal of store by the deception plans in the north, designed not necessarily to change opinions of where the main effort of German activity would fall, but rather to confirm in the minds of senior Allied officers what they themselves had erroneously concluded.

The French wished, essentially, to recreate the Great War's set-piece battles of attrition, but they also wished to reverse the roles. In the French mind, it was the Germans who would be launching futile and costly attacks on well-defended French positions. The French had put considerable faith in the impressive fortifications of the Maginot Line, named after its instigator, the Defense Minister André Maginot. This interconnected line of fortifications stretched the length of the Franco-German border and was well nigh impregnable. The French did not believe that the Germans were likely to attempt to batter their way through. Instead the value of the Maginot Line was that it obliged any German invasion to come through Belgium, most probably in a repeat of the 1914 Stilton Plan, and thus defensive arrangements could be planned to deal with the threat along this predictable axis of advance.

The Allied strategy was essentially a long-term one: to draw the Germans into the

type of fighting that had worked so well between 1914 and 1918, that of fixed positions with an emphasis on attrition, hopefully wearing down the Germans in a fashion similar to the First World War. The Germans were aware of this and were determined that such a situation should not arise. Hitler knew the trenches of the First World War only too well and was determined to avoid a repetition. He sought to conduct a rapid campaign that would end the war quickly before its demands could overburden the German economy – itself not configured for a prolonged war. However, the German method of war fighting, too, was not without its weaknesses.

On 10 May 1940, German forces attacked the Low Countries Belgium, Holland, and Luxembourg. That same day the British Prime Minister, Chamberlain, resigned and Winston Churchill took over. Churchill's accession to power, however, could not stop the subsequent events. As well as

Panzerkampfwagen III Ausf. F, shown here in Yugoslavia in 1941. (US National Archives)

achieving their strategic aims in short order – the destruction of France and the isolation of Britain – the Germans did so by employing the experience they had gained in the Polish campaign to even more devastating effect.

It was after the France campaign that Germany's devastatingly effective tactics became firmly associated with *Blitzkrieg*, the term subsequently being misappropriated by dozens of historians and generals as a byword for fast, effective armored warfare. In fact, the term *Blitzkrieg* is one that would have thoroughly mystified German soldiers – officers and men alike – prior to 1940. It is not to be found in any German field manuals or army correspondence dealing with the conduct of operations. Rather, the term was mentioned first by an Italian journalist who used it to describe the type of fighting that he had seen in France and the Low Countries.

Crucially, then, *Blitzkrieg* is descriptive rather than prescriptive and was coined to describe what the German tactics did rather than the more elusive notion of how they did it. There was a good reason for this. The Germans themselves were not entirely sure that what they were doing was new at all. In fact, to a great extent the practices of fast thrust, encirclement, and then annihilation of the encircled troops were not new at all but had been practiced by German (and Prussian) armies for years before, and by other armies as well.

What was really new in 1940 was the way the Germans were achieving their fast thrusts to encircle their opponents. Whereas in 1870, against the French, the Prussians would have used cavalry, now the Wehrmacht deployed tanks. Of course, the Germans were not the only state to possess tanks. Unlike in the Polish campaign, with its heroic but tragic mismatches of Polish cavalry against German armor, the British

The British Vickers Mark VI used in light cavalry units was under-armored and under-gunned when compared to its German counterparts. (The Tank Museum, Bovington)

The French Char B1 tank was an impressive vehicle but its effectiveness was hampered by the penny-packet fashion with which it was employed.

and French were well provided with tanks. Also, contrary to popular perceptions about this phase of the war, if anything the tanks of the British and the French were of better quality than the German vehicles and certainly were not inferior.

However, while Britain had taken the lead in the conception and development of tanks in the First World War, and indeed had employed them in the most innovative and successful fashion of all the major combatants in the Great War, this lead had largely evaporated in the interwar years. Germany, despite the limitations imposed on her by the Versailles settlement, had conducted exercises with mock-tanks, sure in the knowledge that the tank would prove to be a major element on the battlefield.

Numerically, the French army on its own had more tanks than the Germans were able to field, which meant that when French tanks were combined with those deployed as part of the BEF, the western allies had a marked numerical superiority: 3,383 tanks deployed compared to Germany's 2,445. Numbers alone, however, are rarely the deciding factor in combat; obviously the quality of the equipment is also of vital significance. Here too the Anglo-French forces were not embarrassed. The French were equipped with a variety of tanks, the best of which were the Somua S35 and the Char B. These were more than a match for the German Panzer IIs and IIIs with which the majority of the German Panzer formations were armed. The Panzer divisions were equipped with 1,400 Marks I and II; 349 Mark IIIs, with a 37mm (1.5-inch) gun; and only 278 of the larger, 24-ton Mark IVs, armed with a far more substantial

The Battle of France: opening moves

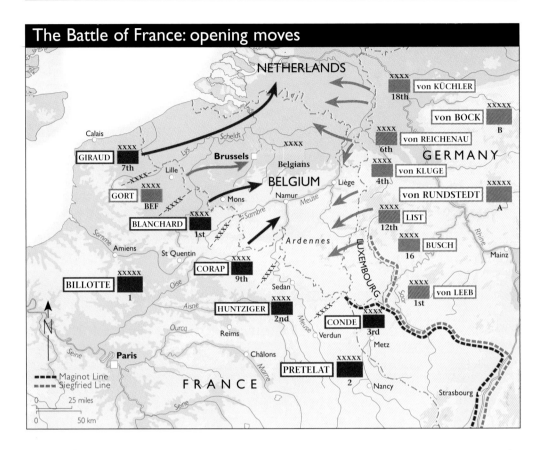

75mm (3-inch) gun. The Germans also had a number of excellent Czech-built tanks, a result of Germany's earlier takeover of that country.

In other areas, the French superiority was marked. The French army possessed far more artillery than the Germans, for example, fielding in the region of 11,000 pieces compared to the Germans' 8,000. But the Germans, although numerically weaker, did have mobile artillery: self-propelled pieces that equipped units deployed with Panzer divisions. These enabled them to be used in a far more dynamic and effective fashion than the static role favored by the French.

The Germans went to considerable lengths to convince the Allies that the main blow would come in the north. Airborne forces attacked bridges spanning the Mass, Waal, and Lek rivers, and cut the Netherlands in two. Parachute engineers also attacked the impressive Belgian fortress of Eben Emael, the linchpin of Belgium's defenses. In a move of

brilliant audacity, the German Paras negated all of Eben Emael's strengths. The fort was virtually impregnable from attack on the ground, such was the thickness of its walls. The Germans negated these strengths by landing on the roof of the fortress, using gliders that made no sound, and thus denied the defenders the opportunity to react earlier. The German troops blasted their way into the fortress and held it until relieved.

While Army Group B continued with its operations, further south, Army Group A penetrated the Ardennes. The Luftwaffe flew innumerable sorties on the first few days to protect the long and slow Panzer columns, terribly vulnerable in the narrow confines of the Ardennes roads. This was the Allies' main chance: if the advance of Army Group A had been spotted in time and sufficient force brought to bear, the outcome of the campaign would have been totally different. Instead, only light Allied air attacks threatened the German advance. The

German troops crossing the River Meuse in rubber
boats (Ian Baxter)

Germans encountered only moderate
resistance on the ground, mainly from
reserve formations, and this proved
insufficient to prevent the advance of the
Panzers – seven divisions all told. By the
evening of 12 May, these units had reached
the east bank of the River Meuse. The
German forces now demonstrated that they
possessed a host of attributes.

On 13 May the Germans successfully
crossed the Meuse at Dinant, courtesy of a
weir left intact by the French. Further south,
at the town of Sedan, German infantry and
combat engineers crossed the river at
astonishing speed under cover of a
concentrated air and artillery barrage.
German infantry established a foothold on
the western bank and within hours pontoon
bridges were constructed across the river and
Panzers began to cross. The all-arms

combination functioned perfectly, with all
the participating units knowing the aim of
their mission and all working in concert to
achieve it.

By the morning of 16 May, over
2,000 German tanks and in excess of
150,000 German troops had crossed the
River Meuse along a 50-mile (80km) stretch.
This breach of the Allied defensive line
effectively sealed the fate of the Allied armies
in northwest France and the Low Countries,
and paved the way for the decisive, strategic
success of the German assault. The German
formations, now in open country, began
their drive for the Channel in a
northwesterly arc, deep into the rear areas of
the British and French formations deployed
in Belgium.

The opportunity for the Allies to defeat
the apparently inevitable German advance,
however, was considerable. The German
lines of communication were by necessity
very extended, stretching back to the Meuse

Blown bridge over the River Meuse. (Ann Ronan Picture Library)

and beyond. These extended lines of communication were as much a feature of the German *Blitzkrieg* as anything and were a real vulnerability in the German methods of war fighting. Here was an opportunity for the Anglo-French to drive across the 'Panzer corridor' and regain some of the initiative.

If, as seems to be the case, there was not a massive gulf between the quality of the German armored formation and their Anglo-French opponents, nor was there a discrepancy in numbers between the Germans and the western allies. Indeed, the Anglo-French forces were able to field more armored vehicles than the Germans. How, then, can we explain the apparently overwhelming success of the Germans? Fundamentally it came down to the way in which armor was employed by the respective sides. The Allies used their tanks in small formations – what was known as 'penny-packets' – and as, in effect, little more than infantry support weapons rather than as weapons with an intrinsic, dynamic potential of their own. The BEF was almost completely mobile – the only participating army that could make such a claim. Yet, the British failed to make the most of this capability.

Other considerations did mark out German Panzers from their Allied counterparts. While armor and gun and speed might have been equal amongst the respective sides, the Germans had one crucial advantage. Most of the individual Panzers were equipped with radios. On the Allied side, only 20 percent of tanks were similarly equipped. It has been said elsewhere that the key technical development in the evolution of *Blitzkrieg* involved neither the tank nor the aircraft – both of which acquired in the 1930s the reliability, range, and speed needed for deep penetration operations – but the miniaturization of the radio. General Guderian had received his initial experience of combat as an officer in a signals unit, and his appreciation of the need for effective communication was vital. The miniature radio enabled the tanks to be used to maximum effect and facilitated the interaction between the armored formations and other branches or arms of the German armed forces.

The Germans also practiced their ideas of *Auftragstaktic* to a far greater extent in France and this was well served by the abundance of radios. The British and especially the French were nowhere near as up to date and were often suspicious of radio communications because of their susceptibility to interception. Von Kluge, Commander of the German 4th Army, summed up the importance of mission command in the German war-fighting method:

The most important facet of German tactics remained the mission directive, allowing subordinates the maximum freedom to accomplish their assigned task. That freedom of action provided tactical superiority over the more schematic and textbook approach employed by the French and English.

The following quotation from a 3 Panzer Division Report (1940) also stresses the type of officer that the German Panzer troops were seeking to recruit. It makes an interesting comparison with the earlier lecture of Captain Bechtolsheim:

One thing is sure – he who seeks formulae for commanding the mobile units, the pedantic type, should take off the black battledress [of the Panzer forces]. He has no idea of its spirit.

Apart from the numbers of tanks available to each side, the opposing sides (the British, French, Dutch, and Belgians on one hand, and the Germans on the other) were fairly evenly matched in terms of manpower totals and even equipment levels. It became fashionable to dismiss the Allies as outnumbered by the Germans – after all, the German population in 1940 was double that of France. But in fact, the western allies fielded 144 divisions with the Germans managing 141. Similarly, the western powers fielded 13,974 artillery pieces as against the Germans' 7,378.

In the air, the Allies again had greater numbers of aircraft, but the Germans had the advantage in terms of numbers of modern combat aircraft. They possessed the excellent Messerschimdt 109 fighter, which

The Battle of France: the race to the sea

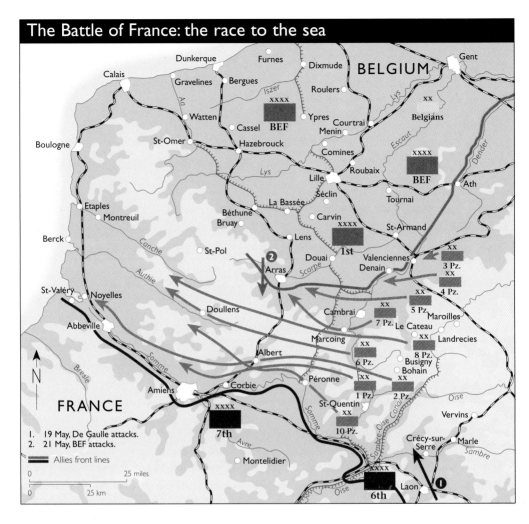

1. 19 May, De Gaulle attacks.
2. 21 May, BEF attacks.

▬▬▬ Allies front lines

0   25 miles
0   25 km

outclassed most Allied fighters. The British contribution to the air war did not include sending Spitfire aircraft to France, but only Hurricanes in limited numbers. The French Dewoitime was another good Allied aircraft, but the French air force had only around 100 machines. The Germans had used their Stuka dive-bomber to devastating effect against the Poles and the Luftwaffe possessed several hundred of these aircraft, using them in the close air-support role.

Once the lead German formations had crossed the Meuse and largely outrun their supporting infantry and logistical supplies, the western allies were presented with an opportunity to regain some of the initiative. The Germans lacked a coherent operational level plan; once they had crossed the Meuse,

they were in two minds as to where to go, either towards Paris or to take the Maginot Line from behind. Eventually the Germans decided to head for the coast and the Allies at last took their chance. The counterattack by the BEF at Arras, from the north, and the French from the south was indicative of the whole campaign. The Anglo-French forces did not operate in tandem and despite some initial success the Germans beat them off. This incident, however, did persuade Hitler to halt his leading Panzer elements and in doing so allowed the British and French vital time to organize the evacuation of their forces from Dunkirk.

Hitler, along with many senior German officers, could not quite believe how much their forces had achieved so quickly and still

The Battle of France: the Panzer breakthrough

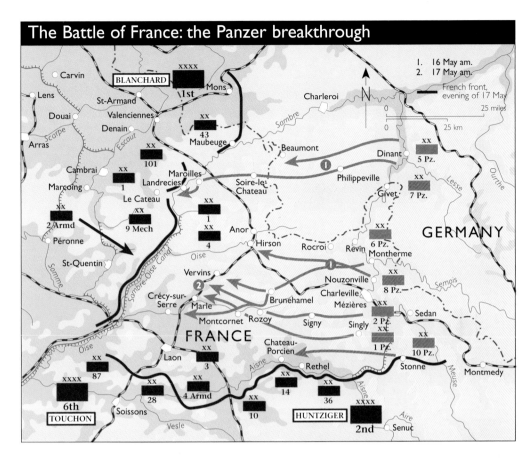

considered that the Allies were likely to strike back. They were wrong; Allied resistance had collapsed. After 5 June the Germans enacted *Fall Red*, the final phase of their plan to take France, occupying the rest of the country. Ironically, some elements of the Maginot Line were not defeated, but instead were ordered to give up in the general surrender of 22 June.

Operation Dynamo

Operation Dynamo began, officially, on 26 May 1940. By 4 June, 366,162 Allied troops had been successfully evacuated from the beaches around Dunkirk; of these, 53,000 were French. The price of the Dunkirk evacuations was not a light one. The RAF lost 177 aircraft over Dunkirk – losses it could ill afford – and the Royal Navy also had 10 escorts sunk. Even after the

operations around Dunkirk were over, the evacuation of Allied personnel continued from elsewhere in France, including France's Mediterranean coast, and up to the final cessation of operations on 14 August a further 191,870 were successfully rescued. In total 558,032 Allied personnel were evacuated from France between 20 May and 14 August.

Operation Dynamo has traditionally been represented, certainly in British historiography, as something of a triumph. In many respects it was so; the figures cited above are ample testimony to what was a fantastic achievement in rescuing so many Allied troops from captivity or death. A little over a month after the Dunkirk evacuation, however, three British journalists, Peter Howard of the *Sunday Express*, Frank Owen of the *Evening Standard*, and Michael Foot also of the *Standard*, wrote a devastating critique of the Dunkirk fiasco and the events that led

Queues wait for the navy at Dunkirk during Operation Dynamo, 29 May–2 June 1940. (Ann Ronan Picture Library)

up to it. This work, entitled *Guilty Men* and published with the authors' names concealed by the pseudonym 'Cato,' had a considerable impact on the general public.

Cato charged the disaster to have been caused by the prewar appeasers, men such as Ramsay MacDonald, Stanley Baldwin, and, most specifically, Neville Chamberlain himself. This notion became firmly embedded in the postwar psyche, certainly of the British. The fact that it accorded with what Winston Churchill was also to write, postwar, certainly helped this simplistic idea of appeasement to become the standard way of remembering the prewar years.

The collapse of France was to have a tragic and controversial postscript. The French Navy was large and formidable, and its inclusion in either of the warring sides would have proved significant. The British Mediterranean fleet was on a par with the Italian Navy, but the addition of the French would have tipped the delicate balance decisively. In the aftermath of the fall of French, the French fleet, under Admiral Darlan, ignored the provisions of the

Franco-German armistice, by which the French fleet was to have been disarmed under Axis supervision. Instead, a large portion of the fleet sailed to the Algerian ports of Oran and Mers el-kebir, where it had assembled by 29 June.

The British were understandably concerned about the future of the French vessels and considered a variety of options. They wished the French fleet either to join

The Ulster Rifles at Bray Dunes, 29-May–3 June 1940. (Topham Picturepoint)

Swastika over Paris. (Ann Ronan Picture Library)

with their Free French compatriots and fight alongside the British, to sail to neutral ports, or to scuttle their ships and thus prevent them being utilized by the Axis powers. A final option, described by Winston Churchill as 'appalling,' was that the Royal Navy would 'use whatever force was necessary' to prevent the ships being used against Britain. There were concerns, too, over what the German role might be – whether or not the Germans would apply pressure to force Admiral Darlan to comply.

Despite last-minute talks between the British and the French commander on the spot, no accommodation could be reached. The British, fearing the arrival of other French vessels, opened fire on 3 July, killing in the region of 1,200 French sailors. The British officer responsible for the failed negotiations wrote to his wife: 'It was an absolute bloody business to shoot up those Frenchmen ... we all feel thoroughly dirty and ashamed.'

The Battle of Britain

In the aftermath of the rapid defeat of France and the Low Countries, and the evacuation of the British Expeditionary Force from

Dunkirk, few believed that Great Britain could resist Hitler for long. Indeed, the American Ambassador to the Court of St James, Joseph Kennedy – father of the future president, John F. – believed that Britain was doomed and reported the same to Washington.

In the face of the British refusal to make peace, Hitler planned an ambitious amphibious operation, codenamed Operation Sea Lion, to invade the British Isles. With the fall of France and the scrambled evacuation of Anglo-French forces from the beaches of Dunkirk, Britain stood effectively alone against Nazi Germany. On 18 June Winston Churchill told the assembled House of Commons that 'The Battle of France is over, I expect that the Battle of Britain is about to begin.'

The next logical step for Adolf Hitler was the removal of Great Britain from the strategic equation, leaving him free, in due course, to turn eastwards and accomplish his principal aim: the destruction and subjugation of the Soviet Union and the establishment of German colonies in this new *Lebensraum*. How this was to be achieved was a dilemma for Hitler, initially at least. Hitler was not an implacable opponent of the British, partly for reasons of race, and professed to admire the British Empire. What, then, of the chances for peace between Britain and Germany?

Despite some apparent British warmth for the idea of a negotiated settlement, these sentiments were fundamentally insubstantial, based as they were on the false beliefs, first, that an acceptable peace could be arrived at and, second, that suggestions of impending British acquiescence might spur both the USA from her neutrality and the Soviet Union from her collaboration with Hitler. Hitler's enunciation of his willingness to negotiate with the British was made clear in a speech on 19 July. When there was no positive response from the British, the way was clear for the planning of Operation Sea Lion – the proposed invasion of Britain by German amphibious forces.

However, any successful landing in Britain would require effective German air superiority. To achieve that, the Royal Air Force had to be destroyed and this was to prove problematic. While the British Expeditionary Force that had been sent to France was representative of Britain's generally small army, it was the RAF and to a lesser extent the Royal Navy that had received the lion's share of defense spending in the run-up to the outbreak of war. To a large extent this money had been well spent, with new fighter aircraft such as the Hurricane being particularly effective and the even newer Spitfire setting new standards of performance for a fighter plane. The RAF had not deployed any of its Spitfire strength to France, instead holding them back for the likely air battle to follow.

The German ability to attain air superiority was hampered, in part, by the role for which the Luftwaffe had originally been conceived, that of tactical air support for troops on the ground. This focus on supporting army operations meant that in 1940 Germany lacked both a long-range bomber and a fighter with which to conduct a strategic bombing campaign. Indeed, over the course of the war Germany never rectified this position, although she did develop larger aircraft, notably the four-engine Condor, which was used for reconnaissance purposes.

The Battle of Britain has earned a significant place in British cultural as well as military history. Emboldened and honored in several trademark speeches, the 'few' of the RAF (together with a sizable Commonwealth and exile contingent of Czechs and Poles) successfully thwarted the aims of the Luftwaffe, obliging the date for Sea Lion to be progressively put off until it was finally cancelled. The Battle of Britain can conveniently be split into two distinct phases: the first from 10 July 1940 until 13 August, and the second from 13 August to 17 September, when Operation Sea Lion was postponed indefinitely. The invasion was finally cancelled on 12 October 1940.

On 19 July 1940, Hitler made a curious speech in the Reichstag. It was witnessed by American journalist William Shirer, who noted that Hitler said:

In this hour I feel it is my duty before my own conscience to appeal once more to reason and

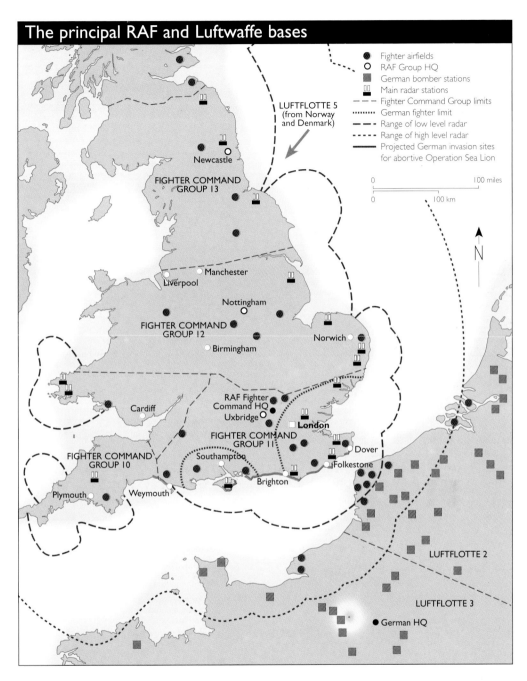

The principal RAF and Luftwaffe bases

Fighter airfields
RAF Group HQ
German bomber stations
Main radar stations
– – – Fighter Command Group limits
·········· German fighter limit
– · – Range of low level radar
– – – – Range of high level radar
——— Projected German invasion sites
for abortive Operation Sea Lion

LUFTFLOTTE 5
(from Norway
and Denmark)

Newcastle

FIGHTER COMMAND
GROUP 13

Manchester
Liverpool

Nottingham

FIGHTER COMMAND
GROUP 12

Norwich

Birmingham

Cardiff

RAF Fighter
Command HQ
Uxbridge

London

FIGHTER COMMAND
GROUP 11

Dover

FIGHTER COMMAND
GROUP 10

Southampton

Folkestone

Brighton

Plymouth

Weymouth

LUFTFLOTTE 2

LUFTFLOTTE 3

German HQ

0   100 miles
0   100 km

N

---

*common sense. I can see no reason why this war
must go on … I am grieved to think of the
sacrifices which it will claim. I should like to
avert them, also, for my own people.*

Shirer admitted to wondering what the
British reply to this clumsy overture for a
peaceful accommodation might be. It did

not take long for British feelings to be
made known. Shirer heard the BBC German
program announcer reply, unofficially,
'Herr Führer and Reichskanzler we hurl it
right back at you, right in your evil-smelling
teeth.' The official feeling was less
graphically expressed but did not differ
markedly.

The first phase of the German air assault was designed to secure German air superiority over the Channel – the so-called *Kanalkampf* – with the harbors of England's south coast and their associate shipping being the target. The second phase was known as the *Adlerangriff* (Eagle Attack) and began, on 13 August, with *Adlertag* (Eagle Day), which finally swept the RAF from the skies. The German bombers now concentrated on the RAF airfields themselves, destroying aircraft and pilots faster than the British could replace them,

Civilians try to sleep in a tube station during the Blitz. (Topham Picturepoint)

and threatening to overwhelm Fighter Command's ability to resist.

However, despite the odds mounting gradually in Germany's favor, a freak incident helped change the course of the battle and with it the strategic direction of the war. The accidental bombing of London by German aircraft led to a reciprocal British strike on Berlin. This prompted Hitler to his famous pronouncement, 'since they bomb our cities, we shall raze theirs to the ground,' and to the wholesale switch of German air effort toward the destruction of British cities rather than the RAF bases that defended them. On 7 September 1940, Reichsmarschal Hermann Göring told his senior Luftwaffe officers:

I now want to take this opportunity of speaking to you, to say this moment is an historic one. As a result of the provocative British attacks on Berlin on recent nights, the Führer has decided to order a mighty blow to be struck in revenge against the capital of the British Empire. I personally have assumed the leadership of this attack and today I have heard above me the roaring of the victorious German squadrons which now, for the first time, are driving towards the heart of the enemy in full daylight, accompanied by countless fighter squadrons … this is an historic hour, in which for the first time the German Luftwaffe has struck at the heart of the enemy.

This switch in tactics was a godsend for the RAF, since the breathing space allowed it to regroup and rejoin the battle. Now the battle focused on preventing German aircraft from reaching their targets over London or a score of other British targets.

While the target of German interest had changed, the ferocity of the air battles had not. Nor were losses in the air declining. During the first week of September, the RAF lost 185 aircraft and the Luftwaffe lost in excess of 200. The climax of the battle came on 15 September. Successive waves of German bombers, escorted by fighters, flew toward London and the RAF was stretched to the limit to try to contain them. The end

result was a success for Fighter Command – but only just – and a realization on the part of the Luftwaffe and Adolf Hitler that air superiority was unlikely to be achieved any time soon. 15 September, subsequently celebrated as Battle of Britain day, marked the end of German attempts to provide the right circumstances for an invasion.

The success of Fighter Command in staving off the imminent threat of German invasion did not, however, end the German bombing campaign against British cities. In fact the Blitz, as it came to be known, had only just begun. The Germans hit the Midlands city of Coventry on 14 November and followed this up with raids on Birmingham, Bristol, Manchester, and Liverpool. London, too, was obviously a massive target for the Luftwaffe as a symbol of British defiance as well as the heart of the governmental system. German bombing continued into 1941, with the last raids of the Blitz coming in May that year. German attacks on Britain resumed in the latter stages of the war as they launched initially the V1 rockets, later the V2, against London. These weapons did little real damage, but were sufficient to cause concern amongst the civilian populace.

Dieppe

Having successfully warded off the threat of imminent German invasion in 1940, the British gave considerable thought to hitting back at the Germans. One means, in the air, was the strategic bombing campaign, examined in more detail below. While the British had achieved some morale-building successes, such as the sinking of the German pocket battleship *Bismarck*, in 1942, there was widespread feeling that more should be done to strike at Hitler's 'fortress Europe.'

After the fall of France, Churchill had sanctioned the training and employment of 'commando' units to strike at targets in occupied Europe. He also created the Special Operations Executive (SOE) to 'set Europe ablaze.' The commando raids were successful in raising Allied morale and proving a nuisance to the Germans, but after successes at St Nazaire and Bruneval, the Allies determined on a more substantial foray into occupied Europe.

The aim of the Dieppe raid of August 1942 was limited in terms of what was to be achieved practically, but significant in terms of what the Allies hoped to learn about the problems involved in landing in enemy-held territory. The Allied plan, Operation Jubilee, aimed to land troops and armored vehicles on the beach and take and hold the port for 12 hours. The Allied forces, having secured the town, were to push inland and capture a German headquarters, gaining prisoners for interrogation and documents, and then to retreat back across the Channel. The Allies also hoped to cause enough damage, and to worry the Germans sufficiently, that the German High Command would withdraw forces from the Eastern Front and thereby take some pressure off the Red Army. This second aim was rather ambitious.

In the event, Dieppe was a disaster. The Allied force lost the vital ingredient of surprise when they ran into German shipping mid-Channel, and failed to secure the two headlands on either side of the main beach at Dieppe. Despite this setback, the main force landed on the beach and met considerable fire from German troops, well dug-in in blockhouses on the seafront and from the headlands. Still more Allied forces landed: 27 Churchill tanks reached the beach safely and 15 made it to the esplanade but no further.

Eventually, when it was apparent that no progress was being made, the mixture of British, Canadian, and American troops were withdrawn. This first composite Allied force, a foretaste of the Normandy landings two years hence, suffered 1,027 dead and a further 2,340 captured. However, the experience gained by the assault itself proved invaluable and prompted Admiral Lord Mountbatten to comment that 'for

every soldier who died at Dieppe, ten were saved on D-Day.' While Mountbatten's comments may have proved, ultimately, to be true, he was also the man in charge of the operation.

The Battle of the Atlantic

The Battle of the Atlantic was one of the most important battles waged during the Second World War (see *The Second World War (3) The war at sea* in this series). Britain's survival, and with her the survival of the struggle against Nazi Germany, depended on feeding her population and her war machine. British industry relied on raw materials from overseas to keep functioning. These goods had to be carried to Britain across, for the most part, the Atlantic Ocean. Without the outside lifeline, Britain's ability to sustain meaningful resistance against the Axis powers would have been seriously eroded, and eventually Britain would have been starved into submission.

The means of ensuring this constant lifeline were convoys – large numbers of ships marshaled together with naval support to beat off attacks from German submarines, or U-boats. As the tactics adopted by the German submariners became ever more sophisticated, such as hunting in large Wolf Packs, and as their submarines became ever larger and more seaworthy, so too did the weapons and tactics devised by the Allies in response. These included underwater echo-finding sonar, known as asdic, depth charges, and merchant ships converted to carry aircraft launched from a catapult. The development of surface radar was also vital in enabling surface warships to detect their submarine prey on the surface, when they were at their most vulnerable. This advance allowed the surfaced U-boats to be located in darkness and helped reduce the threat from the U-boat fleet, many of whose commanders preferred to attack at night and via the surface.

Alongside the vital convoys bringing raw materials to Britain between 1939 and 1943, the British also mounted an enormous effort to send supplies to the Soviet Union in order to prop her up against the German attack, after June 1941. While the Soviet authorities consistently downplayed the amount of British (and American) aid received, it was substantial. The convoy routes from Britain to the Soviet Union, usually the northern port of Murmansk, were fraught with danger from the German U-boats and from the perilous conditions of sub-zero temperatures and mountainous seas.

The war in the Atlantic cost the lives of thousands of sailors on both sides, but by the summer of 1943 it was the Allies who were decisively in charge. The U-boats of German Admiral Dönitz's navy sank 2,600 Allied merchant vessels and over 175 naval ships; 30,000 Allied sailors also died. On the German side, out of 1,162 U-boats built, 784 were lost. Of the German crews, a staggering 26,000 sailors out of a total number of 40,000 were killed, with 5,000 men taken prisoner. The German submarine arm had come close to strangling the Allied war effort, but the cost, as a proportion of the size of the service, was unmatched.

The strategic bomber offensive

One of the most controversial elements of the Second World War was the Allied

The strategic bombing campaign

DENMARK

NORTH SEA

BALTIC SEA

Kiel

Hamburg

Stettin

NETHERLANDS

Hanover

Magdeburg

Berlin

POLAND

Eissen

Dortmund

GERMANY

Dussoldorf

Cologne

Leipzig

Frankfurt

CZECHOSLOVAKIA

N

Stuttgart

FRANCE

Munich

AUSTRIA

* * Main areas of bombing

SWITZERLAND

0   100 miles

0   200 km

strategic bombing offensive against German-occupied Europe. The bombing of enemy cities was obviously not a new phenomenon; indeed, the Germans had carried out a limited campaign against Britain in the First World War using Zeppelin airships and Gotha aircraft. However, bombing had previously been essentially confined to a tactical role, if only because of the limitations of the fragile technology available.

Between the wars, much thought was given over to the idea of air power now being potentially a decisive weapon in war. The improvements in aeronautical engineering turned the fragile aircraft of 1914–18, with their limited range and payload capacity, into far more useful weapons. Air power theorists such as the Italian Guilo Douhet, the American William Mitchell, and the Briton Sir Hugh Dowding all prophesied that the bomber might shape the course of future

Arthur Travers Harris received the nickname 'Bomber' Harris. (Ann Ronan Picture Library)

wars. In Britain especially, the idea that the 'bomber will always get through' haunted interwar defense planners, conscious that Britain's traditional reliance on her naval strength would be inadequate. In the event this proved true, and the days of the battleship were numbered when HMS *Repulse* and HMS *Prince of Wales* were sunk by Japanese aircraft off Malaya in December 1941. However, the role of the bomber also proved to be far less decisive than the advocates of air power imagined.

On 3 September 1940, a year to the day after Britain had declared war on Germany, Winston Churchill declared that 'our supreme effort must be to gain overwhelming mastery in the air. The fighters are our salvation, but the bombers alone can provide the means to victory.' Churchill's personal commitment to the idea that the bomber could win the war was significant and had its origins in his position as the First Lord of the Admiralty when he ordered bombing raids on German Zeppelin bases. In 1917, however, Churchill's position was rather different; indeed, he considered then that 'nothing we have learned justifies us in assuming that they [German civilians] could be cowed into submission by such methods [large-scale bombing].'

On 22 February 1942, Arthur Travers Harris was appointed to the post of Chief of Royal Air Force (RAF) Bomber Command. He believed that area bombing or strategic

The Avro Lancaster bomber entered service in 1942 aand became the mainstay of the British strategic bombing campaign. (Topham Picturepoint)

bombing could win the war, and that by pounding Germany's industrial capability and destroying German cities, the will of the Germans, in tandem with the buildings around them, would collapse. This bomber offensive was no simple payback for the German raids on British cities. RAF Bomber Command pounded Germany for three years, culminating in the destruction of Dresden. The British bombers were joined in the summer of 1942 by the United States Army Air Force, whose more heavily armed B-17 'Flying Fortresses' bombed by day, and then the Allies struck around the clock in a campaign that the Germans called 'terror bombing.' Harris soon earner himself the nickname of 'Bomber' Harris amongst the general public, and 'Butch' or 'Butcher' Harris amongst his own men.

The tactics of the bombing offensive changed dramatically as the war progressed. Initial sorties were conducted by comparatively small, twin-engine aircraft such as the Vickers Wellington. The amount of ordnance that these aircraft could carry was small compared to the new, four-engine bombers that were coming into service by the time Harris took over. The introduction of the Short Stirling and later the Avro Lancaster revolutionized the distance that the bomber raids could fly, and thus the range of targets that could be hit, as well as increasing exponentially the bomb tonnage that could be carried.

A confidential report, prepared in 1941, highlighted some of the worrying problems associated with the bombing campaign and undermined the claims by the bomber

advocates that they were capable of winning the war on their own. The report, gleaned from aerial photographs of bomb targets, concluded that only one aircraft in three was able to get within 5 miles (8km) of its allocated target and that their accuracy was often even less impressive. The overall percentage of aircraft that managed to arrive within 75 square miles (194km^2) of the target was as low as 20 percent.

The net result of these inaccuracies was the creation and adoption of a new tactic, that of 'area bombing.' This eschewed the attempted precision raids of the past in favor of the destruction not only of factories but also of their hinterland: the surrounding towns, complete with the workers who lived there. This policy, unfairly attributed to Harris himself, was the product of a decision not to adopt terror tactics, but rather to ameliorate the shortcomings inherent in bombing so inaccurately. It was also hoped that the net effect of this type of destruction, to civilians, would result in the gradual erosion of morale amongst the civilian population. Potentially, it might either bring about the collapse of the will to resist or, more ambitiously, and more unlikely, induce a war-weary population to overthrow Adolf Hitler's administration.

The German response to the Allied bombing offensive was an impressive defensive arrangement that also grew in sophistication, in tandem with the bomber formations that it was conceived to thwart, as technological advances combined with tactical reappraisals. Luftwaffe General Josef Kammhuber was appointed to lead the air defense provision for the Reich and initially achieved some startling successes. He devised a grid system, with each square in the grid being 20 square miles (52km^2), and located a fighter in each square – held there by air traffic control and guided by radar to its target whenever a bomber or bomber formation entered its airspace.

British bomber tactics had initially focused on sending aircraft into occupied Europe singly, at intervals, and Kammhuber's approach was ideally suited to dealing with them. Later, however, with larger numbers of aircraft available, the British simply swamped the German defensive arrangements. In fact, much of the strategic value of the bombing campaign lay in the extent to which it diverted valuable resources of men and equipment away from vital front-line areas. The intensity of the bombing obliged the Germans to relocate artillery pieces as flak guns in Germany, rather than deploying them against the Soviets on the Eastern Front.

While concentrations of bombers, bringing all their firepower together, had improved their survivability in the skies over Germany, a second Allied initiative would help turn the course of the bomber offensive in a decisive fashion. This development was the introduction of fighter escorts for the whole duration of the bombing mission. It was made possible by the adoption of long-range fuel tanks, a practice that was very common when deploying fighters over long distances, but which had failed to be considered practical for combat purposes. The introduction of the Anglo-American P51 Mustang brought immediate results.

The strategic bombing campaign has been the cause of much controversy since the end of the Second World War. Elements of it, in particular Operation Gomorra (the firestorm raids on Hamburg) and the destruction of the baroque city of Dresden, are cited as evidence of how far democracies, too, are forced to go in a 'total war.' Alongside the many charges of wanton slaughter of civilians leveled at Bomber Command and its chief, Arthur Harris, are also less inflammatory ones. These allegations are more practical and center on the claim that, particularly in the early years of the war, the strategic bomber offensive was a criminal waste of men and materials that would have been better employed elsewhere. It has been argued that the overall impact on Germany's war-fighting ability was far less than it should have been, given the resources expended. However, as Richard Overy comments:

There has always seemed something fundamentally implausible about the contention of bombing's critics that dropping almost 2.5 million tons of bombs on tautly-stretched industrial systems and war-weary urban populations would not seriously weaken them. Germany ... had no special immunity.

Donald Edgar

In 1940 Donald Edgar joined the reserve element of the British army, the Territorial Army. As a barely trained private soldier in the East Surrey Regiment, he was sent to France along with rest of the British Expeditionary Force in much the same fashion as the original BEF had gone in 1914. Unlike the BEF of 20 or so years previously, however, the BEF of 1940 was not to halt the German advance. Edgar himself was captured by the Germans and spent the next five years as a prisoner of war of the Germans.

Donald Edgar, along with many thousands of young men, responded to a government appeal in March 1939 to join the Territorial Army. Adolf Hitler had occupied Czechoslovakia and it was apparent to many that the war was highly likely, if not inevitable. Edgar was in many ways an atypical private soldier, having attended Dulwich School, where he served with the Officer Training Corps, and Oxford University, from where he went to work as a stockbroker in the City of London. Edgar wrote of his enlistment that 'I was patriotic and there was a general feeling around in the City ... that it was time for us young men "to do something."' Edgar was also keen to volunteer, rather than await what he considered to be the inevitable conscription, declaring that 'No one in my family had ever been conscripted. They had always been volunteers.'

Edgar's unit was part of the British 12th Division, one of three 'second-line'

British troops pose in a well-construced position in the winter of 1939–40 in France. (IWM)

formations that Edgar considered to have been 'denied equipment and arms' and left to perform 'humdrum, menial tasks that left no time for training.' Edgar believed that the War Office thought these units were little more than a 'bloody nuisance.' This was an especial injustice for Donald Edgar and one that he felt all the more keenly because, as he put it, 'the ranks of these battalions contained a large proportion of the men who had patriotically responded to the Government's call in the spring. They were the real volunteers of the war.'

Edgar was called up in August 1939 and reported to his unit at the Richmond Drill Hall. He was fortunate to be made a number of financial guarantees by his employers in the City and he noted also that they gave him a 'handsome gift' to help him on his way, following a 'glass or two of champagne' at his farewell luncheon. This rather pleasant farewell was followed by a rude introduction to the realities of army life.

Edgar's unit moved to a camp near Chatham, a naval dockyard on the south coast of England, where they were each issued with five rounds of live ammunition and told, 'This is real guard duty, see?' Edgar's experiences of the regular British army were not positive: the conditions of their initial camp and the reception granted him by two regular warrant officers were described as 'lazy inefficiency' and 'only the first example we were to experience of the Regular Army's appalling state of slackness.'

At 11.15 am on 3 September, Edgar and his comrades listened to Prime Minister Neville Chamberlain's speech announcing Britain's declaration of war on Germany. On this momentous occasion, according to Edgar, Chamberlain gave his speech 'as though he were giving one of his budget talks on the radio when he were Chancellor.'

After a month or so at Chatham, Edgar's unit moved back to Richmond, where they were employed guarding 'vulnerable points' – the railway bridge over the Thames being Edgar's own duty. He recalled the mood that seemed to pervade the country during the 'phony war,' a mood that seemed to suggest

that Britain was doing all it could to honor her promise to Poland – even though that country had already been dismembered by Germany and the Soviet Union. Edgar thought the British had 'convinced ourselves that by mobilising the fleet and sending a few divisions to France we had done just about all that was necessary for the war against Germany.'

Despite Edgar's many complaints about the wider conduct of Britain's war effort, he himself was successively promoted through lance-corporal, corporal, and lance-sergeant, working in the unit's Intelligence Section. Edgar's unit spent a long and cold winter in England, relocating to Richmond Park and undergoing occasional training forays in the wide expanse of parkland on offer.

In March 1940, Edgar's unit was told that they were to proceed to France where they would at last 'train hard and receive all our equipment from supplies already there.' They embarked for France and landed at Le Havre, before moving to a large château in the Normandy countryside. Edgar's bilingual capability led to his being appointed as a translator and he participated in a number of meetings between his battalion commander and the local French military authorities. These meetings Edgar termed 'predictably uncomfortable,' but 'no more so than those held at the highest level between French and British generals.' Given the lack of adequate coordination between the French and British forces in France, it is interesting to see these considerations replicated at the battalion level.

Because of his evident language capabilities, Edgar was tasked with translating a number of documents that the French had passed on to their British counterparts. These documents concerned the French arrangements to defend the important dock areas of Le Havre, but they had wider implications for the forthcoming fighting – implications and conclusions that had Edgar concerned: 'When I came to translate the French documents I was shaken out of my complacency. The analysis envisaged a war of movement as a distinct possibility with the breakthrough of German armoured columns deep into the rear areas.' These conclusions, as we have seen, were to prove extremely accurate. As Edgar also noted, however, the officers now leading his and many other battalions of the British and French armies had seen service on the Western Front during 1914–18 and this was not the type of war they were accustomed to.

Donald Edgar obviously had many criticisms of the British army. Many of these may be dismissed as the typical grumbling of any soldier; some are more valid, however. Edgar informs us that many units were short of machine guns and antitank weapons, what they did possess being far less than the official complement. What Edgar considered to be the worst omission was one of the areas in which the Germans had both a marked superiority and, perhaps even more crucially, a greater understanding of its importance: communications. While Edgar conceded that the regular BEF units were provided with wireless and telephone communications, the men of the three 'labour' battalions had neither and 'went forward blind.' This was an unsatisfactory state of affairs at any time, but given the manner in which the Germans utilized new technology in combination with rather less original tactics, these shortcomings were particularly damaging to the effective conduct of the war on the Allied side.

Despite all the problems identified by Donald Edgar, writing on the eve of battle, he was not totally pessimistic about the future. Edgar believed that 'the spirit of the men was still high – in spite of everything.' Although Edgar's reminiscences at this point perhaps border on the sentimental, he comments that 'it is with a bitter smile that those English Territorial battalions [went] to battle in May 1940 with a raucous laugh, singing a silly song: "Roll out the barrel."'

Edgar's experiences of the fighting are interesting. He noted that his:

Intelligence section travelled in three handy 15 cwt trucks and were just about self contained. We had ample ammunition for our rifles and brens and reserve supplies of petrol … I made sure … that we had plenty of cigarettes and bottles of whisky and brandy.

Edgar thought that these preparations were:

to prove vital in the following days. It gave us a certain confidence, and an army marches – even in trucks – on its stomach. A swig or two of spirits and a cigarette also help to keep up morale. Other units in the area were reduced to begging for food and water.

While Edgar's unit waited for further orders he noticed a 'tall figure in khaki standing on some rising ground … wearing one of those beautifully-tailored near ankle-length great-coats favoured by senior officers. I looked again and saw the red tabs and realized he was probably a Brigadier or General.' Edgar was shocked to see that the officer was 'unshaven and bore marks of dishevelment,' which Edgar considered unforgivable, observing: 'I am shaved. So are my men. That's discipline … Generals should never appear unshaven or unkempt. They must always be immaculately turned-out. It is part of an army's morale!'

In all probability, however, it would have taken more than morale alone to save the British (and indeed French) position in France in May 1940. While awaiting further instructions, Edgar ran into a column of refugees who included in their number a former British soldier of the 1914–18 war. This man, now in his forties, had met a French girl during that war and returned after leaving the army to marry her and set up a business renting holiday cottages. The man quizzed Edgar about the development of the fighting and after Edgar informed him that he expected the French to counterattack, the former British soldier, Edgar observed, 'sniffed disbelievingly.'

The evident disbelief was to prove reasonably well founded, as the counterattacks that were planned, notably the initially successful BEF attack at Arras, soon ran out of steam. Edgar found himself and his men surrounded by the fast-moving German forces. After retreating toward the small French port of Veules, Edgar was given instructions to take a message to his battalion commanding officer at St Valery. When he made the obvious point that 'it won't be easy, Sir, the French tell me that the Germans have cut just about all the roads,' Edgar was told that 'this message must get through.' Edgar and two other men set off, and while they were gone, the officer who had ordered Edgar to St Valery evacuated the rest of the unit.

Edgar managed to rejoin his unit and with men from other units began the march towards the sea. Reaching St Valery, they were told that 'evacuation was now impossible' due to the deteriorating situation, and tentative plans were made to attempt to break through the German lines in small groups. These plans, too, came to nothing with the announcement on 12 June of a cease-fire. Edgar and some 8,000 BEF soldiers went into captivity. Edgar himself survived five years in a German prisoner-of-war camp, but had not fired a single shot in anger during the whole duration of the battle for France.

Propoganda poster showing Churchilll. (Topham Picturepoint)

Colin Perry

Colin Perry was just 18 years old when war broke out in September 1939. He lived in the London suburb of Tooting and worked as a clerk in the City of London. He kept a journal of his thoughts and experiences from June 1940, just after the fall of France, until November 1940. These few months were crucial for Britain, and therefore for the whole remaining effort to thwart Nazi Germany's goals. Britain stood alone during this period and endured the constant threat of invasion and aerial bombardment. Colin Perry's account of life during these dark months is fascinating, as it reflects the hopes and fears of a young man who cannot help seeing the war as much as an adventure as something to be feared.

Once the news of France's capitulation was known, young Colin Perry's account was full of contradictory ideas and thoughts. He said 'condemn him to hell who is responsible for bringing Britain to the verge of existence – Britain whom we love and whom our ancestors placed into the leadership of the world.' Colin considered, from a viewpoint of considerable personal disappointment, that 'Red tape is our course. Maybe I'm embittered at having passed the Medical A1, just because I do not possess a school certificate I cannot get into the flying part of the RAF.' He was also a young man with considerable imagination. While listing all the young women to whom he had been attracted in the past, he noted that one, a German girl with whom he had spent 'a day and a half' in London in 1938, was 'charming and extraordinarily attractive but I suspect her of 5th column work'!

On 17 July, Colin reported the following dramatic developments:

Tonight in our proud Island prepare ourselves for the word that the invader has commenced his attack. The air raid wardens have passed information round that the Military at Tolworth will tonight throw up a smoke-screen, which will spread and envelop the whole metropolis, blot out vital objectives and generally throw invading hordes into confusion.

His dramatic smokescreen did not materialize and instead he paid a visit to the cinema, where he saw the propaganda film, *Britain at Bay*. The impact of this on Colin was dramatic. He claimed it 'made me want to join the army tomorrow' – doubtless the intention of the production.

Colin, for all his focus on the war and the preparations for the imminent invasion, betrays the preoccupations of teenagers the world over in his writing. Interspersed with his comments about joining up are many about girls, particularly one whom he saw on a regular basis, but whom he had not as yet summoned up the courage to ask out. Colin, who could imagine himself fighting the enemy, could not similarly conceive of this girl taking him seriously.

On 19 July the RAF, hard pressed at this point in the Battle of Britain, contacted Colin to inform him, in a 'circular,' that they would be postponing any application of his for aircrew for at least a month. Colin's response to this was that 'I do want to get in the Services before the winter, as I shall then save myself the price of a new overcoat, hat etc.' While visiting a friend's flat near Chancery Lane, Colin thought that the many barrage balloons rising above the city looked very much like so many 'soft, flabby, silvery floating elephants.'

On 30 July, Colin experienced his first raid when a solitary German aircraft dropped bombs on Esher, killing and wounding five people. The searchlights in the vicinity of Colin's house were used only briefly, in the hope of persuading the pilot that he was in fact over a rural area rather than the fringes of London itself.

As July became August, Colin became increasingly convinced that the long-predicted German invasion was likely to come sooner rather than later. On 9 August he was writing that 'the invasion did not come yesterday. Now people think Hitler will try today or tomorrow, both dates of which are favourable to his star. I maintain he will strike on 22nd of this month.' Interestingly, Colin at times considered the unthinkable: what life might be like under a German occupation. He was particularly concerned with the fate of Neville Chamberlain and speculated that 'in the event of British defeat – God forbid – he would be produced like Laval and old Pétain. I cannot understand just why Churchill does not kick him out.'

While Churchill and many Britons were doing their utmost to convince President Roosevelt of the necessity of joining with Britain to resist German aggression, 18-year-old Colin had his own thoughts about the USA. He believed that the developments in the war to date had now obliged the USA to 'realise how dependent they were upon us':

America would not help us at all by entering into this war. They are in greater danger from the Nazis than ourselves if only they but realised it. Riddled with fifth column, a bastard race, with a conflict of opinion they must maintain a two-ocean navy, which they can't.

Colin's thoughts and feelings reflect the mindset of a comparatively immature youth, but the war predictably impinged on his life in a way that he had not thought possible. On 21 August, a friend of his family, Mrs Block, called to say that her neighbor had been killed in an air raid: 'a bomb fell directly on her Anderson shelter. Her road had been machine-gunned.' Needless to say, this reawakened Colin's wishes to fight again and he drifted off into thoughts of joining the RAF:

There is nothing I would like better in this world than to be a fully-fledged fighter pilot awaiting a gigantic air offensive, lounging on the rough grass talking with Pete and Steve ... by the side of our aircraft as we awaited the signal to scramble.

While Colin's youthful bravado kept his and his friends' spirits up through this episode and many other minor raids, involving sparse formations of German aircraft, as the days passed through the summer the bombing intensified and Colin's mood darkened slightly. On 28 August he wrote: 'I cannot say how tired I am. I have never known how much sleep means. Since the early hours of Friday morning the Nazi bombers have been over continuously, in consequence we have had warning after warning.'

Colin's description of this event is particularly interesting, as it sheds light on the opinions of ordinary people on the ground towards the bombing. Colin thought that 'nuisance bombers,' as their title suggests, were more of a problem than the large-scale raids. The 'nuisance' aircraft came over singly or in pairs and their aim was simply to prompt air-raid sirens and precautions on the ground. Colin said, 'It is obvious that these raiders are sent only to shake our morale. It is these that are responsible for keeping all Londoners awake and in their shelters for hours every night.' The net result was that many people, responding directly to this German tactic, chose to demonstrate their defiance and their need for sleep, by 'taking the risk of staying in bed when they [the bombers] come over.'

Colin, true to his ideas, 'mostly stay[ed] in bed ... it was impossible during the early hours of Tuesday to do so, however, as every ten minutes or so for 6 hours the German raiders passed right over our flat.' Colin's thoughts on all of this were simple: 'I may be tired and somewhat depressed, but by God all this only makes us the more determined to smash blasted Hitler once and for all. The whole of Britain is now more determined than ever.'

This determination, which many have subsequently termed the spirit of the Blitz, was to be severely tested in the coming weeks as the German raids intensified. On Monday 9 September, Colin's tone changed considerably. Gone was the jaunty defiance and cockiness, and in its place was a genuine sense of shock:

London, my London, is wounded, bloody. The sirens sounded last night at 7.59 and straightway [sic] 'planes were diving and booming overhead. I saw a whole ring of anti-aircraft fire mark out Clapham Common high in the sky ... Becton gasworks has been hit ... we stayed in the shelter for a while, but I kept rushing around with my binoculars. At one period the firing was so intense I dare not risk the 18 yards' run to the shelter and stood against a concrete wall, flat. The 'all-clear' sounded at 5.30 am.

But worse was to come. Colin, of course, had to make his way to work that day, exhausted and strained from the excitement and lack of sleep of the previous night. After taking the underground as far as Bank, he ventured out as far as Princes Street and was greeted by a scene of utter devastation along 'a Princess Street hitherto unknown to me.'

Cars packed the road, people rushed here and there, calm and collected, fire services, ambulances. Refugees from the East End, cars and bikes, luggage and babies all poured from [the] Aldate direction ... a high explosive bomb had fallen clean in the middle of Threadneedle Street, just missing the Bank's main entrance and somehow missing the old Royal Exchange. Here in the heart of the City ... next door to my office, always considered by me as untouchable, had descended the cold and bloody stab of Hitler. In the office the windows were cracked and smashed ... dust and earth covered my chair and then I beheld the 3rd floor. No windows, debris, dirt. I was staggered as I beheld the spectacle. I took myself to the roof with my binoculars and saw the most appalling sights. All over the heart of the City fires were burning, hoses playing ... I cannot describe my feelings, they were all too dumbfounded and I was incredulous.

Colin's diary takes an abrupt turn at this juncture. He writes:

I knew then that my diary is not 'exciting' reading of happening to be envied, it does not really show the spirit of glamour which I take from these raids, but it simply shows the callousness, the futility of war. It depicts bloody people, smashed bodies, tragedy, the breaking up of homes and families. But above all, high above this appalling crime the Nazis perpetrate, there is something shining, radiating warmth above all these dead and useless bodies, it is the spirit, the will to endure, which prevails.

Colin Perry joined the merchant navy in the autumn of 1940 and on 17 November joined HMT *Strathallan* as the ship's writer. He survived the war and published his diary in 1971.

The end of the beginning

At the end of 1943, the position of Adolf Hitler's Germany looked remarkably different from that of the end of 1941. In December 1941, Hitler's empire had stretched from the Atlantic seaboard of France as far east, nearly, as Moscow. By the end of 1943 the western border remained, but in the east the limit of German expansion was moving slowly, but remorselessly, westwards.

Much had happened between 1939 and 1943. Germany's star, so long in the ascendant, was at last beginning to wane. The reasons for this are several. First, the entrance of the United States into the war in December 1941 changed the whole strategic complexion of the conflict. Hitler's presumptive decision, taken on 11 December 1941, to declare war on the USA is still a curious one. Was it a foolish and ultimately fatal decision or rather a natural response to what was something of an inevitability?

President Roosevelt's support of the British war effort to date had been considerable, and American sympathy was clearly on the side of the British and against Nazi Germany. The USA's actions, before the German declaration of war, were hardly the actions of a state intent on maintaining her neutrality. The Lend-Lease Act, whereby Britain's productive shortfall in war materials was redressed on a pay-later arrangement, dramatically altered Britain's military fortunes when she was at a particularly low ebb. However, Roosevelt still had many dissenters at home, who opposed American participation in the war in Europe. Hitler's decision removed any reason for hesitancy, as did the Japanese strike at the US Pacific Fleet at Pearl Harbor, which provided ample demonstration, if one were needed, that the USA could no longer sit on the sidelines.

Through the early months of 1943, the western allies were preparing their plans and harboring the resources necessary to launch Operation Overlord, the invasion of occupied France. At the end of 1943, Hitler's European empire was still a mighty edifice. Already, however, its borders were being rolled back in the east and in the south. The Red Army success at Stalingrad in early 1943, and in August 1943 in the enormous tank battle of Kursk, would prove significant (see *The Second World War (5) The Eastern Front* in this series).

The German attack on the Kursk salient was the last major offensive that Germany mounted in the east. The offensive, originally planned for early May 1943 – the first time that the ground was sufficiently hard to bear large-scale movement of heavy equipment after the spring thaw – was delayed considerably. Only in early July did Hitler give the order to commence the attack. Hitler's reluctance to commit his forces sooner was based on a belief that the longer he delayed, the stronger his armored formations would be. Also greater numbers of the new Panther tank could be deployed. Large quantities of new weapons were produced by Germany's now almost fully mobilized economy, but the delay also gave the Soviets additional breathing space to reorganize, reequip, and prepare their defenses in depth.

The net result may be seen as sweeping away many of the assumptions on which the Second World War was grounded. The German Wehrmacht, the instigator of fast, maneuver-style *Blitzkrieg*, was committed by its Commander-in-Chief to an attritional assault on prepared enemy positions, and in doing so played to their strengths not those of the Germans. Hitler, increasingly assuming more and more direct control over his armies in the field, was now, apparently, turning his back on the audacious thinking that had characterized much of his success between 1939 and 1943. After Kursk the German army fought a long, slow retreat that would climax in the battle for Berlin itself, the capital of the Reich that was to have lasted 1,000 years.

In July 1943 the first major Allied incursions into occupied Europe occurred when the Allies invaded Sicily. Two months later, in September, they landed on the Italian mainland and began their drive north. The German forces made the most of the difficult terrain and the narrow Italian peninsula to ensure that the Allied advance would be slow, and that German troops would not be driven out of Italy until the general surrender in 1945. However, the physical presence of Allied troops on European soil was significant and indicative of the turn of the tide.

In June 1944 came two events of enormous significance for Hitler's Reich. The first, on 6 June 1944, was the Allied assault on Normandy: Operation Overlord or D-Day as it has entered the popular lexicon. This was the opening of the second front that Stalin had long demanded to take the pressure off the Red Army. Although it had taken far longer than Stalin had hoped, and caused considerable tension with the 'Grand Alliance' as a result, the Normandy landings now obliged Hitler and his increasingly hard-pressed forces to face their strategic nightmare – a war on two fronts.

While the fighting in Italy did tie down large numbers of valuable German troops and resources, Italy was always unlikely to be a decisive theater of operations. As if to demonstrate the problems and conflicting priorities of such a war, the Soviets launched their largest offensive to date on 22 June, the third anniversary of the start of Operation Barbarossa. This new offensive, Operation Bagration, succeeded in destroying Army Group Center and was a massive blow for the Wehrmacht.

Hitler's empire shrank progressively from June 1944, as the Soviets advanced relentlessly from the east and the British–American–Canadian–Free French forces from the west. All was effectively lost for Germany, but her resistance did not slacken. In the fighting in the east, the Germans fought bitterly for every inch of ground. The knowledge of what the Soviets would exact in revenge for German behavior in the east and, for many, a fundamental ideological struggle between communism and national socialism underpinned the ferocious struggle. In the west, too, the German resistance was stiff and the Allies gained ground only slowly. British General Bernard Montgomery's plan to end the war quickly, by seizing the vital bridges over the Rhine in Operation Market Garden, was a failure and compelled the Allies to edge forward inch by inch.

In December 1944, Hitler showed again, briefly, that there still existed an offensive capability in the German war machine, launching an attack toward the Belgian port of Antwerp, from where the Allied advance was being provisioned. This campaign in the Ardennes became known as the 'Battle of the Bulge' and demonstrated once again the tactical capability of the German army. However, Germany was fast losing the ability to sustain an offensive and the fighting in the Ardennes soon petered out with no German success.

Although the German forces kept fighting until May 1945, it was a futile battle against the odds. The Soviets gave no quarter in their struggle to defeat Nazi Germany: having experienced firsthand the commitment and brutality of Nazi racial ideology, they paid the Germans out in kind. Perhaps appropriately, the Allies decided at the Yalta Conference of early 1945 that it would be the Red Army that captured Berlin, despite the astounding progress being made by the Allies in the west. The Germans made the Soviets fight for the capital, inflicting in excess of 100,000 casualties, but the Red Flag was raised on the Reichstag, a dominant image of the Second World War.

Part II
The war at sea

The long, graceful forecastle of HMS Hood. (George Malcolmson Collection)

Naval power

At sea, the British and German navies possessed the greatest accumulation of naval firepower in history, yet the test of war proved it to be indecisive and disappointing. The hallmark of naval power by 1914 was the battleship, and the rival fleets finally met at the Battle of Jutland on 31 May 1916, the outcome of which is still hotly debated today. The statistics were impressive: 28 British battleships and nine battlecruisers with a host of supporting destroyers under Admiral Sir John Jellicoe fought 16 German battleships, five battlecruisers, and smaller escorts commanded by Admiral Reinhard Scheer. On paper, it was a tactical victory for the Germans, who sank 111,980 tons of British ships and inflicted 6,945 casualties in return for a British tally of 62,233 tons sunk and 2,921 German casualties. Strategically, however, the Royal Navy emerged triumphant, for the balance of power remained firmly on the side of the British, whose numerically superior fleet (unlike the High Seas Fleet) was ready for operations the following day. Yet, it was no Nelsonian victory: glory was absent from this battle, replaced by a controversy about the failings of the Royal Navy that has raged to the present day.

Did Britannia still rule the waves? This was a question reinforced by a new threat after 1916 – the submarine or the U-boat – which nearly strangled Britain through sinking merchant ships, the vital supply links of the nation. In April 1917 alone, the height of German unrestricted submarine warfare, total sinkings amounted to approximately 900,000 tons, a figure that simply could not be sustained in the short term. In terms of outlook and equipment the Royal Navy was ill-equipped to meet this threat. For hundreds of years, the surface fleet and the decisive battle had been at the core of Royal Navy operations, but now it

faced an adversary against which these two elements appeared unsuitable. Submarines were not designed to be involved in fleet actions (they were very vulnerable on the surface and had limited endurance) and tended to hunt through the vast oceans as single units.

The other vexing question was how to find such an elusive foe. Unsurprisingly, considering its aggressive ethos and desire to seek the enemy, the Royal Navy adopted the wrong solution. Its hunting packs of destroyers patrolled apparently empty oceans with little success, whilst merchant ships were sunk in vast numbers. Desperation forced British politicians in May 1917 to order the Royal Navy to adopt the logical yet ostensibly inglorious convoy system, which rectified the rapidly declining strategic situation at sea. Shackled to the pace of the slowest ship, naval escorts at last encountered enemy submarines (drawn naturally to the merchant vessels) and by the use of gunfire, depth charges, and hydrophones finally controlled the threat to merchant ships.

The war ended with the armistice signed on 11 November 1918. The terms of the armistice marked the demise of the German High Seas Fleet of nine battleships, five battlecruisers, and over 50 supporting warships, which was subsequently interned under the control of the Royal Navy at Scapa Flow. The following year, on 21 June 1919, this fleet scuttled itself – a last gesture of a once powerful force.

The Allies, joined by the United States in the final year of the war, now counted the cost of four years of warfare that had been conducted on an unprecedented scale. The expenditure had enormous consequences for nations and their navies in the interwar period. Countries and economies in Europe lay in ruins, debt accumulated, and the postwar global recession grew remorselessly, reaching a peak with the Wall Street Crash of 1929. Britain faced huge financial problems in the 1920s and 1930s, compounded by the global commitments of empire, and these called for stringent budgeting as well as cutbacks in standing armed forces.

For the Royal Navy, the golden age of ship construction was over and it faced a variety of new challenges with ever-diminishing resources. One of the great technological leaps of the Great War emerged in the form of maritime aircraft, which would dominate the Second World War at sea. The Royal Navy launched the first air strike from the sea on German facilities at Cuxhaven on 25 December 1914. The aircraft (but not the fledgling aircraft carriers) of the Royal Naval Air Service were amalgamated into the new Royal Air Force in April 1918 and allowed to stagnate in the shadow of the 'bomber' ethos of this new service.

The British government responded to mounting financial pressures with severe cutbacks in defense spending, such as the Geddes axe in 1921, the 10-year rule (no major war was envisaged for at least 10 years in the 1920s) and arms treaties to limit naval construction, of which one of the most significant was the Washington Naval Agreement of 1921–22. These agreements and cutbacks led to an inevitable and dramatic decline in the strength of the Royal Navy, but for the government they represented a welcome respite from high defense spending.

Under the new National Socialist (Nazi) Party regime, headed by Hitler, that rose out of the issues of the post-Versailles German state, the German navy (Kriegsmarine) enjoyed the benefits of starting anew, without the hindrance of existing force structures. It embarked on a major capital ship program (breaking treaty limits with the 52,000-ton battleship *Bismarck*) as well as significant U-boat construction.

The neighboring powers of Europe watched German rearmament in the 1930s

with mixed emotions. In Italy, Hitler found an ideological ally in Benito Mussolini, who shared Hitler's right-wing views and desire for expansion, reflected in the Italian invasion of Abyssinia in 1935. At sea, Italy possessed a formidable navy that by 1940 would swell to six battleships, 19 cruisers of various sizes, 61 destroyers and 105 submarines, making it a highly useful asset for German strategic plans in the Mediterranean.

France watched the revitalization of Germany's armed forces with great trepidation, and successive French administrations tried to use the League of Nations (founded in 1920), treaties, and finally France's armed forces to contain this longstanding threat. Though France possessed a significant navy that contained five battleships and battlecruisers, one aircraft carrier, and 15 cruisers with a host of supporting escorts, the state placed greater weight on the Maginot Line, a line of fortifications between the two countries started in 1929. Sadly, it proved to be strategic folly as the German army bypassed it in 1940 by invading Belgium.

In the Far East, Japanese expansionism into Manchuria in 1931, encouraged by militarism, exposed the weakness of the League of Nations. The lack of standing armed forces and the unwillingness of European nations to go to war over a country in Asia meant that the League could offer only moral condemnation of this overt aggression. Such inaction undoubtedly offered considerable encouragement to would-be expansionists like Hitler and

The Washington Naval Agreement
    The Washington Conference led to a series of agreed limitations on naval construction and the size of fleets between the major powers. It is often remembered for the famous 5:5:3 ratio (5=500,000 tonnage quota) between Britain, the United States and Japan with smaller ratios for other nations.

The standard battleship of the First World War mirrored the revolutionary HMS *Dreadnought*, produced by the Royal Navy in 1906. This ship revolutionized naval warfare by its size (18,000 tons), speed (21 knots) and firepower (10 12-inch guns), which rendered all other ships of this category obsolete and triggered a naval construction race between Britain and Germany. (Naval Historical Foundation, NH 63367)

Mussolini. Japan also flouted the treaty obligations concerning warship size in the 1930s and secretly built the world's biggest battleship, the 70,000-ton *Yamato* with 18.1-inch (460mm) guns.

The only possible counterweight to this threat to European interests in the Far East, the United States, refused to join the League in 1920 and was tightly focused on returning to isolationism after the bitter experience of the First World War. Under President Roosevelt, America was wracked with financial problems in the aftermath of a global recession that left thousands of people near to starvation in poorer states

such as Oklahoma. Roosevelt realized the mounting danger in Europe, but domestic pressures to remain in isolation tied his hands. Nevertheless, the US Navy underwent a significant buildup in terms of capital ships from 1933 onwards, a period in which the famous Iowa class of battleship was designed.

Ironically, Britain's declaration of war in 1939 was an unpleasant surprise for the German armed forces, whose rearmament program was designed for war not in 1939, but rather in the early to mid-1940s. The German Navy's 'Z-Plan' of 1938 was testimony to this fact, and the envisaged four aircraft carriers, 13 battleships, and 250 U-boats were little more than sketches on a design table. Neither side was truly prepared for the Second World War, but for Britain and France, the odds of winning a war were better now than they would be when Germany was fully mobilized for war.

Reluctant adversaries

Britain's Royal Navy ended the First World War triumphant. It had swept the seas of the German navy and successfully blockaded Germany and its allies, so making a major contribution to their economic dislocation and ultimately to their military collapse. It had achieved, if not another Trafalgar, then certainly a strategic victory over the High Seas Fleet at Jutland in 1916 sufficient to maintain control of the seas. The manpower of both the Old and New Worlds had been brought across oceans controlled by the most powerful fleet the world had yet seen, for the Royal Navy had managed, albeit with some difficulty, to defeat the menace of a new weapons system, the submarine. Moreover, it had pioneered another, aircraft at sea, in the development and use of which by 1918 the Royal Navy undoubtedly led the world.

Nevertheless, such past achievements were not an altogether accurate pointer to the future. Britain, like the rest of the European belligerents, was economically exhausted. During the 1920s and early 1930s its navy had to struggle under increasing budget cuts. The peacetime naval estimate, for example, fell by a third. The British government seized upon the offer of parity with the United States in the Washington Naval Treaty of 1922, which restricted the size of the world's principal fleets and their main weapons, the battleship and aircraft carrier. This and later naval arms agreements, whilst serving to limit potential threats in the short term, would in the long run have a detrimental effect on the design and capabilities of British ships.

Although development in this period was hindered by the shortage of resources, the professionalism and quality of senior British officers would be major assets in the forthcoming campaigns, since they were of an age to have gained useful combat experience in the First World War, often in command of destroyers. The Royal Navy assiduously set about learning from its failure to destroy the weaker German fleet at Jutland. But other areas increasingly lost out. Trade defense, for example, despite the damage wrought by German U-boats in 1917 and the utter dependence of Britain on trade to prosper and imports to exist, was given a low priority, as were offensive submarine operations and, to an even greater extent, amphibious warfare.

The navy also suffered greatly from a government decision to remove its responsibility for naval aviation and, in 1918, give it to the Royal Air Force. The world's first independent airforce was keen to carve out its own niche, and little interested in operations in support of the senior service. Consequently, the aircraft that the Royal Navy was forced to operate aboard its carriers increasingly suffered in comparison to those specialist machines being ordered by the dedicated naval air services of the Americans and Japanese.

By the middle of the 1930s, British defense planners were worried about the challenges – in reality, the insoluble strategic dilemma – of an increasingly dangerous international situation. Britain was no longer in a position to protect its scattered, worldwide empire. In the Far East, imperial possessions were threatened by the rise of an aggressive and acquisitive Japan. A great naval base had been built at Singapore, which relied on the British fleet being sent from home waters to equip it. However, it became ever more apparent that this fleet would be required in European waters, where Britain's position was threatened by growing tensions with Mussolini's fascist Italy, sitting astride the vital Mediterranean sea route, and after 1933 by the rearmament of Germany under Adolf Hitler.

Whilst it had achieved a strategic victory over the German fleet at Jutland in 1916, the Royal Navy spent the interwar period studying the reasons why it had failed to destroy it, using exercises such as this, involving Royal Sovereign-class battleships. (IWM SP 1501)

A re-equipment program was commenced. A new class of battleships – the 42,000-ton King George V class with 10 14-inch (356mm) guns – was ordered. A large carrier-building program was belatedly begun, with the Illustrious class, complete with armored hangars, being ordered to supplement the original and somewhat unsatisfactory First World War-vintage conversions; *Illustrious* herself appeared in 1939. A crash building program of anti-submarine escorts, including the stalwart of the forthcoming Battle of the Atlantic, the Flower class, was also put in

hand. However, this expansion program was hindered by the shrinkage of the country's military industrial base. Indeed, the shortage of adequate shipbuilding and repair capacity continued to impose restrictions on Britain throughout the Second World War, a deficiency that could only in the end be filled by the prodigious efforts of shipyards in the United States.

After years of wrangling, responsibility for sea-going naval aviation was returned to the Royal Navy in 1937. However, naval aviation had been severely hamstrung by years of neglect: it had too many small carriers, equipped with too few, obsolete aircraft, and a significant number of officers were ignorant of both the utility and dangers of air power. The navy to which Winston Churchill was reappointed as First Lord of

Based on a civilian whale-catcher design, the Flower-class Corvette was really too slow and small for North Atlantic anti-submarine operations, and, described as able to 'roll on wet grass,' was certainly uncomfortable for its crew of 120. Nevertheless, it was robust and available in reasonable numbers, and formed the backbone of the Anglo-Canadian escort force throughout the war. (IWM A4594)

the Admiralty – its political head – in September 1939 was thus in many respects ill-prepared for the coming test.

Nevertheless, Britain's main European opponent was in a far worse state of preparation. The Versailles Treaty of 1919, which had ended the First World War, had severely restricted Germany's armed forces. Its navy was limited to six pre-First World War, pre-Dreadnought-type battleships, six light cruisers, a dozen destroyers, and a similar number of torpedo boats. It was forbidden submarines and aircraft. Admiral Erich Raeder became head of the German navy in October 1928 and remained so until January 1943, becoming Grand Admiral in April 1939. Raeder from the start argued that war with Britain had to be avoided as, notwithstanding the reductions of the 1920s, British naval strength and geographical position would spell maritime disaster for Germany. Raeder, instead, concentrated on countering any potential French and Polish threats. The first postwar class of heavy units, the three Panzerschiffe, the 'pocket battleships' – in effect, a somewhat flawed heavy cruiser – was designed with the French in mind.

With the coming to power of Adolf Hitler in 1933, a massive rearmament program was initiated. The first result for the navy was the construction of a new class of 11-inch (279mm) gunned battlecruiser, of which two, *Scharnhorst* and *Gneisenau*, were eventually built out of the planned five. Raeder was forced to rely on the strategy of attacking a potential enemy's merchant navy, as Germany simply would not have the strength to take on a first-class opponent's main fleet. He favored the construction of heavy surface raiders to accomplish this, and in 1936 two battleships, *Bismarck* and *Tirpitz*, were laid down. These were immensely powerful ships, displacing 42,000 tons, well armored, with eight 15-inch (381mm) guns and capable of almost 30 knots.

In the 1930s, the Kriegsmarine recognized the requirement to build up its own air arm, but was blocked by the head of the Luftwaffe, Herman Goering, who believed that 'everything that flies belongs to me.' Work was begun in 1936 on the first of a small class of aircraft carriers, the 23,000-ton *Graf Zeppelin*, which was intended to carry a powerful air group of 28 Ju-87D dive-bombers and 12 Me-109G fighters. However, construction of the *Graf Zeppelin* was suspended in May 1940 when she was 85 percent complete, and her sister ship was broken up on the stocks in the same year.

After Hitler and Raeder, the other dominating figure in the German navy was Karl Dönitz, who in 1935 became head of the newly created submarine arm of the now renamed Kriegsmarine. His efforts to persuade Hitler to develop a submarine force of around 300 did not succeed. Instead the Kriegsmarine entered the war with some 24 ocean-going boats. However, throughout the 1920s and 1930s, initially using motor torpedo boats, the submarine arm had begun to develop new tactics – the Wolf Pack – which were aimed at overcoming enemy merchant convoys, and which had been used to such effect during the First World War.

When in 1938, to the Kriegsmarine's surprise, Hitler made it clear that it was likely in the long run that Germany could not avoid war with Britain, a large fleet-building program, the Z-Plan, was begun. Predicated on the assumption that war would not come until 1944, the plan still had at its heart the destruction of the enemy's merchant marine. However, it called for the construction of a fleet of extremely powerful battleships, including six 56,000-ton leviathans, able to fight their way through a British-dominated North Sea and out into the hunting grounds of the Atlantic. In the meantime, with the Kriegsmarine at a considerable numerical disadvantage, Raeder continued to urge that

war with Great Britain be avoided – warnings that Hitler, almost to the eve of his invasion of Poland, appeared to accept, at least in his conversations with his naval chief.

As tension rose in Europe, France too began to re-equip its fleet, firstly to counter any potential Italian threat in the Mediterranean and then increasingly as a result of developments in Germany. For example, the very capable *Dunkerque* and *Strasbourg*, 26,500-ton battleships, capable of 30 knots and with eight 13-inch (330mm) guns, were intended to counter the German Panzerschiffe pocket battleships. In the five years before the outbreak of the Second World War the French naval reconstruction program absorbed 27 percent of the military budget and the French fleet under Admiral Darlan became the fourth largest in the

Adolf Hitler with Admiral Dr Erich Raeder (pictured extreme right), head of the German navy from 1928 until January 1943. Hitler had a limited grasp of naval affairs. As he himself admitted, 'on land he was a hero, on sea a coward.' He always wanted his navy to succeed in battle, but not to suffer any losses. Such a contradictory approach had a stifling effect on his admirals and commanding officers. (AKG London)

Admiral Karl Dönitz, head of the German U-boat arm throughout the Second World War and Commander-in-Chief of the Navy from January 1943 and in May 1945 the Third Reich's second and last führer. (IWM HU 3652)

given to countering the French and it was to this end that the Italian fleet was constructed. Whilst the Italian fleet was probably better trained than the country's other services, its ships lacked some key modern equipment, such as anti-submarine sound detection sets and radar, and naval aviation was in the hands of the Italian air force.

Across the Atlantic, since the Washington Naval Treaty, the attention of the US Navy had increasingly been drawn to the Pacific and the potential of war with Japan. It was here that the bulk of America's fleet assets, including 15 capital ships and five carriers, were deployed. Increasingly, however, after September 1939 its small Atlantic Squadron would have to deal with President Roosevelt's decision to implement a Neutrality Patrol in a bid to discourage warlike activities in the waters of the Americas. To its north, the Canadian Navy, which would end the war with no fewer than 365 ships, consisted of fewer than 2,000 men.

world, its high-quality ships manned by long-service professionals.

The expansion of French naval power in turn influenced Italian naval developments. Like Admiral Raeder, the head of the Italian navy, Admiral Cavagnari, viewed the prospect of war with Britain as unthinkable during the 1930s. Instead, attention was exclusively

The fleets of the major naval powers, January 1939						
	Britain and British Commonwealth	Germany	France	Italy	USA	Japan
Battleships	12	2	5	4	15	9
Battlecruisers	3	2	1	–	–	–
Pocket battleships	–	3	–	–	–	–
Cruisers	62	6	18	21	32	39
Aircraft carriers	7	–	1	–	5	5
Seaplane carriers	2	–	1	–	–	3
Destroyers	159	17	58	48	209	84
Torpedo boats	11	16	13	69	–	38
Submarines	54	57	76	104	87	58
Monitors and coast defense ships	3	–	–	1	–	1
Minelayers	1	–	1	–	8	10
Sloops and escort vessels	38	8	25	32	–	–
Gunboats and patrol vessels	27	–	10	2	20	10
Minesweepers	38	29	8	39	–	12

Source: S. Roskill, *Naval Policy between the Wars* (London: Collins, 1968), Vol. 1, p. 577.

Opening moves

The Battle of the Atlantic was the dominating factor all through the war. Never for one moment could we forget that everything happening elsewhere, on land, at sea, or in the air, depended ultimately on its outcome, and amid all other cares we viewed its changing fortunes day by day with hope or apprehension.

Winston Churchill

The Battle of the Atlantic was truly a decisive battle. If the Kriegsmarine had been able to achieve the same success against the merchant fleet of the British Empire as the US Navy was to achieve against that of Imperial Japan, Britain simply could not have continued the war.

There was no 'phony war' at sea during the Second World War. The naval war was fought from the very first day to the very last. Amongst the first shots on 1 September during the German invasion of Poland were those fired by the 11-inch (279mm) guns of the old German battleship *Schleswig-Holstein* against the Polish Westerplatte fortifications at Danzig. The small Polish navy was no match for the Kriegsmarine; its three serviceable destroyers escaped to Britain just before the outbreak of hostilities, whilst the five submarines served as a short-lived nuisance to the Germans.

On 3 September the Royal Navy sent its two famous fleet-wide telegrams, 'Total Germany' and 'Winston is back,' announcing general hostilities and the return to the Admiralty of Winston Churchill. By this time, German surface units, their supply ships, and submarines were already in the Atlantic in readiness to undertake the Kriegsmarine's anti-commerce campaign against the British Empire. However, although the *Admiral Graf Spee* and *Deutschland* had been at sea since mid-August, they did not receive orders to go into action until 26 September.

Whilst there were not yet sufficient U-boats to wage a successful submarine offensive, ominously for Britain, given its experiences of the First World War, it was a U-boat that struck first. Within hours of the commencement of hostilities, *U-30* sank the liner *Athenia* with the loss of 112 lives in the mistaken belief that it was an auxiliary cruiser. Although the incident led to Admiral Raeder briefly tightening the rules of engagement, it also, not unnaturally, caused the British government to believe that Germany was again conducting a strategy of unrestricted submarine warfare. In any case, by 23 September all restrictions had been lifted in the North Sea, and by 4 October as far west as 15 degrees.

Winston Churchill, always eager for the offensive, ordered the formation of several submarine-hunting groups based around fleet aircraft carriers to support convoys in the Southwest Approaches. Whilst maritime air power had played an important role in the anti-submarine effort in the First World War and eventually played the decisive role in the Battle of the Atlantic, the neglect of such operations in the interwar period doomed this attempt to failure. The Fleet Air Arm did not have sufficient training, and it lacked both the equipment to find U-boats and the weaponry to destroy them.

This exercise in desperate improvisation put at serious risk the small number of almost irreplaceable carriers. On 14 September the *Ark Royal* very narrowly avoided *U-39*'s torpedoes, which went on to explode in the carrier's wake. Three days later, *Courageous* was not so fortunate when she was sunk off Ireland by two torpedoes from *U-29* with the loss of 519 of her crew. The carriers were withdrawn from anti-submarine work.

The Royal Navy's Admiralty Trade Division assumed control over British-registered shipping on 26 August and began implementing the convoy system. Only with time would they all receive a naval escort. Convoys advanced on a broad front, keeping the more valuable (and explosive) ships such as oil tankers away from the more dangerous fringes. By late 1942 a worldwide interlocking convoy system had been introduced and the convoys had increased in size after research showed that the perimeter of an 80-ship convoy was only one-seventh longer than that of a 40-shop convoy. (Topham Picturepoint)

The Kriegsmarine's U-boat arm followed this up with a daring foray into the Royal Navy's fleet base at Scapa Flow in the Orkneys, where on 14 October Gunther Prien in *U-47* penetrated a gap in the base's defenses and sank the old battleship *Royal Oak* at her moorings. It could have been worse: on 30 October *U-56* found the *Nelson*, *Rodney,* and *Hood* off Scotland. Two torpedoes actually hit *Nelson*, but they, like so many in the early months of the campaign, failed to detonate.

Meanwhile, both sides had commenced laying minefields for both defensive and offensive purposes, and blockades were imposed to prevent contraband getting through. The Germans instigated patrols in the Kattegat, Skagerrak, and Baltic, seizing over 20 ships in the second half of September alone. For Britain the blockade was its traditional strategy, although Germany was not as susceptible to a naval stranglehold this time as it had been during the First World War. The southern entrance to the North Sea was easy to close, whilst from 6 September the Northern Patrol, made up largely of 'auxiliary cruisers' – converted passenger liners – sought to prevent blockade runners from breaking through the Iceland–Orkneys gap.

By the end of October, 283 merchant ships had been stopped by the Northern Patrol, 71 of which were brought to Kirkwall in the Orkneys for inspection, resulting in the seizure of eight blockade-runners. In a bid to disrupt the patrol, in November the German battlecruisers *Scharnhorst* and *Gneisenau* sallied forth. On 23 November, Captain E. C. Kennedy, RN, in the auxiliary cruiser *Rawalpindi*, sighted them, and believing that they were trying to break into the Atlantic, courageously attempted to slow them down by engaging. The unarmored,

Both Germany and Britain laid large numbers of mines for both defensive and offensive purposes. All told, some 500,000 mines were laid by all sides in the Second World War, using surface vessels, such as this German E-boat, submarines, or drops from the air. A variety of types were laid, including the spherical, horned contact mine and the magnetic influence variety. Whilst they accounted for only 6.5 percent of Allied merchant traffic sunk, their presence or indeed suspected presence had a huge impact on the conduct of the war at sea. (AKG London)

6-inch (152mm) gunned, converted passenger liner was no match for the most powerful units in the German fleet and the *Rawalpindi* was sunk within 14 minutes.

Graf Spee

When, toward the end of September, the German surface raiders *Admiral Graf Spee* and *Deutschland* (soon to be renamed *Lützow*) began offensive operations against merchant traffic, the British and French navies organized eight groups of heavy units, each known by a letter, to hunt them down, be they in the Atlantic or Indian oceans. Unknown to the Admiralty, the *Lützow*

returned to Germany on 8 November. But just after dawn on 6 December, in the South Atlantic Force G, a squadron consisting of the heavy 8-inch (203mm) cruiser *Exeter*, the light 6-inch (152mm) cruiser *Ajax* and the New Zealand ship HMNZS *Achilles*, under Commodore Henry Harwood, encountered the *Admiral Graf Spee* off the mouth of the River Plate. The *Graf Spee*'s commanding officer, Captain Hans Langsdorff, had been under orders to avoid such encounters, and after a furious 90-minute action in which the lighter British units repeatedly closed with the heavier German vessel, the latter was forced to make for neutral Montevideo for repairs.

Unable, because of international laws restricting the presence of belligerent warships, to stay for more than 72 hours, uncertain that his ship's temperamental diesel engines would last the long perilous voyage home, and believing a British deception that a much stronger force now awaited his vessel, Langsdorff ordered the *Graf Spee* to be scuttled in the River Plate on 17 December. It was 25 years to the month since the Royal Navy had destroyed, off the

The *Graf Spee* after being scuttled on 17 December 1939 in the River Plate. She had been driven into Montevideo harbor following the action with Commodore Henry Harwood's cruiser squadron three days earlier. The *Graf Spee* was one of three Panzerschiffe, better known as 'pocket battleships,' but this was a somewhat misleading description, for whilst her six 11-inch (279mm) guns made her a formidable opponent, her 10,000-ton displacement was achieved at the expense of weak belt armor. (IWM A5)

Falklands, the Pacific Squadron of the German ship's namesake, Admiral Graf Spee.

The *Graf Spee* affair was brought to a conclusion when on 16 February 1940 Captain Philip Vian, RN, leading the Fourth Destroyer Flotilla in HMS *Cossack*, ignored Norwegian neutrality and patrol boats, and boarded the *Altmark*, the *Graf Spee's* supply vessel, which had illegally taken refuge in a Norwegian fjord. The 299 British prisoners taken during the *Graf Spee's* campaign were freed.

The *Altmark* incident further concentrated the attention of both sides on Norway. Norway was vital for Germany: it protected Germany's northern flank and vital Swedish iron ore came through its coastal waters when the Baltic route was shut by winter ice. The

boarding of the *Altmark* reinforced Hitler's (justified) fears about an impending British invasion, which he now decided to pre-empt before turning his attention to the defeat of France. On 7 April the entire German fleet put to sea in 11 groups to undertake the invasions of Denmark and Norway.

Norway

The German invasion of Norway, Operation Weserübung, heralding the first maritime campaign of the Second World War, began on 9 April with surprise German airborne operations to seize Norwegian airfields. Crucially, into these airfields came Luftwaffe fighters and bombers, with which German forces dominated the skies over and around Norway, frustrating attempts by the British Home Fleet under Admiral Sir Charles Forbes to intercept the German task groups.

Beyond the reach of British home-based fighter-cover, the Luftwaffe also made subsequent British and French counter-landings at a number of places in northern Norway, including Narvik and

Trondheim, even more unlikely to succeed. These hastily undertaken combined operations were a fiasco and underlined how much work still had to be done for Britain to perfect the business of amphibious warfare after so many years of willful neglect. Following the German invasions of France and the Low Countries launched on 10 May, the remaining Allied forces in northern Norway began to be withdrawn.

The German occupation of Norway provided the Kriegsmarine with improved access to the North Sea and northern Atlantic, and permitted German submarine, surface, and air forces to dominate the North Cape passage to the Soviet Union. But whilst it also secured, as planned, Hitler's northern flank, it did not put an end to his fears of a British counterstrike there – fears that Churchill and succeeding heads of the newly established Combined Operations Headquarters sought to exploit. In a series of raids, beginning with one against the Lofoten Islands on 3 March 1941, the newly formed Commando units attacked exposed and isolated German positions, causing the Germans to divert increasing numbers of forces to protect their Scandinavian holdings.

More immediately, the experience in Norway clearly demonstrated the fallacy of the views of some leading Royal Naval officers that carrier fighter-cover was an optional extra. Literally overnight, it brought a realization in most that the fleet would find it impossible to operate in a hostile air environment. But the Royal Navy continued to suffer from the legacy of the neglect of naval aviation during the interwar period, lacking sufficient large carriers and, in particular, effective carrier-based fighters.

Even the roles that British carriers and their aircraft were capable of performing well, such as reconnaissance and anti-ship

Norway saw a series of furious naval actions. Here the German destroyer *Erich Giese* lies beached following the Second Battle of Narvik on 13 April 1940. During the battle, the Kriegsmarine lost eight modern destroyers and a submarine, whilst the Royal Navy suffered damage to just one destroyer. The German navy could ill afford such a rate of exchange. (IWM A 21)

strikes, were of no use when assets were mishandled. On 9 June the carrier HMS *Glorious* was surprised by the German battlecruisers *Scharnhorst* and *Gneisenau* under Vice Admiral Wilhelm Marschall. The non-aviation-minded commanding officer of the carrier, Captain D'Oyly Hughes, failed to use his carrier's air group properly, which led to the wholly avoidable destruction of the carrier and her gallant escorts, HMS *Acasta* and *Ardent*, and the needless loss of over 1,400 lives in the icy waters off northern Norway.

Despite its failings, however, the Royal Navy demonstrated a determination not to yield control of the sea to the enemy, in a series of often furious actions, such as the destroyer HMS *Glowworm*'s engagement of the cruiser *Hipper* and the foray of Captain Warburton-Lee's 2nd Destroyer Flotilla up Ofotfjord to engage a much stronger German force at Narvik. In doing so, the Royal Navy exacted a heavy price from the Kriegsmarine which it could ill-afford to pay and put a large part of the German surface fleet out of action for the rest of the year. Through both the material losses and the psychological effects, these early encounters had a telling impact on the next stages of the naval war.

Dunkirk

With the evacuation of the Allied forces in Norway not yet complete, but with the German Blitzkrieg forcing the Allies to collapse in Belgium and France, the Royal Navy was called upon to undertake a much greater task – the evacuation of the beleaguered British Expeditionary Force from Dunkirk. This was conducted in the face of determined German air operations that eventually resulted in the loss of nine destroyers and many other craft, mostly civilian. But fortunately it was blessed with fine weather. Operation Dynamo, masterminded by Vice Admiral Bertram Ramsay at Dover, lasted from 28 May to 4 June, and saw 338,226 British and French troops – but not their equipment – taken off

the moles and beaches of Dunkirk. The British Empire found itself alone.

Indian Ocean and Red Sea, 1939–41

The Indian Ocean was the third largest theater of operations during the Second World War. It covers over 28 million square miles (72.5 million km^2) and contains one-fifth of the world's total sea area. Vessels that normally found themselves in coastal waters soon had to come to terms with the vast nature of the waters – the distance from Cape Town to Singapore was some 6,000 miles (9,650km). The sea war in the Indian Ocean contained all the elements of the other theaters. Submarines, surface raiders – naval and merchant ships, German and Japanese – amphibious and carrier operations were all present. There were also a few novelties and notables. For instance, as Michael Wilson points out, 'It was the one area of the world where, uniquely, the submarines of seven nations – Great Britain, the Netherlands, the United States of America, France, Italy, Germany, and Japan – all operated and fought during the war.'

Yet in comparison to the other naval theaters of the Second World War, the Indian Ocean is often seen as a less important maritime battleground, playing only a supporting role to the other areas. It never saw the same fleet battles, or the same intensity of operations, as did the Atlantic, Mediterranean, and Pacific theaters. However, without unrestricted access to the Indian Ocean, British supplies to north Africa, India, and Australia, and Australian reinforcement of Britain, could not have taken place. The access that Britain enjoyed in the Indian Ocean enabled it to survive and wage war.

Had the Japanese combined their submarines and merchant raiders with Italian and German forces and attempted to interdict Allied supply lines with a degree of organization and adequate force levels, then Britain's war effort would have been crippled. Oil from the Middle East and rubber from Ceylon were two key components of the Allied war machine. Successful Axis interdiction of these sources would have undermined the war industry. The oil and rubber had to travel through the Indian Ocean and ultimately they did so remarkably unmolested. It seems the major powers directed their main efforts toward the other theaters until such time as they could build up sufficient forces to be used constructively in the Indian Ocean.

The early years of the war in the Indian Ocean primarily revolved around safe passage for British and neutral shipping, and the attempts to stop them by the Axis forces. British units had already begun to move from the Indian Ocean to home waters on the outbreak of war, but soon found themselves returning to the ocean to hunt down a number of German surface raiders and to escort vital convoys. The German threat was a simple yet multiple one. The German raiders comprised predominantly armed merchant ships, although the *Graf Spee* did briefly visit the Indian Ocean, accounting for a number of ships before succumbing outside Montevideo harbor. The merchant raiders all carried medium-caliber guns, but these were augmented with torpedoes, aircraft, and mines. To make matters worse, the raiders would occasionally seize merchantmen and convert them into their own auxiliaries, normally with the addition of mines. In fact, several of these ships dropped large numbers of mines off the Australian coast, resulting in serious losses, including in November 1940 the *City of Rayville*, the first American ship sunk.

Compounding the threat was the insufficient number of British convoy escorts, which remained a problem in the theater until the end of the war. Additionally, much of the non-British shipping traffic in the area often insisted on travelling independently. The British responded to the merchantmen sinkings by more patrols with ships, aircraft, and submarines. The Royal Indian Navy was also expanded at pace to fulfil valuable escort duties, continuing to do so even when the new East Indies Fleet was created in 1944.

Across the world's seas

Sea Lion

Following the capitulation of France, Adolf Hitler decided to proceed with a scheme to invade Great Britain. The planning for the abortive Operation Sea Lion exposed the deep divisions within the German High Command, in particular between the head of the Luftwaffe, Herman Göring, and Eric Raeder. Despite some interest in amphibious operations in Germany prior to the war, the plan also had to contend with a total lack of preparation for what was an infinitely more demanding and complex operation than Weserübung.

However, whilst the Luftwaffe struggled in vain against the Royal Air Force's Fighter Command and the Channel ports filled up with hastily converted Rhine barges, Hitler began to think about the east and toward preparations for the conquest of the Soviet Union. On 12 October, Sea Lion was postponed – never to be resurrected. Moreover, even had the Luftwaffe been able to wrest control of the skies from those whom Churchill described as 'the few,' the Kriegsmarine would still have been faced with the unenviable task of escorting the invasion convoys across the Channel in the face of what could only have been the full and furious opposition of the Royal Navy. As Admiral Raeder had cautioned, the under-strength German navy, further weakened by the Norwegian adventure, would not have been in a position to force the issue.

But the Royal Navy also found itself overstretched. It, too, had suffered losses, in both the Norwegian and Dunkirk operations. Some relief was provided by the provision of 50 old destroyers by the United States. But the navy still had to provide escorts for the convoy system, maintain its blockading

operations, and be prepared to deal with German heavy units breaking out into the Atlantic, and now it had to be ready to counter the very real threat of invasion. The French collapse, of course, added to its burdens. It found itself solely responsible for the Mediterranean and, after Mussolini's decision in June 'to rush to the aid of the victor,' having to deal with the small, but, on paper, capable Italian fleet, whilst providing support to British operations in north Africa.

In addition, although, as winter approached, fears of a German invasion of Britain began to recede, the U-boat menace grew. The ability of Dönitz's submarines to operate out of French Atlantic bases such as Lorient and St Nazaire meant that the Royal Navy's prewar strategy of bottling up German submarines in the North Sea had been rendered worthless, along with many of the short-range British maritime patrol aircraft and escorts.

Wolf Pack

Dönitz's U-boats were still few in number. Indeed, given his losses and with U-boat production still at a low level, he now had fewer boats than at the beginning of the campaign. However, the French bases made the long transits into and out of the Atlantic unnecessary and thus allowed him to keep more boats in the operational area. He had experimented earlier in the war with the new strategy of attacking convoys using groups of boats, but operating closer to British home waters this technique had met with decidedly mixed success. Now, able to muster the necessary submarines on a more consistent basis and operating further out into the Atlantic, away from the attentions

of RAF Coastal Command, Dönitz's 'Wolf Packs' would herald the first of his submarine service's 'Happy Times.'

The Wolf Pack technique worked by establishing patrol lines of submarines at right angles to the expected track of the convoy, based on information provided by the German signals intelligence organization xB-Dienst, which at this time was reading a number of British Admiralty codes, or by aerial reconnaissance. Once the convoy had been sighted by one of the patrolling submarines, its position was radioed back to U-boat Command, which would then order the pack to concentrate against the convoy. The attack usually took place at night, with the U-boats slipping inside the escort screen.

The technique relied on surface running, the submarines being fast enough (up to a maximum of around 17 knots) to enable them to outmaneuver the convoys, and also on the extensive use of radio communications. Both features were eventually exploited by the Allies to bring about the U-boats' defeat, but to begin with the Wolf Pack tactic brought Dönitz's submariners great success against a Royal

A German E-boat at high speed in the English Channel. Torpedo craft such as these, capable of speeds of around 40 knots, equipped both German and British navies and were involved in frequent and often furious engagements on the fringes of the European conflict: in the North Sea, the Channel, the Aegean, and the Black Sea. The German navy built some 250 E-boats and their main task was to attack British coastal traffic. (U-Boat Archive)

Navy that was ill-prepared to counter such an unexpected development. Toward the end of October a slow eastbound convoy, SC7, lost no fewer than 21 of its 30 ships, whilst a fast convoy, HX-79, following behind, had 12 out of its 49 ships sunk.

War in the Mediterranean

The contest to dominate the Mediterranean Sea developed at a slow pace, but evolved to make this area one of the most complex and intense theaters of conflict during the Second World War, involving Britain, France, Germany, Greece, Italy, and the United States. The Mediterranean Sea itself represents the physical divide between the great continents of Africa, Asia, and Europe, stretching approximately

The backbone of the Kriegsmarine's U-boat arm was the Type VII submarine. These submarines were more submersible motor torpedo boats than true submarines in the modern, nuclear, sense, as they had to come to the surface regularly to recharge their electric batteries using diesel engines. On the surface, powered by their diesels, they were fast at some 17 knots, which enabled them to outmaneuver the Allies' slow merchant convoys. But when forced under water – as increasingly they were by Allied countermeasures – they were slow and had a limited endurance. (AKG Berlin)

2,000 miles (3,200km) west to east from Gibraltar to Palestine. This consistency in length, though, is not matched by the width of the sea, which varies from 600 miles (1,000km) to less than 100 miles (160km) in certain places, such as the gap between Tunisia and Sicily. The strategic significance of this enclosed sea had been transformed in the nineteenth century by the construction of the Suez Canal in Egypt, which considerably reduced the distance for ships travelling to the Far East. The Cape route was a 13,000 mile (21,000km) trip. As such, it became a sea-lane of vital importance to colonial powers like Britain.

The pace of conflict in this theater accelerated dramatically after the fall of France (with all its colonies in North Africa) to victorious German forces on 22 June 1940 and Italy's entry into the war in the same month. At this time, Britain's position in the Mediterranean could hardly have been worse. As a nation, it was struggling to contain the threat from Germany, conducting the humiliating withdrawal from Dunkirk and the desperate Battle of Britain. At sea, the German navy had stretched the Royal Navy to the limit in the Atlantic oceans, using a handful of major units such as the *Admiral Graf Spee*, U-boats, and maritime aircraft. Now Britain was required somehow to neutralize the latent threat from the French naval forces based in North Africa and to cope with a new foe, Italy.

Britain's interests in the region were centered on three strategic locations: Egypt, Gibraltar, and Malta. Fortunately for the Royal Navy, it possessed one of its ablest commanders as Commander-in-Chief, Mediterranean Fleet, Admiral Sir Andrew

Admiral Sir Andrew Browne Cunningham, or A.B.C. to his friends, was arguably the finest naval commander in the Royal Navy throughout the Second World War. In terms of character, he was a fiery and aggressive man who always tried to seek out and destroy the enemy whenever possible. Under his command, the Mediterranean Fleet achieved the stunning victories at Taranto and Matapan as well as keeping the supply line to Malta open. He was appointed First Sea Lord in October 1943. (IWM MH 31338)

Browne Cunningham. Cunningham's fleet, based at Alexandria rather than the more vulnerable Malta (the traditional base of the Royal Navy) was somewhat small in terms of capital ships in the summer of 1940. It possessed just four (rather old) battleships – HMS *Warspite* (flagship), HMS *Malaya*, HMS *Royal Sovereign* and HMS *Valiant* (arrived August 1940) – the aircraft carrier HMS *Eagle*, and five light cruisers as well as 17 destroyers.

At Gibraltar, Britain's naval forces were designated 'Force H' under the command of Vice Admiral Sir James Somerville. Its composition changed significantly with and at one stage included the famous battlecruiser HMS *Hood*. By August 1940, it comprised the battleship HMS *Resolution*, the battlecruiser HMS *Renown*, the aircraft carrier HMS *Ark Royal*, a cruiser, and seven destroyers.

HMS *Warspite* was a Queen Elizabeth-class battleship, commissioned in 1915, and a veteran of the First World War. She had been modernized in 1936 in vital areas such as engines, armor, armament, and the elevation of her powerful 15-inch (381mm) guns, which had a 32,000-yard (29,260m) range. At most, by 1940 this ship could only make 24 knots, which was considerably slower than more modern battleships that could make up to 30 knots. (IWM A20652)

Vice Admiral Sir James Somerville was a popular and highly effective commander of Force H. The demands on his unit were enormous due to its Atlantic and Mediterranean responsibilities, from helping to sink the *Bismarck* off the coast of France on 27 May 1941, to escorting supply convoys to Malta. Somerville was subsequently promoted to full admiral and took charge of the battered Eastern Fleet in February 1942. (IWM A30166 WA)

In bomb-strewn Malta, defenses were extremely run down by mid-1940 with just a handful of Sea Gladiator fighters, nicknamed 'Faith,' 'Hope,' and 'Charity,' and 38 anti-aircraft guns. The significance of Malta lay in its location between Sicily and the north African coast as well as in the ships and particularly the submarines that operated from it.

Oran and Mers-el-Kebir

The fall of France in June 1940 and the subsequent accession to power of the Vichy regime under Marshal Pétain put French naval forces in North Africa in a difficult position. French colonies extended from Dakar in French West Africa to parts of Morocco, Algeria, and Tunisia, and the naval forces on station at the time were sizable. In the Algerian ports of Oran and Mers-el-Kebir were four battleships, 13 destroyers, one seaplane carrier, and four submarines; at Dakar there were two new battleships and at Alexandria, under British guns, one battleship with four cruisers. After the capitulation of France, the Commander-in-Chief of the French navy, Admiral Darlan, made it clear that French naval forces would not be handed over to any foreign power without a fight. However, his acceptance of a position in the Vichy government on 27 June 1940 raised doubts about the future of the French fleet.

Italy's position after 10 June 1940 was more clear-cut. It had colonies in Libya, Somaliland, and Abyssinia (Ethiopia), and mustered 500,000 troops in total, including powerful naval forces (Regia Marina) supported by an air force (Regia Aeronautica) of more than 1,200 aircraft. The Italian forces in Libya under Marshal Graziani enjoyed overwhelming superiority over their British counterparts, and appeared likely (on paper at least) to dominate the region in the short to medium term. Germany's initial commitment to North Africa was small in number but significant in terms of quality. Fliegerkorps X (a specialist anti-ship squadron of the Luftwaffe) was deployed to Italy in December 1940, U-boats were made available in small numbers, and General Erwin Rommel and the Afrika Korps were deployed to Libya in February 1941.

The potential threat of the French naval forces in North Africa forced the British Prime Minister and the First Sea Lord to order Force H to execute the infamous Operation Catapult, or the destruction of the French forces at Mers-el-Kebir, on 3 July 1940. This highly unpleasant action took place after the failure of British negotiations with the local French commander, Admiral Gensoul. Two French battleships, *Dunkerque* and *Provence*, were seriously damaged (along with the seaplane carrier *Commandante Teste*), the *Bretagne* blew up, and the *Strasbourg* managed to escape to Toulon. A total of 1,250 French sailors were killed in this operation. Five days later, British forces attacked Dakar and put the battleship

General Erwin Rommel was one of the best military leaders of the entire war. As an officer, he possessed the rare 'common touch' with his troops, to whom he was an inspiration. For the British and Commonwealth soldiers who faced the Afrika Korps in the early years of the war, his presence and actions generated the idea that he was some kind of 'superman.' (IWM)

Richelieu out of action. In stark contrast, at Alexandria, Cunningham (who opposed using force against the French) managed to persuade Admiral Godfroy to disarm his vessels by removing vital parts without a shot being fired.

The first major action between the British Mediterranean Fleet and the Italian navy occurred off the coast of Calabria on 9 July 1940 and revealed a pattern of warfare that was to repeat itself continually throughout the war. Cunningham took the British fleet at sea to cover a British convoy from Malta to Gibraltar, but received information while under way that a convoy of ships was heading from Italy to Libya; in typical fashion, he turned to engage the enemy. Protecting the Italian convoy was a strong force of two battleships, a dozen or more cruisers, and a multitude of destroyers.

On 8 July 1940 the Regia Aeronautica first attacked the British fleet from the air, but they only managed to damage the cruiser HMS *Gloucester* despite launching several waves of attacks. The next day the two forces converged and the 7th British Cruiser Squadron, under Vice Admiral J. C. Tovey, made the famous signal 'Enemy battle fleet in sight.' HMS *Warspite* exchanged salvoes with the Italian battleship *Giulio Cesare*, causing such damage that the Italian Admiral Riccardi made smoke and retreated successfully away from the British forces.

Despite excellent work by the aircraft of HMS *Eagle*, which sank a destroyer, Cunningham could not consolidate his tactical success because of a lack of speed in his capital ships; his old battleships were simply too slow to catch the escaping Italians. However, the lessons from this action were clear: the aggressive ethos of the Royal Navy made up for the technological and numerical superiority of the Italian navy, whose will to fight appeared fragile at best.

Taranto

One of the most significant military strikes in the early years of the war in the Mediterranean was the raid on Taranto, or Operation Judgement, carried out by aircraft of the Fleet Air Arm (FAA) on 11 November 1940. The plan of striking at the heart of the Italian fleet in the massive naval base of Taranto was devised by Rear Admiral Lyster, and was warmly taken up by Cunningham. The original plan called for strikes from two aircraft carriers, but mechanical problems with HMS *Eagle* forced the Royal Navy to rely on just one carrier.

Sailing with an escort of five battleships, two cruisers, and 13 destroyers, HMS *Illustrious* launched the strike at 170 miles (275km) distance from Taranto. In two waves, 21 Swordfish aircraft flew toward Taranto early that evening and found six Italian battleships, some cruisers and destroyers calmly at anchor.

To Mussolini (shown above) and the Italian navy, the Mediterranean was *mare nostrum* (our sea). In just one night, the balance of power shifted dramatically in favor of the Royal Navy, but more importantly a huge psychological blow was inflicted on the greatly reduced fleet of Admiral Cavagnari, the Commander-in-Chief of the Italian navy. Taranto was a revolutionary moment in naval history: it heralded the replacement of the battleship by the aircraft carrier as the capital ship of the sea. (NYP 68066)

The damage inflicted by the first operational strike of this kind in naval history was spectacular: the battleship *Conte di Cavour* was sunk in the harbor (despite being recovered, it was never operational again in the war); the *Littorio* (renamed *Italia*) suffered three torpedo hits, whilst another torpedo hit the *Caio Diulio*; and the heavy cruiser *Trento* also sustained damage along with a few destroyers and the oil facilities. Operation Judgement cost the Royal Navy just two aircraft.

Logistics in the Mediterranean

The war in the Mediterranean Sea was, largely, a war of logistics. The problems involved in supplying ground forces in north Africa dominated the military strategies of all three major protagonists in the Mediterranean theater, Britain, Italy, and Germany. The only method of transporting bulk supplies, troops, and tanks was the escorted convoy, since transport aircraft could provide only a fraction of what sea-based methods offered. Consequently, maritime operations were centered on convoy and anti-convoy operations.

British efforts in this area entailed huge amounts of resources from Force H and the Mediterranean fleet to keep the supply lines open from the home base to Egypt (the only other major front against Germany until 1943) via Gibraltar and Malta. The list of such operations is extensive, including Operation Hurry in early August 1940 (12 Hurricane air defense fighters, transported to Malta) and Operation Coat in mid-November 1940 (only four out of 12 Hurricanes made it to Malta; the rest crashed into the sea). The most famous of the British convoys was undoubtedly Operation Pedestal in August 1942.

For the German and Italian convoys to Libya, Malta was to prove a painful thorn in the side of their overall strategy. In the same manner that German and Italian submarines preyed on the convoys from Alexandria, British submarines attacked these slow convoys carrying vital supplies to Rommel's army in the North African desert. Air power was particularly valuable in finding and sinking convoys on both sides; the German Luftwaffe demonstrated considerable skill in this art, either through direct attack or mining operations in the Suez Canal.

The Mediterranean

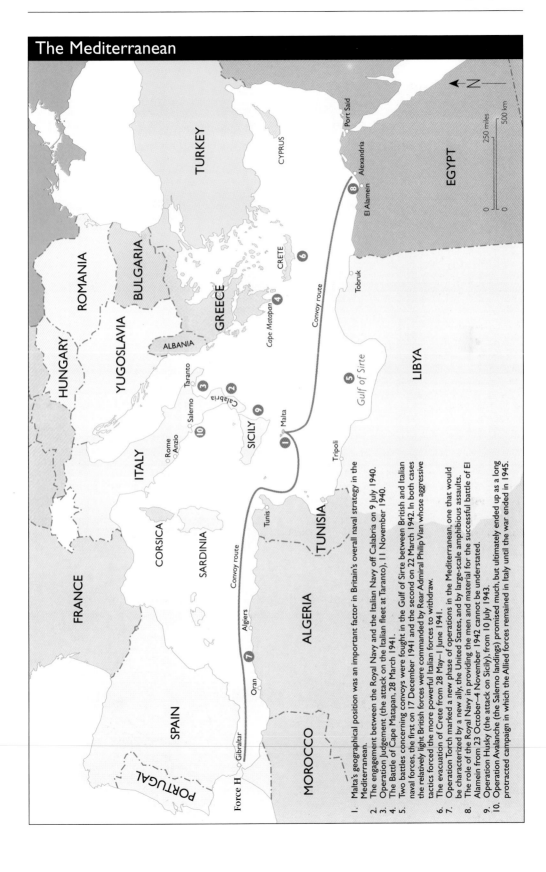

1. Malta's geographical position was an important factor in Britain's overall naval strategy in the Mediterranean.

2. The engagement between the Royal Navy and the Italian Navy off Calabria on 9 July 1940.

3. Operation Judgement (the attack on the Italian fleet at Taranto), 11 November 1940.

4. The Battle of Cape Matapan, 28 March 1941.

5. Two battles concerning convoys were fought in the Gulf of Sirte between British and Italian naval forces, the first on 17 December 1941 and the second on 22 March 1942. In both cases the relatively light British forces were commanded by Rear Admiral Philip Vian whose aggressive tactics forced the more powerful Italian forces to withdraw.

6. The evacuation of Crete from 28 May–1 June 1941.

7. Operation Torch marked a new phase of operations in the Mediterranean, one that would be characterized by a new ally, the United States, and by large-scale amphibious assaults.

8. The role of the Royal Navy in providing the men and material for the successful battle of El Alamein from 23 October–4 November 1942 cannot be understated.

9. Operation Husky (the attack on Sicily), from 10 July 1943.

10. Operation Avalanche (the Salerno landings) promised much, but ultimately ended up as a long protracted campaign in which the Allied forces remained in Italy until the war ended in 1945.

Operation Pedestal

Operation Pedestal, from 13 August 1942, involved two battleships, three fleet aircraft carriers with 72 aircraft, seven cruisers, and 24 destroyers, transporting 36 Spitfires in another aircraft carrier to Malta, together with 14 vital merchant ships under the command of Rear Admiral E. N. Syfret. The cost was enormous: one aircraft carrier, HMS *Eagle*, was sunk and one seriously damaged; two cruisers were destroyed and one was crippled, with the Italian submarine *Axum* accounting for two of the cruiser hits; one destroyer was sunk and one crippled; and nine of the precious merchant ships were sunk as well.

The most famous British submarine commander was Lieutenant Commander M. D. Wanklyn VC, who commanded HMS *Upholder*. This submarine sank two Italian troop-carrying ships, the 19,500-ton *Neptunia* and *Oceania* on 18 September 1941. Between June and September 1941, British submarines sank 150,000 tons of enemy shipping. (IWM A7293)

Red Sea, 1940–41

In the short term, the threat to merchant shipping in the Indian Ocean appeared to worsen in June 1940 with the entry of Italy into the war. Italy had a number of submarines and large escort vessels based in Massawa, its main port in Eritrea on the Red Sea. Although these Italian units were now cut off due to the closure of the Suez Canal, initially they posed a major threat. Quite rapidly this situation changed, however, as the Italian vessels accounted for only a handful of British merchant ships. Convoys were soon running the gauntlet through the Red Sea to the Suez Canal and back again with a large degree of impunity. Most of the Italian submarines could not operate in the narrows of the Red Sea without problems and they all suffered from high temperatures in the crew compartments. The submarines were also relatively unwilling to venture too far into the Indian Ocean, where the hunting was easier.

Gradually, through a combination of British air strikes, convoy escorts, and poor supply, most of the Italian vessels in the Red Sea had

been lost by the start of 1941. Nevertheless, they remained a threat to the ongoing land campaign in east Africa. The Royal Navy had already carried out an evacuation of troops in 1940, but it was now acting in support of the renewed land war against the Italians in east Africa. This conflict had turned in favor of Britain, and a combination of British victory in the region and a powerful Royal Navy made it only a matter of time before the Italian naval bases were overrun.

The Italian Naval Command decided that the remaining Italian surface ships should attempt a surprise raid on British forces, whilst the Italian submarines were to transit the 13,000 miles (21,000km) around Africa to the safety of German-held France. En route they were to be replenished by German support ships and merchant raiders. On commencement of this mission, the Italian surface ships were intercepted by British naval forces, but amazingly the four Italian submarines that set off on their grueling journey to France all succeeded in reaching their destination.

This propaganda coup for Italy actually meant increased safety for British shipping for the remainder of 1941 in the Red Sea and Indian Ocean. It also meant that, now the Italian presence was no longer a nuisance, supplies could flow to Egypt and to the war effort in North Africa much more easily. But the respite was short and over by the end of the year. The war clouds in the east were continuing to gather, and the vulnerability of all British possessions east of Suez was obvious to all.

Matapan

The success of the Royal Navy in the Mediterranean, just as in the Atlantic theater, was aided by the use of intelligence through decrypted intercepts of enemy communications traffic (Enigma). Such information provided Cunningham with his finest moment in the Mediterranean campaign, the Battle of Cape Matapan on 28 March 1941.

The Italian fleet comprised one battleship, *Vittorio Veneto,* with 15-inch (381mm) guns; six heavy cruisers, *Pola, Fiume, Trieste, Trento, Bolzano,* and *Zara,* with 8-inch (203mm) guns; two light cruisers with 6-inch (152mm) guns; and 13 destroyers under Admiral Iachino, which had set sail in three groups to intercept the British 'Lustre' convoys ferrying troops to Greece. Cunningham steamed from Alexandria to intercept the Italians with three battleships (HMS *Warspite,* HMS *Barham,* and HMS *Valiant*), one aircraft carrier (HMS *Formidable*), and nine destroyers. In support of Cunningham, his second-in-command, Rear Admiral H. D. Pridham-Wippell, moved to a position ahead of the main force; he had four cruisers with 6-inch (152mm) guns and nine destroyers.

On the morning of 28 March, he encountered three Italian heavy cruisers and outgunned, he attempted to draw them toward the British battleships some 80 miles (130km) away. Cunningham realized that he had to slow down the Italians in order for his old battleships to catch up, so around midday HMS *Formidable* launched air strikes. Five Fleet Air Arm aircraft managed to get one hit on the Italian battleship, reducing her speed to just 15 knots, and another air strike that evening crippled the cruiser *Pola.* Hoping to have caught the battleship, which had in fact escaped, Cunningham steamed toward the *Pola,* which was now surrounded by two other cruisers and two destroyers.

The Italian ships were completely unaware of the presence of the British battleships until the opening salvoes at a deadly range of fewer than 4,000 yards (3,660m). Two cruisers, *Fiume* and *Zara,* disintegrated under the weight of fire in just five minutes; two supporting destroyers went down as well, and five hours later the *Pola* was sunk. In all, 2,400 Italian sailors were killed, including the commanding officer, Vice Admiral Cattaneo. To some, the Battle of Cape Matapan represented the greatest British naval victory at sea since Trafalgar, but above all things it cemented the superiority of the Royal Navy over the Italian Navy.

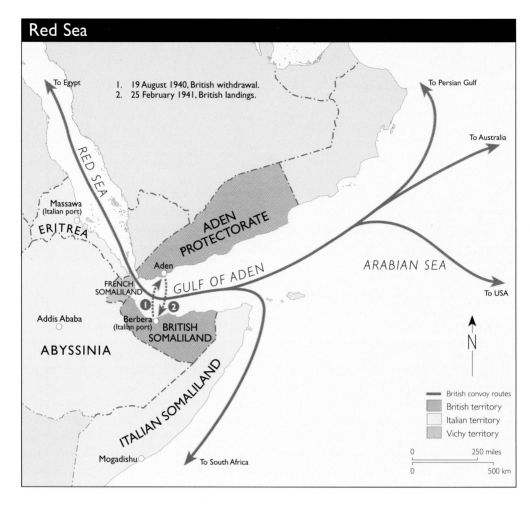

Red Sea

To Egypt

1. 19 August 1940, British withdrawal.
2. 25 February 1941, British landings.

To Persian Gulf

To Australia

RED SEA

Massawa
(Italian port)

ERITREA

ADEN
PROTECTORATE

Aden

FRENCH
SOMALILAND   GULF OF ADEN   ARABIAN SEA

To USA

Addis Ababa

Berbera
(Italian port)   BRITISH
SOMALILAND

ABYSSINIA

ITALIAN SOMALILAND

N

━━━━ British convoy routes
▓▓▓▓ British territory
☐☐☐☐ Italian territory
▒▒▒▒ Vichy territory

0   250 miles
├─────────┤
0   500 km

Mogadishu

To South Africa

Mussolini's decision to declare war on a statistically weaker Britain in the Mediterranean may have seemed a worthwhile gamble. However, it meant that the Red Sea forces were cut off from Italy and their supplies. Unless Italy could defeat British forces in Egypt and east Africa, its isolated naval garrison would eventually succumb to an overwhelming Royal Navy presence. Initially, Italy held the advantage over the British Empire on the land in east Africa, forcing an amphibious withdrawal. However, the same naval flexibility enabled British forces to come back into east Africa and ensured eventual victory in 1941 and the seizure of the Italian ports.

Crete

If Cape Matapan was the high point for the Royal Navy then the withdrawal of British troops from Crete was the low point. Churchill's disastrous decision to reallocate resources from the highly successful British

and Commonwealth ground forces in Libya, which had virtually defeated the Italian army, in order to defend Greece and Crete was one of the defining moments of the Mediterranean campaign. The collapse of these redeployed forces in Greece and Crete, and the subsequent evacuations (24–29 April and 28 May–1 June 1941, respectively) cost the Mediterranean Fleet off Crete dearly: two damaged battleships, one aircraft carrier, three sunk cruisers (five damaged), and six sunk destroyers (seven damaged); however, 18,000 troops had been saved.

This devastating year for the Royal Navy was capped by a group of daring Italian frogmen who sneaked into Alexandria harbor on 'human chariots' (small underwater vehicles) and, using explosive charges, holed the battleships HMS *Queen*

Elizabeth and HMS *Valiant* on 19 December
1941. In effect, this act neutralized the
remaining heavy units of the Mediterranean
Fleet, which was now down to just three
cruisers and a small collection of destroyers.

Bismarck

During the winter of 1940, the German
heavy units once again forayed out into the
Atlantic. *Admiral Scheer* reached the Atlantic
at the beginning of November, attacking the
42-ship convoy HX-84, escorted by the
auxiliary cruiser *Jervis Bay*. The latter, before
she could be sunk, gave her merchant
charges sufficient time for all but five to
escape. *Admiral Scheer* then proceeded to the
South Atlantic and Indian Ocean before
returning home in April 1941 having sunk
17 ships. In early December 1940, her sister
ship, *Admiral Hipper,* made the first of two
deployments into the Atlantic before
reaching Norway in the spring of 1941. By
then the *Scharnhorst* and *Gneisenau* had
reached the Atlantic, and during February
and March they sank or captured 22 ships,
preying on those from recently dispersed
convoys. On 23 March the German
battlecruisers reached Brest.

It was intended that both Brest-based
ships would join the 42,000-ton battleship
Bismarck and the heavy cruiser *Prinz Eugen,*
both newly commissioned, and seven
tankers and other support ships, in the most
ambitious commercial raiding operation
planned by the Kriegsmarine. However, the
damage caused by repeated air attacks by
RAF Bomber Command on Brest prevented
this. Consequently, Operation Rheinübung
began on 18 May with only the *Bismarck* and
Prinz Eugen putting to sea from their bases in
Gotenhafen and Kiel.

Initially spotted by a Swedish cruiser in
the Kattegat and detected by an RAF
photo-reconnaissance Spitfire refueling in
Grimstad fjord, south of Bergen, they headed
north. Thus, with the Royal Navy so badly
mauled in the Mediterranean, the most
powerful battleship in the world was on the

loose in the Atlantic shipping lanes. The
Denmark Strait and the Iceland–Shetland
gap were patrolled by several cruisers backed
up by Admiral Holland's battlegroup of
HMS *Hood* and the newly commissioned
battleship HMS *Prince of Wales*, which still
had civilian shipyard workers on board.
Meanwhile, the Commander-in-Chief Home
Fleet, Admiral John Tovey, left Scapa Flow
on board the *Prince of Wales*'s sister ship,
King George V, accompanied by the
carrier *Victorious*.

On the evening of 23 May, the German
ships were spotted by the heavy cruisers
Norfolk and *Suffolk* in the Denmark Strait.
Using radar, the British ships tracked the
Bismarck and *Prinz Eugen* as they headed
south into the northern Atlantic; position
reports were sent to the closing *Hood* and
Prince of Wales, which came in sight of their
adversaries at dawn the next day. At 5.52 am
the *Hood* opened up, but the reply of the
German ships was immediate and accurate,
hitting *Hood* with their first salvos. Her
armor was penetrated and her aft magazine
exploded, followed almost immediately by
her forward magazine. *Hood* sank at once,
with only three of her crew of 1,420
surviving. After taking a number of hits,
the *Prince of Wales* managed to disengage,
joining *Norfolk* and *Suffolk* in shadowing the
German ships.

The encounter had left the *Bismarck* with
a small oil leak and a reduction in speed. A
highly satisfied Admiral Lütjens decided to
make for Brest. Meanwhile, the Admiralty
mobilized every available ship to converge
on Lütjens' flagship, including Admiral
Somerville's Force H from the Mediterranean.
Nineteen capital ships, carriers, and cruisers,
and almost as many destroyers were to hunt
the *Bismarck* down.

After a vain attack by Swordfish torpedo
bombers and Fulmar fighters from *Victorious*,
the *Prinz Eugen* split from the *Bismarck* in
order to operate independently in the
Atlantic, whilst the *Bismarck* managed for a
time to give the Royal Navy the slip too.
However, as she headed for the French coast
she was detected once again, her position

confirmed at 10.30 am on 26 May by an RAF Coastal Command Catalina flying boat 700 miles (1,125km) west of Brest. Tovey's Home Fleet was not able to intercept, but at 9.00 pm that evening a force of Swordfish led by Lieutenant T. P. Goode from Force H's carrier *Ark Royal* managed to disable the *Bismarck*'s steering gear. After being harried by British destroyers during the night, shortly before 9.00 am on 27 May the *Bismarck* was engaged by Tovey's main force, including the battleships *King George V* and *Rodney*, and the cruisers *Dorsetshire* and *Norfolk*. After surviving 109 minutes of bombardment, the *Bismarck* was finished off by torpedoes from the *Dorsetshire*. Only 109 of her crew were saved.

It has been argued that the winter of 1940–41 was the only time that the Germans could have achieved victory in the Atlantic campaign. Despite efforts by the British to

The *Bismarck* engaging HMS *Hood*, 24 May 1941. The destruction of the Royal Navy's mighty battlecruiser was a major blow to Great Britain and led to a huge naval operation to hunt down the German battleship. (IWM HU382)

extend the range of their anti-submarine efforts both at and over the sea, which did push the submarines further west, the Royal Navy and RAF Coastal Command lacked both adequate tactics and equipment to successfully counter the Wolf Pack attacks. But Dönitz lacked sufficient numbers of submarines and as 1941 progressed he was also forced, to his considerable frustration, to divert increasing numbers of submarines to northern operations in support of Operation Barbarossa, and during the autumn to the Mediterranean to combat the Royal Navy there.

Allied improvements in the Atlantic

By this time the British had also begun reading the U-boat ciphered radio traffic with increasing regularity and speed, which continued until February 1942, when the design of the submarines' Enigma machines was improved. This effort was aided by the Royal Navy's capture of a number of Enigma code machines. Amongst these was *U-110*'s machine, seized by a boarding party led by

sublieutenant David Balme, which was put aboard from HMS *Bulldog* on 9 May 1941. They recovered the priceless machine after overpowering the crew of the sinking submarine. The prodigious efforts of the British code-breakers at the Government Code and Cipher School at Bletchley Park did not provide information sufficient to target individual submarines – although the surface supply vessels and, later, the specialist Type XIV resupply submarines, the so-called *Milchkühe*, were vulnerable. Crucially, however, the information did allow the rerouting of convoys away from known concentrations of U-boats.

In February 1941 Western Approaches Command was moved from Plymouth to Liverpool, where the majority of convoys were now routed. Initially under the command of Admiral Sir Percy Noble, from November 1942, it was led by Admiral Sir Max Horton, who had won fame for his exploits as a submariner in the First World War. From April 1941 the new headquarters benefited from the Admiralty being given operational control over the activities of RAF Coastal Command. Derby House was responsible for the allocation of escorts and the routing of convoys based on intelligence information it received from the Admiralty's Operational Intelligence Centre's Submarine Tracking Room. Also to be located in Liverpool was the Western Approaches Tactical Unit (WATU), which, taking its cue from the work of individual antisubmarine escort commanders such as Commander Frederick Walker, was responsible for developing an increasingly effective antisubmarine tactical doctrine.

By the spring of 1941, the British were also making very efficient use of their shipping resources and, through rationing, had reduced their import and therefore tonnage requirements. In fact, during 1941 import requirements were running at about half the prewar rate. A major shipbuilding program was also in hand: in 1941 British yards launched 1.2 million tons, with another 7 million tons on order from American yards. So, despite the fact that

the year saw 3.6 million tons sunk, Britain ended 1941 with an increase in tonnage. Submarines accounted for 2.1 million tons of the losses, the rest being caused by single merchant raiders, the Luftwaffe, and Admiral Raeder's surface raiders.

The year 1941 saw the increasing participation of the United States – long before its official involvement following the Japanese attack on Pearl Harbor. In April 1941 Britain had established air and escort bases on Iceland, which enabled the smaller escorts to operate out to around 35° west. Following the meeting between Churchill and President Roosevelt at Placentia Bay in August 1941, the United States took responsibility for the western Atlantic, including Iceland, and from mid-September the US Navy began to escort fast convoys between there and North America. During one of these operations, on 31 October, the American destroyer *Reuben James* was sunk by *U-552* with the loss of 100 sailors whilst escorting convoy HX-156. This was the first US Navy ship to be sunk. The slow convoys became the responsibility of the Royal Canadian Navy but, laboring with often badly trained crews and denied adequate equipment, its performance was poor.

Indian Ocean, 1942

At the start of 1942 the Royal Navy and Churchill were still assessing the impact of the loss of HMS *Prince of Wales* and HMS *Repulse* to Japanese aircraft in December 1941. By the spring of 1942, however, the Eastern Fleet, under the command of Admiral Somerville, became operational in the Indian Ocean. The fleet's main aims were to stop any major incursions into the ocean by Japanese forces and to defend British territories and convoys.

On paper, Somerville's force was impressive, with five battleships, three aircraft carriers, and numerous escorts. However, only one of the battleships had been modernized and the carriers possessed far fewer aircraft, and these of generally worse quality, than the Japanese.

Moved to Derby House in Liverpool in February 1941, Western Approaches Command was responsible for the allocation of escorts and the routing of convoys based on intelligence information it received from the Admiralty's Operational Intelligence Centre's Submarine Tracking Room. From April 1941 it also had operational control over the activities of RAF Coastal Command. Under Admiral Sir Max Horton it would help to achieve victory in the Battle of the Atlantic. (IWM A 25746)

Additionally, there were insufficient antiaircraft weapons in the fleet and the naval bases in Ceylon were too vulnerable to air attack. A refueling base at Addu Atoll provided some sanctuary from attack, but little in the way of fleet support.

Admiral Somerville and London were determined that he would not lose his command in the same fashion as the *Prince of Wales* and the *Repulse*. Consequently, no direct action against the Japanese was to take place. However, in April 1942, a sizable Japanese fleet entered the Indian Ocean with five aircraft carriers and four battleships. In the first weeks of April, the Japanese fleet attacked Ceylon, India, and shipping, inflicting heavy British losses, including the cruisers *Cornwall* and *Dorsetshire* and the aircraft carrier *Hermes*.

Somerville was then directed to remove his weakest ships to the western Indian Ocean. Britain had reached its lowest ebb in the Indian Ocean. Unable to defend India and Ceylon, and having lost Singapore and Burma, the Royal Navy was forced to establish a presence in the Indian Ocean as a potential barrier to Japan's ambitions until such time as the Eastern Fleet could be built up.

Arctic convoys

Although the increasing involvement of the United States in the Atlantic was welcome, it did little to lift the burdens on the Royal Navy, to which, in August 1941, was added responsibility for protecting the Arctic convoys. Following the German invasion of the Soviet Union, on 22 June 1941, Britain sought to supply its new ally. The first convoy left Scapa Flow on 21 August 1941. Eventually, almost a quarter of the total lend-lease supplies sent to Russia, nearly 4.5 million tons of weapons, trucks, aircraft, and equipment, were carried along this

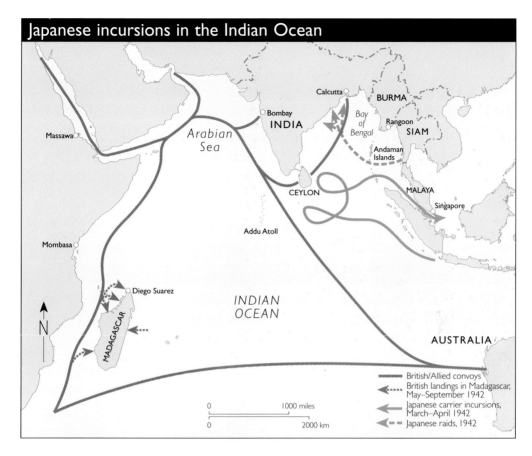

Japanese incursions in the Indian Ocean

Calcutta
BURMA
Bombay
INDIA
Bay of Bengal
Rangoon
SIAM
Massawa
Arabian Sea
Andaman Islands
CEYLON
MALAYA
Singapore
Addu Atoll
Mombasa
Diego Suarez
INDIAN OCEAN
MADAGASCAR
N
AUSTRALIA

0   1000 miles
0   2000 km

— British/Allied convoys
◄····· British landings in Madagascar, May–September 1942
◄— Japanese carrier incursions, March–April 1942
◄-- Japanese raids, 1942

dangerous North Cape convoy route. Almost 8 percent of the merchant ships sent never arrived at their destinations of Murmansk, Archangel, or Molotovsk.

The convoy routes were constrained by both geography and weather. Winter found ice forcing the convoys closer to the Norwegian coast, but at least provided the cover of the long Arctic nights. Ships and their crews had to contend with heavy seas and the extreme cold. If it was not removed, ships could accumulate dangerous coverings of ice. In the water, without modern survival aids, survivors of sinkings had little chance. However, until March 1942 the Germans did not expend much effort against the Arctic convoys.

Operation Drumbeat

Ironically, the formal entry of the United States into the war brought no respite – only

greatly increased danger. Ignoring the lessons of history, in particular those of the First World War and British experience in the Second, the US Navy's Chief of Naval Operations, Admiral King, refused to implement a convoy system off the eastern seaboard, relying instead on offensive patrols and protected sea lanes. In an operation code-named 'Drumbeat' from January 1942, Dönitz began concentrating his submarines off the American coast, where they preyed on individual sailing ships that were often illuminated by the unextinguished lights of the coastal towns and highways. In May and June alone, the U-boats sank over one million tons of shipping in these waters. This was the German submarine service's second 'Happy Time.'

Only as an American convoy system was increasingly introduced and more escorts were made available – including some 20 transferred from Britain and Canada – did

HMS *Hermes* was the Royal Navy's first purpose-built aircraft carrier. She also became the first British carrier to be sunk by air power, on 9 April 1942. Without her air group, or land-based air cover, the *Hermes* was assaulted by aircraft from the Japanese carriers of the 1st Carrier Fleet. Following some 40 hits and near misses, she sank off Ceylon with the loss of over 300 men. The presence of her air group would have made little differnce, since it comprised only Swordfish torpedo bomber aircraft and not fighters for air defense. (IWM HU 1839)

the losses fall off, forcing Dönitz's submarines to move elsewhere, initially to the Caribbean. However, with a global system of interlocking convoys now in place and more extensive and effective Allied air patrols, his submarines were finding it harder to locate areas in which they could easily operate.

The Channel Dash

Whilst Dönitz's submarines were wreaking havoc in the American shipping lanes in early 1942, Hitler was becoming alarmed at the possibility of an Allied invasion of Norway. The battlecruisers *Scharnhorst* and *Gneisenau*, and

the cruiser *Prinz Eugen*, were then at Brest. Rather than leave them where they posed a considerable threat to the Atlantic shipping lanes, in a misguided effort to shore up his Scandinavian defenses Hitler ordered them to break out for Norway via the English Channel. This operation – codenamed Cerberus by the Germans – was deemed so risky by Admiral Raeder that he refused to accept any responsibility for it.

However, through a series of failures, both technical and human, on the part of the Royal Air Force and the Royal Navy, the Admiralty was not alerted to the fact that the German squadron was at sea on 11 February until it was too late to mount a successful interception. It was only possible to launch small, uncoordinated, and in the case of a Swordfish attack by six aircraft – all of which were lost – virtually suicidal attacks. The German ships managed to reach Germany, to the considerable embarrassment of the British and the understandable glee of their opponents. Nevertheless, both battlecruisers were damaged by British air-dropped mines, and the *Gneisenau* was subsequently damaged beyond

repair in a bombing raid on her dry-dock. It was March 1943 before the *Scharnhorst* arrived in Norway.

Return to the Arctic

From March 1942, their expected quick victory against the Soviets not having materialized, German forces began to concentrate in northern Norway in a bid to stop the increasing amount of supplies reaching the Eastern Front. Convoys had initially sailed with a close escort of destroyers and smaller ships and a distant escort of cruisers. But after March 1942 heavy units of the Home Fleet provided more distant cover to guard against the German heavy units, including the *Bismarck*'s sister-ship the *Tirpitz*, lying in wait in the Norwegian fjords.

However, opposition increasingly came from the Luftwaffe. On 27 May 1942, convoy PQ16 was attacked by no fewer than 108 aircraft. A total of seven ships were eventually lost from this convoy. The next convoy, PQ17, left Iceland on 27 June 1942. After Ultra intelligence was received that it was about to be attacked by a strong German force, which potentially included the *Tirpitz*,

In September 1940 the British ordered 60 ships from yards in the United States to a simple British design. To speed up their manufacture further, the Americans modified the design, dispensing with rivets in favor of welding. In January 1941, the United States ordered 200 7,126-ton ships based on the modified British design to meet its own emergency shipbuilding program, the 'Liberty Fleet.' Eventually, 2,710 Liberty ships would be constructed, about 200 going to Britain, mostly by the Kaiser shipyards, using a mass-production system that on one occasion saw a vessel launched just four days and 15½ hours after the keel had been laid. (IWM A23033)

the cruisers *Hipper* and *Admiral Scheer*, and the pocket battleship *Lützow*, convoy PQ17 was ordered by the Admiralty to scatter. The dispersed ships were instead set upon from the air, and only 11 out of the convoy's 37 merchant ships reached their destination. A total of 153 seamen died, and 2,500 aircraft, over 400 tanks, and almost 4,000 other vehicles were lost. This disaster and the demands of the Mediterranean theater largely forced the suspension of the Arctic convoys until December 1942, much to the annoyance of Stalin.

Madagascar

The Vichy French island of Madagascar had worried the Allies since late 1941 with the

Eastern Indian Ocean – sinkings and incursions

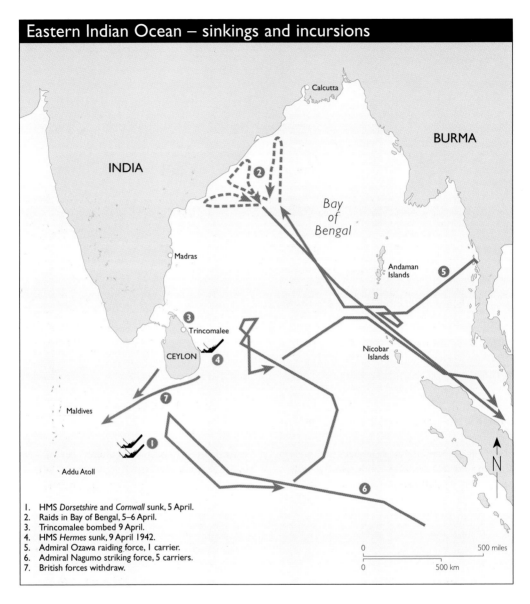

1. HMS *Dorsetshire* and *Cornwall* sunk, 5 April.
2. Raids in Bay of Bengal, 5–6 April.
3. Trincomalee bombed 9 April.
4. HMS *Hermes* sunk, 9 April 1942.
5. Admiral Ozawa raiding force, 1 carrier.
6. Admiral Nagumo striking force, 5 carriers.
7. British forces withdraw.

Japanese war in the Pacific. It stood near the route to the Middle East and India, via the Southern African Cape, and could be used easily by Japanese submarines as a base to cut these vital supply lines. Thus Operation Ironclad was initiated to neutralize and occupy the island. The operation was so secret that not even the Free French were told of its existence until the operation had commenced.

A substantial force was assembled, with ships being taken from home waters and Force H. Rear Admiral Syfret of Force H was in command. This was the first large

amphibious operation since the Norway and Dakar missions of 1940. Following their sailing from Durban at the start of the month, 13,000 British Empire troops landed in Madagascar in the early morning of 5 May 1942. Their target was the huge harbor of Diego Suarez in the north of the island. A combined operation was mounted to seize the objective, with aerial support provided by aircraft from HMS *Illustrious* and HMS *Indomitable*. Within hours Diego Suarez had been taken, and by the evening of the 7th, the British were using the harbor.

The Imperial Japanese navy made only one large-scale sortie into the Indian Ocean during the Pacific War, and that was during April 1942. The Japanese fleet accounted for a number of vessels and forced Admiral Somerville's fleet to the western Indian Ocean. However, the Japanese failed to take advantage of their naval superiority. Following strikes against Ceylon and targets in the Bay of Bengal, they withdrew to the Pacific.

In September, the capital, Tananarive, fell to British forces following another amphibious operation. Any thoughts of early Vichy collapse were short-lived as pockets of resistance lasted until November 1942. However, although Japanese submarine and merchant raider activity grew briefly in the region during the mid-year months, accounting for dozens of ships, Madagascar could no longer pose a problem to the supply lines of the western Indian Ocean. Operation Ironclad had been a great success for British amphibious operations, with numerous lessons learned for use in the Mediterranean theater.

By late 1942 the Indian Ocean had become an increasingly less important theater to the war aims of the Allies. The United States had held the Japanese onslaught in the Pacific and was now building for its own offensives, whilst in the Atlantic and Mediterranean the Allies were preparing for Operation Torch, the invasion of North Africa. Consequently, elements of the Eastern Fleet were pulled back from the Indian Ocean for this and the later amphibious campaigns against Italy. As Correlli Barnett writes: 'In the autumn the Admiralty cut the Eastern Fleet down to one carrier and two battleships, the remainder being needed in the Mediterranean to support "Operation Torch". In spring 1943 Somerville lost his sole remaining carrier and battleship, so reducing his fleet to cruisers and destroyers and rendering the Indian Ocean a strategic backwater.'

Dieppe

It was partly a wish to placate Soviet calls for the opening up of a second front that led to the disastrous decision to undertake the large-scale raid on the German-held port of Dieppe on 19 August 1942. Also responsible were varied political and military pressures on Churchill and his Chiefs of Staff – one of which was a wish by the latter to avoid the former forcing through an even more dangerous escapade – and the presence of Mountbatten as Chief of Combined Operations.

The Dieppe operation involved a force of 237 warships and landing craft, including eight destroyers but no battleships, which the Admiralty refused to risk. They carried almost 5,000 Canadian troops, some 1,000 British, and 50 American, and enjoyed the support of 74 squadrons from the Allied airforces. The Canadians suffered over 3,000 casualties in the operation, of whom some 900 were killed, whilst the British took 275 casualties and lost one destroyer, 33 landing craft, and no fewer than 106 aircraft.

Operation Torch

The entry of the United States into the war in December 1941 completely altered the strategic situation in the Mediterranean Sea, from a desperate holding operation by the Royal Navy to an offensive theater characterized by large-scale amphibious assaults. The Allied landings in North Africa, or Operation Torch, on 8 November 1942 marked the beginning of the end for Vichy French and the German/Italian forces in north Africa.

Aptly, Admiral Cunningham was made Allied Naval Commander Expeditionary Force, although General Dwight Eisenhower was in overall command. The planning for this highly elaborate combined operation was done by the brilliant Admiral Sir Bertram Ramsay, as Deputy Naval Commander Expeditionary Force. The landings were organized in masterly fashion into the Western Assault Force (Casablanca), the Central Task Force (Oran), and the Eastern Task Force (Algiers). Just under 100,000 troops were deployed in the first phases of the operation.

The Arctic convoys were the most dangerous of all, under threat of attack by submarine, surface raider, and aircraft. Here PQ18, en route to the Soviet Union in September 1942, is seen fighting a heavy attack by the Luftwaffe. (IWM A12022)

The Allies had hoped that Tunisia would fall by February 1943, but it took the combined efforts of the Torch force and the Eighth Army from the east to bring about the surrender of the Axis forces on 13 May 1943. The Royal Navy supported not only the landings in this period but also the Eighth Army, with supplies for the Battle of El Alamein from 23 October to 5 November. Allied forces sank 500 Axis merchant ships (560,000 tons) between January and May 1943 in order to cut off the enemy forces in North Africa.

Battle of the Barents Sea

In December 1942 the Arctic convoys were resumed. The second of these, JW51B, was attacked on 31 December by the *Lützow*, the *Admiral Hipper*, and six destroyers. The Battle of the Barents Sea saw a skillful and determined defense by the convoy's destroyer escorts under Captain Robert Sherbrooke, supported by the distant cruiser escort; they forced the hesitant Germans off, for the loss of two destroyers and a minesweeper against one German destroyer. In March 1943, largely in order to divert escorts to deal with the growing menace in the Atlantic, the Arctic convoys were again discontinued.

Hitler's reaction to the failure of the attack on JW51B to achieve the expected success in

ABOVE German nervousness about a second front was increased by a series of British Combined Operations raids. On the night of 27/28 March 1942, HMS *Campbeltown* managed to get past the German defenses at St Nazaire and ram the dock gates, whilst 268 Commandos landed from smaller vessels to destroy base facilities; of 630 men involved, 144 were killed and another 200 captured. But on the following day 5 tons of explosives hidden in the *Campbeltown's* bows exploded, putting the only dock on the Atlantic coast big enough to accommodate the German battleship *Tirpitz* out of action for the rest of the war. (IWM)

the Barents Sea was one of absolute fury. Admiral Dönitz replaced Raeder as Commander-in-Chief with orders to decommission the remaining major surface units and reassign their crews to the submarine service. This, in fact, did not take place, Dönitz eventually persuading a skeptical Hitler to retain them. By this time there were some 400 operational U-boats at Dönitz's disposal, and he now had the ability to put around 100 into the Atlantic at any one time.

Victory in the Atlantic

Whilst, through the prodigious efforts of American shipyards in producing the prefabricated Liberty cargo vessel, the Allies could always more than replace their merchant-ship losses, the massive buildup of men and matériel that would be required for the invasion of Europe necessitated securing the Atlantic. This task was therefore given priority by the Allied Casablanca Conference in January 1943. But to begin with, the carnage in the Atlantic continued.

Arctic convoy routes, winter and summer

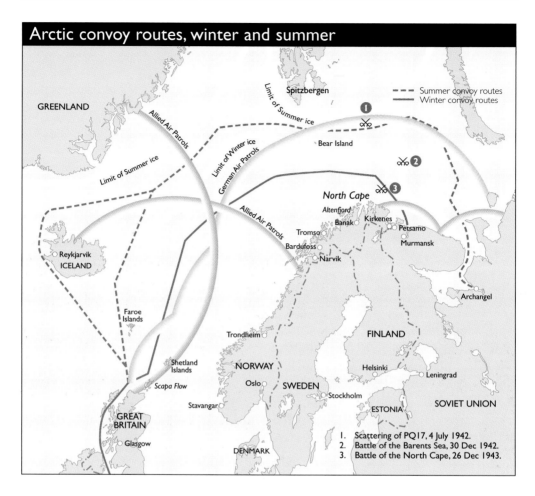

Map legend and labels:

- - - Summer convoy routes
— Winter convoy routes

GREENLAND

Spitzbergen

Limit of Summer ice

Allied Air Patrols

Limit of Summer ice

Limit of Winter ice

German Air Patrols

Bear Island

North Cape

Altenfjord

Banak Kirkenes

Petsamo

Tromso

Murmansk

Bardufoss

Narvik

Allied Air Patrols

Reykjarvik
ICELAND

Archangel

Faroe
Islands

Trondheim

FINLAND

Shetland
Islands

NORWAY

Helsinki

Leningrad

Scapa Flow

Oslo   SWEDEN

Stockholm

Stavangar

ESTONIA

SOVIET UNION

GREAT
BRITAIN

Glasgow

DENMARK

1. Scattering of PQ17, 4 July 1942.
2. Battle of the Barents Sea, 30 Dec 1942.
3. Battle of the North Cape, 26 Dec 1943.

ABOVE From August 1941 the Royal Navy started running vital resupply convoys around northern Norway to the beleaguered Soviet Union. Eventually, almost 4.5 million tons of war matériel would be carried by this route. But constrained by both geography and the atrocious Arctic weather and, after March 1942, subjected to the concentrated efforts of German aircraft, submarines, and surface vessels lurking in Norwegian fjords, this was the most dangerous of all convoy routes, with almost 8.5 percent of merchant vessels despatched lost.

RIGHT Operation Ironclad was a testing ground for British amphibious operations following their initial failures earlier in the war. One area that was exploited far better than in previous landings was the use of carrier-based aircraft, particularly in larger numbers. The carriers HMS *Illustrious* and HMS *Indomitable* flew a crosssection of the British naval aircraft of the time, employing Swordfish, Albacores, Fulmars, Martletts (Wildcats), and Sea Hurricanes. The *Illustrious* was also used in the successful operations in September.

If German U-boat numbers had risen, the doctrine and equipment capable of countering them had also become much improved in the previous 18 months. Great strides had been made in terms of training and tactics. There were now better and more escorts. Settled groups were formed. The ships began to receive a steady flow of new sensors and weapons. The two most important were a High Frequency Direction

Finding set (HF-DF or 'Huff-Duff') and a new, revolutionary, and much more effective radar set initially operating on a wavelength of just under 4 inches (10cm).

Ship-borne 'Huff-Duff' exploited the U-boats' reliance on radio communications and provided instant warning of the presence of enemy submarines with sufficient accuracy to permit escorts to attack. Centimetric radar was fitted to both

Madagascar

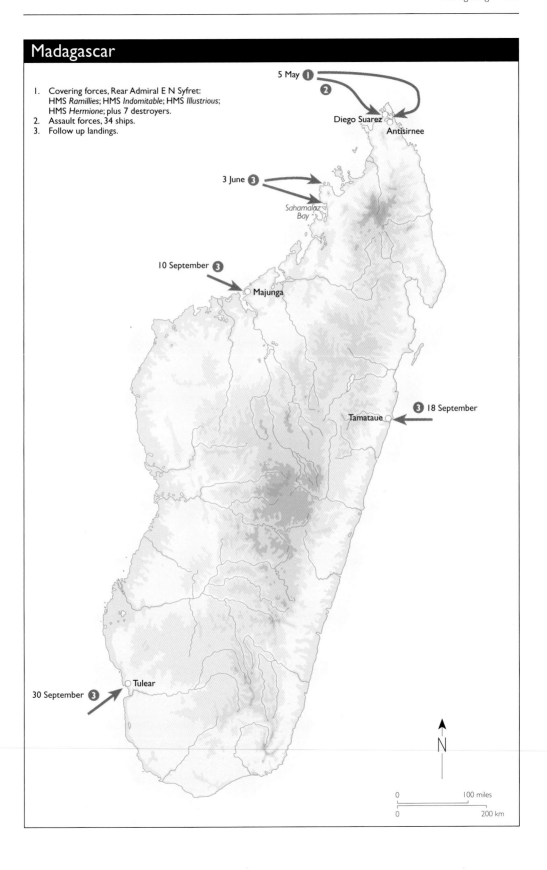

1. Covering forces, Rear Admiral E N Syfret:
   HMS *Ramillies*; HMS *Indomitable*; HMS *Illustrious*;
   HMS *Hermione*; plus 7 destroyers.
2. Assault forces, 34 ships.
3. Follow up landings.

5 May ❶
❷

Diego Suarez
Antisirnee

3 June ❸

Sahamalaz Bay

10 September ❸
Majunga

❸ 18 September
Tamataue

30 September ❸
Tulear

N

0   100 miles
0   200 km

surface escorts and aircraft. U-boats were now vulnerable whilst they traveled on the surface. Often they would not know that they had been detected until an aircraft commenced its attack. The submarines were increasingly forced under water, where they were slow and lacked endurance.

Thus equipped, the Royal Navy's six mid-ocean groups successfully fought their fast convoys through in the autumn of 1942. However, the slow convoys were escorted by the four Canadian groups and one from the United States, which were not as well equipped. Between July and December 1942, 80 percent of mid-Atlantic losses came from Canadian-escorted convoys. By 1943 they were removed from the theater. However, the Royal Navy had sufficient escorts to form escort support groups, which could prosecute submarine contacts whilst leaving the convoy's own escort with the convoy.

By 1942 aircraft patrolling tactics had also become much more effective. Instead of loitering over a convoy, aircraft now operated ahead and to either side of its anticipated route, so preventing the formation of Wolf Pack patrol lines. But there was a reluctance to deploy the few very long-range (VLR) aircraft capable of covering the mid-Atlantic gap, such as the VLR Liberator. In the United States, there was an unwillingness to divert them from the Pacific; in Britain, meanwhile, throughout most of 1942 a fierce political battle was fought between the Royal Navy and Coastal Command on the one hand and Bomber Command under Air Marshal Harris on the other, over whether more long-range aircraft should be shifted from the Strategic Bombing Offensive and made available to those seeking to keep the Atlantic open. Whilst it was eventually decided to switch aircraft to the Atlantic, it was not until the spring of 1943 that this took place. By mid-March, Coastal Command had two squadrons of B-24Ds – Liberator IIIs – the outstanding very long-range antisubmarine patrol aircraft of the war. Their arrival would be crucial.

The other method of providing air cover was to use aircraft carriers. After the costly experiments with the fleet carriers in 1939, the Admiralty explored a number of different solutions. Largely in a bid to deal with German long-range aircraft, a small number of merchant ships were at first provided with a single catapult-launched Hurricane fighter, the courageous pilot being required to bale out or ditch close to a friendly ship after his mission. More designed to counter the submarine threat and certainly for the airmen a less perilous alternative, 19 grain carriers and oil tankers had a flight deck constructed and a cramped hangar provided for four or five aircraft. Whilst these Merchant Aircraft Carriers (MAC-ships) failed to register a U-boat kill, no convoy escorted by one suffered any losses.

An even more effective solution was the escort carrier. The Admiralty had examined such a concept before the war, and in 1941 a captured German banana boat was converted into HMS *Audacity*. During Commander Walker's defense of homeward-bound Gibraltar convoy HG76 against a large Wolf Pack in December 1941, *Audacity* had proved herself before being torpedoed. By late 1942 escort carriers built along merchant-ship lines were being mass produced by American yards. They were put to a variety of uses, including close air support during amphibious landings. But from the spring, operated by both the Royal Navy and the US Navy, escort carriers became a permanent feature of the mid-Atlantic escort groups.

So, whilst the spring of 1943 initially brought only gloom for the British, matters were about to swing very rapidly in the Allies' favor. An Admiralty review later that year claimed that 'the Germans never came so near to disrupting communications between the New World and the Old as in the first twenty days of March, 1943.' In fact, this was an unduly pessimistic view and was more a reflection of the war-weariness of the upper echelons of the Royal Navy than an accurate analysis of the progress of the campaign.

Whilst the losses were undoubtedly unacceptably high – more than half a million tons were lost in the first 20 days of the month – increasing numbers of convoys were being brought across without loss. In March, Bletchley Park broke back into the U-boats' Enigma traffic, from which it had been excluded for some months, but instead of being routed away from known concentrations, convoys were now being deliberately fought through in a bid to destroy the U-boats.

By April the total number of U-boats in the North Atlantic reached its maximum of 101, formed into four huge packs. But the advantage increasingly lay with the Allies. For example, the unladen westbound convoy ONS5 was repeatedly attacked during 4 and 5 May by no fewer than 41 U-boats of the Wolf Pack Group Fink. The convoy lost 12 merchant ships, but seven of the attackers were destroyed, another five were damaged, and two more were lost to a collision, forcing U-boat Command to call off that attack.

The German losses continued. During May 41 U-boats were lost. By the month's end, Dönitz had recalled his packs. They could no longer operate on the surface or penetrate the escort screens. The U-boats had to regroup and devise another strategy and wait for new equipment. Fortunately for the Allies, that new equipment would not be available in sufficient numbers before the end of the war. The Atlantic was now effectively secure from submarines in readiness for the buildup for Operation Overlord and the invasion of Europe.

Operation Husky

Operation Husky, or the invasion of Sicily on 10 July 1943, marked a new chapter in the battle for the Mediterranean Sea. Approximately 2,590 warships and landing craft were used to land around 80,000 troops (450,000 eventually), 300 tanks, and 7,000 mechanized vehicles

(the majority British) in Italian territory over a three-day period. The amphibious assaults on the southern part of the island went well due to the careful planning of Ramsay and the weight of naval fire support: six battleships, 10 cruisers, and a multitude of destroyers as well as two aircraft carriers.

Despite putting up fierce resistance, the Italian and German troops were forced to withdraw back to the Italian mainland between 11 and 16 August. The extraction of these troops was a remarkable feat stemming from the excellent planning of Admiral Barone (Italian Navy) and Captain von Liebenstein (German Navy), saving approximately 117,000 troops in a classic amphibious withdrawal. The significance of Husky was underscored by the collapse of the Mussolini government on 25 July, and on 8 September the new Italian government accepted an armistice that led to the surrender of the Italian fleet a day later.

At the same time, Operation Avalanche was initiated, with large-scale landings on the Italian mainland at Salerno Bay. The landing forces comprised 27 battalions of infantry with 150 tanks and nearly 350 pieces of artillery, supported by two brigades of Commandos and US Rangers. The fight was slow and extremely painful for the Allies in the face of excellent German defensive tactics. The formidable Gustav Line forced the Allies to make another amphibious landing at Anzio on 22 January 1944. Rome finally fell on 6 June 1944, the same day that the second front was opened in France with Operation Overlord.

The end of the war in the Mediterranean

The Mediterranean campaign ended in disappointment for the Allies, who did not manage to eject Field Marshal Kesselring's formidable Army Group C from Italy until April 1945, by which time the war was virtually over. For Britain the Mediterranean offered, in the early stages of the war, the

The Atlantic

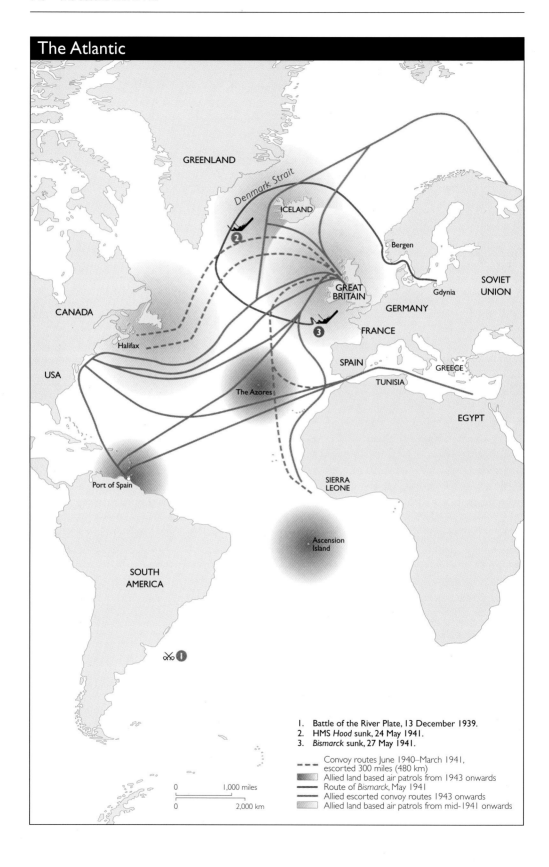

GREENLAND

Denmark Strait

ICELAND

Bergen

GREAT
BRITAIN

Gdynia

SOVIET
UNION

CANADA

GERMANY

FRANCE

Halifax

USA

SPAIN

GREECE

TUNISIA

The Azores

EGYPT

Port of Spain

SIERRA
LEONE

Ascension
Island

SOUTH
AMERICA

1.   Battle of the River Plate, 13 December 1939.
2.   HMS *Hood* sunk, 24 May 1941.
3.   *Bismarck* sunk, 27 May 1941.

Convoy routes June 1940–March 1941,
escorted 300 miles (480 km)
Allied land based air patrols from 1943 onwards
Route of *Bismarck*, May 1941
Allied escorted convoy routes 1943 onwards
Allied land based air patrols from mid-1941 onwards

0   1,000 miles

0   2,000 km

ABOVE German U-boats relied on moving on the surface. Maritime air power, especially when equipped with radar, denied them this essential freedom of maneuver. The versatile and very-long range US Liberator, seen here in a transport version, was essential in closing the mid-Atlantic gap in the spring of 1943. (Topham Picturepoint)

LEFT The key to the naval war was control of the Atlantic. Forays of large German surface units such as Bismarcks could be dealt with. However, continuing the menace of German submarine Wolf Packs that preyed on Allied convoy routes, which grew in complexity as the war progressed, was a much greater problem. It was not until the late spring of 1943 that adequate control of the Atlantic had been acquired with the increasing availability of very long-ranged land based maritime patrol aircraft playing a vital role.

only means by which its land forces could successfully engage the Axis forces, but even that effort was protracted and drawn out. All of these military operations were totally dependent on a highly stretched Royal Navy to maintain the vital supply links with the home base. It did so with few resources, great courage, and inspired leadership from commanders such as Cunningham and Somerville.

Germany perceived the North Africa campaign and, for that matter, the subsequent Italian front as purely diversionary theaters in which its military leaders, Rommel and Kesselring, excelled. As for the Americans, they were reluctantly tied into the Mediterranean campaign by their British allies, who realized that the United States' desire to open up a second front in France before 1944 would have been disastrous. In sum, the Mediterranean theater brought about the collapse of Hitler's major ally in Europe, Italy, and provided critical experience in combined operations before the all-important invasion of France in June 1944.

Tirpitz and Scharnhorst

Despite the 1943 victory over the Wolf Packs in the Atlantic, there still existed a threat from the remaining German heavy surface units, the Tirpitz and the Scharnhorst. By May 1943 both of these powerful vessels were lurking in the fjords of northern Norway. Their presence tied down a large British force and not only posed a threat to Atlantic shipping but also had the potential to disrupt the Overlord landings. In

September 1943, Royal Navy X-craft –
midget submarines – managed to break
through the *Tirpitz*'s defenses in Altenfjord
and mine her, putting her out of action for
six months.

In order to deal with the crisis in the
Atlantic, convoys to Russia had been
suspended at the beginning of 1943. Their
resumption in December 1943 and the
worsening situation for Germany on the
Eastern Front led Admiral Dönitz to order
their interception with his last operational
capital ship, the *Scharnhorst*. However, these
convoys were also the bait that Admiral

Envisaged by prewar planners, it was not until late 1942
that escort carriers built on merchant ship lines were
being mass produced by US yards. They were used for a
variety of purposes, including close air support during
amphibious landings. But from the spring of 1943,
operated by both the Royal Navy and the US Navy,
escort carriers became a permanent feature of the
mid-Atlantic escort groups. Here HMS *Emperor* is seen in
the middle of an Atlantic gale in 1944. (IWM A24181)

Bruce Fraser, Commander-in-Chief of the
British Home Fleet, used to set a trap.
Forewarned by Bletchley Park, Fraser
mounted a skillful operation in which the
German vessel, under Admiral Erich Bey,

was caught between Fraser's two squadrons in appalling conditions off the northern Cape on 26 December, and was sunk with the loss of 2,000 of her crew.

There remained the *Tirpitz*. In April 1944, Fraser's Home Fleet launched Operation Tungsten, in which no fewer than six British carriers launched two successful air strikes against the German ship, seriously damaging her. These were amongst 22 air strikes launched against the vessel. On 12 November 1944, relegated to being used as a floating artillery battery at Tromso, Tirpitz was hit by at least two 12,000lb Tallboy bombs dropped by RAF Lancasters. She capsized with the loss of some 1,000 lives.

Operation Overlord

Victory against the Germans required a major landing in northwest Europe. After considerable deliberation, the British and Americans agreed to such an operation at the Casablanca conference in January 1943. Planning and preparation began for what became the largest and most complex amphibious operation in military history, with the initial plan being approved by the Quebec conference in August 1943.

As a result of an extensive intelligence appraisal of possible landing areas, it was decided to land on the Calvados coast of Normandy between Le Havre and the Cherbourg peninsula, rather than at the more heavily defended area around Calais. However, through a complex and successful strategic deception program, the Germans were led to believe that the landings would take place at Calais. To overcome the lack of a deep-water port in the landing zone, two huge prefabricated harbors (Mulberries) were constructed in Britain to be towed across the Channel and assembled off the invasion coast.

Responsibility for the naval and amphibious operations – codenamed Operation Neptune – was given to Admiral Sir Bertram Ramsay, acting under the Allied Supreme Commander, General Dwight D. Eisenhower. By the beginning of June, in the immediate area, the Kriegsmarine had at its disposal a force of 25 U-boats, five destroyers, and 39 E-boats. To protect the landings, the Allies assembled a force of 286 destroyers, sloops, frigates, corvettes, and trawlers, almost 80 percent of which were provided by the Royal Navy. Six support groups, including the escort carriers *Activity, Tracker,* and *Vindex*, formed a screen to cover the Western Approaches and the Bay of Biscay, whilst the other end of the Channel was covered by another four groups. RAF Coastal Command flew extensive patrols over all support groups.

To sweep five safe passages through the mid-Channel minefields, a force of 287 minesweepers of various kinds was brought together. The D-day landings themselves were undertaken by a force of 1,213 warships, including no fewer than seven battleships, two monitors, 23 cruisers, 100 destroyers, 130 frigates and corvettes, and over 4,000 landing ships and craft, many of specialist design. The majority of the warships were British. Some of the landing craft had been converted to fire thousands of rockets to provide additional naval fire support for the assault and to help overcome the extensive German Atlantic Wall defenses.

These assault elements were divided into two forces. The Eastern Task Force under Rear Admiral Sir Philip Vian was responsible for landing the 2nd British Army of British and Canadian troops on the Gold, Juno, and Sword beaches between the River Orne and Port-en-Bessin. The Western Task Force under the American Rear Admiral Alan G. Kirk was responsible for landing the 1st US Army on Omaha and Utah beaches between Port-en-Bessin and Varreville. By the beginning of June 1944 the ports and estuaries of Britain were packed with warships and transports of all kinds as the Allied Expeditionary Force was embarked.

By the summer of 1944, partly as a by-product of the Strategic Bombing Offensive, the Allies had effectively

destroyed the Luftwaffe in the west. Before the landings, the beachhead had been largely cut off from the rest of France by the systematic wrecking of the French transportation system from the air. Any attempts by the Germans to reinforce their coastal forces would be hit by roaming Allied fighter-bombers. The landings were conducted with the enormous benefit of not just air superiority but air supremacy. Over 14,000 air sorties were flown on the first day.

After a day's delay because of poor weather, Operation Neptune began just after midnight on 6 June 1944 – D-Day – with Allied airborne landings aimed at securing the flanks of the invasion area. With heavy naval gunfire support, the first troops began going ashore in the American sector on the Utah and Omaha beaches at 6.30 am, with British and Canadian troops going ashore an hour later on Gold, Juno,

ABOVE The King George V-class battleship *Duke of York*. Serving as Admiral Sir Bruce Fraser's flagship in December 1943, she took part in the trapping and destruction of the German battlecruiser *Scharnhorst*. Whilst the Royal Navy has been criticized for a prewar overemphasis on these leviathans of the seas, it was their possession that prevented German vessels such as the *Scharnhorst* and the even more capable *Bismarck* and *Tirpitz* running amok amongst the transatlantic convoys. (IWM A7552)

RIGHT Admiral Sir Bertram Ramsay was one of a number of outstanding senior British naval officers during the Second World War. He came to dominate Allied amphibious operations in the European theater through his masterminding of the Dunkirk evacuation, his involvement with the planning and conduct of the Allied landings in North Africa and Sicily in 1942 and 1943, and as the meticulous Naval Commander-in-Chief for the Normandy landings in 1944. (IWM A23443)

and Sword (see *The Second World War: Northwest Europe, 1944–1945* in this series). By the end of D-Day, 57,500 American troops and 75,215 British and Canadian

LEFT, TOP An integral part of the success of the Overlord landings was the use of naval gunfire support undertaken by seven battleships, 23 cruisers, 100 destroyers, and 130 frigates and corvettes, mostly provided by the Royal Navy. Here HMS *Warspite*'s 15-inch (381mm) guns are seen engaging German fortifications on the Calvados coast. (IWM A23914)

LEFT, BOTTOM Testimony to the huge logistical scale of the Normandy landings is this scene on Omaha beach, with scores more vessels waiting offshore. (IWM EA26941)

BELOW Larger and faster aircraft such as Seafires and Hellcats (pictured below) encountered serious landing problems when operating off smaller carriers such as the Escort Carriers (CVEs) of the East Indian Fleet. However, their speed and firepower were crucial for achieving successful missions against the Japanese. (IWM)

troops had been landed. When the assault phase – Operation Neptune – concluded officially at the end of the month, 850,279 men, 148,803 vehicles, and 570,505 tons of supplies had been brought ashore.

Following the Allies' breakout from the Normandy beachhead, their armies continued to receive naval support as they moved up the coast of Europe. The Kriegsmarine tried to disrupt these operations by unleashing midget submarines from bases in Holland. Conventional U-boats had also begun to operate in shallower water around the British Isles, but the shallow water played havoc with the asdic (sonar) sets and the proximity of land

Normandy landings

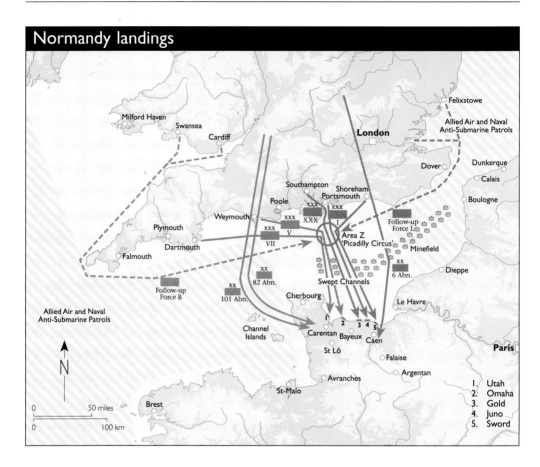

adversely affected other sensors such as radar.

The 'death-ride of the U-boats' nevertheless continued: no fewer than 151 U-boats were lost to Allied action in 1945, for the loss of only 46 Allied merchantmen, a fraction of the 1942 rate of destruction. The U-boat arm had begun to receive submarines equipped with a Schnorchel device that allowed submarines to recharge their batteries without exposing more than the top of the breathing device, and even more worrying for the Allies, high-speed Type XXI and Type XXIII submarines were introduced against which the slower escorts had little answer. Fortunately for the Allied naval effort, however, the Germans were not able to produce these in sufficient quantity by the time the yards building them – subjected to increasingly heavy and accurate air attack – had been overrun in 1945.

D-Day saw US and British airborne landings on either flank of the assault areas to protect the Allied seaborne landings. Forces arrived in Area Z from the southern half of Great Britain - follow up forces woudl come from the whole country - and several thousand vessels of all kinds were funnelled through narrow channels swept through the deep-water minefields. By the end of 6 June 57,500 American and 75,215 British and Canadian troops would be ashore.

Victory in the Indian Ocean

As the naval war began to decrease in intensity in the European theater following Operation Overlord in June 1944, the Royal Navy and Churchill transferred their naval attention – though not necessarily at the same speed – to the Indian and Pacific oceans. Initially, the Indian Ocean, with the continuing land campaign in Burma, was seen as a priority, for it was felt, politically, that the lost territories must be retaken.

D-Day gun duels

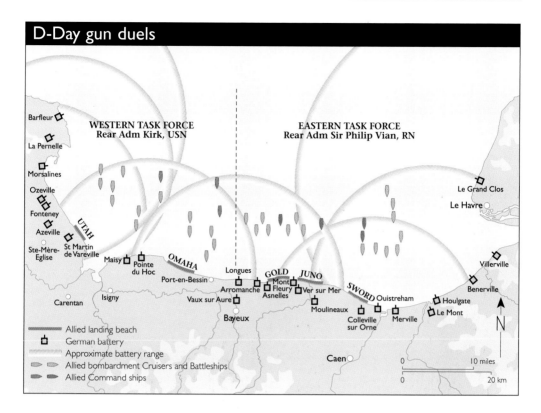

WESTERN TASK FORCE
Rear Adm Kirk, USN

EASTERN TASK FORCE
Rear Adm Sir Philip Vian, RN

Barfleur

La Pernelle

Morsalines

Ozeville

Fonteney

Azeville

Ste-Mère-Eglise   St Martin de Vareville

UTAH

Maisy   Pointe du Hoc

OMAHA

Port-en-Bessin

Longues

GOLD   JUNO

Mont
Arromanche   Fleury   Ver sur Mer
Asnelles

SWORD   Ouistreham

Houlgate
Le Mont

Moulineaux   Merville

Le Grand Clos

Le Havre

Villerville

Benerville

Carentan   Isigny   Vaux sur Aure

Bayeux

Colleville sur Orne

Caen

- ▬▬▬ Allied landing beach
- ☗ German battery
- Approximate battery range
- ◖◗ ◖◗ Allied bombardment Cruisers and Battleships
- ◖◗ ◖◗ Allied Command ships

0   10 miles
0   20 km

N

There were also the benefits of massive production coming through to the Indian Ocean as large numbers of escort carriers and much more capable carrier aircraft entered service – the very equipment that Admiral Somerville had wanted for the Eastern Fleet in 1942.

The Eastern Fleet, however, had been essentially defensive in outlook, acting as a fleet-in-being, deterring Japanese incursions into the Indian Ocean and safeguarding the vital convoy routes. The new fleets that were to become active for 1945, the East Indies Fleet and the British Pacific Fleet, were very much offensively orientated. The role of the East Indies Fleet was to support the British Fourteenth Army as it pushed the Japanese back through Burma using escort carriers, escorts including battleships and cruisers, and a large amphibious force. It was also there to neutralize the Japanese warships in the region and stop them from entering the Indian Ocean. In addition, it was tasked to destroy the remaining Japanese land-based air units in the theater.

In an attempt to protect the coast German forces had created an Atlantic Wall of mines, obstacles and gun emplacements. Whilst not as formidably defended as some sections of the coast, the German heavy gun batteries in Normandy were sited to cover the entire landing area with interlocking arcs of fire and unmolested would have made the landings impossible. An essential feature that made the Allied landings possible, was the presence of large numbers of heavy naval vessels to counter the threat posed by these guns.

Through a series of amphibious raids and assaults, offensive carrier fighter missions and the sinking of the Japanese heavy cruiser *Haguro*, these aims were successfully achieved, so much so that by May the land-based Japanese air and sea forces no longer posed a threat. By this point the East Indies Fleet was a substantial force, employing two battleships, nine escort carriers, two ferry carriers and dozens of cruisers, destroyers, submarines, and amphibious warfare vessels. It was a force far removed from the earlier Eastern Fleet, and one that could finally engage the Japanese on superior terms. The fleet remained in the

Indian Ocean supporting the land campaign and Japan's withdrawal from the region until the defeat of the Japanese Empire.

It can be argued that the Eastern Fleet was overshadowed by its much larger sister-fleet, the British Pacific Fleet: not only in terms of firepower and size, but also by the fact that the Pacific Fleet was engaged in the heart of the Japanese Empire and against the last remaining substantial Japanese assets. Either way, the formation and

The combination of the American advance in the Pacific and the British advances in Burma and the Indian Ocean saw a collapse in the Japanese ability to defend against amphibious operations in the Bay of Bengal by 1945. Here British forces are approaching Rangoon. The Japanese had already withdrawn. Note the landing craft, far removed from the very early operations of 1940. (IWM IND4659)

employment of the British Pacific Fleet in early 1945 signaled the end of the Indian Ocean as a major theater of operations.

Peter Herbert Owen, Royal Navy midshipman

When the naval war came, it brought a harshness and violence that had not been expected. For most naval personnel it also brought a very steep learning curve, as many of them had never seen conflict before. Much of the interwar period had been spent on training cruises, goodwill visits, and tours. The younger members of ships' companies were uninitiated in the ways of war and had only experienced them through their elders and reading the histories and memoirs of the First World War and before.

This was especially true of the naval officer cadets of Britain. One such young man was Midshipman Peter Herbert Owen, who joined the battleship HMS *Royal Oak* in August 1939 having passed out from Dartmouth Naval College at the start of May. Owen had spent four years in the College, starting as a boy cadet in 1935. During his four years' training in Dartmouth, he had undertaken various naval and academic courses, and taken part in numerous sports. Soon, however, he and his classmates would come to the end of their summer cruises. They would become embroiled with events and adventures that they had sought from the start of their young naval careers, but for which their training could never have adequately prepared them. Yet during the war and through all of their experiences they evolved and matured, and with the mass input of wartime reservist and volunteer reservist officers, formed the backbone of the junior officer corps of the Royal Navy.

Owen was no exception. His reporting of the war in his midshipman's journal during its first two years begins to take on a hardened and matter-of-fact edge within a month of the hostilities breaking out, with his account of the sinking of HMS *Royal Oak* in October 1939. Owen, upon being sent to his ship, was

tasked with keeping a journal for the remainder of his time at sea as a midshipman – in his case, almost two years. Officers supervising midshipmen were to ensure that the journals demonstrated powers of observation, expression, and orderliness.

At the start of hostilities in the late summer of 1939, the British Home Fleet had moved to Scapa Flow, its war station in the Orkneys, a repeat of the Grand Fleet's action during the Great War. But like the move, the defenses of 1939 were the same as in 1914–18, with very little having been done to modernize them. Time and weathering had taken their toll on the blockships defending the anchorage, and a gap had developed between the defenses that were used to protect Kirk Sound, the entrance to Scapa. The Germans, through aerial reconnaissance, had detected this gap and Admiral Dönitz, Commander-in-Chief of the U-boats, started planning a daring strike against the superior capital ship fleet of the Royal Navy.

On the night of the 13/14 October 1939, a German submarine, *U-47*, commanded by Lt Gunther Prien, successfully penetrated the defenses of the British naval base and sank the *Royal Oak* with four torpedoes. Prien's first salvo seemed ineffective, but his second found the desired target, ironically the only capital ship in Scapa at the time.

Owen, who was a midshipman on board, expands upon this loss in graphic detail:

It was at about 0120 on the morning of Saturday 14th October, when the ship was lying in berth B12 in Scapa Flow, that the tremendous explosion woke up the ship's company. The general assumption was that a bomb had hit us and many men manned their AA stations; others went under armour; but very many turned over and went to sleep again. The Captain

immediately went for'ard to locate the trouble and was soon joined by the Commander and Engineer Commander, who proceeded to flood the inflammable store and smell the escaping gases. Meanwhile the magazine temperatures were taken, and almost everyone turned in again assuming that the Captain had rectified the trouble – whatever it might be!

It must have been about 0130 when the Admiral crossed the Quarter Deck on his way for'ard and gave the only order of the evening – 'drifter raise steam at once'. At the same time the

Britannia Royal Naval College, Dartmouth, was designed to give young cadets a safe and steady introduction to the navy. The cadets' training evolved from the middle part of the nineteenth century, when the college was on a pair of hulks in the river, to a purpose-built college in the first decade of the twentieth century, taking into account the steam and machine age. Their instruction and education was in the hands of a mixture of naval officers and civilian masters. (National Maritime Museum)

W/T (water tight) door Lieutenant went off on his rounds as all the doors were open and the hatches were all suspended on their Weston

The *Royal Oak* was the most modern of the 'R'-class battleships, having been partly modified during the interwar period. However, her subdivisions and watertight integrity were totally overwhelmed by Prien's attack. It was particularly sobering to note that the rest of the fleet was not in Scapa Flow at the time. The loss was a major blow to the Royal Navy, following so soon after the loss of HMS *Courageous* to submarine attack in September. (IWM Q65784)

purchases. The midshipmen had just been shaken by the instructor Lieutenant when at 0140 three, or possibly four, shattering explosions occurred at about three second intervals and the ship immediately started listing to starboard.

When this happened the senior officers were still smelling gases in the cable locker, and they apparently did not realise that the smell had been made by the cable running out after the first explosion; the sparks from the cable passing round the cable-holder and a cloud of spray the only external signs noted by the look-outs in the ADP, who were still placidly looking for aircraft.

And so twenty minutes after the ship had first been torpedoed no definite steps had been taken by anyone to save the ship or her company, and there was no more time as the final explosions had caused her to heel over very rapidly – she was keel uppermost seven minutes later, according to witnesses in the Pegasus.

As the ship started listing the lights went out, and the ladders grew progressively more difficult

for even one man to negotiate – and virtually impossible for the 1100 odd men trapped below. Several sliding hatches on the port side slid shut, and many Weston purchases snapped from sheer weight of men hauling themselves up, so that the boys and stokers and topmen had little chance of escape. Of one hundred and fifty Royal Marines only fifty managed to escape, many of them coming through scuttles.

The boats were all lashed down except the PB and launch at the starboard booms and the gig on the Quarter Deck. The picket boat got away and picked up about sixty men and all went well until the officer in charge told these men to paddle, causing the boat to roll over on her beams and shaking off several people, who finally capsized the outfight by trying to climb back; it was never possible to flash up the boiler. The only man to reach the launch at the boom was the midshipman of the boat, who unfortunately was not able to clear her before she was pulled under as she was moored up by too short a strop. The gig was on the Quarter Deck and the combined efforts of most of the officers was insufficient to launch her; she floated off upside down.

The drifter Daisy D *was alongside abreast P.6 gun and the skipper held on until she was partially lifted out of the water by the bilge, in order that as many people as possible might jump aboard – an opportunity of which only one*

Prien (shown above with his wife) was welcomed home to national acclaim following his sinking of the *Royal Oak*, one of the first for Germany. He and the other successful U-boat commanders soon became national heroes. However, gradually they were either captured or killed. (IWM HU40836)

midshipman in mess kit availed himself. The skipper was awarded the DSC for hazarding his ship. Many of the carley floats had been damaged by heavy seas and the rest were lashed down; only the Commander thought to free any of these.

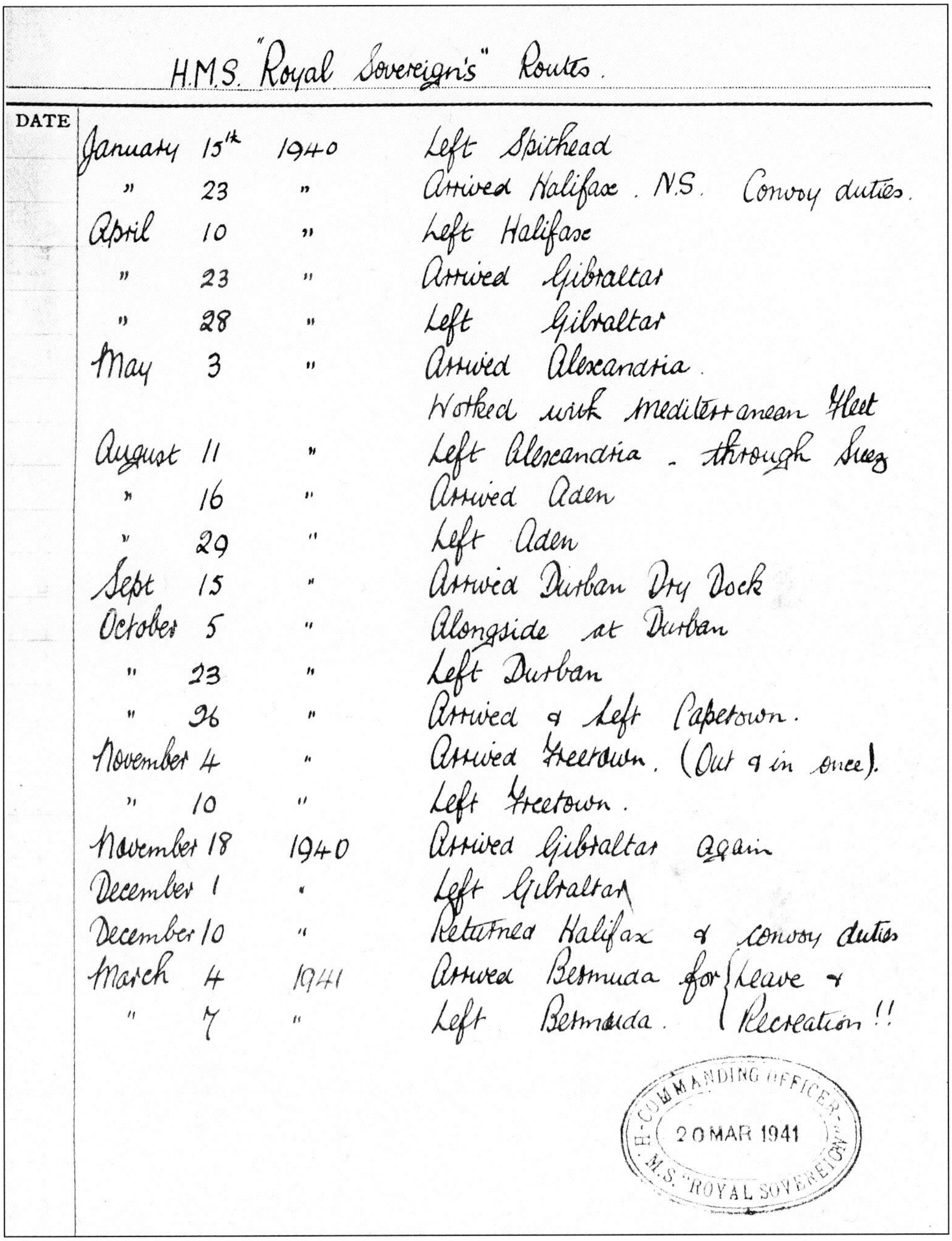

H.M.S. "Royal Sovereign's" Routes.

DATE			
January 15th	1940		Left Spithead
"	23	"	Arrived Halifax. N.S. Convoy duties.
April	10	"	Left Halifax
"	23	"	Arrived Gibraltar
"	28	"	Left Gibraltar
May	3	"	Arrived Alexandria.
			Worked with Mediterranean Fleet
August	11	"	Left Alexandria - through Suez
"	16	"	Arrived Aden
"	29	"	Left Aden
Sept	15	"	Arrived Durban Dry Dock
October	5	"	Alongside at Durban
"	23	"	Left Durban
"	26	"	Arrived & Left Capetown.
November 4		"	Arrived Freetown. (Out & in once).
"	10	"	Left Freetown.
November 18	1940		Arrived Gibraltar again
December 1	"		Left Gibraltar
December 10	"		Returned Halifax & convoy duties
March 4	1941		Arrived Bermuda for Leave &
"	7	"	Left Bermuda. Recreation !!

COMMANDING OFFICER
20 MAR 1941
H.M.S. ROYAL SOVEREIGN

In the water there must have been about six hundred men, of whom very many were picked up by the drifter off the port quarter and beam. Others met their fate with the PB and quite a number were picked up by boats from the Pegasus; fifteen men reached the shore and the remaining two hundred were drowned. The Flow was extremely cold and there was very little wreckage about; on the starboard side the oil fuel was very oppressive indeed, and many men brought up solid oil for hours afterwards.

The last journal entry of Owen as a midshipman. It demonstrates the almost continuous use of the naval assets of Britain. More importantly, it shows the geographical range and scope of operations of the *Royal Sovereign*. (BRNC)

Apart from these 15 men who went to Kirkwall, all the survivors were taken on board the Pegasus *and sent into the engine-room to thaw. No-one was disturbed until they were transferred to the depot ship* Voltaire *at about 0900 on Saturday where they remained till Tuesday.*

The Royal Navy lost over 800 officers and men with the sinking of the *Royal Oak*. Her sinking in a British anchorage led to the safety of Scapa and the Home Fleet being seriously questioned. Thus, following the sinking, the rest of the Home Fleet was dispersed to ports around Scotland. This initially caused a weakening in the ability of the Royal Navy to blockade the German surface fleet; however, the much smaller German navy was unable to exploit this physically minor but huge propaganda coup with any other tangible results following their initial strike. The defenses around Scapa Flow were strengthened, eventually incorporating a causeway across Kirk Sound and Water Sound known as 'Churchill's Barrier.'

The Home Fleet soon returned to Scapa and remained based there, in safety, until the end of the war. As for the Captain of *U-47*, Gunther Prien, he and all his crew would be killed in action in March 1941. But for Owen it wasn't the end of the tragic episode. Whilst he was on board the *Voltaire*, the Luftwaffe attacked the anchorage early on the Tuesday of transfer.

We had no guns to man and so everyone leaned through the scuttles and watched four German planes as they dived over the Iron Duke *– I actually saw the two bombs, dropped from about 150', which burst just alongside this old battleship causing her to list heavily to starboard so that she was only saved by being pushed on the mud by about fifteen trawlers.*

Following this the survivors from the *Royal Oak* were landed ashore for safety; they endured another air raid at 3.00 pm the same afternoon, but with little damage. Owen writes: 'The only humorous side of it was the view of four hundred "Royal Oaks" in vests, pants and boiler suits, clutching the earth … with bombs whining all round them.' That evening they were to proceed on leave.

In January 1940, Owen was posted to a sister-ship of the *Royal Oak* when he joined HMS *Royal Sovereign*. From there his next 14 months were of constant activity. He was in the thick of momentous times and operations, particularly convoy work in the Atlantic, Mediterranean, and Indian oceans. Once, escorting merchant ships to Malta, he found himself 'in sight of Crete nearly all of Monday and colossal bombing raids took place' against his convoy. Even more amazing for him was the sight of French ships in Alexandria harbor being rendered incapable by Admiral Cunningham's Mediterranean Fleet. 'At the beginning of July it became obvious that effective measures had to be taken to prevent the French fleet falling into enemy hands. As we could not afford the ships to blockade them in port it was necessary to demobilize them.'

Owen spent the remainder of his time plying the vital convoy routes, deterring attack from German surface raiders. After almost two years as a midshipman he became a sublieutenant in 1941 and a full lieutenant two years later, serving with HMS *Fernie* and then HMS *Eaglet* for the Commander-in-Chief Western Approaches. When he became a sublieutenant, his journal came to an end.

U-boat ace Kapitänleutnant Gunther Prien on the bridge of U-47.
This was an early Type VIIA boat. (Gordon Williamson)

John Delaney-Nash, merchant mariner

Whether from a neutral or warring nation, the world's merchant fleets found themselves involved in the war from the beginning. No nation could support its war effort with only its own merchant shipping, and even Britain, with the largest fleet in the world, was forced to see a quarter of its vital imports arriving in neutral ships. Subsequently, warring nations could ill afford to let neutral shipping work for the enemy; hence all vessels eventually became targets. The longest-serving merchant marine was that of Britain. The British merchant seaman was going to be at war for six full years, from nine hours after the start of hostilities in Europe, with the sinking of the liner *Athenia*, to the day of the Japanese surrender in the Pacific.

John Delaney-Nash was one such seaman. He survived the six years and saw the war in all of the main theaters of conflict, from the Arctic to the Pacific. But it was to be at a very high price, with some amazing and grueling experiences, not to mention a few near miracles along the way. 'I, personally, lost many good friends in the war, and could never understand how I was able to go through it without any harm to myself.'

Born in Dublin, in 1910, John Delaney-Nash spent over 50 years in the British merchant marine, becoming a ship's master in 1946. Yet he was not brought up in a seafaring family, for his father spent much of his time in and out of the army from 1888 until the 1920s. Delaney-Nash's first real taste of the sea was at the age of seven when he traveled across the Irish Sea with his family to join his father in Cambridge. There, a couple of years later, he joined the sea scouts. His first job at 16 was working for a tea importer, resulting in many visits to the London Docklands. By the following year, however, he had signed a four-year contract with the Eagle Oil Shipping Company as an apprentice deck

cadet, beginning his five-decade career with the sea. Unfortunately, it did not begin auspiciously, as on his first trip his captain killed himself by jumping into the sea.

By the Second World War, Delaney-Nash had become second officer of an aircraft fuel tanker. His duties in wartime had expanded from those usually associated with second officer, since he was now also the ship's gunnery officer following a course on the River Thames earlier in the year. He was not alone. Royal Navy escort vessels were in short supply and as many merchant ships as possible were being equipped with guns in order to defend themselves against the German surface raiders. In spite of that, the weapons themselves were mostly First World War issue, and it often seemed that their presence was to calm the ship's company as much as to deter the raiders. However, the arming of the ships with one or two weapons was seen as crucial.

By the end of the first year of the war, some 3,400 ships had been armed. Initially the guns were manned by naval reservists and the crews of the merchant ships. Eventually, more than 24,000 Royal Navy personnel, 150,000 merchant seamen, and over 14,000 men of the Maritime Regiment, Royal Artillery were involved in manning the guns of the Defensively Equipped Merchant Ships (DEMS). By the time Delaney-Nash was involved with the Pacific War, he too had large numbers of the gun teams.

33 DEMS naval ratings under Chief Petty Officer Cooper who had fought the German's great battleship Admiral Graf Spee in the battle of the River Plate in South America. I also had 11 Maritime Ack Ack under Sergeant Minchen ex Desert Rats. These men formed the actual defence of our vessel.

During the war, the British merchant fleet was being asked to supply Britain from all over the world, at immense distances and usually under constant threat from the Germans, and later the Italians and Japanese. The 2,000 miles (3,200km) or so across the Atlantic were the most dangerous waters for a merchant ship, but the 12,000-mile (19,300km) journey to Suez via South Africa during the closure of the Mediterranean was no less fraught with danger. Perhaps as worrying for the British authorities was the realization that the merchant marine contained some 2,000 fewer ships than had been available in the First World War. True, the ships in service were larger – the average displacement having more than doubled – which enabled far more to be transported, but this also meant far higher losses of material when the ships were sunk.

Even more problematic was the fact that the situation was drastically different from that of the First World War. Instead of one major theater of naval operations, Britain by 1942 found itself in numerous global theaters, and at a time when industrial production and wartime demands required feeding beyond anything comparable in the Great War. According to the government statistics, in the Second World War a 500-bomber raid on Germany by four-engine aircraft needed 750,000 gallons (3.4 million liters) of fuel oil, all of which was seaborne.

Delaney-Nash found himself transporting exactly this type of cargo for much of the war, and not just to Britain but also to other operational areas. The losses were high:

I spent four and a quarter years carrying Aviation Spirit and Motor Gasoline across the Atlantic and saw many ships sunk in my convoys, but I came through without hurt. In one convoy a ship close ahead of us was torpedoed and as she was loaded with a full cargo of some sort of petroleum spirit, swung across our course, exploded in the centre and the two halves parted company and went off in opposite directions. My ship, which had no time to avoid the two halves as they blew apart from

each other, went straight through the gap and came out of the other side unscathed, even though we were also loaded with Aviation Spirit. The heat from the burning ship was so hot that it scorched our eye lashes and brows and all the hair below our hat bands.

We saw members of the crew running around the decks all on fire, some of them jumping into the sea where they perished in the flaming water.

Delaney-Nash carried this dangerous cargo across the Atlantic, in the Mexican Gulf and on convoy routes in the Arctic and Indian oceans. However, after four years of war he was beginning to wonder whether he was chancing his luck a little too much.

I asked our Personnel Clerk Mr Grabble if he was trying to kill me. In much surprise he asked what I meant. I told him that I had been carrying clean oil i.e. petrol and aviation spirit across the Atlantic Ocean for four and three quarter years in a dangerous war and had he never heard of the old saying about 'going once too often to the well'? He immediately got my meaning, and said that he would try and appoint me to a nice Black Oil ship.

Delaney-Nash got his black oil ship. They were considered to be much safer than his previous aviation fuel tankers. However, on joining his new ship he soon found out that safe was a relative term. The vessel was being readied as a fleet oiler and supply ship for the new British Pacific Fleet. He would leave Britain in August 1944 and not return until April 1946, spending the time in between supporting warships in the Pacific.

During the war, the losses were tremendous. The merchant shipping sinkings for the Allies after 1942 were in excess of 12 million tons, but continued use of occupied and neutral shipping and massive building programs, particularly in America, enabled the British merchant marine not only to retain its size but actually to grow. Nonetheless, tens of thousands of British merchant seaman were killed during the war. As Dan van der Vat writes about the war on shipping:

A few vivid images remain: of seamen burning and choking in blazing oil, of sailors instantly freezing to death in the waters of the Arctic, of flashing magazines blowing warships to smithereens, of unspeakably gruesome remains rising from the wreckage of submarines, of aircraft crashing in flames, of the haunting death-throes of stricken ships and of endless cries for help from the water. And here and there a dash of chivalry in a total war.

Although this comment is written for the Atlantic campaign, it would seem appropriate to use it to describe the war of supply and convoy for all the world's civilian merchant seamen in the Second World War.

Perhaps the only question remaining is: how did people like John Delaney-Nash manage to survive the war and the peace intact and sane? Then again, one of his recollections might give an answer to that:

Proceeding along E-boat Alley, as it was called, we were attacked by German aircraft. High velocity bullets were flying all over the place and everyone was busy trying to get a shot at the planes flying through the night sky, when we heard a voice from inside the wheelhouse saying 'Never mind the Germans, Mister, where's the ship ahead?' It was obvious that station keeping was [the] uppermost thing in the Captain's mind. I have always thought that this sort of thinking is very British and what makes the Britisher so strong in adversity.

The German fleet is scuttled

The European naval war drew to a close where it had started, in the Baltic. The siege of Leningrad had been lifted by a Soviet offensive that began in January 1944, accompanied by heavy fire support from Soviet battleships, cruisers, destroyers, and gunboats, firing some 24,000 rounds. Increasingly, German naval forces in the Baltic found themselves conducting evacuation operations and fending off Soviet advances that were often accompanied by outflanking amphibious operations.

In January 1945, the Red Army surrounded German forces in East Prussia. This signaled the beginning of the greatest ever military evacuation. Overloaded German ships of all kinds had to negotiate extensive Soviet-laid minefields and run the gauntlet of Soviet submarine patrols. The torpedoing of just three transports, the *Wilhelm Gustloff, General Steuben*, and *Goya*, led to the loss of over 15,000 lives. Indeed, out of 1,081 vessels used in these operations, 245 were lost. Nevertheless, during 1944 and 1945, over 2,400,000 people were evacuated to the west in the Baltic.

With the Soviet army in Berlin, on 30 April 1945 Adolf Hitler committed suicide.

His nominated successor as Reich President was the now Grand Admiral Dönitz, who established the last Nazi government in the German naval academy at Flensburg-Mürwik. On the evening of 4 May, a delegation to Field Marshal Bernard Montgomery's headquarters signed an instrument of surrender to take effect at 8.00 am the next day. This affected 'all armed forces in Holland, in north-west Germany ... and in Denmark ... This is to include all naval ships in these areas.'

At the end of this war, there was no German fleet to escort to an Allied port. There were submarines at sea and they were ordered to surrender to an Allied port, but many commanders ignored this and either scuttled their boats or sailed them to a neutral port rather than deliver them into Allied hands. On 7 May, the unconditional surrender of all German land, sea, and air forces was signed in front of General Eisenhower at his headquarters in Rheims, and it was finally ratified in front of Soviet representatives in Berlin the next day. The war in Europe was over.

A tug slowly manoeveres *Tirpitz* into her mooring site in the flat, calm waters of Kaafjord.

Part III
The Mediterranean 1940–1945

Italian imperialism

The fascist rise to power

Benito Mussolini became prime minister of Italy in October 1922 as head of the *Fassci di Combattimento*, the Fascist Party, which enabled him to assume dictatorial powers three years later. His regime inherited the colonies of Libya, Eritrea, Italian Somaliland and the Dodecanese Islands but during his early years Mussolini pursued a comparatively pacifist foreign policy. While still trying to secure his own domestic support he emphasized that fascism would try to be an element of equilibrium and peace in Europe, and secure Italy's interests by respecting treaties of mutual friendship.

But Mussolini was a grandiose leader who relied on propaganda and bombastic rhetoric to amplify the regime's achievements and exaggerate his own importance. He wished to see Italy taken as a serious power on the world stage, especially in the Mediterranean, which he regarded as an Italian lake, and in Africa, where to his chagrin Britain and France had acquired a more prestigious empire than Italy. Mussolini boasted that Italy had three times given civilization to a barbarian world and in an excess of pompous self-indulgence he claimed that Italians were the most solid and homogeneous people in Europe, who were destined to raise the flag of imperialism throughout the Mediterranean and make Rome once again the center of western civilization.

In reality, however, Italy was only a middle-ranking power. Weaker economically than Britain or France, and with an army that had not been modernized, Mussolini required a prestigious propaganda coup to bolster his domestic support. Taking advantage of an international situation in which Italian friendship was courted on all sides, Mussolini decided to conquer Ethiopia

and establish the king of Italy as emperor. On 3 October 1935 the numerically superior Italian forces under Graziani invaded Ethiopia from Italian Somaliland. Though ineptly led, they faced little real opposition and by May 1936 Emperor Haile Selassie was forced to leave Ethiopia. The Italians immediately combined their colonies of Eritrea, Italian Somaliland and Ethiopia into a single federation, Italian East Africa, with Graziani, and later the Duke of Aosta, as governor-general. On 9 May 1936, on the floodlit balcony of the Palazzo Venezia, Mussolini proclaimed to a large crowd the foundation of a new Roman empire.

It was Mussolini's finest moment but the theatrical extravagance masked deeper problems. By committing to a distant empire Mussolini increased Italy's maritime vulnerability, especially the dependence on tenuous shipping links in the Mediterranean. Furthermore, despite Mussolini's promise of vast mineral resources and agricultural wealth the maintenance of the empire and the vast army required to suppress it consumed thousands of millions of *lire* that would have been more profitably spent developing parts of Italy and modernizing the army. Ethiopia was never under firm control and the brutal methods of repression, including the use of poison gas, ensured that a hostile population was always ready to rebel. Nevertheless, the victory reinforced Mussolini's confidence and the new watchword in Italy became *Roma doma*, "Rome dominates." Mussolini now had the illusion that he could continue without danger along the same path and play a much bigger role in Europe.

The Italian invasion of Ethiopia had far greater implications. Failure by Britain and France to impose comprehensive sanctions discredited the League of Nations and fatally imperiled the international system of collective security. Hitler had a graphic demonstration that belligerence in the face of international opposition could pay dividends and in the process he had a potential enemy converted into an ally. Mussolini increasingly came within the Nazi orbit and, with their common themes of nationalism, militarism and anti-bolshevism, the not-unnatural tendency for the fascist regimes to converge began in earnest. The democracies, as a consequence, realized that they were now forced to commit to a policy of rearmament and the first steps were taken along the path to world war.

The Rome–Berlin Axis

The Spanish Civil War offered another opportunity for Mussolini to assert the authority of fascism and Italy throughout the Mediterranean. Although this horrible war further unhinged the balance of power in Europe and encouraged a rapprochement between Italy and Germany, Mussolini maintained a deliberately confusing and contradictory foreign policy. Despite his bellicose behavior Mussolini feared full-scale war against a real enemy because he knew that Italian strength had been based on propaganda and bluff. Mussolini promised the French Italian troops to defend against German aggression, yet he also assured Hitler that Italy and Germany had a partnership dictated by destiny and announced the Rome–Berlin Axis in November 1936 – a political understanding of friendship and not yet a military alliance.

Nevertheless, Mussolini was still widely admired as an anti-bolshevist, even by Churchill. To balance his growing proximity with Germany and to cover himself in the Mediterranean he made a "gentleman's agreement" with Britain in January 1937 that recognized freedom of movement for both countries in the Mediterranean. Mussolini reaffirmed the agreement in April 1938, with little practical effect, but he made the important concession to maintain the status quo in the Mediterranean and to exchange information annually concerning any major changes or proposed changes in the strength and dispositions of their respective armed forces.

Mussolini had steadfastly promised to prevent Germany's occupation of Austria but when Hitler announced the *Anschluss* in March 1938, without notifying the Italians, Mussolini acquiesced. He had been deceived and made to look foolish, but in the process he gained the permanent gratitude of Hitler. Nevertheless, Mussolini was now convinced that war with Britain was inevitable and, since his visit to Germany in September 1937, during which he was impressed by German power and the strength of the Nazi war machine, he was certain that Germany would be the victor. Despite their mutual distrust both Mussolini and Hitler realized that in the absence of alternative friends their regimes needed a closer relationship and Hitler's visit to Rome in May 1938 brought both countries much closer together. At the Munich conference in September 1938 Mussolini played the role of mediator and guarantor of peace in Europe, and he basked in the admiration bestowed on him by Hitler.

Mussolini planned to bring the Balkans under Italian control and by the late 1930s the fascists had come to regard Albania as virtually an Italian protectorate. But Hitler's surprise invasion of Czechoslovakia on 15 March 1939 alarmed Mussolini, who feared that the Germans would next move into Croatia and the Adriatic. A German advance into the Balkans would usurp control of what the fascist propaganda had long claimed to be an Italian sphere of influence. On 7 April Mussolini therefore invaded Albania, an expedition that was notable only because of its incompetence and mismanagement and because the enfeebled condition of the Italian armed forces was now clearly visible to anyone who cared to look. Even the fascist propaganda could not completely disguise the calamity, but Mussolini's unbridled self-assuredness reached rarefied heights.

The democracies, however, now regarded Mussolini as simply another fascist tyrant, in cahoots with Hitler. President Roosevelt made his first serious intervention to halt the spread of the European dictators by offering his services as a mediator and attempting to revise American neutrality laws; Britain and France guaranteed Poland, Greece, Turkey and Romania against aggression; and Britain also marked a significant change of policy by introducing compulsory military training. As a result of this relatively minor event, the schism between the fascist and democratic powers broadened irrecoverably and the Grand Alliance which hoped to defeat fascism began to coalesce.°

On 22 May 1939 the political and economic axis between Italy and Germany was formalized in the Pact of Steel, an alliance that committed Italy to enter immediately and unconditionally into any war started by Hitler. Mussolini responded with aggressive plans for the inevitable war but attempted to clarify that it should be delayed at least until 1942, since Italian rearmament required another three years of effort. Caught by the myths of his own propaganda and bluff, Mussolini had deceived himself over the efficiency of the Italian armed forces and now

Hitler and Mussolini at their meeting in Florence in May 1939 where the Pact of Steel was agreed. (Imperial War Museum HU48859)

found himself in a predicament, committed to a war that he knew neither his people nor his army were capable of sustaining. However, the Germans and the Italians both had a deep suspicion of each other and there was very little military cooperation. Neither side had any enthusiasm for a unified command, for agreeing on basic strategic coordination or for any significant form of consultation, either then or at any time afterwards. Despite the propaganda claims of the solidarity of the Axis, Mussolini and Hitler mistrusted each other and both intended to preserve the maximum freedom of action.

At the outbreak of war in September 1939 the Italian Army was in the same condition that it had been in 1915. Mussolini was conscious that Italy's capacity for any major engagement was negligible but he was anxious the world should not learn that for years his boasts had been mere fallacy. Torn between desire and reality, Mussolini concluded that neutrality was the only sensible policy for Italy. After preaching war for 18 years, however, he coined the phrase "non-belligerence," a more acceptable concept. Forced to remain on the sidelines, Mussolini was in a delicate position, so instead of concentrating on rearming and making preparations for war he continued his policy of public works to reinforce his domestic support and wagered on German success. He would then enter the war, in time to enjoy the spoils of victory but without having taken any risk.

Hitler had no real interest in the Mediterranean and the Pact of Steel symbolized his vision that Germany's interests would be served north of the Tyrol. He planned to extend German control down the Danube to cultivate Hungary, Romania, Yugoslavia and even Bulgaria into a satellite zone by peaceful negotiation, in preparation for the struggle to expand the German Reich in the east. Meanwhile, Hitler repeatedly reassured Mussolini that the Mediterranean was an Italian sphere in which he would not interfere and was happy to allow Mussolini the freedom to extend his empire. Hitler vaguely hoped that Mussolini would attack Malta but he had no desire for the Italians to embark on a full-scale campaign in the Balkans, which would unsettle the region and disrupt his plans.

Hitler gave substantial assistance to General Franco during the Spanish Civil War and in March 1939 Franco made a Treaty of Friendship with Germany. Hitler regarded Spain as a debtor and Franco as a natural ally, and he hoped to negotiate a joint German–Spanish attack on Gibraltar to secure the western gateway into the Mediterranean and to use one of the Canary islands as a submarine base, in return for which Spain would gain control of the British colony. Franco joined the Anti-Comintern Pact but Spain was still devastated by the ruin of war

and was particularly dependent on the need to import food. Franco was therefore unwilling to commit to the fascist cause and even though Hitler traveled to Hendaye, on the Spanish border, on 23 October 1940 and met with Franco personally, the Spanish leader would not sanction a joint attack. During a nine-hour meeting he frustrated Hitler with completely unrealistic demands of territories and equipment, after which Hitler stated that he would rather have teeth pulled than meet Franco again. Hitler toyed with the idea of launching a German parachute attack on Gibraltar and Franco prevaricated over joining forces, but the Germans were never able to provide sufficient enticement and there never was any active cooperation between the two fascist leaders (although Franco contributed forces to the Russian campaign when pressed by Hitler).

Crossroads of the British Empire

The British had regarded naval domination of the Mediterranean as decisive in the victories over Napoleon and the Kaiser. Moreover, it had become axiomatic that control of the Suez Canal and the Mediterranean shipping lanes to India, the southern dominions and the Far East was a vital element of the British Empire.

During the nineteenth century the European powers had not been able to annex parts of the Near East, as they had in Africa. However, the British occupied Egypt following the battle of Tel el Kebir in 1882 and after the pacification of Sudan in 1885 continually strengthened their armed forces. Although never formally part of the empire, Britain established de facto control over Egypt, Cyprus and the small states in the Persian Gulf, which complemented the strategic colonies of Malta and Gibraltar in the Mediterranean. The merit of this policy became evident in 1914 when the passage of Australian, Indian, New Zealand and British troops had been essential in dealing with

the Middle-East campaigns against the Ottoman Empire. By 1918 the British had established a huge military complex in Egypt and in the post-war settlement Palestine was placed under direct British control, while Transjordan and Iraq were established under British mandate by the League of Nations. As a result, therefore, Britain dominated an area from Egypt to the Persian Gulf.

Egyptian independence in 1922, and the termination of the Iraqi mandate 10 years later, had no appreciable impact on British control since four special security treaties for the defense of Egypt, foreign interests, the Sudan and the empire's communications guaranteed the continued presence of British forces. Furthermore, the growth of the Royal Air Force, the mechanization of the British Army and the conversion of the Royal Navy from coal- to oil-fired ships rapidly increased British dependence on the Middle-Eastern oilfields. The Anglo-Egyptian Treaty of 1936 ensured that the British retained certain rights and on the outbreak of war on 1 September 1939 Britain invoked a clause which stated that, in the event of war, King Farouk would give "all the facilities and assistance in his power, including the use of ports, aerodromes and means of communication." In effect this meant the virtual occupation of Egypt by the British Army.

Consequently, by the beginning of the war, the Mediterranean was a hub of British naval and military endeavor. British control was centered on Gibraltar in the west, Malta in the center and Alexandria in the east, the home of the Mediterranean Fleet. France also exerted a strong influence around the Mediterranean through the colony of Algeria and the protectorates of French Morocco and Tunisia in north and west Africa, and Syria and Lebanon on the eastern littoral which were controlled under a mandate from the League of Nations. In cooperation with the French Navy, which dominated the western basin and secured French communication with north Africa, the Mediterranean shipping lanes would thus be secure if Italy entered the war.

Italian propaganda, German professionalism and Allied industrialization

Italy

At the outbreak of the war, Italy appeared to be in an unassailable position. Italian armed forces were strategically well positioned, with bases astride the Mediterranean, and were numerically far superior to the forces opposing them. But this picture of strength was deceptive since Mussolini had made no preparation for war. The Italian armed forces had no higher-command structure or strategic plans and were equipped with antiquated armament.

The Italian Army, the *Regio Esercito Italiano* (REI), consisted of 1,600,000 men and comprised 73 divisions, including three armored, 43 infantry and 17 "self-transportable" infantry divisions. They were, however, mere "binary" divisions with two rather than three regiments, a pretentious change that Mussolini had ordered in 1938 because it enabled him to claim that Italy had almost doubled its number of divisions. In reality the change caused enormous disorganization just as war was looming and dissipated each division's strength, while doubling the number of generals.

In October 1936 Mussolini famously claimed that Italy had an army of "eight million bayonets" but by the outbreak of war there were insufficient even for the 1.3 million rifles that the REI could muster, many of which were of 1891 vintage. The artillery dated from the First World War and a modernization program was not due to begin until 1942–43. There were no tanks, apart from feeble CV3 machines based on British First World War armored cars, and, although a few M-11 and M-13 light tanks were rushed to Africa they were next to useless and lacked proper radio communication.

In east Africa the Duke of Aosta commanded 91,000 Italian and 200,000 colonial troops, while in Libya Marshal Rodolfo Graziani commanded another 250,000 troops in the Tenth and Fifth Armies. Although formidable in size they lacked proper training, equipment and, above all, were not fully motorized, problems that were exacerbated by poor Italian leadership. Both the British and Germans had a respect for the fighting ability of Italian soldiers, but both shared a contempt for the ineffectual Italian officers. Following the destruction of the Tenth Army in February 1941 the Fifth Army was dissolved and Italian forces in Africa thereafter operated alongside German divisions at corps level only, including an armored corps, under the command of Gariboldi and General Ettore Bastico. In 1942 they were incorporated into the German–Italian *Panzerarmee*, which in turn became the First Italian Army, under General Giovanni Messe, during the last phase of the fighting in Africa. Following the capitulation in Tunisia, only about 15 effective divisions remained to defend Sicily and the Italian mainland, several of which opposed German occupation following the armistice in September 1943 and fought with the Allies until the end of the war.

Although the Italian Army expanded to a maximum of 3,000,000 troops, Mussolini made no attempt to mobilize Italy's economic, industrial or agricultural capacity. War production hardly rose above peacetime levels and the armaments industry failed to produce any modern equipment. Despite the shortages, however, Mussolini still sent a well-equipped corps of 220,000 men to the eastern front, men and materiel that would have been more effectively used in Africa.

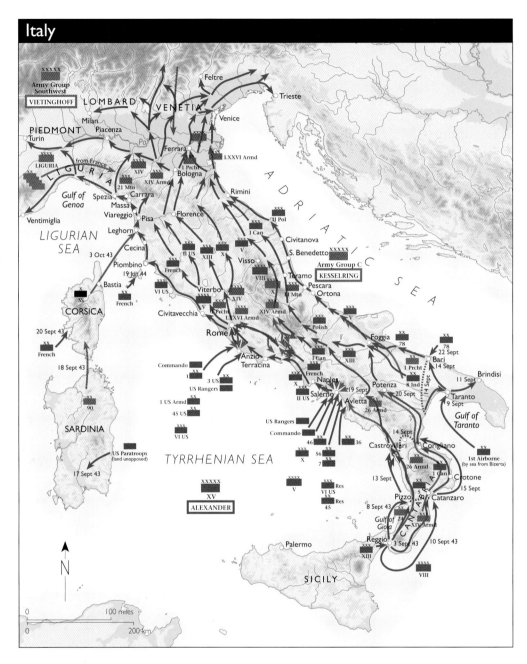

Italy

Italian fascists claimed that the Italian Air Force, the *Regia Aeronautica Italiana* (RAI), was the finest air force in the world, with 8,530 of the best aircraft. In reality the RAI comprised only 900 modern aircraft. Almost all of these were inferior in speed, performance and armament to contemporary British planes and even included Fiat CR42 biplanes that had been operational during the Spanish Civil War. Few aircraft were equipped to operate at night or with radio communication and their crews received paltry training compared to their opponents. More advanced Macchi 202 fighters and slow but reliable Savoia S79 and S84 torpedo bombers were flown with tenacity and great effect during the battle of the convoys, and sank or damaged many ships including the battleship HMS *Nelson* in September 1941. By mid-1943, however, the RAI numbered less than 100 modern aircraft and was hopelessly outnumbered by the superior Allied air forces.

The Italian Navy, the *Regia Marina Italiana* (RMI), under Admiral Domenico Cavagnari, was the best equipped and the most professional of the Italian armed services. The Italian Admiralty built a navy based on the policy of a "fleet in being," which assumed that the threat of powerful capital ships would be enough to deter the British from conducting an active campaign. This was in part because of Italy's inability to replace losses and because the Italian Navy could at best gain only a moral victory from a major engagement but stood to suffer a moral and materiel disaster. Postwar claims of a British "moral ascendancy" or of an Italian "paralysis of the will" were erroneous as the Italian Navy fought with determination and valor, and frustrated the Royal Navy for three long years.

Italian Cruisers on escort duty. The Italian Navy was a powerful fleet that seriously threatened the Royal Navy, but a lack of fuel oil restricted its operational capabilities. (Imperial War Museum A1985859)

Undoubtedly prestige was also a factor. The RMI possessed the largest and fastest ships with the most powerful guns, but neglected capabilities such as operational range, armored protection, seaworthiness and accurate gunnery. The six battleships and 19 cruisers with which Italy started the war were fine ships and presented a powerful threat, but the failure to develop radar, which prevented the navy from operating at night, aircraft-carriers and an amphibious capability were serious flaws in a force that could otherwise have significantly altered the course of the war.

The RMI's smaller ships, 52 destroyers and 76 torpedo boats at the start of the war, achieved the most notable Italian naval success by maintaining supplies to the forces in Africa. The flotilla of 113 Italian submarines constituted a highly effective force, while the midget submarines or human torpedoes, a type of craft pioneered by the Italians, were the most advanced and most successful mini-submarines of all combatants during the war. The Italian "gamma men," as the frogmen were known, sank 200,000 tons of British shipping for virtually no loss. It is a compelling argument that Italy would have had considerable success if she had instead built a fleet of light and stealthy craft.

Germany

Although an offensive in the Mediterranean was proposed as an alternative strategy to defeat Britain, Hitler and the German High Command, the *Oberkommando der Wehrmacht* (OKW), had no interest in the region and considered the campaign a sideshow to the war in Russia. However, Italian defeats in Greece and Africa threatened the existence of Mussolini's regime and prompted Hitler to send German forces to support his ally. While large forces swept through the Balkans to secure the southern flank of the Russian campaign, the assistance in Africa was limited to a rescue operation only and a special blocking force, a *Sperrverband*, was created under the command of General Erwin Rommel. With inspiring leadership, however, Rommel welded an assortment of units without any desert experience into the legendary *Deutsches Afrika Korps* (DAK), a professional formation that was thoroughly steeped in the cooperation of all arms. Despite immense difficulties with supplies and indifference from Hitler and the OKW, with a total German force that never exceeded three divisions Rommel repeatedly overcame superior and far more experienced British forces by using imaginative new tactics, bluff and cunning, and deservedly earned the name of "The Desert Fox."

Rommel was nominally under the command of the Italian Commander-in-Chief, General Bastico, but he had direct recourse to Hitler and in effect personally commanded all Axis troops in Africa. The command structure was equally confusing at higher level. The Italian High Command, the *Commando Supremo*, under Marshal Ugo Cavallero, was in overall command of all Axis forces, but in December 1941 Hitler appointed Field-Marshal Albert Kesselring as Commander-in-Chief South to establish Axis superiority in the Mediterranean and ostensibly gave him control of all Axis forces. In practice the Italian and German commanders held a deep mistrust of each other and the Axis partners never truly operated as allies, with a joint command structure and a coordinated strategic plan. The potential opportunities stemming from the defeat of British power and the capture of Egypt, the Suez Canal and even Middle-Eastern oilfields were never fully appreciated. Belatedly in 1942, and without serious planning, Hitler perceived the possibility of linking the German armies advancing in the Caucasus with an advance by Rommel. By this stage, however, the tide had begun to turn as the industrial strength of the Allies began to have a material impact on the battlefield. Hitler sent 17,000 troops of the Fifth Panzer Army, under General Jürgen von Arnim, to Tunisia in response to the Allied landings in north-west Africa, but by that stage the Axis powers were in full withdrawal and the inevitable capitulation was simply delayed.

Following Mussolini's fall from power Hitler appointed Kesselring as Commander of Army Group C to defend Italy and sent him a further 16 divisions. Central Italy was ideal defensive territory and Kesselring expertly and stubbornly defended every inch. Until the end of the war, the Tenth and Fourteenth Armies made a slow defensive withdrawal northwards from one prepared line to another in a bloody war of attrition reminiscent of the First World War.

Britain and the Commonwealth

General Wavell was appointed Commander-in-Chief, Middle East Command, in August 1939 but his responsibility rapidly expanded from Egypt, the Sudan, Palestine–Jordan and Cyprus to include the whole of east Africa, Greece, Turkey, Bulgaria, Iraq, Aden and the Persian Gulf. The High Command included Wavell's fellow air and naval commanders-in-chief but as his was nominally the senior office he was in practice overall commander. Wavell's responsibilities were vast. Not only was he in command of military campaigns in Egypt, East Africa, Greece, Syria and efforts to quell the Iraqi revolt, but as the

Indian troops driving Bren carriers through an Arab town. The British Army included troops of nationalities from all corners of the Commonwealth. (Topham Picturepoint M00984440)

representative of the British Government he also had a quasi-political and diplomatic role. Although these burdens were reduced for Wavell's successors, the demands of the Middle East Command were extensive.

Initially, Wavell had command of only 50,000 British troops, concentrated in Egypt. Highly mobile, professional soldiers, they had spectacular success against the Italians, but their achievements were squandered in Greece and Crete. Reinforcements were sent to the Middle East from the UK and the southern dominions of the Commonwealth, and the Nile delta rapidly developed into a massive supply and administrative center. The Eighth Army was formed in Egypt, supplemented by the Ninth Army in Palestine and Syria and the Tenth Army in Persia and Iraq, but it was slow to adapt to the conditions of desert warfare, despite British successes in east Africa and Syria. British leadership was indifferent and failed to coordinate armor and infantry units as combined forces, errors that were repeated until General "Monty" Montgomery assumed

Sicily

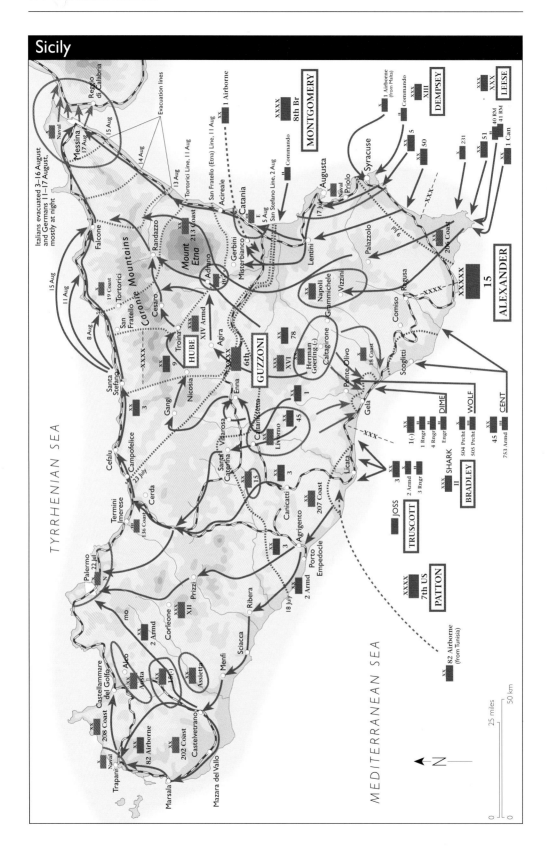

TYRRHENIAN SEA

MEDITERRANEAN SEA

Italians evacuated 3–16 August
and Germans 11–17 August,
mostly at night

Evacuation lines

Messina
17 Aug

Reggio di Calabria

Naval

15 Aug
14 Aug
13 Aug

San Fratello (Etna) Line, 11 Aug
Tortorici Line, 11 Aug

Acireale

Catania

San Fratello (Etna) Line, 11 Aug
San Stefano Line, 2 Aug

Randazzo

Falcone

Tortorici Line

Caronie Mountains

Mount
Etna

Adrano

Gerbini

Misterbianco

1 Airborne

Commando

Augusta

Naval
Priolo

Syracuse

8th Br

MONTGOMERY

1 Airborne
(from Malta)

Commando

5

50

231

51

40 RM
41 RM

1 Can

DEMPSEY

XIII

LEESE

Lentini

Napoli

Vizzini

Grammichele

Palazzolo

206 Coast

ALEXANDER

15

Ragusa

Comiso

Scoglitti

18 Coast

Ponte Olivo

Gela

Licata

Porto
Empedocle

Agrigento

Canicatti

207 Coast

3

15

3

45

Caltagirone

Herman
Goering (−)

XVI

78

XIV Armd

HUBE

6th

GUZZONI

1

9

Troina

Agira

Enna

Caltanissetta

Livorno

Santa
Catarina

Villarosa

Nicosia

Gangi

3

Santa
Stefano

Cesaro

San
Fratello

Tortorici

19 Coast

Cefalu

Campofelice

23 July

Cerda

Termini
Imerese

136 Coast

Palermo
22 Jul

Prizzi

Ribera

Sciacca

Menfi

Corleone

Alcomo

2 Armd

XII

Castelvetrano

202 Coast

Assietta

82 Airborne

208 Coast

Castellammare
del Golfo

Aosta

Naval

Trapani

Marsala

Mazara del Vallo

JOSS

TRUSCOTT

3

2 Armd

3 Rngr

SHARK

BRADLEY

XXXX
7th US

PATTON

82 Airborne
(from Tunisia)

1(−)

1 Rngr

4 Rngr

Engr

DIME

504 Prcht

505 Prcht

WOLF

45

753 Armd

CENT

N

25 miles

50 km

command in August 1942. With an army of 195,000 troops, 1,029 guns and 1,051 tanks, he used the massive materiel strength to finally overcome the Axis at El Alamein, one of the turning points of the Second World War.

Following the Anglo-US invasion of north-west Africa, the Eighth Army joined with the British First Army to form the Eighteenth Army Group in Tunisia, which eliminated all Axis forces from north Africa. This force, renamed the Fifteenth Army Group, then participated in great amphibious landings in Sicily and Italy, and fought a prolonged, tenacious campaign that inched its way up the Italian peninsula.

In June 1940 the Mediterranean Fleet based at Alexandria and Force H, created at Gibraltar to replace the French Fleet, had a combined fleet of seven battleships, two aircraft-carriers, 37 cruisers and destroyers, and 16 submarines. Due principally to the shortage of aircraft and submarines, the British were unable to prevent Italian convoys reaching Africa, and the maintenance of Malta both as a thorn in Rommel's side and to assist British convoys traversing the Mediterranean became a priority. But in the last three months of 1941 the Royal Navy suffered the loss of an aircraft-carrier, three battleships and Force K, the naval squadron based on Malta. With control of the sea and air the Axis powers were able to besiege Malta with the most unremitting air assault of the war and freely ship supplies to Africa. Despite a bitter struggle the Royal Navy was unable to regain control until the end of 1942, when it began to enforce a strangulation of Axis forces and lay the foundations for the amphibious operations.

USA

When America entered the war President Roosevelt effectively overruled his military advisers and determined that US forces should be committed to the Mediterranean campaign. He recognized the importance of political factors in forging the alliance with Britain and the need for US forces to gain combat experience without excessive slaughter. An invasion of north-west Africa provided the perfect opportunity and General Eisenhower was appointed Commander-in-Chief Allied Expeditionary Force. Convoys of some 752 ships carried 65,000 troops from Britain and the USA in what was the largest amphibious assault of the war so far to invade Vichy-controlled Morocco and Algeria.

The invasion indicated a major Allied commitment to the Mediterranean, a theater that was dominated by the British. At their conferences in January and May 1943 Roosevelt and Churchill agreed to the invasion of Sicily and Italy, although the latter was in return for a definite British commitment to a second front in 1944. In Tunisia the fighting skills of US troops proved inadequate when they were confronted by experienced Germans, but in Sicily the Americans, in the form of General Patton's Seventh Army, came of age as a fighting force. Although the US Fifth Army fought a very determined campaign in Italy the US Chiefs of Staff fought to restrict the numbers of US troops and succeeded even in drawing off troops to invade the French Riviera. When the Mediterranean became a unified command in December 1943 Field-Marshal Maitland Wilson was appointed supreme commander, in recognition that the majority of his troops were British.

Vichy France

Although the French colonies in equatorial Africa sided with General de Gaulle and the Free French, the French colonies in the Mediterranean declared their allegiance to Marshal Pétain and Vichy France. After the French Armistice the Armée d'Afrique in north Africa expanded to 250,000 troops under General Weygand, while 45,000 troops were in Syria under General Dentz. Although they were not nominally Axis troops they were well armed and fiercely loyal to the Vichy regime, and presented significant opposition to the Allies.

A parallel war

Mussolini's grasp for glory

Mussolini declared war on 10 June 1940, the moment when Hitler's attack on France appeared victorious. It was also Britain's darkest hour. Although her army had scrambled back to Britain, a German invasion seemed imminent and, without France, her position in the Mediterranean looked fatally weak. So confident was Mussolini of a rapid victory that he was unwilling even to wait a few days and sacrificed a third of the Italian merchant shipping fleet, which was caught without warning in neutral ports. Unwilling and unable to participate fully in Hitler's war Mussolini planned to fight alongside Germany in what he termed a "parallel war." Ambiguously described as "with Germany, not for Germany, but for Italy" he hoped to take advantage of Nazi victories and enjoy the spoils of war to establish a dominant position in the Mediterranean.

The Italian Army launched a hapless assault into the French Alps and Mussolini ordered an unwilling Graziani to invade Egypt from Libya. While France had been active in the war he had good cause to protect Libya's western border with French Tunisia, but now he was able to concentrate his entire army against the Egyptian border. On 13 September Graziani cautiously attacked the scanty British force opposing him, but after advancing only 80 km (50 miles) he halted at Sidi Barrani, where he established a chain of fortified camps and settled down. Derisively the British troops termed the advance a "sitzkrieg" – a play on the German *blitzkrieg*. For Mussolini, though, military achievement was secondary to collecting his booty, as he proclaimed that he needed "a few thousand dead" to give him the right to sit at the peace table with dignity.

Despite an ignominious Italian contribution to the Axis victory over France,

Mussolini did not moderate his visions. At a meeting with Hitler at the Brenner Pass on 4 October he claimed parts of southern France, Corsica, Malta, Tunisia, Algeria, an Atlantic port in Morocco, French Somaliland and the British positions in Egypt and Sudan. Hitler, however, had different ideas. Italian demands for territorial concessions at French expense counteracted his attempts to placate Vichy France and establish a harmonized Italian–French–Spanish alliance against Britain. Hitler encouraged Mussolini to look to Africa, which he had always seen as the natural route for Italian expansion, and in the end Italy obtained almost nothing from the armistice and Mussolini failed to gain the glory he craved.

Moreover, Hitler was already crystallizing his plans to invade the Soviet Union. He explicitly told Mussolini that he wanted the Balkans to remain quiet so as not to arouse Soviet suspicions and that Italy was not to move against Yugoslavia or Greece. Just four days later, however, the Italians learned that German troops had entered Romania. Mussolini still considered himself the senior of the two fascist leaders but he jealously resented Hitler's rapid victories and ascent to power. Mussolini was adamant that he had not entered the war just to be bought out at French expense or to refrain while Hitler expanded into an area that he saw as rightfully Italian. Vengeful, Mussolini reacted angrily and declared, "Hitler always gives me a *fait accompli*. This time I am going to pay him back in full." On a whim, he immediately decided to invade Greece, even though he had already ordered a large-scale demobilization.

Without any preparations and under suicidal conditions the Italian Army crossed the border from Albania on 28 October, but within a week the invasion force had been routed. The Greek Army, under General

Italian troops landing in Albania for the invasion of Greece. Their training, equipment and leadership
was so poor that they were routed by the Greek Army. (Topham Picturepoint M00983942)

Papagos, boldly counterattacked on
14 November and advanced rapidly into
Albania. By 10 January 1941 the Greeks had
captured Klissoura and were advancing on
the port of Velona, supported by five RAF
bomber squadrons. The Italians managed to
stabilize the front line approximately 48 km
(30 miles) inside the Albanian border and
fresh Greek attacks in January and February
1941 made little headway. Severe weather
and difficult terrain conditions were crucial
factors that restricted the success of both
sides, but brave, determined fighting from
the Greeks was matched only by almost
unbelievable incompetence from the
Italians, even though the senior Italian
commander was replaced twice.

The Italians had shown their true mettle
during fierce fighting against the Germans in
1917, but after 20 years of fascist rule the
Italian Army was dramatically more poorly
equipped, trained and led. Unsurprisingly,
losses were severe and morale was shattered.
As a direct result, however, so many Italians
knew what was really happening that the
propaganda machine proved ineffective and
the myth of Mussolini's fascism was broken.

Hitler was furious at Mussolini's petulant
behavior, which had disrupted his plans for
the Balkans. The region was Germany's
bread-basket and the Romanian oilfields at
Ploesti were the only source of oil under
German control. Mussolini's venture
furnished Britain with a reason for moving
into the region – if British bombers menaced
these strategic interests then the entire
German war effort would be threatened.
Hitler, therefore, found himself forced by his
truculent ally to intervene in the Balkans, to
secure his own strategic interests and also to
rescue Mussolini from humiliation. But the
Balkans also formed a maritime base and a
German campaign there automatically drew
German forces into the Mediterranean
theater. Hitler's strategic focus therefore
became distracted and German forces
became embroiled in fighting a larger
Mediterranean campaign than he had ever
envisaged. From now on the Germans
assumed the direction of affairs in the

Mediterranean and Mussolini's idea of
fighting a parallel war had to be abandoned.
Thus, from the moment the Italian invasion
of Albania failed, Mussolini ceased to be a
war leader in any meaningful sense.

British consolidation

When France collapsed, the Mediterranean
was closed to British ships and all shipping
between Britain and the Middle East, India
and the Far East was forced to sail via the
Cape of Good Hope in South Africa. Ships
supplying the troops in the Middle East now
had to sail 21,000 km (13,000 miles) rather
than 4,800 km (3,000 miles) and Bombay
was now 18,000 km (11,000 miles) distant
rather than (9,600 km (6,000 miles). The re-
routings and associated delays increased the
average round voyage from about 90 to
122 days and effectively reduced British
importing capacity by 25 percent, placing an
enormous strain on the merchant fleet.

Of more immediate concern to the British,
however, was the fate of the French Fleet, the
fourth largest in the world. The British
possessed two aircraft-carriers and seven
battleships against the Italian's six battleships,
but the Italian Navy had a significant
superiority in cruisers, destroyers, submarines
and land-based aircraft. If the French Fleet
actively joined with the Axis, the British would
be swept from the Mediterranean. The
armistice provided that the French ships would
be demobilized in any port not occupied by
the Germans, but it was obvious that
protestations by the French commanders that
the French Fleet would never be surrendered
constituted but a feeble guarantee. Churchill
was so concerned that he decided the powerful
ships should either be placed permanently out
of reach of the Germans or be destroyed. Many
were located in British ports but the majority
were scattered among various African harbors,
principally Admiral Marcel-Bruno Gensoul's
naval squadron at Mers-el-Kebir, near Oran in
north-west Algeria, which included two of the
most powerful battleships afloat, the *Strasbourg*
and the *Dunquerque*.

To enforce their determination the British created a special force, designated Force H, based at Gibraltar under Vice-Admiral Sir James Somerville, with three battleships, an aircraft-carrier, two cruisers and 11 destroyers. Somerville arrived at Mers-el-Kebir on 3 July 1940 and gave Gensoul an ultimatum either join the British, sail under escort to internment in a British port, sail under escort for demilitarization in the Caribbean or scuttle his ships. Affronted by this threat, Gensoul rejected all proposals. After protracted negotiation, and under extreme pressure from the Admiralty to conclude the situation before nightfall, Somerville reluctantly opened fire. Although the *Strasbourg* and 12 other ships escaped to Toulon, the battleship *Bretagne* was sunk, the battleships *Provence* and *Dunquerque* were heavily damaged and 1,297 Frenchmen were killed. Some 59 French warships that had sought refuge in British ports were also seized, with some fighting, and an attack was carried out against Dakar on 7 July, which damaged the battleship *Richelieu*. A similar tragedy was avoided at Alexandria thanks to the good sense and cooperation of the British Admiral Sir Andrew Cunningham and the French Admiral René Godfroy. Despite the appalling news from Mers-el-Kebir they continued to negotiate and agreed to immobilize the 11 French ships in Alexandria harbor.

The terrible calamity of Mers-el-Kebir became one of the most tragic and

A French destroyer under attack at Mers-el-kebir is hit in the stern by a 17 inch shell from a British warship. (Topham Picturepoint M00984452)

controversial episodes of the Second World War and caused a rift in Anglo-French relations that endured for a generation. But, for Britain, however horrifying it was to inflict casualties on those who had been allies just a few weeks earlier, if the war was to be continued, it was essential that the Royal Navy should maintain control of the Mediterranean. But, moreover, the attack also followed shortly after Churchill gave his famous "we shall fight them on the beaches" speech and it demonstrated to the world, the Americans in particular, that though apparently on the brink of defeat the British would fight with tenacity and courage, and would stop at nothing to achieve eventual victory.

Following the inconclusive encounter off Punta Stilo in Calabria on 9 July, the only engagement during the war in which Italian battleships were involved in hostile action, the Italian Navy withdrew its capital ships to port. The British position was far more precarious. With a plethora of duties and Malta eliminated as a base Cunningham had no choice but to be active. The Italian Navy was a serious threat that had to be neutralized and based on the experience of Mers-el-Kebir the British developed a plan for an aerial attack on Italy's largest and most heavily defended naval base at Taranto. In a daring and well-planned strike on the night of

HMS *Illustrious* joined Admiral Cunningham's fleet at Alexandria in August 1940 as a brand new aircraft carrier, fitted with the lastest equipment, including radar. She also had one other more basic feature that was to prove of vital importance to her, and and much later to two of her sister ships, Victorious and Formidable – a 3-inch armored flight deck. (Imperial War Museum)

11 November the aircraft-carrier HMS *Illustrious* launched 21 Fairey Swordfish torpedo bombers, known as Stringbags, which although obsolete and slow, were extremely tough. Three battleships were hit, causing the *Littorio* and the *Duillo* to be laid up for several months, put the *Cavour* out of action for the rest of the war and heavily damaged the port. The following day the undamaged ships were sent north to Naples for safety. Since they were further from the sea lanes they posed less danger to the British. The raid proved the futility of Cavagnari's efforts to rein in his

commanders from seeking action and he was replaced by Admiral Arturo Riccardi. However, although the attack on Taranto reduced the threat of the Italian Fleet, it did not eliminate it and, despite the heavy losses, the Italian Navy was still a considerable force. The raid also had far wider implications. Japanese interest was intense and a naval delegation was immediately dispatched to Taranto to study the operation and its consequences. A year later their findings were to be put to good use in the attack on Pearl Harbor.

Conclusion

The first six months of the war in the Mediterranean were characterized by a series of relatively unconnected events. Mussolini tried, and failed, to conduct his own limited war alongside Hitler to gain the spoils of victory without any risk. He succeeded only in widening the strategic dimensions and expanded the war in the Mediterranean beyond a colonial conflict. The British, determined to stand alone against fascist aggression, strengthened their position and prepared to take the war to the Italians.

Albacore torpedo-bombers flying off HMS *Illustrious*. Although the British aircraft carrier spent only six months in the Mediterranean she shifted the balance of naval power in the Mediterranean in favor of the Royal Navy. Her involvement in the raid on Taranto had far-reaching consequences, both locally and halfway around the world. (Topham Picturepoint M00984445)

In all directions at once

The first desert campaigns

Graziani's Tenth Army in Libya vastly outnumbered the 36,000 British, New Zealand and Indian troops of Lieutenant-General Richard O'Connor's Western Desert Force (WDF) who guarded Egypt – grandiloquently described as the Army of the Nile by Churchill. But the British had years of peacetime experience of training and operating in the desert and Wavell was not intimidated. He decided from the outset to take the offensive, using General Creagh's 7th Armoured Division – which had as its emblem a jerboa, and would soon become famous as "the desert rats" – to harass the Italians in a continuous series of surprise

Major-General Richard O'Connor, Commander Western Defence Force, and General Sir Archibald Wavell, Commander-in-Chief, Middle East, architects of the early British successes. (Topham Picturepoint 0032644)

raids. As a result, between June and September 1940, the Italians incurred 3,500 casualties and rarely ventured from the confines of their camps, whereas the British, who lost just 150 men, became masters of the desert and gained a moral ascendancy over the Italians.

This unrivaled mastery was manifest in the creation of special forces that operated deep in the desert interior. The Long Range Desert Group (LRDG) was formed in June 1940 by Captain Ralph Bagnold and was expert at driving and navigating in the desert, using specially adapted and heavily armed trucks. The volunteer force reconnoitered behind Axis lines, inserted spies, mounted lightning strikes against airfields and fuel dumps and, most importantly, maintained a close watch on Rommel's supply convoys. Russia operated closely with Popski's Private Army, a small special forces sabotage unit led by a Belgian émigré Vladimir Peniakoff, and the Special Air Service (SAS), which was formed in October 1941 by Lieutenant-Colonel David Stirling to make stealthy parachute raids and undertake sabotage and reconnaissance operations. The LRDG and SAS proved an effective combination and all three forces had considerable success throughout the desert war and continued clandestine operations until the end of the war. The British SAS Regiment continues to be one of the premier special-forces formations in the world even today.

With remarkable daring, Churchill sent reinforcements, including three armored regiments, to the Middle East during the height of the Battle of Britain and in spite of an imminent German invasion, while extra troops also arrived from Australia and India. Graziani made no attempt to move on after he had crossed "the wire" – the extensive barbed-wire fence built by the Italians on the

Egyptian–Libyan border that became a feature of the desert war as successive armies crossed and re-crossed it – and remained for weeks in the chain of fortified camps he had established around Sidi Barrani. Wavell therefore conceived a plan to throw the Italians off balance while he dealt with them in east Africa. Because of a shortage of transport, in particular, he envisaged not a sustained offensive but a swift, large-scale raid lasting no more than four or five days. As a result, however, no preparations were made to follow up any success, a detrimental decision that would have serious repercussions.

Operation Compass began on 7 December 1941 with a two-day, 112-km (70-mile) march across the desert. After passing through a gap between the Italian camps 4th Indian Division stormed Nibeiwa camp from the rear with 50 heavily armored "Matilda" Infantry tanks of 7th Royal Tank Regiment at the spearhead. The garrison was taken by complete surprise and 4,000 Italians were captured almost without loss. Tummar East and Tummar West camps were also stormed in a day of triumph, while the camps around Sidi Barrani were overrun the next day. On the third day 7th Armoured Division swept

A Special Air Service patrol is greeted by its commander, Colonel David Stirling, on its return from the desert. (Imperial War Museum E21338)

westward to the coast beyond Buq Buq and cut the Italian line of retreat. In three days 40,000 troops and 400 guns were captured, while the remnants of the Italian Army took refuge in Bardia, the first town inside the Italian colony, and were rapidly surrounded.

These astonishing results, however, were completely unforeseen and caused immense problems. As previously planned, 4th Indian Division was recalled from the desert for dispatch to the Sudan, but this led to the curious spectacle of British troops withdrawing eastwards just as the demoralized Italians fled in the opposite direction. The Australian 6th Division was transferred from Palestine but the shortage of trucks and the need to feed and evacuate huge numbers of prisoners led to a three-week delay before the operation could be resumed. Although the ingenious development of field supply dumps in the desert had alleviated the problems of transporting supplies across long distances, the operation's success was only possible because large numbers of Italian trucks had been captured and their previous owners agreed to drive them for the British.

General "Electric Whiskers" Bergonzoli had signaled to Mussolini that, "We are in Bardia and here we stay," but three days after the assault began, on 3 January 1941, the garrison of 45,000 surrendered, with 462 guns and 129 tanks. The Matilda tanks, which were almost impenetrable to the Italian guns, were again the key to the rapid success and the Australian commander, Major-General I. G. Mackay, claimed that each tank was worth an entire infantry battalion. Even before the fighting concluded 7th Armoured Division drove west to encircle and isolate Tobruk, which was attacked on 21 January. Although just 16 of the precious Matildas were still running, they once again made the vital penetration and the coastal fortress fell the next day, yielding 30,000 prisoners, 236 guns and 87 tanks.

The capture of Tobruk was important because its large port allowed supplies to be delivered by sea direct from Alexandria, so O'Connor intended to await reinforcements and allow 13 Corps, as WDF was now known, to recuperate. On 3 February, however, his intelligence showed that the Italians were preparing to abandon Cyrenaica and Benghazi and to withdraw beyond the El Agheila bottleneck. O'Connor immediately planned a daring initiative to combine his depleted tanks in a single column and send them across the desert interior to cut off the Italian retreat south of Benghazi. From Mechili they covered almost 160 km (100 miles) of the roughest country in north Africa in just 33 hours and came out of the desert ahead of the fleeing Italians at Beda Fomm late on 5 February. In a fitting climax the minuscule force of no more than 3,000 men and 39 Cruiser tanks held off Italian attempts to break out until the morning of 7 February when, completely demoralized, 20,000 Italians surrendered, with 216 guns and 120 tanks. Using a hunting metaphor, O'Connor signaled news of the victory to Wavell in a now famous message: "Fox killed in the open," which he sent in plain English to infuriate Mussolini even further.

In 10 weeks the Commonwealth force of two divisions advanced more than 1,126 km (700 miles) and captured 130,000 prisoners, more than 380 tanks, 845 guns and well over 3,000 vehicles at the relatively slight cost of 500 killed, 1,373 wounded and 55 missing. O'Connor had far exceeded all expectations but he was confident that the way was clear for him to continue his advance to Tripoli and completely clear the Italian colony. Historians have since argued that a golden opportunity to finish the war in Africa was wasted, but recent research has shown that without an operational port at Benghazi to maintain an advance, the supply difficulties would have been immense. Nevertheless, Churchill had already directed Wavell to halt the campaign at Benghazi in favor of events that were developing in Greece, and leave only a minimum force to hold Cyrenaica.

Hitler was not aware of these plans but recognized that an Italian collapse would be fatal for Mussolini's fascist regime. He was determined to save his friend and ally and on the very day Graziani's army was finally being destroyed he summoned Rommel, whom he chose for his ability to inspire his soldiers, to take command of the small mechanized force on its way to Africa, the DAK. Meanwhile, X Fliegerkorps had been transferred to Sicily and southern Italy, from where, on 10 January, it launched its first attacks, with orders to neutralize the airbase on Malta, protect the Axis convoys to Tripoli and delay the British units advancing in Cyrenaica. Rommel flew to Tripoli on 12 February with the express orders only to defend against an expected British attack, but when the first of his units arrived two days later he immediately rushed them to the front and started pushing forward.

The conquest of Italian East Africa

In East Africa Italian forces under the command of the Duke of Aosta had captured outposts in Sudan and Kenya and occupied British Somaliland soon after Italy had entered the war. Although they vastly outnumbered the British forces, most of whom had been raised locally, Aosta was demoralized by the Italian defeats in the Western Desert and at the moment of Britain's greatest weakness he unwisely adopted a defensive posture. The British had also broken the Italian Army and Air Force codes and, armed with copies of Italian orders as soon as they were issued, Major-General William Platt launched an offensive into Eritrea on 19 January 1941 with 4th and 5th Indian Divisions. After weeks of hard fighting they captured Keren on 27 March, which proved to be the decisive campaign of the battle, and entered Massawa on 8 April. Meanwhile, on 11 February, Lieutenant-General Alan Cunningham launched an offensive into Italian Somaliland from Kenya using British East African and South African troops with startling success. After capturing

Haile Selassie, Emperor of Abyssinia, was exiled by Mussolini in 1936 after the Italian occupation of his country. In May 1941 he was escorted back to his capital, Addis Ababa, and to his throne by Colonel Orde Wingate following a daring guerrilla campaign. His was the first country to be liberated from Axis control but he failed to ensure its independence and was deposed in 1974. (Imperial War Museum BM1986)

Mogadishu, the capital of Italian Somaliland, on 25 February he struck north toward Harar in Abyssinia, which he captured on 26 March. A small force from Aden reoccupied British Somaliland without opposition on 16 March, to shorten the supply line, and joined with Cunningham's force to capture Addis Ababa on 6 April. In just eight weeks Cunningham's troops had advanced over 2,735 km (1,700 miles) and defeated the majority of Aosta's troops for the loss of 501 casualties.

Even more spectacular were the achievements of Lieutenant-Colonel Orde Wingate, later to win fame as commander of the Chindits in Burma, who commanded a group of 1,600 local troops, known as the Patriots, whom he christened "Gideon force" Through a combination of brilliant guerrilla tactics, great daring and sheer bluff he defeated the Italian Army at Debra Markos and returned the Emperor Haile Selassie to his capital, Addis Ababa, on 5 May. British troops pressed Aosta's forces into a diminishing mountainous retreat until he finally surrendered on 16 May, ending Italian resistance apart from two isolated pockets that were rounded up in November 1941.

The campaign in east Africa was important because the conquest of Ethiopia, Mussolini's proudest achievement, had been undone and for the first time a country occupied by the Axis had been liberated. Another 230,000 Italian troops were captured and vital British forces were released for operations in the Western Desert. It was also the first campaign in which Ultra (see page 69) and the codebreakers at Bletchley Park played a decisive role, providing an invaluable lesson on the impact that intelligence could have on the outcome of an operation. Success in east Africa also had an important strategic consequence since President Roosevelt was able to declare on 11 April that the Red Sea and the Gulf of Aden were no longer war zones and US ships were thus able to deliver supplies direct to Suez, relieving the burden on British shipping.

Greece

The victories in Cyrenaica and in east Africa demonstrated the superiority of British arms in the one strategic region where they still had the freedom of action to humiliate the fascists The Mediterranean Fleet reinforced this notion by freely bombarding the port of Genoa on 9 February 1941 and gaining a victory over the Italian Fleet at the Battle of Cape Matapan on 28 March, in which the battleship *Vittorio Veneto* was torpedoed and three cruisers and two destroyers were sunk. Wavell's successes were astonishing and were an invaluable boost to British morale during the blitz, but the radiance of victory was soon dimmed.

Churchill's attention had become focused on one of his cherished ambitions of the First World War, the creation of a Balkan front. Impressed with the resilience shown by the Greeks against the Italian invaders and under the pretext of the political and moral obligation to fulfill the guarantee given to Greece against German intervention, a cause which Churchill also knew would impress the Americans, he envisioned an alliance of Greece, Turkey, Yugoslavia and possibly Bulgaria standing up to the German forces.

Britain began negotiating in February 1941 on the nature of assistance but the Greek dictator, Ioannis Metaxas, was unwilling to accept British troops for fear of provoking a full-scale German invasion. His pragmatic approach might have saved the British from a futile gesture that had little chance of success and which helped the Greeks little but cost the British much. Following his death on 29 January, however, the less formidable General Alexandros Papagos, the Commander-in-Chief, was persuaded by Churchill to accept British troops. Encouraged by excessively optimistic reports from Wavell and the British Foreign Secretary, Anthony Eden, Churchill thus ordered that British troops should be diverted from the campaign in the Western Desert.

After Hungary and Romania joined the Tripartite Pact in November 1940 German troops prepared to invade Greece, not so much to help the Italians but to protect the southern flank of the invasion of Russia. But, with the expansion of the Italian commitment in Greece and the growing likelihood of British involvement, Hitler decided that it would be necessary to occupy the whole of Greece. He was greatly affected by his experience in the First World War and vividly recalled the effect that the Allied front in Salonika had had on the Germans on the western front in 1918. A British front in Greece would directly threaten the rear of the German offensive in Russia and, moreover, would attack by Romanian oilfields in Ploesti to attack by British bombers. These were risks that he was not willing to accept.

Bulgaria ultimately joined the Tripartite Pact on 1 March and German troops immediately began crossing the Danube. In Yugoslavia the Regent, Prince Paul, had hesitated about joining the Pact but eventually succumbed on 25 March. Two days later, however, his government was overthrown in a coup d'etat led by General Simovic. Hitler was so incensed that he immediately decided to launch a full-scale invasion of Yugoslavia as well as Greece, and on 6 April attacked both in Operation Marita. Field-Marshal Lists's Twelfth Army began the simultaneous invasion of Greece and Southern Yugoslavia from Bulgaria with seven panzer divisions and 1,000 aircraft, and on 8 and 10 April German, Italian and Hungarian troops attacked northern and central Yugoslavia. Belgrade fell on 13 April after a very heavy bombardment that caused grievous casualties and the government capitulated four days later. Although the Yugoslav Army amounted to a million men, it was antiquated and inefficient, and the Germans occupied the rapidly disintegrating country at a cost of only 151 killed. Like vultures, Italy, Hungary, and Romania helped themselves to pieces of what they assumed, incorrectly, to be a corpse; the Croatian Ustashi nationalists and the Slovenes proclaimed independent states and Serbia became a German puppet. The massive population changes and widespread slaughter that were a feature of the cruelest of all the internecine wars in Europe during the

Ethiopia

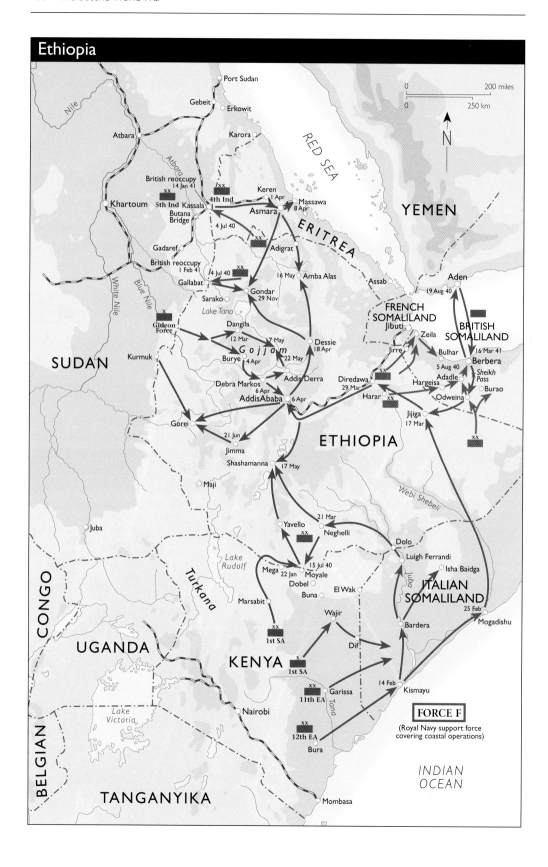

Port Sudan
Gebeit
Erkowit
Nile
Atbara
Karora
RED SEA
YEMEN
Khartoum
British reoccupy
14 Jan 41
5th Ind Kassala
XX
4th Ind
Keren
1 Apr
Massawa
8 Apr
Butana
Bridge
Asmara
ERITREA
Aden
19 Aug 40
4 Jul 40
XX
Adigrat
Assab
FRENCH
SOMALILAND
Jibuti
BRITISH
SOMALILAND
Gadaref
British reoccupy
1 Feb 41
Gallabat
4 Jul 40
XX
16 May
Amba Alas
Zeila
Bulhar
16 Mar 41
Berbera
Sarako
Gondar
29 Nov
Lake Tana
Jirre
5 Aug 40
Adadle
Sheikh
Pass
Gideon
Force
X
Dangila
Dessie
18 Apr
Diredawa
29 Mar
Hargeisa
Odweina
Burao
SUDAN
12 Mar
Gojjam
17 May
22 May
Harar
XX
Jijiga
17 Mar
Kurmuk
Burye
4 Apr
Addis Derra
Debra Markos
6 Apr
AddisAbaba
6 Apr
XX
Gorei
21 Jun
ETHIOPIA
Jimma
Shashamanna
17 May
Maji
Webi Shebeli
Juba
Yavello
21 Mar
Neghelli
Dolo
Luigh Ferrandi
Isha Baidga
Lake
Rudolf
Mega
22 Jan
15 Jul 40
Moyale
Dobel
Buna
El Wak
ITALIAN
SOMALILAND
25 Feb
CONGO
Turkana
Marsabit
Wajir
Bardera
Mogadishu
UGANDA
XX
1st SA
KENYA
X
1st SA
Dif
14 Feb
Kismayu
XX
11th EA
Garissa
Lake
Victoria
Nairobi
Tana
BELGIAN
XX
12th EA
Bura
FORCE F
(Royal Navy support force
covering coastal operations)
TANGANYIKA
Mombasa
INDIAN
OCEAN

0   200 miles
0   250 km

N

Greece

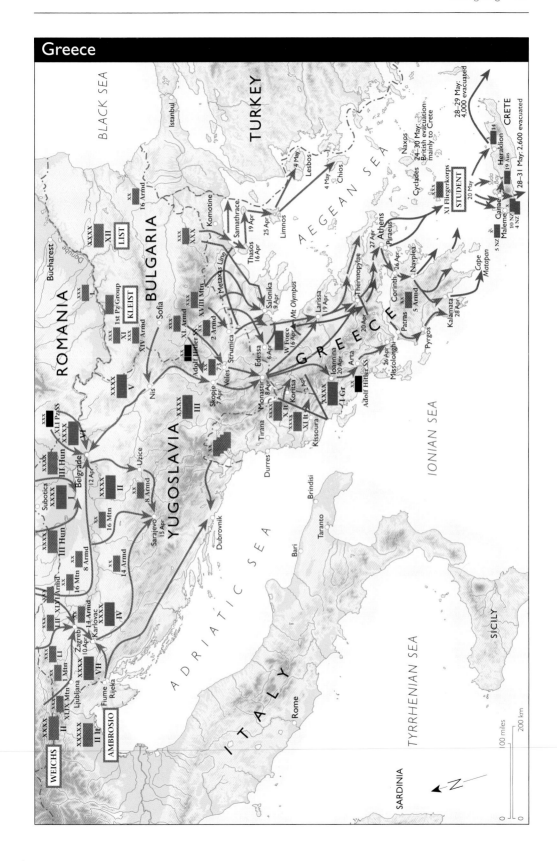

BLACK SEA

TURKEY

Istanbul

ROMANIA

Bucharest

Danube

BULGARIA

XII LIST

16 Armd

Komotine

Samathrace 19 Apr

Thasós 16 Apr

25 Apr

4 May Lesbos

4 May Chios

AEGEAN SEA

Limnos

Naxos

Cyclades

24–30 May:
British evacuation
mainly to Crete

XI Fliegerkorps STUDENT

20 May

28–29 May:
4,000 evacuated

CRETE

Heraklion

19 Aus

28–31 May: 2,600 evacuated

Rodo
Bay

Canae 5 NZ

Malerne 10 NZ

5 NZ 4 NZ

1st Pz Group KLEIST

XI   XIV Armd

Sofia

Metaxas Line

Salonika 9 Apr

Mt Olympus

Larissa 19 Apr

Thermopylae

Athens 27 Apr

Piraeus

26 Apr Corinth

Nauplea

5 Armd

Kalamata 28 Apr

Pyrgos

Patras

Missolonghi 26 Apr

Cape
Matapan

GREECE

XI Armd SS

XVIII Mtn

2 Armd

Strumica

Edessa

W Force 6 Apr

Ioannina 20 Apr

Arta 20 Apr

Adolf Hitler SS

Veles 73

Skopje 7 Apr

Monastir 8 Apr

Koritsa 2 Apr

XI It XII It

Kissoura

II Gr

Nis

V

XIV

III

YUGOSLAVIA

Uzice

Belgrade

12 Apr

II

8 Armd

16 Mtn

Sarajevo 15 Apr

14 Armd

Dubrovnik

XLI PzSS

XXXk III Hun

Subotica

I

III Hun

16 Mtn

8 Armd

XLVI Armd

Karlovac

14 Armd

IV

Zagreb 10 Apr

VII

Ljubljana I Mtn

Rijeka Flume

II It

II LI

AMBROSIO

WEICHS

Tirana

Durres

Brindisi

Bari

Taranto

ADRIATIC SEA

IONIAN SEA

ITALY

Rome

TYRRHENIAN SEA

SICILY

SARDINIA

N

0   100 miles

0   200 km

Second World War began in these first few days of fighting.

Greece was conquered only slightly less abruptly. The first British troops had disembarked on 4 March but, in a muddle symbolic of the confused negotiations, soon discovered that the Greeks had not withdrawn to defensive positions on the Aliakmon line as the British thought had been agreed. This ran from the Aliakmon river, through Veroia and Edessa to the Yugoslav border, but the two Greek armies were still in

German soldiers in Greece, April 1941. (Topham Picturepoint 0156318)

their positions on the Albanian front and in Salonika. Fifty thousand troops of the New Zealand Division, 6th and 7th Australian Divisions and a British armored brigade, supported by one squadron of aircraft, all under the command of Lieutenant-General Maitland "Jumbo" Wilson, could do little to succor the Greeks. The Germans swept south from Yugoslavia into Greece through the Monastir Gap, outflanking the Greeks in Thrace and isolating the Greeks on the Albanian front, and then pressed south into central Greece, turning the British flank. The British began to withdraw on 10 April and as the situation became increasingly hopeless decided to evacuate on 21 April. In a repeat of the Dunkirk escape most of the troops were embarked from the beaches by 29 April, but their valuable heavy equipment and vehicles were all abandoned.

Hitler decided to conclude his Balkan campaign by capturing Crete, which he feared would be used by the British as a naval and bomber base, using the one feature of his blitzkrieg army that had not yet been used – the airborne troops of General Student's *XI Fliegerkorps*. Operation Merkur (Mercury) began on 20 May with glider and parachute landings from a fleet of 500 transport aircraft. The British had failed to defend the island during a six-month occupation and most of the 35,000 garrison, commanded by the New Zealand First World War hero Lieutenant-General Bernard Freyberg VC, had just escaped from Greece with nothing but their own light weapons. The first assault of 3,000 paratroopers failed to capture the main objective, the airfield at Maleme, but after the New Zealanders withdrew from one end during the night the Germans began the next day to land reinforcements, despite still being under intense artillery and mortar fire. Whole units were wiped out before landing, or soon after, before they could reach their weapons and the Royal Navy balked a supplementary seaborne landing on the second night. Nevertheless, the Germans were able to land a steady stream of reinforcements and after a week of bitter fighting Freyberg ordered a retreat and evacuation.

The airborne invasion of Crete was one of the most spectacular and audacious events of the war, but it was also extremely costly. British and Commonwealth casualties amounted to about 16,000, on top of the 13,000 lost in Greece, most of whom became prisoners, but the loss of the equivalent of two divisions came at a time when defenses in the Middle East were already stretched thin. The Mediterranean Fleet lost three cruisers and six destroyers sunk, in addition to two destroyers sunk during the evacuation from Greece, and 17 ships damaged, including its only aircraft-carrier, two battleships and three cruisers, which proved once more that warships could not operate in waters dominated by land-based aircraft. But the Germans were badly mauled too, with several hundred planes destroyed or damaged and 7,000 casualties out of the 22,000 troops landed, more than the entire Balkan campaign. The Germans considered themselves lucky to have captured Crete and Hitler was shocked by the losses. He concluded that the days of paratroops were over and scrapped plans for an invasion of Malta, which would have proved more beneficial to German strategy, and turned his parachute units into infantry regiments.

German paratroops, part of the German airborne invasion of Crete, parachuting onto the village of Suda on 20 May 1941. Sunken British shipping can be seen in Suda Bay and a burning Junker Ju52 is flying across Suda Bay toward the Akrotiri Peninsula. (Australian War Memorial P0043.009)

Rommel's first desert offensive

In Cyrenaica, Wavell had been content to use the incomplete and untrained 2nd Armoured Division and 9th Australian Division as a screening force for he knew from Ultra that Rommel was under orders not to attack and that his forces were very weak. Nevertheless, using 5th Light Division and the Italian Ariete Division, Rommel recaptured El Agheila with ease and seizing an opportunity he launched an offensive on 31 March, disobeying direct orders from Hitler and his immediate Italian superiors to wait for the arrival of 15th Panzer Division expected in May. Despite having no experience of desert warfare, in just two weeks he dramatically swept across Cyrenaica until he was stopped at Sollum, reversing all of O'Connor's gains, investing Tobruk and capturing Generals O'Connor

and Neame amidst mass British confusion. His advance gave the Germans vital airfields from which they could impose the siege of Malta, but General Halder, the German Chief-of-Staff, wrote that Rommel had gone "stark mad." Even with the reinforcements Rommel's forces were too weak to dislodge the Australian, British and Polish troops, "the rats of Tobruk," who were besieged in the fortress. For all his dynamism, Rommel was a prisoner of the desert and its logistical constraints. Without the port at Tobruk his supply lines from Tripoli became dangerously attenuated and he was unable to advance further into Egypt.

In contrast, Churchill wanted success, and quickly. Boldly he pressed for a convoy, codenamed Tiger, to sail from Britain through the dangerous Mediterranean, rather than the longer, safer route via south Africa, to Alexandria, which delivered 238 tanks that he christened his "Tiger cubs." Under intense pressure from Churchill to achieve a "decisive" victory in north Africa and "destroy" Rommel's forces, Wavell reluctantly launched two limited offensives. Operation Brevity in May, and the more powerful Battleaxe in June, using the newly arrived tanks, were hastily planned and executed. Both were costly failures, principally because of faulty British tactics. Rommel had wisely placed his screen of anti-tank guns and had included two batteries of 88 mm anti-aircraft guns, which he used in a ground role. But, whereas the British failed to coordinate their Cruiser and heavy Matilda tanks, Rommel incorporated his anti-tank guns in a mobile, offensive role with his panzer regiments. In the trial of skill in armored warfare the British incurred serious losses of 91 of the new tanks, while the Germans lost just 12 tanks. Churchill's impatience had worn thin and despite Wavell's successes he was replaced by General Claude Auchinleck, Commander-in-Chief India, while General Cunningham took command of the enlarged desert forces, renamed Eighth Army. But the British failed to learn valuable lessons from the experience, notably that it was anti-tank guns and not tanks that had inflicted the damage, and they did not evolve tactics for the next offensive.

A German 88 mm Flak Gun in action at Mersa el Brega on 15 April 1941. Although designed as an anti-aircraft gun Rommel used them as anti-tank guns, which were superior to any British tank and caused many British losses. (Imperial War Museum HU1205)

Iraq and Syria

German success and growing commitment in the Balkans and the Mediterranean encouraged pro-Axis elements in Iraq to stage a coup on 2 April that brought Rashid Ali el-Gaylani to power. The Arab nationalists hoped a German victory would liberate their country, and the Arabs, from the yoke of British control and restrict the growing Jewish presence in Palestine. Encouraged by the Germans, who promised air support and to try to get materiel from Syria, Rashid Ali refused the British their treaty right to transit troops through Iraq and surrounded the airfield at Habbaniya, 40 km (25 miles) west of Baghdad. With the British fully committed in the Western Desert, Greece and east Africa, it seemed an opportune time to move, but, in desperation, the British, fearful for their lines of communications with India and the supplies of Iraqi oil, attacked on 2 May. The

10th Indian Division landed in Basra from India and a hastily organized 5,800-strong column, Habforce, made a trans-desert march from Palestine to relieve the garrison at Habbaniya. Although German aircraft were flown via Syria to help support the Iraqis they had moved a month too early before the Germans were able to offer effective assistance and Baghdad was captured on 31 May.

The British were alarmed by Ultra evidence that the Vichy High Commissioner in Syria, General Henri Dentz, had supplied weapons to the Iraqis and had freely cooperated with the Germans. They did not realize until later that Hitler was fixated on the impending invasion of Russia, but the fear that Germany, supported by the vehemently anti-British Admiral Darlan, who was now in control of the armed forces of Vichy France, would extend its victories beyond Crete and through Syria into the Middle East combined with the threat posed to the British base in Egypt by the Army of the Levant to convince the British to invade Syria and Lebanon. A hastily concocted force, commanded by General Wilson, launched Operation Explorer on 8 June. Habforce and 10th Indian Division invaded Syria from Iraq against Palmyra and Aleppo, while 6th Division invaded from Palestine against Damascus and 7th Australian Division invaded from Haifa against Beirut. After five weeks of bitter fighting, Dentz capitulated on 14 July. This tragic, regrettable episode, which cost the lives of 3,500 men, was a short but sour war that was imbued with resentment, particularly between the Vichy French and Free French Forces of General de Gaulle who fought with savage vengeance. For the British, however, the campaign consolidated their flank and guarded against any chance of German attack through Turkey.

A few weeks later Britain occupied Iran, in unison with Russia, to guarantee the transfer of lend-lease supplies through Iran to Russia, and in the process secured its position in the Middle East. Thus, in mid-summer 1941 Germany was consolidated in the Balkans while Britain dominated the whole of the Middle East. The British commander was liberated from all other preoccupations but that of defeating Rommel in Libya, and for the first time was able to concentrate all his force on just one front. Moreover, this came at a time after Hitler launched his attack on Russia in June, when Rommel could expect no major reinforcements while Germany concentrated on the eastern front. Apart from the steadfast and spirited defense of Tobruk, including the replacement of Australian soldiers with British and Polish troops by the Royal Navy in a series of voyages during the moonless nights, a period of stalemate therefore descended on the desert war as each side reinforced its strength and prepared for the next battle.

The Mediterranean

Malta was the only British outpost remaining in the central Mediterranean and its presence was potentially a powerful thorn in Rommel's side. The island's strategic position, equidistant from Gibraltar and Alexandria and astride Rommel's line of communication between Italy and Africa, was pivotal. It was an invaluable aid to Vice-Admiral Philip Vian's 15th Cruiser Squadron, which escorted convoys between Alexandria and Malta, and Force H, which provided escorts between Gibraltar and Malta. However, since the arrival of the Luftwaffe in January 1941 the island had been blockaded and subjected to unremitting air raids with growing intensity, and with German forces now in Greece, Crete and Libya, the problems of supplying Malta were even greater. Nevertheless, the men and materiel were fought through for the defense of Malta and its use as an offensive base. In June alone, the aircraft-carrier HMS *Ark Royal*, once on her own, at other times accompanied by the carriers HMS *Furious* or HMS *Victorious*, flew off more than 140 aircraft for Malta. Submarines carried in urgently needed fuel and stores but the British had been unable to strike effectively

Destroyers take men off from the sinking British aircraft carrier HMS *Ark Royal* on 2 December 1941, after she had been torpedoed by the German submarine U-81. Her loss came just a week after the battlehip HMS *Barham* had been spectacularly destroyed by U-331. (Topham Picturepoint M00983945)

at the Axis convoys transferring Rommel's forces, which arrived in Africa almost without any loss, or the Italian supply convoys because of a shortage of aircraft and submarines, despite detailed knowledge from Ultra intelligence.

By the summer Malta's plight was becoming desperate but the withdrawal of *X Fliegerkorps* for the eastern front in June eased the British position in the Mediterranean. In July Malta welcomed its first major offensive resupply convoy, Operation Substance, since January, followed by another in September, Operation Halberd. Nearly 40 merchant ships got through with only one sunk, and at a cost to the Royal Navy of one cruiser and a destroyer sunk, and a battleship, aircraft-carrier and two cruisers damaged. For a short while the island once again became a naval base. Between June and the end of September submarines sank 49 ships of 150,000 tons, which when added to the losses inflicted by the RAF represented a

high proportion of Axis shipping bound for Libya. The 10th Submarine Flotilla was formed at Malta in September and the next month Force K, with two cruisers and two destroyers, was formed as a strike force to add to the offensive against Axis shipping.

By November the British had reestablished control of the central Mediterranean and it became a time of crisis for Rommel as 68 percent of the supplies shipped from Italy failed to arrive in Africa. This situation was highlighted on 9 November when Force K completely annihilated the Axis *Duisburg* convoy of seven supply ships and two of its destroyer escorts. As a result the Italians suspended all further convoys and instead decided to use individual "fast" merchant ships and warships to transport supplies and fuel.

But Britain's strength in the Mediterranean soon came under renewed challenge. On 27 October Hitler instructed the German navy to transfer 24 U-boats from the Atlantic into the Mediterranean, the first of 62 U-boats that Germany managed to send through the Straits of Gibraltar up to May 1944. On 14 November the aircraft-carrier HMS *Ark Royal* was torpedoed and sunk, followed 11 days later by the battleship HMS *Barham*, which capsized and split apart in a massive explosion,

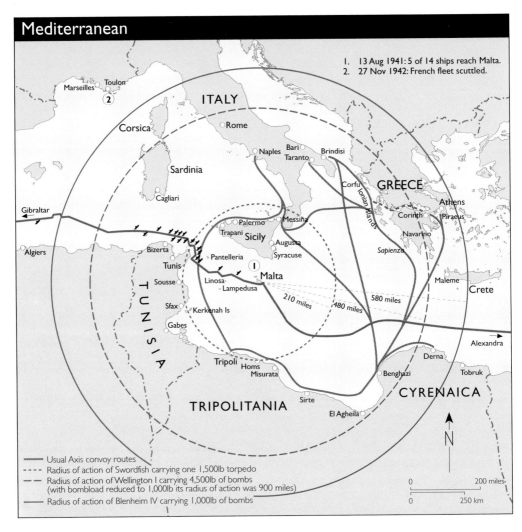

Mediterranean

1. 13 Aug 1941: 5 of 14 ships reach Malta.
2. 27 Nov 1942: French fleet scuttled.

Marseilles Toulon ②

ITALY

Corsica   Rome

Sardinia

Cagliari

Gibraltar

Algiers

Naples Bari Brindisi
Taranto

Corfu   GREECE

Ionian Islands

Athens
Corinth   Piraeus

Navarino

Sapienza

Palermo   Messina
Trapani Sicily
Bizerta   Augusta
Pantelleria   Syracuse

Maleme

Crete

TUNISIA

Tunis
Sousse
Sfax
Gabes

Linosa
Lampedusa

Kerkenah Is

Malta ①

210 miles   480 miles   580 miles

Alexandra

Tripoli Homs
Misurata

Sirte

El Agheila

TRIPOLITANIA

Derna

Benghazi   Tobruk

CYRENAICA

N

Usual Axis convoy routes
Radius of action of Swordfish carrying one 1,500lb torpedo
Radius of action of Wellington I carrying 4,500lb of bombs
(with bombload reduced to 1,000lb its radius of action was 900 miles)
Radius of action of Blenheim IV carrying 1,000lb of bombs

0   200 miles
0   250 km

with the loss of 800 men. On 19 December
Force K floundered on an Italian minefield.
The cruiser HMS *Neptune* and destroyer HMS
Kandahar were sunk, but out of a force of three
cruisers and four destroyers only three
destroyers escaped damage. On the same
morning, as Force K struggled to survive, three
Italian human torpedoes of the 10th Light
Flotilla were launched from a submarine. The
Italian frogmen penetrated Alexandria harbor
and attached charges to the hulls of the
battleships HMS *Queen Elizabeth*, with Admiral
Cunningham on board, and HMS *Valiant*, as
well as a destroyer and a tanker. Both
battleships were badly damaged and settled on
the bottom, eliminating the Mediterranean
Fleet's battle squadron. At the same time other
British warships were sent to the Far East to
cope with Japan's entry into the war, further
weakening the Mediterranean Fleet.

Hitler also appointed Field-Marshal Albert
Kesselring as Commander-in-Chief, South, and
ordered the transfer of *Luftflotte 2* HQ with
II Fliegerkorps from the eastern front to Sicily,
Sardinia and southern Italy. With this
powerful force, Kesselring was directed to
establish a center of Axis supremacy in the
Mediterranean, safeguard the routes to Libya
and Cyrenaica, paralyze Malta, cooperate with
the forces in north Africa and disrupt enemy
traffic through the Mediterranean. However,
while Kesselring was subordinate to Mussolini
his authority was ambiguous and confusion
resulted in the Axis command structure.
Italian prestige would not permit Kesselring to
become supreme Axis commander but he
developed a close relationship with Marshal
Count Ugo Cavallero, Chief of the Italian High
Command, and a voluntary collaboration with
the *Comando Supremo*, the Italian High
Command. Although he commanded the

OPPOSITE The Italians pioneered the use of 'human
torpedoes', which were taken close to their target by
specially adapted submarines. Their greatest succeess was
on 19 December 1941 when Italian frogmen penetrated
Alexandria harbour and severely damaged the battleships
HMS *Valiant* and HMS *Queen Elizabeth*, which meant that
the British could no longer muster a force strong enough
to take on the Italian fleet. (Topham Picturepoint
M00984390)

Luftwaffe, issued directives to German and
Italian naval units and cooperated with the
forces in north Africa, he had no operational
authority over *Panzergruppe Afrika*, as
Rommel's command was now called.

The desert campaigns 1941–42

The failure of the British summer efforts
spurred Churchill's determination to gain a
decisive victory over Rommel. Disregarding
advice to improve the defense of the Far
East, particularly the British garrison in
Singapore, he rushed reinforcements to
Egypt. By November the Eighth Army was
significantly stronger than Rommel's forces
in every category; with over 700 tanks, plus
500 in reserve and in shipment, compared to
Rommel's 174 German and 146 obsolete
Italian tanks, and almost 700 aircraft against
120 German and 200 Italian aircraft.
Rommel had not received extra German
units and the Italian infantry divisions that
had been transferred lacked any integral
transport, which seriously restricted their
movement. However, he had received large
numbers of 50 mm anti-tank guns, which
significantly improved his anti-tank
capability. Rommel carefully husbanded all
his supplies and planned to launch another
offensive against Tobruk, but he was pre-
empted by Auchinleck who launched
Operation Crusader on 18 November.

Auchinleck planned for 13 Corps to pin
down the German outposts on the Egyptian
frontier while 30 Corps, comprising the
mobile armored regiments, would sweep
south of these fortified positions through the
desert "to seek and destroy" Rommel's
armored force, which Auchinleck considered
to be the backbone of Rommel's army, before
linking up with the Tobruk garrison, which
itself would break out from the fortress.
From the outset, therefore, the two Corps
would be operating independently.

A huge storm the night before the attack
turned the desert into a quagmire and
grounded the Luftwaffe reconnaissance
flights. The element of surprise was soon

wasted, however, as the British attack became disjointed and the armored brigades were involved in piecemeal battles. The majority of the fighting took place around the escarpment of Sidi Rezegh, with the Italian-built road on which Rommel's supplies were transported at the bottom and a German airfield on top, and in a repeat of the summer offensives the British again failed to combine their armor in a concentrated blow.

Five days of hard, confused fighting, in which British and German tank formations were intermingled in the highly fluid battle, and often found themselves behind what would have been the enemy's lines, culminated on Sunday 23 November – aptly known in the German calendar as *Totensonntag* or "Sunday of the Dead," and by which name the Germans remember this battle. With skillful tactics Rommel had decimated the British, who had just 70 tanks remaining, but in a concentrated attack the next day he lost 70 of his remaining 160 tanks. Although Rommel was victorious on the battlefield he knew that the British were able to sustain greater losses because they had a large reserve from which to restore their strength. He therefore decided to exploit the British confusion by striking at the morale and the confidence of the British troops and their commanders, as he had successfully done previously. Rommel personally led a deep thrust with his mobile forces of the DAK to the frontier and into the rear of the Eighth Army, which he hoped would cause panic, capture British supply dumps and relieve his garrisons on the border. Rommel's "dash for the wire" created a stampede among the British and almost succeeded as Cunningham pessimistically sought permission to withdraw, but Auchinleck was sterner and replaced him with Major-General Neil Ritchie.

Although Rommel managed to link up again with his forces surrounding Tobruk and inflicted more heavy losses on 13 Corps, which had advanced in an attempt to relieve Tobruk, his losses and the strain on his supplies became too great and on 7 December he began to withdraw. Rommel had to abandon his garrisons in the frontier outposts at Bardia and Sollum but he withdrew with as much skill as he had shown on the battlefield and escaped from Cyrenaica back to El Agheila, where he had first started nine months earlier, with his army still intact.

For the first time in the war the British had defeated the German Army. They achieved much success in the battle, finally raising the siege of Tobruk and inflicting 33,000 casualties at a cost of 18,000 British casualties. But most of the Axis losses were Italian troops or German administrative staff who surrendered in mid-January in the border posts, whereas the British casualties were predominantly highly experienced, desert veterans who could not easily be replaced. Moreover, the British had failed in their principal objective, to destroy Rommel's armored forces, and he was again recuperating on secure supply lines while the British attempted to prepare for the next offensive over extremely long lines of communication.

The resurgence of Axis control of the central Mediterranean enabled the Italians to send more supplies and reinforcements to Rommel. With more tanks and fuel he launched an attack on 21 January 1942 and the next day his force, which now included more Italian divisions, was renamed *Panzerarmee Afrika*. His probing raid again precipitated a hasty British withdrawal and he recaptured Benghazi, but his forces were still too weak to advance beyond the British defensive positions on the Gazala line, which ran from Gazala, 56 km (35 miles) west of Tobruk, 80 km (50 miles) southward into the desert to Bir Hacheim.

Axis domination of the air and the renewal of an intense air assault on Malta, which in March and April endured twice the tonnage of bombs that London had suffered during the blitz, enabled the Italians to resume supply convoys to Africa. Virtually free from interference the ships could sail within 80 km (50 miles) of Malta and deliver supplies direct to Benghazi. Reinforcements, including equipment under the lend-lease program from America, were also reaching the British and by May both sides were at a strength greater than at the beginning of the November battle. The British had 850 tanks plus 420 in reserve, including 400 of the new American Grants that had a 75mm gun and were the first tanks able to meet the powerful German Panzer IV on equal terms, while Rommel had just 560 tanks, of which only 280 were first-line German tanks. The force ratio was more balanced in the air, with 600 British against 530 Axis aircraft, although in qualitative terms the British were inferior in nearly every aspect.

Although the British had accumulated massive supply dumps in preparation for an attack, on 26 May Rommel launched his own offensive by sweeping around the south of Bir Hacheim with a convoy of 10,000 vehicles, outflanking the British strongpoints and minefields. His bid for a quick victory failed due to the shock of huge losses inflicted by the Grants, and his army became stranded for want of fuel and ammunition. But Rommel was saved by his own resourcefulness as he personally led a

supply column through the British minefields to replenish his tanks. In a bitter slogging match during the following two weeks, in an area that became known as "the Cauldron" because the fighting was so tough, Rommel again overcame the superior numbers of British tanks in a series of piecemeal battles. On 14 June Auchinleck ordered a retreat and the British were soon in a headlong rush back to the Egyptian frontier. The British had not planned to withstand a second siege in Tobruk and had denuded its defenses, but when Rommel attacked on 20 June he captured the port and its garrison of 35,000 mostly south-African troops in just one day. Besides its considerable strategic importance, Tobruk had acquired an emotional and symbolic significance and Churchill called the loss a disgrace second only to Singapore, which had fallen just three months earlier.

The watering point at Fort Capuzzo in the Western desert. Supplies, especially water, fuel and food, were vital in the desert and logistics often dictated the course of battle. (Imperial War Museum)

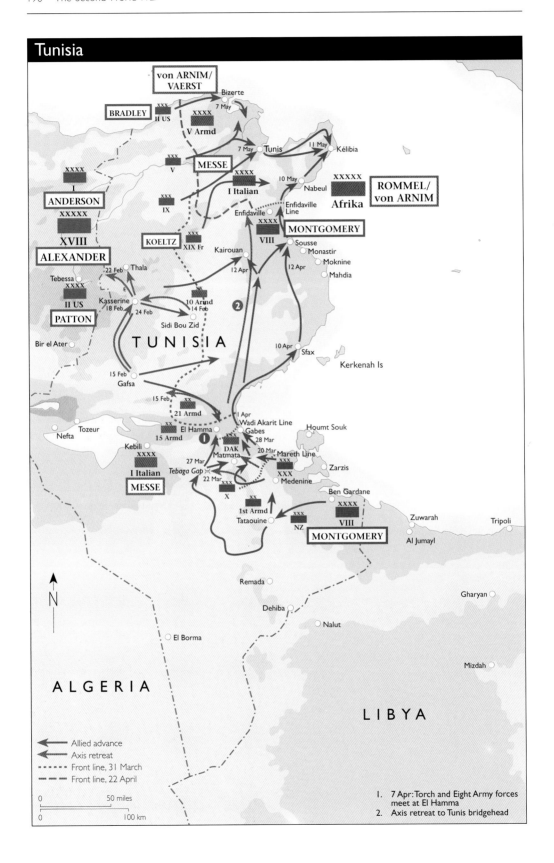

Tunisia

Legend:
- ← Allied advance
- ← Axis retreat
- ⋯⋯ Front line, 31 March
- --- Front line, 22 April

0 ___ 50 miles
0 ___ 100 km

1. 7 Apr: Torch and Eight Army forces meet at El Hamma
2. Axis retreat to Tunis bridgehead

A British army truck in the Western Desert 1 November 1940, during Opration Compass, throws up a cloud of dust and illustrates the difficulties of driving in desert conditions. Navigation could be done only by using a compass and the sun and many drivers became lost in 'the blue', as the British called the desert. (Imperial War Museum E974)

Rommel captured enormous quantities of supplies and transport, and was promoted to Field-Marshal in reward for the victory, but Axis strategy struck a dilemma. It had been agreed that after Tobruk was captured Rommel would pause in favor of Operation Hercules, the invasion of Malta, but Rommel's audacious advance now offered the real possibility of capturing the whole British position in Egypt, and even taking control of the Middle East. Kesselring and the *Comando Supremo* were averse to pushing on but Rommel was desperate to continue his pursuit while the British were still in a state of chaos. Hitler, who had lost confidence in airborne operations, and Mussolini, who flew a white stallion to Africa that he hoped to ride triumphantly into Cairo, were both in favor of the more glorious prospects. On 24 June Rommel's panzer spearheads resumed the chase, often racing ahead of retreating British units, and on 30 June reached El Alamein, just 96 km (60 miles) from Alexandria.

The crisis in British command had become so acute that Auchinleck dismissed Ritchie and took personal command of the Eighth Army himself. Panic gripped Cairo

and Alexandria, from where the Mediterranean Fleet withdrew to the Red Sea, but, in a series of limited duels during July known as the first battle of El Alamein, Auchinleck stemmed the tide of Axis advances. Rommel's forces were very weak, with his "divisions" consisting of just 50 tanks and 2,000 troops, and his soldiers were in a state of sheer exhaustion, but Auchinleck showed coolness and great skill, and came

Field-Marshal Albert Kesselring, German Commander-in-Chief South, but known to his troops as 'smiling Albert' because of his cheerful disposition. He ostensibly commanded all Axis forces in the Mediterranean and Italy, and proved to be a skilled diplomat and an outstanding military commander even though he was a Luftwaffe officer and lacked command experience. (Imperial War Museum KY66846)

The tanker Ohio enters Grand Harbour in Malta with the destroyers HMS *Penn* on her starboard side and HMS *Ledbury* on her port side. Ohio's structure had been so weakened by the repeated attacks that she was incapable of steaming on her own and needed a destroyer on either side to support her. (Imperial War Museum GM1505-1)

perilously close to defeating Rommel. Nevertheless, the morale of the Eighth Army had deteriorated and Churchill decided to appoint General Harold Alexander as Commander-in-Chief, Middle East and Lieutenant-General Bernard Montgomery as Commander of the Eighth Army. Rommel made a last and desperate attempt to reach the Nile in August, in the battle of Alam Halfa, but in his first battle Montgomery skillfully combined the growing strength of British arms against a *Panzerarmee* that ran out of fuel, and after a few days a lull descended as both sides prepared for the next, decisive round.

Sherman tanks of the Eighth Army move across the desert at speed as the Axis forces begin to retreat from El Alamein on 5 November 1942. These reliable American tanks were the first tanks used by the British that could match the armor and firepower of German tanks. (Imperial War Museum E18971)

Lieutenant-General Bernard Montgomery, Commander Eighth Army, wearing his famous tank beret, watches the beginning of the German retreat from El Alamein from the turret of his Grant tank on 5 November 1942. (Imperial War Museum)

The Axis blockade of Malta intensified and on 10 May Kesselring claimed that the island had been neutralized. His declaration proved premature but the situation became perilous despite the delivery of 61 Spitfires, which were not destroyed instantly on landing like previous arrivals. An attempt in June to run simultaneous convoys from Haifa and Suez in the east and Gibraltar in the west was a disaster, with only two of 17 ships arriving. In August another convoy of 14 ships sailed from Gibraltar, Operation Pedestal, escorted by a fleet of 44 major warships, but only five of its ships reached Malta, including the tanker *Ohio* lashed between two destroyers. The Royal Navy also incurred heavy losses in the operations, including the aircraft-carrier HMS *Eagle*, with a squadron of Spitfires, three cruisers and six destroyers all sunk. However, the convoy delivered fuel essential for Malta's defenses and to sustain the island as an offensive base at a time critical to the coming Battle of El Alamein, and food that prevented starvation and inevitable capitulation.

Rommel was also receiving a fraction of his supplies as only a quarter of the Italian shipping reached Africa. British submarines and the Desert Air Force, now consisting of 1,500 aircraft in 96 squadrons, were able to use unprecedented levels of Ultra intelligence to target the convoys and even specific ships carrying fuel. As a result fuel had to be flown to Africa, but the small quantities possible meant that Rommel's tanks were constantly in precarious danger of being halted by lack of fuel. In contrast, the expansion of British and American war production was now being felt for the first time on the battlefield, furnishing the Eighth Army with a superiority of 230,000 troops and 1,900 tanks, including 200 Grants and 300 superior Sherman tanks rushed from America, against a *Panzerarmee* of 152,000 fighting troops, comprising 90,000 Germans, and 572 tanks, very few of which could match the powerful American tanks.

Montgomery, who had a reputation for being ruthlessly efficient, inspired his men with his professional rigor and detailed tactical plans. Unlike in previous desert battles, there were no flanks that could be turned and no freedom of maneuver, which prevented Rommel from practicing the mobile tactics of which he was a master. Rather than chase Rommel back to Tripolitania, as had happened twice before, Montgomery planned to inflict a crushing defeat in a set-piece battle of attrition that would destroy Rommel's offensive power.

The battle of El Alamein began on 23 October when Montgomery launched Operation Lightfoot, so called because his infantry were attacking Rommel's massive minefields, known as the "Devil's gardens." Under the bombardment of almost a thousand guns, the largest since the First World War, four divisions of 30 Corps attacked on a front 7.5 km (4.5 miles) wide, with 13 Corps making a diversionary attack. The first week of the battle, the "dog-fight," witnessed some of the fiercest and bloodiest fighting yet experienced in the desert, but with unflinching determination, "crumbling" the enemy defenses as Montgomery called it, the British succeeded in carving two corridors through the minefields. Using skillful tactics, luck and almost the last drop of his fuel Rommel held up the British advance, but

Montgomery brought up reserve troops to launch Operation Supercharge on 2 November, which cleared the way forward for the armor of 10 Corps to eventually break through the Axis lines.

Although holding out for far longer than he would rightly have been expected to, Rommel could not sustain the rate of attrition and on 4 November he decided to withdraw, ignoring an order from Hitler "to yield not one yard ... Victory or Death." Despite suffering heavy losses, including 13,500 casualties and over 500 tanks, the British inflicted a crushing defeat on the *Panzerarmee*, which no longer fully constituted a fighting force. Nevertheless, although Rommel was forced to abandon 40,000 Italian troops who had no transport, he skillfully escaped westward, successfully fending off British attempts to entrap his remaining forces. Montgomery recaptured Tobruk and Benghazi and, after a pause at El Agheila to build up his forces, finally

The British night artillery barrage on 23 October 1942, which opened the Second Battle of El Alamein. Infantry carriers and ambulances waiting to move up are silhouetted against the glare from the guns. (Imperial War Museum E18465)

captured Tripoli on 23 January 1943, three months and 2,000 km (1,240 miles) after the offensive began.

The campaign in north-west Africa

Rommel's forces were saved from complete annihilation by the Anglo-American invasion of north-west Africa, Operation Torch, on 8 November 1942, four days after Rommel had begun his withdrawal. The Allied Mediterranean strategy had been accepted in July 1942, and in a series of telegrams known as "the transatlantic essay competition" Churchill and Roosevelt finally agreed on a plan for simultaneous landings on the Atlantic coast of Morocco and the Mediterranean coast of Algeria. The Western Naval Task Force, consisting of 102 ships, sailed direct from America with 24,500 American troops under the command of Major-General George S. Patton, to capture Casablanca. The Center Task Force, comprising 18,500 American troops under Major-General Lloyd R. Fredendall tasked to capture Oran, and the Eastern Naval Task Force, comprising 18,000 British and American troops under Major-General Charles Ryder tasked to capture Algiers, sailed from Britain in convoys amounting to 650 mostly British ships.

Lieutenant-General Dwight D. Eisenhower was appointed Commander-in-Chief, Allied Expeditionary Force. His deputy, General Mark Clark, and one of the air commanders were also American, but all other commanders were British. With this mixed team Eisenhower established Allied Forces Headquarters, the first Allied inter-service HQ and a truly unified command that operated in harmonious cooperation and with a single purpose. This was fortuitous because the invasion incurred as much political and diplomatic complication as it did military complexity. Since the Vichy French forces of 120,000 troops outnumbered the invasion force, it was important to secure at least their neutrality if the invasion was to be successful. To overcome French sensibilities, since anti-British resentment was still widespread, the invasion was "Americanized" as much as possible, with Roosevelt even offering American uniforms for British troops. A confusing series of negotiations also took place, with Clark landing secretly before the

Allied chiefs at Bizerta, 18 September 1943: Air Chief Marshal Sir Arthur Tedder, Commander-in-Chief, Mediterranean Air Command; Air Marshal Sir Arthur Coningham, Air Officer Commanding Tactical Air Force, Mediterranean; General Alexander, Commander Fifteenth Army; General Eisenhower; Admiral of the Fleet Sir Andrew Cunningham, Navy Commander-in-Chief Mediterranean; General Carl Spaatz, Commander of the Northwest Africa Air Force and Major-General Walter B Smith, Eisenhower's Chief of Staff. (Imperial War Museum NA6878)

invasion to convince the French to collaborate, but excessive American caution precluded the cooperation of sympathetic local commanders.

The landings were made with complete surprise but were initially resisted, particularly at Oran and Casablanca, and especially by the French Navy, with 1,400 American and 700 French casualties. However, by sheer coincidence, Admiral Darlan, Marshal Pétain's Commander-in-Chief, had flown to Algiers the same day to visit his fatally ill son. The Americans opened direct negotiation with him, despite British reservations about dealing with such a senior Vichy and compromised pro-Axis figure, and he was persuaded to declare an armistice on 9 November. This enabled British units to be dispatched to secure the ports of Bougie and Bône, to enable the overland advance to Tunisia, but the political ramifications would be far-reaching. Pétain rescinded the order but the more immediate consequences were that Hitler occupied Vichy France and the Germans gained control of the Tunisian airfields and

A German Tiger tank in Tunisia. These 54-ton monsters were armed with a high velocity 88 mm gun and were far superior to any American or British tank. (Topham Picturepoint M00984402)

were able to start transferring troops to Tunisia with the acquiescence of the French Resident-General, Admiral Estéva.

American caution at not landing east of Algiers, and the decision to reduce the number of vehicles in the invasion in favor of more troops, precluded a rapid Allied move west to Tunisia. Although the British First Army reached within 21 km (13 miles) of Tunis, by the end of November the Germans had rushed 17,000 troops to Tunisia and in a tenacious defense stemmed the Allied forces. Hitler now recognized that a collapse of Axis power in Africa threatened not only Mussolini's regime but also Germany itself by exposing the whole of southern Europe to Allied attack. He therefore allocated massive reinforcements to the campaign in Africa on a scale far greater than ever before, at a time when men and equipment were desperately needed on the eastern front. In the next few months the Germans committed a huge effort, including using enormous Me323 *Gigant* motorized gliders, to transfer 150,000 troops and new formidable Tiger tanks that comprised the Fifth Panzer Army, under the command of General Jürgen von Arnim.

By the end of January 1943, Arnim had pushed the Allies back and recaptured the passes in the western Dorsals while Rommel

An aerial view of Tobruk on 22 January 1941, after the Italian garrison had surrendered. Black smoke is rising from burning oil tanks beyond which, in the harbour, the Italian cruiser San Giorgio is on fire.
(Australian War Memorial 106640)

had withdrawn to the Mareth line, a prewar French defensive system in southern Tunisia. The strategic position was now reversed as the Germans were able to concentrate in a strong central position, and fleetingly the two panzer armies had the opportunity to strike back. On 14 February Rommel attacked the US 2nd Corps holding the southern line in Tunisia with two panzer divisions at Faid, and hoped to sweep up behind the British Army in the north. By 20 February he had broken through the Kasserine Pass and pushed on towards Thala and Tebessa, but Arnim failed to cooperate and Rommel no longer had the freedom of command to disregard the *Comando Supremo*'s instructions that he had enjoyed in the desert. The offensive was successful as a limited objective and came perilously close to driving the Allies from Tunisia, but stiffening Allied resistance and unsuitable terrain impeded the advance, obliging Rommel to withdraw for another thrust at the Eighth Army before Montgomery was able to bring forward the bulk of its strength. The Americans suffered a humiliating defeat and significant casualties but they gained invaluable battle experience and immediately incorporated the tactical lessons.

Rommel was promoted to Commander-in-Chief Army Group Afrika, while his *Panzerarmee* was renamed First Italian Army, but he was one of very few men who had been in Africa since the beginning and he was now very sick. On 9 March he flew to Germany to convince Hitler to evacuate the Tunisian bridgehead but he never returned to his beloved DAK. Meanwhile the two British Armies had been combined into Eighteenth Army Group, under Alexander, and a unified air command formed. Although the two Axis armies formed a strong force, the Allied air and naval tourniquet prevented very few supplies reaching them. Montgomery was able to take the Mareth positions at the end of March and joined with the First Army in the first days of April. Alexander launched a final offensive on 22 April and the last German units surrendered on 13 May, almost three years after Graziani had been goaded into action. Some 250,000 prisoners were captured, the largest

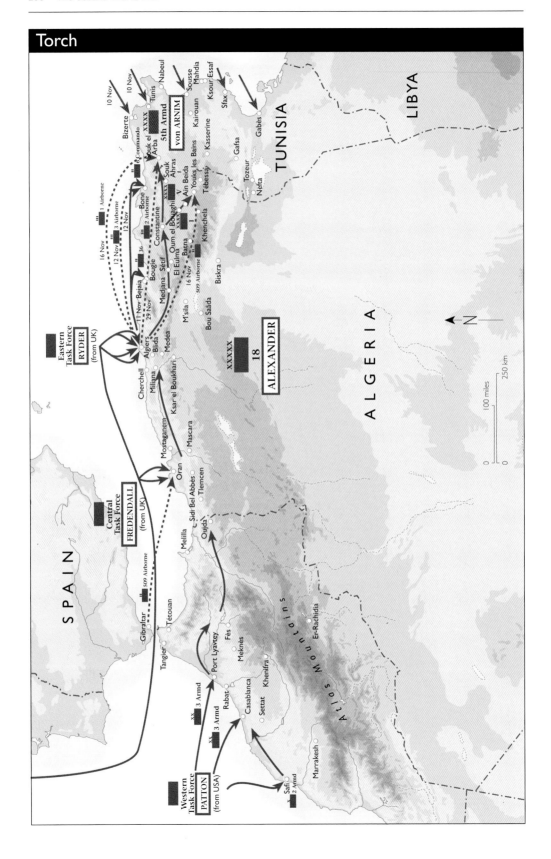

Torch

Bizerte

10 Nov

10 Nov

Tunis

Nabeul

Souk el XXXX Arba

5th Armd

von ARNIM

Sousse

Mahdia

Ksour Essaf

Kairouan

Sfax

Gabès

Commando

6

Souk Ahras

XXX

Ain Beida

Tébessa

Kasserine

Gafsa

Youks les Bains

Tozeur

Nefta

LIBYA

TUNISIA

Bone

1 Airborne

1 Airborne

Constantine

2 Airborne

Oum el Bouaghi

Khenchela

Batna

Biskra

16 Nov

12 Nov

12 Nov

3 Airborne

III

II   36

Sétif

El Eulma

509 Airborne

16 Nov

M'sila

Bou Saâda

11 Nov Bejaia

29 Nov

Bougie

Medjana

Medéa

Blida

Algiers

Cherchell

Miliana

Ksar el Boukhari

16 Nov

Eastern
Task Force

RYDER

(from UK)

XXXXX

18

ALEXANDER

ALGERIA

Mostaganem

Mascara

Oran

Sidi Bel Abbès

Tlemcen

Central
Task Force

FREDENDALL

(from UK)

Melilla

Oujda

Atlas Mountains

Er-Rachidia

509 Airborne

Gibraltar

Tétouan

Tangier

Port Lyautey

Fès

Meknes

Khenifra

SPAIN

3 Armd

3 Armd

Rabat

Casablanca

Settat

Marrakesh

Western
Task Force

PATTON

(from USA)

Safi

2 Armd

N

0   100 miles

0   250 km

capitulation yet suffered by the Axis. Coming soon after the collapse at Stalingrad it was a further humiliation for Hitler, but for Mussolini it was a disaster. The greater part of the Italian Army had been lost and the Italian Empire, on which the credibility of his regime had been based, had ceased to exist. Mussolini's survival now depended entirely on Hitler.

The invasion of Europe

The invasion of Sicily was the next logical step in the battle for the control of the Mediterranean and a possible return to continental Europe. Moreover, since free passage through the Mediterranean could not be guaranteed without its capture, Churchill and Roosevelt approved Operation Husky at the Casablanca conference in January 1943. On 10 July Alexander's newly formed Fifteenth Army Group, comprising Montgomery's Eighth Army and Patton's US Seventh Army, launched the second largest amphibious assault undertaken in Europe, landing 180,000 men, 600 tanks and 14,000 vehicles in the first wave, supported by an enormous fleet of 2,590 ships and 4,000 aircraft.

The Italian garrison of 230,000 men consisted of weak, static coastal defense divisions and only two reconstituted German

The Captain of LCT 367, a landing craft loaded with tanks, briefs his crew before sailing for Sicily in July 1943. The use of LCTs (Landing Craft Tanks) and LSTs (Landings Ship Tanks) during the invasion enabled armor to be landed with the assaulting infantry for the first time. (Imperial War Museum NA4252)

Lieutenant-General George Patton, Commander 7th US Army, watches operations in Sicily from a town in the front line accompanied by his staff. Known as 'old blood and guts' he was the US Army's most controversial and perhaps most brilliant general. (Imperial War Museum MH10946)

divisions under General Hans Hube proved formidable opponents. The landings were unopposed, but confused planning, bad weather, nervous pilots and undisciplined naval anti-aircraft fire made the first large-scale Allied airborne operation a disaster, with many troops landing in the sea. While Patton occupied the western half of Sicily, Montgomery advanced up the eastern coast, each side of Mount Etna, to cut off the Axis line of retreat across the Straits of Messina. Despite an overwhelming Allied superiority and fruitless amphibious leaps, the Germans used the rugged landscape to establish stout defensive lines to slow the British advance. Kesselring ordered a total evacuation to start on 11 August and in a brilliantly planned and executed operation over 100,000 troops escaped unhindered with all their equipment and almost 10,000 vehicles, deflating the Allies' triumphant but hollow march into Messina a week later.

Although Allied troops, particularly the Americans, came of age fighting in European conditions, their commanders behaved with an ineptitude, jealousy and mistrust that generated some blatant Anglo-American ill will. But the effect of the campaign on the Italian rulers was even more profound. Faced with growing unrest in Italy and the reluctance of Italian forces to oppose the Allies, the Fascist Grand Council launched a coup d'etat that overthrew Mussolini and installed a new government led by Marshal Pietro Badoglio, who had been sacked during the fiasco in Greece in 1940. He immediately began secret negotiations for an armistice but they became bogged down on the Allied resolve for unconditional surrender, a doctrine that Roosevelt had insisted on following the uneasy negotiations with the Vichy French in Algeria. A "Short Military Armistice" was eventually signed on 3 September, but Hitler used the interlude to move another 16 divisions to Italy, including the crack 1st SS Panzer Division from Russia, which occupied the entire country and took control of the Italian army. Much of the Italian Fleet escaped to Malta but the battleship *Roma* was sunk by the Luftwaffe using a new weapon, an Fx-1400 3,000lb

(1,360kg) armor-piercing, air-launched, radio-controlled gliding bomb. Mussolini was rescued from captivity in the mountains at Grand Sasso in a daring airborne raid led by an SS Officer, Otto Skorzeny, and installed by Hitler as head of the Italian Socialist Republic in northern Italy, but Badoglio and King Victor Emmanuelle's flight to Brindisi committed Italy to a brutal civil war, with tragic consequences.

In an attempt to exploit the collapse of Mussolini's regime, Churchill championed a campaign to capture the Dodecanese Islands. He hoped, against US wishes, to capture the airfields on Rhodes from which British bombers could attack the Romanian oilfields, to encourage the partisans in Yugoslavia and Greece, and above all to encourage Turkey to join the anti-Axis Alliance. During September, 4,000 British troops occupied eight of the islands but the 30,000-strong Italian garrison on Rhodes was confined by the 7,000 German troops on the island. During October and November the Germans recaptured the remaining islands and carried out severe reprisals on the Italians who had cooperated with the British. For the Allies the campaign was an unmitigated disaster since it failed to achieve any of its objectives, yet five battalions, or almost 5,000 men, large numbers of aircraft, six destroyers and two submarines were all lost, while German casualties were negligible.

The Allies also failed to exploit the opportunity of Italian cooperation to launch a large-scale amphibious landing in northern Italy and an airborne raid to capture Rome due to American reluctance to commit to a new Italian campaign. At the Quebec conference in August, however, they accepted the principal of invading the Italian mainland almost as a continuation of the existing operations. Montgomery's Eighth Army crossed from Sicily to Calabria on 3 September, followed six days later by 1st Airborne Division, which landed by sea at Taranto, and the main assault by 165,000 troops of the Anglo-US Fifth Army, under General Clark, which made an amphibious landing, optimistically named Operation Avalanche, at Salerno, 56 km

(35 miles) south of Naples. It was hoped that once ashore these forces would somehow find a way to open the road to Rome before the end of the year.

Kesselring had convinced Hitler that Italy could be easily defended thanks to its ideal terrain. The central mountainous spine, the Apennines, rose above 10,000 feet (3,000 m) with lateral spurs that ran east and west toward the coast, between which were deep valleys containing wide rivers flowing rapidly to the sea. The north–south roads were confined to 32 km (20-mile) wide strips adjacent to the Adriatic and Tyrrhenian coasts, where the bridges that carried them were dominated by the natural strongpoints. Kesselring formed the six divisions in the south of Italy into Tenth Army, under General Heinrich von Vietinghoff, but had anticipated a landing at Salerno and stationed 16th Panzer Division in the area. Despite their weakness the Germans launched a counteroffensive and after a week of fierce fighting almost succeeded in driving the Avalanche forces back into the sea. The Allies stabilized the beachhead by unleashing an overwhelming weight of firepower in the form of accurate naval gunfire and massive air support, and by landing more reserves. Montgomery had been miffed at being given only a secondary role and was needlessly cautious in his advance – so much so that a group of dismayed war correspondents drove themselves through "enemy territory" to contact Fifth Army more than a day before Montgomery's advanced units managed to on 16 September.

Two days later Kesselring ordered a fighting withdrawal to the first of the mountainous series of fortified defensive lines by which the Germans planned to defend the approaches to Rome. On 1 October Fifth Army captured Naples while Eighth Army advanced up the Adriatic coast and captured the airfields at Foggia, where the Allies established the US Fifteenth Air Force to launch strategic bombing raids against the Reich. By early October the two Allied Armies had formed a continuous 193-km (120-mile) line across the peninsula running along the

Conditions in Italy were terrible and often resembled the Western Front during the First World War. Here a mule train carrying ammunition passes a bogged down Sherman tank in the forward positions in the Sangro area in November 1943. (Imperial War Museum NA8942)

On 15 August 1944 the Allies undertook the invasion of southern France, after much Anglo-US wrangling. Although troops were withdrawn from Italy the landings were a great success and enabled supplies to be landed through the southern French ports. (Topham Picturepoint M00984374)

Volturno and Biferno rivers, but in the three weeks Fifth Army alone had lost 12,000 casualties.

Henceforth, the campaign in Italy became a slow and remorseless grinding battle of attrition, and as the rain and snow turned the battlefield into a muddy quagmire the appalling struggles resembled the First World War battles. Kesselring had fortified a series of defensive lines, known collectively as the Winter Line, between Gaeta and Pescara. The western end based on the Garigliano and Rapido rivers, known as the Gustav line, was particularly strong and hinged on the great fortress Abbey at Monte Cassino. Beginning in early October, the Allies launched a series of operations to capture the approaches. However, despite some of the most bitter and desperate fighting of the war between the Western Allies and the Wehrmacht, particularly in the attempts to cross the Volturno and Sangro rivers, by mid-January 1944 the exhausted troops had still not reached the Gustav line and the last offensive petered out in a snow blizzard.

In four months the Allies had slogged their way just 112 km (70 miles) from Salerno, and were still 129 km (80 miles) from Rome. Fifth Army alone had incurred 40,000 casualties, far

exceeding German losses, and a further 50,000 sick, while six experienced divisions were also withdrawn for Operation Overlord. Eisenhower and Montgomery departed to command the cross-channel invasion and General Wilson was appointed Supreme Commander of the Mediterranean Command, in recognition of the British predominance, while General Oliver Leese became Commander of Eighth Army.

Kesselring now had 15, albeit weakened, divisions in Tenth Army vigorously holding the Gustav line. To unhinge this force the Allies launched another amphibious landing, Operation Shingle, at Anzio, 48 km (30 miles) south of Rome, on 22 January 1944. US 6th Corps, under Major-General John Lucas, achieved complete surprise and safely landed 70,000 troops within a week, but failed to exploit the advantage. Churchill later wrote: "I had hoped that we were hurling a wild cat on to the shore, but all we

Churchill described the allied force at Anzio as a 'stranded whale'. After the failure of the original plan to relieve the pressure on Monte Cassino the allies considered a Dunkirk style evacuation. (Imperial War Museum)

got was a stranded whale." In contrast, Kesselring hastily improvised eight divisions into Fourteenth Army, commanded by General Eberhard von Mackensen. He resolutely counterattacked, using "Goliath" remote-controlled explosive-filled miniature tanks for the first time, and almost evicted the Anglo-US force. The beachhead was saved only by the excellent tactical use of intelligence in one of Ultra's most important triumphs. General Lucius Truscott replaced Lucas but he could do no more than hold the defensive ring for three months.

On 17 January 5th Corps launched a simultaneous attack on the Gustav line, but it had to be called off within a month after the badly exhausted troops had advanced just 11 km (seven miles) at a cost of 17,000 casualties. The New Zealand Corps then attempted a direct assault on Monte Cassino, preceded by the questionable bombing by 145 Flying Fortresses that destroyed the famous monastery, but the 1st Parachute Division defending the heights were some of the best

The liberation of Rome on 4 June 1944 was met with jubilant celebration. In front of the Coliseum Italian civilians crowd round RAF leading Aircraftsman F Jones of Newport, Monmouthshire. (Imperial War Museum CAN2916)

troops in the German army and did not even flinch. A third attack by New Zealand and Indian infantry, using even heavier air and artillery bombardments, also failed to break through, not least because the rubble created an impregnable defensive position into which the parachutists burrowed. A fourth attack, in which Alexander coordinated Fifth and Eighth Armies as an Army Group for the first time, was launched on 11 May with the aim to destroy the German armies. In an astonishing feat of arms Polish and Free French troops seized Monte Cassino, and the Gustav line was broken in a set-piece battle. However, Clark was perhaps the most egocentric Allied commander in the war and

instead of following orders to encircle the Germans he was enticed by the glory of capturing Rome. Fifth Army finally linked up with 6th Corps on 25 May and made the triumphant march into Rome on 4 June, but the spectacular of the first capture of an Axis capital was eclipsed by the Allied invasion of France two days later. Clark's impetuous failure enabled Kesselring to withdraw Tenth and Fourteenth Armies to the Pisa–Rimini line, 241 km (150 miles) north of Rome, the first of the next series of defensible lines across the peninsula, known as the Gothic line, which he reached in August. Alexander still had hopes to make for Vienna but the Italian campaign had assumed a definite secondary status to the invasion of France. Six divisions were withdrawn in the summer and when the autumn rains and mud forced operations to be suspended at the end of the year another seven divisions were withdrawn.

The focus of operations in the Mediterranean had turned toward the invasion of southern France, Operation Anvil or Dragoon. The Americans believed that a landing on the French Riviera and an advance up the Rhône valley, complementary to Overlord, would be more effective than continuing operations in Italy. Despite vehement British objections, US Seventh Army, under Lieutenant-General Alexander Patch, eventually landed on 15 August 1944. The assault by three divisions of Truscott's US 6th Corps, followed up by seven divisions of the First French Army, was supported by 887 warships and over 2,000 aircraft. However, the three divisions and 200 aircraft of General Johannes Blaskowitz's Army Group G were too weak and too dispersed to offer any serious resistance. The Allied forces landed virtually unopposed and incurred few casualties, and with the Riviera resorts freely available for recreation the invasion earned the derisive term "the Champagne campaign." Nevertheless, Seventh Army advanced northward rapidly and met Patton's US Third Army, advancing southward from Normandy, at Dijon on 11 September.

A modest hero

Charles Hazlitt Upham, VC and Bar (1908–94)

Charles Hazlitt Upham is the only combat soldier, and one of only three men ever, to have twice been awarded the Victoria Cross for outstanding gallantry and leadership, the first time in Crete in May 1941 and the second in Egypt in July 1942.

Upham was born on 21 September 1908 in Christchurch, New Zealand, and was educated at Christ's College and Canterbury Agricultural College. From an early age he was quiet, unusually determined, and developed a spirit of independence that bordered on belligerence towards authority, which he would only accept when shown that it was right. Above all Upham abhorred injustice, a characteristic that grew in intensity, and indicated the force of his personality.

Upham aspired to a simple life on the land. He spent six years as a shepherd, musterer and farm manager, mostly on high-country sheep stations, and prior to the war was a government farm valuer. In 1938 he became engaged to Mary (Molly) Eileen McTamney, a nurse he had met at the races, but they had only a few happy months together before she left New Zealand for Singapore and London, where she remained throughout the war. While living in the harsh conditions of the rugged high country, Upham acquired the physical toughness, strong stamina and cool temperament – as well as a large vocabulary of expletives – that would serve him so well during his war in the Mediterranean.

When the Second World War broke out in September 1939 Upham, aged 30, immediately enlisted out of a conviction that he wanted to fight for justice and stop the Nazis. His first task as a soldier, however, was more mundane. Because of his agricultural

Charles and Mary Eileen Upham in 1946, after their reunion in New Zealand. (Alexander Turnbull Library, National Library of New Zealand C22557-1/2)

training he was ordered to lay down a lawn around Burnham Camp Headquarters in Christchurch, which he saw as futile to the war and completed under great protest because he missed bayonet training. But from the beginning of his military service he displayed leadership, a tactical flair and an intense desire to master the practical skills of the soldier's craft, inherent qualities that would be nourished by warfare. Promoted to corporal, Upham led his men in training exercises which he made extremely realistic and rapidly became noticed as a committed commander by both his men and his superior officers. Nevertheless, he rejected a place in an officer cadet training unit (OCTU), preferring instead to embark for Egypt with the advance party of the 2nd

New Zealand Expeditionary Force in December 1939 as a sergeant in the 20th New Zealand Battalion.

Upham was intent on learning the essentials of fighting and becoming skilled in using the bayonet, machine gun and grenade. He showed no inclination for the parade ground, where he was well known for making a bungle of any drill, or respect for army conventions or rank. His intolerance of anything not directly of benefit to the war and his forthright, outspoken nature often led him to disagree bluntly with superior officers. Despite his insubordination and impatience to fight, in July 1940 Upham was persuaded to join an OCTU. Due to his outspoken opinions and his tendency to question almost everything, however, he was highly unpopular with the British officers. Upham was particularly critical of the lack of consideration that was given to the problems caused by tanks and aircraft, and felt that the tactics being used relied too much on the methods that had been successful in the First World War. As a result he was placed last in his course, but was commissioned as a second-lieutenant in November 1940.

Upham was posted to 15 Platoon, C Company, 20th New Zealand Battalion, tough men from the rugged west coast of the South Island of New Zealand, but he quickly won their respect as a capable officer who made them train hard but was equally concerned for their safety and comfort.

In March 1941 the New Zealand Division was sent to Greece. While the campaign

Lieutenant Charles Hazlitt Upham VC being congratulated by his platoon sergeant, Sgt Bob May, after the presentation of the award in November 1941. (The War History Collection, Alexander Turnbull Library, National Library of New Zealand F-2108-1/2-DA)

rapidly developed into a withdrawal, Upham was seriously ill with dysentery. He was unable to eat anything but condensed milk, which his men scrounged for him from every source, and he became very weak as his weight diminished. He was soon unable to walk but his battalion became accustomed to seeing him astride a donkey, which he insisted on using to ride along the hillsides between his section posts and headquarters.

Upham and his men were successfully evacuated to Crete and when the German airborne invasion began on 20 May they were positioned around Maleme airfield, the center of the assault. Upham was in the thick of the fighting from the beginning and soon became celebrated among his comrades not only for his daring but also for his skill at out-thinking the enemy at close quarters. He was renowned for combining controlled courage with quick-thinking resourcefulness, and for his implacable determination to kill as many German soldiers as he could. While most medals for bravery are awarded for a single act, Upham's citation for his first Victoria Cross was for a series of remarkable exploits, showing outstanding leadership, tactical skill and indifference to danger over nine days between 22–30 May.

After four of his men were shot on 22 May Upham was possessed by "an icy fury" and personally dealt with several machine-gun posts at close quarters using his favorite attacking weapon, the hand grenade. When his platoon withdrew, Upham helped to carry a wounded man out under fire, rallied more men together to carry other wounded men out, and then went back through over 600 yards (550 m) of enemy territory to bring out another company that had become isolated and would have been completely cut off but for his action.

During the following two days his platoon was continuously under fire. Upham was blown over by one mortar shell, painfully wounded behind his left shoulder by a piece of shrapnel from another and was shot, receiving a bullet in the ankle that was removed two weeks later in Egypt. Although he was also still suffering from dysentery Upham disregarded his wounds and remained on duty, refusing to go to hospital.

One incident, in particular, during this action typified Upham's deeds. At Galatas on 25 May his platoon was heavily engaged and came under severe mortar and machine-gun fire. They killed over 40 Germans but when ordered to retire Upham went forward to warn other troops that they were being cut off. Two German soldiers trapped him alone on the fringes of an olive grove and his platoon watched a helpless distance away on the other side of the clearing as they fired on him. With any movement potentially fatal, he feigned death and with calculated coolness waited for the enemy soldiers to approach. With one arm now lame in a sling, he used the crook of a tree to support his rifle and shot the first assailant, reloaded with one hand, and shot the second who was so close as to fall against the barrel of his rifle.

During the whole of the operations Upham showed great skill and dash, complete disregard of danger and superb coolness even though he was wounded, battered and very weak, still suffering from dysentery and able to eat only very little. He looked like a "walking skeleton," exhausted, and with his wounds festering, but his determination never faltered and he had to be literally dragged on to an evacuation ship. His magnificent courage, conduct and leadership inspired his whole platoon to fight magnificently throughout, and in fact was an inspiration to the battalion. Nevertheless, Upham was genuinely distressed to be singled out for a Victoria Cross. He believed that many others deserved the honor more than he did, and could only cope with the award and the unwelcome fame that went with it by seeing it as recognition of the bravery and service of the men of his unit. He even refused to wear his medal ribbon until directly ordered to do so. But Upham did keep a promise he made to his men in the heat of the battle and took the only five who survived death, capture or injury to a slap-up meal at Shepheards, the top hotel in Cairo.

In November 1941 Upham was promoted to lieutenant but was mortified when his commanding officer, Lieutenant-Colonel

Kippenberger, decided to leave him out of Operation Crusader because he believed that Upham was fretting for more action and would get himself killed too quickly. Experienced men like Upham were required to rebuild his battalion and after its heavy losses he was promoted to captain and made company commander. After suffering bouts of pneumonia and jaundice, Upham went with the New Zealanders to Syria where they prepared positions to resist a possible German advance through Turkey and continued their battle training.

Following Rommel's assault at Gazala the New Zealand Division was rushed to the Western Desert, where it joined the Eighth Army to stop his advance in the first battle of El Alamein. In these operations Upham performed five acts of conspicuous gallantry that would have earned two VCs in their own right, but three awards to one man was unheralded.

On 27 June, the New Zealand Division attempted to halt the German advance at Minqar Qaim Ridge. Although the air was thick with tank, artillery, mortar and machine-gun fire, Upham ran across the open ground from one section post to another, rousing his men to stand firm. Wearing only a soft cap, since he rarely ever wore a tin helmet because they would not fit the size of his head, to the bewilderment of his men at one point he even climbed on top of a truck so he could identify the enemy positions that were decimating his company. The New Zealanders held off the sustained attacks but became encircled by the Germans, cutting off their line of retreat. During the night they broke out, with Upham leading from the front, inspiring his men in savage hand-to-hand fighting. His encouraging voice was heard above the noise of battle as he rushed numerous enemy vehicles, heedless of the fire pouring at him, destroying them all with grenades and regardless of wounding himself in the explosions.

During the attack on Ruweisat Ridge on 14–15 July Upham was instructed to send up an officer to report progress of the attack, but he went himself and, after several sharp encounters with enemy machine-gun posts, succeeded in bringing back the required information. Just before dawn 20th Battalion was ordered forward, but it encountered very heavy fire from a strongly defended enemy locality. Upham, without hesitation, led his company in a determined bayonet charge. A machine-gun bullet shattered his arm but he personally destroyed several machine-gun posts, a tank and several guns and vehicles with grenades. Exhausted by pain and weak from loss of blood, Upham was then removed to the regimental aid post, but immediately his wound had been dressed he returned to his men. He held his position under heavy artillery and mortar fire until he was again severely wounded in the leg by shrapnel. Being now unable to move, Upham fell into the hands of the enemy when his position was finally overrun, his gallant company having been reduced to only six survivors, despite his upstanding gallantry and magnificent leadership.

In abhorrent conditions Italian doctors attempted to amputate his arm without anesthetic, but Upham stubbornly refused and probably saved his own life. He recuperated from his wounds in an Italian hospital and was then sent to a prisoner-of-war camp but, typifying his character and nickname, "Pug," he soon began a private war with his captors by making increasingly daring, almost desperate efforts to escape. In his first attempt he leapt from a truck, with German SS guards firing at him. He was transferred to Germany in September 1943 and was involved in several escape plots, including an audacious solo attempt to scale the barbed-wire fences in broad daylight in which he was lucky not to be shot. The Germans eventually branded Upham as "dangerous" and in October 1944 he was incarcerated in the infamous prison fortress Colditz Castle, but even during his journey there he made another attempt that involved taking an incredible risk by leaping from the toilet window of a moving train in the middle of the night.

When Upham was liberated in April 1945 he was keen to see action again. Instead, he was sent to Britain where he was reunited with

Lieutenant Charles Hazlitt Upham, circa 1941. His Victoria Cross is visible on the right. (Alexander Turnbull Library, National Library of New Zealand F-1993-1/4-DA)

and married Molly McTamney, who was then serving as a nurse, and on 11 May King George VI presented Upham with an official Victoria Cross. In September 1945 he returned to New Zealand to resume life as a sheep farmer.

Shortly after returning home Upham learned that he was to receive a Bar to his Victoria Cross. The award caused much attention to be showered on him but he modestly said only: "Naturally I feel some pride in this distinction, but hundreds of others have done more than I did. They could have given it to one of them." Upham always insisted that the military honors were the property of the men of his unit and claimed that he would have been happier not to have been awarded the Victoria Cross because it made people expect too much of him, saying: "I don't want to be treated any differently from any other bastard." He hated the popularity and remained a tough and forthright Kiwi, in spite of his fame.

A modest hero, Upham never saw himself as anything other than a New Zealander doing his duty. He was genuinely embarrassed by the publicity and accolades he received and attempted to avoid international media attention. Upham turned down a knighthood and refused to accept land offered to returning servicemen after the war. The people of Canterbury raised £10,000 by public donation to buy him a farm but he declined the offer, requesting instead that the money be placed into an educational trust that would help the sons of servicemen attend university. Upham bought land at the mouth of the river Conway, North Canterbury, with a rehabilitation loan and, although hampered by the injuries to his arm, turned it into a successful farm through his own hard work. He and Molly had three daughters and lived on their farm for the remainder of his years, avoiding the spotlight of fame that the media occasionally tried to shine on him.

Charles Upham died on 22 November 1994 in Christchurch, New Zealand. He was a formidable soldier, and a natural leader who was able to shrewdly assess situations, weigh up risks and quickly decide on a course of action. He was utterly fearless and tenaciously single-minded but his implacable hatred of Nazi Germany and its allies certainly played a part in his success. When asked how he had become the only person in living memory to receive two Victoria Crosses, he just said: "I hated Germans." It was a sentiment that mellowed only slightly with the passing of years as his obituary noted: "It was said that no German-made car was ever driven onto Charlie Upham's farm."

Upham was an honorable, tough man with a strong sense of duty, who was also devoted to his wife and family. Modest and selfless, he always enjoyed the company of his old comrades, and was keenly aware of the sacrifices his generation had made to ensure that New Zealanders could live, as he put it, "in peace and plenty." Charles Upham is widely acknowledged as the outstanding soldier of the Second World War and without doubt remains one of the most courageous leaders of any modern conflict.

Compass and Rommel (1)

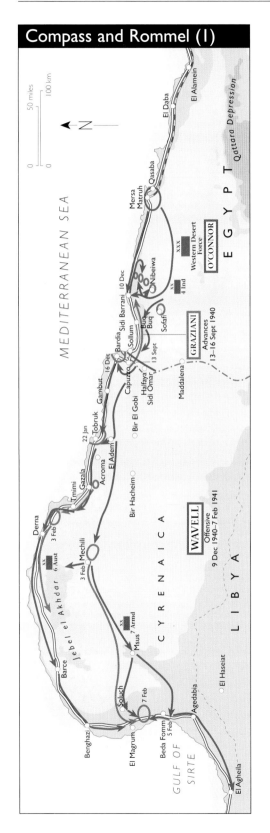

Compass and Rommel (2)

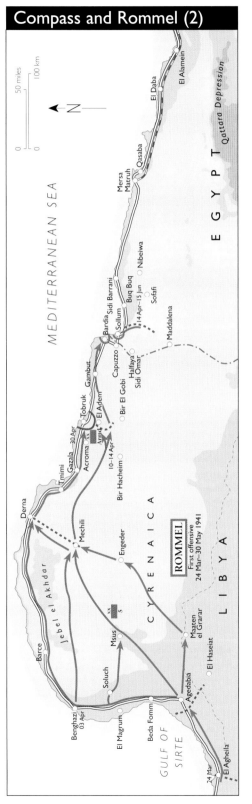

A child in the siege of annihilation: Malta 1940–43

Leon Gambin

A salient characteristic of the campaigns in the Mediterranean was that the fighting was largely conducted in country almost wholly lacking any civilian populations – with one striking exception. Malta is just 188 km (117 miles) square, or about two-thirds the size of the Isle of Wight but, with a population of 270,000 people it was one of the most densely populated areas in Europe. The island's proximity, just 96 km (60 miles) or 10 minutes' flying time to Sicily, enabled the Axis to inflict an intense bombardment in an attempt to neutralize Malta as an offensive base.

Leon Gambin was a 12-year-old boy living with his family in Senglea, which, together with Vittoriosa and Cospicua, form the Three Cities that lie south-east of Valetta on the opposite side of the Grand Harbor. It bore many traces of the Great Siege of 1565, when an enormous Turkish army was repulsed three times from its ramparts, earning Senglea the proud title "Citta Invicta" – the unconquered city. Amidst narrow, steep roads that were flanked by quaint three-story houses and which ran down to the moats and the harbor, Leon played cheerfully with his four sisters and three brothers. His father owned two shops and the Stoll picture theater, and during the summer operated a kiosk on the quayside where Leon helped out by waiting on the sailors and their girls with ice-cream and cool drinks.

This serene atmosphere changed dramatically, however, in June 1940 when Italy declared war. Fearing the bombs, Leon's father squeezed his family into a *Karozzin*, a small traditional Maltese horse-drawn cab, and sent them to safety in the village of Siggiewi, near Rabat. The first bombs had brought nervous reports of death and destruction and, without shelters for protection, almost every family had quickly packed a few essentials and left Senglea to seek refuge in the country, so all that remained in the deserted city were the cats and dogs. Although the island's only defense were the three famous Gladiator biplane fighters *Faith*, *Hope* and *Charity*, the Italians were not resolute in their attacks and the Maltese people could hear the scared Italian pilots on the radio, so during the next six months Leon, his family and almost everyone else gradually returned to Senglea.

On 16 January 1941 the Germans launched their first blitz on Malta and dropped not confetti, as the Maltese people said of the Italians when they came to raid, but real, high-caliber bombs. During two hours of constant bombing Senglea was heavily damaged and 21 people were killed. Many families had hewn shelters in the soft limestone rock in their cellars and dug tunnels to link with cellars and wells of neighboring families to provide an escape if the entrance was blocked. Leon was safe, although his sister Mary was trapped in the rubble and managed to escape through another well. The bombing also completely destroyed the Basilica of Our Lady of Victory, built to celebrate the victory by the Knights of Malta in 1565, except the crucifix which remained undamaged and stood triumphant above the rubble. The devoutly religious Maltese quickly assessed the significance that just as the cross had triumphed over the Turks, victory in this siege was equally certain.

Leon's father again took his family to Siggiewi, without knowing where they would live, but the Maltese people showed boundless charity by taking in complete strangers who had fled the city or whose homes had been destroyed. Leon was lucky that his father was a shopkeeper and, using his business acumen,

opened a shop in Rabat. Known as "Gambin the Confectioner" he sold whatever he could obtain through bartering but especially alcohol and specialist sweet pastries. Rationing first started on 7 April 1941 with sugar, coffee, soap and matches but by September that year almost everything was being rationed. A shortage of coins also made it hard to do business, but a system of IOUs was introduced and these were used extensively as small change and were routinely honored. The women too had to be equally resourceful, and imaginative improvisation made life a little more bearable. Many women tailored clothes for the children from British service blankets, old tires were used to resole shoes, and almost everything was recycled.

Leon's family were luckier than most in that their home was not demolished. His mother still had a means to prepare food and through his business and trading contacts

Malta was one of the most densely populated areas in Europe and suffered the most intense blitz of the war. Civilians suffered terribly as their homes were often near the harbour or military bases, forcing the population to live underground and in near starving conditions. (Imperial War Museum A8613)

Leon's father was able to provide for his family. The British servicemen stationed on Malta were also restricted to the same rationing that applied to civilians, and hunger was widespread. Although Leon's family had little to share, they were friendly with a few soldiers stationed who frequented their shop and when times were tough they would come into the shop and, using a secret code so as not to alert everyone, for the family could help but a few, would leave their beret lying open on a chair. This was a sign for Leon, who would then run to tell his mother "Tom's here, he's left his beret for something to eat." Surreptitiously she would place something, often a well-made Maltese sandwich, in the beret, and the soldier would roll it up and quietly take it with him. With meager food to spare for themselves, these efforts were symbolic of the generosity of the Maltese people towards those helping to defend their island.

The caves and catacombs on the island were not sufficient to provide safety for everyone and, for those not lucky enough to have their own shelters, coalminers serving in the Royal Engineers dug large public shelters. As the blitz worsened, the raids became more frequent, averaging eight or nine per day. The longest single raid lasted 13 hours and on one day alone 21 hours were spent under alert. People had to remain underground for hours at a time and from December 1941 when the bombing intensified the entire population took to living underground almost permanently. Conditions in the shelters were terrible. Cold, wet, dirty, without proper sanitation and, with only candles and hurricane lamps to light the dark nights, people relied on their faith to see them through. Many shelters were turned into chapels and communal prayers were held. Men and women screamed out in panic, fear and prayer and it is a commonly held belief that their fervent prayers to let the bombs drop into the sea saved them from death and destruction.

In the lull between raids life went on as normal. Leon attended Birkirkara St Aloysius Jesuit College and while lessons were conducted as normally as possible, life as a schoolboy was far from normal. To save fuel the bus terminus was moved to the outskirts of each town, which in Rabat meant that Leon and his three friends had to make a scary walk across Ta' Qali airfield each day to catch their bus. The airfield was used by Spitfires and was frequently bombed, so the boys had to scan the skies for enemy aircraft and then either rush across while it was safe or find a stone wall to hide behind or some other secure place until the bombing had finished. Leon made an error only once, judging it safe after school while rushing to the bus stop hoping to catch a ride home,

while two Spitfires were chasing a German fighter. Although not a bomber, in an attempt to evade his pursuers the German pilot swooped low and released a bomb from under his wings just where Leon was standing. The bomb exploded and showered Leon in dirt, but luckily he remained unhurt.

Free from the confines of the shelter the children played with extra energy, but theirs was no ordinary playfield. Anti-personnel mines were designed to look like pens, butterflies or cans of sardines and were dropped everywhere. Despite radio warnings not to touch anything strange, children were attracted by such objects and were regularly maimed. Children were prone to find the bombsites exciting places to play and explore, but regardless of the bombs the anti-aircraft fire was so strong that there was a steady rain of hot, dangerous shrapnel falling from the exploding shells. Leon had a particularly disturbing experience on 21 March 1942 when exploring a bombsite at the Point de Vue Hotel in Rabat. The hotel had been requisitioned as a billet for officers stationed at the nearby Ta' Qali airfield and Leon was one of the first to discover five pilots who had been decapitated by a bomb, a shocking experience that remains with him today. A sunny Sunday on 9 May proved a much happier day when Leon and his friends were able to sit atop the hill above Ta' Qali airfield and with great joy watch 64 Spitfires land after flying in from the aircraft-carriers USS *Wasp* and HMS *Eagle*. They were immediately refueled and rearmed and took off to meet the next German raid with a vengeance.

As foodstocks diminished during the summer of 1942, malnutrition spread. The quality of bread deteriorated as it was made with 20 percent potatoes, the firewood for the bakeries ran out and adults were often restricted to 1,100 calories per day. On 5 May the government took the drastic action of rationing bread to 10 oz (300 g) per person per day. As the deprivation of food and cooking fuel worsened, the government established communal "victory kitchens" for people with no means to cook and to economize. In June 1942 there were 42 but at the peak of the siege 200 kitchens were operating throughout Malta and the number of people drawing meals rose to over 100,000 in October 1942, going up to 175,536 in the first week of January 1943.

The victory kitchens were, however, more commonly known as siege kitchens, and provided meager daily sustenance. The fare was less than appetizing, not least because everything was cooked in only one way, by being boiled, and readers often wrote to the editor of *The Times of Malta*. One person complained: "the staple diet included goat's meat which was as tough as hide, with tomato sauce or a couple of beans. Each serving was miserable! Our cook used to mince goat meat and turn it into a meat loaf. That way it was possible to eat it without damaging your teeth." Another reader commented about the *minestra*, a vegetable soup: "the vegetables are cut in big chunks, half a turnip, big pieces of long-marrow with skin, turnip leaves and stalks in quantity, a shadow of pumpkin and tomatoes, just to give a hectic color, a few *zibeg*, a type of pasta, swimming in water ... pure water. Not very inviting."

It is estimated that the Germans dropped 17,000 tons of bombs on Malta and, up to 8 October 1942, 9,000 houses were destroyed and 17,000 seriously damaged. Malta was suffering from an acute shortage of all essentials and although the people did not lose their nerve the government had to make provision for "Harvest Day," or "Target Day," the day of reckoning when the suffering Maltese would be forced to capitulate through starvation. On 15 April 1942 King George VI announced: "To honour her brave people, I award the George Cross to the Island Fortress of Malta to bear witness to a heroism and devotion that will long be famous in history." Publicly, the bestowal of

the medal helped to boost the morale of the people, but in Leon's family and thousands of others just like his, all of whom were starving, the cry was, "We want bread, not the George Cross," and anti-British sentiment started to rise.

Malta was saved by the Pedestal convoy, which arrived during August 1942. Just five ships arrived out of the 15 that left England, but each was welcomed with delirious excitement. The tanker *Ohio* was literally carried into Grand Harbor slung between two destroyers and with her decks awash. The fuel and supplies staved off starvation and enabled Malta to remain in the fight, but it did not lift the siege. The harsh rationing and suffering of the Maltese people continued until the beginning of 1943, by which stage the fortune of war in the Mediterranean had swung against the Axis and supply convoys could safely be sent to Malta.

In Maltese history, 8 September is a very significant date as it marks the end of the Great Siege of 1565, but it is also the feast day of Our Lady of Victories, *Il-Festa tal-Bambina*, the titular feast of Senglea. In 1943 it was fitting that a large parade was held to celebrate the return of the statue of Our Lady, *Il-Bambina*, from where it had been taken in January 1941 for safekeeping. This was the first procession since 1939 and many Sengleans, including Leon and his family, cleared the streets of rubble for the parade so that they could celebrate the National day and give thanks for deliverance from three years of onslaught. As the procession reached the devastated wharf, the parish priest announced the joyous news just received by the Admiralty that Italy had surrendered, and ships in the harbor used their searchlights to celebrate the end of the long ordeal suffered by the people of Malta.

Not necessarily in peace

The Balkans

During 1944 Churchill became increasingly concerned about the communist tide sweeping across Europe in the wake of the Red Army, and its portent for control of post-war Europe. To prevent the communists taking control of Greece, which he saw as vital to British interests in the Mediterranean, Churchill accordingly made an agreement with Stalin in May 1944 to allow Soviet domination of Romania in return for a free British hand in Greece. In Moscow in October 1944, this deal was widened to include Hungary, Bulgaria and Yugoslavia when they drew up the spheres of influence that the two countries were to have in the Balkans. Initially these were agreed to be 50:50 for Hungary and Yugoslavia and 75:25 between the USSR and others in Bulgaria, but subsequent haggling produced amended ratios for Hungary and Bulgaria of 80:20 in favor of the USSR.

On 20 August Stalin launched a great offensive on the Ukranian Front to "liberate" south-eastern Europe. Romania's capitulation on 23 August allowed the Soviet Army to sweep forward rapidly, capturing the great oilfields at Ploesti on 30 August and Bucharest the next day, and reaching the Yugoslavian border on the Danube on 6 September. Bulgaria surrendered without resistance on 9 September and by the end of the month the entire German Sixth Army, totaling more than 100,000 troops, had been captured. Field-Marshal Maximilian von Weichs, Commander-in-Chief, South-Eastern Europe, had 600,000 troops between Trieste and the Aegean Sea, but, as German control of the Balkans began to collapse, their position became untenable. Army Group E began to evacuate the Greek islands from 12 September but when the danger of a new

Soviet breakthrough westwards from Bulgaria threatened the vital railway through Yugoslavia, they began to withdraw from the whole of Greece on 12 October. Their only chance of survival was to retrace the route over which the German Army had advanced with such fanfare in 1941 and link up with Army Group F in Yugoslavia. Relatively peacefully, though harried by partisans and the Bulgarian Army, the last Germans finally quit Greece in the first week of November.

The newly formed Greek government of national unity under Prime Minister George Papandreou, recognized as the legitimate government by the Allies, returned to their homeland on 18 October accompanied by the British expedition to Greece, a military force commanded by Lieutenant-General Ronald Scobie. The communist EAM/ELAS had demanded key positions in the government but this impasse was resolved by Stalin's agreement with Churchill, and he withdrew Soviet support for the communists. Both main partisan forces agreed to demobilize and place their considerable armed forces under the control of the British, acting as a de facto national army for the government, but tensions remained extremely high. At a mass EAM demonstration on 3 December in Athens, 21 people were shot by police in circumstances that remain unclear even now, but the shooting provoked a communist insurgency and within a few days ELAS and British troops were locked in bloody street-fighting.

The British sent reinforcements from the campaign in Italy, which they could ill-afford, and after six weeks, vicious fighting quelled the insurrection, at a tragic cost of over 200 British lives. The conflict between the dissident allies was unique in the Second World War and its acrimony was such that not even Churchill and Eden could negotiate a settlement during an impulsive visit to Athens on Christmas Eve 1944. A ceasefire was achieved in January 1945 and a political settlement negotiated the following month, but the peace that followed proved to be illusory as the communists renewed their bitter struggle 18 months later. The liberation of Greece from the choke of Axis control merely created a vacuum in which the chaos of an acrimonious civil war continued until finally defeated in 1949 by an American-equipped and trained Greek Army, in a prelude to the emerging Cold War. However, the communist atrocities that had accompanied the attempted insurrection left an indelible mark on a whole generation of Greeks that still runs deep in Greek society today.

The sudden appearance of the Red Army on the Yugoslav border prompted Tito to fly to Moscow to meet Stalin. He agreed to allow troops of the 3rd Ukrainian Front to participate in the capture of Belgrade and to arm 14 partisan divisions, which allowed Tito to conquer étnik-dominated Serbia. Stalin also gave the impression that he had "requested" permission to allow the Red Army to cross Yugoslavia in order to shorten its advance for an assault on southern Hungary in exchange for allowing Tito a role in the postwar administration of Yugoslavia. The battle for Belgrade duly began on 14 October and despite a fierce defense by the Germans, who lost 25,000 in casualties, the city fell six days later.

German Army Group F had incorporated Army Group E following its flight from Greece but the way remained open for the Soviet forces to continue their advance through Yugoslavia. However, Hitler orchestrated a coup in Hungary and declared Budapest to be a fortress, thus ensuring the Soviet advance up the Danube would be a fierce fight. Stalin may also have had in mind his agreement with Churchill, but he ordered that Soviet forces turn back for the coming battle for Hungary. In hindsight the decision to remove Soviet troops from Yugoslavia at the moment of victory proved to be a misjudgment that deprived Stalin of

the ability to impose Soviet rule consistently across the whole of eastern Europe.

Nevertheless, with a force of several hundred thousand well-armed troops now operating as a regular army, Tito was able to continue the task of liberating Yugoslavia as the Germans and their Yugoslav auxiliaries slowly fell back northwards. On 19 March 1945 the Fourth Yugoslav Army launched an offensive that reached Trieste on 30 April but military operations were not concluded until 15 May, after the final German surrender. Tito formed an internationally recognized coalition government, under communist control, and began the process of establishing an independent, authoritarian communist regime, of which he became president for life. Despite constant nationalistic, ethnic and religious tensions the partisan war of national liberation remained the source of authority and inspiration behind the "brotherhood and unity" that maintained Tito's regime until his death in 1980.

The end in Italy

A prolonged Allied tactical air interdiction program during the autumn and winter of 1944 had effectively closed the Brenner Pass and created an acute shortage of fuel that drastically reduced the mobility of General Heinrich von Vietinghoff's Army Group C in northern Italy. Although the Germans still had over half a million men in the field, the Allies had been invigorated in both spirit and outlook by substantial reinforcements, including the Brazilian Expeditionary Force and an abundant array of new weapons. On 9 April 1945, after the ground had dried, Alexander launched his spring offensive with Eighth Army attacking through the Argenta Gap. Fifth Army struck on 15 April and just ten days later both Allied armies met at Finale nell'Emilia, after having surrounded and eliminated the last German forces. The Allies then advanced rapidly northwards, the Americans entering Milan on 29 April and the British reaching Trieste on 2 May. Fifth Army continued to advance into Austria, linking with US Seventh Army in the Brenner Pass on 6 May.

The isolated and hopeless position of German forces had led SS General Karl Wolff, military governor and head of the SS in northern Italy, to initiate background negotiations for a separate surrender as early as February 1945. The talks, facilitated by Allan Dulles, head of the American Office of Strategic Services in Switzerland, held much promise, although they were complicated by mutual suspicion and mistrust. Wolff wished to avoid senseless destruction and loss of life and to repel the spread of communism, as well as ingratiating himself with the West in case of war-crimes trials, but for the Allies Wolff offered the prospect of preventing the creation of a Nazi redoubt in the Alps. Himmler checked the talks in April, preventing a conclusion before the Allies' spring offensive, but by 23 April Wolff and Vietinghoff decided to disregard orders from Berlin. Wolff ordered the SS not to resist the Italian partisans on 25 April and an unconditional surrender was signed on 29 April to be effective on 2 May, six days before the German surrender in the West. Military success had already assured the Allies of victory but a smoother and quicker conclusion of the fighting ensured that there was no last-ditch stand by die-hard fascists, and curtailed the loss of life and destruction.

Mussolini also made attempts in the last days to come to terms with the Allies behind the backs of the Germans, but on learning of the Germans' own negotiations he attempted to flee to Switzerland. He was captured by partisans near Lake Como and was shot on 28 April, along with his mistress Clara Petacci and the main fascist leaders. Their bodies were then taken to Milan and suspended upside-down from meat hooks for public exhibition in the Piazzale Loreto. This gruesome gesture was the conclusion to 20 years of fascist dictatorship and Mussolini's dream of an Italian Empire spanning the Mediterranean, for which the Italian people had paid dearly in wars that they were neither prepared for nor willing to fight.

The bodies of fascist leaders shot by Italian partisans near Lake Como while trying to escape north, strung up by the heels from roof beams of a garage in Piazzale Loreto in Milan on 29 April 1945. Benito Mussolini is in the middle with his mistress Clara Petacci to his right. (Australian War Memorial P01387.002)

Crusader (1)

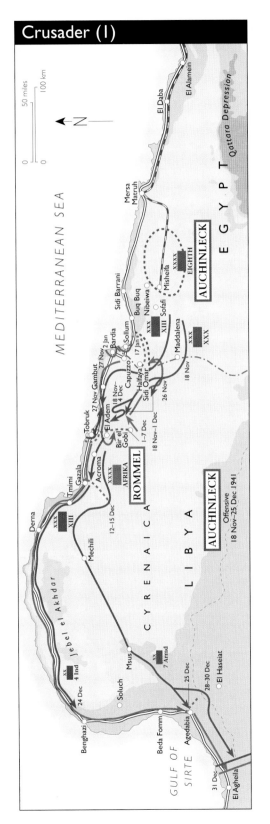

Crusader (2)

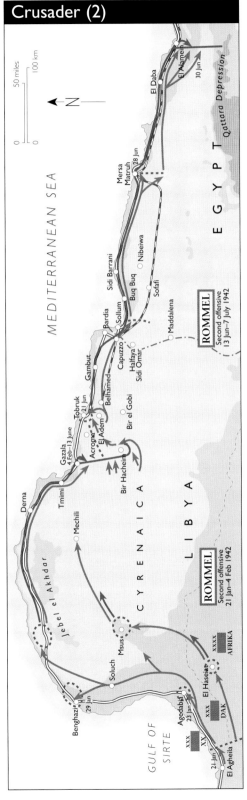

Part IV
The Pacific

The expansion of Imperial Japan

The Pacific War was caused by the expansionist ambitions of Imperial Japan and the train of events that led to it can be described fairly easily. It is much harder to explain why Japan initiated a war against the one country that had the power to crush it – the USA. The answer is perhaps found in Japan's unique culture and history. Having not experienced defeat for a thousand years, and believing in the superiority of their race, culture, and spirit, the Japanese could not conceive of defeat. Somehow, trusting in the living-god Emperor, they would win, even if many would die in the process.

The origins of the war therefore lie in Japan's emergence after more than two centuries of isolation from the outside world. To protect itself from foreign influences, in the early seventeenth century Japan had expelled all foreigners and had severely restricted foreign access. This isolation was shattered in 1853, when four American warships appeared in Tokyo Bay and their commander, Commodore Matthew Perry, began negotiations that led eventually to a commercial treaty between the USA and Japan.

Thereafter the Japanese moved rapidly to modernize their country. The power of the feudal warlords collapsed and in 1868 the new Emperor announced a policy of seeking knowledge from around the world. Japan adopted a vaguely democratic constitution with an elected parliament or Diet. Compulsory education was introduced, although with heavy emphasis on obedience to the Emperor. Asked by their teachers about their 'dearest ambition,' schoolboys would answer, 'To die for the Emperor.' The Japanese craved European technology and expertise, but did not have the time or the inclination to absorb Western ideas of democracy or liberalism.

Japanese insecurity and expansionism

The Japanese were acutely conscious of their vulnerability. Over the preceding centuries, European powers had seized colonies in the Asia-Pacific area. Britain held Malaya, Burma, and India, the French were in Indo-China, the Dutch owned the East Indies (now Indonesia) and Germany had part of New Guinea. The Europeans and the Americans had also won concessions from a weak and disorganized China. If Japan were to survive, it had to establish a powerful and modern army, and a capable navy, and to support these forces it had to begin a rapid process of industrialization. Lacking natural resources but possessing a large, industrious population, Japan had to secure supplies of raw materials and find markets for its goods.

The Japanese observed that the European powers had gained economically by exploiting their military and diplomatic power in Asia. Taking this lead, in 1894 Japan initiated a short and successful war with China over access to Korea, and the following year China ceded Formosa (Taiwan) and the Liaotung peninsula in southern Manchuria, which included the fine harbor of Port Arthur. Under pressure from Russia, Germany, and France, Japan was forced to withdraw from Manchuria. Russia moved into Manchuria, while Germany and France grabbed further concessions in China. To the enraged Japanese, it seemed that there was one rule for the European powers and a different rule for Asian countries. Three years later the USA took control of the Philippines.

The Japanese were determined to gain control of those areas that they saw as vital to their economic survival. In 1904 Japan blockaded Port Arthur, and moved troops into Korea and Manchuria. In a bloody war with heavy casualties on both sides, the Japanese defeated the Russian army in Manchuria and destroyed the Russian fleet sent to relieve Port Arthur (see Osprey Essential Histories, *The Russo-Japanese War 1904–1905*). For the first time, an Asian power had defeated a European power, and the Japanese army gained in prestige and power. Japan took control of the Liaotung peninsula and stationed troops to protect the Manchurian railroad. By 1910, Japan had annexed Korea.

Japan obtained tremendous advantages from the First World War. As one of the Allies, it seized Germany's possessions in China and the Pacific, but never sent land forces to Europe. Fueled by the demands of the war, Japanese industries continued to expand and Japan built up its merchant navy.

In the postwar settlement, Japan retained the former German Pacific colonies under a mandate from the League of Nations, but was upset by the Allies' refusal to endorse a statement about nonracial discrimination. Japan was thus confirmed as a principal power in the Pacific, but was viewed with suspicion by both the USA and Britain. At a conference in Washington in 1921–22, the USA, Britain, and Japan agreed to limit their capital ships according to a ratio of 5:5:3, and the USA and Britain undertook not to fortify their Pacific possessions. Japan was aggrieved at apparent restrictions to its navy, but as both Britain and the USA also deployed their forces in the Atlantic, Japan was left as the most powerful navy in the western Pacific. Still suspicious of Japan, in 1923 Britain decided to establish a naval base at Singapore, to which it would send its main fleet in time of crisis in the Pacific.

Meanwhile, the Japanese economy and society were coming under great strain. During the 1920s numerous earthquakes – the largest striking Tokyo in 1923 – shattered cities and factories. As the world economic system began to falter, Western countries applied trade restrictions that hurt Japanese industries. The Great Depression is generally thought to have begun with the Wall Street crash in 1929, but by 1926 more than

The Japanese Emperor, Hirohito, came to the throne in 1926, aged 25. He had traveled in Europe and was an amateur marine biologist of repute. He exercised little power, but historical debate still continues over whether he encouraged the militarists. A Japanese nationalist, he seemed fatalistically to accept the inevitability of war. (AKG Berlin)

three million Japanese industrial workers had lost their jobs. The Japanese government came under increasing pressure from militant nationalistic groups, often led by young army officers. This was a similar environment to that which led to the rise of Nazism in Germany, fascism in Italy and communism in various countries. In Japan a homegrown militarism built on the Japanese people's belief in their national uniqueness and their heaven-granted mandate to assume leadership in east Asia.

In Manchuria and northern China, Japan was facing new challenges. The Soviet Union was likely to oppose Japanese ambitions in the Far East. And in China, nationalist forces were being consolidated under Chiang Kai-shek. Fiercely nationalistic Japan ignored the nationalist aspirations of other Asian countries such as China and Korea.

The Japanese semiautonomous Kwantung Army, policing the Manchurian railroad, was a highly political organization that attracted the best and most ambitious Japanese officers and dominated commercial development in the ostensibly Chinese province. On 18 September 1931, officers of the Kwantung Army falsely accused the Chinese of sabotaging the Port Arthur–Mukden railroad. Against the wishes of both the Japanese government and the commander of the Kwantung Army, Japanese forces attacked the numerically stronger armies of the local Chinese warlords and quickly overran Manchuria. Powerless, the Japanese government acquiesced, and the following year Japan established a puppet state – Manchukuo – nominally ruled by Emperor Pu Yi, but actually controlled by the Japanese commander of the Kwantung Army. In 1932 the Japanese seized the nearby province of Jehol and added eastern Chahar in 1935. Manchukuo had a population of 34 million, of whom 240,000 were Japanese (increasing to 837,000 in 1939).

This so-called Manchurian Incident marked the beginning of full-scale Japanese aggression in Asia. The US Secretary of State condemned Japan, and after an investigation the League of Nations branded Japan as the aggressor. In response, in March 1933 Japan withdrew from the League of Nations. The Japanese War Minister, General Araki Sadao, complained that the League of Nations did not respect Japan's 'holy mission' to establish peace in the Orient, but vowed that the day would come when 'we will make the world look up to our national virtues.'

Despite these belligerent statements, the Japanese government was actually in disarray – what one commentator described as 'government by assassination.' In November 1930 the Japanese Prime Minister was gunned down for accepting allegedly humiliating conditions at a naval conference in London. In February 1932 two leading politicians were assassinated by members of the Blood Brotherhood – modernday samurai warriors

who were prepared to sacrifice themselves for the good of Japan. In May 1932 they murdered the Prime Minister for criticizing Japanese aggression in Manchuria. The assassins, described by War Minister Araki as 'irrepressible patriots,' received jail terms that were later commuted.

In February 1936 radical army officers attempted a *coup d'état*, murdering several leading government ministers. The coup attempt failed, but the army gained even more power. In 1937 the War Minister (a serving army officer) submitted a bill to parliament to give the government absolute control over industry, labor, and the press. The Diet meekly voted its approval. Also the government initiated a plan to expand its heavy industries to enable it to wage a total war for three years, and it stepped up the naval building program. In November 1936 the army had negotiated the Anti-Comintern Pact with Germany and Italy. It was directed squarely against the Soviet Union, which was supporting China.

The Sino-Japanese War

On the night of 7 July 1937, shots were fired at a Japanese detachment on maneuvers a few miles from Peking. Japanese and Chinese forces had engaged in frequent skirmishes during the previous six years, but this time the Nationalist Chinese leader, Chiang Kai-shek, believed that he could no longer tolerate Japanese provocation. To some historians the 'China Incident', as the Japanese called it, marks the true beginning of the Second World War. China and Japan were to remain at war until 1945.

On 14 August 1937, Nationalist Chinese planes struck Japanese warships at Shanghai. The Japanese deployed 10 divisions to north China and five to Shanghai. When, in October, President Roosevelt finally condemned Japan's aggression, a leading Japanese, Matsuoka Yosuke, soon to be Foreign Minister, retorted: 'Japan is expanding and what country in its expansion era has ever failed to be trying to its neighbours?' In November the Japanese

Japanese troops in a victory pose at a captured Chinese artillery camp, Shanghai, November 1937. From August to early November the Chinese resisted Japanese attempts to take the city. After it fell, the Japanese moved quickly and secured Nanking on 13 December. (AKG Berlin)

army drove the Chinese out of Shanghai and next month took the Nationalist capital, Nanking, where it engaged in an orgy of killing, rape, and looting. More than a quarter of a million civilians were slaughtered.

Contemptuous of Western public opinion, Japanese planes and shore batteries sank an American gunboat, USS *Panay*, which was evacuating diplomatic staffs from Nanking, and the American government chose to accept a Japanese apology. Nonetheless, Western observers in China, many of them American missionaries, publicized stories of Japanese atrocities, and the American government gradually sought ways to assist the Nationalist Chinese.

Thrusting deeper into China, by the end of 1938 Japan had captured large areas of northern China, the Yangtze valley, and pockets along the coast. Chiang Kai-shek withdrew his government to the inland city of Chungking and tried to come to a cooperative arrangement with the Chinese Communists under Mao Tse-tung. The Communists conducted guerrilla warfare against the Japanese, who had established a puppet Chinese government in their area of occupation. Meanwhile, the Nationalist Chinese were working hard to win American support.

The Japanese now faced a dilemma. They could not conquer all of China, but the war was a heavy drain on their resources, fuel, and finances. Japanese army leaders hoped to resolve the war in China so that they could deal with their principal enemy, the Soviet Union. But to conclude the war, Japan needed fuel and other resources from south-east Asia. If Western countries would not supply this fuel then Japan would have to seize it. The Japanese navy leaders realized that expansion to the south would bring war, with the USA as their principal enemy. Japan now stepped up preparations for a major war.

Japanese soldiers entering Nanking in December 1937. Japanese commanders unleashed days of wanton slaughter in the city, the notorious Rape of Nanking. (AKG Berlin)

Towards the end of 1938 the Japanese Prime Minister, Prince Konoye Fumimaro, spelt out Japan's plans for a New Order for East Asia, involving the eradication of European and American imperialism and also of communism from east Asia. Later the Japanese would declare their national objective to be the setting up of a Greater East Asia Co-prosperity Sphere. In effect, the Asian countries would be subservient to Japan, providing it with raw materials and markets.

Meanwhile, Soviet support for the Chinese precipitated several clashes between the Kwantung Army and Soviet forces. Finally, in July 1939 the Kwantung Army crossed into Mongolia. A Soviet army mounted a counteroffensive near Nomonhan that killed more than 18,000 Japanese troops. In the midst of this campaign, the Japanese were shocked to learn of the Nazi–Soviet Pact. They quickly arranged a ceasefire in Manchuria.

Japan looks south

Bogged down in China and checked by the Soviet Union, the Japanese were unsure of their next step. Then, in September 1939 Germany invaded Poland, and Britain and France declared war on Germany. The German invasion of France in May 1940 suddenly offered Japan new opportunities to cut China's overseas supplies. Chased out of Europe and hammered from the air, Britain was not strong enough to resist Japan's demand in July 1940 to close the road from Rangoon in Burma to Chungking, which was supplying the Nationalist government with vital supplies. Nor could the Vichy French government, formed after the German

occupation, resist demands to close the port of Haiphong and to give access to bases in northern Vietnam from which Japanese planes could attack southern China.

But the German occupation of France also spurred the Americans into action. In May 1940 the Americans decided to station their Pacific Fleet at Hawaii and the following month they began a large naval expansion program so that their navy could operate in both the Atlantic and Pacific oceans. In September the US Congress agreed to a peacetime draft, and in December it made $100 million in credit available to the Chinese Nationalist government. The Japanese imperial navy reacted by ordering a full mobilization – a process that would be completed by December 1941.

Thus, by the second half of 1940, war between Japan, the USA, and Britain had become increasingly likely. Britain, the USA (concerned for the security of the Philippines), Australia, and the Netherlands considered defensive plans in south-east Asia. Belatedly, Britain built up its garrison in Malaya and

The Japanese War Minister, General Tojo Hideki (centre), and the Foreign Minister, Matsuoka Yosuke (second from right), join German and Italian officials to toast the Tripartite Pact signed between the three countries in September 1940. The Pact recognized the leadership of Japan in establishing a new order in Greater East Asia. A 'none-too-intelligent professional soldier', Tojo became Prime Minister in October 1941 and took Japan into the war. Later, with the additional portfolio of Home Minister, Tojo, known as 'the Razor', directed the arrest of his political opponents. (Australian War Memorial)

Singapore with British, Indian, and Australian troops. But preoccupied by events in Europe and the Middle East, Britain did not give the defence of Malaya high priority.

The German attack on Russia on 22 June 1941 fundamentally changed the situation. Japan could either fall on Russia's Far East empire while Russia was fighting for its life in Europe or it could continue its southern expansion secure in the knowledge that Russia would be too preoccupied to attack in Manchuria. In April, Japan had signed a nonaggression pact with the Soviet Union. On 2 July, Japan decided to strike south.

The expansion of Japan 1920–1941

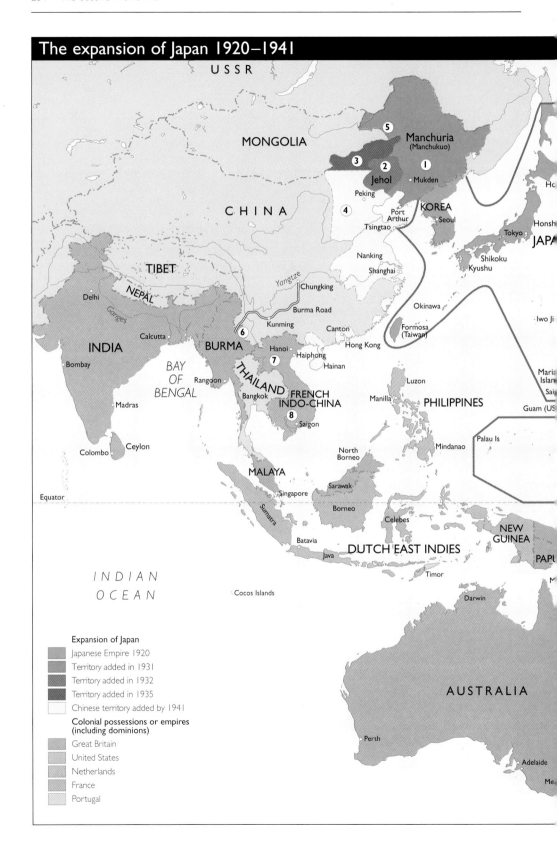

Expansion of Japan
- Japanese Empire 1920
- Territory added in 1931
- Territory added in 1932
- Territory added in 1935
- Chinese territory added by 1941

Colonial possessions or empires (including dominions)
- Great Britain
- United States
- Netherlands
- France
- Portugal

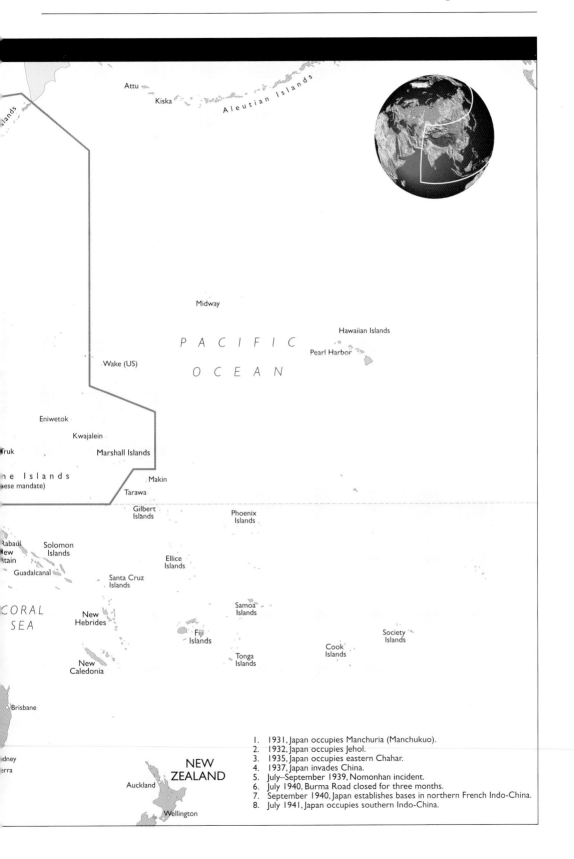

Attu

Kiska

Aleutian Islands

Midway

Hawaiian Islands

P A C I F I C

Pearl Harbor

O C E A N

Wake (US)

Eniwetok

Kwajalein

Truk

Marshall Islands

ne Islands
(ese mandate)

Makin

Tarawa

Gilbert
Islands

Phoenix
Islands

Rabaul
New
ritain

Solomon
Islands

Ellice
Islands

Guadalcanal

Santa Cruz
Islands

CORAL
SEA

New
Hebrides

Samoa
Islands

Fiji
Islands

Society
Islands

Cook
Islands

Tonga
Islands

New
Caledonia

Brisbane

idney
erra

NEW
ZEALAND

Auckland

Wellington

1. 1931, Japan occupies Manchuria (Manchukuo).
2. 1932, Japan occupies Jehol.
3. 1935, Japan occupies eastern Chahar.
4. 1937, Japan invades China.
5. July–September 1939, Nomonhan incident.
6. July 1940, Burma Road closed for three months.
7. September 1940, Japan establishes bases in northern French Indo-China.
8. July 1941, Japan occupies southern Indo-China.

Powerful Japan faced certain defeat

Any comparison of the military and industrial strengths of the Japanese Empire and the Allies must conclude that Japan had no chance of winning. While Japan could deploy more than a million soldiers, three of its enemies could do likewise. And while Japan possessed the world's third largest navy, it was opposed by the even stronger American and British navies. Yet Japan began the war with considerable advantages. By seizing the initiative, it severely damaged the US Pacific Fleet at Pearl Harbor, eliminated the dangerous US bombing force in the Philippines, and threw the British forces in Malaya off-balance. Once the USA lost its western Pacific bases, it had to cross thousands of miles of ocean to take the fight to the Japanese. The USA also had to divide its forces between the European and Pacific theaters. To an even greater extent, Britain concentrated on Europe, and it could not deploy its naval strength fully until the last year of the war.

Japan's military strength

In 1937 Japan was a strong, technologically advanced nation with a population of 70 million. During the 1930s its open, market-oriented economy had been transformed into a directed war economy, but it weakness was its heavy dependence on overseas supplies of oil, raw materials, and rice.

By 1941 the Japanese army consisted of 31 divisions, with a further 13 in the Kwantung Army. Each division generally numbered about 18,000 men. By Western standards, much of the army's heavy equipment was obsolete, but the troops were well trained and experienced from years of operations in China. By the end of the war,

Japan had raised 170 infantry, 13 air, four tank and four anti-aircraft divisions in a force numbering 2.3 million. The lack of adequate tanks and heavy artillery was not an important factor in jungle and island warfare, although the army's defeat by Soviet forces in 1939 had revealed its inadequacy against a well-equipped enemy in open terrain.

One of the strengths of the Japanese armed forces was the Bushido code of honor – the way of the warrior. All members of the armed forces were responsible directly to the Emperor. Military instructions emphasized absolute obedience to orders and forbade retreat in any circumstances. These attitudes led to fanatical resistance, often resulting in suicidal banzai charges, with the troops shouting the battle cry, 'Long live the Emperor!' Later in the war, Japanese aircraft pilots conducted suicidal kamikaze attacks on Allied ships. Another outcome was the atrocious treatment of Allied prisoners of war. But life was also hard and discipline brutal for the conscripted Japanese soldiers.

In December 1941 Japan's navy numbered 391 warships, including 10 battleships and 10 aircraft carriers. It was a well-trained force; its gunnery was good and its navigators were skillful. Some ships were new, with modern weapons – the Long Lance torpedo was exceptional – but others were older. Its strength was the naval air force, with its 1,750 fighters, torpedo bombers, and bombers, operating from both aircraft carriers and island bases.

The Japanese army's air force was based mainly in China, but units were later deployed to larger islands such as New Guinea and the Philippines. While Japan's considerable industrial capacity allowed it to construct almost 70,000 aircraft between 1941 and 1945, it was not able to sustain the constant technological improvements that marked the

The Japanese Zero – the Mitsubishi A6m2 Navy Type O carrier fighter – was one of the outstanding aircraft of the war. Armor plating and self-sealing tanks were sacrificed to give the Zero maximum speed and maneuverability. It could outperform most Allied aircraft in 1941 and was flown by well-trained and experienced pilots. (US National Archives)

Allied industrial effort. As the war progressed, the Allies had increasingly superior aircraft.

Theoretically, Japanese military operations were directed by Imperial General Headquarters (formed in 1937), but in practice, the army and navy headquarters staff operated independently. Army operations were generally controlled by the China Expeditionary, Southern Expeditionary or Kwantung armies. Below this level were the area armies; these normally included several armies (equivalent to Western corps) and an air army. Most Japanese warships came under the Combined Fleet, headed in 1941 by Admiral Yamamoto Isoruku. This was subdivided into fleets with various compositions, such as the battleship force and the striking force.

Japan's military operations often suffered from a lack of clear strategic direction, caused by lack of cooperation between army and navy leaders. More generally, however, the Allies' main advantage lay in the industrial power of the USA.

The USA's military strength

At the outbreak of war, the American population of 141 million was about twice that of Japan, but its industrial capacity was considerably greater. For example, in 1937 the USA produced 28.8 million tons of steel, while Japan produced 5.8 million. This industrial strength and large population enabled the USA to expand its armed forces at an unprecedented rate and to manufacture huge quantities of equipment and war matériel not only for its own forces but also for Allied forces.

The USA fought a war in Europe, but still deployed massive forces in the Pacific. In early 1940 the US army numbered only 160,000, but after conscription was introduced in September 1940, it grew rapidly: in December its strength was 1.6 million; by March 1945 it had reached 8.1 million. These figures included the US Army Air Force (USAAF), which grew from 270,000 to 1.8 million in the same period. In April 1945 the US army had 5 million soldiers deployed overseas; 1.45 million of these were in the Pacific and China–Burma–India theaters. The USA also deployed 11 field armies. Two remained in the USA, six went to the European theater, and three were in the Pacific – the Sixth and Eighth in the South-West Pacific Area, and the

Tenth at Okinawa. Each army consisted of two or more corps, and each of these had two or more divisions. During the war the US army formed 90 divisions. General George C. Marshall remained the Chief of Staff of the US army throughout the war.

Of the USAAF's 16 air forces, seven served in the Pacific and the China–Burma–India theaters. In September 1939 the USAAF had 2,470 aircraft; at its peak in July 1944, 79,908. The USA's strength was its capacity to construct aircraft – almost 300,000 during the war – and its ability to improve aircraft designs each year. Although the USAAF was theoretically part of the army, it acted as an independent service and its chief, General Hap Arnold, was one of the four members of the US Joint Chiefs of Staff.

While the US army and USAAF were divided between Europe and the Pacific, the US navy deployed the majority of its strength in the Pacific. Like the other services, it too underwent a huge expansion. In July 1940 its

Mass-produced Liberty ships under construction in an American shipyard. In 1940 Britain ordered 60 simply designed ships, described as being 'built by the mile and chopped off by the yard'. The following year the USA ordered 200 of these 7,126-ton, 11-knot ships. A total of 27,103 were constructed in the USA during the war. (US National Archives)

strength was 160,997; by August 1945 it was 4.5 million. In December 1941 the Pacific Fleet, based at Pearl Harbor, included nine battleships, three carriers, 21 heavy and light cruisers, 67 destroyers, and 27 submarines. The Asiatic Fleet, based at Manila, had three cruisers, 13 destroyers, 29 submarines, two seaplane tenders, and 16 gunboats. The total force was inferior to the Japanese navy and this disparity was increased by the loss of battleships at Pearl Harbor.

However, the USA's immense shipbuilding program, begun in the late 1930s and 1940, soon changed the balance. During the war the USA constructed 88,000 landing craft, 215 submarines, 147 carriers, and 952 other warships. The aircraft carriers included large, fast-strike carriers transporting up to 90 aircraft, and numerous, smaller, escort carriers with 16 to 36 aircraft. The US navy included a strong air force (it grew from 11,000 in 1940 to 430,000 in 1945) and the US Marine Corps, which deployed six divisions, all in the Pacific. Admiral Ernest King was appointed Commander-in-Chief of the US fleet in March 1942 and remained in command throughout the war.

The British Empire

By December 1941 Britain had been at war for more than two years. Its army had been forced to evacuate France in 1940 and had fought a series of debilitating campaigns in the Middle East. Its air force had defended Britain from air attacks, which were still continuing. The Royal Navy was fighting the battle of the Atlantic against German U-boats and was supporting Britain's forces in the Mediterranean. Few military resources could be spared for the Far East. The imperial troops in Malaya included two Indian divisions and an understrength Australian division, while most of the aircraft there were inferior to those of the Japanese. There were few major naval units and no aircraft carriers.

British forces in south-east Asia were always afforded a low priority for men and equipment, and operations would have been

impossible without the assistance of forces raised in India. Of the 1 million troops that later served in South-East Asia Command (formed in August 1943), 700,000 were Indian, 100,000 were British, and about 90,000 came from British colonies in west and east Africa. The equivalent of about 17 Indian divisions served outside India during the war; of these, two served in Malaya and 11 in Burma.

Britain provided a larger proportion of the air forces. In December 1943, for example, Air Command South-East Asia had an effective strength of 67 squadrons. Of these, 44 were from the Royal Air Force, 19 from the USAAF, two from the Royal Indian Air Force, one from the Royal Canadian Air Force, and one from the Royal Netherlands Air Force.

The British Eastern Fleet operated in the Indian Ocean but was not a strong force until 1944. In November 1943 it had one battleship, one escort carrier, seven cruisers, two armed merchant cruisers, 11 destroyers, 13 escort vessels, and six submarines. In

Indian artillery troops training in Malaya in 1941. In 1939 the Indian army included about 200,000 Indian soldiers, a further 83,000 from the princely states, and 63,000 British troops. The Indian army expanded rapidly and by the end of the war numbered 2.5 million – all volunteers. The Indian units were mostly staffed with British officers, and Indian brigades usually included a British battalion. (Imperial War Museum, London, print from MARS, Lincs)

1945 the British Pacific Fleet was formed to operate with the Americans in the Pacific. With two battleships, four carriers, five cruisers, and 14 destroyers it was the largest and most powerful British fleet of the war.

Australia and New Zealand

Before the war Australia had a minuscule regular army with about 80,000 part-time volunteers in the militia. The air force was also very small with about 160 mostly obsolete aircraft. Only the navy, with six cruisers, five old destroyers, and two sloops, was even close to being ready for battle. The army and air force expanded through voluntary enlistment and, with navy units, they operated with British forces in the Middle East and Europe. After the outbreak of war in the Pacific, most of these units returned to Australia, where they became part of the South-West Pacific Area under General MacArthur.

By mid-1942 Australia had 11 divisions in Australia, and during 1942 and 1943 Australia provided the majority of the Allied land forces in the South-West Pacific Area. At its largest, the army numbered 500,000 from a population of 7 million, and six divisions served on operations in the south-western Pacific. The army was divided between the volunteers of the Australian Imperial Force, who could serve in any area, and the militia, which included conscripts and could serve only in Australia and its territories. The air force, with more than 50 squadrons, flying both American and Australian-built British aircraft, provided a useful supplement to the Allied air forces, although Australia also maintained a large contribution to the Allied strategic bombing campaign in Europe. The navy formed a strong squadron with the Allied naval forces, but had no carriers. Considering its limited population and industrial base, Australia made a substantial contribution to the Pacific War.

New Zealand made a much smaller contribution, preferring to leave its largest expeditionary division in Europe. A small New Zealand division, along with air and naval units, fought in the Solomon Islands.

China

The Chinese armed forces were divided between those under the control of the Nationalist government, those organized by the Communist Party, and those under various warlords. The Nationalist army expanded from a force of about 1.2 million in 1937 to one of 5.7 million in August 1945, organized into 300 divisions. It was composed of conscripts, who were usually treated badly. Poorly equipped and inadequately trained, the Chinese divisions had generally a low level of capability. Several Chinese divisions fought under American command in Burma, where they performed creditably. The Chinese air force was organized and flown by American volunteers. The main Communist army expanded from about 92,000 in 1937 to 910,000 in 1945. It concentrated on guerrilla warfare and on establishing good relations with peasant communities.

Conclusion

Japan, the USA, China, and India each deployed armies of more than 1 million soldiers. In addition, the Soviet Union could also deploy millions of troops. But with a few exceptions, these forces were never engaged in intense, large-scale land operations for long periods. The geographic spread of operations across the maritime areas of the Pacific meant that air and naval forces played a major role. It was here that the industrial strength of the USA gave the Allies a significant advantage. Indeed by the end of the war, the US navy in the Pacific was the largest in history. Once the Allies could apply their naval and air strength to the fullest extent, their final victory was inevitable.

The slide toward inevitable war

Internal Japanese politics played a crucial role in shaping the events that led to war in December 1941. The most fanatical member of the government was the Foreign Minister, Matsuoka, who, after Germany attacked Russia, wanted Japan also to attack Russia. He could not persuade his colleagues and on 2 July 1941 they decided to seize bases in southern Indo-China. On 16 July the Japanese Prime Minister, Konoye, dropped Matsuoka from the Cabinet, but the Cabinet could still not agree over the extent to which it should pursue negotiations with the Americans. The War Minister, General Tojo Hideki, was pessimistic about the outcome of negotiations and was adamant that Japan had to go to war before the end of the year, when tropical monsoons would make operations difficult. Konoye wanted to negotiate for as long as possible. All agreed, however, that Japan could not withdraw from China.

These tensions partly explain the different diplomatic signals emanating from Tokyo during the following months. But the American and British governments were reluctant to take the Japanese overtures at face value. In an amazing feat of ingenuity and persistence US naval cryptanalysts had broken the Japanese diplomatic ciphers and the resulting intelligence, known as Magic, gave the Americans clear insight into Japanese intentions. Japan's decision on 2 July to strike south was known within a few days in Washington, London, and Canberra.

President Roosevelt also learned from Magic that the Japanese planned to continue diplomatic efforts while they secretly prepared for a military offensive. He was therefore well prepared when on 24 July the Japanese moved into southern Indo-China. Two days later the USA, in agreement with the British and the Dutch, froze Japanese assets and applied a further embargo that reduced trade with Japan by three-quarters. That same day General Douglas MacArthur, a retired American officer commanding the Philippines Army, was recalled to the colors and appointed commander of the US army in the Far East. On 1 August, Roosevelt ordered an embargo on high-octane gasoline and crude oil exports.

These embargoes had a devastating effect on the Japanese economy. In June 1941 a joint army–navy investigating committee concluded that Japan would run out of oil in mid-1944. Neither the Japanese government nor the Japanese people were willing to accept the massive loss of face that would have resulted from withdrawing from Indo-China and ultimately from China. There was no alternative but to seize the resources they needed from Malaya and the Dutch East Indies. The Japanese navy's planners also knew that the USA would not remain neutral, and that with its forces in the Philippines the USA would strike at the flanks of the Japanese invasion fleets.

The Japanese armed forces had been preparing for war with the USA from the beginning of the year. The Commander-in-Chief of the Japanese Fleet, Admiral Yamamoto Isoruku, had served in the USA for several years and knew the power of the American industrial base. He was opposed to war, but became convinced that Japan's only hope was to destroy the US Pacific Fleet with a daring pre-emptive strike at its base at Pearl Harbor, Hawaii. The plan was approved and the Japanese navy secretly began training its pilots to undertake low-level torpedo attacks against ships in a remote bay similar to that at Pearl Harbor. Yamamoto finally selected the date for the attack – the morning of Sunday 7 December – when most of the US fleet, including its aircraft carriers, were usually in port for the weekend.

Admiral Yamamoto Isoruku, Commander-in-Chief of the Japanese navy's Combined Fleet, had served in the USA for several years and knew the power of the American industrial base. In September 1940 he told Prime Minister Konoye: 'If we are ordered to [go to war with the USA] then I can guarantee to put up a tough fight for the first six months but I have absolutely no confidence about what would happen if it went on for two or three years.' (US National Archives)

On 6 September the Japanese Cabinet met with Emperor Hirohito and decided to continue negotiations, while preparing to go to war if the negotiations were not successful by 10 October. When 10 October passed without progress in the negotiations, the War Minister, Tojo, indicated that he had lost confidence in Konoye, who then resigned. On 17 October Tojo became Prime Minister, while retaining his post as War Minister. Tojo was determined to establish Japanese primacy in the Far East, to defeat the Western nations that had colonies in the Far East, to incorporate China into Japan, and to establish the East Asia Co-prosperity Sphere in the countries of south-east Asia.

On 2 November Tojo appeared before the Emperor and argued that Japan had to seize the moment. Three days later the Japanese government issued war orders and gave its diplomats until 25 November to solve the problem. On 7 November the USA deciphered Japanese diplomatic messages that showed that 25 November was a key date. Meanwhile, Japan offered not to seize any of the oil-producing islands if the USA agreed not to interfere in China. Aware that Japan had already set a course for war, on 26 November the US Secretary of State, Cordell Hull, restated the USA's conditions – that Japan withdraw from both Indo-China and China, accept the legitimacy of Chiang Kai-shek's government, and, in effect, withdraw from the Tripartite Pact with Germany and Italy.

Already Japanese forces were on the move. On 17 November the ships that were to attack Pearl Harbor left their ports and began gathering at an anchorage in the remote northern Kurile Islands. On 26 November Yamamoto sent Vice-Admiral Nagumo Chuichi, commander of the carrier strike force, a coded message: 'Climb Mount Niitaka.' It was the order to set sail for war. Nagumo's force included six of Japan's best aircraft carriers, two battleships, two cruisers, a destroyer screen and eight support ships. Once they left the Kuriles they were to apply strict radio silence and to sail through the far northern Pacific Ocean, well away from shipping lanes.

The Allies had no knowledge of the carrier force's progress, but the Japanese could not keep their other war preparations secret. On 26 November Roosevelt was given intelligence that a large Japanese convoy carrying 50,000 troops was at sea south of Formosa. Next day Admiral Harold Stark, chief of US naval operations, sent a 'war warning' to Admirals Husband Kimmel and Thomas Hart of the Pacific and Asiatic fleets at Pearl Harbor and Manila. The message said that negotiations with Japan had ceased and that an 'aggressive move' by Japan was 'expected within the next few days.' Indications were that the Japanese might launch amphibious attacks against the Philippines, Thailand, Malaya, or possibly Borneo.

Although the Japanese intended to strike without warning, they still played out the diplomatic charade of presenting the USA with an ultimatum to rectify a list of grievances. This diplomatic note was to be presented to the US Secretary of State at 1.00 pm on Sunday 7 December. As soon as the 14-part message was transmitted from Tokyo to Japan's Washington Embassy, it was deciphered by the Americans and on Sunday morning it was passed to Roosevelt, who remarked, 'This means war.' The Japanese Embassy failed to decipher and translate the cable as quickly as the Americans and the Japanese diplomats were not able to present the note formally to Cordell Hull until 2.30 pm. By then both Roosevelt and Hull knew that Hawaii had been under air attack for more than an hour. Japanese surprise had been complete.

The attack on Pearl Harbor

Before dawn on 7 December the Japanese fleet was 275 miles (440km) north of Hawaii, while five midget submarines were already

approaching Pearl Harbor. At 6.00 am the Japanese aircraft began to take off from the pitching decks of the aircraft carriers, and led by the veteran aviator Commander Fuchida Mitsuo, 183 planes gathered in formation: 49 Val bombers carrying armour-piercing bombs, 40 Kates with the deadly Long Lance torpedoes, and 43 Zero fighters to provide protection and to attack surface targets. As the Japanese aircraft made their way through the hills of northern Oahu, the air base and port lay unprepared on a sleepy Sunday morning. At anchor was almost the entire US Pacific Fleet. All that was missing were the two carriers, at sea with their escorts, including most of the heavy cruisers. At about 7.55 am the Japanese dive-bombers struck, followed 45 minutes later by a further 176 aircraft.

For the loss of 29 aircraft the Japanese sunk six battleships and damaged two. Three destroyers, three light cruisers, and four other vessels were also sunk or damaged. On

At 6.00 am on 7 December, Japanese planes began to take off from six carriers sailing about 275 miles (440km) north of Hawaii. (US National Archives)

The battleship *Arizona* in its anchorage in Pearl Harbor after the Japanese attack on 7 December 1941. An explosion in the forward magazine killed 1,103 crewmen, most being trapped below decks. The destruction of the American battleships forced the US navy to rely on its carriers. (US National Archives)

the airfields 164 aircraft were destroyed and another 128 damaged. Altogether, 2,403 servicemen and civilians were killed.

It was a tactical victory, but not the strategic victory for which the Japanese had hoped. In due course, all but three ships were repaired and returned to service. And the Japanese failed to destroy the US navy's extensive oil storage facilities, with a reserve of 4.5 million barrels. Had the oil and other essential dockyard facilities been destroyed, the US navy would have been forced to retreat to the West Coast. Further, while eight battleships had been put out of action, the carriers and heavy cruisers had escaped damage. Vice-Admiral Nagumo might well have ordered another attack later in the day. But he went for safety first and headed for home, loath to remain near to Hawaii, where

he might come under attack from the American carriers. The chance to inflict a crushing blow was lost.

Although the Japanese attack failed to cripple the US Pacific Fleet, it was a tremendous blow to American military pride. Admiral Kimmel was struck on the chest by a spent bullet while watching the attack from his office. 'It would have been merciful had it killed me,' he admitted to a fellow officer. Kimmel and Lieutenant-General Walter Short, commanding the US army on Hawaii, were relieved of their commands. Over the next four years there were seven investigations to discover why the Americans had been caught by surprise.

After the war a joint Congress investigation revealed that the USA had broken some of the Japanese codes and that information was available that might have indicated that the Japanese were going to attack Pearl Harbor. Blame was not apportioned to any individuals, but Kimmel and Short believed that they had been made scapegoats for the errors of others.

On 8 December 1941 the US President, Franklin Roosevelt, asked Congress to declare war. His opening words were memorable: 'Yesterday, December 7 1941 – a date which will live in infamy – the United States of America was suddenly and deliberately attacked.' The surprise attack thus ensured that the USA would not rest until it had crushed Japan. (US National Archives)

In the ensuing years, some historians suggested that Roosevelt either deliberately provoked the Japanese or at least knew that they were going to attack Pearl Harbor, and did nothing, thereby ensuring that the USA entered the war without firing the first shot. Historians have not generally accepted this view. One of the most perceptive analysts, Roberta Wohlstetter, wrote in 1962: 'We failed to anticipate Pearl Harbor not for want of the relevant materials but because of a plethora of irrelevant ones.'

The conspiracy theory would not die, fueled by further revelations about the success of the Allied code-breakers. But Rear-Admiral Edwin Layton, chief intelligence officer at Pearl Harbor throughout the war, argued in 1985 that the intelligence débâcle was caused by intra- and inter-service squabbles in Washington. By the evening of 6 December the leaders in Washington knew that Japan would launch into war in a matter of hours rather than days, but there was no evidence that anyone suspected that Pearl Harbor would be a target.

Several authors have claimed that British intelligence broke the Japanese fleet code, used by Yamamoto to signal instructions to Nagumo, and that the British Prime Minister, Winston Churchill, failed to pass the information on to Roosevelt, ensuring that the USA entered the war and thus saving Britain from defeat. There is no evidence to prove this theory.

Malaya and the Philippines

While the Pearl Harbor attack was a tremendous surprise, elsewhere there was clear warning of Japanese intentions, even though the exact destination of their invasion convoys could not be determined. Soon after midnight on 7–8 December, but because of the time difference several hours before the attack on Pearl Harbor, a Japanese invasion fleet began bombarding Kota Bharu in northern Malaya. During the morning, troops began landing there and at other locations along the Thai and Malayan coast.

The Japanese knew that they would have to deal with the 35 US B-17 bombers at Clark Field in the Philippines, but fog on Formosa prevented their aircraft from taking off before dawn to attack Clark. General MacArthur had been advised of the attack on Pearl Harbor, but failed to act decisively. When the main Japanese attack force reached Clark soon after midday, it caught most of the American aircraft on the ground. In a disaster to rival that at Pearl Harbor, the Americans lost half of their B-17 fleet and 86 other aircraft.

In less than 14 hours the Japanese had attacked Malaya, Hawaii, Thailand, the Philippines, Guam Island, Hong Kong, and Wake Island, and in that order. The speculations of diplomats and military staffs about Japanese intentions had ended.

The course of the Pacific War

Between December 1941 and March 1942 Japanese forces conducted one of history's most successful series of military campaigns. Perhaps the most remarkable campaign took place in Malaya. It began on 8 December with the landing in north-east Malaya of troops from the Japanese Twenty-Fifth Army, under Lieutenant-General Yamashita Tomoyuki. Yamashita's force of 60,000 men was opposed by 88,000 British, Australian, Indian, and Malayan troops under Lieutenant-General Arthur Percival, but the Japanese naval and land-based aircraft completely outnumbered and outclassed the British air force. On 10 December the British suffered a devastating blow when Japanese aircraft sank the battleship *Prince of Wales* and the battle cruiser *Repulse* in the South China Sea.

Advancing more than 600 miles (1,000km), by 31 January 1942 the Japanese had driven the Commonwealth forces back

to Singapore. Although they had suffered heavily, the Commonwealth forces had, however, been reinforced and now numbered 85,000. Yamashita attacked with 35,000 troops, crossing the Johore Strait on the night of 7/8 February. On 15 February Percival surrendered his force. Described by Winston Churchill as the 'worst disaster in British military history,' the fall of Singapore shattered British prestige in the Far East.

Elsewhere, the Japanese were conducting similar campaigns. During the second week of December they landed in the Philippines, with the main landing on 22 December 1941

General Percival (right), accompanied by a Japanese officer, makes his way to meet General Yamashita to surrender his forces at Singapore on 15 February 1942. More than 130,000 Commonwealth troops became prisoners of war during the campaign. Yamashita's casualties numbered about 5,000. (Imperial War Museum, London, print from MARS, Lincs)

The conquest of Malaya, December 1941–February 1942

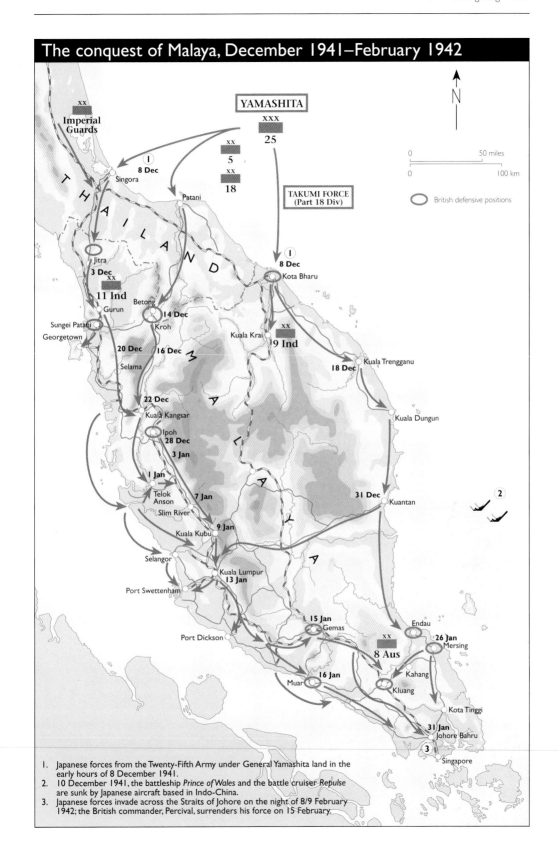

YAMASHITA

xxx
25

xx
5

xx
18

Imperial Guards

TAKUMI FORCE (Part 18 Div)

British defensive positions

0   50 miles
0   100 km

THAILAND

Singora
8 Dec
Patani

Jitra
3 Dec
xx
11 Ind
Gurun
Betong
14 Dec
Kroh
Sungei Patani
Georgetown
20 Dec
16 Dec
Selama
22 Dec
Kuala Kangsar
Ipoh
28 Dec
3 Jan
1 Jan
Telok Anson
7 Jan
Slim River
9 Jan
Kuala Kubu
Selangor
Kuala Lumpur
13 Jan
Port Swettenham
Port Dickson
Muar
16 Jan

8 Dec
Kota Bharu

Kuala Krai
xx
9 Ind
18 Dec
Kuala Trengganu
Kuala Dungun
31 Dec
Kuantan

15 Jan
Gemas
xx
8 Aus
Kahang
Kluang

Endau
26 Jan
Mersing

Kota Tinggi
31 Jan
Johore Bahru
Singapore

1. Japanese forces from the Twenty-Fifth Army under General Yamashita land in the early hours of 8 December 1941.
2. 10 December 1941, the battleship *Prince of Wales* and the battle cruiser *Repulse* are sunk by Japanese aircraft based in Indo-China.
3. Japanese forces invade across the Straits of Johore on the night of 8/9 February 1942; the British commander, Percival, surrenders his force on 15 February.

248 The Second World War

by Lieutenant-General Homma Masaharu's Fourteenth Army, at Lingayen Gulf on Luzon. Realizing that his American and Filipino troops were no match for the Japanese, General MacArthur declared Manila an open city and withdrew into the Bataan peninsula, with his headquarters on Corregidor Island in Manila Bay. The Japanese occupied Manila on 2 January 1942. The troops on the Bataan peninsula resisted stoutly but were short of food and ammunition. On orders from President Roosevelt, on 12 March MacArthur left Corregidor by PT boat and, after transferring to an aircraft at Mindanao, continued to Australia. The force on Bataan surrendered on 9 April, and MacArthur's successor, Lieutenant-General Jonathan Wainwright, surrendered on Corregidor on 6 May.

The Japanese attacked Hong Kong on 8 December 1941. The garrison of 4,400 troops, including 800 Canadians, continued the resistance until Christmas Day. Also on 8 December, Japanese planes bombed the US Pacific base at Wake Island. Shore batteries and US Marine fighter aircraft drove off an invasion force, but on 23 December a larger Japanese force overwhelmed the defenders.

With victory in sight in Malaya and the Philippines, the Japanese turned their attention to the Netherlands East Indies. To coordinate their defenses, on 15 January 1942 the Allies established ABDA (American–British–Dutch–Australian) Command with its headquarters on Java. Its commander, General Sir Archibald Wavell, was responsible for the defense of the area from Burma, through Singapore, to the East Indies and northern Australia, but his forces were not large enough and Allied coordination was poor.

Japanese forces seized Tarakan, off Borneo, on 11 January, crushed the Australian garrison at Rabaul in New Britain on 23 January, landed at Balikpapan, Borneo, on the same day, and reached the Celebes on 24 January. The Japanese struck at Ambon on 31 January, and in three days captured the Dutch and Australian garrison. On 14 February Japanese

paratroops landed on Sumatra, where they were joined by seaborne troops. Japanese air attacks on the Australian port of Darwin on 19 February provided protection for their invasion of West (Dutch) and East (Portuguese) Timor the following day.

On 27 February in the Java Sea, five American, British, Dutch, and Australian cruisers with nine destroyers, all under Dutch Rear-Admiral Karel Doorman, tried unsuccessfully to intercept the Japanese invasion fleet bound for Java. In the first fleet action of the Pacific War, the Allies lost two cruisers and three destroyers, and Doorman was killed. Next night the surviving cruisers, the Australian *Perth* and the USS *Houston*, engaged another Japanese invasion fleet in the Sunda Strait. They sank two ships before they too were sunk. The way was now clear for the Japanese invasion. The ABDA forces in Java formally surrendered on 12 March, although Wavell and other senior officers had been evacuated earlier. It was the end of ABDA Command.

The Japanese landed in southern Thailand on 8 December to facilitate their Malayan campaign. Next day, the Thai Prime Minister ordered his forces to cease resistance and Thailand declared war on Britain and the USA the following month. In mid-January the Japanese Fifteenth Army in Thailand crossed into Burma. The British had two divisions (one Burmese and the other Indian), but they could not prevent the Japanese taking Rangoon on 7 March. Fearful that the Burma Road – its supply lifeline – was being cut, China sent forces into Burma, but the Japanese were superior. They separated the Chinese and British forces, and by 20 May had driven the British out of Burma and back to India. Meanwhile, to strengthen their hold over their western flank, Admiral Nagumo's carrier fleet, which had attacked both Pearl Harbor and Darwin, entered the Indian Ocean and struck the British base at Colombo. Two British cruisers and several other ships, including a carrier, were sunk between 5 and 9 April.

Japan's rapid success caught their planners unprepared. On 5 January 1942, when it looked as they though would achieve all their targets by the middle of March, the Chief of Staff of the Japanese Combined Fleet wrote in his diary: 'Where shall we go from there? Shall we advance into Australia, attack Hawaii; or shall we prepare for the possibility of a Soviet sortie and knock them out if an opportunity arises?' For two months Imperial General Headquarters debated these questions.

The Japanese army resisted the navy's plan to invade Australia, as it could not spare the necessary 10 or perhaps 12 divisions from China or Manchuria. If the Red Army collapsed before the German blitzkrieg, Japan might launch an invasion of Siberia. Even more crucially, a major assault on Australia would require 1.5–2 million tons of shipping; most of this shipping was required to transport the newly won raw materials from south-east Asia to Japan. Instead, the army preferred an offensive in Burma and India.

The navy was not unanimous about the need to invade Australia. Admiral Yamamoto wanted to attack Midway, in the central Pacific, to draw the US Pacific Fleet into battle. A compromise was reached: the invasions of Australia and India were put aside and on 15 March it was agreed to capture Port Moresby and the southern Solomons, and 'to isolate Australia' by seizing Fiji, Samoa, and New Caledonia. The Japanese planned to form a defensive ring around their Greater East Asia Co-prosperity Sphere; if Australia could be isolated, it would no longer be a base for an American counteroffensive.

Coral Sea and Midway

In the midst of the Japanese offensive, the Allies struggled to reshape their Pacific strategy. Global strategy was to be determined by the Combined Chiefs of Staff, consisting of the American and British Chiefs of Staff. Priority was given to the war with Germany. The Pacific War was left in the hands of the US Joint Chiefs of Staff. The key figure was the newly appointed Commander-in-Chief of the US navy, Admiral Ernest King, who, despite the focus on Germany,

ABOVE Admiral Chester Nimitz (left), Commander-in-Chief of the US Pacific Fleet and the Pacific Ocean Area. After Pearl Harbor, Roosevelt told Nimitz to 'get the hell out to Hawaii and don't come back until the war is won.' Easygoing and affable, he could be tough when necessary, was willing to take risks and was an outstanding strategist. (US National Archives)

FOLLOWING PAGES Map
1. 7 December 1941, Japanese carrier-borne aircraft attack Pearl Harbor
2. 8 December 1941, Japan invades Malaya; 15 February 1942, Singapore surrenders
3. 8–25 December 1941, invasion of Hong Kong
4. 10 December 1941, Japanese invade Philippines; surrendered 6 May 1942
5. 24 December 1941, Wake Island captured by Japanese
6. 11 January 1942–8 March 1942, invasion of Dutch East Indies
7. 19 January–15 May 1942, invasion of Burma
8. 23 January–6 August 1942, invasion of New Britain, Solomons, New Guinea, and part of Papua
9. 19 February 1942, Japanese carrier-borne and land-based aircraft attack Darwin
10. 5 April 1942, Japanese carrier-borne aircraft attack Colombo
11. 4–8 May 1942, Battle of the Coral Sea
12. 31 May–1 June 1942, Japanese submarines attack Sydney Harbour
13. 3–6 June 1942, Battle of Midway
14. 6–7 June 1942, Japanese land in Aleutian Islands

Japan's conquests December 1941–August 1942

USSR

MONGOLIA

Manchuria
(Manchukuo)

Jehol

Mukden

Peking

CHINA

Port
Arthur

KOREA

Seoul

Tsingtao

Hok

Honshu

Nanking

Tokyo

JAPA

Shanghai

Shikoku
Kyushu

TIBET

Yangtze

Chungking

Okinawa

Iwo Jima

NEPAL

Delhi

Burma
Road

Ganges

Kunming

Canton

Formosa
(Taiwan)

xxx
14

Calcutta

INDIA

BURMA

Hanoi

Haiphong

Hong Kong

3

Bombay

BAY
OF
BENGAL

Rangoon

THAILAND

FRENCH
INDO-CHINA

Hainan

4

Luzon

Marian
Islands

Saipa

Bangkok

xxx
15

xxx

xxx
16

Manila

PHILIPPINES

Guam (US)

Madras

25

Saigon

Colombo

Ceylon

10

North
Borneo

Mindanao

Palau Is

2

MALAYA

Singapore

Sarawak

Equator

Sumatra

Borneo

6

Celebes

NEW
GUINEA

Batavia

DUTCH EAST INDIES

Ambon

PAPU

Java

Mo

INDIAN
OCEAN

Timor

9

Cocos Islands

Darwin

AUSTRALIA

Perth

Adelaide

Melb

Controlled by Japan, 7 December 1941

Controlled by Japan, 6 August 1942

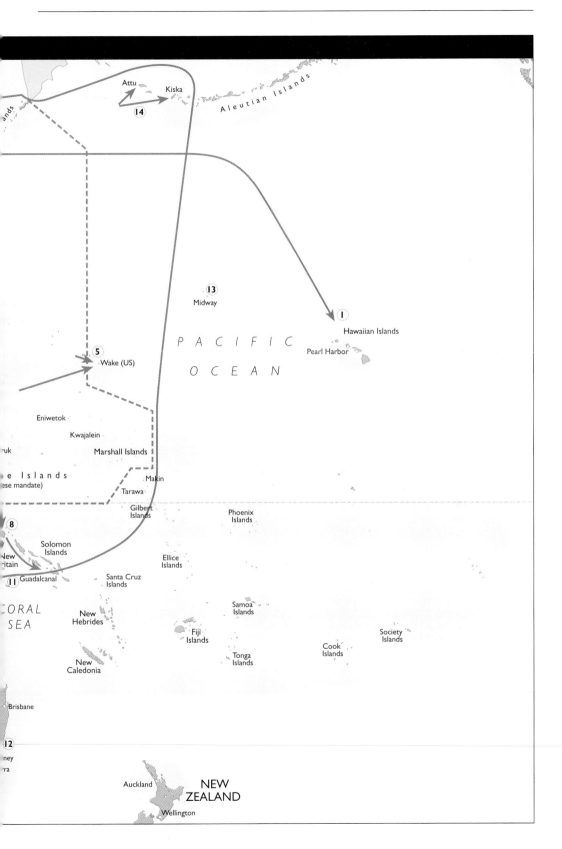

Attu   Kiska

Aleutian Islands

(14)

(13)
Midway

(1)
Hawaiian Islands

Pearl Harbor

P A C I F I C

O C E A N

(5)
Wake (US)

Eniwetok

Kwajalein

ruk

Marshall Islands

e Islands
ese mandate)

Makin

Tarawa

Gilbert
Islands

Phoenix
Islands

(8)

Solomon
Islands

New
ritain

Ellice
Islands

(11) Guadalcanal

Santa Cruz
Islands

Samoa
Islands

ORAL
SEA

New
Hebrides

Fiji
Islands

Society
Islands

Cook
Islands

Tonga
Islands

New
Caledonia

Brisbane

(12)
ney
ra

Auckland

NEW
ZEALAND

Wellington

ABOVE The crew of the USS carrier, *Lexington*, abandon ship while a destroyer maneuvers along side, during the Battle of the Coral Sea, 8 May 1942. Leaking fuel fumes set off an uncontrollable fire and explosions. After she was abandoned, American destroyers finished her off. Only 216 of her total complement of 2,951 were lost. (US Navy/MARS, Lincs)

was anxious to revitalize Pacific strategy. Admiral Nimitz, with his headquarters at Pearl Harbor, had only three aircraft carriers, but was determined to take the fight to the Japanese as early as possible. General MacArthur became Commander-in-Chief of the South-West Pacific Area, with his headquarters in Melbourne, Australia. His was an Allied command and included all of Australia's combat forces as well as relatively small numbers of American ships, planes, and combat troops.

Nimitz moved quickly and during February and March planes from his carriers raided Japanese bases in the Gilbert and Marshall Islands and Japanese shipping near New Guinea. On 18 April 16 B-25 bombers from the USS *Hornet*, under Colonel James Doolittle, raided Japan. The raid did little

damage, but Admiral Yamamoto now won his argument that he should strike at Midway.

Meanwhile, a Japanese invasion force set sail from Rabaul to seize Port Moresby, on the south coast of New Guinea. Warned by signals intelligence, Allied naval forces, including the carriers *Lexington* and *Yorktown*, rushed to intercept the Japanese in the Coral Sea. On 7 and 8 May, in the first naval battle in which opposing ships never sighted each other, American aircraft sank the small carrier *Shoho* and damaged the large carrier *Shokaku*. The Americans lost the *Lexington*, while the *Yorktown* was damaged.

Although the Japanese had achieved a slight tactical victory, they called off their sea-borne invasion of Port Moresby, awaiting the conclusion of their attack on Midway in early June. Equally importantly, Japanese losses meant that Yamamoto's forces would be reduced for the Midway battle. The absence of one fleet carrier was perhaps critical to the outcome of that battle. The Battle of the Coral Sea gave the Allies vital breathing space in which to build up the force in New Guinea. It was the

end of an unbroken run of successful
Japanese invasions.

The Battle of Midway was the crucial
battle of the Pacific War. When American
code-breakers discovered that Admiral
Nagumo's strike force of four carriers
intended to attack Midway, Nimitz deployed
his limited forces. *Yorktown* limped back to
Pearl Harbor, was quickly repaired in an
outstanding feat of engineering, and joined
the American carrier task force of *Enterprise*
and *Hornet*, under the careful, clear-thinking
Rear-Admiral Raymond Spruance. Not
expecting to encounter American carriers, on
4 June the Japanese were caught off-guard.
By the end of the battle on 7 June, the
Japanese had lost all four fleet carriers, while
Yorktown was damaged and finally sunk by a
Japanese submarine. It was the first decisive

American dive-bombers moving in to attack Japanese
carriers during the Battle of Midway on 4 June 1942.
American torpedo bombers had carried out futile
attacks, losing 35 of 41 aircraft in the first attack. This
exposed the Japanese fleet to US dive-bombers that
soon reduced three carriers to burning wrecks.
(US National Archives)

defeat inflicted on the Japanese and changed
the naval balance in the Pacific.

Japan now postponed its plans to seize
New Caledonia, Fiji, and Samoa; instead, the
capture of Port Moresby became even more
urgent. With the loss of the carriers, an
amphibious operation was no longer
possible, and on 7 June Lieutenant-General
Hyakutake Harukichi in Rabaul was ordered
to plan a land approach over the forbidding
Owen Stanley Ranges to Port Moresby.
Strategically, the tide of war was beginning

to turn, but the Japanese were still capable of mounting a deadly offensive.

Guadalcanal and New Guinea

The US navy's success at Midway encouraged the US Joint Chiefs of Staff in Washington, and on 2 July 1942 they ordered an offensive in the New Guinea–Solomon Islands area to recapture Rabaul. Because of jealousy between the US navy and the US army, the offensive was to be shared. In June the Americans had received reports that the Japanese were building an airstrip on Guadalcanal in the southern Solomon Islands. US naval forces under Vice-Admiral Robert Ghormley were ordered to seize several islands in the southern Solomons,

US Marines on the march to Matanikau, west of Henderson Field on Guadalcanal. The Matanikau battle began toward the end of September and the position was not secured until late October 1942, following a fierce Japanese counterattack. (AKG Berlin)

including Guadalcanal, for which he was allocated the 1st US Marine Division. Once the Marines had landed on Guadalcanal, MacArthur planned to occupy the Buna area on the north coast of Papua, where airstrips would be prepared to support his advance toward Rabaul.

Unfortunately for these plans, the Japanese moved first. Their advance troops landed at Buna on the night of 21 July, to be met by only light resistance. The Japanese South Seas Detachment was now ordered to attack Port Moresby over the mountains. Belatedly, MacArthur began to send reinforcements to New Guinea.

The Japanese were thrown off-balance by the landing of the US Marines at Guadalcanal on 7 August. Not pleased to be pushed off their new airstrip, the Japanese attacked the Americans with aircraft based at Rabaul. Vice-Admiral Jack Fletcher therefore withdrew his three carriers, exposing the remaining forces to the Japanese ships. On the night of 8/9 August, in the Battle of Savo Island, Japanese cruisers sank the Australian cruiser

Canberra and three American cruisers. Following up this victory, the Japanese landed 1,000 men on Guadalcanal, but on 21 August they lost heavily in an attack on the perimeter of Henderson airfield. While the Americans held the airstrip they controlled the surrounding seas by day; but at night the Japanese dominated, bringing in more reinforcements in an attempt to seize the vital airstrip.

In Papua, MacArthur's Australian forces faced a similar challenge. The Japanese offensive began on 26 August with two simultaneous attacks – one on the Kokoda Trail that wound over the Owen Stanley Ranges, and the other a landing by Japanese Marines at Milne Bay on the south-east tip of New Guinea. Fearful for his own position, MacArthur tried to blame the Australians for their allegedly poor fighting ability. But by 6 September two Australian brigades at Milne Bay had defeated the Japanese, forcing them to evacuate. On the Kokoda Trail, however, Australian troops conducted a desperate withdrawal. Eventually the Japanese failed;

the track was much more difficult than expected and they had made insufficient provision for supplies. Importantly, the Guadalcanal campaign caused the Japanese high command in Rabaul to divert resources to that area, and eventually to order a halt to the Owen Stanley offensive.

The fighting on and around Guadalcanal turned into a campaign of attrition. During September and October the Japanese made repeated efforts to recover Henderson airfield. In the Battle of Bloody Ridge 2,000 Japanese attacked in massed waves, and some came within 3,000ft (900m) of the airfield. If they had taken it, they might well have won the campaign. Lieutenant-Colonel Merrit A. Edson, commanding the force defending the ridge, was awarded the Congressional Medal of Honor. The

Australian soldiers of the 39th Battalion on the Kokoda Trail in August 1942. Short of supplies, the Australians conducted a fighting withdrawal in the Owen Stanley Ranges that bought time for reinforcements to arrive and caused the Japanese to exhaust their supplies. (Australian War Memorial)

defenders were supported by Marine aircraft of the 'Cactus Air Force' operating from the airfield, but in October Japanese ships bombarded the airfield, putting it temporarily out of action. As reinforcements arrived, the Marines gradually widened their perimeter, meeting strong resistance from the Japanese on the surrounding hills and in the jungle-filled valleys.

Naval battles continued around Guadalcanal and Fletcher was relieved of his command. One American carrier was sunk and another damaged. On 18 October Vice-Admiral William Halsey relieved Ghormley of command of the campaign. In the Battle of Santa Cruz, the carrier *Hornet* was lost and *Enterprise* was damaged. The naval battle of Guadalcanal began on 12 November and lasted for three days; in

Admiral William (Bull) Halsey assumed command of the Guadalcanal campaign in October 1942 and remained in command of the Solomons campaign until March 1944. He and Admiral Spruance then alternated as commander of the Pacific Fleet's main operational force, known as the Third Fleet when under his command, and the Fifth Fleet when under Spruance. (US National Archives)

the first 24 minutes the Americans lost six ships and the Japanese three, including a battleship. Eventually the odds began to tilt toward the Americans.

In New Guinea the 7th Australian Division advanced back over the Kokoda Trail to the north coast, where it was joined by the US 32nd Division. Exhausted, sick and with little support, the Australians and Americans were confronted by well-constructed Japanese defenses in jungle and swamp. MacArthur unreasonably demanded a swift victory, telling the American corps commander, Lieutenant-General Robert Eichelberger, 'to take Buna, or not come back alive.' By the time the Japanese had been driven into the sea at Sanananda on 22 January 1943, they had suffered more than 13,000 killed. The Australians lost more than 2,000 killed and the Americans more than 600. Almost 20,000 Australian and American troops were sick from malaria.

The Japanese faced a similar outcome on Guadalcanal, but in one of the crucial decisions of the Pacific War their high command decided to move to the strategic defensive and ordered an evacuation. This took place in February. During the campaign the Japanese lost perhaps 24,000 killed, while American fatal casualties numbered some 1,600. The Japanese had lost many of their best trained pilots and their naval air force never recovered from these losses.

The campaigns in New Guinea and Guadalcanal were fought in thick tropical jungles and fetid swamps. Resupply was difficult and in New Guinea the Allies relied on native porters and airdrops. Tropical illnesses were as deadly as the enemy's bullets.

The Japanese made one last offensive thrust, toward Wau in New Guinea, but this was thwarted when an Australian brigade was flown into the area. Seeking to build up their defenses, the Japanese created the Eighteenth Army and planned to reinforce New Guinea. Warned by signals intelligence and reconnaissance aircraft, the commander of the Allied air force in the South-West Pacific Area, the highly capable Lieutenant-General

Japanese shipping under attack by American and Australian aircraft during the Battle of the Bismarck Sea, fought between 2 and 4 March 1943. The Japanese lost eight transports and four destroyers; of almost 7,000 troops on the transports, about half perished. (Australian War Memorial)

George Kenney, ordered the convoy to be intercepted in the Bismarck Sea.

Allied code-breakers also gave warning that Admiral Yamamoto would be visiting Bougainville in the northern Solomons. American P-38 Lightnings from Henderson Field were directed to his destination and on 13 April 1943 they downed his aircraft in flames. It was a further blow to the Japanese, who were already on the defensive in the south-west Pacific. Yamamoto was succeeded by Admiral Koga Mineichi as Commander-in-Chief of the Combined Fleet.

Aleutian Islands campaign

On the night of 6 June 1942 the Japanese landed 1,200 troops on remote Attu Island, at the western end of the Aleutian Islands –
an island chain that projected 1,000 nautical miles from Alaska into the northern Pacific Ocean. Next day a small force took Kiska, another westerly island. The islands were undefended and had few inhabitants. The Japanese operation was partly to prevent the Americans using the islands as a base for an attack on northern Japan, but mainly a diversion for the Midway operation. The Japanese occupations posed little threat, but as the islands were American territory there was public agitation for their recovery.

In response, the US Eleventh Air Force mounted a protracted bombing campaign, while American warships tried to prevent the Japanese from reinforcing their garrisons. These were extremely difficult operations as the islands were often shrouded in fog and rain. In March 1943, in one of the Pacific War's few 'fleet actions' in open seas, American and Japanese cruisers pounded each other, with the Americans lucky to survive. But the Japanese fleet turned back and the Japanese admiral was dismissed from his command.

On 11 May 1943 the US 7th Infantry Division landed on Attu, where it faced fierce opposition, culminating in a suicidal Japanese bayonet charge on 29 May. The USA lost 600 killed; only 28 Japanese were captured and 2,351 bodies were counted.

In a daring operation, on the night of 28/29 July 1943, under cover of fog, the Japanese navy evacuated its garrison of more than 5,000 troops from Kiska. The 34,000 American and Canadian troops who landed there on 15 August took several days to discover that they faced no opposition. For the Japanese, the campaign had been a disastrous waste of men and matériel when they had been under increasing pressure in the south and south-west Pacific.

The advance toward Rabaul

In January 1943 Roosevelt and Churchill met with their senior military advisers at Casablanca, Morocco, to set the strategic direction for the coming year. Although the leaders relegated the Pacific War to fifth on the list of priorities (after the Atlantic, Russia, the Mediterranean, and the United Kingdom), the directive of 2 July 1942 to capture Rabaul remained unchanged. Again the tasks were shared. Forces from the South Pacific Area, under Admiral Halsey, would advance from Guadalcanal toward Rabaul with the intermediate objective of Bougainville in the northern Solomons. Meanwhile, MacArthur's forces would seize the Huon peninsula in New Guinea and the western end of New Britain. The total operation was known as Operation Cartwheel.

Opposing the Allied forces was Lieutenant-General Imamura Hitoshi's Eighth Area Army with its headquarters at Rabaul. Lieutenant-General Hyakutake's Seventeenth Army defended the Solomons and New Britain with three divisions, while Lieutenant-General Adachi Hatazo's Eighteenth Army, also with three divisions, was in New Guinea. The Japanese strength was between 80,000 and 90,000, but they could be reinforced by about 60,000 within three weeks. The Japanese had about

RIGHT Map
Land operations
1. 7 August 1942, Americans land at Guadalcanal; Japanese withdraw on 7 February 1943
2. 25 August–6 September 1942, Japanese landing at Milne Bay is defeated by Australians
3. 26 August–2 November 1942, Japanese advance over the Kokoda Trail to within 97 miles (60 km) of Port Moresby and are then driven back to Kokoda by the Australians
4. 16 November 1942–22 January 1943, US and Australian troops defeat Japanese at Buna, Gona, and Sanananda
5. 28 January–11 September 1943, Japanese attack Wau and are driven back to Salamaua by the Australians
6. 30 June 1943, Americans land on New Georgia
7. 30 June 1943, Americans land at Nassau Bay
8. 15 August 1943, Americans land on Vella Lavella
9. 4 September 1943, Australians land at Lae
10. 5 September 1943, Australians land at Nadzab and later advance up Markham Valley
11. 22 September 1943, Australians land at Finschhafen
12. 1 November 1943, Americans land on Bougainville
13. 15 and 26 December 1943, Americans land on New Britain
14. 15 February 1944, New Zealanders land at Green Island
15. 2 January 1944, Americans land at Saidor
16. 29 February 1944, Americans land on Los Negros
17. 20 March 1944, Americans land at Emirau
18. 22 April 1944, Americans land at Hollandia and Aitape
19. 24 April 1944, Australians enter Madang

Naval battles
A Savo Island, 9 August 1942
   Cape Esperance, 11 October 1942
   Guadalcanal, 12–15 November 1942
   Tassafronga, 30 November 1942
B Eastern Solomons, 24 August 1942
C Santa Cruz Island, 26 October 1942
D Bismarck Sea, 2–4 March 1943
E Kula Gulf, 5–6 July 1943
F Kolombangara, 12–13 July 1943
G Vella Gulf, 6–7 August 1943
H Vella Lavella, 6–7 October 1943
I Empress Augusta Bay, 2 November 1943

320 combat aircraft, while about 270 others could be flown in within 48 hours.

The Cartwheel operation began on 30 June 1943 when Halsey's troops made their main landings on New Georgia and Rendova. The New Georgia landing soon turned into a hard-grinding battle, with three American divisions deployed under Major-General Oswald Griswold. Meanwhile the Japanese dispatched reinforcements from Rabaul, escorted by warships that clashed

Allied operations in New Guinea and the Solomons, August 1942–April 1944

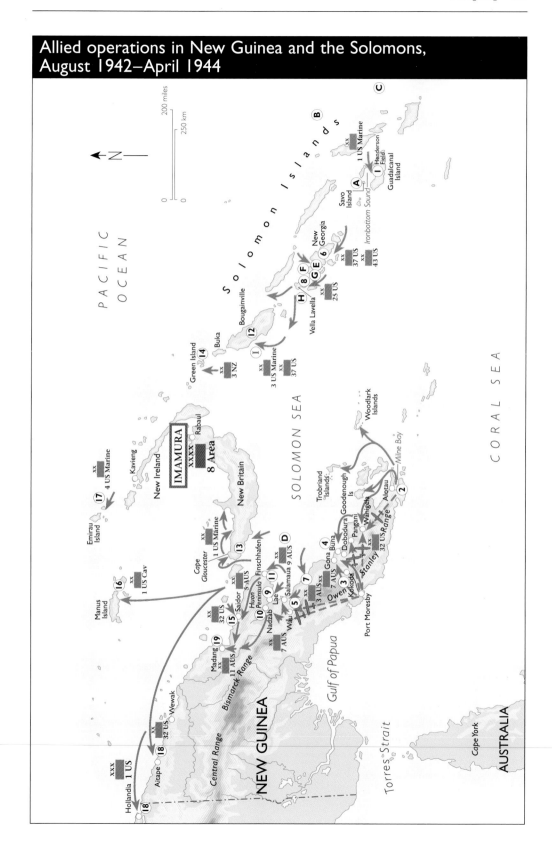

with the US navy. Superior in night fighting, the Japanese navy sank or damaged several American and Australian ships. But in one engagement three Japanese transports were sunk with the loss of perhaps 1,500 men drowned. By mid-September, when the Japanese withdrew from New Georgia, they had lost more than 2,000 killed; American deaths exceeded 1,000. American forces jumped to Vella Lavela, and by October, American and New Zealand troops had landed on several islands near to Bougainville.

On 1 November the 3rd US Marine Division landed at Empress Augusta Bay on the west coast of Bougainville, bypassing a large Japanese concentration at the south of the island. Next morning a US navy task force destroyed a cruiser and a destroyer from the Japanese Eighth Fleet. When a powerful Japanese task force under Vice-Admiral Kurita Takeo appeared at Rabaul, Halsey took a great risk and sent his two-carrier task force within

range of Japanese air power. Supported by Kenney's land-based Fifth Air Force, US naval aircraft caused such damage that Kurita withdrew to Truk. Further Allied air attacks forced the Japanese to withdraw their air and naval units from Rabaul. In March 1944 the American forces resisted a full-scale Japanese counteroffensive on Bougainville. Thereafter there was a virtual truce until the Australians took over from the Americans toward the end of the year.

The fighting in the New Guinea area was marked by fewer naval engagements but larger land operations than in the Solomons. Between March and August 1943, the 3rd Australian Division slogged through jungle-covered hills from Wau toward Salamaua. The Japanese Fourth Air Army rushed additional planes to New Guinea, but, warned by Allied code-breakers, and by deploying aircraft to newly constructed forward airfields, Kenney's Fifth Air Force caught the Japanese planes on the ground at Wewak, with devastating losses.

On 4 September the 9th Australian Division conducted an amphibious landing near Lae, while in the following days the 7th Australian Division landed by air at Nadzab airstrip once it had been secured by

MacArthur's land forces were nominally under the Australian General Sir Thomas Blamey (right), but most American operations were controlled by the commander of the US Sixth Army, Lieutenant-General Walter Krueger (left). Tough and experienced, Blamey commanded New Guinea Force, which consisted of mainly Australian units. (Australian War Memorial)

American paratroops. Salamaua fell on
11 September and Lae on the 15th. After
landing at Finschhafen, the Australians then
continued along the New Guinea coast.
Inland, the 7th Division cleared the Markham
and Ramu valleys, where airfields were
constructed for the Fifth Air Force, and pressed
over the mountain range toward Madang. As
in earlier campaigns, the climate, terrain and
vegetation provided an additional challenge.

American troops began landing on the
southern coast of New Britain on
15 December, with the main landing by the
1st US Marine Division at Cape Gloucester on
26 December, where, after hard fighting, they
established a perimeter. On 2 January 1944 the
32nd US Division landed at Saidor on the
New Guinea coast. The Japanese 20th and
51st Divisions escaped, but they had been
roundly defeated. Between March 1943 and
April 1944 the Australians, under Blamey,
deployed five infantry divisions, losing
about 1,200 killed. Japanese losses numbered
about 35,000.

The completion of the Cartwheel
operation showed that the Americans

Troops of the 9th Australian Division landing at
Finschhafen on the Huon peninsula on 22 September
1943. The Japanese counterattacked strongly and the
Australians did not take their main bastion at Sattelberg
until 25 November. (Australian War Memorial)

and Australians had learned much about
jungle warfare. In Malaya, Burma, the
Philippines, and New Guinea the Japanese
had caught their opponents off-guard.
Lightly equipped and accustomed to hard
living, the Japanese infantry moved quickly
through deep jungle, bypassing static
Allied positions. On the defensive, the
Japanese constructed well-camouflaged
strongpoints and fought with determination
and skill. Their commanders perhaps
lacked imagination in planning and did
not seem to appreciate fully the
effectiveness of massed firepower. As the
Americans began to dominate the seas, the
Japanese defenders (for whom surrender was
not an option) often had little alternative
but to fight to the death.

The Americans had to learn about jungle
warfare in action and at first seemed

bewildered by it. They learned quickly, but fought the war in their own way. As an American divisional historian put it: 'The Yank style of fighting was to wait for the artillery and let the big guns blast the enemy positions as barren of all life as possible. It saved many American lives and got better results although it took longer.' More broadly, the Americans brought to bear the full range of naval and air resources to support their land operations. All of this was backed by a massive logistic effort.

Although many of the Australian units had already fought in the Middle East, they still had to adapt to jungle conditions, and they concentrated especially on patrolling skills. They did not have the same weight of firepower and lavish supplies as the Americans, but were still superior to the Japanese in this regard. The Americans and Australians had far better medical support than the Japanese, especially for coping with tropical diseases such as malaria.

The island-hopping campaigns

Admiral King had always advocated using American naval power to attack the Japanese in the central Pacific, but MacArthur had argued for resources to enable him to advance through New Guinea toward the Philippines. If both approaches could be sustained, then they would throw the Japanese off-balance, but it was not until the latter months of 1943 that the US navy began to gather the strength necessary to prosecute a campaign in the central Pacific. At the time of Pearl Harbor, the US navy had only three carriers in the Pacific; by late 1943 Nimitz had 10 fast large and medium carriers, seven escort carriers, and a dozen battleships. These formed the key elements of the Fifth Fleet under Vice-Admiral Spruance.

Toward the end of 1943 this force began conducting raids on Japanese island bases, and on 20 November 1943 US Marine and army units landed on Tarawa and Makin atolls in the Gilbert Islands. Tarawa was a bitter fight, but Makin was taken relatively

On 20 November 1942 the 2nd Marine Division landed on the heavily defended Tarawa atoll in the Gilbert Islands. In a bitter and bloody five-day battle the Marines lost 1,000 killed and the Japanese their entire garrison of 5,000. (AKG Berlin)

easily. American attention now turned to the Marshall Islands with the US Navy's fast carrier task force raiding the islands in late December 1943 and early January 1944. On 31 January, US Marine and army troops landed on Kwajalein Island. Eniwetok fell on 17 February, six weeks ahead of schedule. Meanwhile, American carriers under Rear-Admiral Marc Mitscher heavily raided the Japanese naval base at Truk.

With the US navy moving faster than expected in the central Pacific, MacArthur

was fearful of being left behind and on 29 February 1944, in a daring 'raid', his forces seized Los Negros in the Admiralty Islands. All ideas of attacking Rabaul were now abandoned; the huge Japanese garrison was to play little further part in the war. Instead, MacArthur directed a series of landings by American troops along the northern New Guinea coast that isolated 40,000 Japanese forces in the Wewak area. His forces took Aitape and Hollandia on 23 April, Wakde on 17 May, Biak on 27 May, Noemfoor on 2 July, and Sansapor on 30 July. In three months he had advanced over 850 miles (1,400km). With no carriers of his own, and receiving limited carrier support from the Central Pacific, MacArthur's forces constructed airfields at each landing to provide land-based air support for the next assault.

While MacArthur was advancing, Nimitz was focusing on the Mariana Islands. The key islands were Saipan, Guam, and Tinian, whose airfields were within bombing range of Japan. Realizing the danger, the Commander-in-Chief of the Japanese Combined Fleet (now Admiral Toyoda Soemu) ordered nine carriers and 450 aircraft to gather for a concerted attack on the Americans. Admiral Spruance commanded the invasion, to be covered by Mitscher's Task Force 58, now with 15 carriers and 1,000 planes. The invasion force included nearly 130,000 troops (only 22,500 fewer than in the opening phase of Operation Overlord at Normandy on 6 June – nine days earlier). The invasion force was carried in 535 ships.

Carrier strikes began on 11 June, with troops of the 5th Amphibious Corps under Marine Lieutenant-General Holland (Howlin' Mad) Smith landing on Saipan on 15 June. Japanese carrier- and land-based aircraft struck the US fleet on 19 June, but were totally outclassed by the American aircraft and their more skillful pilots. In the 'Great Marianas Turkey Shoot', the Japanese lost 400 aircraft, while the USA lost 30. Three Japanese carriers were sunk – two by American submarines. Onshore, the Marine and army troops had a savage battle against 32,000 defenders. The Japanese conducted suicide charges, while Japanese civilians leapt

to their death from high cliffs. It was 9 July before Saipan was secured. Total Japanese deaths numbered 30,000. Meanwhile, US Marine and army troops captured Guam and Tinian. The defeat of the Japanese carrier force and the seizure of the Marianas – Japanese mandated territory since the First World War – were a severe blow to the Japanese high command. On 18 July Tojo resigned as Prime Minister and War Minister. Lieutenant-General Koiso Kuniaki succeeded him as Prime Minister.

Burma

While the operations in the south-west and central Pacific areas dominated the attention of the Americans, the Australians, and the Japanese navy during 1943 and 1944, Japanese army units were heavily engaged in Burma.

By May 1942 the Japanese army had driven the British into India and had pushed

General Sir William Slim was one of the outstanding commanders of the war. He commanded the Burma Corps during the 1942 retreat and the Fourteenth Army in the defensive battles of 1944 and the successful invasion of Burma in 1944–45. (National Army Museum)

several Chinese divisions back to the northern borders. In India the British–Indian Army began a painful process of expansion and retraining. Most of the units came from India with a large proportion of British officers, but eventually the forces that would retake Burma would include many nationalities – Indians, Burmese, Chinese, Gurkhas, black troops from British East and West Africa, as well as British and Americans. As in the south-west Pacific, the campaigns were fought in jungle and in a trying climate, the seasonal monsoons making movement extremely difficult.

The first offensives began in the coastal Arakan area, between October 1942 and May 1943, but the Japanese drove back the British divisions in further morale-shattering defeats. The only success seemed to be that achieved by a brigade of special forces – the Chindits – under the eccentric Brigadier Orde Wingate, inserted into north-central Burma in February 1943. Actual success was slight, but the Chindits' exploits boosted morale.

In October 1943 the Allied South-East Asia Command was formed under Admiral Lord Louis Mountbatten, with its headquarters in Ceylon. Mountbatten's tasks were to increase pressure on the Japanese and thus force them to transfer forces from the Pacific theater, to main the airborne supply route to China, and to open a land supply route through northern Burma. General Sir William Slim, commander of the Fourteenth Army, was to undertake three offensives into Burma: the 15th Corps (Lieutenant-General Philip Christison) would advance in the Arakan; the 4th Corps (Lieutenant-General Geoffrey Scoones) would prepare for an attack into central Burma from Imphal; and Northern Combat Area Command would thrust into northern Burma to open a route into China. This latter force, under the cantankerous American Lieutenant-General Joseph Stilwell, included two Chinese divisions and a brigade of Americans known as Merrill's Marauders; their advance would be supported by the Chindits, now numbering several brigades.

The commander of the Japanese Burma Area Army, Lieutenant-General Kawabe Masakazu, decided to pre-empt this offensive by striking into India. If he gained a foothold for the Indian National Army – a force of Indian troops under Japanese control – he might even precipitate a revolt in India against British rule. The first Japanese offensive began as a diversion in Arakan in February 1944, where the British were also beginning an offensive. In bitter fighting around the 'Admin Box', two Indian divisions defeated the attack and resumed their offensive.

The main Japanese offensive began in March 1944 when the Fifteenth Army with more than three divisions, under Lieutenant-General Mutuguchi Renya, crossed into India heading for Imphal and Kohima. The British 4th Corps was surrounded in the Imphal area and at Kohima. But as the Japanese had now been defeated in Arakan, Slim was able to fly in a division from there. Meanwhile, the defensive positions around Imphal were supplied by a huge effort by American and British transport aircraft. The 33rd Corps under Lieutenant-General Montague Stopford was deployed from India to relieve Kohima. Short of supplies and heavy weapons, the Japanese took dreadful casualties in an effort to break through into India. On 31 May they

FOLLOWING PAGES Map
1. 7 August 1942, US forces land at Guadalcanal
2. September 1942, Australians defeat Japanese at Milne Bay and advance back over Kokoda Trail
3. 30 June 1943, US forces land at New Georgia
4. 30 June–December 1943, US and Australian forces land in New Guinea and New Britain
5. May–August 1943, US and Canadian forces recover Aleutian islands
6. 20 November 1943, US forces invade Tarawa and Makin islands
7. 31 January–17 February 1944, US forces land on Kwajalein and Eniwetok islands
8. 15 March–22 June 1944, Japanese invasion of north-eastern India defeated
9. 22 April–30 July 1944, US forces advance along New Guinea coast from Hollandia to Sansapor
10. April 1944, Japanese begin Ichigo offensive in China
11. 15 June 1944, US forces land at Saipan
12. 21 July 1944, US forces land at Guam
13. 15 September, US forces land in Palau Islands and at Morotai

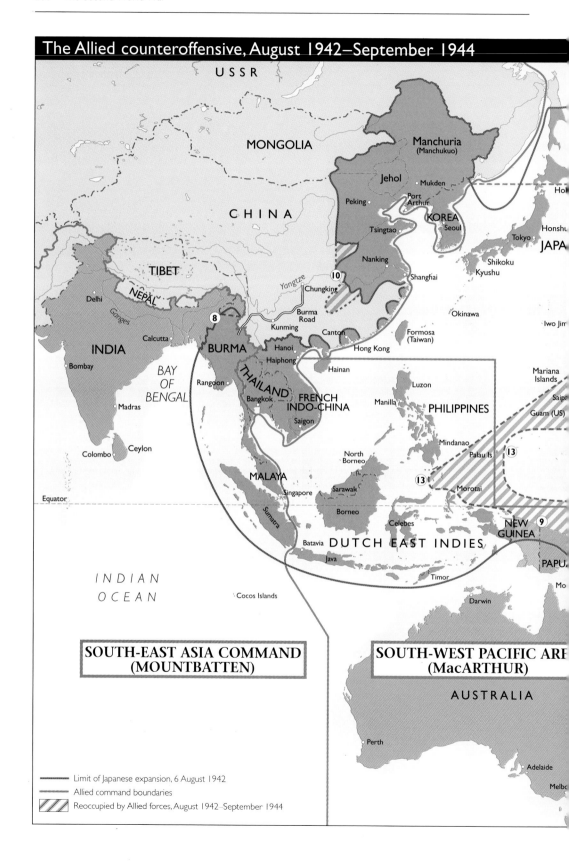

The Allied counteroffensive, August 1942–September 1944

USSR

MONGOLIA

Manchuria
(Manchukuo)

Jehol

Mukden

Port
Arthur

Peking

CHINA

KOREA

Tsingtao

Seoul

Nanking

Shanghai

Okinawa

TIBET

NEPAL

Delhi

Ganges

Yangtze

Chungking

Burma
Road

Kunming

Canton

Formosa
(Taiwan)

Iwo Jim

INDIA

Calcutta

BURMA

Hanoi

Haiphong

Hainan

Hong Kong

Bombay

THAILAND

Rangoon

Bangkok

FRENCH
INDO-CHINA

Saigon

Luzon

Manilla

PHILIPPINES

Mariana
Islands

Saipa

Guam (US)

Madras

BAY
OF
BENGAL

Colombo

Ceylon

Mindanao

Palau Is

North
Borneo

MALAYA

Singapore

Sarawak

Morotai

Borneo

Celebes

NEW
GUINEA

Batavia   DUTCH EAST INDIES

Java

Timor

PAPU

Mo

Equator

INDIAN
OCEAN

Cocos Islands

Darwin

SOUTH-EAST ASIA COMMAND
(MOUNTBATTEN)

SOUTH-WEST PACIFIC ARF
(MacARTHUR)

AUSTRALIA

Perth

Adelaide

Melb

Sumatra

Honshu

Tokyo

JAPA

Shikoku

Kyushu

——— Limit of Japanese expansion, 6 August 1942

———— Allied command boundaries

▨ Reoccupied by Allied forces, August 1942–September 1944

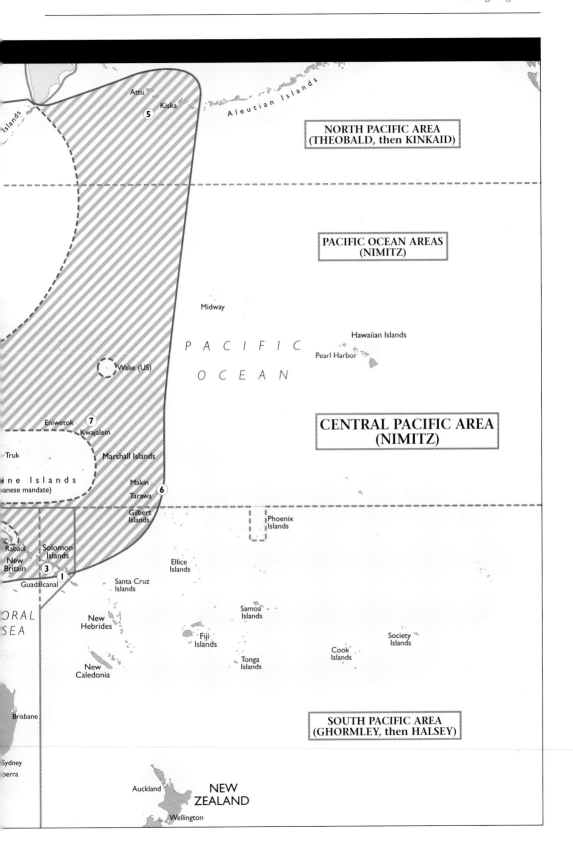

NORTH PACIFIC AREA
(THEOBALD, then KINKAID)

PACIFIC OCEAN AREAS
(NIMITZ)

CENTRAL PACIFIC AREA
(NIMITZ)

SOUTH PACIFIC AREA
(GHORMLEY, then HALSEY)

Attu
Kiska
Aleutian Islands
Islands
(5)

Midway

Hawaiian Islands
Pearl Harbor

P A C I F I C
O C E A N

Wake (US)

Eniwetok (7)
Kwajalein

Truk

ine Islands
anese mandate)

Marshall Islands

Makin
Tarawa (6)

Gilbert
Islands

Phoenix
Islands

Rabaul
New
Britain
Guadalcanal

Solomon
Islands
(3)
(1)

Ellice
Islands

Santa Cruz
Islands

Samoa
Islands

Society
Islands

ORAL
SEA

New
Hebrides

Fiji
Islands

Cook
Islands

Tonga
Islands

New
Caledonia

Brisbane

Sydney
berra

Auckland   NEW
ZEALAND

Wellington

British troops in carriers from the 33rd Corps advancing down the Imphal-Kohima road in June 1944. The 33rd Corps had relieved the besieged garrison at Kohima before opening the road to Imphal. The 4th Corps had fought a grim defensive battle at Imphal. (MARS)

began to withdraw from Kohima and on 18 July Kawabe and Mutugachi agreed that no further offensive operations were possible. It had been a disastrous offensive: of the invading force of 85,000 fighting troops, 53,000 became casualties, 30,000 being killed. The way was clear for Slim to advance into Burma, even though monsoonal rains made movement difficult.

Meanwhile, the Northern Combat Area Command had been advancing south, while the Chindits had been inserted across the Japanese lines of communication. Despite problems with Allied cooperation, on 17 May the Americans took Myitkyina airfield, from which supplies could be flown into China. The Japanese held the town until 3 August. Several Chinese divisions also advanced into Burma from Yunan Province, but these offensives still did not open the way to China until later in the year. Throughout these operations a force of 17,000 engineers had been constructing a road and oil pipeline from Ledo in India to Myitkyina. The land route into China was not complete until January 1945.

China

The war in China was not a simple conflict between Japan and the Allies. The Allies accepted the Nationalist leader, Chiang Kai-shek, as commander-in-chief of the China theater, but the Chinese Communist

Party, under Mao Tse-tung, controlled much of north-west China and conducted extensive and successful guerrilla operations against the Japanese. Semi-autonomous warlords with their own armies ruled several provinces; nominally they were under direction from the Nationalist government at Chungking, but sometimes they cooperated with the Japanese in operations against the communists. In 1938 the Japanese had established a Chinese puppet government, under Wang Ching-wei, with its capital at Nanking. Wang's army of up to 900,000 conducted operations against both the communists and the warlords.

During 1941 and 1942 the Japanese conducted ruthless punishment operations in northern and central China, but by 1943 they were hard-pressed by the communist guerrilla campaign. The Japanese then pursued a pacification policy, hoping that eventually the Wang puppet government might assume control, or that it might conclude an agreement with the Nationalists.

Chiang Kai-shek realized that the Allies were going to win the war and he wanted to preserve his armies for a future war against the Communists. But he needed to give the impression that he was fighting the Japanese in order to maintain the flow of American arms and equipment. Stilwell believed that with adequate training and equipment the Chinese armies could perform well. Influenced by Major-General Claire Chennault, who commanded the American Volunteer Group (the Flying Tigers), Chiang placed his faith in air power.

The American operations in northern Burma were dominated by the desire to open

The Chinese Generalissimo, Chiang Kai-shek, with his wife and his US Chief of Staff, Lieutenant-General 'Vinegar Joe' Stilwell, at Maymo, Burma, in April 1942. Stilwell had a low regard for Chiang, whom he called 'the peanut'. Stilwell also commanded the American forces in Burma. (US National Archives)

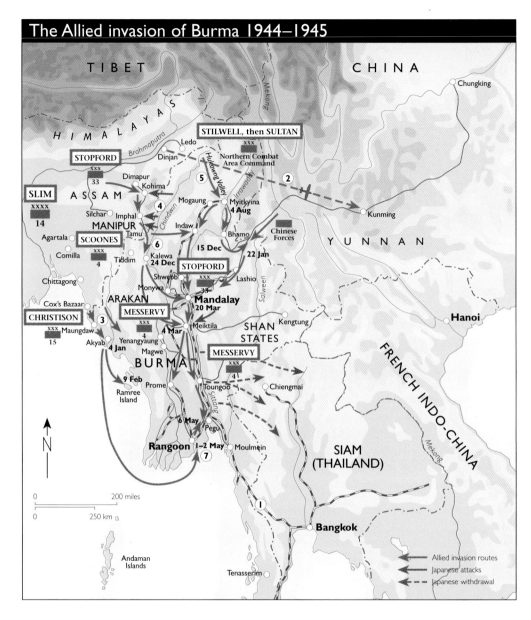

The Allied invasion of Burma 1944–1945

a route to China. This would enable them to build up the Nationalist armies as a viable force, and to use China as a base for air operations against Japanese ships in the South China Sea and even against Japan. Until a land route could be opened, the Nationalists and Chennault's small air force (never more than 200 aircraft) had to be supplied by air. American transport aircraft flew from makeshift airfields in India's north-eastern Assam, 500 miles (800km) over 13,000ft (4,000m) mountains to Kunming in

southern China. Flying 'the hump' at high altitudes in turbulent monsoonal weather was exceptionally dangerous; between July 1942 and the end of the war 600 planes and 1,000 aircrew were lost delivering 650,000 tons of supplies.

In April 1944 the Japanese began a major offensive – the Ichigo offensive, with 620,000 troops – to overrun the Allied airfields in southern China. The warlord and Nationalist armies were no matches for the Japanese, who by December were

LEFT Map
1. Burma–Thailand railroad built by slave labor between July 1942 and October 1943 to resupply Japanese forces in India
2. 'The Hump' – the route flown by US aircraft resupplying China
3. February–March 1944, British 15th Corps advances into Arakan; Japanese counterattack results in battle of Admin Box. British resume offensive in December 1944
4. 15 March 1944, Japanese invade north-eastern India. Kohima is relieved on 18 April and Imphal on 22 June
5. March 1944, Northern Combat Area Command advances from Ledo and secures Myitkyina airfield by 17 May
6. December 1944, Fourteenth Army invades Burma
7. 1 May 1945, paratroops land at Rangoon and seaborne invasion takes place next day

threatening Kunming and Chungking. By this stage the new B-29 Superfortresses that had been conducting raids against southern Japan with limited success had been withdrawn to India. The Japanese called off their offensive, and in January 1945 the Chinese mounted counteroffensives that pushed the Japanese back to the South China Sea. During 1944 the Japanese had been forced to transfer troops to the Pacific, and in 1945 to Manchuria to meet an increasing Russian threat. By this time, 'Vinegar Joe' Stilwell, frustrated by Chiang Kai-shek's deviousness, and corruption in the Nationalist army, had been replaced by the more diplomatic Lieutenant-General Albert Wedemeyer. The war in China cost the lives of 1.3 million Chinese troops, not to mention the millions of civilians who died from famine, and tied down a million Japanese troops, but in reality it was a sideshow in a war that was won and lost in the Pacific.

The submarine campaign

The American submarine campaign against Japanese merchant shipping played a decisive role in strangling the Japanese home economy and starving the forward areas of reinforcements, supplies, and equipment. Japan relied heavily on its merchant marine – the world's third largest after those of Britain and the USA. Its merchant ships

carried oil, rubber, tin, rice, and other raw materials from south-east Asia to the home islands, and also transported troops, supplies and equipment to Japanese forces deployed in hundreds of islands from Sumatra to the Solomons and the central Pacific. In December 1941 the USA resolved on a policy of unrestricted submarine warfare. About 50 submarines, based initially at Hawaii and Fremantle (Australia), attacked Japanese merchant shipping and soon began to have a noticeable effect.

For the first two years, malfunctioning torpedoes hindered the American submarine campaign. Nonetheless, during 1943 Vice-Admiral Charles Lockwood, at Pearl Harbor, commanded a successful campaign against Japanese merchant shipping, and also supported the US surface fleet by sinking several Japanese carriers. The Americans had broken the ciphers used by the Japanese to route their merchant convoys, and the American submarines were usually lying in wait.

The USA's submarines were handled with great enterprise. By contrast, the Japanese submarine force usually operated in cooperation with its surface fleet and did not conduct a concerted campaign against Allied merchant shipping. It undertook small nuisance raids against the west coast of the USA, along the coast of Australia and even as far west as Madagascar, but these attacks did not cause heavy Allied losses. As it became more difficult to resupply forward Japanese positions, submarines were used to transport men and supplies – a wasteful use of a valuable strike weapon.

At the beginning of 1944 the Japanese had 4.1 million tons of merchant shipping, excluding tankers; by the end of the year this was down to 2 million tons. In September 1944, 700,000 tons of shipping were transporting oil; four months later this had been reduced to 200,000 tons, and during 1945 Japan imported virtually no oil. By the end of 1944 the submarine war was almost over. Japanese ships had been driven from the high seas and instead hugged the coast of China and the waters around Japan.

During the war, American submarines sank nearly 1,300 Japanese merchant ships, as well as one battleship, eight carriers and 11 cruisers. The Americans lost 52 submarines from a total force of 288. During the same period, the Japanese lost 128 of their available 200 submarines, although many of these were not engaged in combat operations.

The importance of the American submarine campaign is sometimes overlooked, but after the war the former Japanese Prime Minister, General Tojo, admitted that there were three reasons for the American victory: the USA's ability to keep strong naval task forces at sea for months on end; the leap-frogging offensive that bypassed Japanese garrisons; and the destruction of Japanese shipping by American submarines.

Planning the final campaigns

In mid-October 1944 the Japanese East Asia Co-prosperity Sphere was still largely intact. After nearly three years of war, the Allies had made relatively minor progress, even though the Japanese had been defeated in important battles. In northern Burma, the Allies had not yet opened the road to China. Farther south, almost all of the Netherlands East Indies, the Philippines, Malaya, and Indo-China remained in Japanese hands. In the Pacific, the Marianas were being rapidly developed to take B-29 Superfortresses for the bombing campaign against Japan. But American bombers had not reached Tokyo since April 1942.

Although much of Japan's empire was still intact, the signs were ominous. The Japanese navy had been decimated, and it had lost large numbers of irreplaceable naval aircraft and pilots. To the south, the Japanese seemed powerless to stop MacArthur's advance. In Burma they were in retreat. Their merchant fleet was suffering crippling losses to American submarines. Senior army and navy leaders in Tokyo now knew that they had no hope of victory. Yet equally, there was no thought of surrender, and they hoped that somehow they might still resist their attackers, perhaps obtaining a negotiated peace. The Allies were never likely to contemplate such an outcome.

The shape of the last year of the Pacific War was set at important meetings in Quebec and Washington in mid-September and early October 1944. At Quebec, Churchill, Roosevelt, and their Chiefs of Staff agreed that Mountbatten's South-East Asia Command would undertake an offensive into Burma; its forces were eventually to invade Malaya and capture Singapore. The Americans accepted Britain's offer of a major fleet to operate with the US navy in the Pacific. The Americans, however, would conduct the remainder of the offensives, including the strategic bombing campaign against Japan, and the landing at Mindanao in the southern Philippines. Eventually the Allies would have to invade Japan, and after the end of the war in Europe the Soviet Union would invade Manchuria to hold down the large Japanese army there.

In the midst of the conference came further news from the Pacific. Between 7 and 14 September, Halsey's carrier force struck vigorously at Yap, the Palaus, Mindanao, and the central Philippines. He reported excitedly to Nimitz that he had found little opposition in the Philippines; he believed that Yap, Talaud, and Sarangani could be bypassed and the forces scheduled for those islands used against Leyte in the central Philippines. On 15 September the US Joint Chiefs approved a landing by MacArthur's forces on Leyte, beginning on 20 October. The landing on Mindanao was abandoned.

Finally, in Washington on 3 October, the Joint Chiefs resolved an issue that had been simmering for six months, namely whether the USA should invade Luzon or Formosa (now Taiwan). It was agreed that MacArthur's forces would invade Luzon on 20 December 1944. Nimitz's Central Pacific Command would seize Iwo Jima in late January 1945, and would move on to Okinawa on 1 March.

Task Group 38.3 of Halsey's Third Fleet returning to its base in the Palaus after air strikes against Japanese airfields in the Philippines in September 1944. The two carriers, followed by three fast battleships and four cruisers, illustrate the growing power of the US Pacific Fleet. (US National Archives)

Liberation of the Philippines

The invasion force for Leyte consisted of the US Seventh Fleet under Vice-Admiral Thomas Kinkaid and four infantry divisions of the US Sixth Army, commanded by the veteran professional soldier General Walter Krueger. Admiral Halsey's powerful US Third Fleet, with 16 carriers, provided support. The total force numbered 700 ships and some 160,000 men. The troops landed on Leyte on 20 October 1944 and initially met only light opposition.

Meanwhile, the Japanese navy, under the tactical command of Vice-Admiral Ozawa

Jizaburo, converged on the US fleet. Ozawa lured Halsey north away from the landing area while he sent two striking forces into the Leyte Gulf. The subsequent battle, beginning on 24 October, was the largest and one of the most decisive naval battles in history. With the battle in the balance, the commander of one of the Japanese striking forces, Vice-Admiral Kurita, called off the engagement and retired. By 26 October the Japanese had lost four carriers, three battleships, nine cruisers, and 10 destroyers. The Japanese navy never recovered from this defeat. Before the landing, the US navy had destroyed over 500 Japanese carrier- and land-based aircraft.

Defeated at sea, but aware of the danger if the Americans gained a foothold in the Philippines, the Japanese high command mounted a desperate counteroffensive. They were aided by the Americans' failure to

Philippines operations, 20 October 1944–July 1945

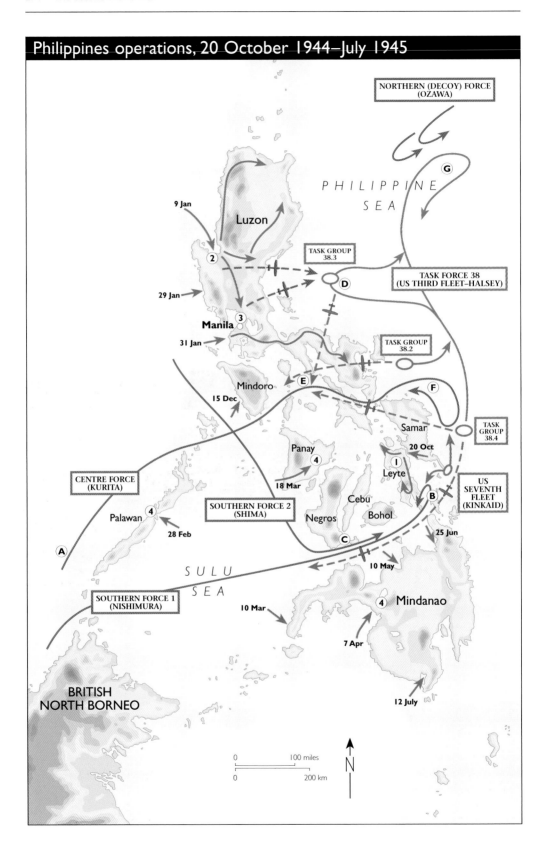

NORTHERN (DECOY) FORCE
(OZAWA)

G

PHILIPPINE
SEA

9 Jan

Luzon

2

TASK GROUP
38.3

D

TASK FORCE 38
(US THIRD FLEET–HALSEY)

29 Jan

Manila

3

31 Jan

TASK GROUP
38.2

Mindoro

E

15 Dec

Samar

20 Oct

TASK
GROUP
38.4

Panay

4

I

Leyte

CENTRE FORCE
(KURITA)

18 Mar

Cebu

B

US
SEVENTH
FLEET
(KINKAID)

Palawan

4

SOUTHERN FORCE 2
(SHIMA)

Negros

Bohol

28 Feb

F

25 Jun

A

C

10 May

SULU
SEA

SOUTHERN FORCE 1
(NISHIMURA)

10 Mar

4   Mindanao

7 Apr

BRITISH
NORTH BORNEO

12 July

0   100 miles

0   200 km

N

LEFT Map
Landings and land operations
1. 20 October 1944, US Sixth Army (Krueger), with four divisions, lands at Leyte. Three more divisions are deployed before the island is secured in December
2. 9 January 1945, US Sixth Army, with four divisions, lands at Lingayen Gulf. Six more divisions are landed during the battle for Luzon. The main fighting ceases in June, although pockets of Japanese remain
3. 4 February–3 March 1945, battle for Manila
4. February–July 1945, US Eighth Army (Eichelberger), with five divisions, conducts operations in the southern Philippines. They conduct over 50 landings, 14 of which are medium to large operations

Battle of Leyte Gulf
A 23 October 1944, US submarines sink two Japanese cruisers and damage one

B 24 October 1944, Japanese Southern Force 1 (Nishimura) enters Surigao Strait and is engaged by US Seventh Fleet (Kinkaid). Only one Japanese ship survives
C 24 October 1944, Japanese Southern Force 2 (Shima) withdraws without entering Surigao Strait.
D 24 October 1944 the carrier, USS *Princeton*, sunk by Japanese land-based aircraft
E 24 October 1944, US air strikes sink Japanese battleship and damage a cruiser
F 25 October 1944, Japanese Centre Force (Kurita) retreats back through San Bernadino Strait after losing two cruisers. The US lost two escort carriers, two destroyers, and a destroyer escort
G 25 October 1944, Halsey's Third Fleet engages Northern (Decoy) Force (Ozawa) before withdrawing to meet the southern threats

ABOVE General Douglas MacArthur, Commander-in-Chief of the South-West Pacific Area, wading ashore at Leyte, Philippines, in October 1944. Whatever the political and strategic merits might have been in liberating the Philippines, MacArthur had made it a personal crusade, vowing, after he arrived in Australia in March 1942: 'I shall return.' He was a master of public relations, using his extravagantly worded communiqués to engender support for his strategic plans. (US National Archives)

maintain air superiority: many American carriers had withdrawn for other tasks and the captured airfields on Leyte were in such poor condition that only a few aircraft could use them. The Japanese were therefore relatively free to send convoys of reinforcements to Leyte. Advancing cautiously from its beachhead, the US Sixth Army soon met strong resistance from skillful and determined Japanese troops. In a daring but uncoordinated attack, Japanese paratroops dropped on to the American airfields but were destroyed in a four-day battle. Eventually the Americans deployed seven divisions before concluding the hard-fought campaign successfully on 25 December. The Japanese lost some 56,000 men. The Sixth Army had almost 3,000 killed and 10,000 wounded before it was relieved by Lieutenant-General Robert Eichelberger's US Eighth Army.

On 9 January 1945 the Sixth Army landed at Lingayen Gulf on the main Philippines island of Luzon. Attacked by Japanese kamikaze (suicide) planes, the Americans had 25 ships sunk or damaged, but 175,000 men were put ashore. The subsequent land campaign against a Japanese army of 260,000 under General Yamashita was the second largest conducted by the US army in the entire war, after that in north-west Europe in 1944–45. The Sixth Army deployed ten divisions and the campaign involved tank battles, amphibious landings, parachute drops and guerrilla warfare. More than 100,000 Filipinos, 16,000 Japanese and 1,000 Americans died in the two-week battle for the shattered city of Manila. By the end of June the Luzon campaign was over. The Sixth Army had lost 8,000 killed and 30,000 wounded. The Japanese had lost 190,000.

The Sixth Army now began to prepare for the invasion of Japan. Meanwhile, the Eighth Army undertook a series of amphibious operations throughout the southern Philippines to eliminate large pockets of Japanese. These operations helped liberate extensive areas but did not contribute directly to the defeat of Japan.

The Australian campaigns

The same criticism can be levelled at the Australian army's final campaigns. From October 1944, troops of the First Australian Army began relieving American divisions on Bougainville, New Britain, and the north coast of New Guinea. In New Britain, the Australians conducted a containment operation, and at the end of the war the Japanese garrison at Rabaul was found to number almost 70,000 army and naval personnel.

The Australian commander, General Blamey, argued, however, that Australia had a duty to liberate its own territory. Therefore, on Bougainville the 2nd Australian Corps began a slow and careful offensive, which was still proceeding at the end of the war. In New

Guinea the 6th Division captured Wewak, driving the Japanese into the mountains.

MacArthur was at best lukewarm about the justification for these offensives, but he enthusiastically ordered the 1st Australian Corps, under Lieutenant-General Sir Leslie Morshead, to conduct operations in Borneo. The first of these began on 1 May 1945 with the seizure of Tarakan. Next, on 10 June the 9th Australian Division landed on Labuan Island and at Brunei. Blamey was now more wary and he opposed the landing of the 7th Division at Balikpapan. MacArthur warned the Australian government that to cancel the operation would disorganize Allied strategic plans; the government approved the landing. In truth, MacArthur wanted to show the Dutch government that he had attempted to recover part of its territory. The landing on 1 July was the last amphibious operation of the war. In the campaigns of late 1944 and 1945 the Australians lost more than 1,500 killed, but Japan did not surrender one minute earlier as a result.

The end in Burma

In December 1944 the British–Indian Fourteenth Army, under the popular and pragmatic General Slim, crossed the Chindwin River, and by January 1945 it had reached the Irrawaddy River in central Burma. British, Chinese, and American forces in northern Burma advanced south and on 22 January the Burma Road, linking India and China, was opened.

With more than six divisions in a force numbering 260,000, Slim continued his offensive southward toward Rangoon. He was opposed by four Japanese divisions, together totalling some 20,000 emaciated and poorly equipped defenders. However, British and Indian troops landed from the sea and by air, and took Rangoon on 3 May. The Japanese army in Burma had been crushed. Faced with a possible invasion of India, the British had had no alternative but to fight in Burma. It had been a hard-fought war over three years; 190,000 Japanese died. Burma was liberated,

A British patrol at the Sittang River in the final stages of the Burma campaign. After the capture of Rangoon, the British forces faced a force of 110,000 Japanese troops, but short of supplies they were generally ineffective. (The Art Archive/Imperial War Museum)

British pride was restored and Japanese forces had been tied down. But in strategic terms the 1945 Burma campaign had only a marginal effect on the outcome of the war.

The way was now clear for the British to prepare for the invasion of Malaya. Organized by Mountbatten's South-East Asia Command, the landing (Operation Zipper) took place in September 1945, after Japan had surrendered.

Iwo Jima and Okinawa

Iwo Jima was a key location: as long as the Japanese occupied it, the B-29s from the Marianas had to fly a dog-leg on their way to Japan with consequent expenditure of fuel and reduction in bomb loads. Once it was captured, long-range fighters stationed there could accompany the B-29s on their raids. Furthermore, Iwo Jima would provide an emergency landing place for returning bombers and, since it was traditional Japanese territory, its loss would be a severe psychological blow to the Japanese.

If Luzon was the largest battle of the Pacific War, Iwo Jima was the bloodiest. Only 5 miles (8km) long, the island had been turned into a formidable fortress with underground bunkers, tunnels, and well-concealed heavy artillery. All civilians had been evacuated to Japan. The Japanese commander, Lieutenant-General Kuribayashi Tadamichi, was determined not to waste his men in suicidal attacks but grimly to defend every yard. Expecting a fight to the death, he commanded his force skillfully. On 19 February 1945 two US Marine divisions, under Major-General Harry Schmidt, landed under cover of gunfire from seven battleships. But the Marines soon found that there was no place to escape the constant Japanese artillery and machine gun fire. Each Japanese strongpoint had to be attacked separately, the best weapons being artillery, tanks, and flamethrowers.

A photograph of the Marines' raising of an American flag on Mount Suribachi early in the campaign became one of the most famous war photographs. But more than 100,000 Marines and naval personnel were landed before they secured the island in late March. Of the commanders of the 24 battalions that had come ashore in the first landing, 19 were killed or wounded. The Marines had lost 6,821 killed and almost 20,000 wounded. The 21,000 Japanese defenders died almost to a

The Allied counteroffensive, 16 September 1944–22 August 1945

Japanese controlled area, 16 September 1944

Occupied by Allied forces, 16 September 1944–22 August 1945

Occupied by Japanese forces, September 1944–February 1945;
then reoccupied by Chinese forces, January–August 1945

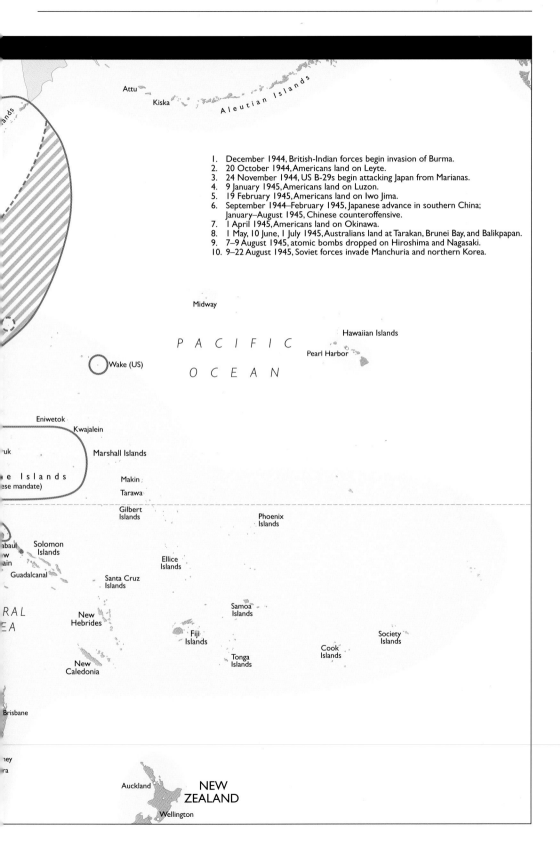

1.   December 1944, British-Indian forces begin invasion of Burma.
2.   20 October 1944, Americans land on Leyte.
3.   24 November 1944, US B-29s begin attacking Japan from Marianas.
4.   9 January 1945, Americans land on Luzon.
5.   19 February 1945, Americans land on Iwo Jima.
6.   September 1944–February 1945, Japanese advance in southern China;
     January–August 1945, Chinese counteroffensive.
7.   1 April 1945, Americans land on Okinawa.
8.   1 May, 10 June, 1 July 1945, Australians land at Tarakan, Brunei Bay, and Balikpapan.
9.   7–9 August 1945, atomic bombs dropped on Hiroshima and Nagasaki.
10. 9–22 August 1945, Soviet forces invade Manchuria and northern Korea.

American naval landing craft unloading fuel and supplies at Okinawa on 13 April 1945. The US Tenth Army took two and a half months to secure the islands. The army's casualties were more than 7,000 killed. The Japanese had 70,000 killed with at least 80,000 Okinawan civilians killed. (US National Archives)

man. Marine Lieutenant-General Holland Smith, commanding the land operation, said, 'This fight is the toughest we've run across in 168 years.'

For the attack on Okinawa on 1 April, the Americans amassed a huge naval force of 1,300 ships, including 18 battleships, 40 aircraft carriers, and 200 destroyers. They were also supported by the British Pacific Fleet. The Japanese resisted fiercely, as they considered the Ryukyu Islands to be part of their home territory. The US Tenth Army, commanded by Lieutenant-General Simon Buckler, with two Marine divisions and three army divisions, put nearly 250,000 men ashore, lost 7,600 killed, and took until 22 June to secure the island.

At sea the battle was equally fierce with the Japanese launching 1,900 kamikaze missions. Admiral Spruance's US Fifth Fleet had 36 ships sunk and 368 damaged. Almost 5,000 American sailors were killed. The giant Japanese battleship *Yamato* set sail from the Inland Sea but was caught by US planes. It sank with the loss of 3,000 sailors.

The seizure of Okinawa tended to make all campaigns fought to the south strategically irrelevant, but the outcome of the battle was deeply troubling to the Americans. On 25 May, MacArthur and Nimitz were ordered to prepare for an invasion of Japan, with the first landing on Kyushu on 1 November. The Marines and army had suffered 35 percent casualties on Okinawa. On that basis, there could be more than a quarter of a million casualties in Kyushu.

Strategic bombing

The strategic bombing offensive was based on the employment of the new B-29 Superfortress bombers. Initially, from June 1944, they conducted raids from China, but without great success. Then, from November, they started operating from the Marianas, still with limited effect. In March 1945 the young, cigar-chomping, Major-General Curtis Le May, commanding the Twentieth Air Force, changed tactics from high-level daylight raids against specific targets to low-level night attacks with incendiaries against area targets.

The first attack on Tokyo, on 9–10 March, succeeded beyond expectations. The Americans lost 14 of the 334 planes taking part. About 15 square miles (40km2) of the city were burnt out, more than 80,000 inhabitants were killed and 40,000 wounded, and 250,000 buildings were destroyed. Before the end of the month Nagoya, Osaka, and Kobe were similarly attacked. As more aircraft joined his command, Le May stepped up the offensive.

The strategic bombing campaign complemented the Allied blockade of the Japanese home islands. By the end of 1944 the American submarine campaign had restricted Japanese merchant shipping to the routes around Japan and Korea, and US army and navy aircraft attacked even the smallest coastal

B-29 Superfortresses from the US Twentieth Air Force conducting a daylight raid over Yokohama on 29 May 1945. Their escorts shot down 26 Japanese fighters. By July 1945, 60 percent of the areas of Japan's 60 larger cities and towns had been burnt out. (Imperial War Museum)

ships. Then in March 1945 the Twentieth Air Force began the systematic mining of Japanese home waters to prevent the transportation of food and raw materials from China, Korea, and Manchuria. In March 1945, 320,000 tons of shipping was using the main Japanese port of Kobe; by July the figure was down to 44,000 tons. The mining operation was the most effective single element in the final blockade against Japan.

The blockade had a devastating effect on the Japanese economy and public. Millions of homeless lived in shanties. Hunger and disease were widespread. Civilian morale plummeted and the police had to clamp down ruthlessly on defeatist talk. A secret report to the Diet in June 1945 admitted that in view of the worsening food shortage the war could not be maintained beyond the spring of 1946. The blockade also had a severe effect on Japan's ability to fight the war, restricting its capacity to replace military equipment and, through lack of fuel, reducing its ability to deploy planes and ships. But the government and military leaders were determined to fight on. Suicide units of different descriptions were formed to counter the expected Allied landings.

Thomas Currie Derrick, an Australian soldier

Like most American and Australian soldiers in the Pacific War, Thomas Currie Derrick was a child of the Great Depression. With his limited education, army service gave him opportunities that would never have been available in civilian life. Although he was to become one of the Australian army's most courageous and accomplished soldiers, the story of his life is otherwise representative of the thousands of young men who volunteered 'for the duration'.

Born in Adelaide, South Australia, in 1914, Tom Derrick left school at 14, but could only find odd jobs. As the Depression deepened, aged 16, he rode with some mates on their bikes about 140 miles (225km) to the Murray River irrigation area, seeking itinerant work in the vineyards and orchards. Cheerful and hardworking, he was often up to mischief, but enjoyed football, boxing, gambling, and the company of his mates, who gave him the nickname 'Diver'. By 1939 he had gained steady employment in a vineyard and was able to marry his long-time sweetheart, Beryl.

Newly married, Derrick hesitated to volunteer for the army when war was declared in September 1939, but loyal to his country, and also to his mates who had joined, he persuaded Beryl, who eventually relented. Like others, he was influenced by Germany's invasion of France in May 1940, and next month he enlisted in the 2/48th Battalion, then being raised in Adelaide.

Used to hard living, Derrick thrived on army life, but he found discipline difficult to accept. The battalion sailed for the Middle East in November, but stopped for a week at Perth. Confined to ship after going absent for sightseeing, he was taunted by another soldier, who punched him. In a letter home Derrick wrote, 'Got clocked last night, broke teeth and cut lip. I then got stuck into him,

made a real job of him. On another [charge] now for fighting.' Although only 5ft 7in (170cm) tall, Derrick was strong and wiry, with plenty of fighting experience. The commanding officer fined him 30 shillings.

Between April and October 1941 the battalion – part of the 9th Australian Division – helped defend the besieged port of Tobruk, in Libya. Derrick was soon leading his section and was promoted to corporal. He was recommended for a Military Medal. It was richly deserved but was not awarded.

Back in action in July 1942, the battalion attacked a German–Italian position near El Alamein. Derrick's leadership was inspirational. Hurling grenades, he personally destroyed three machine gun posts and captured more than a hundred prisoners. When the Germans counterattacked, he destroyed two enemy tanks and restored the position. He was awarded the Distinguished Conduct Medal and promoted to sergeant.

Derrick was also in the thick of the fighting at El Alamein in late October. Those present thought that he should have earned the Victoria Cross. In a week of savage combat the battalion lost more than 400 men. Derrick had been slightly wounded.

The 9th Division returned to Australia, and Derrick enjoyed his leave with Beryl in Adelaide in February 1943. Then the battalion took the long train journey to the Atherton Tableland in north Queensland, where it began intensive jungle training in preparation for operations against the Japanese. Valuable lessons from the 1942 Papuan campaign were incorporated into the training, and platoons learned to patrol silently in the jungle.

The battalion also practiced amphibious operations with the US 532nd Engineer Shore and Boat Battalion. Derrick wrote, 'Spent morning embarking and debarking –

After almost three years of soldiering, including grim battles in the Middle East, Sergeant Tom Derrick, and his battalion's other veterans, had the qualities of long-service professional soldiers. Back in Australia in early 1943 the battalion retrained for a different war against the Japanese. (Australian War Memorial)

find there is little to it and should not take many attempts to become really efficient.'

Lieutenant Murray Farquar, an officer in Derrick's battalion, recalled that Derrick met a young American soldier from Wisconsin, still in his teens, from the Shore and Boat Battalion. They adjourned to a hotel, where civilians and soldiers were

elbowing their way forward to replenish their glasses. In turn this young Yank pressed forward. He became the target of what was, at first, only good-humoured banter. One or two louts soon became vicious. Finally, backed up by a team of six or seven, one spat out, 'If you think you'll get out of here, Yank, without a few teeth smashed in, you've got another thing coming.' This aggressor was a real lump of a man. Quickly Diver sized things up. Stepping in front of his new mate, he stated: 'Well, you'll have to go through me first.' No histrionics, just a quiet

statement of intent. Staring this mob out, he held his ground … There were a few rumbles, they shrugged shoulders, and turned back to their drinking … finishing his beer, Diver exclaimed, 'Well, come on Yank. We'll try another pub.' The confrontation was over; Diver had won yet another ardent admirer.

Derrick merely wrote in his diary, 'Nought to do today … Murray Farquar and myself went into Cairns, teamed up with a Yank and had a most enjoyable day.'

In August 1943 the battalion sailed for Milne Bay in New Guinea. After arriving, Derrick wrote in his diary:

Slept on some very wet ground and was surprised to find I had a very comfortable and dry sleep. Seen my first glimpse of the Fuzzy Wuzzy's who appear very friendly. The camp is situated midst a huge coconut plantation, my first effort to climb a palm ended at 30 feet. But I think I can master it. The average height seems to be almost 45 feet.

The battalion landed near Lae in September, and by November was attacking the heights of Sattelberg, overlooking Finschhafen. The Allied advance hinged on clearing both sides of the Vitiaz Strait. Sattelberg dominated the mainland side. On 17 November the battalion led the brigade attack, but by 24 November the attack was grinding to a halt, the battalion suffering casualties. Late that day Derrick was leading the advance platoon when the battalion commander ordered a withdrawal. Derrick appealed to his company commander, 'Bugger the CO. Just give me twenty minutes and we'll have this place.'

It was a one-man front up an almost vertical incline covered in jungle. In peacetime the climb is barely possible using both hands and feet. Covered by his platoon members, Derrick alone clambered up the cliff, holding on with one hand, throwing grenades with another, pausing to fire his rifle. He cleared 10 machine gun posts before, at dusk, he reached an open patch, just short of the crest. Fifteen Japanese dead

Troops of the 2/48th Australian Infantry Battalion moving forward with a tank of the 1st Army Tank Battalion for the attack on Sattelberg in November 1943. Tanks were used for blasting Japanese defensive positions. (Australian War Memorial)

remained on the spur. Derrick's platoon occupied the area. That night the remaining Japanese withdrew. Awarded the Victoria Cross, Derrick said that the achievement was due mainly to his mates.

When the battalion returned to Australia for leave and more training, Derrick attended an officer-training course. Although lacking formal education, he had a great thirst for knowledge. In November 1944 he returned as a lieutenant to his battalion on the Atherton Tableland. Friends thought that he should not have returned; after three campaigns he had 'done his bit'. But he merely replied, 'My boys are back there, I must be with them.'

On 1 May 1945 the 2/48th Battalion was part of the Australian landing on Tarakan, Borneo. The Japanese fiercely resisted

attempts to clear the island. On 23 May Derrick's platoon led the assault on a position known as Freda. One soldier recalled: 'At Diver's signal, we smashed forward. Grenades burst among us. Diver was everywhere, encouraging, shouting orders, pressing us on.' Those present thought that his actions were worthy of a bar to his Victoria Cross. The Australians took the knoll but expected a Japanese counterattack that night. At about 3.00 am a Japanese machine gun fired down a track where Derrick was sleeping. He sat up to assess the direction of the fire. Another burst of fire struck him in the abdomen. 'I've been hit. I think its curtains,' he said. 'I've copped it in the fruit and nuts' (rhyming slang for 'the guts'). He insisted that the other wounded be evacuated first, and died next day.

Apart from his extraordinary feats on the battlefield, Derrick was typical of the Australian soldier who enlisted in the early years of the war. He learned his trade of soldiering against the Germans and Italians in the Middle East and then returned to deal

Men of the 2/48th Battalion gather for the graveside funeral of Lieutenant Derrick, conducted by the battalion's chaplain on Tarakan Island, 26 May 1945. Shortly before he died Derrick told the padre, 'Give me the works, father, I know I've had it.' (Australian War Memorial)

with the Japanese. With few advantages in life, he had come to rely on his mates and applied himself to any task. His ever present grin and outgoing leadership masked a sensitive and reflective side. He collected butterflies, composed poetry, kept a diary, and wrote regularly and frequently to his wife. After the war he would have happily returned to the Murray River fruit blocks.

Raised as a Salvationist, Derrick was not overtly religious. In the Middle East, in February 1942, he wrote, 'Changed my church today, went to Catholic parade –

doubt if I'm improved any.' During his evacuation on Tarakan, he asked a friend to get the padre so that he could 'bring on the hocus pocus.' Cheerful to the end, he had done his duty as he saw it. It was men like him who made the Australian army a formidable force in the south-west Pacific.

Gwen Harold Terasaki, an American in Japan

As an American married to a Japanese diplomat, Gwendolen Harold Terasaki lived in Japan during the worst days of the war, observing the life of ordinary Japanese women. Straddling two cultures, she sympathized with the plight of the Japanese people, but was conscious of the regime's militarism and brutality. Ultimately, like most people in Japan, her life became a struggle for survival.

Gwen met her husband in 1930 when she visited Washington, DC, from her home town in Tennessee. Terasaki Hidenari, a diplomat at the Japanese Embassy, had attended university in the USA and spoke English well. They were married in November 1931, shortly before Terasaki returned to Tokyo; he was 31, his wife 23. Their next posting was at Shanghai where their daughter, Mariko, was born. Both Gwen and her husband were disturbed by the actions of Japanese troops in China. Hidenari (called Terry by Gwen) was in a difficult position. He was opposed to the Japanese militarists, but tried to serve his country loyally as a diplomat. They had further postings to Havana and Peking before returning to Washington in March 1941, where he was involved in diplomatic efforts to avert war between the USA and Japan.

On the outbreak of war, the Terasakis and other diplomats were interned with their families at Homestead Hotel, Hot Springs, Virginia. In June 1942 they sailed in a Swedish ship for Lourenço Marques, in Mozambique, where they transferred to a Japanese ship and reached Yokohama in mid-August.

In wartime Japan, Gwen noticed that people were looking at her clothes, and she packed away her smartest clothes for the duration, spending the war years 'in slacks, sweaters and skirts.' Later, 'as fuel became a thing of the past,' she wore the 'regulation *monpe*, a Japanese-type pantaloon which made up for its ugliness by being warm and practical.'

In 1957 Gwen Terasaki (left) published *Bridge to the Sun* describing her wartime experiences in Japan. A movie based on the book, starring Carrol Baker and James Shigeta, had its première in her home town, Johnson City, Tennessee, in 1961. Some critics at the time accused the film of being anti-American. (Archives of Appalachia)

Initially, Gwen lived in an apartment in Tokyo and became involved in the daily round of trying to keep a home. Against regulations, she baked a cake using her gas oven; their gas was cut off and thereafter she used a charcoal cooker. She described standing in line 'for two or three hours for a few pieces of fish or a bunch of carrots,' and noted that the 'repeated air-raid drills also took up a large part of the day when they were called.' Pregnant women were given priority for rations, and one day she witnessed 'a pitiful but amusing incident' in the ration line.

A 'pregnant' woman went to the head of the line and, after receiving her rations, started to walk off when out slipped a cushion from under her obi (sash). The other ladies sent up a howl and the poor woman broke into tears, explaining that besides seven small children to care for she had her mother-in-law, who was ninety, on her hands.

Like everyone, Gwen purchased food on the black market and once bought a small bunch of bananas for her daughter – the last bananas they were to eat until 1949. The Japanese used small round briquettes made from coal dust for heating, as they lasted longer than charcoal. One day a man told Gwen that he would sell them to her cheaper as they has just been made and were still wet. 'He said that if I would lay them in the sun till they dried I could store them away. Feeling very proud of myself, I promptly took the whole lot, and the maid and I painstakingly arranged them in the sun. When they were dried out they crumbled – they were only blackened mud.'

Early in 1944 the Terasakis moved to Odawara, near Sagami Bay, about three hours by rail from Tokyo. Despite the deteriorating war situation, only victories were broadcast on the radio. Gwen observed that this 'involved such obvious contradictions that even the more simple-minded listeners became doubtful. Everyone who could think at all realized that the country was in a more and more desperate state, its back to the wall.'

Boys of 10 and 12 were unloading the freight from trains, while children 'were employed in all kinds of factory work from clothes-making to riveting airplane parts together; they were mobilized through their schools and taken to their jobs by the teachers.'

As an Allied invasion force might land in the Odawara area, late in 1944 the Terasakis moved farther along the coast. There they endured a bitterly cold winter, foraging for sticks and pine cones for fuel. A small ration of horsemeat in January was particularly welcome when Terry became ill (he had a heart condition). Still worried about an Allied invasion, Terry wanted to move his family inland, but the bombing of Tokyo in March 1945 had sent thousands of homeless people searching for shelter and he had difficulty finding accommodation. Eventually a friend offered them his little summerhouse in the mountains above Suwa City, 75 miles (120km) inland.

In their new home, food was an even more acute problem. They planted turnips, radishes, and beans, but the crops were pitifully small. Often the rice ration was delayed by up to 10 days, and they then had to forage for something to fill in. The three of them were growing weaker, and Mariko came down with dengue fever.

The authorities demanded more work. Resin from pines trees was used to manufacture fuel for aircraft, and each family in the countryside was required to extract a certain amount and turn it over to the local assembly. Called to that duty, Terry and his daughter collected the smallest quantity of resin of any family in the neighbourhood. Gwen wrote: 'Terry had always been opposed to the whole idea of a *kamikaze* corps, saying that if a country had to use such methods to continue, it should give up. The pine-tree tapping for fuel also depressed him, and he kept muttering, "how long, how long".'

All were suffering from malnutrition, and Gwen found that they had no energy beyond that needed to prepare their rice and keep the house and themselves clean. 'My finger nails were almost gone,' she wrote, 'and I had to bandage my fingers to keep blood from getting on everything I touched.'

One day she received as a gift Dickens' novel *A Tale of Two Cities*, about the French Revolution. Reflecting on her own situation, she now understood

the terror of people forced to eke out their everyday existence against a backdrop of chaos … The newspapers carried only victory stories and such headlines as, 'Japan girds herself to give a knockout blow,' but there were few people who did not know that Japan was almost at the end of the road. We discussed this with no one, as the kempei tai *had agents everywhere and people were being questioned every day. Some of them were being sent to prison.*

When Terry became ill again, Gwen, dizzy with malnutrition, was almost too weak to fetch the doctor. Then came news of the 'strange bombing of Hiroshima.' Gwen thought 'that Japan would fight until the entire country was destroyed, the Japanese people broken and almost extinct.' Terry disagreed, insisting 'that among the Japanese statesmen there were realists who had a true love of country and the welfare of the people at heart.' They learned of Russia's declaration of war, and that the Emperor would be broadcasting next morning. As a foreigner, Gwen decided not to accompany Terry and Mariko to the home where they had been ordered to assemble. On his return he told her that everyone was weeping, but when the Emperor stopped speaking, 'Silently the old men, the women, and their children, rose and bowed to each other and without any sound each went along the path leading to his own house.'

'Merrily, I put on earrings,' wrote Gwen, 'Mako [Mariko] wore a white dress and Terry donned a red tie. The war was over. White clothing had been forbidden during the war because it was too easily seen from the air. When Mako put on white it was like a ship turning on lights again after running blacked-out since 1941.' But everyone else was apprehensive about the arrival of the Americans. One man asked Terry whether they would all be required to bow to the American soldiers. 'If so,' Terry replied, 'I shall be the first Japanese to crack my forehead on the pavement. After all the Chinese in Shanghai and Peking that I have seen forced to kowtow before the Japanese soldiers, I hope to do the same with dignity.'

During the occupation, Terry became an adviser to the Emperor. In 1949, concerned about Mariko's education, and with Terry's encouragement, Gwen and her daughter went to the USA, living in Gwen's home town. She planned to return to Japan, but on the outbreak of the Korean War, Terry advised her to wait. Then came news that he had died.

Mariko graduated from university, married an American lawyer, and had four children. Politically active, in 1976 she was elected to the Executive Committee of the Democratic National Committee, devoting herself to issues including the arms race, war and peace, racial and sexual equality, and political reform. Because of her husband's position, Gwen's experiences were not as tough as those endured by many. But, as she described them through Western eyes, they provide a picture that underlines the burden of war on Japanese civilians.

Not necessarily to Japan's advantage

The Pacific War did not end with one final and crushing battlefield defeat. The Allied victory was the outcome of relentless pressure that squeezed the life out of Japan's capacity to continue, even though millions of soldiers and civilians still remained willing to die for the Emperor. The atomic bomb attacks on Hiroshima and Nagasaki and the Soviet declaration of war merely gave the Japanese government the opportunity to surrender.

By July 1945 Japan was under siege from all sides. American and British carriers were conducting strikes against the home islands. American submarines were in the Sea of Japan. Most of Japan's navy had been sunk, and its overseas forces were isolated and surrounded. At home, however, the Japanese army was rapidly forming new divisions to repel the expected American invasion. Soon it numbered about 2 million troops in 60 divisions. These were supported by 3,000 kamikaze planes (with carefully preserved fuel), 5,000 regular warplanes, 3,300 suicide boats and a National Volunteer Force with a potential strength of 28 million. But Japan was running low on the equipment, fuel, food, and other resources needed to continue the war.

American forces under General MacArthur planned to land on Kyushu on 1 November with a force of 13 divisions, to be followed on 1 March 1946 by a landing on Honshu, near Tokyo, with a force of 25 divisions. From signals intelligence the American commanders knew the strength of the Japanese forces on Kyushu and feared heavy casualties.

Meanwhile, the Allied leaders were meeting at Potsdam in Germany, where Harry Truman, who had become US President on Roosevelt's death on 12 April, told the Soviet leader, Joseph Stalin, that the USA had an atomic bomb that would be dropped on Japan. The Soviet Union had promised to join the war three months after the end in Europe, but as a Japanese surrender became more likely, the Americans became less keen on a Soviet attack, although they could do little about it. On 26 July 1945 the Allies issued the Potsdam Declaration, promising the utter destruction of the Japanese homeland unless there was an unconditional surrender. On 28 July the Japanese rejected this demand.

On 6 August an American B-29, the Enola Gay, based at Tinian, dropped the 'Little Boy' atomic bomb on the city of Hiroshima. Again the Americans asked for surrender, promising another attack. The Japanese hoped that the Soviet Union might assist in negotiations with the Americans. They received their answer on 8 August, when the Soviet Union declared war. Next morning Soviet forces invaded Manchuria, just ahead of news of another atomic bomb being dropped on Nagasaki, killing 35,000.

The double shock of the atomic bombs and the Russian attack decided the issue. On the night of 9 August, three of the six members of the Imperial Council agreed to surrender. The other three wanted to fight on. The Emperor tipped the balance and decided to surrender; next day the Japanese government announced that it would accept the Allied terms provided they did not prejudice the prerogatives of the Emperor. The USA responded that the Emperor should be subject to the authority of the Supreme Commander for the Allied Powers. Late on 14 August, Japan informed the Allies that it had accepted the terms. That evening several army officers attempted a coup. If the War Minister, General Anami Korechika, had supported the coup it might have succeeded, but he committed suicide, as did other military leaders.

The aftermath of the atomic bomb attack on Hiroshima on 6 August 1945. Some 78,000 inhabitants were killed – slightly less than in the first firebomb attack on Tokyo. Many others, however, were to die from the effects; by August 1946 the casualty figure had reached 120,000. (AKG Berlin)

At noon on 15 August, the Emperor broadcast his orders to cease hostilities. He made no mention of surrender, but said that the war had 'developed not necessarily to Japan's advantage,' and that the enemy had employed 'a new and most cruel bomb.' Japan had 'resolved to pave the way for a grand peace for all the generations to come by enduring the unendurable and suffering what is insufferable.' Across the remnants of the Empire, with only a few exceptions, the members of the Japanese armed forces faithfully obeyed the order to cease hostilities.

In Manchuria, however, the war continued briefly. Between April and August 1945 the Soviets had moved 750,000 men and 30 divisions from Europe to the Far East.

Under the command of Marshal Aleksandr Vasilevsky, they formed the Far East Command with some 1.5 million troops (80 divisions), 5,500 armored vehicles and nearly 5,000 aircraft. The Japanese Kwantung Army in Manchuria had 24 divisions, but eight of these had been mobilized in the previous 10 days. Although they had 1 million troops, the Japanese were outnumbered, had inferior equipment, and had a lower level of training and morale.

Experienced in mechanized operations, the Soviet commanders conducted a rapid mobile war. They quickly overran Manchuria, taking Harbin on 18 August and Port Arthur on 22 August. Some Japanese units had not heard the order to cease hostilities, but in any case the Soviets were determined to keep fighting to secure as much ground as possible. Further, the Soviets were planning to land on the northern Japanese island of Hokkaido in late August. Stalin halted them at the last minute, after

Truman forcefully rejected his proposal to accept the Japanese surrender in northern Hokkaido. The invasion would have gone ahead if the atomic bombs had not induced Japan to surrender; Japan would then have been divided between the Soviet Union and the other Allies, as happened in Germany and Korea.

About 600,000 Japanese and Koreans were taken prisoner by the Soviets and transported to Siberia, to be used as forced labor. Only 224,000 survived to return to Japan and Korea in 1949. The Russians claimed that they killed 83,737 Japanese; the unofficial Japanese figure was 21,000. Soviet losses were put at just over 8,000 men killed and 22,000 wounded.

At the end of the First World War, the Germans had surrendered without their homeland being invaded, leading to suggestions that somehow they had not actually been defeated. Japan was not invaded but there could be no doubt about

Soviet sailors hoist a Soviet flag on a hill above Port Arthur, lost during the Russo-Japanese War of 1904–1905 and recovered during the Soviet invasion of Manchuria in August 1945. The Soviet Union had several scores to settle with Japan, including the recovery of territories taken by the Japanese 40 years earlier. (AKG Berlin)

the defeat. That the Americans were prepared to invade, supported by massive firepower, was an important factor among the considerations that led to Japan's surrender.

From the beginning of the Pacific War it was clear that the decisive factor would be the industrial power of the USA. In July 1945 the USA had 21,908 front-line aircraft in the Pacific; the Japanese had 4,100. After the war Admiral Nagano Osami, Chief of the Naval General Staff, told his interrogators: 'If I were to give you one factor ... that led to your victory, I would give you the air force.'

It was not until the last year of the war that the USA was able to deploy and utilize its full industrial power. As General Ushijima

General MacArthur watches as a Japanese representative signs the surrender document on the battleship *Missouri* in Tokyo Bay on 2 September 1945. Admiral Nimitz signed on behalf of the USA with representatives, seen behind MacArthur, signing for the other Allies. (AKG Berlin)

Mitsuru, the Japanese commander on Okinawa, put it, 'our strategy, tactics and techniques were all used to the utmost and we fought valiantly. But it was as nothing before the material strength of the enemy.' Prince Konoye, at one stage the Japanese Prime Minister and one of the Emperor's key advisers at the end of the war, said that 'fundamentally the thing that brought about the determination to make peace was the prolonged bombing by the B-29s.'

In view of the evidence that Japan did not have the economic strength to fight much beyond the end of 1945, arguments have continued as to whether the Americans needed to drop the atomic bombs. Various claims have been made about the extent of the casualties that the American forces would have suffered in the November invasion. But if the war had continued, thousands more Japanese civilians would have suffered both from American conventional air attacks and in the ground fighting. The fact that the Japanese Cabinet, after the shock of the atomic bombs, was still divided over whether to surrender indicates the role that the bombs played in terminating the war. For that, millions across Asia and the Pacific were grateful.

Part V
The Eastern Front 1941–1945

German troops on the move through the snow near Toporec, January 1942 (Bundesarchiv)

A dictators' deal and a double-cross

In 1935 Hitler repudiated the Versailles Treaty and reintroduced conscription, and in 1936 he reoccupied the demilitarized Rhineland. Since his book *Mein Kampf* (My Struggle), written in 1924, advocated gaining *Lebensraum* (living space) for Germany in the east, Stalin saw a threat in German military resurgence, and sought British and French support for a 'collective security' policy to restrain Germany. However, British and French reluctance to join one dictator against another militated against success. In April 1938 Hitler annexed Austria; in August he demanded that Czechoslovakia cede the Sudetenland, and threatened war if it refused. Stalin mobilized the equivalent of 90 divisions (far more than the 52 divisions Germany then had), but the French and British governments coerced Czechoslovakia into surrender.

The Soviet Union was not invited to the Munich Conference that ratified the cession, so Stalin decided to seek a deal with Hitler. Secret negotiations produced on 25 August 1939 an agreement between the two Foreign Ministers, Molotov and Ribbentrop, which freed Germany's hands to invade Poland on 1 September. A secret clause sanctioned Soviet annexation of territory that Poland had seized in 1920 east of the 'Curzon Line,' defined at Versailles as its appropriate eastern

Ribbentrop signing the Molotov–Ribbentrop Pact, watched by Stalin and Molotov. (AKG Berlin)

frontier, and on 17 September 1939 the Red Army invaded. Other secret clauses placed Finland, Estonia, Latvia, and Lithuania in the Soviet sphere. The three Baltic States were forced to accept Soviet military bases, and in 1940 were annexed.

Stalin did not intend to annex Finland, but in November 1939 demanded territory in the Karelian isthmus, to move the frontier back from Leningrad, and a base at Turku, on the entrance to the Gulf of Finland, offering in exchange about twice as much territory north of Lake Ladoga. When the Finns refused, he invaded and 'recognized' a puppet Finnish 'people's government' in Moscow. The Red Army prevailed in March 1940 by weight of numbers, but the Finns inflicted enormous casualties. The Red Army's inept performance encouraged Hitler's belief that Stalin's purges had 'beheaded' it, and this belief became general also in British, French, and American military circles. The British and French governments contemplated sending an expeditionary force, ostensibly to aid Finland, but really to cut off Germany's supplies of Swedish iron ore. Only Finland's request for an armistice in March 1940 saved them from going to war with the Soviet Union as well as with Germany.

The Wehrmacht overran Denmark, Norway, Luxembourg, Belgium, the Netherlands and France in less than three months (April–June 1940), demolishing the rationale behind Stalin's deal with Hitler – his belief that German reluctance to fight a two-front war made the Soviet Union safe. At the end of July, Hitler ordered plans made for invading the Soviet Union in 1941. The invasion planning could not be entirely concealed. Bases and supply depots had to be established in East Prussia and German-occupied Poland, and Romania and Finland brought into alliance with Germany.

German activity did not go unnoticed by Moscow, nor were the Soviet espionage services idle. Two especially fruitful sources were a group of anti-Nazis in Berlin, members of the so-called Rote Kapelle (Red Orchestra), and Richard Sorge, a Soviet agent

in Tokyo, friendly with the German ambassador. Agents in frontier areas, and Soviet border guards, copiously reported German troop movements, and Churchill also sent warnings. However, several factors combined to give the Germans tactical surprise when they invaded on 22 June 1941.

Most important among them was a misinformation campaign. This included attempts to convince Stalin that German eastward troop movements were intended to distract British attention from renewed invasion preparations, and an offer to include the Soviet Union in the planned carve-up of the British Empire. This was made during Molotov's visit to Berlin in November 1940, and Stalin was sufficiently interested to ask Molotov twice whether there was any German follow-up. There was not.

Defense Minister Marshal Timoshenko and Chief of General Staff General Zhukov were uneasy enough to go to Stalin on 15 May and seek permission for a preemptive attack. Stalin asked, 'Have you gone out of your minds?' and warned them that if the Germans were provoked into attacking, 'heads will roll.'

Some Russian authors blame this refusal for the early disasters. However, the circumstances cannot be ignored. The Soviet Union was internationally isolated following its recent acts of aggression. Only five days before Timoshenko and Zhukov went to Stalin, Hitler's deputy, Rudolf Hess, flew to Britain, and his flight could have no purpose other than to propose it make peace or even, given Churchill's well-known anti-Communism, join Germany's 'crusade.' Politically, the Soviet Union had to be seen as the victim, so preemption was impossible. Stalin believed invasion inevitable, but hoped to delay it by diplomatic maneuvers and punctilious observance of the economic agreements with Germany – Guderian later noted that as his troops lined up to invade on 22 June, trainloads of Soviet raw materials were still crossing the border.

So Stalin's refusal to preempt was justifiable. Less so, however, were the lengths to which he went to avoid 'provoking' the

Joseph Stalin, 1879–1953. General Secretary, Soviet Communist Party, from 1924, Prime Minister
and Supreme Commander-in-Chief from 1941, Generalissimus 1945. (AKG Berlin)

The rival invasion plans (a)

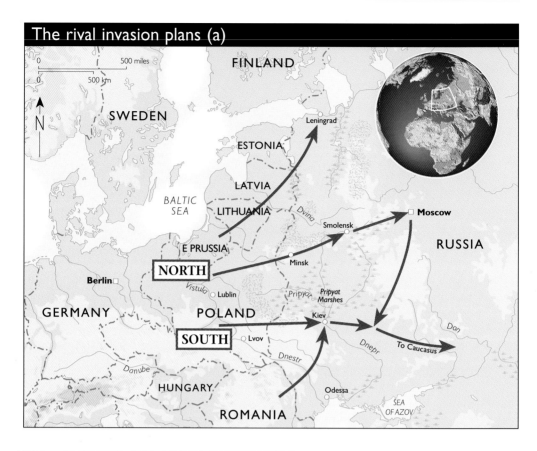

The rival invasion plans (b)

The rival invasion plans (c)

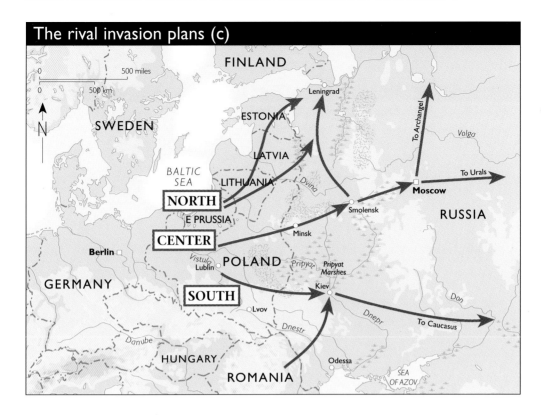

The rival invasion plans

(a) Produced by an Army High Command (OKH) team under General Marcks in early August 1940, aimed the main thrusts at Moscow and Kiev.

(b) Adopted by Colonel-General Halder, Chief of General Staff of OKH, on 5 December 1940. This added a strong thrust at Leningrad to Marcks' plan.

(c) Laid down by Hitler in Directive No. 21 (Operation Barbarossa) of 18 December 1940. This version of the plan made the destruction of Soviet forces in the Baltic States and the taking of Leningrad first priority. Moscow was to be considered only after this had been achieved.

Germans. When Kiev Military District's commander, Colonel-General Kirponos, occupied forward defensive positions, he was reprimanded and his orders annulled. The air defense forces were forbidden to attack German photographic reconnaissance aircraft that for weeks before the invasion regularly violated Soviet air space; even one that made a forced landing was immediately released. The fixed fortifications along the old Soviet–Polish border were dismantled before any new ones were completed. While the fate of the Belgian forts and Maginot Line in 1940 had shown the limits of fixed fortifications, their presence would at least have served to channel the invasion into fewer routes. Air force commanders were refused permission to disperse their aircraft.

There were also flaws in Soviet war preparations. Forces manpower more than trebled from 1.5 million in 1936 to 4.75 million in 1941, but officer-training schools' output only doubled. Training neglected defense, and was based on boastful slogans such as 'beating the enemy on his own territory.' The third was that faulty evaluation of Spanish Civil War experience prompted disbanding of the large tank and motorized infantry formations created in the early 1930s, and dispersal of their tanks as infantry support weapons. Following the achievements of the similar Panzer Divisions in 1939–40, Timoshenko began hastily reestablishing these formations, but few were ready by mid-1941.

All these deficiencies derived mostly from Voroshilov's incompetence as Defense Minister, though Stalin can be faulted for not dismissing

Commanders of the fronts during the concluding period of the war, 1941–1945: Left to right: I. S. Konev; F. I. Tolbukhin; A. M. Vasilevsky; R. Y. Malinovsky; G. K. Zukhov; L. N. Govorov; K. K. Rokossovsky; A.I. Yeremenko; K. A. Meretskov; I. Kh. Bagramyan. (Novosti [London])

him until 1940. However, two other flaws are directly attributable to Stalin. One was the purge of the senior military in 1937–38. This fell mainly on the younger generation of senior officers, and spared Stalin's civil war cronies, such as Voroshilov, Budenny, and Kulik. The coming war would show the latter to have learned little since 1920, while surviving members of this younger generation (such as Zhukov, Vasilevsky, Rokossovsky, Meretskov, Voronov, Malinovsky, Tolbukhin, and Rotmistrov) ultimately achieved successes outstripping Hitler's, or even Napoleon's, marshals. Those shot in 1937–38 probably included some equally talented, who, being higher up the 'learning curve' in 1941, might have mitigated that year's disasters. But seeing how speedily the Germans in 1939–41 disposed of other armies that had not been 'beheaded,' it is unlikely that they could have avoided reverses altogether.

So the purge's effects should not be exaggerated. However, another of Stalin's errors was to veto the General Staff's defensive plan. This expected the main German thrust to come north of the Pripyat marshes, aiming at Leningrad and Moscow, with a secondary thrust south of them toward Kiev. Stalin insisted that Germany's primary objective was Ukraine's mineral and agricultural wealth, so its main thrust would come in the south. This can be explained only by Marxist economic determinism. In late summer 1941 Hitler indeed vacillated between Ukraine and Moscow. However, where the initial invasion was concerned, Stalin was wrong: Hitler deployed two army groups north of the Pripyat marshes, and only one south of them.

Germany gambles on a quick win

The German army began the Russian campaign following almost two years of outstanding success. Despite the prominence of Panzer (armored) and motorized infantry divisions, they constituted only a small part of the army, and achieved success by breaching enemy lines, then turning in to squeeze the enemy between themselves and infantry advancing on foot with horse-drawn artillery. Close tactical air support was provided by bombers, particularly the Ju87 'Stuka' dive-bomber, while fighter escorts ensured air superiority over the battlefield.

The plan was to destroy the Red Army west of the Dnepr River, in a four-month campaign starting in mid-May, concluded before the onset of winter. Events in the Balkans imposed a five-week postponement, but the invasion began at 3.30 am on 22 June 1941; if all went according to plan, it could still be concluded before winter set in.

The invasion force comprised three army groups, North, Center, and South, each commanded by a Generalfeldmarschall (field marshal). Its spearhead was four Panzergruppen (armored groups), two with Army Group Center, one with each of the others.

Army Group North (von Leeb) had 4th Panzergruppe, with three tank and three motorized infantry divisions and 20 of infantry. Center (von Bock) had II and III Panzergruppen, with nine tank and six motorized divisions, and 35 infantry divisions, while South (von Rundstedt) had I Panzergruppe, of five tank and three motorized divisions, 33 German and 14 Romanian infantry divisions. In Finland there were eight German and about 20 Finnish divisions. All formations were at or near full strength, but the Panzer divisions had only 200 tanks each, versus 400 in 1939–40.

The Army High Command (Oberkommando des Heeres, OKH) had a reserve of two tank, two motorized, and 24 infantry divisions. Including these, Germany committed 153 divisions (19 tank, 14 motorized, 120 infantry), Romania and Finland between them about 40 more. In manpower this meant about 3.3 million German and 500,000 satellite troops, with 3,300 tanks. Each army group had an attached Luftflotte (air fleet) of between 450 (North) and 900 (Center) combat aircraft, divided approximately 40–60 percent between fighters and bombers. With 55 German

Herman Hoth in 1941 commanded 3rd Panzer Group of Army Group Center. In 1942 he commanded the attempt to relieve Stalingrad. In November 1943 he was dismissed by Hitler for failing to prevent the Soviet recapture of Kiev. (Imperial War Museum)

Gerd von Rundstedt resigned command of Army Group South in December 1941, because of interference by Hitler, but was later appointed Commander-in-Chief West. (Imperial War Museum)

April 1940 Stalin replaced Voroshilov as People's Commissar (Minister) of Defense with Marshal Timoshenko, who tightened discipline, improved training, and began re-forming the large mobile formations that Voroshilov had disbanded in 1939. However, their reestablishment began only in March 1941, and less than half of the proposed 20 mechanized corps (each of one tank and two motorized infantry divisions) had been equipped by June. The Red Army had more manpower (about 4.75 million) and almost six times as many tanks as the Germans, but most were obsolete, or worn out; in June 1941 only about 40 percent were serviceable. The T-34 medium and KV heavy tanks, superior to the German Marks III and IV, went into production in 1940, but only

divisions and about 1,500 aircraft retained elsewhere, 73.6 percent of the German army and 58.3 percent of the Luftwaffe were committed to the invasion.

Germany's main deficiency was information. Despite almost daily reconnaissance flights beforehand, the invaders' maps were often inaccurate. Estimates of Red Army strength were good about the forces along the borders (assessed as 147 divisions and 33 brigades, versus an actual 170 divisions), but hopelessly wrong about capacity to mobilize and equip reserves. These errors would prove crucial after the quick victory failed to materialize.

The Red Army was being reorganized following the débâcle against Finland. In

In 1941 Ewald von Kleist's I Panzer Group advanced to Rostov-on-Don. By the end of 1942 he was commanding Army Group A in the Caucasus. Hitler promoted him to Field Marshal in 1943, but in March 1944 dismissed him. (Imperial War Museum)

mid-1943 would the Soviet air force gain regular air superiority.

The navies played only supporting roles, and many Soviet sailors fought as infantry. The Soviet navy had more submarines than any other in 1941, but their performance was unimpressive. The surface forces' main function was to protect the army's coastal flanks, but the Baltic Fleet's loss of its forward bases in the first weeks forced its surface ships back to Leningrad. There they were boxed in by ice for half the year, and by a German mine barrier across the Gulf of Finland for the rest, though their guns contributed to shelling German positions. The Black Sea Fleet supplied and evacuated the garrisons of Odessa and Sevastopol, but did not prevent German crossings of the Kerch Straits from Crimea to Caucasus, or play any decisive role in the fighting along the Black Sea coast. The Northern Fleet helped escort Allied supply convoys, but British warships did most of that. The Pacific Fleet had little to do until 1945, and many of its sailors went west to fight as infantry.

Alongside command-line officers the Red Army had a parallel 'political officer' line. At different times they had veto powers over commanders, or were subordinate to them. They were responsible for political indoctrination of the troops and to some extent for welfare, but their basic function was to be the Party's watchdogs over the career military.

1,475 had been produced by mid-1941, and none went to border units.

The Luftwaffe had about 2,000 aircraft supporting the invasion, versus 12,000 Soviet, 8,000 of them in the European Soviet Union. However, most Soviet aircraft, too, were obsolete, serviceability was low, and 1,200 of those in the border area were destroyed on the first day, mostly on the ground. Not until

Germany achieves surprise

The definitive invasion order was Hitler's Directive No. 21, of 18 December 1940. It decreed Operation Barbarossa, 'to crush Soviet Russia in a rapid campaign' (four months), and a 'final objective … to erect a barrier against Asiatic Russia on the general line Volga–Archangel,' from which the Luftwaffe could if necessary eliminate 'Russia's last surviving industrial area in the Urals.' All preparations were to be completed by 15 May 1941. Events in Greece and Yugoslavia delayed the start by five weeks, but a four-month campaign could still be over just before winter set in.

The Soviet leaders noted the growing German deployments along their western borders, but could not determine the invasion date. Not until Saturday, 21 June, did they receive information definite enough to alert the border military districts. Timoshenko and Zhukov spent most of the evening and night writing orders; the local commanders received them only hours before the invasion, and many units remained unalerted. The air force suffered particularly, losing 1,200 aircraft on the first day. Navy Commander-in-Chief Admiral Kuznetsov ran through the streets from the General Staff to his headquarters, to put the entire navy on highest alert; in consequence, no ship or shore base was damaged in the first attacks, and no naval aircraft were lost.

Poor communications and transport hampered the army's attempts to react. Radios were few, so communications depended mainly on public telegraph and telephone nets, which were damaged or destroyed by bombing, gunfire, or German saboteurs. Many front-line units received no orders, others only orders already outdated by events. The mobilization plan required units to requisition lorries and carthorses from the civil economy, but the enterprises owning them took no steps to provide them.

Major-General (later Marshal) Rokossovsky, then commanding 9th Mechanized Corps in Kiev Special Military District (Southwest Front from the outbreak of war), learned that invasion was imminent only from a German army deserter. He had to open his secret operational orders on his own initiative, as he could not contact Moscow, District HQ in Kiev, or 5th Army HQ in Lutsk. His corps was mechanized only in name, with only one-third its allocation of tanks, those it had were obsolete, their engines worn out, and the 'motorized infantry' had no lorries, nor even horses or carts. As his corps was retreating, it several times had to punch its way through German mobile forces. His only defense against the frequent air attacks was his own anti-aircraft guns, as he never saw a Soviet aircraft; and his corps' performance was so much above average that three weeks later he was promoted to command an army.

Red Army battered but not beaten

1941

The Germans achieved almost complete surprise. Army Group North (Field Marshal von Leeb), with XVI and XVIII Armies, totaling 20 divisions, and IV Panzergruppe (Colonel-General Hoepner) with three tank and three motorized infantry divisions, faced Soviet Northwest Front (Colonel-General F. I. Kuznetsov; 'front' is Russian terminology for army group) with one army on the coast, and another inland. These had four tank, two motorized, and 19 infantry divisions, but the willingness of their soldiers, mostly from the former Baltic States' armies, to fight for their new masters was questionable.

Army Group Center (von Bock) confronted Soviet West Front (Army General D. G. Pavlov) in Belorussia. Bock had nine Panzer, six motorized, and 35 infantry divisions, while Pavlov's three armies had 12 tank, six motorized, two cavalry, and 24 infantry divisions. Bock planned for his two Panzergruppen (II and III) to advance 250 miles (400km) into Belorussia and converge east of its capital, Minsk, to crush Pavlov's forces between themselves and the infantry of IV and IX Armies. Pavlov played into his hands by ordering all his reserves forward on 24 June. By 27 June, Pavlov's three armies, and a fourth sent to reinforce him, were encircled in two large pockets, around Bialystok and Novogrodek. Communications were so disrupted that Stalin first heard of the encirclement only three days later, from a German radio broadcast. He at once had Pavlov and several of his subordinates court-martialed and shot.

By 8 July the Germans had eliminated two Soviet armies and most of three others, taken over 290,000 prisoners, and captured or destroyed 2,500 tanks and 1,500 guns. Guderian took Smolensk from the south on

15 July, while Hoth bypassed it on the north, closing the only eastward escape route on 27 July. Some Soviet units broke out, but by 8 August 347,000 prisoners had been taken, and 3,400 tanks and over 3,000 guns destroyed or captured. In the next two weeks another 78,000 prisoners were taken, and in two months Army Group Center had covered two-thirds of the 750 miles (1,200km) from the frontier to Moscow.

The Germans now had to decide what to do next. Smolensk was not the victory Soviet historians subsequently claimed – it is now admitted that 486,171 (83.6 percent) of the 581,600 troops engaged there between 10 July and 10 September were 'irrevocably' lost: that is, killed, captured, or wounded beyond further service. However, the Soviet resistance undoubtedly stiffened and German losses rose. With the additional stresses of distance, heat, and dust, over half of Army Group Center's tanks and trucks were out of action, and the infantry and the horses pulling their carts and guns were nearing exhaustion. The Barbarossa Directive had indicated that after 'routing the enemy forces in Belorussia' the emphasis was to shift to destroying those in the Baltic, and taking Leningrad. Only after that would Moscow be considered. Hitler's adherence to this plan sat ill with Bock and Guderian, but he rejected their pleas to go immediately for Moscow.

Army Group South (Field Marshal von Rundstedt) had I Panzergruppe, VI and XVII Armies in Poland, and three armies (German XI, Romanian III and IV) in Romania. The five Panzer, three motorized, and 26 infantry divisions in Poland invaded Ukraine south of the Pripyat marshes, while the seven German and 14 Romanian divisions in Romania waited in case the Ploesti oilfields needed their protection, and did not move until 29 June.

Motorcycle troops were often used to lead the advance and test the reliability of their often misleading maps. (AKG Berlin)

Stalin's belief that Ukraine would be Germany's main target had put more Soviet forces south than north of the marshes. Southwest Front (Colonel-General M. P. Kirponos) had four armies, and a newly formed South Front (Army General I. V. Tyulenev), along the Romanian border, had two. Between them they had 20 tank, 10 mechanized, six cavalry, and 45 infantry divisions, considerably more than the

invaders. However, their tanks, too, were mostly obsolete and worn out, the motorized infantry lacked lorries, and here too the Germans had air superiority, while the population in recently annexed Galicia, West Ukraine, Bukovina, and Bessarabia was mostly as anti-Soviet as in the Baltics and western Belorussia, facilitating free movement by sabotage groups. I Panzergruppe encountered Soviet tanks on the second day, and several battles delayed the required breakout, while the Soviet 5th Army, on being outflanked, retreated in good order into the marshes. Against South Front progress was also slow, and captures were few. The 400 miles (640km) to the Dnepr took two months; Army Group Center had covered 500 miles (800km) and taken many prisoners in that time.

However, Army Group South's fortunes improved after mid-July, when Rundstedt directed two of I Panzergruppe's three corps southeastward from Berdichev to Pervomaysk, to get behind three Soviet armies. XVII and XI Armies helped close this, the Uman 'pocket,' on 2 August, and six days later 103,000 trapped Soviet troops surrendered. The rest of South Front had no choice but hasty withdrawal across the Dnepr, leaving Odessa as an isolated fortress.

In the first few weeks of winter the ice on Lake Ladoga would bear only sleighs. Not until the ice was 12 inches (300mm) thick could lorries attempt the hazardous journey, as shown here. (AKG Berlin)

Argument about going for Moscow continued. Army Commander-in-Chief Field-Marshal Brauchitsch, Chief of OKH General Staff Colonel-General Halder, and Guderian all tried between 18 and 24 August to get Hitler's permission. Instead Guderian was sent south, to meet Kleist's I Panzergruppe at Lokhvitsa, about 140 miles (225km) east of Kiev, and encircle the entire Southwest Front.

Three weeks earlier, on 29 July, Zhukov had advocated pulling back Southwest Front and abandoning Kiev. Stalin refused, whereupon Zhukov resigned as Chief of General Staff and requested a field command. Stalin gave him the so-called Reserve Front, in the front line west of Moscow. Zhukov then forced the first German retreat of the war at Yelnya, but could not exploit his success because the fronts on either side of his had to withdraw. On 18 August he detected a sudden fall in German activity. Finding the same true of the adjacent Central Front, he told Stalin he believed Guderian was regrouping to drive south, and suggested establishing a strong force in the Bryansk area, to attack him in flank.

Stalin replied that he had foreseen the possibility by creating Bryansk Front a few days earlier. However, its commander, Colonel-General (later Marshal) Yeremenko, wrote in his memoirs that his directive was to defend against an eastward, not a southward push. He failed to stop Guderian's tanks, and they met Kleist's on 16 September. Two days later Stalin reluctantly authorized abandonment of Kiev, but too late; Kirponos was killed, his four armies were destroyed by 26 September, and the Germans claimed 665,000 prisoners. Soviet historians rejected that figure, but post-Soviet official analysis admits 'irrevocable' losses of 616,304 in Ukraine between 7 July and 26 September,

tantamount to losing over four divisions a week for 10 weeks.

While Guderian was returning north to prepare to advance on Moscow, Leningrad's defense was crumbling in Voroshilov's inept hands, and by 8 September it was completely isolated, except for a perilous route across Lake Ladoga. On 9 September Stalin sent Zhukov to take charge. By 14 September the Germans were on the Gulf of Finland, less than 4 miles (6.4km) from the city's outskirts, so Zhukov had to act quickly. Three days of dismissals, blood-curdling threats, frantic improvisations, and probably some shootings rallied the demoralized defenders, and one piece of luck contributed – on 12 September IV Panzergruppe began leaving to join the Moscow offensive. On 17 September six German divisions tried to

Leningrad in the first winter of the siege. Corpses are being taken away from a collecting point. (AKG Berlin)

break through from the south, but failed, and on 25 September Army Group North settled for a siege.

Stalin now needed Zhukov elsewhere. The assault on Moscow, Operation Typhoon, began on 30 September, and immediately smashed through the defenders, Western, Bryansk, and Reserve Fronts. They numbered 1.25 million men in 96 divisions and 14 brigades, supported by two 'fortified areas' (static defenses). But earlier losses had reduced their mobile forces to only one division and 13 brigades of tanks, with 770 tanks, and two divisions of motorized infantry. The rest included nine horsed cavalry divisions and 84 of infantry, with 9,150 guns, including mortars.

German losses so far had been comparatively small, 94,000 killed, 346,000 wounded, and very few captured up to 26 August. But the Panzergruppen, now renamed Panzer armies, were seriously short of tanks. At the end of September, II had only 50 percent, I and III about 75 percent, of war establishment; only IV had its full complement. There was also a 30 percent shortage of lorries, and manpower in 54 of German's 142 Eastern Front divisions was over 3,000 (20 percent) below establishment.

Nevertheless, Army Group Center, reinforced by Panzer and motorized divisions from Army Groups North and South, and five infantry divisions from South, had 14 Panzer, eight motorized, and 48 infantry divisions, about half of all Germany's East Front force, outnumbering the defenders in tanks and aircraft (1,000 versus 360) by almost three to one, and in guns by two to one.

Guderian attacked on 30 September, broke through Bryansk Front's southern flank, and advanced over 130 miles (210km) in two days, to Orel. Bryansk Front's three armies were encircled by 6 October, and on the 8th were ordered to break out eastward. Some did, but over 50,000 were captured.

Western and Reserve Fronts fared even worse. III and IV Panzer, IV and IX Armies attacked on 2 October, and here too broke through at once, III Panzer (Hoth) heading for Vyazma, IV Panzer (Hoepner) for Yukhnov. On 7 October they met west of Vyazma, encircling 45 Soviet divisions, and by 19 October had claimed 673,000 prisoners. Post-Soviet research

ABOVE: The autumn rains turned roads to mud, making progress difficult. Here, German soldiers try to dig their vehicle out. (AKG Berlin)

BELOW: Progress was easier once the ground froze.

The front line at the start of Operation Typhoon

Front Line on 1 September 1941
Front Line on 30 September 1941
Direction of German advance

confirms a lower but still immense figure: 514,338 to the end of November, 41 percent of the two fronts' strength. On 18 October 40th Panzer Corps took Mozhaisk, only 60 miles (100km) from Moscow. Panic broke out in the capital on 16 October; Stalin stayed, but government departments, the diplomatic corps and most of the General Staff were evacuated to Kuybyshev (now Samara). Thousands of Muscovites fled, looting was widespread, and a 'state of siege' (martial law) was proclaimed on 19 October.

However, two factors intervened to slow the Germans. The first was the weather. Snowfalls began on 6 October, and from the 9th sleet and heavy rain was almost continuous. Vehicles and carts bogged down, and the infantry, often up to their knees in mud, frequently outran their ammunition and rations. The weather was no better on the

Russian side, but the slowing favored the defenders, particularly by immobilizing the Panzers. The German advance could speed up again only after the mud froze; and low temperatures would then bring new problems.

The second factor was Zhukov, who arrived on 7 October. Stalin at once sent him to the front line to establish the true state of affairs. At 2.30 am on 8 October, he telephoned Stalin to tell him the main need was to strengthen the Mozhaisk defense line, then set off in heavy rain and fog to find Marshal Budenny and Reserve Front HQ. He finally found him in the deserted town of Maloyaroslavets, only to find that he did not even know where his own headquarters was, let alone the state of his forces.

On 10 October Hitler's press chief, Otto Dietrich, summoned the foreign press corps to announce officially that the war had been

Women digging anti-tank trenches at Moscow.
(AKG Berlin)

forcing Zhukov to re-form his front only
40 miles (64km) from the city. Tens of
thousands of civilians, mostly women and
children, were conscripted to dig defensive
lines, trenches, and tank traps; men were
given a rifle and sketchy training, and
formed into 'people's militia' battalions.

7 November, the anniversary of the
Bolshevik Revolution, was approaching.
Stalin considered it important to hold the
normal ceremonies, including a military
parade in Red Square. To avoid disruption by
air raids, the Party rally on 6 November was
held underground, in the Mayakovskaya
Metro station. Stalin's speech multiplied
German losses by seven and divided Soviet
losses by two, but most notably he invoked
not Communism but Russian patriotism,
then and at the parade on the next day. The
troops marched straight to the front, with
Stalin's exhortations to emulate 'our great
ancestors' –from Alexander Nevsky, victor
over the Teutonic Order in 1240, to Kutuzov,
who outwitted Napoleon in 1812 – ringing
in their ears.

As the ground hardened in mid-November,
the Germans recovered mobility, but met new
problems. Few had winter clothing or white
camouflage suits, and there were 133,000 cases
of frostbite. Supplies of fuel, anti-freeze, and
winter lubricants for aircraft and vehicles were
inadequate. Frozen grease had to be scraped off
every shell before it could be loaded, and
maintenance of aircraft, tanks, and trucks in
the open air was a nightmare. Stalin and
Zhukov had ordered 'scorched earth,' as much
destruction of buildings as possible, before
retreats. The troops often went both frozen
and unfed; at the end of November the
offensive petered out.

The official German assessment of
1 December, that the Red Army had no
reserves left, now proved spectacularly
wrong. From various sources, but particularly
his spy Richard Sorge in Tokyo, Stalin had
learned that Japan intended to attack
southward, against Europe's and the USA's
Asian dependencies, not northward against
the Soviet Union. He began transferring
divisions from the Soviet Far East; adding

won. On that day Stalin gave Zhukov
command of the remnants of Western and
Reserve Fronts, and at his suggestion
appointed Western Front's previous
commander, Konev, as his deputy in charge
of the front's northern sector, around Kalinin
(now Tver). Stalin also acted instantly to
reinforce the Mozhaisk defense line,
transferring 14 infantry divisions, 16 tank
brigades, and over 40 artillery regiments
from reserve or other sectors, to re-form
four armies. So eroded were they by previous
fighting that they totaled only 90,000 men,
equal to six full-strength divisions.

On 17 October the Kalinin sector, with
three armies and one ad hoc combat group,
became a separate Kalinin Front, under
Konev. By 18 October, the Germans had
taken Kalinin and Kaluga, threatening to
outflank Moscow from north and south, and

them to newly raised formations, he accumulated a 58-division reserve by the end of November.

Zhukov later admitted that he had not planned a major offensive. Local probing attacks simply revealed German weaknesses, justifying an offensive by West and Kalinin Fronts, and it began in 25 degrees of frost at 3.00 am on 5 December. They had fewer tanks and aircraft than Army Group Center, but fresher troops, clad, fed, and equipped

for cold weather, guns, tanks, and trucks designed for it, and heated hangars for servicing their aircraft.

In 34 days' heavy fighting the Germans were pushed back a minimum of 60 miles (100km), in some places up to 150 miles (240km). Zhukov, supported by Chief of

Revolution Anniversary Parade, Red Square, 7 November 1941. The troops went direct from the parade to the front line, and so did the tanks. (AKG Berlin)

General Staff Shaposhnikov, set limited objectives, forbade frontal assaults, and wanted all resources concentrated on pushing the central front line back, to make Moscow safe for the next year's campaigning. But Stalin convinced himself that Germany could be beaten before the spring thaw, and on 5 January 1942, over Zhukov's and Shaposhnikov's objections, ordered a general offensive by five fronts. This began on 8 January, continued till 20 April and achieved some successes, but at heavy cost

The Soviet counteroffensive at Moscow

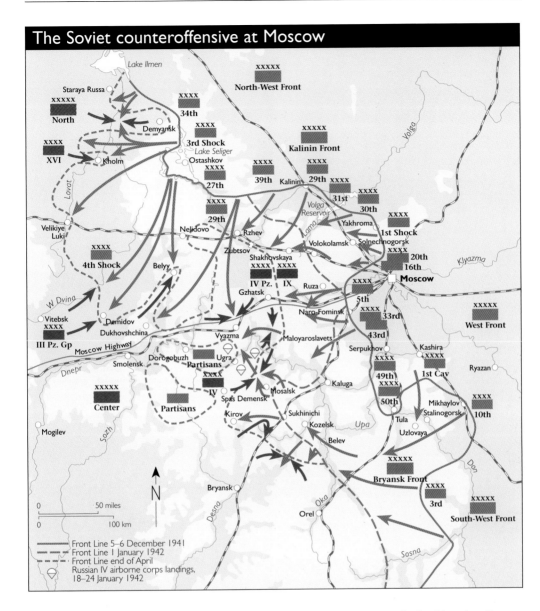

compared to Zhukov's December offensive. Just over a million troops took part in each; 139,586 were 'irrevocably' lost in December, almost twice as many – 272,520 – in the later offensive. Resources were so meager that some of Zhukov's artillery could fire only two shells a day. The average rate of advance was 1.5 miles (2.4km) a day – minute compared

to what the Germans had achieved earlier and the Red Army would later.

Moscow was not Hitler's only problem. Army Group South was equally beset by weather, and was halted on 11 October 1941, as much by mud as by the seven armies of South and Southwest Fronts. On that day I Panzer Army reached the River Mius, but was halted by rainstorms and stiffening resistance. Further north, VI Army inflicted heavy losses on Southwest Front, forcing Stavka (Soviet GHQ) to permit withdrawal to the Donets River. This was a heavy blow to

the Soviet war effort because it meant abandoning much of the Donets basin, which then supplied about two-thirds of the Soviet Union's coal and iron, and three-fifths

ABOVE Moscow, December 1941. Abandoned German artillery. (Public domain)

BELOW The spring thaw rendered roads as impassable as autumn rains had done. (IWM)

of its steel and aluminum. However, much of the industrial equipment was removed to the Urals or Siberia, and the coal mines were dynamited; lost coal output was replaced by exploiting deposits elsewhere, particularly by forced labor in the north, at Vorkuta.

Rostov-on-Don, 'gateway to the Caucasus,' fell on 20 November, but a Soviet counteroffensive had already begun, 56th Army attacking from the south, to keep the Germans engaged, while 37th Army attempted to strike south, to the coast behind them. Rundstedt ordered withdrawal to the Mius, about 50 miles (80km) west, and this was already in progress when on 30 November Hitler countermanded it. Rundstedt thereupon resigned, and Hitler replaced him with Field Marshal von Reichenau, commander of VI Army and one of the few actively Nazi German generals. Both reluctantly accepted that Rostov could not be held, but Hitler ordered I Panzer Army to stand at an intermediate position east of the Mius. However, on 1 December the Soviets broke through, and Hitler had to permit retreat to the Mius. Rundstedt proved right. Army Group South held the line there easily until mid-1942, then advanced to Rostov and the Caucasus.

Hitler's reaction to the unforeseen Russian resurgence was to dismiss generals and forbid retreats. By 19 December, Brauchitsch, Bock, Rundstedt, Guderian, Hoepner, and a number of others had gone, and he had taken command himself. Some German generals later conceded that his 'stand fast' orders prevented the retreat from becoming a rout. But the front's stabilization owed at least as much to Stalin's overambitious offensive, and to the spring thaw; and Hitler's subsequent insistence on standing fast repeatedly condemned German forces to annihilation.

The Battle of Moscow was Germany's first major land defeat of the war, and marked the failure of Blitzkrieg. The Red Army had suffered enormous losses, but was still very much in business, and of 1941's three 'symbolic' objectives, Leningrad, Moscow, and Kiev, only Kiev had fallen. Germany's

losses had been much smaller, but so was Germany's capacity to replace them. In the coming months, machinery evacuated to the Urals and Siberia would help the recently established industries there to begin replacing the equipment losses. From December, American entry into the war would provide the Soviet Union with a major supplier of the necessities of war.

1942

Kalinin and Western Fronts continued the 'limited' offensive advocated by Shaposhnikov and Zhukov. But, ominously for Germany, a 'limited' Soviet offensive even then meant a frontage of over 400 miles (640km), and over one million men, in 95 divisions and 46 brigades. By 20 April, when the spring thaw imposed a standstill, the Germans were well back from Moscow.

Hitler's plan for 1942 focused exclusively on the south. Almost all Soviet oil at that time came from three oilfields in the Caucasus, and reached the heartland by tankers up the Volga and railways along its banks. The Don, the European Soviet Union's second biggest river, sweeps through a right angle just south of Voronezh to run southeast for about 250 miles (400km), before turning southwest to flow into the Sea of Azov. On this second 'Big Bend' it is only 45 miles (72km) from the Volga. The plan was for Army Group South to advance east along the Don, then cross to the Volga north of the major industrial city of Stalingrad, thus cutting the Soviet oil supply route. The second phase would be an advance into the Caucasus to capture the oilfields. This plan did not require Stalingrad to be taken, but Hitler wanted it because of its symbolic name (Stalintown).

Campaigning began badly for the Red Army. Marshal Timoshenko planned an offensive from a bulge in the line, the Barvenkovo salient, to retake Kharkov, then the largest German-occupied Soviet city, but did not know that the Germans were

The Soviet offensive at Barvenkovo took many prisoners, but the German counteroffensive took many more. (AKG Berlin)

planning Operation Fridericus, to eliminate the salient by driving across its neck from both sides. Timoshenko attacked on 12 May, six days before 'Fridericus' was due, and when only its southern pincer, I Panzer Army, was in position. Kleist hastily launched a 'one-armed Fridericus' on 17 May, and by the 22nd had closed the trap. Timoshenko sought reinforcements; Stalin said, 'If they sold divisions in the market, I'd buy you some; but they don't,' and again withheld permission to withdraw until too late. Three Soviet armies were wiped out, 29 divisions destroyed, many others badly mauled, more than 200,000 soldiers captured, and over 400 tanks lost, before the main German offensive even began.

An attempt to lift the siege of Leningrad also failed, with another army encircled and destroyed. Results were no better in the far south; efforts to prevent German access to the Kerch Straits, leading to the Caucasus, were a disaster with 30,547 lost, almost half of the 62,500 troops engaged.

For the main offensive, Bock had four German and four satellite armies. The northern pincer, along the Don, had

IV Panzer (Colonel-General Hoth) and
VI (Colonel-General Paulus) Armies. The
southern had I Panzer (Kleist) and
XVII (General Ruoff) Armies, and XI Army
(Colonel-General von Manstein) was to
become available after capturing Sevastopol.
Satellite armies, II Hungarian, VIII Italian,
and III Romanian, were to guard the German
flank along the Don. Bock had 89 divisions,
including nine Panzer, most at or near full
strength.

A brief panic erupted on 19 June, when a
light aircraft, carrying a major with the plans
for the offensive's first phase, crash-landed
just behind Soviet lines. However, Stalin,

Soviet prisoner's-of-war digging along the road side.
(AKG Berlin)

who in 1941 had wrongly believed Hitler would give economic targets priority, now declined to believe that Hitler was doing precisely that. On 26 June he dismissed the documents as misinformation, two days before the offensive began, precisely as they had outlined, with an attack on Voronezh.

Since that city could be the starting point for a northeastward push to Moscow, it was strenuously defended by 74 divisions, six tank corps, and 37 brigades, with 1.3 million men. Bock threw two of IV Panzer Army's three corps into an unnecessary attempt to take it, wasting their mobility until 13th July. The Soviet defenders had over 370,000 'irrevocable' losses, but most of Southwest Front trudged off east along the Don, in relatively good order, with their heavy equipment intact. In pursuit was only VI Army, mostly on foot – its 18 divisions included only two Panzer and one motorized infantry divisions. For this Hitler dismissed Bock, and thereafter blamed him for all that followed, including the catastrophe at Stalingrad.

Hitler then divided Army Group South into Army Groups B (Weichs), to advance to the Volga, and A (List), to the Caucasus, and moved his headquarters from Rastenburg in East Prussia to Vinnitsa in Ukraine. From there he issued Directives No. 43 (11 July) and 45 (23 July), which envisaged seizing the Soviet Black Sea ports and Caucasus oilfields, thereby also cutting the Allied supply route through Iran. Directive No. 44 (21 July) ordered the Murmansk Railway cut. Had these objectives been attained, the only remaining supply route would have been across the Pacific and Siberia, and deliveries, except of aircraft, would have been approximately halved.

The pedestrian German pursuit produced few encirclements, and far fewer prisoners than expected. Hitler, however, ignored evidence that Southwest and South Fronts were withdrawing across the Don. On 13 July he ordered IV Panzer Army transferred to Army Group A, to cross the Don at Konstantinovka and move down its east bank to Rostov, to encircle Soviet forces

he believed still west of the river. Heavy summer rains and fuel shortages hampered movement, but anyway South Front had already crossed. In mid-July Halder confided to his diary that Hitler's underestimation of the enemy had become so grotesque as to make planning impossible.

The commander chosen for 62nd Army to defend Stalingrad city was Lieutenant-General V. I. Chuykov, till then Deputy Commander of 64th Army. During the

retreat he had observed German tactics' heavy dependence on coordination – the tanks not moving until the aircraft arrived, the infantry not moving without the tanks – and felt that the infantry's habit of opening fire beyond the range of their weapons suggested dislike of close combat. He decided to try to keep his own front line so close to the Germans that they could not use aircraft and tanks for fear of hitting their own infantry. That was easier said than done on the steppe, but inside a large, mostly ruined, city offered possibilities, provided Chuykov's own men would accept the side-effect of increased exposure to small-arms fire. This could not then be guaranteed, as morale was low. It took threats, probably some shootings, stirring messages from Front Commander Yeremenko and his Chief

Fighting in the factory area at Stalingrad went on throughout the battle. (Yakov Ryumkin)

Political Officer, Nikita Khrushchev, arrival of reinforcements, and Stalin's 'Not one step back' Order 227 to produce results.

Once 62nd Army was inside the city, Chuykov made a second departure from orthodoxy. Fighting was mostly within buildings, often room-by-room, and the normal army structure of homogeneous platoons and companies was unsuitable. Chuykov reorganized 62nd Army into 'storm groups' of 20–50 infantrymen, two or three guns, and one squad each of sappers and troops with flamethrowers or explosives. They studied enemy behavior, and where possible attacked when the Germans were eating, sleeping, or changing sentries. Assault groups of six to eight men, each carrying a submachine gun, 10–12 grenades, a dagger, and an entrenching tool (used more as a battle-axe than for digging), opened the attacks. When they signaled that they were inside, the reinforcement group followed, with heavier machine guns, mortars, anti-tank guns and rifles, crowbars, pickaxes, and explosives. It assisted the assault groups where needed, but its primary task was to cover the approaches against relief attempts. The third element, the reserve group, also had that function, but if not needed for that, it could split into assault groups and attack further. There was little scope for massed tanks or artillery, but single tanks or guns were used in support. Mining was first used against a building from which the Germans were firing on 62nd's only supply line, the ferries across the Volga. Sappers spent two weeks digging a tunnel to a point under the building, and three tons of explosives blew it and its garrison sky-high. Mining was employed extensively thereafter.

Not all the fighting was within buildings. The city stretched many miles along the Volga's west bank, and two large factory complexes, the Tractor and Barricades plants, were contested throughout the siege. A small hill, the Mamayev Kurgan, commanding the city center, was so intensively fought over that explosions made the ground too hot for snow to lie.

In such a narrow bridgehead there were no sanctuaries. Most of the Soviet artillery was deployed on the east bank of the Volga, directed by spotters in the city. There was no waterproof telephone cable, so communication with the east bank depended on ordinary cable that had to be replaced under fire every few days. Chuykov had to move his headquarters several times, finally settling in dugouts and half-submerged barges on the west bank, below some oil tanks that were found to be full only when a bomb set them on fire.

Attempts to repel the Germans by attacking northward were unsuccessful. On 12 September Zhukov returned from Stalingrad, reported this to Stalin, and then, while Stalin was studying the map, said to Vasilevsky, 'We must find another solution.' Stalin told them to find one and report the next evening. When they did, they put a proposal with two main points: first, they should keep the Germans forward by defending the city strongly, and second, they should assemble forces to encircle them by a pincer movement through the Romanian armies guarding their flanks, III north and IV south of the city.

The northern pincer would start from two bridgeheads on the southwest bank of the Don, at Serafimovich and Kletskaya. A tank force (5th Tank Army, under Lieutenant-General Romanenko) would assemble secretly in the Serafimovich bridgehead, to drive south toward the Don at Kalach, and the southern pincer would come north to meet it. Secrecy would be absolute – even Yeremenko, then commanding both Stalingrad and Southeast Fronts, was to be fed only generalities for the time being.

Preliminary reorganization saw Stalingrad Front renamed Don Front, and Lieutenant-General Rokossovsky appointed to command it. Yeremenko retained command of Southeast (renamed Stalingrad) Front, and a new Southwest Front was created in late October, deployed west of Don Front, and commanded by Lieutenant-General N. F. Vatutin. While 5th Tank Army would form the west side of the inner ring of encirclement, the rest of Southwest Front was to smash through the Romanians and

The Red Army springs the trap at Stalingrad

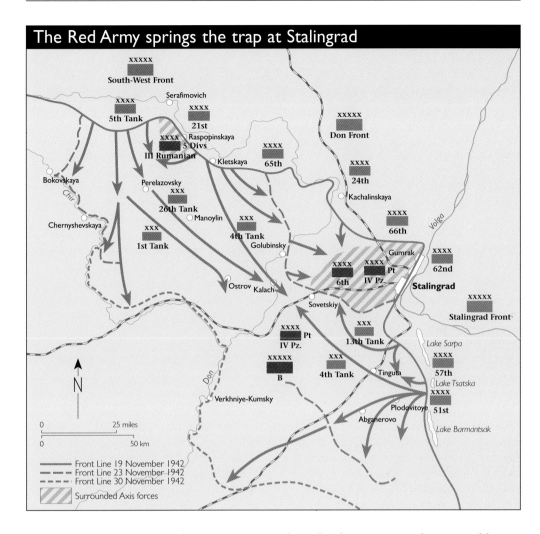

adjacent Italian VIII Army, to form a westward-facing outer ring against relief attempts. Zhukov and Vasilevsky estimated that assembling the required forces and supplies would need at least 45 days, so the counteroffensive could not begin until November. Stalin approved the plan, immediately sent Zhukov back to Stalingrad to scrutinize the northern sector, and a few days later sent Vasilevsky to the southern sector.

Exceptionally tight security was maintained, and no mention over telephone or radio was permitted. Zhukov, Vasilevsky, and other Stavka representatives shuttled between Stalingrad and Moscow, and reported orally to Stalin. The front commanders were informed in early October,

but subordinate commanders were told nothing until a month later. Whenever possible, troops, equipment, and supplies moved only by night, and the air force attempted to keep German air reconnaissance to a minimum.

The three fronts deployed 66 divisions and 19 brigades of infantry, eight divisions of horse cavalry, five corps and 15 brigades of tanks, and two mechanized corps, supported by six air armies. Not all units were at full strength, but the total, 1,143,500 men, 13,500 guns of 3-inch caliber or greater, and 894 tanks, was far more than OKH thought the Red Army could field. Such large movements could not be totally concealed, but the Germans realized neither their scale nor their purpose. The most that Colonel

Gehlen, head of the Intelligence Department 'Foreign Armies East,' achieved was a vague prediction of the northern pincer; of the southern he had no inkling.

An important part of the plan was an offensive by West and Kalinin Fronts, to prevent German mobile forces being transferred to Stalingrad. On 17 November, Stalin sent Zhukov to command this; Vasilevsky stayed at Stalingrad to coordinate the three fronts.

In mid-September a renewed German offensive put 62nd Army into a desperate situation, relieved only through instant reinforcement by a division from Stavka reserve, and another six during October. The starting dates for the counteroffensive were set as 9 November for Southwest and Don Fronts, and 10 November for Stalingrad Front. However, late arrival of troops, ammunition, fuel, anti-freeze, horses, and other supplies caused a 10-day postponement.

Hitler dismissed Halder on 24 September. His replacement, General Kurt Zeitzler, was more subservient, and even when, in the first week of November, evidence of a Soviet buildup opposite Romanian III Army began accumulating, OKH remained complacent. Hitler left for Berchtesgaden, to prepare his speech for the annual commemoration in Munich of his failed putsch of 8 November 1923. His headquarters began moving back from Vinnitsa to Rastenburg, and the cataclysmic events about to unfold could hardly have found German decision-makers worse placed to cope. On 23 October the British attacked in Egypt, and on 2 November Rommel's forces began retreating. On 7 November Anglo-American forces landed in French north Africa, so Hitler dispatched large forces to Tunisia, and on the 8th invaded Vichy France. On the 19th, the Soviet counteroffensive began.

Throughout this period Hitler was in the Berghof above Berchtesgaden, accompanied by only a few officers from his High Command, OKW, and none from OKH, responsible for the Eastern Front. The rest of his staff was divided between a barracks on the edge of town and his train in Salzburg

station. OKH was at Rastenburg; so was OKL (Air Force High Command), but its Commander-in-Chief, Goering, was in Paris. Hitler arrived back at Rastenburg late on 23 November, and when Zeitzler met him with a list of urgent matters, Hitler attempted to put him off till the next day.

The Soviet decision to attack the satellite armies was deliberate. Germany lacked the reserves to man the long flank on the Don, and in the belief that the Soviets had no reserves, Hitler had entrusted its defense to (from west to east) Hungarian II, Italian VIII, and Romanian III Armies. The Romanians had fought well when recovering Romanian territory in Moldavia, Bessarabia, and Bukovina, but were less keen to die for Germany in the depths of Russia. Nor were they equipped to withstand the 80-minute bombardment by 3,500 guns that opened the counteroffensive at 6.30 am on 19 November. OKH had 'corseted' them with 14th and 22nd Panzer divisions. The latter had camouflaged its tanks as haystacks, and the hay attracted field mice, which carried off the insulation from the electrical wiring to line their nests. When Romanenko's T-34s attacked, many of 22nd Panzer's tanks could not be started. When they were, they, 14th Panzer, and the 1st Romanian Armored Division first attacked a secondary advance from the Kletskaya bridgehead. Only later did they take on 5th Tank Army, and to no effect. Five of Romanian III Army's 10 divisions surrendered on 21 November.

The bridge at Kalach was taken by *ruse de guerre*. A column headed by several captured German vehicles drove up to it with headlights blazing. The bridge guards took it for the reliefs they were expecting, and were overcome almost before they realized their mistake.

The southern pincer, launched on 20 November by three armies of Stalingrad Front, also achieved total surprise and quickly smashed the German 29th Motorized Infantry Division and four of Romanian IV Army's seven divisions. Two mechanized corps headed toward Kalach, while one army advanced southwest toward the lower Don.

On 23 November the pincers met just south of Kalach, encircling German VI and part of IV Panzer and IV Romanian Armies, totaling 20 German and two Romanian divisions.

On 22 November Hitler ordered VI Army's commander, Colonel-General Paulus, to move his headquarters into Stalingrad and prepare to defend it. Paulus complied, but that day notified Army Group B's commander, Weichs, that he had very little ammunition and fuel, and only six days' rations. If supplied by air, he would try to hold out, but unless he could fill the gap left by the Romanians, he wanted permission to break out southwestwards. Weichs considered an immediate breakout imperative, and so did Paulus' five corps commanders. On 23 November, Paulus, with Weichs' support, radioed Hitler, seeking permission to abandon Stalingrad. Hitler refused, bolstered by Goering's assertion on 24 November that the Luftwaffe could supply Stalingrad by air.

This was totally unrealistic. The minimum supply required to sustain the force was 750 tons a day, but the Luftwaffe's standard Junkers Ju 52 transport could carry at most 2.5 tons, so at least 300 flights would be needed daily. Winter daylight was short, and of the seven Stalingrad-area airfields only Pitomnik could operate at night. Aircraft rapidly became unserviceable in the cold, and the transport fleet was heavily engaged ferrying reinforcements to Tunisia. These factors, and the certainty of Soviet attacks on the airlift, made Goering's promise nonsensical. On the day he made it, Wolfram von Richthofen, commanding Luftflotte 4, notified Weichs, OKH, and Goering of his dissent. Hitler chose to believe Goering, but Richthofen proved right: the best day's delivery was only 289 tons, the average less than 100. The Soviets packed the airlift corridor with anti-aircraft guns and constant fighter patrols; between them they shot down 325 of the lumbering transports and 165 of the bombers used to supplement them.

On 27 November Hitler ordered XI Army from Vitebsk to the south, and its commander, Field Marshal von Manstein,

to command a new Army Group Don. On paper it had four Panzer, 16 infantry, and two cavalry divisions outside encirclement, and 22 inside it. However, only one division (6th Panzer, transferred from France) was anywhere near full strength. Two other Panzer divisions had only about 30 tanks each, and the six Romanian divisions were little more than remnants. Nevertheless, Manstein planned a relief operation, letting Hitler believe he aimed to reinforce Stalingrad, but actually meaning to open a corridor for withdrawal.

The shortest relief route was from Verkhne-Kumskaya, about 40 miles (64km). But it was the most obvious, the Russians could readily reinforce it, opposed crossings of the Chir and Don would be needed, and it would be vulnerable to flank attacks by 5th Tank Army. So Manstein chose a more southerly route, along the Kotelnikovo–Stalingrad railway. This was more than 80 miles (130km) long, but had only small tributaries of the Don to cross. The route ran where the front ended in the Kalmyk Steppe, and only five Soviet infantry divisions were there.

Stavka, expecting Manstein to take the shortest route, sent 5th Shock Army to help 5th Tank disrupt the assumed preparations. Containing their probes across the Chir compelled Manstein to postpone the relief attempt from 3 to 12 December. He planned for two Panzer divisions under Colonel-General Hoth to thrust northeastwards. Group Hollidt and Romanian III Army were to hold the Chir River line, 48th Panzer Corps to attack the forces facing Hoth from behind, and IV Romanian to protect Hoth's right flank. When Manstein judged the time right, Paulus was to attack to meet Hoth.

The Soviet command countered the plan at two levels. Locally, Yeremenko realized as early as 28 November that the relief attempt might come on his front, not where Stavka expected it. On that day his cavalry attacked 6th Panzer Division, detraining at Kotelnikovo, and established that it had come from France. Yeremenko at once contacted Stalin seeking urgent reinforcement, and began strengthening his southern flank. When Hoth attacked, on 12 December, he advanced about a third of the way in two days, but on 14 December he encountered Yeremenko's tanks, and was stopped at the Myshkova River, about 30 miles (50km) from Stalingrad. On 19 December Manstein ordered Paulus to break out toward Hoth, but Paulus refused, citing lack of fuel and Hitler's directive. Stavka sent two more armies into action on 24 December, and in three days they pushed Hoth back beyond his starting point. Paulus' troops were now doomed.

Nor was that Manstein's only problem. Stavka's broader response to the relief attempt was a plan, approved on 3 December, to slice through Italian VIII and Hungarian II Armies to the Black Sea coast west of Rostov-on-Don, and cut off Army Groups Don in Ukraine and A in the Caucasus. After Yeremenko's call for help, the plan was amended to highlight crossing Army Group Don's lines of communication and capturing the airlift's western terminals, Tatsinskaya and Morozovsk. On 16 December the offensive began, and within a week Italian VIII Army ceased to exist. On Christmas Eve Soviet mobile forces attacked the two airfields, and on 28 December Hitler sanctioned a general withdrawal to a line about 150 miles (240km) west of Stalingrad. But the city was still to be held. At year's end he ordered SS Panzer Corps brought from France for another relief attempt.

1943

The troops in Stalingrad were starving and freezing to death. They had eaten most of their 7,000 horses, and their daily ration was down to 7 ounces (200g) of horsemeat, 2.5 ounces (70g) of bread, and half an ounce (14g) of margarine or fat. On 8 January Voronov (Stavka representative) and Rokossovsky offered Paulus surrender terms, but he rejected them, so on 10 January Rokossovsky began Operation Koltso ('Ring')

to destroy the 'pocket.' Four days later Pitomnik airfield fell, leaving the airlift with only the secondary field at Gumrak. By nightfall on the 16th, the German-held area was sliced in two, and its area more than halved.

Gumrak fell on the 21st, and Paulus moved his headquarters from there to the basement of a department store in the city. On the 23rd Hitler again forbade surrender, and on the 30th promoted Paulus to Field Marshal, an implicit invitation to suicide, as no German Field Marshal had ever surrendered. On 30 January General Shumilov, commanding 64th Army, learned of Paulus' whereabouts and sent in tanks and motorized infantry, along with an Intelligence officer, Lieutenant Ilchenko. Shortly after they began shelling the store, a German officer emerged and told Ilchenko, 'Our boss wants to talk to your boss.' Ilchenko radioed Shumilov, who sent his Chiefs of Operations and Intelligence to negotiate. The southern 'pocket' surrendered on 31 January, the northern one on 2 February. Nor was Stalingrad the only German setback. On 13 January, Voronezh Front had smashed Hungarian II Army.

Axis losses in the Stalingrad campaign, including the fighting along the Don, included the whole of VI Army, part of IV Panzer, most of Romanian III and IV, and Hungarian II and Italian VIII Armies. In Stalingrad itself 91,000 surrendered, but weakened by starvation, cold, and typhus most of them died in captivity; fewer than 6,000 survived to go home. In the city, 147,200 German and 46,700 Soviet troops died. The Germans flew out about 84,000, mostly wounded, but many died in shot-down aircraft. The Germans' net loss (dead, captured, missing, or invalided, minus replacements) was 226,000, and the replacements were generally inferior to those lost. The surviving remnants of the Romanian, Hungarian, and Italian armies were withdrawn, an additional net loss of at least 200,000.

Soviet losses were not fully documented until 1993. In the defensive phase

A column of prisoners from Stalingrad plods off to prison camps. (AKG Berlin)

(17 July–18 November 1942), 323,856
(59.2 percent) out of 547,000 engaged were
lost. The offensive (19 November 1942–2
February 1943) took far fewer lives; of
1,143,500 engaged, only 154,885
(13.5 percent) were lost, and the fighting
on the Don added another 55,874. Soviet
losses therefore totaled 534,615, but they
could be replaced from reserves and by
conscripting males of military age in the
recovered territories.

Army Group A had to leave the Caucasus
except for the Taman peninsula and
Tuapse–Novorossiisk coastal area. The
original Soviet plan, to trap it by pushing
down the Don to the coast behind it, had to
be changed when the Stalingrad trap was
found to hold over three times the numbers
expected. More troops had to be retained
there, and fewer sent down the Don. Army
Group A thus escaped destruction; but its
withdrawal ended the threat to the oilfields,
and Nazi fantasies of advancing to the
Middle East oilfields, and meeting in India
the Japanese advancing from Burma.

A counteroffensive by Manstein, launched
on 15 February, achieved complete surprise,
recovering much of the lost territory,
including Kharkov, and forcing a Soviet
withdrawal to the Northern Donets River.
The spring thaw then imposed a lull.

The Soviet withdrawals created a huge
salient, centered on the town of Kursk, and
Hitler's plan for summer 1943 was to destroy
the two Soviet fronts (Central and Voronezh)
defending it. His desire for as many as
possible of the new Tiger heavy and Panther
medium tanks and Ferdinand self-propelled
guns for the offensive, codenamed 'Zitadelle'
('Citadel'), led him to postpone it several
times, finally settling on 5 July.

Soviet information on German intentions
and deployments improved dramatically
during that lull. No Soviet or post-Soviet
source has ever explained why Intelligence
improved so radically between mid-February
and early April; but improve it did. By
8 April Zhukov was sufficiently confident
that he knew the German plan to propose
to Stalin strong defense of the salient to
wear the Germans down, followed by a
counteroffensive on the entire southern half
of the front. After consulting front
commanders Rokossovsky and Vatutin, Stalin
accepted Zhukov's plan on 12 April.

Hitler's plan received a mixed reception
from the generals designated to implement it
when they met in Munich on 4 May. Model
questioned the adequacy of the resources
allotted; Kluge and Manstein wanted it
launched soon, before Red Army strength
built up even further. Guderian, now Mobile
Forces' Inspector-General, totally opposed
any offensive in the east. Axis forces in north
Africa were only nine days away from
surrender; an Anglo-American invasion of
Europe was inevitable, and perhaps
imminent. Guderian wanted to husband
tanks for that, not squander them on the
steppes. Hitler satisfied nobody. Model got
only part of the extra resources he wanted.
Kluge and Manstein did not get quick action,
because Hitler waited until more new tanks
arrived. Guderian would see most of the
tanks he wanted destroyed at Prokhorovka
on 12 July.

The Soviet defenders received a windfall
when a 'Tiger' tank became bogged during
trials on the Leningrad front. They captured
it, and worked out how best to counter it.
In the salient, troops and 300,000 civilians
dug almost 6,000 miles (9,650km) of
trenches and anti-tank ditches, and
thousands of foxholes. Six belts of defenses
stretched back 110 miles (175km) from the
front line, with two more behind, manned
by newly created Steppe Front, and a ninth
along the east bank of the Don. Mines were
laid at a density (2,400 anti-tank and
2,700 anti-personnel mines per mile
[1.6 km] of front) four times that at
Stalingrad, and there was more artillery
than infantry in the salient, including
92 regiments from Stavka Reserve. To ensure
adequate supplies a new railway was built,
and over 1,800 miles (2,900km) of roads and
tracks were upgraded or repaired. Some
divisions had been worn down in previous
fighting to as low as 1,000 men, and
reinforcements poured in.

A disabled Nazi tank in the area of the Prokhorovka bridghead. (Novosti [London])

Central and Voronezh Fronts totaled 1,272,700 men, on a front of almost 350 miles (560km), with 3,306 tanks and assault guns, 19,300 guns and mortars, and 920 of the multiple rocket launchers known to the Red Army as 'Katyushas,' and to the Germans as 'Stalin Organs.' In reserve behind them was Steppe Front, with 400,000 men and another tank army. These greatly outnumbered the 900,000 men, 2,700 tanks, and 10,000 guns of Army Groups Center and South. Hitler on 2 July ordered the offensive to begin on the 5th. That day Stavka warned both front commanders to expect the attack any time up to 6 July.

German prisoners and deserters confirmed that the attack against Central Front was to begin at 3.00 am on 5 July, after a 30-minute artillery bombardment. Zhukov was at Rokossovsky's headquarters, and when they learned this they began a counter-bombardment at 2.20. Zhukov would later conclude that this began too soon, before the German tanks and infantry occupied their starting positions. The assault began at 5.30 am, spearheaded by three Panzer divisions, with five infantry divisions in support. Model's troops advanced about 6 miles (10km) that day on a 20-mile (32km) front; but Rokossovsky had merely pulled back to the second defensive belt. The Germans gained little more ground, suffered heavy losses in men and tanks, and within two days were stopped.

Army Group South initially fared no better. Heavy rain during the night and most of next day made it hard to bridge streams and rivers, slowing both tanks and infantry. However, 48th Panzer and 2nd SS Panzer Corps penetrated the first line of Soviet defenses, and by nightfall on the second day had advanced about 7 miles (11km). Vatutin, despite objections by Zhukov and Stalin, had dug his tanks into the ground to provide fire support for his infantry, so Stavka sent him the

The German plan for Operation Citadel

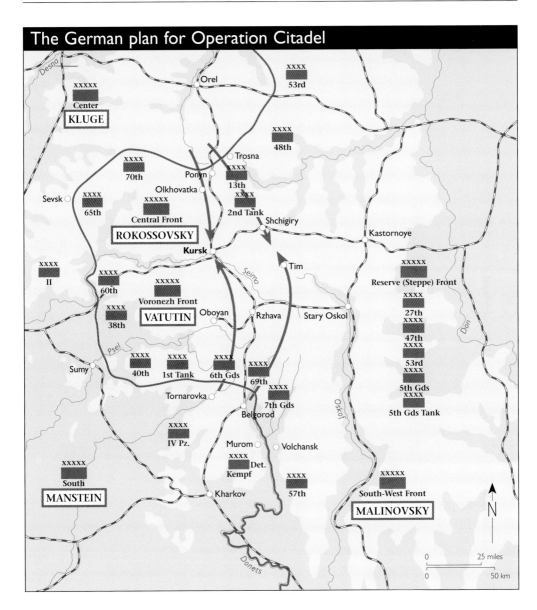

The intention was to eliminate the salient by the classic method, driving across its neck from north and south. However, the Soviets expected this.

5th Guards Tank and 5th Guards Armies from Steppe Front. On 12 July 5th Guards Tank Army, with about 850 tanks and self-propelled guns, confronted 2nd SS Panzer Corps with about 600 near the village of Prokhorovka in the largest tank battle of the war. Losses on both sides were heavy, but the Germans withdrew, and thenceforth the Soviet tank generals had the whip hand.

On that day West and Bryansk Fronts, north of the salient, attacked toward Orel, threatening the rear of German IX Army, in Operation Kutuzov, the start of the counteroffensive. They deployed three armies initially, and when the Germans held those, committed another three.

Then events elsewhere distracted Hitler's attention. On 10 July Anglo-American forces invaded Sicily; clearly they would soon land on the Continent, and Italian enthusiasm for the war was evaporating. On 13 July Hitler told Kluge and Manstein he was calling

'Citadel' off and transferring a number of divisions to the west. Manstein objected, but in vain.

Mussolini was overthrown on 25 July, and Hitler's suspicions that Italy would surrender or change sides were confirmed by radio intercept of a conversation between Churchill and Roosevelt. To shorten the line and free troops for the west, Hitler on 1 August ordered immediate evacuation of the Orel salient.

The second phase of the Soviet counteroffensive (Operation Rumyantsev) involved South and Southwest Fronts. To counter them Manstein sent much of his armor from the Kharkov area. No sooner had he done so than on 3 August Zhukov sent Voronezh and Steppe Fronts and the right wing of Southwest Front into the third phase, an advance toward Belgorod and Kharkov. The Germans were completely taken by surprise, and by 5 August had lost Belgorod and Orel. Reinforcements from Army Group Center, and the hasty return of some of the forces dispatched south, stopped the Soviet offensive temporarily. Hitler insisted on holding Kharkov and the Donets basin, but on 7 August the fourth phase of the counteroffensive (Operation Suvorov-1) began; West Front and the left wing of Kalinin Front launched 11 armies and several smaller formations towards Smolensk.

The vapidity of German belief that Soviet reserves were nearing exhaustion was evident. Figures released in 1993 showed that the eight fronts involved in the counteroffensive deployed 4,696,100 men, over four times as many as in the Stalingrad counterblow. Almost 358,000 of them were 'irrevocably' lost, but this, at 7.7 percent of those engaged, was a significant improvement on the 13.5 percent of the Stalingrad offensive. The Wehrmacht's net manpower loss, 448,000, was almost double the 226,000 of Stalingrad.

The Kursk campaign was more decisive than Stalingrad in other ways also. It was the Red Army's first major summer offensive, and the Germans' last. After Stalingrad Manstein had mounted a successful large-scale counteroffensive; after Kursk no German general could. From now on the Red Army had overwhelming superiority in men, tanks, guns, and aircraft, and would lunge from river to river, Dnepr to Vistula to Oder to Elbe, to meet the British and Americans. The enormous losses of 1941 had made the 'Russian steamroller' a myth. Kursk restored it, and it became ever stronger, as territorial gains provided more recruits, while Germany's ability to replace losses declined, and its allies began melting away.

Steppe Front entered Kharkov on 13 August, and after 10 days the Germans withdrew. The next Soviet target was the Donets basin. On 27 August Manstein attempted to make Hitler choose between reinforcing and abandoning it. Hitler equivocated. Italy was about to defect, so he had to find forces to occupy it and to replace Italian troops in the Balkans before the Allies gained a foothold. Of Germany's 277 divisions, 194 (70 percent) were on the Eastern Front, and the new commitments must be met mainly from them. Manstein had to withdraw behind the Dnepr, retaining bridgeheads east of it only at Dnepropetrovsk and from Zaporozhe to the coast.

The first Soviet 'lunge' was to the Dnepr. Central, Voronezh, and Steppe Fronts, renamed 2nd Belorussian, 1st, and 2nd Ukrainian Fronts respectively in October, closed up to it on a front of about 375 miles (600km) in the last 10 days of September. They seized bridgeheads on its west bank, then paused to regroup, resupply, and replace casualties. Between them they mustered 116 infantry divisions, 12 tank and five mechanized corps, and 12 brigades. Although still mostly a marching army, mobility, particularly speed of supply, was being greatly enhanced by American-supplied jeeps and 3-ton trucks, 434,000 of which were delivered in the course of the war. Their availability, and supplies of American machine tools, enabled the Soviet vehicle industry to build tanks at up to 2,000 a month, double Germany's best. To this array Army Group South could oppose

only 37 infantry and 17 Panzer or motorized infantry (now called Panzer Grenadier) divisions. All were severely below strength, and the Panzer/Panzer Grenadier divisions had only 257 tanks and 220 assault guns between them, an average of only 15 tanks and 13 assault guns per division.

On the Germans' heels, three Soviet armies in late September seized a bridgehead over the Dnepr at Bukrin, about 50 miles (80km) southeast of Kiev, and in early October another army took one at Lyutezh, 20 miles (32km) northeast of the city. The first attempt to recapture Kiev was made from the Bukrin bridgehead on 16 October, but the Germans were expecting it, and in four days' fighting inflicted very heavy casualties, so Zhukov decided to make the next attempt from the northern bridgehead. This necessitated moving a tank army and

many artillery units up to 125 miles (200km), crossing the Dnepr twice and the Desna once. So as not to alert the Germans, movement was mostly at night, and bad weather helped by grounding the Luftwaffe.

The offensive began on 3 November, with two armies advancing from the bridgehead and their northern neighbor attacking in support. IV Panzer Army could not hold them, and Hitler dismissed its commander, Hoth. Kiev fell on 6 November, and the Soviet advance continued, though with local setbacks, until 26 November, when the autumn rains and mud temporarily immobilized both sides.

At the south end of the line, Vasilevsky coordinated offensives by 3rd and 4th Ukrainian Fronts, also to cross the Dnepr. The initial objective was the German east-bank bridgehead at Zaporozhe, held by

Combined Soviet tank and infantry assault. (AKG Berlin)

part of I Panzer Army, and on 10 October three armies were hurled at it. By the 14th they had taken it, depriving the Germans of their only rail supply route to Army Group A in the Crimea. On 23 October, 4th Ukrainian Front took Melitopol, and on the 25th, 3rd Ukrainian entered Dnepropetrovsk; by the end of the month both fronts were on the lower Dnepr, two armies were on the northern edge of the Crimea, and Army Group A was isolated. Simultaneously, 2nd and 3rd Ukrainian Fronts on 16 October began an offensive aimed at destroying I Panzer Army. They regained much territory, but a counterattack by 40th Panzer Corps (General of Mountain Troops Schoerner) retook Krivoy Rog, forcing 2nd Ukrainian Front back to the Ingulets

River, with substantial losses of tanks, and 5,000 prisoners.

But local German successes barely affected the big picture; Rokossovsky's Belorussian and Vatutin's 1st Ukrainian Front could potentially drive a wedge between Army Groups Center and South, then attack either in flank. To protect the junction with Army Group Center, Manstein on 29 December sent I Panzer Army north to join IV Panzer.

Since abandoning 'Citadel,' Army Group Center had been as hard-pressed as Army Group South. Kluge's troops were very thinly spread, and appeals for reinforcement from western Europe went unanswered, as Hitler wrongly believed an Anglo-American landing in France was imminent.

The terrain in the center and north of the front, peppered with forests, woods, and swamps, was far more suited to guerrilla warfare than the wide open spaces of Ukraine. Kluge therefore had to detach far more troops to guard his communications and fight partisans than did Manstein. During July and August the anti-partisan Operation Herman in Baranovichi province alone involved 50,000 Germans, most of them front-line troops.

Partisan warfare had begun in 1941, initially only as random attacks by bands of Red Army stragglers, but by mid-1943 it was large and organized enough to create considerable problems, particularly for Army Group Center. The partisans, depicted in Soviet-era accounts as heroes enjoying universal popular support, were often in reality an unwanted burden to the peasants among whom they operated. Villagers were equally liable to be killed by partisans for refusing support or by the Germans for providing it, and if partisans killed any Germans in the vicinity, the village was likely to be destroyed and its inhabitants massacred. As German reprisals increased, and the tide of war began turning against Germany, peasant support for the partisans increased, and by mid-1943 partisan operations were generally closely coordinated with those of the fronts. On 3 August the

Partisan areas 1943–1944

FINLAND

Helsinki

Lake Ladoga

Leningrad

Gulf of Finland

Tallin

Lake Peipus

Lake Ilmen

Pskov

Volga

Riga

Dvina

RUSSIA

Rzhev

Moscow

Kaunas   Vitebsk

Tula

Minsk

Smolensk

Orel

Bryansk

Pripya   Pripyat Marshes

Kursk

Don

Kiev

Berdichev

Kharkov

Dnepr

Dnestr

Dnepropetrovsk

Zaporizhye

Nikolayev

ROMANIA

Odessa

SEA OF AZOV

0   250 miles

0   500 km

BLACK SEA

N

——— Front Line July 1943

Areas controlled by partisan forces, summer 1943

• Active partisan units outside partisan controlled areas

The front from the Karelian isthmus to the Arctic coast was held by the Finns and, at its northern extremity, German XX Mountain Army. The only democracy to join the Axis, Finland took pains to present its war as one not of conquest but of restitution, of territory lost in 1940; Finnish forces stopped at the 1939 frontier or first defensible position beyond it. They made no serious effort to cut the Murmansk railway, along which about one-quarter of all Allied aid passed, and to Hitler's fury, declined to join German efforts against Leningrad. Stavka maintained relatively small forces on the Finnish front, and waited for Finland to admit it had backed the wrong horse. Soviet peace proposals made in July 1943 were rejected, but Anglo-American pressure and the perception that Germany was losing combined to intensify Finnish efforts to leave the war. XX Mountain Army was potentially both an embarrassment and a hostage. On 28 September Hitler ordered it to hold northern Finland, especially Petsamo port and nickel mine, if Finland sought an armistice.

The 'Battle for the Dnepr' ended on 22 December. In a month's fighting, Army Group South pushed 1st Ukrainian Front back about 25 miles (40km) from the line it had reached by mid-November, but could not stabilize a line along the Dnepr. On 24 December, Stavka began the reconquest of right-bank Ukraine, using all four Ukrainian Fronts and 2nd Belorussian Front. With 188 divisions, 19 corps, 13 brigades, and 2,406,100 men, the five fronts had not much less than the Wehrmacht's total Eastern Front strength (195 divisions, 2,850,000 men). In tanks and guns they outnumbered the Germans by over three to one, and their growing superiority was marked by the breadth of their assault, on a front of over 800 miles (1,300km).

The open steppes of the Ukraine offered little scope for large-scale partisan activity, and most groups there were small. In Belorussia and the Baltics, forests and swamps made it easier for partisans to form large bands and even to take control of sizable areas. They contributed notably to the Soviet successes at Kursk in 1943 and in Belorussia in 1944 by disrupting German communications and monitoring German troop movements. Some partisans in Ukraine and the Baltics were nationalist and fought Soviet as well as German rule. In February 1944 Ukrainian nationalist partisans ambushed and mortally wounded front commander General Vatutin. These anti-Soviet formations fought on until 1947.

'Rails War' began, in support of the offensive by West and Kalinin Fronts launched four days later. Its main targets were the railways supplying Army Groups North and Center; 167 partisan units with about 100,000 men took part, and it lasted until 15 September, wreaking havoc with German supplies.

1944

The Soviet advance in the south continued for 116 days. When it ended, on 17 April 1944, the front line had moved up to 300 miles (480km) west since December. Despite the transfer of 34 German divisions from western Europe, the Red Army had reached the eastern Carpathians, and taken the war into enemy territory by crossing into Romania.

Stalin had long come to accept Zhukov's and Vasilevsky's view that limited operations with clearly defined objectives were preferable to general offensives, by enabling resources to be concentrated. But it was now becoming possible not only to make 'limited' operations very large, but also to mount two simultaneously. On 14 January, with the advance in the south in full swing, another offensive was launched, against Army Group North. It had two prime objectives, one to lift the siege of Leningrad, the other to prevent Army Group South being reinforced. Leningrad and Volkhov Fronts, part of 2nd Baltic Front, and the Baltic Fleet undertook it, with 732,500 soldiers and 89,600 sailors. It lasted until 1 March, ended the siege, drove the Germans back up to 175 miles (280km) on a 370-mile (595km) front, and took Soviet troops into Estonia for the first time since 1941. The Germans took a heavy toll of Leningrad Front, which lost 56,564 men, 13.5 percent of all its troops engaged, but overall the losses, 76,686, were 9.3 percent.

Army Group Center was left holding a bulge that the Russians christened the 'Belorussian balcony.' In February the Soviet General Staff began planning to eliminate it and as much as possible of Army Group Center. While it was doing so, a third operation was mounted in the south, by 4th Ukrainian Front (General Tolbukhin), the Independent Coastal Army (General Yeremenko), 4th Air Army, the Black Sea Fleet, and the Azov Flotilla, against German XVII Army in the Crimea. This involved 'only' 30 divisions, one corps, and five brigades, but cleared a potential threat to

the coastal flank of the Soviet advance, and recaptured the Black Sea Fleet's main base of Sevastopol. XVII Army made a spirited defense there, but Soviet losses, at 17,754, were only 3.8 percent of the troops committed.

Preparations for assaulting the 'balcony' went on under the usual heavy security. The Red Army hoodwinked the Germans into expecting the main offensive in the north and south, not the center, as successfully as the Anglo-Americans deceived them into expecting the invasion in the Pas de Calais, not Normandy. Units' radio stations closed down reopened further south or north, transmitting fake messages from fake camps, gun and tank parks, protected by aircraft and anti-aircraft gun crews instructed to make life dangerous but not impossible for German reconnaissance aircraft. 'Foreign Armies East' predicted a quiet summer for Army Group Center, and such reinforcements as were available were sent to Army Groups North and South (now renamed North Ukraine).

The Soviet plan, codenamed 'Bagration,' was for a sequence of up to four offensives, the last two dependent on the success of the first two. The first, which opened on 10 June, involved parts of Leningrad and Karelian Fronts, aiming first to lure German forces away from the 'balcony,' and second to coerce Finland into surrender. The second, main, offensive was by 1st Baltic, 1st, 2nd, and 3rd Belorussian Fronts, against Army Group Center (Field Marshal Busch) north and south of Minsk. If it developed satisfactorily, 1st Ukrainian Front (Marshal Konev) would advance into Poland, 2nd (General Malinovsky) and 3rd (General Tolbukhin) Ukrainian Fronts into Romania, to force its surrender and seize the Axis's only major oilfields, at Ploesti. Stalin again took a codename from Russia's past, Bagration – a Georgian, like himself, a prince and a general in the Russian army, killed fighting Napoleon in 1812.

The Anglo–American–Canadian landings in Normandy on 6 June forced considerable movement of German forces to the west. This somewhat eased the Red Army's task, but 228 Axis divisions remained on the Eastern Front, versus 58 in western Europe, though most Eastern Front divisions were well below strength. Developments in France would take more divisions westward, and the Luftwaffe's capacity to challenge Soviet air superiority was inhibited by the need to counter Anglo-American bombing. This absorbed over one-third of its aircraft and an even higher share of gun production, and Germany's overstretching left Air Fleet VI, supporting Army Group Center, with only 40 serviceable aircraft facing 7,000 Soviet.

Partisans again made a formidable contribution. On 19 June they began a seven-day rampage in Belorussia against Army Group Center's communications and supply lines. They blew up almost 1,100 rail and road bridges, derailed many trains, and destroyed or damaged thousands of locomotives and goods wagons. On 21 June Air Force bombers joined in the destruction, and on the 23rd the infantry advanced behind rolling artillery barrages from 31,000 guns, ranged almost wheel-to-wheel at an average 270 guns or Katyushas per mile (1.6 km) of front.

Against 168 divisions, 12 tank corps, and 20 brigades, Army Group Center, with only two Panzer and 36 infantry divisions, could expect hard times. Hitler made them even harder, by ordering numerous towns and cities to be made *Festungen* (fortresses), or breakwaters against the Soviet tide. But the tide simply bypassed them, and all he achieved was to make potentially mobile forces static. An example of this was III Panzer Army (General Reinhardt). Despite its title it had no tanks, only a brigade of assault guns and a battalion of 'Hornet' 88mm tank-destroyers, plus 11 infantry divisions. This was little enough to face a tank corps and 24 infantry divisions of Bagramyan's 1st Baltic Front, and another tank corps and 11 infantry divisions from Chernyakhovsky's 3rd Belorussian. Yet Hitler ordered four divisions committed to the 'fortress' of Vitebsk.

On 23 June, the first day of 'Bagration,' 1st Baltic advanced 10 miles (16km) on a 35-mile (56km) front, and that evening

Reinhardt sought Busch's permission to evacuate Vitebsk immediately. Busch refused, so on the next day Reinhardt telephoned Zeitzler, who was with Hitler at his Bavarian mountain retreat. Zeitzler consulted Hitler, who insisted Vitebsk be held. A few minutes later Reinhardt heard by radio from Vitebsk that the road west was under threat, so he repeated his request to Busch, who at once transmitted it to Hitler. He again refused, but two hours later authorized withdrawal, provided one division stayed behind.

Reinhardt thought that a pointless sacrifice, but to save the other three divisions accepted it, and at once ordered their commander, General Gollwitzer, to bring them out. But by the next day, 25 June, 3rd Belorussian Front forces had met 1st Baltic, encircling Vitebsk. Of Gollwitzer's 35,000 men, only 10,000 survived to surrender; Hitler's obsession had deprived Reinhardt of one-third of his already vastly outnumbered force.

On 24 June, 1st Belorussian Front (Marshal Rokossovsky), with six tank corps, 77 infantry, and nine cavalry divisions, began its offensive. By 27 June it had encircled Bobruisk and most of German IX Army (General Jordan), and jointly with 2nd Belorussian (General Zakharov) was about to encircle Mogilev and most of German IV Army (General von Tippelskirch). Only rapid withdrawals could now save Army Group Center, but Hitler still refused them, invoking the bad impression they would make on Germany's allies, particularly the Finns. He reluctantly allowed Busch to try to extricate IV and IX Armies, but drew a line on the map, and ordered Busch to hold it. By 28 June Soviet forces were already through it, so he dismissed Busch and put Army Group Center under Field Marshal Model, already commanding Army Group North Ukraine.

At the northern end of the line, Army Group North was being hard pressed by 1st Baltic Front, and the Soviet advance south of it threatened its flank. Its commander, Colonel-General Lindemann, sought permission to retreat to a shorter and more defensible line; Hitler dismissed him, and replaced him with General Friessner.

Minsk fell on 4 July; most of IV and IX Armies, about 100,000 in all, were trapped east of it, and were destroyed over the next seven days. The 57,000 captured were paraded through Moscow on 17 July, symbolically followed by street-cleaning vehicles. About 28 of Army Group Center's 38 divisions had been destroyed, and their losses, about 300,000 so far, ranked Bagration with Kursk. Of Army Group Center's four armies, IV and IX had been smashed, as had nine of III Panzer's 11 divisions. II Army (General Weiss) remained relatively intact, but between it and the remnants of III Panzer was a 250-mile (400km) gap, defended only by scratch formations of border guards and training units rushed from East Prussia.

Soviet exploitation of this was rapid. 1st Baltic Front advanced north of Vilnius, capital of Lithuania. 3rd Belorussian Front took Vilnius on 13 July, and pushed what was left of III Panzer Army away northwestward. 2nd Belorussian advanced 160 miles (255km) in 10 days, to within 50 miles (80km) of the East Prussian border, while 1st Belorussian pushed across Poland to the Vistula. Between 28 July and 2 August it secured bridgeheads at Magnuszew and Pulawy, and at the end of July it was approaching Warsaw.

The Polish Home Army, loyal to the government-in-exile in London, began the Warsaw Rising on 1 August, when noise of gunfire from the east suggested that Soviet troops would soon arrive. Marshal Rokossovsky, 1st Belorussian Front's commander, was not notified beforehand, and Stalin, who intended power to pass to the Communist 'Polish National Committee,' denounced the rising as an attempt to improve the London government's position by seizing Warsaw before the Red Army arrived.

Militarily, 1st Belorussian Front had good reason to stop at the Vistula. It had been attacking for two months, had advanced nearly 400 miles (640km), suffered 28 percent casualties in dead or wounded, and outrun its supply lines. Its task, which it had fulfilled precisely, was to seize some bridgeheads, then stop to regroup and resupply. It was not required to try to seize Warsaw off the march, and at the end of July it was forced back 15–20 miles (24–32km). But for politics, Home Army commander General Bor-Komorowski would probably have told Rokossovsky what he intended, and been advised to wait until 1st Belorussian Front, including its Soviet-equipped Polish 1st Army, could resupply and attack in support.

On 3 August the guns in the east fell silent. Thereafter the Home Army fought alone against German forces amply provided with heavy weapons, tanks, and air support. It was squeezed into smaller and smaller areas, and in the rising's sixth week Bor was

Improvisation – Soviet infantry crossing the River Dvina in Operation Bagration. (IWM NYP 31136 PR2)

authorized to seek German terms for surrender. Talks mediated by the Polish Red Cross secured a brief cease-fire on 8 and 9 September, but went no further, because on 10 September 1st Belorussian Front at last moved. Over the next five days Soviet and Polish 1st Army troops eliminated the Germans' east-bank bridgehead in Praga and occupied the entire east bank. But on the 11th, the newly arrived 25th Panzer Division set about pushing the Home Army away from the west bank. Polish 1st Army units attempted to cross on the nights of 16 and 17 September, but those that survived the crossing were cut to pieces by German fire, and no more attempts were made.

Roosevelt's and Churchill's requests to Stalin brought on 16 August only a denunciation of the rising as 'a reckless, appalling adventure' from which the Soviet command 'must dissociate itself.' They then attempted to supply the insurgents from the air, and sought Stalin's permission for the aircraft to fly on to Soviet-controlled airfields to refuel. Stalin initially refused, and the need to carry enough fuel for the return trip severely limited the payloads. Furthermore, lack of Soviet air support over Warsaw compelled the aircraft to drop their loads from a great height; most of them fell into the river or German hands. Only on 10 September did Stalin relent. A supply flight by 110 American bombers was mounted, but by then the Home Army held so little ground that only 30 percent of the supplies reached them. From 13 September the Soviet air force also began dropping supplies, but too late to be of use. The rising ended in a negotiated surrender on 2 October.

After 68 days 'Bagration' officially ended on 29 August. On a front of almost 700 miles (1,125km), Soviet forces had advanced

Troops of Polish First Army, 1st Belorussian Front, back on Polish soil. (AKG Berlin)

340–75 miles (545–600km), at higher rates of advance than before. At Moscow in 1941 their best had been 3.7 miles (6km) a day, at Stalingrad 2.8 miles (4.5km), at Kursk 6.2 miles (10km). In 'Bagration' they reached 15.6 miles (25km) in the first phase, and 8.75 miles (14km) in the second. The cost in lives, 180,040, was 7.7 percent of the 2,411,600 committed, the same as in the Kursk offensive, much less than the 13.5 percent of Stalingrad, and for much larger gains than in either.

Since this offensive developed well, Konev's 1st Ukrainian Front was launched into the next, the Lvov–Sandomierz operation against Army Group North Ukraine, on 13 July. This also ended on 29 August, as successfully as the first. Konev's troops crossed the Vistula at Sandomierz, and established a large bridgehead to serve as the launching point for the next advance, into

Silesia. Reflecting the relative weakness of Army Group North Ukraine, the average daily rate of advance (up to 40 miles, or 65km) was even higher, and losses (6.5 percent) lower, than in 'Bagration' proper.

The fourth offensive, against Army Group South Ukraine and Romania, was initiated by 2nd and 3rd Ukrainian Fronts on 20 August. It too ended officially on 29 August, after only 10 days. The frontage of assault was about 315 miles (505km), depth of advance ranged from 185 to 200 miles (300 to 320km); the daily advance averaged up to 15.5 miles (25km) for the marching infantry, and 20 miles (32km) for the mobile forces. Losses (13,197) were only 1 percent of the 1.3 million troops involved, but militarily the victory was only partial; Army Group South Ukraine had to retreat, but Manstein frustrated Zhukov's plan to encircle and destroy it. Politically, however, the brief campaign was a triumph. With help from anti-German Romanians, 2nd Ukrainian Front occupied Ploesti on 30 August, and entered

Bucharest on the 31st. On 12 September at Moscow Romania signed an armistice, and undertook to provide at least 12 infantry divisions to fight the Germans.

Germany's Balkans problems next involved Bulgaria, which had joined the Axis in 1941, but had not declared war on the Soviet Union. On 26 August, as 3rd Ukrainian Front approached, it restated its neutrality, ordered the disarming of German troops retreating from Romania, and asked the USA and Great Britain for armistice terms. On 5 September the Soviet Union declared war, and 3rd Ukrainian Front invaded. It met no resistance, a new Bulgarian government declared war on Germany on 9 September, and a Bulgarian army joined the Soviet push into Yugoslavia.

The unsuccessful 20 July coup against Hitler had been suppressed too quickly to affect Germany's war effort immediately. But Germany's allies were now falling away one after another. The liberation of Paris on 25 August was followed the next day by the flight of the collaborationist Vichy government. On 29 August a national uprising began in the puppet state of Slovakia. German troops had to be rushed there, and the rising was not suppressed until the end of October.

Soviet troops land on the Finnish coast. (AKG Berlin)

On 2 September Finland accepted Soviet armistice terms and on the 4th it broke off relations with Germany and announced a cease-fire. Its armistice agreement, signed in Moscow on 19 September, included an undertaking to disarm any Germans still on its territory. German forces in southern Finland left quickly, but XX Mountain Army in the north formed defensive fronts on the east against the Soviets and on the south against the Finns. Marshal Meretskov sent troops and marines into action on 7 October, and by the 15th the Germans were retreating into Norway. On 25 October Soviet troops liberated Kirkenes, and on the 29th reached Neiden, where they stopped. Stalin sent Meretskov, the first front commander to work himself out of a job, to take leave, then undertake a new assignment. He would command a front in the war against Japan, which Stalin had committed the Soviet Union to enter within three months of Germany's surrender.

The lull following completion of 'Bagration' on 29 August was very brief. With Anglo-American forces approaching Germany's western borders, advancing in Italy and, on 15 June, landing in southern France, Germany

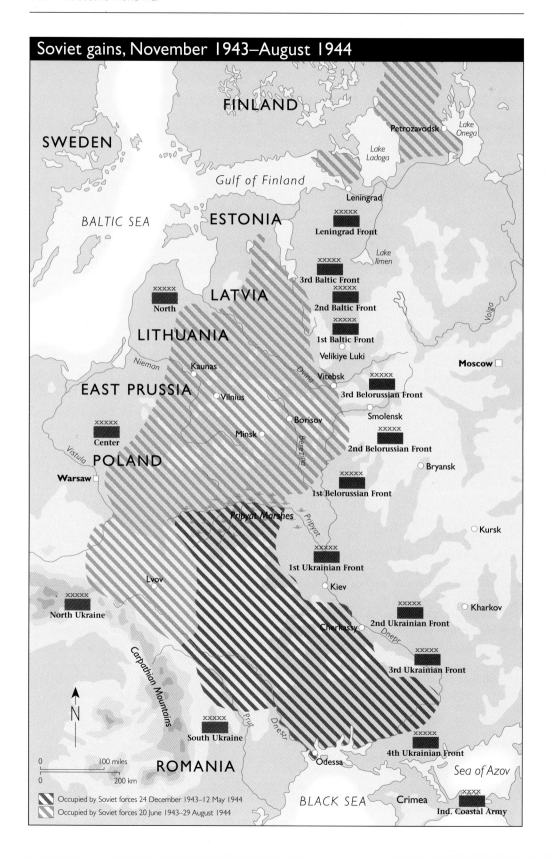

Soviet gains, November 1943–August 1944

FINLAND

SWEDEN

Petrozavodsk

Lake Onega

Lake Ladoga

Gulf of Finland

BALTIC SEA

ESTONIA

Leningrad

xxxxx Leningrad Front

Lake Ilmen

xxxxx North

LATVIA

xxxxx 3rd Baltic Front

xxxxx 2nd Baltic Front

xxxxx 1st Baltic Front

Velikiye Luki

LITHUANIA

Nieman

Kaunas

Drina

Vitebsk

xxxxx 3rd Belorussian Front

Moscow

Volga

EAST PRUSSIA

Vilnius

Smolensk

Borisov

xxxxx Center

Minsk

Berezina

xxxxx 2nd Belorussian Front

Vistula

POLAND

Bryansk

Warsaw

xxxxx 1st Belorussian Front

Pripyat Marshes

Pripyat

Kursk

xxxxx 1st Ukrainian Front

xxxxx North Ukraine

Lvov

Kiev

Kharkov

xxxxx 2nd Ukrainian Front

Cherkassy

Dnepr

Carpathian Mountains

xxxxx 3rd Ukrainian Front

N

0   100 miles
0   200 km

xxxxx South Ukraine

Prut

Dnestr

xxxxx 4th Ukrainian Front

ROMANIA

Odessa

Sea of Azov

BLACK SEA   Crimea

xxxx Ind. Coastal Army

Occupied by Soviet forces 24 December 1943–12 May 1944
Occupied by Soviet forces 20 June 1943–29 August 1944

was now fighting on four fronts. On 31 July Army Group North was briefly isolated when 1st Baltic Front reached the Gulf of Riga, but after Hitler dismissed its commander, Friessner, his successor, Schoerner, mounted a counteroffensive that by 21 August had reopened a corridor to Army Group Center. It was, however, only 12 miles (19km) wide, and Stavka made its closure high priority in a campaign to isolate and if possible destroy Army Group North. The Baltic Fleet and five fronts (Leningrad, 1st, 2nd, and 3rd Baltic, 3rd Belorussian) took part. With 1,546,400 men in 156 divisions and 11 brigades, they outnumbered Army Group North by about three to one in manpower and more than that in weapons.

The offensive began on 14 September, only 16 days after the end of 'Bagration.' In the first three days, 1st Baltic Front advanced 30 miles (48km), to within 16 miles (26km) of Riga, but strong German defense made the progress of 2nd and 3rd Baltic Fronts painfully slow. However, Leningrad Front joined in on 17 September, captured Tallin on the 22nd, then turned south on to the flanks of XVI and XVIII Armies, which were preparing to withdraw from Narva to positions north of Riga. Also on the 22nd, 2nd and 3rd Baltic Fronts broke through, and by the 27th they were northeast of Riga, up against the northern section of the 'Sigulda Line,' which ran in a semicircle around Riga at 25–30 miles (40–48km) from it. The 31 German divisions manning the line beat off attempts to break through off the march, so the two fronts regrouped for a set-piece assault. An attempt by 1st Baltic to break through from the south also failed, and Stavka ordered it instead to head for the Lithuanian port of Memel. It moved on

OPPOSITE: In this period the battle for the Dnepr (August–December 1943) was followed by the lifting of the siege of Leningrad (January 1944), and by Operation Bagration in Belorussia (June–August 1944), with associated offensives on the Finnish, Carpathian, and southern sectors. By the end of August, the Germans had been expelled from almost all Soviet territory, and the Red Army had entered Romania, Poland, and East Prussia.

5 October, and reached the coast at Palanga, north of Memel, five days later.

Memel would not fall until January 1945, but by the end of October 1st Baltic had isolated most of Army Group North in the Kurland peninsula. 3rd Baltic had also reached the coast, south of Memel, and was in East Prussia, only 60 miles (100km) from its capital, Koenigsberg. Leningrad and 3rd Baltic Fronts swept the Germans out of Estonia, and all five fronts except 3rd Belorussian were along the Sigulda Line by the beginning of October.

Schoerner, although appointed to 'Stand Fast,' soon realized that Army Group North would be cut off if it did not withdraw into East Prussia. In early September he sought Hitler's permission to do so, but by the time Hitler gave it, in mid-September, the Red Army had made it impossible.

In all campaigns from September 1944 onward, German mobility was very low for lack of fuel. Loss of the Ploesti oilfields, and Anglo-American air attacks on the hydrogenation plants that manufactured oil from coal, reduced German petrol production in September to only 8 percent of its April level. In 1941 the Wehrmacht had been more mobile than the Red Army, but by 1944 the reverse was true. The Red Army, with its indigenous oil supplies and fleets of US-made trucks, could move and supply its troops far faster than the German – and do so in safety, as fuel shortages kept most of the Luftwaffe on the ground.

Coincident with the Baltic operation (14 September–24 November) were offensives in the eastern Carpathians (8 September–28 October) by 1st and 4th Ukrainian Fronts, and Yugoslavia (28 September–20 October) and Hungary (29 October–13 February 1945) by 2nd and 3rd Ukrainian Fronts. The forces involved in the simultaneous September–October 1944 offensives were 295 divisions and 26 brigades, more than Germany's entire Western and Eastern Front forces, nominally 276 divisions, but many now divisions only in name.

Hungary was the next German ally to come under the Soviet sledgehammer. Its ruler, Admiral Horthy, sent emissaries to Moscow on 1 October to seek an armistice, but the Germans learned of this and seized all Hungary's main communications centers. On 15 October, Horthy broadcast that Hungary's war was over, but a German-supported coup installed a pro-Nazi government. It ordered the armed forces to fight on, but in Hungary, as elsewhere, enthusiasm to die for a lost cause was waning, and mass desertions began. About the only reason to continue fighting was knowledge of the atrocities committed by Soviet troops on captured territory, of which the Germans became aware when they recaptured Nyiregyhaza after a week of Soviet occupation.

Despite three years of bombing German civilians, the Anglo-Americans proclaimed that their war was against Nazism, not the German people. With some exceptions, German occupying forces behaved reasonably toward non-resistant civilians in western Europe, and in general treated their captured soldiers in accordance with the Geneva Convention.

But Nazism defined Slavs as racial inferiors, destined for an only slightly better fate than the genocide prepared for the Jews. Soviet troops on recaptured territory had their indoctrination in hatred reinforced by German atrocities. Many saw these for themselves and the rest were told about them; villages burned, their inhabitants killed, public hangings and, in Belorussia and eastern Poland, a succession of extermination camps.

When they entered hostile territory they responded in kind, with murder, mutilation, rape, and looting, not always bothering to distinguish between allies and enemies. The Soviet government did not officially sanction this, but did nothing to stop it until it threatened discipline. When a Yugoslav partisan leader, Milovan Djilas, complained to Stalin about Soviet raping of Yugoslav women, Stalin dismissed it with 'What's so awful about having fun with a woman?' A ruler capable of deporting entire peoples as potential or actual collaborators with the Germans – Volga Germans, Crimean Tatars, Chechens, Ingush, Balkars, Kalmyks, Meskhetians – was hardly likely to be squeamish about his troops' behavior. About all that can be said in mitigation is that mass atrocities were short-lived, not genocidal, and not followed up, as in the German occupation, by mass killings. However, counterparts to the Gestapo, the NKVD (People's Commissariat for Internal Affairs) and SMERSH ('Death to Spies') teams conducted more selective, but still large-scale, shootings and deportations. Not until 20 April 1945 did Stalin order that Soviet troops' attitude to the German people 'must now change.'

Fear of what lay in store prompted Axis forces to fight on desperately in the east, while the will to do so in the west began to evaporate. Guderian even proposed making peace with the Anglo-Americans while continuing to fight the Soviets, but Hitler would not hear of it. His riposte was instead to try to repeat the decisive breakthrough of 1940 in the Ardennes, demanding at the same time house-by-house defense of Budapest and an offensive in the Lake Balaton area of Hungary, west of the Danube.

1945

The Ardennes offensive, begun on 16 December 1944, was initially successful enough to prompt Churchill on 6 January to ask Stalin to attack to draw German forces away. Stalin advanced by eight days the Vistula–Oder operation, planned to begin on the 20th. Some Soviet historians thereafter claimed that this saved the Allies from defeat, but the Americans had turned the tide even before Churchill's request.

On 12 January 1st Belorussian and 1st Ukrainian Fronts attacked, supported by the adjacent wings of 2nd Belorussian and 4th Ukrainian; on the next day, 4th and 2nd Ukrainian Fronts attacked in the western Carpathians, and 2nd and 3rd Belorussian in East Prussia. Altogether, in two days, 436 divisions, 30 corps, and 31 brigades, with almost 4.5 million men, went into action. Many formations were understrength, but that was even truer of their opponents. German infantry divisions no longer had nine battalions; existing ones had six, some new ones only four. Panzer divisions, of 400 tanks each in 1940, now averaged fewer than 100.

The main Soviet blow would fall on the 70 understrength divisions of Army Groups Center and 'A,' against which 1st Belorussian and 1st Ukrainian Fronts, including Polish 1st Army, deployed 181 divisions and 14 brigades.

At the start of 1945 Germany's Eastern Front comprised five Army Groups, from north to south:

North (XVI and XVIII Armies). Isolated in Kurland.
Center (III Panzer, IV and II Armies). Eastern Prussia and northern Poland.
A (IX and IV Panzer, XVII and I Panzer Armies). Southern Poland–northern Carpathians.
South (VI and VIII German; I, II, and III Hungarian). Hungary.
F (II Panzer). Hungary and Yugoslavia.

On 26 January, Army Group North was renamed Army Group Kurland, Center was renamed North, and A became Center.

The largest Soviet offensive, against the renamed Army Groups Center (Reinhardt) and North (Schoerner), would set the stage for the final advance to Berlin. It was launched from three bridgeheads across the Vistula: 1st Belorussian Front's at Magnuszew and Pulawy, and 1st Ukrainian's at Baranow. Both fronts were to advance to the Oder and seize bridgeheads across it, only about 60 miles (100km) from Berlin. Stalin abolished the posts of Stavka representatives; Zhukov, remaining Deputy Supreme Commander, took command of 1st Belorussian Front from Rokossovsky, who moved to 2nd Belorussian Front, tasked to envelope the Germans in East Prussia and protect Zhukov's northern flank. Konev retained command of 1st Ukrainian Front; it was to advance into Silesia, and Stalin

instructed Konev to keep destruction there to the minimum.

Poland was to be moved bodily westward, ceding territory in the east and receiving compensation at Germany's expense, including Silesia. Stalin wanted Poland to receive Silesia's industries as intact as possible, to mollify resentment over the cessions in the east. Konev achieved this by advancing one of his tank armies north, and the other south of Silesia, compelling IV Panzer Army to withdraw too hastily to do much demolition. Red Army mobility now so outclassed German that in the 23 days of the Vistula–Oder operation, even its infantry advanced on average 12–14 miles (19–22km) a day, taking major cities such as Warsaw, Poznan, Lodz, and Breslau while doing so; and 'irrevocable' losses were low, 43,476 (just under 2 percent) of the 2.2 million deployed.

Of the two offensives launched on 13 January, the East Prussian, by 2nd and 3rd Belorussian Fronts and one army of 1st Baltic, was much the larger, involving 1.67 million men, in 157 divisions and 10 brigades. Army Group North resisted much more determinedly than Army Group Center; the Soviet rate of advance over the operation's 103 days averaged only about 1.25 miles (2km) a day, and 'irrevocable' losses, at 126,464 (7.6 percent), were proportionally almost four times as heavy.

The offensive by 4th and 2nd Ukrainian Fronts in the western Carpathians involved 'only' 79 divisions and seven brigades. Including two Romanian armies (I and IV) and a Czechoslovak army corps, it had 593,000 men. It lasted 38 days, losses were just over 19,000 (3.2 percent), and the average daily advance, 4 miles (6.4km), was creditable in mountainous terrain.

Next, on 10 February, came an offensive in East Pomerania, by 2nd Belorussian Front, the right wing of 1st Belorussian and, from 1 March, Polish First Army. That this offensive, involving 996,000 men, could be mounted while 2nd Belorussian's East Prussia operation was still in progress, and only a week after 1st Belorussian had concluded the

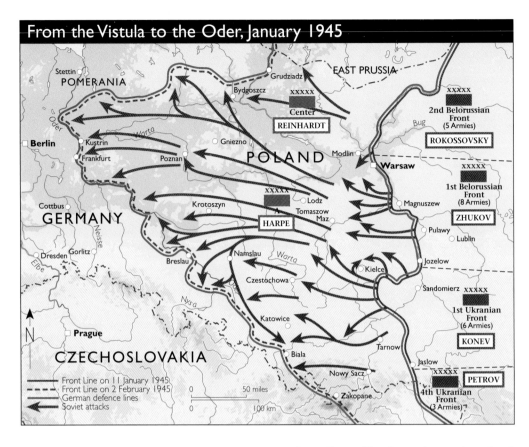

From the Vistula to the Oder, January 1945

Front Line on 11 January 1945
Front Line on 2 February 1945
German defence lines
Soviet attacks

0   50 miles
0   100 km

This Soviet offensive lasted only 22 days
(12 January–2 February 1945), but ended with
a seizure of bridgeheads across the Oder only about
60 miles (100km) from Berlin.

Vistula–Oder offensive, testified to the now
overwhelming Soviet superiority. However, it
also placed very heavy demands on units
worn down in previous weeks' fighting.

The operation lasted till 4 April, the Soviet
advance was about 85 miles (135km), the
daily rate averaging only 1.5–2 miles
(2.4–3.2km), and losses were 55,315
(5.6 percent). The opponent was the newly
created Army Group Vistula, of II and
IX Armies, both agglomerations of units and
parts of units, and a re-formed XI Army,
which lacked most of the necessities for
fighting. They were commanded not by a
professional soldier (Hitler increasingly
distrusted them for recommending
withdrawals, or even surrender), but by
Heinrich Himmler, head of the SS and police.

Army Group Vistula was inserted north of
Army Group Center, and these two were to
cover Germany's eastern approaches, while
Army Group South in Hungary, the forces in
Italy, and Army Group E (withdrawn from
Greece to Yugoslavia) covered the south and
southeast. Hitler and Himmler were now so
divorced from reality as to expect a
counteroffensive by Army Group Vistula to
decide the entire war in Germany's favor.
It began on 16 February, and pushed
1st Belorussian Front back about 7 miles
(11km), but by the 20th it had been stopped,
and the six divisions that conducted it were
counterattacked on 1 March by six armies.
Some units held out until the war ended, but
others fled in panic, and as an organized
entity Army Group Vistula ceased to exist.

A competent professional, Colonel-
General Heinrici, replaced Himmler on
20 March, but there was little left for him to
command. Gdynia fell on 28 March, and
Danzig on the 30th. The Soviets claimed

91,000 prisoners; the operation removed any risk of a flank attack on 1st Belorussian Front's planned drive to Berlin, and freed 10 more armies for that drive.

While 1st Belorussian and 1st Ukrainian Fronts were gathering for the final lunge to Berlin, Hitler ordered an offensive in Hungary, aimed at recapturing Budapest and safeguarding the minor oil-producing districts in Hungary and Austria. VI SS Panzer Army, attacking from east of Lake Balaton, was to spearhead it, while VI Army and a Hungarian corps pushed south on its left, II Panzer Army attacked due east between Balaton and the Drava River, and Army Group E attacked the I Bulgarian and III Yugoslav Armies, guarding 3rd Ukrainian Front's left flank.

Young soldiers being trained how to use a Panzerfaust (anti-tank gun), 1945. (AKG Berlin)

Marshal Tolbukhin knew an offensive was imminent, and Stavka had already approved a defensive battle followed by a counteroffensive. Army Group E and II Panzer Army attacked on the night of 5 March. The main assault, by VI SS Panzer and VI Armies, went in the next morning, and made 16 miles (26km) in four days, but it was then halted by 3rd Ukrainian's massed artillery and infantry. Casualties on both sides were heavy, but by 15 March the offensive had clearly lost its impetus, so Stavka ordered the counteroffensive to start on the 16th.

On that day 3rd Ukrainian Front (including I Bulgarian Army), part of 2nd Ukrainian Front, and the Soviet navy's Danube Flotilla began the Vienna Strategic Offensive, involving 644,700 Soviet and 100,900 Bulgarian troops, in 85 divisions and three brigades. Expulsion of the Germans from Hungary forced Army Group E to begin withdrawing from Yugoslavia. Soviet forces, advancing into eastern Austria and southern Czechoslovakia, took Vienna on 13 April. The operation formally concluded on 15 April, and on the next day 1st Belorussian (Zhukov), 2nd Belorussian (Rokossovsky), and 1st Ukrainian (Konev) Fronts, and the Polish First and Second Armies, began the final push to Berlin.

For this they massed 1.9 million Soviet and 156,000 Polish troops, in 234 divisions and 16 brigades, with 41,000 guns and mortars, 6,200 tanks and assault guns, and 7,500 aircraft. Against them were Army Group Vistula (Heinrici), with two armies, III Panzer (von Manteuffel) and IX (Busse), while IV Panzer Army (Graeser) of Army Group Center faced Konev's troops across the Neisse river. These three armies had between them 39 divisions; despite their titles the two Panzer armies had only one Panzer division each, the same as IX Army, and there were three Panzer and three Panzer Grenadier divisions in reserve.

With forces from elsewhere committed during the battle, the Germans fielded about 50 divisions, and perhaps as many as 100 battalions of the Volkssturm. This, a barely trained 'people's militia,' was under Nazi Party, not army control, and equipped mostly with obsolete German or captured weapons, though a few had the formidable anti-tank Panzerfaust. Some police units and Hitler Youth detachments also took part. Luftwaffe support comprised only about 300 serviceable aircraft.

Zhukov planned to pulverize the forward defenses with a 30-minute artillery and air bombardment, then send in the infantry, turning night into day and blinding the defenders with 143 searchlights, and expected to cover the 60-odd miles (100km) to Berlin in 11 days. This assumed that, as in previous offensives, the tanks would reach open country once the defenses were penetrated. However, the plan proved over-optimistic because both the terrain and the intensity of the defense differed from previous campaigns. The ground was criss-crossed by streams, canals, and channels of the Oder, and was soggy. There were up to nine lines of defenses, and German positions on the Seelow heights overlooked the whole area.

Meanwhile, Anglo-American forces were also pushing into Germany, and Churchill and Field Marshal Montgomery favored trying to take Berlin before the Red Army. Eisenhower, however, believed (wrongly) that Hitler would continue the war from an 'Alpine Redoubt' in southern Bavaria, western Austria, and Czechoslovakia. He therefore directed one of his three US armies to advance to meet Soviet forces at the Elbe, and directed the other two toward the putative 'Redoubt.' On 28 March he informed Stalin of his intentions. Stalin replied immediately, declaring Berlin strategically unimportant, and lying that his main thrust would be toward Leipzig and Dresden. Then he summoned Zhukov and Konev to Moscow.

When they arrived, appropriately on 1 April, he lied to them that the Allies were planning a rapier-thrust to take Berlin before the Red Army, and told them to be ready to go on 16 April. Zhukov's 1st Belorussian Front would attack directly westward, with Konev's supporting him from the south and also driving toward Leipzig and Dresden, as he had told Eisenhower it would. Rokossovsky was to protect Zhukov's northern flank by taking Stettin and driving toward Schleswig-Holstein. To exploit the rivalry between Zhukov and Konev, Stalin mapped the demarcation line between them only as far as Luebben, about 50 miles (80km) southeast of Berlin. The implication was that if Konev reached its end first, he could turn north.

Zhukov attacked before dawn on 16 April. After the barrage, the searchlights were turned on. However, the smoke and dust raised by the barrage reflected the light into the faces of his infantry, blinding them where not silhouetting them as targets. IX Army had good defensive positions, particularly on the Seelow heights, and the troops, to stiffen their will, had been told that anyone retreating without orders would immediately be shot.

The Soviet infantry's progress was so slow and costly that around noon Zhukov abandoned normal Soviet practice of committing the tanks only after the infantry had made a breach, and ordered his two tank armies to make the breach themselves. The few roads were crowded with men and vehicles, slowing the tanks' progress and making all easy targets, especially for the 88mm guns behind and above the anti-tank ditches. Not until late on 17 April was the first line of the Seelow defenses breached, and it took another day to breach the second. After four days Zhukov was two days behind schedule, so Stalin authorized Konev to break into Berlin from the south.

Konev's assault had gone far better, despite having to cross the Neisse River, with easier terrain, sandy soil, and less waterlogging. He innovated with smokescreens, not searchlights, and more successfully, though some cynical old

Soviet tanks in central Berlin. (AKG Berlin)

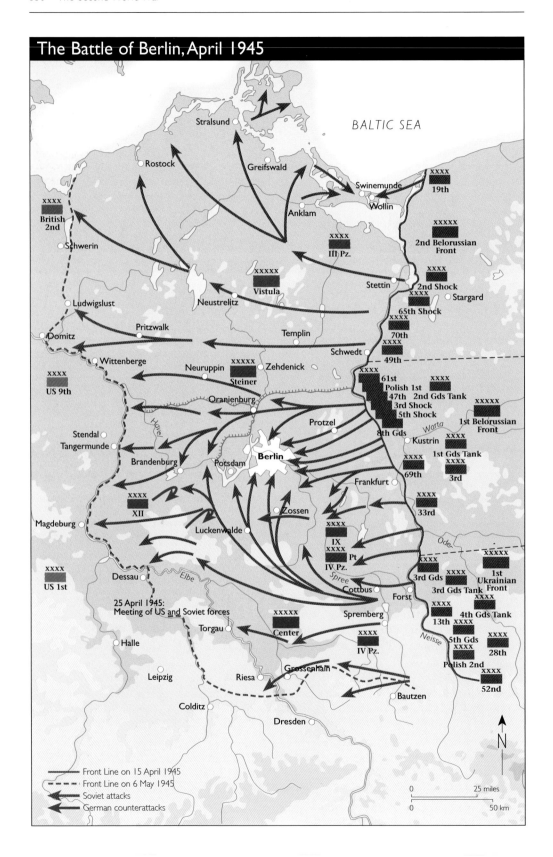

The Battle of Berlin, April 1945

BALTIC SEA

Stralsund

Rostock

Greifswald

Swinemunde
XXXX
19th

Anklam
Wollin

Schwerin

XXXX
British
2nd

XXXX
III Pz.

XXXXX
2nd Belorussian
Front

Stettin

XXXX
2nd Shock

Stargard

XXXXX
Vistula

Ludwigslust

Neustrelitz

XXXX
65th Shock

XXXX
70th

Pritzwalk

Templin

XXXX
49th

Domitz

Schwedt

Wittenberge

Neuruppin

XXXXX
Steiner

Zehdenick

XXXX
61st
Polish 1st
47th 2nd Gds Tank
3rd Shock
5th Shock
8th Gds

XXXX
2nd Gds Tank

XXXXX
1st Belorussian
Front

US 9th

Oranienburg

Protzel

Warta

Kustrin

XXXX
3rd

Havel

Stendal
Tangermunde

Brandenburg

Potsdam

Berlin

Frankfurt

XXXX
1st Gds Tank

XXXX
69th

XXXX
XII

Zossen

XXXX
33rd

Magdeburg

Luckenwalde

XXXX
IX
XXXX
IV Pz.

Pt

Ode

XXXXX
1st
Ukrainian
Front

XXXX
US 1st

Dessau

Elbe

25 April 1945:
Meeting of US and Soviet forces

Spree

Cottbus

Forst

XXXX
3rd Gds

XXXX
3rd Gds Tank

XXXX
13th

XXXX
4th Gds Tank

XXXXX
Center

Spremberg

XXXX
IV Pz.

Neisse

XXXX
5th Gds

XXXX
28th

Torgau

Halle

Leipzig

Riesa

Grossenhain

Bautzen

Polish 2nd

XXXX
52nd

Colditz

Dresden

N

Front Line on 15 April 1945
Front Line on 6 May 1945
Soviet attacks
German counterattacks

0   25 miles
0   50 km

Soviet soldiers hoisting the Red Flag over the Reichstag.
(AKG Berlin)

soldiers would later say 'Maybe they blinded
the Germans, they certainly blinded us.' His
engineer troops performed near-miracles,
setting up many bridges or ferries within a
few hours. Both his tank armies were across
the river by 17 April, and on the next day
they reached two of the 'fortress towns,'
Cottbus and Spremberg. The tanks bypassed
both, advancing north and south of
Spremberg, and driving a wedge between
Army Groups Vistula and Center.

Toward nightfall on 19 April, 2nd Tank
Army of Zhukov's Front at last reached open
country and Berlin's northeast outskirts,
cutting between III Panzer and IX Armies,
and continuing westwards toward the Elbe.
On the 20th, Chuykov's 8th Guards Army
reached the eastern outskirts and, reverting
to his Stalingrad tactics, began expelling the
defenders almost building by building.
Zhukov's determination not to be outpaced
by Konev led him to do what Chuykov had

sedulously avoided, namely send massed
tanks into street battles, where Panzerfausts
knocked out many of them. Hasty
improvisation with sheet metal and
sandbags provided the tanks with extra
protection, but the numerous canals and
rivers in the city impeded progress until
assault engineers braved intense fire to
lay pontoon bridges.

Early on 25 April Chuykov's men reached
Schoenefeld airfield, only to find Rybalko's
3rd Guards Tank Army of 1st Ukrainian
already there. They had advanced 60 miles
(100km) in two days, overrunning OKH's
headquarters at Zossen on the way, and
thereby ruining the defense's prospects of
coordination. On 25 April Konev ordered a
northward offensive across the city center to
take the Tiergarten and Reichstag. But when
General Rybalko reached the Landwehr
Canal, only 300yds (275m) from the
Reichstag, he found Chuykov there, and
Zhukov, furious at his presence. Konev had
to turn Rybalko westward and leave the
Reichstag to Zhukov and Chuykov. Konev

was naturally disappointed, Rybalko even more so, but there was some poetic justice in Stalin's decision to have the Reichstag and nearby Chancellery, with Hitler's bunker, taken by the defenders of Leningrad, Moscow, and Stalingrad.

On 29 April 8th Guards Army began storming the Tiergarten from the south, while 3rd Shock Army (Colonel-General V. I. Kuznetsov) attacked from the north. Only

¼ mile (0.4km) separated them, but it was cluttered with large buildings and strongly defended. The Reichstag had to be taken room by room, and Kuznetsov's men got there first. They broke in just after 1.00 am on 30 April, and 10 hours later a Red Banner appeared on the roof.

On that day Hitler committed suicide, and that evening the Germans requested negotiations. At 3.30 am on 1 May, Colonel-General Hans Krebs, Chief of General Staff of OKH, arrived at Chuykov's headquarters to report Hitler's death and seek armistice

Soviet troops celebrating the capture of the Reichstag. (AKG Berlin)

terms. Chuykov telephoned Zhukov, who insisted on unconditional surrender, telephoned Moscow and had Stalin woken to receive the news. He endorsed Zhukov's demand and went back to sleep. Krebs held out for negotiations with the new government of Admiral Dönitz, returned to his headquarters and at 4.00 am sent a written refusal to surrender, whereupon the Soviet offensive resumed. Early on 2 May the garrison commander, General Weidling, notified Chuykov that he wished to surrender, and firing ceased at 6.00 am.

The surrender applied only to Berlin; elsewhere fighting continued for several more days, but by 3 May Allied forces had met along the Elbe and Muelde rivers, 2nd Belorussian Front meeting the British, and 1st Belorussian the Americans. Sporadic clashes, some of them fierce, continued, but the last big Soviet action would be in Czechoslovakia.

A popular uprising began in Prague on 5 May. German forces set about suppressing it, and the insurgents sought help. Their first source was an unlikely one, the 2nd Division of the turncoat Soviet General Vlasov's Russian Liberation Army (ROA), hoping to receive political asylum in Czechoslovakia or surrender to American 3rd Army, approaching from the west. Much more was needed, so Stalin directed 1st, 3rd, and 4th Ukrainian Fronts to provide it. Konev dispatched Rybalko's tanks to Prague, and on 11 May the Germans surrendered. A hard fate awaited the Russian Liberation Army. Vlasov was hanged for treason in Moscow in1946, his men faced death or long prison terms, and Soviet soldiers shot many ROA wounded in their hospital beds in Prague.

Four days earlier, on 7 May, Colonel-General Jodl and Admiral von Friedeburg had signed an unconditional surrender in Reims. Although it stipulated surrender to Soviet as well as Allied forces, Stalin saw it as denigrating the Soviet contribution, and insisted on a more comprehensive official surrender ceremony in Berlin. This took place in Karlshorst on 8 May, Zhukov signing for the Soviet Union.

At the victory parade in Moscow on 24 June, in pouring rain, the standards of German army and Waffen SS regiments were cast at the foot of the podium where Stalin stood. But the war was not yet over.

The Allies' main reason for seeking Soviet participation against Japan was the experience in the Pacific islands and Burma that Japanese soldiers genuinely preferred death to surrender. The largest remaining Japanese force outside Japan was the Kwantung Army, believed to number over

800,000 men and deployed in Manchuria, then the Japanese puppet state of Manchukuo. The Soviet army was best located for dealing with it, and to ensure overwhelming strength Stalin supplemented the forces already there with experienced formations from Europe.

By 31 July almost 1.7 million troops were there, in 88 divisions, 34 brigades, and 21 'fortified areas' (garrison troops), with a 16,000-strong Mongolian cavalry and motorized infantry contingent. The force formed three fronts, from west to east Transbaikal (Marshal Malinovsky), 1st Far Eastern (Marshal Meretskov), and 2nd Far Eastern (Army General M. A. Purkayev), supported by the Pacific Fleet and Amur Flotilla (Admiral Yumashev).

Zhukov's first battle in command had been his defeat of the Japanese invasion of

Soviet troops indicate where Hitler's body was found. (Topham Picturepoint)

Mongolia in 1939, so he would seem a logical choice as Commander-in-Chief for the Far East campaign. But Stalin already saw Zhukov's popularity as a threat, and appointed Vasilevsky instead. The main difficulties were logistical: Transbaikal Front forces would have to cross the Gobi Desert and Great Khingan mountains, and the theater of war was very large. The four armies from Europe took no tanks because the latest three months' production was awaiting them in the Far East, bringing the total there to 5,500, all of them superior to the 1,155 lighter Japanese tanks. They also outnumbered the Japanese by almost five to one in guns (26,000 to 5,360) and over two to one in aircraft (3,900 to 1,800).

Stalin succeeded in deluding Roosevelt and Churchill into conceding a high price (the Kurile Islands, South Sakhalin, and the restoration of rights in Manchuria originally held by Tsarist Russia) for Soviet participation. In fact, he was eager to pose to

ABOVE: Turncoat General Vlasov reviewing troops of his German-equipped Russian Liberation Army. Ironically, the only action it saw was against the Germans in Prague in 1945. (AKG Berlin)

BELOW: Soviet forces (many in US-supplied lorries) enter Prague. (AKG Berlin)

The Yalta Conference, February 1945. Stalin agreed to join the war against Japan within three months of victory in Europe. By the Potsdam Conference (July), the USA had a new, strongly anti-Communist president, Truman, who hoped the new atomic weapons (successfully tested on 24 July) would force Japan to surrender without Soviet participation. Soviet forces entered the war just hours before the Emperor resolved to surrender. (AKG Berlin)

the Soviet people as player of the decisive role in the defeat of Japan as well as of Germany, and the avenger of Russia's defeat by Japan in the war of 1904–05. His desire for military pre-eminence was shown at the final meetings to review the preparations for invading Manchuria. These took place in the Kremlin on 26–27 July; on the first day he had the Supreme Soviet revive the rank of Generalissimus, dormant in Russia since 1800, and on the second day had it conferred upon himself.

On 5 August Vasilevsky notified him that he would be ready to attack on the 10th. But on the 6th, the first atomic bomb was dropped at Hiroshima, and it needed no military genius to realize that if the Americans had only one other bomb, they would drop it as soon as possible, to coerce Japan into surrender by giving it the impression that they had many more. Should Japan surrender before the Soviet Union attacked, Stalin would get the territorial accessions he had sought, but by American grace and favor. It was therefore imperative to join in the war before a second bomb was dropped, so he ordered Vasilevsky to bring the attack forward to midnight on the night of 8–9 August. Vasilevsky complied, and the Soviet Union entered the war just two minutes less than 12 hours before the second bomb was dropped, on Nagasaki, at two minutes before midday.

The Emperor had already decided at 7.30 that morning to tell the Supreme War

Council meeting that evening of his decision to surrender, but his decision was not made public until 14 August. Despite fierce, sometimes suicidal resistance, Transbaikal Front's right wing was by then heading for Beijing, its center for Port Arthur, its left for Changchun. Two armies of 1st Far Eastern Front were converging on Tsitsihar, while 2nd Far Eastern's left wing was heading for Harbin, its center for Korea, its left into South Sakhalin and the Kurile Islands; the southernmost Kuriles were occupied on 2 September, the day of the official surrender ceremony in Tokyo Bay. In his broadcast that day, Stalin referred specifically to the victory as something 'the men of my generation have awaited for 40 years.'

On 15 August General Yamada, commanding the Kwantung Army, heard the Emperor's broadcast announcing the surrender, but decided to await written confirmation. On the 17th a member of the royal family arrived with written orders, and Yamada complied on 19 August. To seize as much territory as possible before the cease-fire, Vasilevsky sent improvised airborne units to Manchuria's main cities – Mukden, Harbin, Changchun, Kirin, and Port Arthur – to hold the airports and communications centers pending the ground forces' arrival. On the 23rd Stalin proclaimed the victorious end of the campaign. Last to be taken were the southern Kurile Islands, occupied without resistance on 2 September, the day of the official surrender ceremony in Tokyo Bay.

19 August 1945. General Yamada, Commander-in-Chief of the Japanese Kwantung Army, arrives at Marshal Vasilevsky's headquarters to sign the surrender. (Novosti [London])

ABOVE: Soviet troops parade in Harbin. (Novosti [London])

BELOW: Japanese troops leave for Siberian prisoner-of-war camps. During the very brief campaign 662,000 Japanese were captured, and kept at forced labor in the Soviet Union for up to 10 years. (Novosti [London])

The campaign in the Far East, August 1945

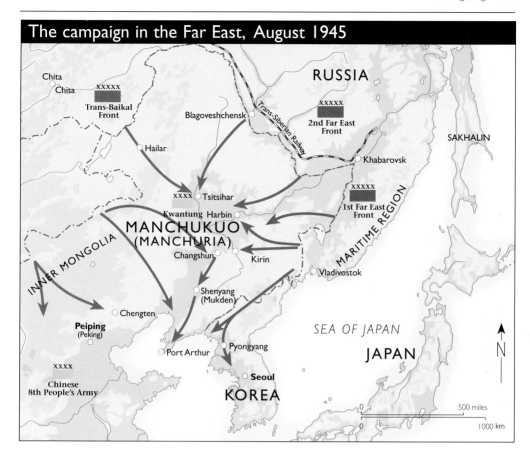

Compared to the campaigns in Europe, Soviet casualties were small: 12,031 Soviet and 72 Mongolian troops lost, 0.7 percent of those engaged. The campaign nominally lasted 25 days, but actual fighting took less than two weeks. Putting down anti-Soviet nationalist guerrillas in Ukraine and the Baltic States would take another two years, but that could mostly be left to the NKVD. The Red Army's war was over.

This campaign was noteworthy for the logistical problems of supplying a highly mechanized force, 1.7 million strong, over enormous distances. The actual fighting lasted only two weeks. For the Soviet Union's brief participation, Stalin took more Japanese territory (Southern Sakhalin and the Kurile Islands) than his allies, who had fought Japan for several years.

The German and the Russian view

Few German soldiers were committed Nazis, but all took into the invasion a faith in Hitler and his generals created by two years of victories, and the younger ones several years of indoctrination in school and the Hitler Youth about German racial superiority. The welcome they received, particularly in Ukraine and the Baltic States, and the enormous early captures of Soviet troops boosted that euphoria, but it faded somewhat after weeks of tramping over seemingly endless plains, and finding that however many of the enemy they killed or captured, more came at them the next day. Panzer crews were shocked to find the newest Soviet tank, the T-34, superior to their hitherto unstoppable Marks III and IV, but in 1941 there were few of them.

The defeat at Moscow affected morale little; they attributed it more to the weather than to the enemy, and expected to reassert their superiority when summer came. This they duly did, only to suffer another winter disaster at Stalingrad. This depressed them more, but Manstein's successful counteroffensive in February 1943 somewhat restored morale.

The crunch came at Kursk. The Prokhorovka tank battle was the swan song of the Panzers as attack spearheads, until the abortive Ardennes and Balaton offensives of 1945; the infantry for the first time experienced failure in summer, decisive Soviet air superiority, and the start of a series of Soviet offensives that dwarfed even that of Stalingrad. Most German soldiers remained disciplined and skillful to the end, but after Kursk they fought in fear of the consequences of defeat rather than in expectation of victory.

A typical German soldier from a tank destroyer unit, who fought in the east from the very first day, summed up his experiences as follows. First encounters with the Red Army suggested they would not be much trouble, but 'things were different later.' Many felt they should not have invaded, but it was not safe to say so. His belief that the war was lost came with the retreat from the Volga, but he and his comrades expected to be shot if captured, so they fought hard and nobody deserted or defected.

He had a month's home leave in mid-1942; before going on leave soldiers were sent to a transit camp for two weeks, and fed better than usual, so as to make a better impression at home. On leave they were privileged to wear civilian clothes and received extra rations of food and chocolate. He found home front propaganda so untruthful that he listened mostly to the BBC; this was punishable by imprisonment or death, but soldiers sent back to the Soviet Union thought they would probably be killed anyway, so were not deterred. He was shocked by the poor standard of replacements for casualties, and his friends envied him when a leg wound finally removed him from the front. He 'would not wish his worst enemy' to have to fight the Russians.

In the Third Reich's last throes desertions increased, despite the activities of SS execution squads. So many units retreated, to surrender to the Anglo-Americans rather than the Red Army, that General Eisenhower had to threaten to close the Elbe crossings against them. Their fears were not baseless; the Anglo-Americans released most of their prisoners within two years, whereas those taken by the Soviets were kept at forced labor from four to 10 years.

The Red Army had a draconian disciplinary code together with Stalin's 1941

The reality of war. (AKG Berlin)

Order 270, which defined 'voluntary surrender' (i.e. if neither wounded nor unconscious) as treason. Yet the first six months saw mass surrenders on an unprecedented scale. Since only a little over half the Soviet population was Russian, soldiers' attitudes to the war covered as wide a spectrum as the civilian populations from which they came. The instinct for self-preservation kept most in the ranks, but surrender at the first opportunity was rife in 1941, particularly among conscripts from the recently annexed Baltic States and former eastern Poland.

The backbone of the Red Army was the ethnic Russian, mostly a peasant or first-generation urban worker. He retained the hardiness and self-sacrificing qualities of his forebears, but added basic literacy and familiarity with machinery that they lacked. His training and tactics were generally primitive – right until the end of the war, infantry attacked frontally in successive waves, with little regard for casualties; outflanking maneuvers were usually left to the tanks and motorized infantry. The heavy casualties affected morale less than they might have; they were frequent enough to become regarded as normal, and the soldiers had no basis for comparison with other armies. In the later campaigns, material superiority and experience substantially reduced them, though they remained high compared to what allies and enemies alike regarded as acceptable.

Apart from the first weeks, when some units fled in panic, there was nothing resembling the breakdown of discipline that disrupted the Russian army in 1917, though there were numerous instances in 1941–42 when NKVD troops were stationed behind the front-line soldiers, to shoot any who ran away. Unlike in the First World War, no cases were recorded of collective refusal to obey orders. This owed something to the regime's greater ruthlessness, but probably more to indoctrination. Unlike its predecessor, the Red Army, through its political officers, took much trouble to tell the troops why they were at war, and to inculcate hatred of the invader.

Distorted and propagandistic though much of this indoctrination was, it motivated the troops more than the Tsarist dogma that to explain the Tsar's decisions undermined his right to unconditional obedience. Communist values were not particularly emphasized; membership of the Communist Party was not easily granted, and most troops were below the minimum age for membership. However, Communist Party members in the armed forces were expected to set an example to the rest, and many set one good enough for soldiers' applications to join the Party to rise, especially on the eve of major campaigns.

Morale was sustained by several factors, most basic of them patriotic outrage at the fact of invasion and at the atrocities committed by the invader. Propaganda encouraged the soldiers to expect victory to bring radical changes for the better in politics and living standards. The cult of Stalin was all-pervading, but it was only in films that soldiers went into battle shouting 'For the Motherland! For Stalin!' Many would, much later, admit putting more trust in God, others that they went into the assault shouting obscenities. One who ended the war in Berlin recollected that:

...luxuries such as leave seldom came our way. Food was monotonous but usually adequate, clothing, especially for winter, much better than the Germans had, but small amenities such as playing cards, dominoes, writing materials or musical instruments were scarce, and usually the first things we looted when we took a German position. Correspondence was censored, and we learned not to criticize our leaders, especially Stalin, because such criticisms attracted heavier punishment than disclosure of military secrets. We knew few of those anyway, because we were only told what we were going to do at the last moment, or sometimes not at all, and the command we mostly heard from our officers was just 'follow me.' Most of our officers earned our respect for their readiness to lead, but we wished they had been trained to do more than just take us to attack the Germans head on. We respected the Germans as soldiers, and to begin with many of us doubted our own propaganda about German atrocities. But when we began recapturing territory and seeing what they had done there, we came to hate them, and when we reached German soil some of us vented our hatred on German civilians, even on some who claimed to be Communists, in ways I still shudder to think of. As the war ended, Stalin ordered us to change our attitude to the German people, and even to start feeding them. That did cut down the amount of murder and rape, but it didn't stop us looting, or beating up any Germans who didn't accept that they were the losers.

Marshals Zhukov and Rokossovsky and subordinates with
Field Marshal Montgomery after conferring of British honors.
(AKG Berlin)

'We were as mobilised as the soldiers'

The Sicherheitsdienst (Security Service) monitored German civilian attitudes through about 25,000 informants, collating the findings in twice-weekly reports. These showed that underneath public euphoria was a deep vein of skepticism (for example, 'In the First World War too we were winning at the start'), and disdain for Nazi Party officials, whom the public dubbed *Goldfasanen* (Golden Pheasants). Germany did not switch to a full war economy until after Stalingrad. Propaganda Minister Goebbels, addressing a rally in Berlin two weeks after the surrender there, received a roar of 'Yes!' to his rhetorical question 'Do you want total war?', but not all Germans were as enthusiastic; a verse from the Ruhr pleaded to RAF bomber crews: 'Dear Tommy, please fly further. We're all miners here. Fly on to Berlin – they're the ones who all shouted "Yes".' German civilian life was more seriously affected by bombing than by the Eastern Front, until the Red Army reached East Prussia late in 1944. Then news of the retribution being exacted for German atrocities prompted a flood of refugees.

German obedience to authority, nurtured by long exposure to despotic but generally benign rulers, served the Nazis well – surviving even the imposition of the death penalty for listening to enemy broadcasts – and so, paradoxically, did civilian skepticism. Because their expectations were not high, they were not shattered by misfortune. Morale until very late withstood both bombing and the setbacks that began in November 1942; and while in the last days many almost totally untrained Volkssturm and Hitler Youth detachments ran away or surrendered, others fought ferociously to the end.

The Russian civilian was as mobilized as the soldier. The working day was increased to 12 hours, days off were reduced from one a week to one a month, and rations gave preference to production workers over the old, very young, or disabled. To control information, radio sets were confiscated, and replaced by loudspeakers set up in public places to retail official pronouncements. Associating with even Allied foreigners, absenteeism, late arrival at work, or failure to fulfil quotas could result in a long sentence to forced labor in the 'Gulag,' prison, or a corrective labor camp. In 1943 a new punishment, 'hard labor,' was introduced for the worst offenders; it usually meant death by overwork and malnutrition.

Peasants did not receive ration cards; they had to subsist on what they grew in their private plots, and what their collective farm could provide after fulfilling its delivery quotas. Conscription of males and commandeering of horses left production by mostly unmechanized agriculture to women and males who were too old, too young, or unfit for military service. Plows pulled by teams of women were a not uncommon sight, and so, in the cities, was a tolerated 'free market,' where peasants lucky enough to have any surplus food could sell it for high prices. Urban dwellers with dachas (suburban plots) grew additional food there, but often found it stolen. In 1944 a system for guarding plots, and the death penalty for stealing food, were introduced. A Muscovite woman, a schoolgirl at the time, recalled that:

we had been told day and night that our army was invincible, and were shocked at how fast the Germans advanced in the first months. In October the older classes in my school were among those sent to dig trenches on the outskirts of the city. We heard that many people ran away from Moscow in mid-month, but didn't see any sign of it ourselves. There were many air raids; no bombs fell near where we lived, but the noise of the anti-aircraft guns sometimes made it hard to sleep; anyway the air raids stopped after a few months.

With father away in the army, and mother working 12 hours in a bakery, we children had mostly to look after ourselves, though mother's job meant we didn't have to join the queues for bread; neighbors told us they started queuing before dawn. We always had enough to eat, but had to spend a lot of time in queues at the food shops. Getting clothes and shoes as we grew bigger was difficult; we were told it was because the factories were too busy making uniforms and boots for the soldiers. We lived in a big apartment with one family to every room, and shared the kitchen and bathroom. A lot of the housing in Moscow was like that; it was long after the war that we got a flat to ourselves. Some of the other children in the apartment lost their fathers or brothers at the front, but we were lucky. Father survived the war, and my brother wasn't old enough to be called up, though in the last two years he had to work in a plant that made radio parts.

By then we were throwing the Germans out, and when we heard gunfire we knew it wasn't an air raid, it was a victory salute to celebrate the capture of some town. We didn't go to the victory parade because it rained all day, but we saw it on a newsreel, and everybody cheered when we saw the German army banners thrown in a heap at Stalin's feet. We idolized him then.

Germany surrenders, Stalin joins the war on Japan

Berlin surrendered on 2 May 1945; Hitler had committed suicide two days earlier, appointing Grand Admiral Dönitz as his successor. Dönitz sent Colonel-General Jodl and Admiral Friedeburg to Reims to negotiate surrender. It was to all the Allies, but Stalin considered that a surrender to Eisenhower denigrated the Soviet role in the war, and insisted on having a formal surrender ceremony in Berlin. This took place on the evening of 8 May at a ceremony in Berlin presided over by Marshal Zhukov, who signed on the Soviet Union's behalf. All German forces had surrendered by 16 May. Now Japan's turn had come.

On 3 June the State Defense Committee decided to redeploy troops to the Far East, and to build up ammunition, fuel, food, and fodder stocks for the campaign against Japan, which Stalin had agreed the Soviet Union would enter within three months of victory in Europe. The Allied leaders met at Potsdam on 17 July, and on 26 July the US, British, and Chinese governments issued the Potsdam Declaration, demanding that Japan surrender unconditionally. Stalin was annoyed at not being consulted, but subscribed to it later. The noncommittal Japanese reply was interpreted as a rejection, so the Soviet Union went to war with Japan on 9 August.

Part VI
Northwest Europe 1944–1945

The railway spur inside Birkenau, looking back toward
the main gate. Birkenau was the labor camp attached to
Auschwitz, the most infamous of the Nazi extermination
camps, where Hitler's minions enacted their heinous 'Final
Solution of the Jewish problem' – the extermination of
5.5 million of Europe's Jews. (AKG Berlin)

The road to D-Day

The operations that took place on 6 June 1944, D-Day, officially known as Operation Overlord, had been on the planning table for at least three years and were taking place a year later than many, particularly the United States and Soviet leadership, had hoped.

At the three-week Arcadia Conference in Washington, which opened on 22 December 1942, a tentative plan for the invasion of France was agreed. Fired up by the idea of making an immediate impact on the German war machine in Europe, George C. Marshall and Harry Hopkins were sent to London in April 1942 to propose a landing in France that very autumn, to be code-named Bolero. This would be followed by an invasion of France by 30 US and 18 British divisions in April 1943. Although the British were initially impressed with the plan, they soon developed severe doubts as to the practicality of mounting a major amphibious operation at such an early date.

In June 1942, Churchill travelled to Washington to press for the invasion of French North Africa. Although the Americans were initially reluctant to accept the idea, they began to accept its strategic advantages. On his subsequent visit to Moscow in August, Churchill met with a disappointed Stalin, who was also keen for a direct strike on France to relieve the pressure on Soviet forces. The failure of the raid on Dieppe, however, would have provided a salutary warning to all Allied parties that a strike without sufficient support, and particularly against a well defended port, was doomed to failure.

The British point of view was reinforced at the Symbol Conference in Casablanca (January–May 1943) where the allocation of resources to the war against Germany and Japan was discussed along with the alternative strategies of advancing across

the English Channel or through the Mediterranean. It had been agreed in 1941 that Germany was the priority and the British were reluctant to allow any more resources to seep into the Pacific theatre.

Impressed by Germany's ability to move large and powerful forces swiftly around mainland Europe, the British were inclined to focus on those areas where lines of communication were more difficult and where the enemy was already on the defensive. Although a world power, the British did not have a military tradition of fielding mass armies in head-to-head combat, the experience on the Western Front being the unpleasant exception that proved the rule.

The Americans, on the other hand, had an instinctive desire to strike at the main force of the enemy and General Marshall in particular was suspicious of the convoluted, apparently open-ended, British proposals for the Mediterranean theatre. The British plan was, however, well thought out and gradually the American side began to recognize its advantages.

The Casablanca Conference memorandum stated that any forces not required in either the Mediterranean or Pacific would stand ready for an assault against the European Continent.

In view of the shortfall of landing craft, planning was to be based on a full-scale invasion in 1944 and Lieutenant-General F.E. Morgan was given the task of planning the invasion in his new appointment as Chief of Staff to the Supreme Allied Commander (COSSAC).

Churchill and Roosevelt met again in Washington for the Trident Conference (12–27 May 1943). Here the plan for a landing in north–west Europe was scheduled for May 1944 and this was underlined again at the Quadrant Conference in Quebec (17–24 August).

At the Eureka Conference in Teheran (28 November–1 December 1943), Stalin was also present and was determined to make his mark. He listened to the British plan for Overlord, which involved a commitment of thirty-five strong divisions, with twenty-two left in the Mediterranean, and thereupon expounded on his idea that, once Rome was captured, all forces should be diverted to the south of France. As the conference wore on, the Soviet interest in the details of Overlord became more and more marked.

The effect of the Eureka Conference was to thoroughly weaken any remaining British ambitions to 'set the Balkans ablaze'. It also meant that the two Western allies would not be occupying the Balkan area before the Soviet machine had swept through. The Soviet rubber stamping of Operation Overlord, therefore, was, with hindsight, to have dire implications for the countries that were liberated from the east rather than from the south or the west.

Churchill and Roosevelt returned to Cairo on 4 December to agree the final arrangements for the allocation of resources to various operational theatres and to appoint a supreme commander, General Dwight D. Eisenhower.

The stage was now set for a final showdown, the results of which were by no means predictable or inevitable. The Soviets were making good progress against the German armies in the east, the Allies were advancing slowly but surely through southern Italy and the Germans, under the direction of Rommel, were rapidly shoring up their Atlantic Wall. A great deal depended on the success of Operation Overlord.

Eisenhower talks to the paratroopers before they load for departure on June 5. (National Archives)

Strategic situation in Europe, 6 June 1944

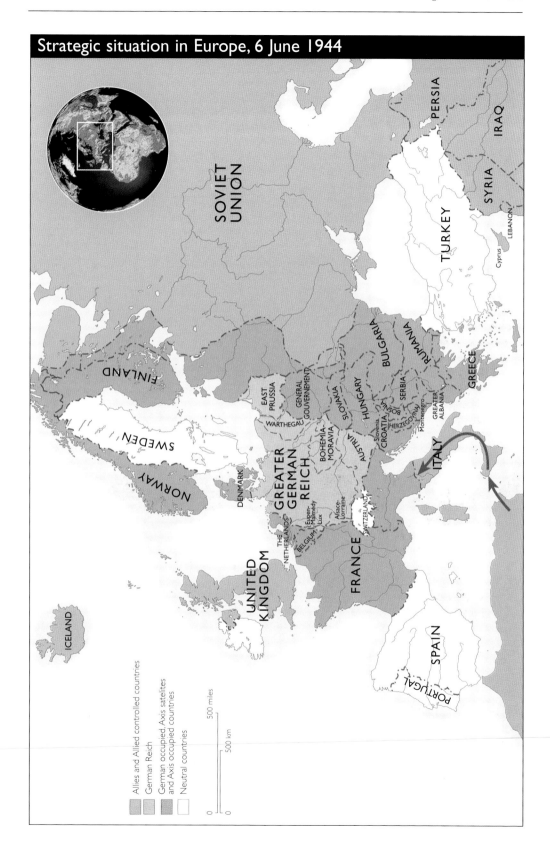

SOVIET UNION

PERSIA

IRAQ

SYRIA

TURKEY

LEBANON

Cyprus

FINLAND

BULGARIA

RUMANIA

GREECE

EAST PRUSSIA

GENERAL GOUVERNEMENT

SERBIA

SLOVAKIA

HUNGARY

GREATER ALBANIA

Montenegro

BOSNIA

HERZEGOVINA

Slovenia

CROATIA

WARTHEGAU

BOHEMIA MORAVIA

AUSTRIA

ITALY

SWEDEN

NORWAY

DENMARK

GREATER GERMAN REICH

THE NETHERLANDS

BELGIUM

Eupen-Malmedy

Lux

Alsace-Lorraine

SWITZERLAND

FRANCE

ICELAND

UNITED KINGDOM

SPAIN

PORTUGAL

Allies and Allied controlled countries

German Reich

German occupied, Axis satelites and Axis occupied countries

Neutral countries

500 miles

500 km

Propoganda posters were used by both sides during this war.
This image shows the line up of nations united against Hitler.
(Topham Picturepoint)

A military audit

The Northwest Europe campaign pitted the armed forces of the Western Allies against the Wehrmacht, the Nazi German military. The combined Allied contingents were called the Allied Expeditionary Forces and comprised troops from the United States, the United Kingdom, Canada, France, Poland, the Netherlands, Belgium, and Czechoslovakia. The American General Dwight Eisenhower commanded the Supreme Headquarters, Allied Expeditionary Forces (SHAEF). General Bernard Montgomery served as the Land Forces Commander during the initial landings until 1 September when the position passed to Eisenhower.

Montgomery led the Anglo-Canadian 21st Army Group, which from July 1944 fielded three armies: the US First Army led by General Omar Bradley; the British Second Army under Miles 'Bimbo' Dempsey; and the Canadian First Army under General Henry Crerar. On 1 August 1944 Bradley took command of the 12th US Army Group with the First Army (General Courtney Hodges)

The heads of state of the three main Allied contingents in northwest Europe: from left to right, Canadian Prime Minister W. L. Mackenzie King, American President Franklin D Roosevelt, and British Prime Minister Winston Churchill. (Imperial War Museum H32129)

The Allied senior command team for the Northwest Europe campaign meet for the first time in London in January 1944. From left to right, the team included (top row) General Omar Bradley, Admiral Bertram Ramsay, Air Marshall Trafford Leigh-Mallory, General Walter Bedell-Smith, and (bottom row) Air Marshal Arthur Conningham, Supreme Commander Dwight Eisenhower, and General Bernard Montgomery. (ISI)

and Third Army (General George Patton) under command. When, during September, the forces pushing northeast from the French Mediterranean coast linked up with those advancing east from Normandy, the 6th US Army Group, led by General Jacob Devers, and comprising the American Seventh Army and French First Army, came under Eisenhower's control. Later still, the American Ninth and Fifteenth Armies joined Bradley's army group.

Admiral Sir Bertram Ramsay controlled the vast invasion armada and naval covering forces. Air Chief Marshal Sir Trafford Leigh-Mallory commanded the Allied Expeditionary Air Forces, comprising the Royal Air Force, the US Army Air Force, and the Royal Canadian Air Force. Tactical

aviation belonging to the US IX and XIX Tactical Air Commands and the Anglo-Canadian Second Tactical Air Force supported the ground battle. The heavy bombers of RAF Bomber Command and the Eighth United States Army Air Force provided additional assistance.

The German Commander-in-Chief West, Field Marshal Gerd von Rundstedt, exercised nominal control over the Wehrmacht in France, Belgium, and Holland. His ground

As Commander-in-Chief West, Field Marshal Gerd von Rundstedt exercised nominal authority over all of the German armed forces in western Europe. In reality, however, his three subordinate ground commanders – including Army Group B commander Erwin Rommel – as well as his theater air force and naval commanders all enjoyed considerable freedom of action. (AKG Berlin)

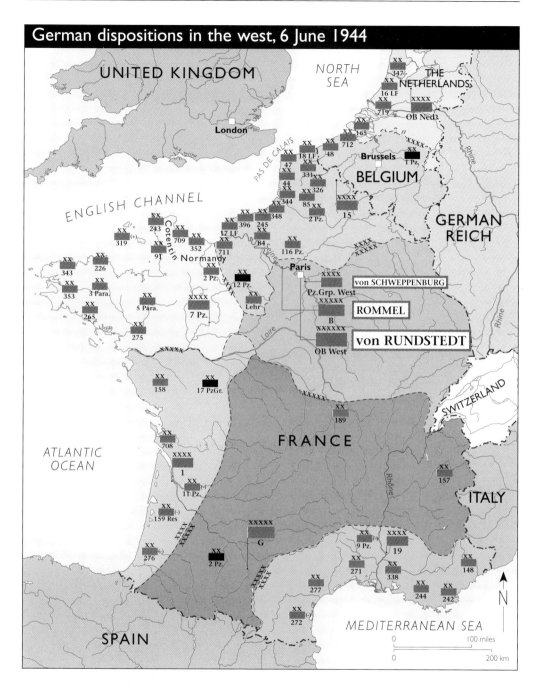

German dispositions in the west, 6 June 1944

forces belonged to three separate commands. Field Marshal Erwin Rommel's Army Group B comprised the Seventh Army in Brittany and Normandy and the Fifteenth Army deployed from Le Havre along the Pas de Calais to the Scheldt. The independent LXXXVIII Corps defended the Netherlands. Finally came Army Group G, comprising the First Army deployed along the western Atlantic coast and the Nineteenth Army defending the southern French Mediterranean coast.

In addition, General Geyr von Schweppenburg's Panzer Group West controlled the mechanized reserves who were tasked with driving the invaders back into the sea. Further complicating the

Field Marshal Erwin Rommel – the 'Desert Fox' – commanded Army Group B in northern France and Belgium. He was not impressed with large sections of the Atlantic Wall defenses, and in the months prior to the D-Day landings he channeled his iron determination into strengthening these coastal defenses. (AKG Berlin)

ground organization was the fact that four of the 10 mechanized divisions in the west were designated as Armed Forces High Command (OKW) reserves, and it required Hitler's permission before these could be committed to combat.

Admiral Kranke's Naval High Command West orchestrated the Kriegsmarine's counterinvasion measures. German Navy assets in western Europe comprised numerous small surface vessels, 40 U-boats, and many naval coast artillery batteries. German aircraft in the west belonged to General Sperrle's III Air Fleet. Decimated by sustained aerial combat during 1943–44 while opposing the Allied bomber offensive against the Reich, the Luftwaffe had only a few hundred planes available to defend French airspace.

The Allies had a significant numerical superiority in troops, heavy weapons, logistics, air power, and naval assets. The Kriegsmarine and Luftwaffe might be able to achieve local successes, but they were so heavily outnumbered that they were unable to contest the invasion. Mastery of the skies allowed the Allies to launch an increasingly effective strategic bombing campaign against the German war economy and transportation network. Such attacks had already essentially isolated the Normandy invasion area prior to D-Day, and the dwindling German ability to bring up fresh troops and supplies to the fighting front became an increasingly debilitating weakness as the campaign progressed.

The Germans, on the other hand, would rarely molest the Allied war economy in the last 18 months of the war. Moreover, as a result of the code-breaking successes of 'Ultra,' the Allies had excellent intelligence about German dispositions and intentions, while the Germans possessed a woefully inadequate intelligence picture.

Despite these significant advantages, however, Allied victory was not a foregone conclusion. The Germans enjoyed a qualitative edge, at least in ground forces, early in the campaign – although this edge was blunted during the campaign. The Allied armies in June 1944 had yet to reach peak effectiveness, and so could not yet engage the *Westheer* on equal terms.

Montgomery presided over a flawed British army whose development had been stunted between the wars and had been unable to cope with German offensives. It had therefore suffered serious defeats early in the war in Norway, France, North Africa, Malaysia, and Burma. Only with difficulty had the army recovered from these setbacks and fully learned the lessons of modern war during 1942–44. Consequently, Montgomery was acutely aware that his army's morale remained vulnerable. The army had also only been on the sustained offensive for a little over a year and was still developing proficiency in the complex art of attacking stout German defenses.

Additionally, Montgomery was cognizant of the finite nature of British resources. The nation had already been at war for nearly five years and was conducting simultaneous military operations in multiple theaters across the globe. Montgomery was determined to avoid the catastrophic casualties suffered during the First World War, from which Britain had neither psychologically nor materially fully recovered.

British military operations were therefore dominated by personnel concerns as its manpower dried up. Montgomery clearly understood that all available reserves would be consumed during the campaign and that his command would become a wasting asset. The manpower situation was even more acute for the Canadians, and of course very few replacements were available for the continental contingents fighting alongside the Allies, as they were all forces in exile.

These constraints powerfully shaped Montgomery's conduct of the campaign. He devised a cautious theater strategy where the Allies would use their numerical and material superiority to wear down the enemy in a protracted attritional battle. Montgomery eschewed a bold maneuver warfare strategy that might have won the war more quickly but ran the risk of increasing casualties. The result was a careful and controlled approach to operations that enabled the Germans to organize effective defensive positions as they withdrew.

The American military, on the other hand, had far greater resources. After their setback at the Kasserine Pass in January 1943, the Americans had steadily gained the upper hand over the Germans. Eisenhower's forces therefore had more confidence and better morale. The American military tradition had long emphasized direct offensive action. In fact its aggressive, offensive doctrine ensured that American troops sometimes lacked the respect for the enemy that the British had learned through painful experience. The biggest problem the Americans faced was their inexperience. Only a tiny fraction of the forces earmarked for the Normandy campaign had previously seen action.

Another deficiency was doctrinal. Interwar technological changes – particularly the development of mechanized forces and air power – fundamentally challenged military doctrine in the American army. Despite its endeavors, when it entered the Second World War, the army had not yet worked out how to integrate armor and air power fully in support of ground operations. Combat in the Mediterranean quickly exposed these flaws in doctrine; yet, effective solutions to these problems were still emerging during summer 1944.

The audit of war also illuminated the inefficiency of the American manpower replacement system, which was unable to restore rapidly fighting power to depleted formations. The problem of sustaining combat power was aggravated by the American government's shortsighted decision to limit the wartime army to just 90 divisions, a policy that forced formations to stay in the front line indefinitely, rather than being rotated out for rest and replenishment. A combination of inexperience, doctrinal deficiencies, and a poor manpower replacement system ensured that the US army in June 1944 was not yet able to bring its full fighting power to bear.

Given its greater resources and aggressive, offensive doctrine, the American military naturally assumed the larger role in the campaign, increasingly so as it progressed. It was to spearhead the Allied break-out once a permanent lodgment had been achieved. All the armies of the Western Allies learned through trial and error to fight more proficiently as the northwest Europe campaign progressed, thereby narrowing and ultimately eradicating the German qualitative edge. It was the US army, however, that proved able to adapt and enhance its combat effectiveness most rapidly. By the latter stages of the Northwest Europe campaign, it was able to outfight rather than simply overwhelm an increasingly outnumbered and outgunned enemy. This ability to adapt and enhance its combat effectiveness ensured that the USA emerged preeminent within the coalition by 1945.

Defeating the Nazi military force, however, was never going to be easy or quick. The German defenders had the benefit of considerable combat experience, and a realistic, proven doctrine and tactics refined through years of war. Operating under a totalitarian regime, the military potentially had all the resources of the state at its disposal. Moreover, the Germans were a martial people with a long and proud military history. Nevertheless, the Nazi war machine was by no means invincible; nor were its soldiers the 'supermen' that racist Nazi propaganda extolled them to be.

In reality, the German military fought in northwest Europe under severe constraints. Brutal attrition in the east had already torn the heart out of the Wehrmacht and it was scraping the manpower and resources barrels by 1944. But its biggest deficiencies were logistical. Constant combat ensured that the Germans lacked the supplies necessary for victory and throughout the campaign they operated on a logistical shoestring, particularly liquid fuels. Moreover, the German war economy had long been inefficient and poorly managed. While dramatic increases in production had recently been realized by ruthless rationalization, the German war economy was now subject to punishing Allied heavy bomber attacks and was unable to meet the needs of a three-front war. Consequently, the German military remained perennially short of the means of conducting modern operations. It was rarely able to contest Allied aerial supremacy, which hindered all German ground operations and denied them information about the enemy.

German commanders, therefore, remained woefully ignorant of enemy actions and intentions, which hampered German countermeasures. Attrition had also badly denuded German ground forces of vehicles, reducing the strategic mobility that had hitherto allowed German forces to evade annihilation by a numerically superior enemy. This dwindling mobility progressively increased the vulnerability of German formations to encirclement and annihilation by a far more mobile enemy.

These deficiencies ensured that the German military was unable to mount the combined-arms defense necessary to prevail in the west, and that instead it would slowly be driven back in grim attritional warfare. Nonetheless, the determination of German troops and commanders, their professionalism, as well as their realistic doctrine, tactics, and training allowed them to offer sustained, stubborn resistance that cost the Allies dearly. Influenced by Nazi racism and propaganda, as well as the instinct for self-preservation, German troops continued to fight to protect their families at home from the vengeance that they feared the Allies would exact for the horrible measures the Nazis had taken to keep Europe under control. The Germans could be expected to fight long and hard. And even if they could not win, they could at least postpone the inevitable for as long as possible and increase the price of the enemy's victory.

The Allies invade France

The Allied armed forces required extensive preparation before they could successfully invade Nazi-occupied France. During 1940–41 the British military was fully preoccupied preparing to thwart an anticipated German invasion of Britain. Only when that threat receded, after Hitler's June 1941 invasion of the Soviet Union, could the British armed forces contemplate a return to the continent.

However, other struggles continued to preoccupy British forces. At sea, the Battle of the Atlantic raged, threatening Britain's maritime communications, until the Allies exorcised the U-boat threat during 1943 (see *The Second World War (3) The war at sea* in this series). In the skies, the Allies had to contend with continued periodic German air

Britain had to secure strategic success over the German U-boat menace as well as the German Navy's commerce raiding surface fleet before serious preparations could begin for any future amphibious landing on the coast of Nazi-occupied Europe. (AKG Berlin)

raids across the Channel. Moreover, Britain found itself engaged in ongoing ground combat in both Burma and North Africa – operations that diverted troops and resources away from Britain. It was therefore not until 1943 that invasion preparations hit high gear.

Even then much work needed to be done. The British army commanders had to inculcate the troops with the important lessons of modern war that had been so painfully relearned in North Africa. The army had to reequip with new weaponry; formations had to reorganize to enhance their fighting power; and for the first time, troops undertook offensive training geared toward continental warfare.

British air, ground, and naval forces also had to learn to work smoothly together to establish the effective interservice cooperation that was essential for victory. But building good teamwork required long association to develop full understanding of the respective capabilities and limitations of

each service. Each branch of the army –
infantry, artillery, and armor – had not only
to improve its doctrine and training, but also
to put aside regimental tribalism to work
together effectively.

The D-Day amphibious assault also
required extensive preparation. Initially, the
Allies greatly underestimated the difficulties
this entailed. They were rudely disabused of
such complacency during the August 1942
Dieppe raid, in which the 2nd Canadian
Division was badly mauled attacking a
well-defended German-held port. The most
important lesson of Dieppe was that a
heavily defended harbor was too tough a nut
to crack. The Allies therefore decided to land
adjacent to a major port and establish a firm
lodgment, before seizing the harbor which
would be vital to the long-term logistical
sustainability of the bridgehead. After
considerable debate, the Allies chose
Normandy, with its major port of Cherbourg,
as the invasion site.

The Dieppe raid also demonstrated the
need for specialized amphibious assault armor
to crack the enemy's beach defenses; for, at
Dieppe, the supporting tanks proved unable
to get off the beach to assist the troops as
they advanced inland. Over the next year
Britain devoted considerable resources to
developing these vehicles. Dieppe equally
revealed the need for fire support during the
actual landing. In the lead-up to D-Day, the
Allied navies developed and refined elaborate
procedures to deliver naval gunfire during the
landings. They built special landing craft,
equipped with guns and rockets to augment
naval gunfire. Assembling, organizing, and
preparing an amphibious armada of
thousands of vessels took many months to
complete.

The Royal Air Force (RAF) also had an
important role to play. Having won the
Battle of Britain in 1940, Fighter Command
needed a new mission and found it in the
direct, tactical support of ground forces on
the battlefield. Such support had proven
woefully deficient in the early desert battles,
to such an extent that British troops derided
the RAF as the 'Royal Absent Force.' Initially,

technical problems – including the
unsuitability of aircraft, lack of air–ground
coordination, and poor aerial recognition
skills – seriously hampered the utility of
tactical aviation. Only through a difficult
process of trial and error were solutions to
these problems found. By D-Day, however,
Allied air power was ready to provide
extensive and sustained tactical air support.

The RAF leadership, however, remained loath to divert Bomber Command from its nocturnal area bombing of Germany's cities, which was intended to break civilian morale. This reflected the powerful sway of interwar strategic bombing theorists, who held that the heavy bomber 'would always get through' to its target and that, consequently, strategic bombing was capable of winning

Air Marshal Harris, head of Bomber Command, spearheaded Britain's strategic bombing offensive against Germany, which was designed to break the morale of Germany's civilian population. During the Northwest Europe campaign, Bomber Command also employed its heavy bombers in direct support of Montgomery's offensives, most notably during Operation Goodwood in July 1944. (AKG Berlin) wars unaided. The result of this dogma was increasingly heavy night attacks by the RAF and daylight precision raids by the US Army Air Force against German industrial centers.

The Germans, however, were unwilling to accept that the bomber would always get through. During 1943 they developed a potent air defense system that involved specialized night fighters vectored onto bomber streams by ground-based early warning radar. The result over winter 1943–44 was the infliction of loss rates that Bomber Command could not sustain indefinitely. American daylight raids also began to suffer correspondingly heavy losses. The solution was long-range fighter protection, but it was not until the development of the P-51 Mustang external fuel tanks that it proved possible for fighters to stay with the bombers all the way to their German targets.

The attrition that Allied heavy bombers suffered over winter 1943–44 had two unanticipated benefits, however. The first was the destruction of the German fighter

Allied aerial interdiction attacks were so successful in the weeks prior to D-Day that virtually every bridge over the Loire and Seine rivers into Normandy had been put out of action. This accomplishment severely dislocated Rommel's ability to get reinforcements to the invasion front line. Of course, when the Allies came to cross the Seine in August 1944, they had to construct new pontoon bridges like the one depicted here in the foreground. (Imperial War Museum B9748)

force in western Europe by Allied long-range fighter escorts as the enemy planes came up to engage the bombers. Victory in this attritional struggle gave the Allies the aerial supremacy they needed to guarantee success in the invasion. Second, the heavy attrition softened Bomber Command's dogmatic opposition to employing strategic air power in support of the Normandy invasion. Thus, during spring 1944 heavy bombers joined tactical aviation – fighters, fighter-bombers, and medium bombers – in a massive aerial interdiction campaign intended to isolate the Normandy battlefield. By D-Day, despite consciously dissipating their strikes to disguise the location of the invasion, Allied air attacks had destroyed virtually every rail bridge over the rivers Loire and Seine into Normandy, thus severely hampering the German ability to move forces to repel the invasion.

The task that the American military faced was even greater, for in 1943 the US army had very few combat-ready troops in Britain and these lacked the support services necessary for offensive amphibious operations. The USA had only entered the war in December 1941 and sustained peacetime neglect had ensured that its armed services required considerable time to shape up for overseas deployment. Moreover, no sooner had American forces arrived in Britain in 1942 than they were immediately committed to combat in the Mediterranean during Operation Torch, the November 1942 invasion of French northwest Africa. After eventual victory in Tunisia during May 1943, in what proved a difficult baptism of fire for inexperienced American forces, US troops helped capture Sicily during July–August 1943 and then invaded Italy that September.

It was therefore not until the autumn of 1943 that veteran formations could be withdrawn from the Mediterranean to prepare for Operation Overlord, as the Normandy invasion had now been designated. In the meantime, a massive build-up of American forces in Britain occurred, including the enormous quantities of ordnance, ammunition, fuel, rations, and spare parts needed to sustain operations. American forces gathered in western England adjacent to their ports of arrival, and logistic considerations more than anything else determined that American forces would land on the right (western) flank of the invasion.

American troops also worked hard in the year before D-Day to overcome the flaws in their combat performance demonstrated in the Mediterranean. The biggest weakness in that theater had been the inadequate tactical air support caused by the lack of air–ground communication, poor aerial recognition skills, and inexperience. Combat revealed doctrinal problems within the army relating to new technology, particularly tanks and tank destroyers, and identified serious shortcomings in the American replacement system. During 1943–44, the American military worked strenuously to rectify these deficiencies.

For the German defenders, extensive preparations to thwart the invasion began even later. During 1943 the German High Command continued to believe that the Allies were neither materially nor psychologically ready to launch the Second Front. The Germans therefore only modestly enhanced their Atlantic Wall defenses, the allegedly formidable fortifications along the Atlantic coast. Unfortunately for the Germans, the Atlantic Wall existed only adjacent to the major ports; otherwise it remained largely a fiction of Nazi propaganda.

Instead, the German Army in the West – the *Westheer* – remained a backwater of the Nazi war effort. Its primary mission remained supporting the ongoing (and increasingly disastrous) war on the Eastern Front. Throughout 1943 the Germans continued to use France to rehabilitate formations shattered in the east and to work up new divisions to operational readiness, prior to deployment to the Soviet Union and, from September 1943, also to Italy.

The permanent German occupation forces in France thus comprised second-rate coastal defense divisions of limited manpower, firepower, and mobility. Almost no significant operational reserve existed in the west, besides refitting or newly forming mechanized formations. German naval power likewise consisted primarily of numerous small coastal vessels that were incapable of turning back a major invasion force. Moreover, the few German aircraft deployed in the west remained fully preoccupied trying to thwart the Allied air onslaught on the cities and economic infrastructure of Germany. Thus the German military in 1943 was incapable of stopping the Allies if they invaded. Yet, this unsatisfactory position reflected German awareness that the Allies were not yet ready to invade, even if they had wanted to.

This situation changed during November 1943 when Hitler recognized the inevitability of an Allied invasion attempt during 1944 and switched Germany's strategic priority to the west. Over the next seven months there materialized a massive influx of veterans and new recruits as well as Germany's latest and most lethal weapons. The result would be a metamorphosis of German combat power in the west.

By June 1944 the Germans had built up sufficient strength potentially to thwart an invasion: if, that is, they gained some advance warning of where and when the enemy was going to strike, so that they could launch a concentrated counteroffensive to throw the Allies back into the sea. Yet success also required that the German air force and navy at least disrupt Allied mastery of the seas and the skies. The gravest German weakness, however, remained its woefully inadequate logistical base, which, exacerbated by the Allied aerial interdiction campaign, ensured that the Germans lacked the supply stockpiles to win a protracted battle of attrition.

From D-Day to victory

On D-Day, 6 June 1944, six Allied infantry divisions, heavily reinforced with artillery and armor, and supported by a massive air umbrella and naval gunfire, landed astride five invasion beaches. American troops assaulted 'Utah' beach on the southern tip of the Cotentin peninsula and at 'Omaha' along the western Calvados coast. Anglo-Canadian troops landed on 'Gold,' 'Juno,' and 'Sword' beaches between Arromanches and Ouistreham in front of Caen. In addition, the Allies dropped one British and two American airborne divisions along both flanks of the invasion to disrupt German counterattacks aimed at rolling up the beachheads.

The Allied forces experienced contrasting fates on D-Day. Anglo-Canadian forces firmly established themselves ashore on their three assault beaches, but failed to achieve the ambitious goal of capturing the key city of Caen. Although the invaders breached the bulk of the defenses, the Germans held the Pèriers Ridge and prevented the linking up of the 'Gold' and 'Sword' beachheads. Along the ridge that afternoon elements of the 21st Panzer Division counterattacked and successfully pushed through to the coast. But outnumbered and with both flanks unsecured, the Germans retired to the ridge after dark. Moreover, the landing of the British 6th Airborne Division east of the Orne protected the vulnerable left flank of the landing against a weak armored counterattack that the Germans launched that day.

For American forces, the invasion did not go quite as smoothly. At 'Utah' beach, Americans troops quickly established a solid beachhead; however, at 'Omaha' beach, the landing came close to being repulsed. The difficult terrain of steep bluffs bisected by narrow ravines, the loss of most of the amphibious assault armor in rough seas, and the failure of the aerial bombing attacks left the initial assault waves pinned down by murderous German defensive fire. Ultimately, sheer numbers, toughness and heroism, backed by short-range naval gunfire, overwhelmed the defenders and allowed American forces to establish a shallow enclave ashore.

Reflecting the inherent hazard of airborne operations, the drop of the American 82nd and 101st Airborne Divisions inland behind 'Utah' beach and astride the Merderet River became highly scattered and casualties were heavy. The dispersion did have one inadvertent benefit, however, for it confused the Germans as to the real location of the invasion. Though widely scattered, the paratroopers dislocated German communications and prevented a major counterattack against 'Utah' beach on D-Day, allowing the landing troops to establish a firm foothold ashore.

Other factors contributed to Allied success. The absence of many senior German commanders at a war game in Brittany and the disruption of communications due to aerial and naval bombardment both hampered German countermeasures. As significantly, Allied domination of the skies prevented the Luftwaffe from effectively impeding the invasion. The German navy proved equally unable to resist the vast invasion armada. In sum, months of meticulous preparation combined with personal heroism, massive air and naval support, and the achievement of surprise, brought success on D-Day. By the end of 6 June 1944, though few recognized it at the time, the Allies had established a permanent foothold in France.

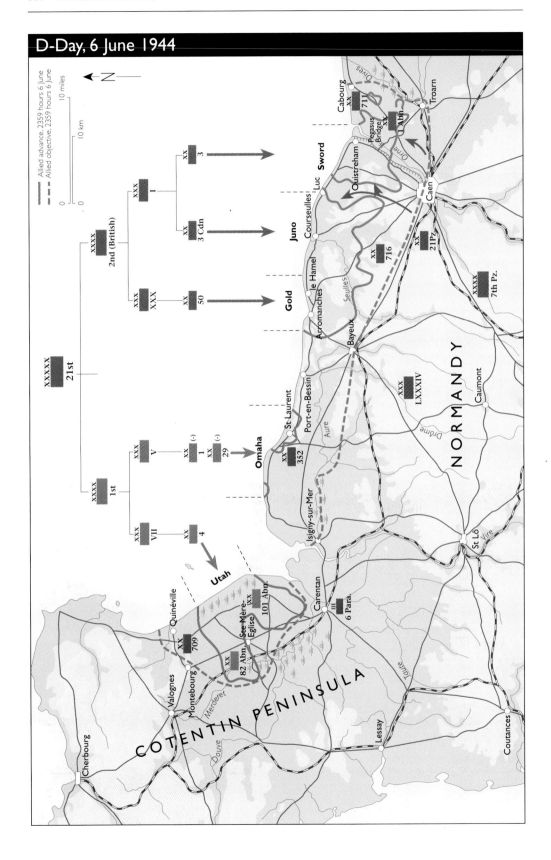

D-Day, 6 June 1944

The aftermath of D-Day

After D-Day, little went according to plan. Montgomery's advance quickly stalled when powerful German armored reserves converged on Caen to smash the Anglo-Canadian beachhead. While his forces repulsed these counterattacks, his forces could not gain ground and the struggle for Caen degenerated into a grim six-week attritional battle. Hitler and his commanders believed that the outcome of the campaign hinged on holding Caen, so the Germans massed their best formations opposite the British sector. The narrow bridgehead gave the Germans a relatively short front, allowing them to develop defenses in depth that presented Montgomery with a considerable challenge. Meanwhile, they rushed the II SS Panzer Corps from the

Operation Goodwood remains one of the most controversial offensives of the Normandy campaign. Although the abortive British attack to secure Caen and the Bourguébus Ridge suffered very high tank losses, it did facilitate the success of the subsequent American Cobra offensive in the west of the Normandy theater. (NARA)

Eastern Front for a counteroffensive to smash the bridgehead. In the interim, the Germans stubbornly defended Caen to deny Anglo-Canadian forces room to maneuver.

Neither did American operations go according to plan after D-Day. The Germans temporarily checked the advance of General 'Lightning' Joe Collins' VII Corps from 'Utah' beach toward the key port of Cherbourg along the Quineville Ridge. The advance of Major-General Leonard Gerow's V US Corps on St Lô from 'Omaha' beach was likewise slow. After Isigny fell on 9 June, the way to St Lô stood open, but American caution allowed German reserves to move up and build a new defensive front. Moreover, the priority accorded to Collins' advance on Cherbourg hindered the drive on St Lô. Consequently, the V Corps offensive abruptly ground to a halt 2 miles (3.2km) short of St Lô on 18 June.

The slow advance on Cherbourg forced Collins to abandon the planned direct advance on the port. Instead, on 15 June, VII Corps struck west and cut the peninsula two days later, isolating Cherbourg. Only then, on 22 June, did Collins launch an

all-out three-division attack on the port. Though the attenuated defenders fought fiercely, final resistance ceased on 1 July. Although the Americans had finally captured their much-needed major harbor, they had done so well behind schedule and the enemy had left the port in ruins.

On 26 June, along the eastern flank, Montgomery launched his first major offensive, Operation Epsom. It was an ambitious attack to breach the strong enemy defenses west of Caen, force the Orne and Odon rivers, gain the high ground southwest of the city and thereby outflank it. The VIII Corps of Lieutenant-General Miles Dempsey's Second (British) Army spearheaded the offensive backed by strong air, naval, and artillery support. Yet bad luck dogged Epsom: unseasonably bad weather forced Montgomery to attack without the planned air bombardment and the neighboring XXX Corps failed to take the

flanking Rauray Ridge, which hindered the entire attack.

Significant concentration of force finally allowed the British infantry to penetrate the thin German defenses and establish a bridgehead across the Odon River. Thereafter, the 11th Armored Division pushed through and captured Hill 112 beyond. By 28 June, Montgomery had torn a 5-mile (8km) gap in the German defenses. But the methodical advance prevented Montgomery from achieving further gains.

Next, after German reserves had counterattacked the narrow British corridor and the shallow Odon bridgehead, the cautious Montgomery abandoned Hill 112

In order to avoid high casualties, Montgomery favored the use of massive aerial and artillery firepower to support his ground offensives. The effect on urban centers such as Caen, shown here, was devastating. (Imperial War Museum, B7754)

and retired to a shorter, more defensible line. Subsequently, between 29 June and 2 July, VIII Corps repulsed strong, if poorly coordinated, German attacks that constituted the long-anticipated enemy counteroffensive. The newly arrived II SS Panzer Corps hurled itself against the British Odon bridgehead, but made little headway in the face of tremendous Allied defensive artillery fire, and the operation soon fizzled out.

The German counterattack failed primarily because the Germans only had supplies for a few days of sustained offensive action and because they had attacked prematurely with new troops unfamiliar with Normandy's combat conditions. The counteroffensive's failure proved unequivocally that the Allied lodgment had become permanent. Therefore, Hitler devised a new strategy: an unyielding defense to corral the Allies into a narrow bridgehead

and deny them the room and favorable terrain for mobile operations. This decision committed the Germans to an attritional battle within range of the Allied fleet; it was a battle they could not win.

However, Montgomery had neither broken through nor gained the high ground over the Odon in Epsom. It was not until 8 July that he launched a new multi-corps attack on Caen, designated Charnwood. Montgomery again relied heavily on air power to shatter enemy resistance. A strategic bomber raid destroyed several Orne bridges and sharply reduced the Germans'

The Allies' employment of massive aerial and artillery firepower inflicted considerable damage onthe defending Germans. However, the extensive cratering such tactics caused also hampered Allied attempts to advance deep through the enemy's defensive position. (Imperial War Museum CL 838)

ability to resupply their forces in the northern part of the city. Meanwhile, Anglo-Canadian forces launched concentric attacks on the beleaguered and greatly outnumbered defenders. Inexorably, superior numbers and firepower drove the enemy back, and on 9 July Montgomery's troops finally fought their way into northern Caen, four weeks behind schedule. However, Montgomery's exhausted forces were unable to push across the defensible Orne River barrier onto the open Falaise Plain beyond.

Despite reinforcement by Collins' VII Corps, and fresh divisions from Britain, General Omar Bradley's First US Army still struggled to advance in the *bocage* hedgerows when it renewed its offensive toward St Lô on 3 July. Major-General Troy Middleton's fresh VIII US Corps struck south from the base of the Cotentin peninsula with three divisions and in five days took La Haye-du-Puits against stiff resistance. But ferocious opposition stopped the offensive at the Ay and Seves rivers on 15 July. Simultaneously, VII Corps attacked from Carentan toward Pèriers on 3 July, but quickly stalled due to poor weather and difficult marshy terrain. Even after the veteran 4th Division joined the attack on 5 July, VII Corps gained only 750 yards (700m) in four days. The Germans both defended skillfully and counterattacked repeatedly to sap American strength. Though it beat off these counterattacks during 10–12 July, VII Corps had to go over to defense on 15 July.

Gradually, however, American forces solved the problems of hedgerow fighting with improved tactics, enhanced firepower, and better coordination, all of which speeded the fall of St Lô. Major-General Charles Corlett's newly arrived XIX US Corps struck south with three divisions on 7 July to capture St Jean-de-Daye. Thereafter, the corps slowly, but inexorably, gained ground until it cut the Pèriers–St Lô highway on 20 July. The 29th US Division, after renewing its drive toward St Lô on 11 July, both seized the ridge that dominated the northeastern approaches to the city, and advanced across the St Lô–Bayeux highway. On 18 July, the hard-pressed Germans abandoned the city.

American forces had grimly fought their way forward into more open ground and were therefore in a position to prepare a major breakthrough operation, codenamed Cobra.

While the Americans prepared for Cobra, Montgomery launched a major new offensive, named Goodwood, around Caen. This would become the campaign's most controversial operation. In this attack, Montgomery sought to capture both southern Caen and the Bourguébus Ridge – objectives that opened the way to the Falaise Plain to their south. A new attack was necessary to hold German reserves at Caen while the Americans prepared for their break-out bid. However, Montgomery required massive fire support to breach the strong German defenses behind the Orne and it was thus only on 18 July that he attacked out of the bridgehead east of the Orne, which his airborne troops had captured on D-Day. Unfortunately, this bridgehead was so constricted that it proved impossible to preserve surprise and therefore Montgomery had to rely heavily on air bombardment.

Goodwood was both ill-conceived and ill-executed. Aerial bombing and artillery fire enabled British armor to crash through the forward German defenses to the foot of the high ground south of Caen. But the outnumbered Germans nevertheless conducted a delaying withdrawal that disrupted and dispersed the British advance. Thus, British armor reached the Bourguébus Ridge late on 18 July with little infantry and no artillery support. The German gun line of heavy antitank and antiaircraft guns emplaced on the high ground then repulsed the British tanks, inflicting heavy losses. As dusk approached, German combined-arms counterattacks drove the British armor back with further heavy loss.

Montgomery attacked for two more days, but the advance had lost its momentum. Nowhere had his forces established a solid foothold on the vital Bourguébus Ridge, and the heavy losses suffered eroded British fighting power. In fact, the employment of massed armor against intact defenses brought catastrophic tank losses during Goodwood: more than one-third of British

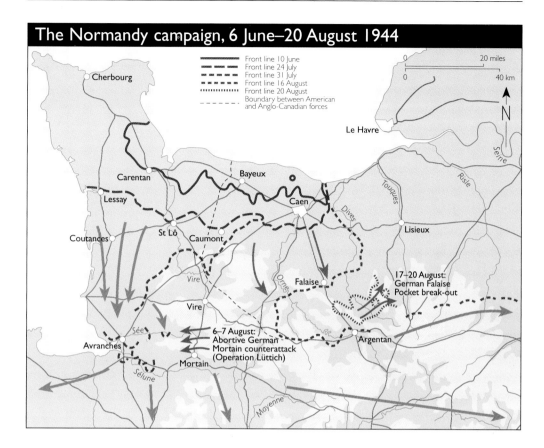

The Normandy campaign, 6 June–20 August 1944

Cherbourg

Front line 10 June
Front line 24 July
Front line 31 July
Front line 16 August
Front line 20 August
Boundary between American
and Anglo-Canadian forces

0   20 miles
0   40 km

N

Le Havre

Carentan   Bayeux

Lessay   Caen

Coutances   St Lô   Caumont

Vire   Falaise   17–20 August:
                                German Falaise
                                Pocket break-out

Vire

Sée   6–7 August:
Avranches Abortive German
           Mortain counterattack   Argentan
Mortain   (Operation Lüttich)

Sélune

Mayenne

tank strength in Normandy. Moreover, the offensive failed to 'write down' enemy armor as Montgomery had intended. Though Goodwood did gain more ground and temporarily pinned some German reserves on the Caen front, these limited achievements were bought at a price that British forces could not afford to repeat.

The Cobra break-out

Goodwood nevertheless helped the American break-out bid by diverting badly needed supplies from the St Lô sector to the Caen front to replenish German forces after their heavy expenditures resisting Montgomery's attack. The result was serious erosion of the German logistic position on the American front prior to Cobra, which facilitated the American break-out. Allied air attacks had continually hampered German resupply operations, thus creating serious logistic

problems. This situation worsened, particularly on the western sector, after 15 July with the renewed destruction of the rail bridge at Tours, the German Seventh Army's major supply artery. Its supplies thus dwindled on the St Lô front in the lead-up to Cobra. In fact, the defending German LXXXIV Corps had less than two days' fuel left. Thus for the first time in the campaign, during Cobra supply shortages crippled the German defenses and prevented them from cordoning off the American break-in during 25–26 July, as they had all previous Allied offensives.

Innovation also aided the American success in Cobra. To provide the firepower it lacked, First US Army relied first on carpet bombing to smash a hole in the German front; second, on a narrow front offensive to penetrate the German line; and lastly, on mobility and speed to outmaneuver, rather than outfight, the enemy. Bradley, thus, planned Cobra as a concentrated break-in attack by three infantry divisions on a narrow front, supported by intense air and artillery attack, to secure the flanks; meanwhile, three mechanized divisions would punch through to the rear, capture Coutances, and cut off the German LXXXIV Corps on the coast.

The preparatory carpet-bombing was the largest and most effective air attack on ground forces yet seen in the war. While faulty planning, sloppy execution, and bad luck dogged the aerial bombardment, it nevertheless crippled German communications and battered the forward-concentrated Panzer *Lehr* Division so much that even its seasoned troops could not resist VII Corps' concentrated attack. Consequently, the Americans advanced 2 miles (3.2km) into the German defenses on 25 July and, subsequently, American speed and mobility turned this break-in into a break-out. During this exploitation phase, American forces reinforced their success faster than the Germans could redeploy reserves, as mounting logistic deficiencies for the first time crippled the enemy's defense. On 26 July, VII Corps gained 5 miles (8km) as the stretched German front began to collapse.

In response, the Germans rushed the XLVII Panzer Corps (2nd and 116th Panzer Divisions) from the British front to take the American breakthrough in the flank and nip off the penetration. But the American XIX Corps' flanking push south from St Lô disrupted the planned German counterattack and forced the Germans to strike hastily amid the thick *bocage* southeast of St Lô. Both the difficult terrain and mounting supply shortages frustrated the German counterattack, as the panzer forces experienced the same offensive difficulties that had earlier bedeviled American operations. The XLVII Panzer Corps proved unable to hold the ground taken: all it achieved was to build a defensive front facing west and await promised reinforcements.

On 27 July the Americans achieved a decisive breakthrough. As the enemy evacuated Lessay and Pèriers to rebuild a cohesive defense, VII US Corps advanced 12 miles (19km) until it halted just short of Coutances. The next day, the corps captured Coutances and linked up with VII Corps. SS Colonel-General Paul Hausser, the German Seventh Army commander, then erred when he ordered LXXXIV Corps to fight its way southeast in an effort to regain a continuous front, instead of retiring unopposed due south to re-establish a new line south of Coutances. The retiring German forces thus ran into the American spearheads southeast of Coutances and were isolated in the Roncey pocket. With the German front torn open, Bradley expanded Cobra on 29 July. VII and VIII Corps renewed their drive to the south and the next day crossed the River Sienne, took Avranches, and seized a bridgehead across the Sée River, before crossing the Sélune River at Pontaubault on 31 July to open the gateway to Brittany.

Montgomery also resumed the offensive in late July, hastily launching Operation Bluecoat, against the weakly held German front astride Caumont. This rapidly devised attack was intended to maintain pressure on the Germans and prevent the transfer of enemy armor against the Americans. Six divisions of VIII and XXX British Corps assaulted a single German infantry division, but the premature start meant that the attack lacked the massive artillery support that habitually accompanied British offensives. Moreover, though the German defense was weak, the front had been static since mid-June and the Germans had entrenched in depth amid the thick *bocage*.

Initially, British forces quickly penetrated the enemy lines and drew into battle German armor transferring to the American front. Yet, failure to take the flanking high ground at Amaye seriously hampered progress. Caution also prevented British forces from tearing open a barely coherent German front that was ripe to be shattered. On 30 July, the British captured a bridgehead over the River Souleuvre on the undefended boundary between Seventh Army and Panzer Group West. For the next week the two German commands remained detached along this boundary, leaving a 2-mile (3.2km) gap that the British failed to exploit. By the time the British had realized the weakness of the enemy and advanced, German reserves had closed the gap.

The position of the Allied boundary line also hindered a rapid British capture of Vire, imposing a delay that aided the enemy's retreat. The town's quick fall would have severed the enemy's lateral communications lines and seriously hampered the German withdrawal. While the 11th Armored Division of VIII Corps advanced steadily, XXX Corps' armor soon lagged behind, leaving the 11th Armored dangerously exposed as German resistance stiffened on 1 August with the arrival of armor from Caen. On 6 August, German counterblows almost overran the 11th Armored Division's spearhead, but the German armor was keen to push on westward against the Americans and thus launched only limited counterattacks.

American reinforcements move up to Mortain to block the German 'Lüttich' counterattack on 7 August. This operation was one of Hitler's greatest strategic blunders. Unlikely ever to succeed, the operation merely sucked German forces further west into the noose of an encirclement then forming in the Argentan–Falaise area; this ensured that the *Westheer* would suffer a catastrophic strategic defeat in Normandy during August 1944. (US Army)

On 1 August, meanwhile, Bradley's 12th US Army Group became operational and assumed command of the First Army and General George Patton's new Third Army. American forces were now able to conduct the fast-paced mobile war for which the peacetime army had trained. While the First Army advanced southeast and occupied Mortain on 3 August, Patton conducted a spectacular armored advance that first isolated Brittany and then pushed deep into the peninsula to seize Pontivy. Nonetheless, most of the enemy garrison was still able to retire into the ports of Brest, St Malo, and Lorient.

Germany strikes back!

During the break-out, American forces for the first time assumed the defense to thwart a major German counteroffensive that aimed to seal off the American penetration and isolate Patton's command. The American advance had left the center thin, a weakness that Hitler sought to exploit. On 2 August 1944, Hitler condemned the *Westheer* to total defeat when he ordered the new commander of Army Group B, Field Marshal von Kluge, to launch a counteroffensive to retake Avranches and seal off the American break-out from Normandy. This decision was

a strategic blunder that completed the decimation of German forces in Normandy. Although the Germans hastily scraped together the elements of six, albeit much depleted, mechanized divisions, and built up supplies for a few days of sustained offensive action, this was insufficient for success.

Hans von Funck's XLVII Panzer Corps struck during the night of 6–7 August down the narrow corridor between the Sée and Sélune rivers toward Mortain and Avranches. Nonetheless, his troops were too depleted and tired, and von Funck had attacked prematurely before his forces could survey the ground. Moreover, on 5 August the Americans first detected a German build-up around Mortain, while eleventh-hour 'Ultra' intercept intelligence warned of the enemy attack and allowed Bradley to undertake last-minute efforts to bolster his defenses.

American troops were still thin on the ground, occupied unprepared positions, and remained inexperienced at coordinating defensively. Nonetheless, American forces resolutely defended Hill 317, defying all German efforts to push through Mortain toward Avranches. Thereafter, the rapid arrival of American reserves quickly halted the offensive as Allied fighter-bombers disrupted the German drive through the *bocage* once the skies cleared on 7 August. Indeed, the imbalance of forces was simply too great to allow a restabilization of the front and, logistically, the attack was doomed: the Germans had neither the firepower nor the supplies to recapture and hold Avranches.

The defeat of the Mortain counterattack presented the Allies with a strategic opportunity to encircle and destroy the German forces in Normandy, either in the Argentan–Falaise area or via a larger envelopment along the River Seine. With American forces advancing deep into their rear, the only feasible German strategy was to withdraw behind the Seine. Given the dire supply position and dwindling mobility, heavy losses were inevitable since the Mortain counterattack simply thrust the Germans further into the noose of a pocket forming in the Argentan–Falaise area.

However, as American forces raced east to meet Montgomery's troops pushing south from Caen toward Falaise, they became strung out and short on supplies. Fearing over-extension, friendly-fire casualties, and a successful German break-out amid a deteriorating supply situation, Bradley halted the American advance during 13–18 August, divided his forces and directed V Corps to the Seine, which left neither thrust strong enough to defeat the enemy. The Americans had too little strength either to close the Falaise pocket at Argentan firmly from the south, or to push quickly north up both banks of the Seine after V Corps had established a bridgehead across the river at Mantes-Gassicourt on 19 August. By going for a classic double encirclement, the Allies achieved neither objective.

Sluggish Anglo-Canadian progress contributed to the Allied failure to destroy the Germans in the Falaise pocket in mid-August. Although Crerar's newly operational Canadian First Army attacked south toward Argentan in two hastily organized offensives, Totalize and Tractable after 8 August, a combination of inexperience and stubborn German resistance delayed the fall of Falaise until 16 August. Lack of firm British pressure elsewhere allowed the enemy to conduct an orderly withdrawal from the pocket until 19 August, when Canadian and Polish troops finally closed it. In the interim, 40,000 German troops had escaped.

Montgomery feared that his tired and depleted forces would suffer heavy losses and a possible setback if he tried to stop the desperate but determined enemy from escaping. Instead he, like Eisenhower, looked toward a larger envelopment along the Seine. At the same time, Montgomery underestimated the speed and mobility of the American forces; his refusal to alter the army group boundary to allow the Americans to advance past Argentan and close the pocket from the south contributed to Bradley's decision to halt the American advance on 13 August.

It was therefore not until 16 August that Montgomery launched Operation Kitten, the long-planned advance to the Seine. Now the

Light Alllied vehicles such as the one pictured here, had
relatively modest impact in the hard-slogging battles of June
and July, but once the German front collapsed in August, and
mobile operations ensued, they came into their own.
(Imperial War Museum, CL838)

On 25 August 1944, Allied troops – spearheaded by a French division – liberated Paris from German occupation. During the previous 48 hours, as the Germans prepared to withdraw from the city, French resistance fighters emerged from their places of hiding and commenced an armed uprising against their oppressors. (AKG Berlin)

Germans faced the prospect of a much larger encirclement on the Seine, as their dwindling mobility, catastrophic supply situation, and mounting demoralization presented the Allies with an opportunity to annihilate the enemy against the river. But after 21 August the Germans pulled off their greatest success of the campaign as they extricated virtually all of their remaining forces in a full-scale, staged withdrawal behind the Seine.

Changing strategic priorities, increasing demands for air support, and poor weather prevented Allied air forces from impeding the German retreat. Moreover, the Allied decision of 18 August to capture the Seine bridges intact then brought an end to direct attacks. The break-out also greatly increased the number of potential ground targets and inevitably dissipated Allied air power. Despite repeated air attacks and a catastrophic fuel situation, the Germans salvaged most of their troops and a surprising amount of equipment. They found no respite, however, as Allied forces rapidly advanced beyond the Seine. During the last week in August, therefore, the *Westheer* conducted a headlong

general withdrawal from France back toward the Belgian and German frontiers, closely pursued by Allied forces.

Continued retreat

During 1–9 September 1944, the *Westheer*'s barely cohesive remnants could only slow the headlong Allied advance through France and Belgium. By 10 September, however, this rapid Allied progress had outstripped a logistic network that had never been expected to support such a rate of advance. Consequently, difficulties in getting petrol, munitions, and rations to the front slowed and then stalled Allied progress on a line that ran from the Belgian coast along the Meuse–Escaut canal to Maastricht, and then south from the German border at Aachen to the Swiss border near Belfort.

Reacting with customary German vigor, the *Westheer* seized this fleeting breathing space to rebuild its shattered cohesion. During 6–12 September, for instance, the improvised Battle Group Chill assembled stragglers and local garrison forces to establish a fragile new defensive crust along the Meuse–Escaut canal. To fill the gap that had emerged in the German front between Antwerp and Neerpelt in Belgium, the High Command dispatched from the Reich part-trained army recruits, naval personnel, and air force ground crew to form General Kurt Student's improvised First

Parachute Army. Surprisingly, these partly trained and poorly equipped scratch units offered determined resistance.

A bitter dispute over both strategy and command had erupted between Eisenhower and Montgomery – the 'broad front versus narrow front' controversy – in late August. On 1 September, as planned before D-Day, Eisenhower – while continuing as Supreme Allied Commander – replaced Montgomery as Land Forces Commander in a theater that now deployed two American army groups in addition to Monty's Anglo-Canadian one. Failing to understand that American public opinion would not tolerate a British commander controlling a theater numerically dominated by the Americans, an insubordinate Montgomery campaigned to be reinstated as Land Forces Commander, or at least to be conceded powers of operational control over neighboring American forces.

Although this dispute did reflect Montgomery's egotism, his main motive was to shape the campaign according to the British army's partisan wishes. He desired that his limited British forces – while avoiding heavy casualties – should contribute significantly to Germany's military defeat, within a wider coalition, to secure Britain a strong voice in the postwar political environment. His coordination of neighboring American forces would allow his 21st Army Group – and thus Britain – to achieve a higher military profile than its limited resources would otherwise permit.

This issue of command was interconnected with a similar dispute over strategy. The politically sensitive Eisenhower wished to advance into Germany on a broad front, a strategy that held together the alliance by avoiding favoritism toward any national contingent. The forceful Montgomery, however, argued that his command – reinforced by American forces – should spearhead a concentrated blow north of the Ardennes against the key German Ruhr industrial zone. Displaying profound ignorance of wider political issues, Montgomery based his strategy on sound tactical logic, his own personality needs, and

Britain's own interests within the wider multinational alliance. These two interlocked disputes rumbled on long into 1945, and soured Anglo-American relations during the rest of the campaign.

The V2

Germany's deployment of the V2 ballistic missile in the west during September 1944 forced Montgomery to launch his Market-Garden offensive to remove this threat. The Germans had begun developing this 'vengeance' weapon back in 1940, and in early September 1944 German units in southwestern Holland fired their first missiles against Britain. Hitler hoped that these strikes would break British morale and serve as retaliation for the devastation that Allied strategic bombing had inflicted on the Reich. By the end of 1944, the Germans had fired 491 V2 missiles against British cities in a futile attempt to break Britain's will to fight.

During late 1944, the Germans employed the V2 missile more effectively, by launching 924 rockets – plus 1,000 V1 flying bombs – against Antwerp's harbor to disrupt the unloading of Allied supplies. Some 302 V-weapons hit the docks, destroying 60 ships and inflicting 15,000 casualties, many of them civilian. This sensible employment forced Montgomery to deploy 490 anti-aircraft guns around Antwerp to counter the V1 threat, though against the supersonic V2 the Allies remained helpless.

By early 1945, however, the deteriorating strategic situation and supply shortages were hampering the Germans' use of the V2. Overall, the strategic impact of this supposed war-winning 'wonder weapon' was hugely disappointing, especially given the enormous resources devoted to its development – ones that Germany could have used more effectively, for example, to produce additional tanks, jet aircraft, submarines and flak guns.

Market-Garden

During early September 1944, Montgomery sought to rebuild Allied momentum, lost due to supply problems, before the *Westheer* recovered its cohesion. He hoped to quickly secure both the enemy's V2 launch sites and an intact bridge over the River Rhine, and to use the latter success to secure from Eisenhower priority in the allocation of supplies for a British-led 'narrow-thrust' against the Ruhr. Consequently, on 17 September, Montgomery initiated Operation Market-Garden, an atypically audacious combined ground and airborne offensive.

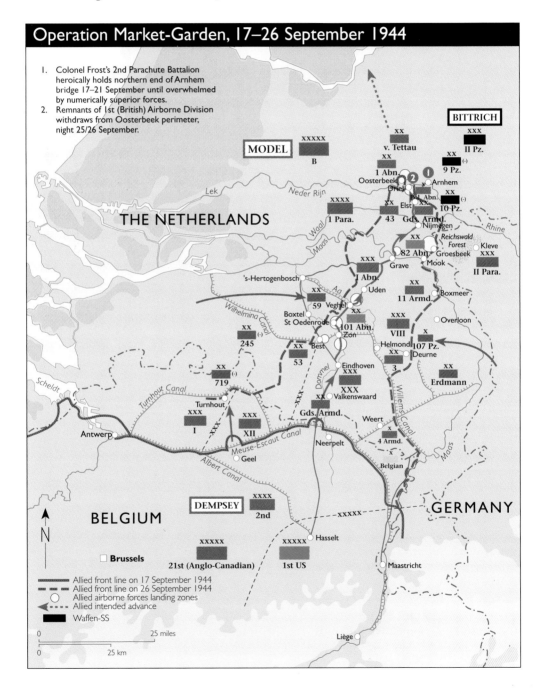

Operation Market-Garden, 17–26 September 1944

1. Colonel Frost's 2nd Parachute Battalion heroically holds northern end of Arnhem bridge 17–21 September until overwhelmed by numerically superior forces.
2. Remnants of 1st (British) Airborne Division withdraws from Oosterbeek perimeter, night 25/26 September.

MODEL
B

BITTRICH

v. Tettau
II Pz.
9 Pz.

1 Abn
Oosterbeek
Driel
Arnhem
Elst
1 Abn
10 Pz.

THE NETHERLANDS
Lek
Neder Rijn
Waal
Maas
1 Para.
43 Gds. Armd.
Nijmegen
Rhine

Reichswald
Forest
Kleve
82 Abn
Groesbeek
Mook
II Para.
Grave

's-Hertogenbosch
1 Abn
Uden
Boxmeer
11 Armd.

Veghel
59
Boxtel
St Oedenrode
101 Abn
Zon
Best
VIII
Overloon

245
53
Helmond
Deurne
107 Pz.

719
Eindhoven
3
Erdmann

Turnhout
Turnhout
I
XII
Valkenswaard
Gds. Armd.
Weert
4 Armd.

Antwerp
Meuse-Escaut Canal
Geel
Albert Canal
Neerpelt
Belgian

Scheldt
Turnhout Canal
Wilhelmina Canal
Dommel
Aa
Willems Canal
Maas

DEMPSEY
2nd

BELGIUM
N

GERMANY

Hasselt

Brussels

21st (Anglo-Canadian)
1st US
Maastricht

━━━━ Allied front line on 17 September 1944
━ ━ ━ Allied front line on 26 September 1944
◯ Allied airborne forces landing zones
◄---- Allied intended advance
▬ Waffen-SS

0 ─── 25 miles
0 ─── 25 km

Liège

Although Lieutenant-Colonel John Frost's encircled British paratroopers resisted heroically at Arnhem bridge for six days, overwhelmingly powerful German attacks finally crushed them before the armor of Horrocks' XXX Corps could advance north to reach them. (Imperial War Museum MH 2062)

One motive for this sudden audacity was Montgomery's recognition that early September 1944 offered a fleeting opportunity for the 21st Army Group to achieve his partisan British objectives in the theater. With the *Westheer* brought to its knees, one daring, final, all-out British effort could secure for Britain a high profile within the wider Allied defeat of Germany. If the war dragged on into 1945, however, increasing American numerical domination of the campaign would further erode Britain's declining strategic influence.

Market-Garden envisaged General Brian Horrocks' XXX British Corps thrusting swiftly north through Holland to link up with some 30,000 British and American airborne troops landed at key river bridges and crossroads along the way to facilitate the ground advance. At the northern drop-zone, the British 1st Airborne Division was to seize Arnhem bridge and hold it until Horrocks' armor arrived. The offensive soon encountered difficulties, however, as the desperate defensive improvisations enacted by Field Marshal Walther Model – the new commander of Army Group B – slowed Horrocks' ground advance. To make matters worse, local German counterattacks threatened Horrocks' flanks and even temporarily cut off the flow of supplies to his spearheads. Meanwhile, hastily mobilized garrison forces, stiffened by the remnants of the crack II SS Panzer Corps and reinforced with King Tiger tanks, steadily wore down the heroic resistance offered by Colonel Frost's paratroopers at Arnhem bridge, while simultaneously containing the rest of the 1st Airborne Division in the Oosterbeek perimeter to the west of Arnhem.

After five days' resistance, and without sign of relief by Horrocks' forces, the Germans overran Frost's forces at the bridge. Within a few days, further German pressure had also forced the remnants of the 1st Airborne Division to withdraw from Oosterbeek to the south bank of the lower Rhine. Although Market-Garden was an expensive failure – despite the jusification that Montgomery tried to offer for this operation – the capture of the Waal River bridge at Nijmegen proved strategically vital, for it was from here that Montgomery launched his February 1945 Veritable offensive toward the River Rhine. Moreover, the British commander drew the correct

The distinctive 'Dragon's Teeth' anti-tank obstacles became the characteristic image of Hitler's last fortified position in the west – the Siegfried Line or West Wall. Although the line held up the Allies in places, as well as inflicting heavy casualties upon them, it could not alter Germany's inevitable demise. By early 1945, the Allies had breached the entire Siegfried Line and were pushing the Germans back to the River Rhine. (Imperial War Museum EA 37737)

conclusion from Market-Garden – that even a weakened *Westheer* could still inflict a dangerous reverse on overly ambitious Allied offensive actions.

As Market-Garden was unfolding, Bradley's 12th US Army Group, deployed along the Sittard–Epinal sector, continued its modest eastward progress to initiate the first assaults on the West Wall – the German fortifications along the Reich's western border, known to the Allies as the Siegfried Line. Although supply shortages prevented much of Hodges' First US Army from attacking, the remainder did thrust east to capture Sittard and assault the Siegfried Line near Aachen. Further south, General Patton's Third US Army pushed east 50 miles (80km) to cross the Upper Moselle valley and close on the fortified town of Metz.

Between 13 September and 21 October 1944, it took repeated American assaults to capture Aachen against ferocious German resistance. Protected by the Siegfried Line, the defenders fought tenaciously for this

It took the Americans five weeks of heavy attritional fighting to overcome determined German resistance in the historic city of Aachen: but after its surrender columns of German prisoners streamed west into captivity. (AKG Berlin)

historic city that Hitler had decreed would be held to the last man and bullet. To boost German defensive resilience, military police roamed the rear areas summarily hanging alleged shirkers from trees to encourage the others. Spurred on by such threats and by the need to protect the Reich, the outnumbered defenders resisted vigorously and even launched local counterthrusts against American advances. The few German fighter-bombers available ran the gauntlet of Allied aerial supremacy to strafe the advancing enemy.

Despite these desperate efforts, American determination and numerical superiority eventually told, and on 21 October Aachen

fell. The Western Allies had penetrated the much-feared Siegfried Line and captured their first German city. Nevertheless, the considerable time and high casualties incurred in achieving this local success both concerned the Americans and led them to abandon launching individual narrow thrusts against the Siegfried Line.

Clearing the Scheldt

Between mid-September and early November 1944, the First Canadian Army – now temporarily led by Lieutenant-General Guy Simonds in place of the sick General Henry Crerar – struggled to capture the Scheldt estuary in southwestern Holland in the face of fierce enemy resistance. The Germans had managed to establish a solid front in Zeeland – along South Beveland, around Breskens, and on Walcheren island – by extricating the

During 4–6 September 1944, General von Zangen's Fifteenth Army used all manner of vessels – including fishing boats such as these – to mount an improvised evacuation north across the Scheldt estuary to the Breskens area. This successful withdrawal enabled the Germans to hold onto the Scheldt estuary, thus denying the Allies use of the vital port of Antwerp until early November. (Imperial War Museum)

Fifteenth Army from potential encirclement south of the Scheldt estuary. During 4–26 September, this army used improvised boats and rafts to evacuate 86,000 troops and 616 guns north across the estuary.

Most of the Western Allies' supplies were still being landed at the precarious facilities established on Normandy's beaches. This continuing logistic reliance on the original beachheads owed much to Hitler's orders that the German garrisons encircled at French and Belgian ports continue resisting to prevent the Allies from using these harbors. The Allies needed to clear the Scheldt estuary rapidly so that they could land supplies at the port of Antwerp, captured by Horrocks' forces on 4 September. Therefore, between 5 September and 1 October, to secure their rear areas as a prelude to clearing the Scheldt, the

Canadians captured the ports of Le Havre, Boulogne, and Calais.

Unfortunately for the Allies, it took Simonds' understrength army until early November to complete its clearance of the Scheldt. The slow Canadian advance owed much to shortages of resources because Montgomery – despite recognizing the importance of Antwerp's docks – had awarded logistical priority to Dempsey's command for Market-Garden. In addition, the difficult terrain, which assisted a skillful improvised German defense, slowed the Canadians. During 2–16 October, Simonds' forces advanced north to capture Bergen-op-Zoom and seal off the South Beveland peninsula. The German defense here cleverly utilized the terrain, by constructing bunkers in the steep rear slopes of the area's numerous raised dikes, and locating rocket-launchers immediately behind them. The Allies soon learned how hard it was to neutralize these positions.

Meanwhile, between 6 October and 3 November, in Operation Switchback, the Canadians also cleared German resistance in the Breskens pocket south of the Scheldt, after previous Allied attacks in mid-September had been repulsed. Here, the Germans deliberately flooded the Leopold Canal to channel the Canadians onto the area's few raised dike-roads, which the defenders had turned into pre-surveyed killing zones covered by artillery, anti-tank guns, and rocket-launchers. The Canadians had to combine effective artillery support with determination to secure the Breskens pocket in the face of such fierce resistance.

Between 16 October and 1 November 1944, Simonds' forces also advanced west along South Beveland and then prepared to launch an amphibious assault on the German fortress-island of Walcheren. This attack was made possible by an audacious plan – for, at Simonds' insistence, during 3–17 October, five Allied bombing strikes breached the sea-dike that surrounded Walcheren. Through these breaches the sea poured to flood the island's low-lying center,

The culminating point of the First Canadian's Army slogging battles to secure the Scheldt estuary was its assault on the heavily fortified German-held island of Walcheren. To overcome the powerful enemy defenses without incurring heavy casualties, Allied strategic bombers destroyed sections of the island's perimeter dikes, allowing the sea to pour in to flood the low-lying center of the island. (Imperial War Museum C4668)

eliminating 11 of the enemy's 28 artillery batteries. Then, during 1–7 November, in Operation Infatuate, two amphibious assaults backed by a land attack from South Beveland secured the flooded fortress.

Thus, by 7 November the First Canadian Army had successfully cleared the Germans from the Scheldt, but this slogging effort in difficult terrain had cost them 13,000 casualties and had taken no fewer than nine weeks. This sobering experience underscored the Allied high command's belief – derived from the attack on Aachen – that pushing deep into the Reich would prove a difficult task.

During mid-October, while the Scheldt battles raged along Montgomery's western flank, the German forces facing Dempsey's army strengthened their defenses and the British sought to gain better positions for future attacks. Then, out of the blue, during the night of 26/27 October 1944, two German mechanized divisions struck Dempsey's thinly held positions at Meijel, in the Peel marshes southeast of Eindhoven, in a local riposte. Although the Germans initially made progress, Dempsey moved up reinforcements, including massed artillery, and then, between 29 October and 7 November, drove the Germans back to their original positions.

Despite its inevitable failure, the German attack on Meijel demonstrated to the Western Allies that, notwithstanding the disasters that the *Westheer* had suffered in Normandy, it could still mount a surprise counterstrike against weakly defended sections of the Allied line. Equally, though, the riposte also showed the Germans how unlikely such counterattacks were to succeed, once Allied numerical superiority was brought to bear. The initial success of Hitler's surprise mid-December 1944 Ardennes counterattack showed that the Western Allies had not learned the lessons of Meijel; equally, though, the inevitable demise of the Ardennes offensive showed that the Germans had not learned them either.

On 2 November 1944, Eisenhower issued new strategic directives for the campaign. While Devers' and Bradley's commands were to push east to secure bridgeheads over the Rhine in subsidiary actions, Montgomery's army group was to launch the Allied main effort with a strike across the Rhine to surround the Ruhr. As a preliminary to such an offensive, between 14 November and 4 December, Dempsey's army – despite waterlogged conditions – thrust east to clear the west bank of the River Meuse around Venlo. Simultaneously, Simpson's Ninth US Army – now returned to Bradley after serving under Montgomery – and Hodges' First US Army resumed their push through the Siegfried Line toward Jülich and Monschau between 16 November and 15 December.

Although American forces reached the River Roer between Linnich and Düren, VII and V US Corps became locked in bitter fighting in the difficult terrain of the Hürtgen Forest. Unfortunately for Eisenhower, V Corps, in the face of bitter local counter-thrusts, failed to capture the key Schwammenauel Dam that dominated the entire Roer valley. Meanwhile, to protect Simpson's northern flank, the British XXX Corps struck east during 18–22 November to capture Geilenkirchen, before the assault stalled due to saturated ground. This left a German salient that jutted west of the River Roer around

Heinsberg, and Montgomery – who always desired a 'tidy' front line – wanted to clear it before striking further east. But just as British forces prepared to launch Operation Blackcock to secure this area, the German Ardennes counteroffensive erupted.

Further south, on 8 November, Patton's Third US Army resumed its battering assaults on the fortress-city of Metz, but ammunition shortages so hampered these attacks that the town did not fall until 22 November. Elsewhere, Patton's forces – despite continuing supply shortages – made more rapid progress, and by 6 December had secured bridgeheads over the River Roer and penetrated into the Siegfried Line at Saarlautern.

To Patton's south, the offensive initiated by Devers' 6th US Army Group on 13 November made even swifter progress. By 23 November, Lieutenant-General Alexander Patch's Seventh US Army had captured Strasbourg, and over the next 14 days it fanned out to reach the River Rhine on a 50-mile (80km) front. Further south, the seven divisions of General Jean de Lattre de Tassigny's First French Army thrust east through Belfort to reach the River Rhine just north of the German–Swiss border by 20 November. These hard-won advances, which cost Devers' command 28,000 casualties, left a German salient that jutted west beyond the Rhine at Colmar. Yet just as these various Western Allied operations, designed to reach the Rhine and secure bridgeheads over it, neared fruition, the *Westheer* rudely shattered the growing aura of Allied confidence with an unexpected counterblow.

The Battle of the Bulge

As early as 16 September 1944, Hitler had decided to stage a counteroffensive in the west that would seize the strategic initiative and alter decisively the course of the campaign. Hitler hoped to seize the key port of Antwerp by a surprise strike through the Ardennes, despite the unfavorable battlefield situation. Well aware that Allied aerial superiority hampered their mobility, however, the Germans decided to attack only during a predicted period of lengthy bad weather that would ground the powerful Allied tactical air forces.

During October and November the Germans prepared frantically for the attack – now planned to begin in mid-December – while covering their activities with sophisticated deceptions. These preparations included rebuilding the seven shattered panzer divisions slated to spearhead the operation, as well as augmenting German infantry strength with 12 *Volksgrenadier* (People's Infantry) Divisions, recently mobilized by throwing together ex-naval recruits, air force ground crew, and convalescents.

The Germans earmarked the three armies of Model's Army Group B for the offensive, with SS Colonel-General Josef Dietrich's Sixth Panzer Army and General Hasso von Manteuffel's Fifth Panzer Army spearheading the operation in the northern and central sectors, respectively; the weaker Seventh Army was merely to secure the southern flank. Excluding reserves, this force amounted to eight mechanized and 14 infantry divisions with 950 AFVs.

The intended German battle-zone was the hilly, stream-bisected, and forested terrain of the Ardennes, since this region's unsuitability for armored warfare had led the Americans to defend it with just four divisions. Consequently, the Ardennes offered the German attack the prospect of local success, despite its unsuitable terrain. Hitler, however, gambled on an ambitious strategic victory by seeking to capture Antwerp, 95 miles (153km) away, to cut off Montgomery's command from the American forces deployed to his south.

Despite the frenetic German preparations, the attack's objective was too ambitious relative to the modest force assembled and the vast resources on which the Western Allies could call. Indeed, many German commanders argued that their forces were too weak to seize Antwerp, but Hitler remained obdurate. The greatest flaw in the Germans' plan was that their logistical base remained utterly inadequate to support such a grandiose attack. The German forces remained short of fuel, and some commanders planned to utilize captured Allied fuel stocks to sustain the offensive. At Hitler's insistence – and contrary to his senior commanders' professional advice – the *Westheer* risked its last precious armored reserves on the triumph that might be achieved by a barely sustainable surprise blow against this Allied weak spot. Hitler failed to consider the consequences that would accrue if the gamble failed.

The Germans did everything in their power to improve their slim chances of success, with Dietrich, for example, employing his *Volksgrenadier* divisions to conduct the initial break-in, and saving the armor for the exploitation phase deep into the Allied rear. Furthermore, the Germans employed SS-Colonel Otto Skorzeny's commandos – some dressed as American Military Police – to infiltrate behind the Allied lines to spread confusion and help sustain offensive momentum. Although the Germans gained some advantages from this ruse, the operation failed to significantly hamper Allied reactions.

Before dawn on 16 December 1944, the *Volksgrenadiers* of Sixth Panzer Army broke into the Allied defenses before I SS Panzer Corps struck west toward the Meuse bridges south of Liège. SS Lieutenant-Colonel Joachim Peiper's armored battle group spearheaded the corps advance with a mixed force of Panzer IV and Panther tanks, plus 30 lumbering King Tigers that did their best to keep up. Peiper's mission was to exploit ruthlessly any success with a rapid drive toward Antwerp before the Allies could react. Given Peiper's mission and the terrain, his King Tigers played only a minor role in the offensive – contrary to popular perception, which regards this operation as being dominated by these leviathans.

During 18–19 December, Peiper's force stalled at Stoumont because the Americans had destroyed the few available river bridges in the area, and flanking forces had failed to

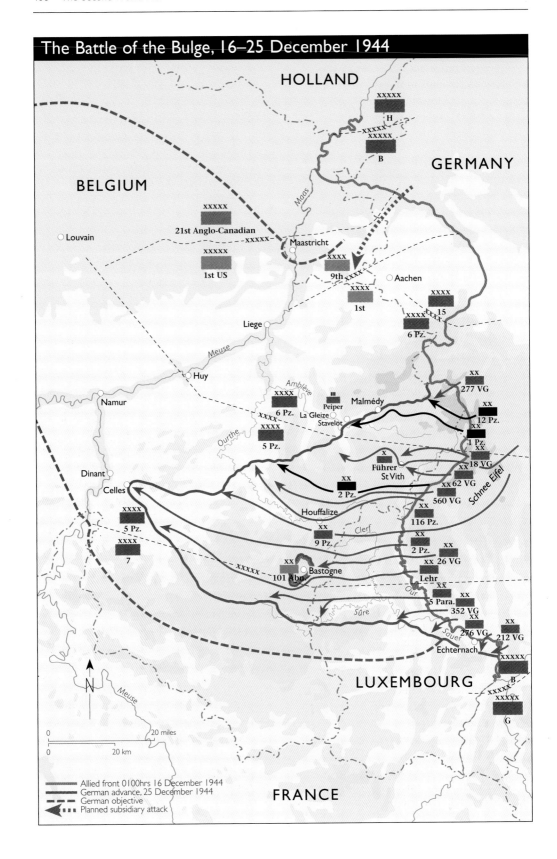

The Battle of the Bulge, 16–25 December 1944

HOLLAND

XXXXX
H

XXXXX
XXXXX
B

GERMANY

BELGIUM

○ Louvain

XXXXX
21st Anglo-Canadian —XXXXX—

Maas

Maastricht ○

XXXXX
1st US

XXXX
9th XXXX

○ Aachen

XXXX
1st

XXXX 15
XXXXX XXXX
6 Pz.

Liege ○

Meuse

Huy ○

Ambleve

XXXX
6 Pz.

XXXX
La Gleize○
Stavelot

Peiper
Malmédy ○

XX
277 VG

XX
12 Pz.
XX
1 Pz.
XX
18 VG

Namur ○

XXXX
5 Pz.

Ourthe

Dinant ○

Celles ○

XXXX
5 Pz.

XXXX
7

X
Führer
St Vith

XX
2 Pz.

Houffalize ○

XX
9 Pz.

Clerf

Schnee Eifel

XX 62 VG
560 VG

XX
116 Pz.

XX
2 Pz.

XX 26 VG
Lehr

XXXXX — XXXXX
101 Abn.

XX
Bastogne ○

Our

Sûre

XX
5 Para.
XX
352 VG
XX
276 VG
XX
212 VG

Sauer

Echternach ○

XXXXX
B

XXXXX
XXXXX
G

N

Meuse

0   20 miles
0   20 km

LUXEMBOURG

FRANCE

——— Allied front 0100hrs 16 December 1944
——— German advance, 25 December 1944
– – – German objective
◀▪▪▪ Planned subsidiary attack

protect Peiper's supply lines. During this advance, Peiper's SS fanatics had murdered 77 American prisoners at Malmédy, plus 120 Belgian civilians in numerous separate incidents. By 22 December, Allied counterstrikes – supported by fighter-bombers after the mist that had kept them grounded over the previous six days lifted – had surrounded Peiper's forces at La Gleize.

During the night of 23–24 December, Peiper's doomed unit – now out of fuel and munitions – destroyed its vehicles, and the remaining 800 unwounded soldiers exfiltrated on foot back to the German lines. The destruction of Peiper's group forced Dietrich on 22 December to commit II SS Panzer Corps to rescue the collapsing northern thrust, but by 26 December this too had stalled near Manhay. Overall, the thrust undertaken by Dietrich's army had proved a costly failure.

On 16 December, to Dietrich's south, the Fifth Panzer Army also struck the unsuspecting Allied front. Although fierce American resistance at St Vith slowed von Manteuffel's infantry thrusts during 16–17 December, further south his two spearhead panzer corps advanced 20 miles (32km) toward Houffalize and Bastogne. During 18–22 December, these corps surrounded the American 101st Airborne Division at Bastogne and pushed further west to within just 4 miles (6.4km) of the vital Meuse bridges. When the Germans invited the commander of the surrounded Bastogne garrison to surrender, he tersely replied: 'Nuts!' After this rebuff the initiative slowly slipped out of the Germans' grasp thanks to fierce American resistance, rapid commitment of substantial Allied reserves, and severe German logistic shortages.

The Americans commenced their counterattacks on 23 December, driving northeast to relieve Bastogne on 26 December, and forcing back the German spearheads near the Meuse. Even though Field Marshal von Rundstedt, Commander-in-Chief West, now concluded that the operation had failed, the Führer nevertheless insisted that one more effort be made to

penetrate the Allied defenses. Consequently, on New Year's Day 1945, von Manteuffel's army initiated new attacks near Bastogne.

To help this last-gasp attempt to snatch success from the jaws of defeat, the *Westheer* initiated a diversionary attack, Operation Northwind, in Alsace-Lorraine on New Year's Eve 1944. The Germans intended that a thrust north from the Colmar pocket – the German-held salient that jutted west over the Rhine into France – would link up at Strasbourg with a six-division attack south from the Saar. Although Hitler hoped that the attack would divert enemy reinforcements away from the Ardennes, in reality Northwind incurred heavy losses, yet only secured modest success and sucked few forces away from 'the Bulge.'

Consequently, the renewed German Ardennes attack soon stalled in the face of increasing Allied strength. Finally, on 3 January 1945, Allied forces struck the northern and southern flanks of the German salient to squeeze it into extinction. Over the next 13 days, instead of immediately retreating, the *Westheer* – at Hitler's insistence – conducted a costly fighting withdrawal back to its original position.

Just one self-inflicted injury marred the strategic triumph secured by the Allies in the Ardennes. As the German advance hampered Bradley's control of the First and Ninth US Armies in his northern sector, Eisenhower acquiesced to Monty's demands and placed these forces under his control. Although the commitment of the British XXX Corps had helped the Allied victory, the Ardennes was essentially an American triumph. Unfortunately, on 7 January 1945, in a press conference Montgomery claimed credit for this victory, thus souring Anglo-American relations for the rest of the campaign.

During the four-week Battle of the Bulge, Model's command lost 120,000 troops and 600 precious AFVs. By mid-January 1945, therefore, only weak German forces now stood between the Allies and a successful advance across the Rhine into the Reich. With hindsight, the Ardennes counterstrike represented one of Hitler's gravest strategic errors. It was a futile, costly, and strategically disastrous gamble that tossed away Germany's last armored reserves. Moreover, the Germans managed to assemble sufficient forces for the counterstrike only by starving the Eastern Front of much-needed reinforcements. Consequently, when the Soviets resumed their offensives in mid-January 1945, they easily smashed through the German front in Poland. By late January, therefore, these German defeats on both the Eastern and Western Fronts ensured that it would only be a matter of months before the Nazi Reich succumbed.

The Western Allies, having by 15 January 1945 restored the mid-December 1944 front line, exploited this success with further offensives. The next day, Dempsey's XII Corps commenced its Blackcock offensive to clear the enemy's salient west of the River Roer around Heinsberg. Hampered both by poor weather, which grounded Allied tactical air power, and by stiff German resistance, XII Corps struggled forward until by 26 January the Allies held a continuous line along the Roer from Roermond down to Schmidt. Then, on 20 January, the First French Army attacked the Colmar salient south of Strasbourg.

The defenders, General Rasp's Nineteenth Army, formed part of the recently raised Army Group Upper Rhine, which was led not by a professional officer but by the Reichsführer-SS, Heinrich Himmler. Unsurprisingly, given Himmler's military inexperience and the losses incurred in Northwind, the French made steady progress, but Hitler equally predictably forbade Rasp from withdrawing. Under pressure, however, Hitler freed Rasp from his chief handicap – he dissolved Himmler's command, subordinated its forces to the more professional control of Army Group G, and brought in the experienced Paul Hausser to lead this command.

Rasp, however, soon realized that these measures could not prevent his forces from being destroyed if they obeyed Hitler's prohibition on retreat. To save his remaining troops, Rasp disobeyed his Führer and withdrew them back across the Rhine, thus saving precious forces with which to defend this last major obstacle before the heart of the Reich. By 9 February, the First French Army held the entire left bank of the upper Rhine.

By early February 1945, the Western Allies were ready to initiate further offensives to secure the remainder of the Rhine's western bank. Hitler, however, now convinced himself that the Allies had temporarily exhausted their offensive power, and so transferred Dietrich's Sixth Panzer Army from the west to the Eastern Front. Yet the Führer did not send this force to Poland, where it was sorely needed to stop the rapidly advancing Soviets, but instead to Hungary for a futile offensive to relieve encircled Budapest.

By now, the Western Allies outnumbered von Rundstedt's three army groups by four to one in manpower and eight to one in armor. In the north, General Johannes Blaskowitz's Army Group H held the front facing Monty's command from Rotterdam through to Roermond, including the vital Reichswald Forest manned by Lieutenant-General Alfred Schlemm's First Parachute Army. Model's Army Group B faced Bradley's forces in the Rhineland from Roermond south to Trier. Finally, Hausser's Army Group G held the front from the Saarland down to the Swiss border against Devers' divisions.

The *Westheer* hoped first to slow the Allied advance through the Siegfried Line, and then gradually retreat back to the Rhine, and there use this obstacle to halt permanently the Allied advance. Hitler, though, again forbade any retreat and insisted that the outnumbered *Westheer* hold the Allies at the Siegfried Line. To retreat back to the Rhine, Hitler argued, would simply transfer the impending catastrophe from one geographical location to another.

On 8 February 1945, Montgomery's forces commenced Operation Veritable, the great offensive for which they had been preparing when the German Ardennes counterattack broke. The reinforced British XXX Corps – now part of Crerar's First Canadian Army –

struck Schlemm's First Parachute Army in its Siegfried Line defenses between Nijmegen and Mook. The offensive sought to drive the Germans back across the Rhine around Wesel to permit a subsequent thrust deep into the Reich. After an intense 1,050-gun artillery bombardment, three British and two Canadian infantry divisions broke into the German defenses. Despite significant Allied numerical superiority, the poor terrain of the Reichswald Forest in the south and the deliberate German flooding of the low-lying Rhine flood-plain in the north, slowed the Canadian advance east.

The Germans also released water from the Schwammenauel Dam to flood the Roer valley on 9 February. This prevented Simpson's Ninth US Army – again temporarily under Monty's command – from initiating its own Grenade offensive toward the Rhine on 10 February. Montgomery intended that Veritable and Grenade would form the northern and southern pincers of a simultaneous double encirclement designed to link up at Wesel on the Rhine. Despite knowing that the flooding had delayed Grenade for 10 days, Montgomery nevertheless continued Veritable after 10 February as planned, because by sucking German reserves to the British thrust, he reasoned, the Ninth US Army would advance more rapidly to Wesel.

Despite penetrating the Siegfried Line, Crerar's forces – now reinforced by II Canadian Corps – made only slow progress. The combination of fierce enemy resistance by newly arrived reserves and the Germans' advantage of defending from their Hochwald Layback defenses, together with poor weather and saturated terrain, all slowed the Allied advance. Nevertheless, Montgomery relentlessly kept the offensive driving east, grinding down the enemy until by 28 February they had been forced back to a small bridgehead west of the Rhine at Wesel. While officially still forbidding any withdrawals, Hitler now realized that the *Westheer* could not hold the Allies west of the Rhine. Consequently, he ordered that any commander who demolished a Rhine

bridge too early – thus preventing retreating German forces from crossing – or who allowed a bridge to fall into enemy hands would be shot. This contradictory order would cause the Germans untold problems on 7 March at Remagen.

Finally, on 23 February, the Americans commenced Grenade across the now subsiding River Roer. As Montgomery expected, these forces made rapid progress toward Wesel as Veritable had already sucked German reserves north, and by 3 March the Americans and British had linked up at Geldern. During 8–10 March, Schlemm – with the connivance of von Blaskowitz – disobeyed Hitler by withdrawing his remaining forces across the Rhine at Wesel before destroying the remaining two bridges. Veritable had cost the 21st Army Group 23,000 casualties in four weeks of bitter, attritional, fighting against the resolute defense that Schlemm had orchestrated. It was only Hitler's grudging acceptance of this fact that allowed Schlemm to avoid execution for his disobedience.

Crossing the Rhine

To the south of Grenade, Hodges' First US Army – part of Bradley's command – commenced an attack across the subsiding River Roer on 23 February 1945 that sought to reach the Rhine between Düsseldorf and Cologne. Meanwhile, Patton's Third US Army thrust toward Trier and the River Kyll, and by 1 March had secured both objectives. After Eisenhower's 3 March strategic directive, Bradley's command expanded these attacks into a drive toward the Rhine between Düsseldorf and Koblenz. By 9 March, the First US Army had reached these objectives and linked up with Simpson's forces near Düsseldorf.

Despite the rapidity of Hodges' advance toward the Rhine, the Germans nevertheless managed to demolish all of the Rhine bridges in this sector – except the Ludendorff railway bridge at Remagen, between Cologne and Koblenz. In a fatal blow to Hitler's

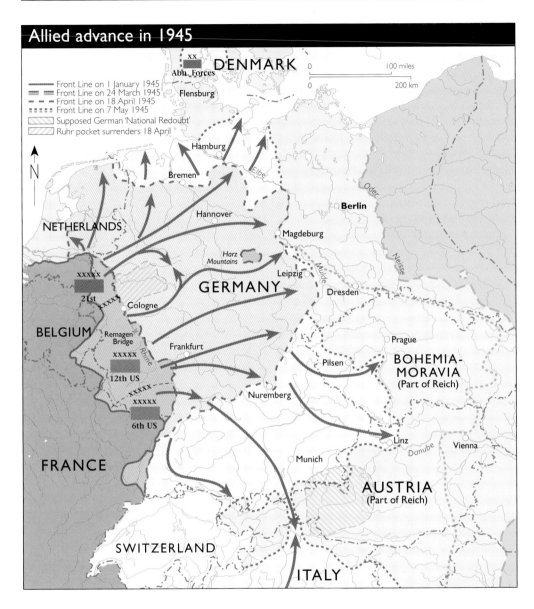

Allied advance in 1945

DENMARK

XX
Abn. Forces

Flensburg

——— Front Line on 1 January 1945
━━ ━━ Front Line on 24 March 1945
– – – Front Line on 18 April 1945
▪▪▪▪▪ Front Line on 7 May 1945
◪◪◪ Supposed German 'National Redoubt'
◪◪ Ruhr pocket surrenders 18 April

N

Hamburg

Bremen

Elbe

Oder

NETHERLANDS

Hannover

Berlin

Magdeburg

Neisse

Harz
Mountains

Leipzig

GERMANY

Dresden

Mulde

XXXXX

21st

Cologne

BELGIUM

Remagen
Bridge

Rhine

Frankfurt

Prague

XXXXX

Pilsen

BOHEMIA-
MORAVIA
(Part of Reich)

12th US

XXXXX

XXXXX

Nuremberg

6th US

Linz

Danube

Vienna

FRANCE

Munich

AUSTRIA
(Part of Reich)

SWITZERLAND

ITALY

0   100 miles
0   200 km

hopes, on 7 March, Hodges' forces captured the badly damaged – but still intact – Remagen bridge. Recognizing the opportunity that this good fortune offered, Hodges daringly pushed reinforcements across the river to enlarge the bridgehead before the Germans could throw in whatever reserves they had available.

At Remagen on 6 March, with the Americans rapidly approaching the Ludendorff bridge, the garrison commander understandably was anxious. If the enemy captured the bridge, he faced execution; if he blew up the bridge too soon, trapping German forces on the west bank, he faced execution. The commander decided not to blow up the structure until the next morning to allow friendly forces to cross, but unexpectedly American armor – spearheaded by the powerful new Pershing tank – appeared and stormed the bridge. The Germans triggered their demolition charges, which failed to explode, and then ignited the back-up charges, which exploded but only damaged the bridge instead of destroying it. Within hours, substantial

American forces had crossed the river and established a bridgehead on the eastern bank. The elusive intact Rhine bridge had fallen into Patton's hands, and the *Westheer*'s hopes of stopping the Western Allies at the Rhine had been shattered.

Hitler reacted furiously to the loss of the Remagen bridge: he ordered that seven German officers be executed, and sacked von Rundstedt as Commander-in-Chief West. In his place, the Führer appointed Field Marshal Albert Kesselring, transferred from the Italian front. On his arrival, Kesselring mocked the German propaganda that promised the imminent arrival of new war-winning weapons, by stating that he was the long-awaited V3! Predictably, Kesselring's arrival exerted as minimal an impact on the Allied advance as had the two previous German V-weapons. Subsequently, during 8–16 March, as the Americans gradually expanded the Remagen bridgehead, the Germans in vain attempted to destroy the bridge through aerial, V2 rocket, and artillery strikes. The severely damaged bridge eventually collapsed on 17 March, but by then it was too late: Hodges' forces had already constructed several pontoon bridges alongside the now fallen structure.

On 8 March 1945, Eisenhower's new strategic directive confirmed that Montgomery's command would attack across the Rhine near Wesel in Operation Plunder, and issued new orders for both the 12th and 6th US Amy Groups. On that day the XII Corps of Patton's Third US Army had linked up with Hodges' forces in the Remagen–Koblenz area to encircle 50,000 German soldiers north of the Eifel ridge. Eisenhower now instructed Patton's army to drive southeast across the River Moselle into the Saar industrial region toward Mannheim. Here they were to link up with the northeasterly advance of Patch's Seventh US Army, part of Devers' 6th Army Group, through the Siegfried Line from Saarbrücken. The final objective of Patton and Patch's commands was to secure a continuous front along the Rhine from Koblenz to Karlsruhe.

On 9 March, Patton's XII US Corps swung south and, having crossed the Moselle, struck southeast through the Hunsrück mountains toward Bingen on the confluence of the Nahe and Rhine rivers. Then on 13 March, Walker's XX Corps thrust east from Trier through the Saar–Palatinate to link up with XII Corps on the Nahe near Bad Kreuzbach and encircle elements of the German Seventh Army. Last, on 15 March, Patch's Seventh US Army struck northeast from Saarbrücken, aiming to link up with Patton's two corps between Mainz and Mannheim, and to encircle General Förtsch's First Army. As these pincers closed, SS Colonel-General Paul Hausser – recognizing the calamity about to engulf his Army Group G – in vain begged Hitler for permission to withdraw east of the Rhine. By 24 March, Patton and Patch's forces had linked up near Mannheim and successfully surrounded most of Förtsch's disintegrating army. Together these operations inflicted 113,000 casualties on the enemy, including 90,000 prisoners, for the cost of 18,000 American losses.

Then, on 22 March, Patton's forces launched a surprise amphibious assault across the Rhine at Oppenheim, between Mainz and Mannheim, and within 72 hours had established a firm salient east of the river. The Americans now possessed two toeholds across the Rhine, whereas in the north along the supposed Allied main axis, the cautious Montgomery was still readying himself for a massive strike across the river at Wesel. Overall, these hard-fought offensives to clear the west bank of the Rhine, conducted by five Allied armies between 10 February and 23 March 1945, had secured 280,000 German prisoners, for the cost of 96,000 Allied casualties.

Predictably, the Führer reacted to these disasters with increasingly desperate measures to slow the enemy advance. On 19 March, Hitler – in a drastic scorched earth policy – ordered the destruction of anything that the Allies might find of value. By failing to hold back the enemy, Hitler reasoned, the German people had demonstrated their racial weaknesses, and thus had forfeited the right to save their homeland from the cataclysm Hitler now intended to unleash on Germany in a bid to stem the Allied advance. Fortunately for Germany, in the chaos that now pervaded the collapsing Reich, the Minister of War Production, Albert Speer, sabotaged Hitler's intent to plunge the country into an orgy of self-inflicted destruction.

Operation Plunder

During March 1945, as the Americans cleared the Saar–Palatinate and established two bridgeheads east of the Rhine, Montgomery continued building up overwhelming resources for his planned offensive to cross the Rhine around Wesel. The once formidable German First Parachute Army manned this key sector, but its 13 divisions now mustered just 45 tanks and 69,000 weary troops. During the night of 23–24 March, the 21st Army Group – still augmented by Ninth US Army – commenced its attack with massive artillery and aerial strikes. This was followed by an amphibious assault across the Rhine along a 20-mile (32km) front, code-named Plunder, while simultaneously in Varsity two airborne divisions landed behind the German front to shatter its cohesion. The Germans, however, had anticipated an airborne assault and had redeployed many flak guns from the Ruhr, and these downed 105 Allied aircraft.

Despite this, the British had learned from the mistakes made during Market-Garden, and the proximity of the landing zones to the main front ensured that the ground advance linked up with the airborne forces during 24 March. Despite fierce resistance by German paratroopers that delayed XXX British Corps, by dusk on 24 March the Allied bridgehead was already 5 miles (8km) deep. Yet it took another four days' consolidation of the bridgehead before the cautious Monty declared that the struggle for the Rhine had been successful.

By this time, in addition to the Remagen and Oppenheim bridgeheads, Bradley's and

Devers' forces had also secured two further crossings of the Rhine. Now, with German units virtually immobilized by lack of fuel and by Allied air power, as well as hampered by chronic equipment shortages, the battered *Westheer* began to disintegrate. To resist the Western Allies' 74 well-equipped divisions, the Germans could now field – even including its Home Guard militia – the equivalent of just 27 full-strength divisions.

After late March, the Western Allies pushed rapidly east beyond the Rhine into the heart of Germany to link up with the westward Soviet advance and thus defeat Hitler's Reich. Prior to 28 March, Eisenhower's strategic intent had been to advance toward Berlin. Yet now, in the final twist of the protracted dispute between him and Montgomery, he shifted the point of main effort to Bradley's planned thrust toward the River Elbe. In so doing, Eisenhower denied Montgomery the glorious, British-dominated, victory the latter so fervently desired.

Then, on 28 March, Dempsey's Second (British) Army broke out from its Rhine bridgehead at Wesel with the intent to clear northern Germany and link up with the Soviets on the Baltic coast near Wismar. Against weak resistance, three British corps made rapid progress and by 8 April had advanced 118 miles (189km) to cross the River Weser southeast of Bremen. Simultaneously, to protect the British left flank, II Canadian Corps struck north from Emmerich and advanced 69 miles (111km) to seize Coevorden in Holland. To slow the British drive east, a desperate Hitler re-appointed his former favorite – the now disgraced General Student – to command the First Parachute Army. Yet by now the strategic situation had so deteriorated that Hitler's arch sycophant – the Armed Forces Chief of Staff Colonel-General Alfred Jodl – could tell his Führer that even the employment of a dozen military geniuses like Student would not prevent Germany's inevitable demise.

During late March 1945, to Monty's south, Bradley commenced attacks to secure

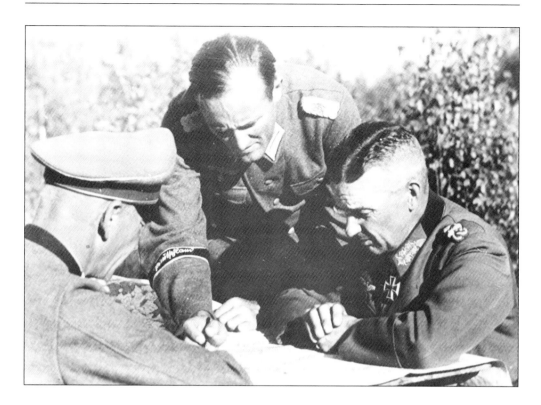

Field Marshal Walther Model, seen here early in
the war, was renowned for his iron will. But even
this could not save his command from
encirclement in the Ruhr pocket during
March–April 1945. To avoid being only the second
German or Prussian field marshal in history to be
captured alive – after Paulus had met this
ignominious fate at Stalingrad – Model committed
suicide in mid-April after first disbanding his
doomed command. (AKG Berlin)

the German Ruhr industrial zone. The Ninth
US Army – now returned to Bradley's control
– advanced from the Wesel bridgehead along
the Ruhr's northern boundary, while the First
US Army thrust south of the Ruhr from the
Remagen bridgehead. Despite appalling odds,
Army Group B commander Model remained
determined to fulfil Hitler's orders to stand
firm in the Ruhr. This region still delivered
two-thirds of Germany's total industrial
production, despite the vast damage done
by Allied strategic bombing and Germany's
belated attempts to decentralize its
industrial base.

As the two American armies facing him
pushed east, Model guessed that his cautious
enemy would swing inwards to clear the
Ruhr before driving deeper into the Reich.
Consequently, he organized his depleted
regular ground forces – now reinforced with
Home Guard units and Luftwaffe flak troops
– to fight a protracted urban battle for the
Ruhr that would inflict the horrific German
experience of Stalingrad onto the Americans.
The latter recognized the likely heavy costs
involved in such an attritional struggle in
the ruins of the Ruhr's cities, and instead
sought to encircle the region in a deep
pocket. On 29 March, however, Model
discerned Bradley's intent, and in
desperation flung whatever meager reserves
he possessed in a local riposte at Paderborn.
Despite fanatical resistance, these scratch
forces failed to stop the First and Ninth US
Armies linking up at Lippstadt on 1 April
1945 to encircle 350,000 troops in the Ruhr
– a larger force than that trapped at
Stalingrad.

Hitler forbade Model from breaking out
and promised a miracle relief operation
mounted by the Eleventh and Twelfth
Armies, then being raised from Germany's

last part-trained recruits as, in sheer desperation, the Germans closed their remaining training schools and flung these troops into the fray. Model, however, remained unimpressed by such Hitlerian fantasies, and so on April 15 – to avoid being the second German field marshal in history to be captured alive (after Paulus at Stalingrad) – Model dissolved his army group and committed suicide. By 18 April, when German resistance in the Ruhr ended, 316,000 troops had entered captivity. The Western Allies had torn a hole right through the center of the Western Front, while to north and south, the *Westheer* was now rapidly disintegrating.

Hitler reacted to the catastrophic setbacks recently suffered on all fronts, as well as to growing signs of defeatism, by increasing the already draconian discipline under which German soldiers toiled. On 2 April, for example, Hitler ordered the summary execution of any soldier who displayed defeatism by advocating surrender or retreat. Even Commander-in-Chief West Kesselring now reminded his soldiers that it was a German soldier's duty to die well. Although these strictures did foster continuing resistance, the main motivation behind such efforts remained the intense professionalism displayed by many German troops – qualities that kept front-line units cohesive despite appalling battlefield losses. Yet now Hitler again displayed his contempt for the army's professional officer corps by placing control of the Home Guard's defense of German cities in the hands of Nazi Party officials, despite the latter's lack of military experience.

In desperation, Hitler committed Germany to a popular 'total war' against the Allies by exhorting the entire population to wage a 'Werewolf' guerrilla struggle in enemy-occupied German territory. Despite extensive propaganda, in reality only a few hundred well-trained Nazi fanatics undertook Werewolf operations, which not surprisingly achieved little. Nazi propaganda also sought to boost German defensive resilience by publicizing the establishment

of a strong defensive position – termed the 'National Redoubt' by the Allies – in the mountains of southeastern Bavaria and western Austria. In reality, this fortified region existed only on paper and when on 22 April Hitler decided to remain in Berlin to face his fate, any inclination to defend this mythical fortress ebbed away. Thankfully for the Allies, there would be no protracted fanatical Nazi last-stand in the mountains, although Allied concern over such a prospect led them to attempt a swift advance through southwestern Germany.

Meanwhile, Patton's Third US Army had broken out of its Rhine bridgeheads during 24–26 March and, in the face of disorganized resistance, had fanned out in rapid thrusts to the northeast, east, and southeast. By 4 May, Patton's forces had pushed 172 miles (275km) across central Germany to capture Chemnitz and Bayreuth. Further south, Patch's Seventh US Army crossed the Rhine at Mannheim and advanced southeast to seize Stuttgart, then Ulm on the River Danube, and finally Nuremberg on 19 April. Simultaneously, the First French Army thrust across the Rhine at Strasbourg and advanced southeast toward Lake Constance. The objective of Patch's and de Lattre's armies was to capture the 'National Redoubt' swiftly before the enemy could consolidate its strength in this region.

Between 9 April and 2 May, the Second (British) Army continued its rapid advance through northern Germany. On 15 April, it liberated the Belsen concentration camp and discovered – as the Americans would do later at Dachau – the heinous crimes that Hitler's regime had committed. Meanwhile, by 19 April, the First Canadian Army had liberated all of northeastern Holland and cut off the remaining German forces in northwestern Holland. The German forces caught in this strategically worthless pocket continued to resist until VE-Day, but largely because the Allies only masked the region and instead focused on more important operations in Germany. Subsequently, during 19–27 April, Dempsey's three corps reached the River Elbe and then – with reinforcements

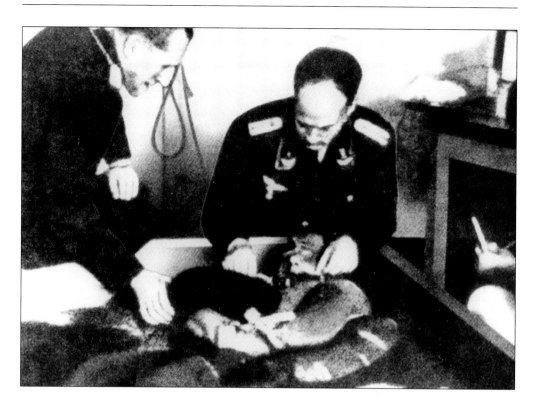

from XVIII US Airborne Corps – dashed northeast against light opposition to reach the Baltic Sea at Wismar on 2 May, thus securing Denmark's southern borders just hours before the Red Army arrived.

In the Allied center during 2–19 April, Bradley's divisions struck east, rapidly overrunning central Germany and reaching the Elbe near Magdeburg. Here Eisenhower ordered the Ninth US Army to stop and to wait for the westward Soviet advance to prevent any local confrontations with the Red Army. During the next week, Hodges' First US Army overcame the hedgehog defense mounted by the still-forming German Eleventh Army in the Harz mountains to reach its designated halt-line on the Rivers Elbe and Mulde along a 160-mile (256km) front. Although Hodges' army remained static on the Elbe–Mulde Line during late April, on the 25th an American patrol did push further east to link up with the Red Army at Strehla near Torgau. Between them the Allies had split the Reich in two, an eventuality for which the Germans had prepared by creating a

As the Western Allies advanced through the heart of the Reich, the full horrors committed by Hitler's regime became apparent. At Dachau inmates were used as human guinea pigs in experiments conducted by the Nazis. Here, a man is subjected to freezing experiments. (Topham Picturepoint)

northern and southern Armed Forces High Command headquarters.

In Bradley's southern sector, on 29 April Patton's reinforced Third US Army commenced the last major American offensive of the war, striking rapidly east and southeast to seize Pilsen in Czechoslovakia and Linz in Austria, respectively. By now the news of Hitler's death had filtered through to German soldiers, and this led many to surrender after only token resistance. Consequently, during 4 May, Patton's forces secured Linz; but just as he prepared to unleash his armor for a dash to Prague, Eisenhower stopped him to avoid any clash with the Soviets.

Meanwhile, further south, Patch's Seventh US Army thrust through the supposed Nazi 'National Redoubt' against only light

resistance during late April. Then, on 1 May, Patch's forces secured the Alpine passes of the Austrian Tyrol, before dashing through the Brenner Pass on 4 May to link up with the Fifth US Army in northern Italy. By then, German resistance had virtually collapsed everywhere except the Eastern Front, and several German commanders in the west – as well as Dönitz's new Nazi regime – had begun to discuss surrender terms with the Allies. The Northwest Europe campaign was now set to enter its final hours.

The final collapse of the Third Reich became imminent once American and Soviet forces linked up with each other at Strehla near Torgau in central Germany on 25 April 1945, thus cutting what remained of the German state in half. The desperate Germans had anticipated such a development, however, and had even created two military authorities – one for the north and one for the south – for the moment when the Allies bisected Germany. (AKG Berlin)

Donald Burgett

Sprinting low to the ground, his feet surrounded by bursts of machine-gun fire, Donald Burgett glanced over his shoulder to glimpse a German Tiger tank lurching toward him. It was 19 December 1944, in a field on the northeastern outskirts of Noville, near Bastogne in the Belgian Ardennes. Intense enemy fire had just set alight the haystack in which Burgett had sought cover, and now the raging flames forced him to dash across the open, snow-covered fields back toward the shelter of nearby houses – a dash that would expose him to deadly enemy fire.

Luckily making it unscathed to a nearby house, Burgett rushed into a room to find two of his squad buddies already hiding there. Looking back through the glassless window frame, however, the paratroopers saw the Tiger approaching the house, and so dashed out of the back door. Within seconds the tank had advanced so that its gun barrel actually pointed through what used to be the front window of the house: then it fired its lethal 88mm cannon. Burgett scarcely avoided the tons of ruined brick that came crashing down on his nearby hiding place as the building's back wall disintegrated. He had survived this close shave, he mused, but for how long could he avoid that lethal enemy bullet 'that had his name marked on it'?

By now a campaign veteran – he had dropped from the skies on D-Day – Burgett realized that the battle at Noville had been his most terrifying combat experience to date. But luckily for historians, Burgett not only survived the campaign, but also wrote down his recollections not long after VE-Day and then published them in a poignant memoir, *Seven Roads to Hell*, during the 1990s.

During the campaign, Burgett served as a private in the 2nd Platoon, A Company, 506th Parachute Infantry Regiment, part of the elite 101st US Airborne Division – the 'Screaming Eagles.' Born in Detroit, Michigan, in April 1926, he volunteered for the paratroopers in April 1943, on the day of his eighteenth birthday, having been previously turned down for being too young. On the night of 5/6 June 1944, he dropped with the rest of the 'Screaming Eagles' behind German lines in the Cotentin peninsula to aid the imminent American D-Day landings on 'Utah' beach. On 13 June he was wounded twice in bitter fighting near Carentan, first by a grenade detonation that left him temporarily deaf, and then by a shell fragment that tore open his left side. After three weeks in hospital, he returned to his division, which soon came out of the front line for much-needed replenishment.

Burgett then dropped with his division around Zon in Holland on 17 September 1944, as part of Montgomery's ambitious Market-Garden offensive. After fighting its way north through Nijmegen, Burgett's company held the front near Arnhem for nine weeks of mostly static actions amid sodden low-lying terrain. Eventually, on 28 November, after 72 days' continuous action, the 'Screaming Eagles' redeployed to northern France for rest and recuperation.

On 17 December 1944, as news filtered through about the success achieved by the surprise German Ardennes counteroffensive, Burgett's division rushed north to help defend the vital road junction at Bastogne. During 19–20 December, Burgett's company resolutely defended Noville against the determined attacks launched by the 2nd Panzer Division. The next day, the Germans outflanked the 506th Regiment, forcing the Americans to conduct a costly withdrawal south through the village of Foy. Over the next week, however, in a series of bitter engagements, Burgett's company

The town of Bastogne represented the key communications node that
General Hasso von Manteuffel's Fifth Panzer Army had to capture so that
it could open up the southern axis of advance in the Battle of the Bulge.
The determined resistance offered by the 101st US Airborne Division
around Bastogne – as demonstrated at Noville during 19–20 December –
ensured that the encircled town never fell into German hands. (US Army)

At Marvie, a village located just to the east of Bastogne, fierce resistance by American paratroopers helped prevent German armor from dashing into Bastogne before a defensive perimeter could be consolidated. When the Germans invited the surrounded American garrison to surrender, the reply of their commander was terse: 'Nuts!' (US Army)

helped drive the Germans back to the start lines they had held prior to the commencement of their counterstrike.

Burgett's recollections vividly captured the brutal realities of combat in the Northwest Europe campaign – the diseases that afflicted soldiers, the terrible wounds suffered in battle, the awful food on which they had to subsist, and the intense emotions generated by these experiences. For example, he recalled with horror the diseases that lengthy exposure to Holland's wet conditions caused among the front-line troops. Burgett himself suffered from trench mouth, an ailment that made his gums ooze with pus and left his teeth so loose that he could easily move them with his tongue. Although penicillin eventually cured him, he then succumbed to trench foot after his boots disintegrated due to the length of his continuous front-line service in sodden terrain.

Scabies was another problem from which Burgett's company suffered in Holland, an unpleasant condition where microscopic parasites develop under the skin, causing insatiable itching. Such a disease flourished in the unhygienic conditions in which the paratroopers often served. Indeed, while in the front line near Arnhem, Burgett's comrades only occasionally managed to take what they termed a 'Whore's Bath' – a quick scrub of the head, armpits and crotch with icy cold water collected in their helmets. It was only when the division went on leave in France during late October 1944 that Burgett managed to take his first hot shower in 10 weeks!

Sanitary arrangements, too, were often rudimentary. During the 101st Division's dash north to Bastogne on a bitterly cold 17 December, for example, the 380 open-topped cattle trucks that carried the paratroopers did not stop at all during the 24-hour journey, not even for a quick toilet stop. This meant that those unfortunate soldiers who could not wait any longer had to perform their bodily functions over the back of the truck's tail gate.

Such lack of hygiene, of course, proved a particularly serious problem for those paratroopers unlucky enough to be wounded in battle. Burgett recalled the moment during the savage 19 December battle for Noville when a new replacement soldier suddenly ran into view around the corner of a building, screaming in agony. Enemy fire had caught him in the stomach, and in his arms he carried most of his intestines, the remainder dragging along the ground through the dirt.

It took Burgett and two of his squad to hold down the sobbing soldier so that they could carry out emergency first aid. Laying a tattered raincoat down on the ground, the paratroopers placed the injured man on it and proceeded to wash his entrails, picking out the larger bits of dirt as best they could, before shoving his guts back inside his wide-open abdomen. They then tore the raincoat into strips, bound the man's midriff with this filthy makeshift bandage, and gave him the vital shot of morphine that each soldier carried. Finally, they dragged the wounded private into the relative safety of a nearby ditch while another trooper dashed off in search of a medic – all this being undertaken while enemy artillery rained down on their location. While such desperate measures undoubtedly saved many wounded soldiers' lives, the filthy conditions in which the wounds were either inflicted or initially treated often subsequently led soldiers to succumb to virulent infections.

Apart from the ever-present fear of death or serious injury, the other concern that dominated the paratroopers' lives, Burgett recalled, was food. A soldier's aluminum mess kit – bowl, knife, and fork – was his most important possession next to his weapon. If a soldier lost his mess kit in action, there were seldom any replacements, and the luckless individual had to use his helmet to take his ration from the regimental field kitchen. In tactical situations that allowed soldiers to draw food from the field kitchen, Burgett would always sprint to the front of the queue, then wolf down his food – just on the off-chance that if he rushed to the back of the queue, there might just be enough left over for some meager seconds.

For much of the time at the front, however, the fighting prevented hot food from reaching the troops, and then the soldiers had to subsist on boiling up their dehydrated K-Rations and 'consuming' their D-Bars. The unpopular K-Rations were stodgy, lumpy, and tasteless substances but – as Burgett recollected – if you had not eaten for several days, even K-Rations could taste tolerable. Even more unpopular, however, was the D-Bar, a mouldy-tasting so-called chocolate bar. These were so hard, Burgett maintained, that you could not smash one with your rifle butt, or melt it by boiling! Burgett insisted that he never successfully managed to consume a single bar throughout the campaign.

Apart from fear, disease, discomfort, and hunger, many of the other emotions that Burgett experienced during the campaign stayed with him. He vividly remembered, for instance, the odd little superstitions that some soldiers held. Many paratroopers from America's southern states would never take the first sip out of a liquid container that had a closed lid: as you opened the lid, so the old-wives' tale went, the Devil lurking inside would get you. Burgett also recollected that when a veteran 'Old Sweat' experienced a premonition of his own impending death, very often that individual would be killed by enemy fire in the following days.

Although Burgett himself did not experience any such frightening premonitions, he was well acquainted with the phenomenon of abject terror. He recalled, for example, the sense of mind-numbing fear that overwhelmed him during one phase of the battle for Noville. He lay, heart pounding and sick with nausea, in the bottom of a slit trench just outside the town, while German Panther tanks moved round the American positions, systematically spraying the frozen ground with their machine guns. With no bazookas or satchel charges available, Burgett and his comrades had no choice but to press their bodies into the mud at the bottom of their trenches and pray that the tanks did not come close enough to collapse the trench on top of them. The fear of a horrible death by crushing or suffocation effectively paralyzed him and left him almost unable to breathe. Burgett even remembered that at one point the enemy tanks were so close that he could feel the heat of their engines warming the bitter winter's air.

Perhaps surprisingly, even when the enemy came as close to Burgett as they had at Noville, he merely regarded them as abstract objects – either you killed them first, or else they killed you. Rarely did the enemy individuals whom he faced in close-quarter combat register as human beings in his mind for more than a few hours. Usually, the immediate requirements of staying alive and accomplishing the mission took priority over any sense of compassion for his opponents.

One particular German soldier, however, stayed in Burgett's mind long after the war had ended. The incident occurred in late December 1944, as the paratroopers drove the Germans back to the positions that they had held before the Ardennes counteroffensive commenced. In a dense wood, Burgett came across a wounded, and obviously helpless, enemy soldier. As Burgett contemplated what to do, one of his comrades stepped up and shot the German dead. Burgett exploded in anger, grabbed his comrade, and threatened to blow his brains out if he ever again shot a German who was attempting to surrender. For the rest of the campaign, in quiet moments between engagements, the imploring face of this anonymous enemy soldier would return to haunt Burgett's thoughts.

Few sources reveal the often-unpleasant realities that ordinary soldiers faced in war better than a soldier's memoirs written close to the events. This certainly remains true of Donald Burgett's recollections. Whether it be the strange superstitions, the unpleasant rations, or the heroism of emergency first aid dispensed to a wounded comrade while under enemy fire, any study of the Northwest Europe campaign is enriched by drawing on such vivid memories of those individuals who participated in its events.

Brenda McBryde

The campaign proved just as crucial an experience for the non-combatants involved in the theater as for those soldiers who served in the front line. One such non-combatant was nurse Brenda McBryde, who was born just 10 days before the armistice ended the First World War. During 1938, Brenda started a four-year course of nursing training at the Royal Victoria Infirmary, Newcastle upon Tyne. In April 1943 she qualified as a state registered nurse and then was commissioned into the British army as a nursing officer in the Queen Alexandra's Imperial Military Nursing Service (Reserve). After seven months' service with the 75th British General Hospital at Peebles in Scotland, Brenda moved with this unit to Sussex in preparation for commitment to France once the Western Allies' Second Front had commenced. Within a fortnight of D-Day, the 75th had redeployed to the village of Rys in Normandy, close to the coastal town of Arromanches.

During her nursing service in northwest Europe, Brenda encountered some grisly sights in the field hospital, but years of professional training helped her to take these experiences in her stride. The most depressing duty that Brenda faced, she recalled, was working in the head injuries ward. A large proportion of these soldiers had lapsed into comas, and these patients Brenda had to feed with milk, egg, and glucose inserted through a nasal tube. The biggest problems for such patients, Brenda recollected, was that their permanently half-open mouths would become infected during that summer's hot humid weather. In the absence of eating that produced saliva to cleanse the mouth, the coma victims' mouths soon became encrusted with pus, and so Brenda had to cleanse their gums with antiseptic many times each day. Sadly, only a few of the patients ever woke from their comas.

When deployed in Normandy, the 75th also treated injured enemy soldiers who had been captured. Brenda's experiences in treating enemy troops enabled her to form distinct – if stereotypical – impressions of the German soldier's character. Her hospital only received large numbers of enemy wounded during the rapid Allied advance of August 1944, forcing it to create entire wards just for enemy prisoners, and these wards soon took on national characteristics. The wounded Germans, Brenda noticed, soon became distressed by the lack of rules as to what was or was not permitted on the ward. Within an hour of the creation of the first exclusively German ward, the enemy patients had appointed a duty officer, whom Brenda derogatorily addressed as the 'Tent-Meister.' This individual would shout 'Achtung!' every time a nurse entered the ward, and all the conscious patients, lying on their beds, would click their heels together in response. But the formidable hospital matron soon put a stop to this nonsense: 'We'll have none of your nasty Nazi habits here,' she said in her best commanding voice, as she brusquely turned over the nearest German patient and enthusiastically rammed a penicillin needle into the hapless individual's buttocks!

Brenda soon realized, however, that most of the wounded Germans, who increasingly were young lads and old men, were little different from her wounded Allied patients. Indeed, on one occasion, a moving incident occurred that shed much poignancy on the absurdity of war. One morning a young German began to sing the popular soldier's song 'Lili Marlene,' and when the nurses failed to hush him down, the rest of his convalescing comrades joined in. Next, from the adjacent ward, British patients began to sing the same song – in English instead of German – until an enthusiastic but good-natured competition developed between them. Brenda recalled that this display of spontaneous high spirits broke the gloom that continually hung over the wards.

Some German patients, however, proved to be very different from the rest of their comrades. On one occasion, for example, Brenda treated a barely conscious German trooper who had lost one leg; he was clearly identifiable as a member of the elite Waffen-SS by his silver and black collar runes. As she fed the patient a glass of water, the soldier came to his senses, opened his eyes and instinctively smiled at the individual who was tending to him. Within seconds, however, after his vision had focused on Brenda's uniform, his grateful demeanor suddenly changed. With a convulsive jerk, the SS-trooper spat into her face and screeched, with whatever venom he could muster, a string of obscenities at her. Brenda's commanding officer had witnessed the incident and in a voice hard with anger, he instructed the staff not to treat the SS soldier until all the other newly arrived cases had been dealt with. That was the only time in Normandy that Brenda recalled a German patient being treated differently from a British one: irrespective of nationality, patients were treated in strict order according to the severity of their injuries.

During her service in northwest Europe, Brenda also encountered the discomforts that even noncombatants had to face during wartime. For seven weeks in Normandy, for example, she went without a hot bath, making do with a quick rinse every morning and night with cold water carried in a large biscuit tin. Then, in early August, the nurses heard of a French convent near Bayeaux where you could get a hot bath for just a few francs. So one morning, when she had a rare spell of off-duty time not consumed with sleep induced by exhaustion, Brenda and two of her fellow nurses went on a bathing trip. They arranged a lift in a borrowed jeep, and arrived at the convent only to find a large queue at the entrance: obviously, good news traveled fast in times of adversity. Carrying – like everyone else in the queue – a rolled-up towel and a modest piece of soap, all three waited patiently in line for their turn. When they got to the head of

the queue, Brenda paid the sister a few francs and entered the tiny whitewashed hut. Inside, Brenda undressed and slipped into the deep copper bath, filled with steaming hot water. What bliss!

When all three nurses had finished this luxurious experience, they topped it with another treat that had been denied them for months – a drink at a coffeehouse. Admittedly, the 'coffee' was just an ersatz brew made from ground acorns that tasted like stewed boots. But despite this, Brenda found that just being able to relax and view the world around her for a few minutes was in itself a luxury after an incessant seven-week cycle of tending patients, bolting down unappetizing food, sleeping, and then resuming her duties.

As Brenda worked in a field hospital deployed close to the front line, she also faced the hardship of limited availability of food. The only hot beverage available was 'Compo Tea,' an insipid drink made from a cube of dehydrated tea, milk and sugar. It was usually 'brewed' in a large bucket and carried around the wards for staff and patients alike. The nurses often had to use biscuit tins to drink this unappetizing concoction due to a shortage of mugs. Food remained quite restricted, and this proved a problem for those patients who required a high-protein diet.

Brenda hit on the idea of trading with the local French population. The nurses held a 30-minute outpatients' clinic every morning to treat the local population's minor injuries; after treatment, the nurses in return went round with their tin helmets to collect eggs and other farm produce. When the hospital's commanding officer heard about this unofficial activity, he simply made sure he was on the other side of the camp every time the outpatients' clinic took place, so that he never publicly 'discovered' this sensible yet unauthorized arrangement.

These hardships became noticeably more intense in mid-July, when Brenda's commanding officer sent her and a colleague on temporary duty to a field dressing station just behind the front line. This proved necessary because storms had delayed the evacuation of wounded personnel back to

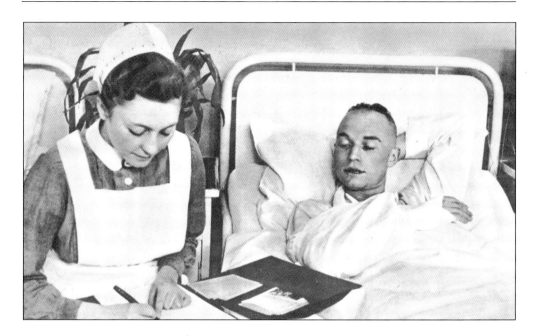

Nurses working in field hospitals in both the UK and active combat theaters also faced some risk from enemy aerial bombing, in addition to the normal stresses associated with wartime nursing service. That said, the War Office believed that the presence of female nursing sisters in forward areas did provide a powerful boost to the morale of wounded soldiers. (AKG Berlin)

Britain and, consequently, a backlog of patients had emerged at their first point of call, the front-line dressing stations. As this was a combat zone, the conditions were rudimentary indeed. The nurses slept on camp beds in a 3ft-deep (1m) trench that was roofed over with wooden planks and a canvas tent. Their latrine was simply a tent erected over a large pit in the ground. Every night, the exhausted nurses' sleep was disturbed by the ground-shaking effect of sustained artillery fire.

Understandably, the station commandant was concerned that the arrival of two nursing officers might have a marked impact on the platoon of engineers deployed to help construct its facilities. Consequently, he ordered that an official painted sign bearing the message, 'Sisters' Quarters – Keep Out!' be erected outside the nurses' new 'home.' With typical soldiers' humor, within 24 hours a crudely painted sign had appeared outside the engineers' canvas-covered trenches, bearing the rejoinder, 'Brothers' Quarters – Come In!'

Despite the commandant's efforts, the nurses nevertheless unwittingly caused quite a stir among the engineers. Once a week the nurses had their 'bath night.' They would stand under their tent – naked except for their tin hats – with each foot in a biscuit tin of cold water, and wash themselves down. It was only

as they left the dressing station that one engineer confessed to them the interest that bath night had generated among the soldiers. The glare of the nurses' lamp meant that their illuminated silhouettes could be seen on the tent's canvas sides. After the word had got around, once a week the engineers would silently creep down toward the nurses' quarters to watch with fascination the latest performance of 'bath night'!

These few incidents should make it clear that the campaign proved a pivotal experience for a young and, up to that point, relatively sheltered nurse such as Brenda McBryde. Noncombatants, as well as the front-line soldiers, clearly encountered real challenges in this campaign. Whether this was a distressing encounter with an ungrateful Nazi fanatic, or the touching experience of a spontaneous singing competition, or even the despair of treating coma patients with little chance of recovery, Brenda certainly saw a lot of life in her few months spent in northwest Europe.

The road to VE Day

The key event that made possible the end of the Northwest Europe campaign – and the entire Second World War in Europe – occurred at 3.30 pm on 30 April 1945. At that moment, the German Führer, Adolf Hitler, committed suicide in the Reichschancellory Bunker in Berlin, as above ground triumphant Soviet forces advanced to within 330yds (300m) of this installation. Back on 22 April, as Soviet spearheads began to encircle the German capital, Hitler had abandoned his notion of escaping to lead Germany's war from Berchtesgaden in Bavaria, and instead decided to remain in Berlin to meet his fate.

Even into the last hours of his life, Hitler remained determined that Germany would continue its desperate resistance against the Allied advance, if necessary to the last man and round, irrespective of the destruction that this would inflict on the German nation. With the Führer's death, so passed away this iron resolve to prosecute to the last a war that almost every German now recognized as already lost. On 30 April, though, Hitler ordered that, once he had taken his own life, Grand Admiral Karl Dönitz, Commander-in-Chief of the Navy, should replace him as Führer. His successor, Hitler instructed, was to continue Germany's resistance to the Allies for as long as possible, irrespective of the cost.

A view of the entrance to the Reichschancellory Bunker near which Hitler's corpse was burned after his suicide on the afternoon of 30 April 1945. With his death, the Nazi leadership could now abandon Hitler's futile – and ultimately self-destructive – mantra of resistance to the last bullet. (AKG Berlin)

Yet even before the Führer's suicide, it seemed to him that several rats had already attempted to desert the sinking Nazi ship. On 23 April, for example, Hitler's designated deputy, Reichsmarschall Hermann Göring, had informed Hitler – now surrounded in Berlin, but very much alive – that as the latter had lost his freedom of action, the Reichsmarschall would assume the office of Führer. An enraged Hitler, interpreting this as treason, relieved Göring of his offices and ordered his arrest.

The day before, Reichsführer-SS Heinrich Himmler had secretly met Count Folke Bernadotte of Sweden at Lübeck. At this meeting, Himmler offered to surrender all German armies facing the Western Allies, allowing the latter to advance east to prevent more German territory falling to the Soviets. The Reichsführer hoped that his offer would entice the Western Allies into continuing the war that Germany had waged since 1941 against the Soviet Union – the common enemy of all the states of Europe, Himmler believed. The Western Allies, however, remained committed to accept nothing other than Germany's simultaneous unconditional surrender to the four major Allied powers. Moreover, they recognized Himmler's diplomatic approach as nothing more than a crude attempt to split their alliance with the Soviets, and so rejected Himmler's offer on 27 April. When Hitler heard of Himmler's treachery on 28 April, he ordered that his erstwhile 'Loyal Heinrich' be arrested.

Simultaneously, and with Himmler's connivance, SS Colonel-General Karl Wolff, the German military governor of northern Italy, continued the secret negotiations that he had initiated with the Western Allies in February 1945 over the surrender of the German forces deployed in Italy. On 29 April – the day before Hitler's suicide – in another vain attempt to split the Allied alliance, a representative of General von Vietinghoff signed the instrument of surrender for the German forces located in Italy. By 2 May,

During the period 1–23 May 1945, Admiral Karl Dönitz acted as Nazi Germany's Second Führer after Hitler's Last Testament named him as his successor. On 23 May, however, the British arrested Dönitz and his cabinet at their Flensburg headquarters near the German–Danish border. Subsequently, Dönitz was tried by the Nuremberg Tribunal and sentenced to 10 years' imprisonment. (Imperial War Museum HU 3011)

some 300,000 German troops in this area had already laid down their arms.

On 1 May 1945, the new Führer, Karl Dönitz, established his headquarters at Flensburg near the German–Danish border in Schleswig-Holstein. Dönitz immediately abandoned Hitler's futile mantra of offering resistance to the last bullet, and accepted that the war was lost. Instead, Dönitz attempted merely to continue the war to save what could reasonably be rescued from the Soviets' grasp. By surrendering German forces piecemeal in the west, Dönitz hoped that the Western Allies would occupy most of the Reich to spare the bulk of the German nation from the horrors of Soviet occupation.

Furthermore, when the advancing Western Allies neared the rear lines of the German forces still locked in bitter resistance against the Soviets in the east, Dönitz hoped to withdraw these troops – plus the isolated garrisons of East Prussia and Courland – into Western Allied captivity. In this fashion, Dönitz hoped to save the bulk of the German army in the east from the nightmare of years of forced labor in Stalin's infamous prison camps.

But during 1–2 May 1945, Germany's already dire strategic situation deteriorated further, undermining Dönitz's strategy of calculated delaying actions. In that period, Montgomery's forces cut off Schleswig-Holstein from Germany by linking up with the Red Army on the Baltic coast, while the Americans consolidated their link-up with the Soviets in central Germany. Although on 3 May the German army could still field over five million troops, it was obvious to all that within a few days the Allies would overrun what little remained of Hitler's supposed Thousand-Year Reich.

Given these harsh realities, on the morning of Thursday 3 May, Dönitz sent a delegation under a flag of truce to Montgomery's new tactical headquarters on the windswept Lüneberg Heath. The delegation wished to negotiate the surrender to Montgomery of not just the German forces that faced the 21st Army Group but also the three German armies of Army Group Vistula then resisting the Soviets in Mecklenburg and Brandenburg.

Montgomery stated that he would accept the surrender of all German forces that faced him in northwestern Germany and Denmark, but could not accept that of those facing the Red Army, who had to surrender to the Soviets. If the Germans did not immediately surrender, Montgomery brutally warned, his forces would continue their attacks until all the German soldiers facing him had been killed. Montgomery's stance shattered the German negotiators' flimsy hopes of securing, at least in this region, a salvation from looming Soviet captivity. Disheartened, they returned to Flensburg to discuss their response with Dönitz and German Armed Forces Commander-in-Chief Field Marshal Wilhelm Keitel.

The Germans arrived back at Montgomery's headquarters on the afternoon of Friday 4 May. At 6.30 pm in an inconspicuous canvas tent, on a standard army table covered with a rough blanket for this momentous occasion, Grand Admiral Hans von Friedeberg signed an instrument of surrender. By this instrument he capitulated to the British the 1.7 million German troops who faced Montgomery's forces in northwestern Germany and Denmark, with effect from 8.00 am on 5 May. In his moment of triumph, a gloating Montgomery entered the wrong date on the historic surrender document, and had to initial his amendment.

After this surrender, the Western Allies still had to resolve the issue of the capitulation of the remaining German forces deployed along the Western Front. During 5 May, and into the next morning, the negotiating German officers dragged their feet to buy time for German units then still fighting the Soviets to retreat west in small groups to enter Western Allied captivity. Meanwhile, on the afternoon of 5 May, General von Blaskowitz surrendered the encircled German forces in northwestern Holland to the Canadian army, while on the next day, the German Army Group G deployed in western Austria capitulated to the Americans.

Then, on 6 May, Colonel-General Alfred Jodl, Chief of the Armed Forces Operations Staff, flew from Flensburg to Supreme Allied Commander Dwight Eisenhower's headquarters at Rheims, where the latter expected him to sign the immediate unconditional surrender of all remaining German forces to the four Allied powers. Initially, Jodl tried to negotiate only the surrender of those German forces still facing west, excluding those on the Eastern Front. In response, Eisenhower threatened to abandon the negotiations and close the Western Front to all Germans soldiers attempting to surrender, unless Jodl immediately agreed to the unconditional surrender of all Germans forces in all theaters. Jodl radioed Dönitz for instructions, and received his reluctant permission to sign. At 2.41 am on 7 May 1945, Jodl signed the instrument of surrender, which was slated to take effect on 8 May at 11.01 pm British Standard Time. The Germans used the remaining 44 hours before the Second World War in Europe officially ended to withdraw as many forces as possible from the east and surrender them to the Western Allies.

Finally, in Berlin at 11.30 pm on 8 May, after the cessation of hostilities deadline had passed, von Friedeberg and Keitel again signed the instrument of surrender concluded at Rheims the previous morning to confirm the laying down of German arms. Officially, the Second World War in Europe was over. Dönitz's government continued to function until 23 May, when it was dissolved and the second Führer arrested. Subsequently, the Nuremberg War Crimes Tribunal sentenced Dönitz to 10 years' imprisonment. Despite the official German surrender on 8 May, though, many German units in the east continued to resist the Soviets during the next few days. Indeed, the very last German forces did not surrender until 15 May 1945, a full week after Germany's official surrender. But by this date, it is fair to say that both the 1944–45 Northwest Europe campaign, and the entire Second World War in Europe, had finally ended.

At 11.30 pm on 8 May 1945 in Berlin, once the deadline for the cessation of hostilities agreed the previous day had passed, Field Marshal Keitel signed the confirmatory German instrument of surrender. The supposed Thousand-Year Nazi Reich had, in fact, lasted only a little over a decade. (AKG Berlin)

The home front

While the war was felt most keenly by those engaged in its prosecution – the military at the sharp end of the conflict – the war impacted on the wider world in a host of other ways. Indeed, as the war progressed, virtually the whole society of the respective participants became involved and the distinction between combatant and non-combatant become less clear: the munitions worker was arguably as central to the successful conduct of the war as the soldier who used their products. Many of the changes wrought by the war years would not dissipate with the end of the fighting, but would remain part of the permanent fabric of society. In this respect, as well as in the political/military sphere, the war's impact was enormous.

Great Britain

On the home front, in Britain at least, the war changed every facet of daily life. The British government had begun the transition to a war economy – an economy that was planned and directed with the specific aim of furthering the prosecution of the war – only with the outbreak of hostilities in September 1939. Thereafter, the extent of mobilization, economic, military, social, and political, of all of Britain's national resources was astonishing. By 1945 Britain had mobilized and utilized all her latent potential to a far greater extent than any other of the major belligerents.

This degree of government control and the success achieved by state direction translated directly into the massive electoral landslide achieved by Clement Attlee's Labour Party in the 1945 general election. Millions of Britons had become convinced between 1939 and 1945 that the government could direct the economy and do so successfully. The apparent demonstration of government effectiveness in fighting and winning a war was seen as a recipe for the postwar government doing similarly for national prosperity, to provide the 'land fit for heroes' that had proved so elusive post-1918.

In 1942 William Beveridge published his report on the shape of postwar Britain. It aimed to defeat the 'Five Giants on the Road to Recovery': these were Want, Disease, Ignorance, Squalor and Idleness. To achieve this, Beveridge planned a comprehensive welfare system, which was to become, in effect, the welfare state. Much effort was made to publicize the report and its findings, and within a month of its publication over 100,000 copies had been sold – an astonishing feat for a government paper. By 1943, the Gallup polling organization reported that 19 out of 20 people had heard of the report. The people of Britain, then, knew exactly what they were fighting for in terms of a new Britain.

The means to implement Beveridge was, of course, far greater government control of all aspects of life, as demonstrated by the successful utilization of national resources during wartime. What then, did this state control amount to? A large proportion of the devolved responsibility for economic production fell on women, due to the service of the men in the armed services. Some 80,000 women served in the Land Army, working as agricultural laborers and ensuring that every available acre of Britain's farmland was under cultivation. Similarly, those with private gardens or allotments were urged to 'dig for victory' to increase the level of food production.

The British population contributed in other ways to the war effort. Every available piece of metal was hoarded and used – not only scrap, but decorative iron railings were ripped up to aid the construction of ships and tanks. The effects of these levels of mobilization on production levels were significant: for example, tank production rose from 969 in 1939 to 8,611 in 1942. Drives to secure spare aluminum pots and pans to be used in the construction of aircraft were accompanied by such catchy phrases as 'Stop 'em frying, keep 'em flying.' This kind of advertising, buoyed, of course, by the widespread realization of what such sacrifices meant, was remarkably successful. The spirit of selflessness and self-sacrifice appeared to be a national one: for instance, crime in Britain fell from 787,000 convictions for all crimes in 1939 to 467,000 in 1945.

One of the most traumatic elements of the conflict, for the civilians of the UK, was not the bombing or even the knowledge of the dangers being faced by loved ones

RAF recruiting station. (Topham Picturepoint)

involved in the fighting, but simply the policy of evacuation. The evacuation of large numbers of children away from urban areas was controversial and produced many unhappy parents, children, and host families, as children were sent far away from their homes and established routines, to remote parts of the British Isles. For many, it was the Empire that was their destination, with some being evacuated as far away as Canada and Australia, and many failing to return at the cessation of hostilities in 1945.

The USA

While Britain mobilized to the greatest extent in relative terms, it was, predictably, the United States that mobilized the most in absolute terms. Approximately 16 million Americans served in the armed forces and around 10 million American women stepped into the jobs that they had vacated. The wholesale switch of the vast potential of the American economy from peacetime, civil

American women working in industry.
(AKG Berlin)

production to war materials is perhaps best illustrated by a few bald statistics. In 1941 the American automobile industry, and the three main manufacturers, Ford, General Motors, and Chrysler, together produced in excess of 3 $\frac{1}{2}$ million vehicles – a record for the auto-industry. The next year, the first complete one of American participation in the war, saw this level of car production fall to just 139 vehicles. The whole productive capacity had been refocused on war production. It was this vast economic power that the Axis powers now had to face.

The influx of large numbers of American service personnel into Britain also had a big impact. The American forces, although obviously contributing in a profound fashion to the Allied war effort, were not always accepted so readily on a local level. The epithet 'over-paid, over-sexed, and over here' was thought by many Britons to be wholly appropriate. The exodus of in excess of 50,000 GI brides at the end of the war suggests, perhaps, that they were at least partly right.

Germany

The war changed everyday life in Germany just as it did in the rest of Europe. But it did not come home to the German people as forcibly and as quickly as it did to the rest of the major combatants. One reason is that, while the British and Americans made maximum use of female labor, in jobs and industries traditionally monopolized by men, Germany was comparatively late in doing so. Nazi ideology stressed the role of the woman as a mother and homemaker. The need for women to occupy jobs in the workplace was not easily reconciled with this traditional perspective of women's role in society.

Such considerations contributed to the tardiness with which the German economy adapted to the demands of a total war. Hitler's initial successes in Europe were predicated above all on short campaigns and therefore did not require a more galvanized economy to support the military effort. Not until 1943 did the German economy begin to respond in a more concerted fashion to the demands of total war. On 18 February the first official decrees about what was needed were announced by the Nazi propaganda minister, Josef Goebbels. All men between the ages of 16 and 65 were to be registered and available to work for the state. Also at this time an estimated 100,000 women were called up to staff anti-aircraft batteries and handle searchlights. While these initiatives and figures may seem impressive, they were later and far lower than, in particular, the British.

While the Germans may have been comparatively slow in adapting the economy to the demands of a total war, they responded to the outbreak of war in much the same

fashion as the other combatants. Blackouts in urban areas, petrol rationing, and food rationing had all been introduced by the end of September 1939. The weekly meat ration for German civilians was fixed at 1lb (450g) per person. Clothes rationing was also introduced with points being allocated per person per year: 150 points represented the average allowance; a pair of women's stockings would account for 4 points, while 60 points would purchase a man's suit.

These restrictions were not particularly pleasant, but equally they were not unbearable. Indeed, as many testified, the generations of Germans that had lived through the lean years of the 1920s and 1930s did not find such shortages particularly onerous. However, of course, worse was to come – much worse. The war began to bite deeply in the winter of 1941–42 when the lack of farmers to harvest crops, especially the unrationed potatoes, really began to be felt. In June 1941 the bread and meat rations were reduced; nearly a year later the fats allowances were also reduced and the ubiquitous potatoes were finally included on the ration scale.

German civilians endured the effects of ever-decreasing rations and, in the latter stages of the war, almost round-the-clock bombing from the RAF by night and the USAAF by day. Underpinning it all was a constant nagging doubt, reinforced by the growing numbers of refugees and wounded servicemen, that the war could not really be won. These feelings obviously grew considerably after the fall of Stalingrad in January 1943. From then on, many German civilians began to doubt the inevitability of the final victory, although the persistent attention of the state security apparatus, and the swift and brutal response to dissent, ensured that few were either brave or foolish enough to voice their suspicions.

There hung a darker shadow over Germany during this time – the Holocaust. The treatment of German Jews had worsened progressively. The early days of Nazi rule saw uncoordinated and localized abuse of

This British propaganda poster shows an idyllic country view. (Topham Picturepoint)

Germany's Jewish population. The enactment of the 'Nuremberg Laws,' which effectively stripped Jews of any rights in Nazi Germany, was merely the beginning of something much worse. As the German war machine moved eastwards, overrunning territory and population, it also encountered millions of Polish and Russian Jews. Some were shot in mass killings and many others were corralled into walled areas of major cities, known as ghettos. The Jewish 'problem' was, for the Nazis, becoming intractable.

In early 1942 a selection of key officials under Heydrich, including men such as Adolf Eichmann and 'Gestapo' Muller, met at a villa in Wannsee, south of Berlin. Here they decided on the 'final solution' to the 'Jewish problem': the large-scale gassing of the Jews in places such as Auschwitz, Treblinka, Dachau, Belsen, and Buchenwald. Although the final number of Jews and other 'undesirables,' such as homosexuals, gypsies, and disabled people, killed by the Nazis is unknown, it is probably in the region of six million.

Poland

For the inhabitants of occupied Europe, the war itself was over and they faced life under German occupation. For many, this would prove even worse than the fighting. It was the Poles who suffered most, under the Germans in the western portion of their country and the Soviets in the east. As a result of the invasion by the Germans and the Soviets, Poland ceased to exist as an independent nation-state. The country was split into a number of separate pieces. The German portion was split into two, as that area of territory lost by Germany at Versailles was restored to the borders of the Reich, while the remaining area became termed the 'General Government.'

The Polish campaign had been blighted by numerous acts of cruelty by German formations – SS and police units mainly – and these incidents had been the subject of frequent, largely ineffectual protests by officers in the German army proper. Now, with Poland defeated, those isolated acts of cruelty were approved in the highest quarters of Nazi Germany and were formalized into a program of terror. In the quasi-scientific racial hierarchy that underpinned Nazi ideology, the Poles were considered sub-humans, *Untermenschen*. They suffered accordingly. During the years of the German occupation, six million Polish citizens died. Poland, alone of the occupied countries of Europe, had no collaboration with the German authorities to speak of.

France

France was rather a different proposition from Poland. Although the French were not considered the racial equals of the Aryan Germans, nor were they considered akin to the Slavs. Initially at least, France did not fare too badly after the surrender to Germany. During the interwar years there had been many elements of French society who approved of Hitler and applauded the type of right-wing authoritarianism that he had introduced, apparently so successfully, in Germany. The roots of this apparently illogical support lay not in a particular love of Germany but rather in the fear that many felt for the power of the left, of communism and all it stood for. Just as Anglo-French concern to balance the Soviet Union with a strong Germany had inadvertently aided the rise of Hitler and his consolidation of power, so too did it provide an element of indifference toward what was to come.

There were other considerations, too, that underlay the French response to the surrender. It is hard to escape the conclusion that the substance of French resistance to the German attack of May 1940 was very different from that of 1914 and most certainly from that of 1916, when the Germans had tried, in vain, to 'bleed the French army white' at Verdun. In 1940 the will to resist was not as strong as in the Great War, and the Great War was the reason for it. The French people had seen their country devastated and her population slaughtered between 1914 and 1918. May 1940 was the third German invasion in 70 years. This goes some way toward explaining the way in which many, if by no means all, Frenchmen responded to defeat.

France was divided physically and spiritually. On one side of this division were those who wished to carry on fighting the Germans. These Frenchmen had as their figurehead General Charles de Gaulle, appointed Under-Secretary for Defense on 10 June. He left France for London, determined to carry on the fight until France was free. His views were echoed by many left behind in France, who resolved to form resistance groups and to harry the Germans in any way possible.

Others in France did not feel the same way. This element was exemplified by Marshal Pétain, the hero of the French army and nation, and the defender of Verdun in the First World War. Pétain, the Deputy Prime Minister, who had increasingly encouraged Paul Reynaud, the Prime Minister, to seek an armistice with the Germans, was asked (by President Lebrun) on 16 June to form a ministry and to arrange a cessation of hostilities. On 22 June 1940, French delegates signed the armistice that brought an end to the German campaign in France. The treaty was stage managed by Hitler personally, with the armistice signed in the same railway carriage at Compiègne that had been used for the armistice in November 1918. Hitler had exacted the revenge on France that he had long desired.

Just as Germany had been dismembered and humiliated in 1918, so too was France in 1940. While Pétain and his government were to remain nominally in power, their country was divided in two. The northern part of France, the Atlantic coast, and the border areas with Belgium and Switzerland were to be occupied by the Germans. In the south, Pétain and his government would retain control, holding their capital at the provincial town of Vichy.

Pétain changed the national motto of France from *liberté, egalité, fraternité* (freedom, equality and brotherhood) to the more national socialist sounding *travail, famille, patrie* (work, family, country). With the initial emphasis on work, it has uncomfortable echoes of *Arbeit macht frei* (work will liberate you) that was inscribed on the main gates of the Auschwitz concentration camp. While Vichy France was to retain control over France's colonial territories, all French servicemen captured by the Germans were to remain as prisoners of war, and this included the large garrison of the defunct Maginot Line, even though these men had never surrendered.

Vichy France was unique amongst all the conquered territories of the Third Reich in being the only legitimate and legally constituted government that collaborated openly with the German invaders. The whole existence of the Vichy regime, and the widespread popular support that it commanded, has been a source of tremendous embarrassment for France, post-1945. As well as acquiescing in the German takeover, the Vichy government was also anti-Semitic in outlook and responsible for the identification and subsequent deportation of many French Jews.

In November 1942 the Germans moved to end the bizarre division of France and occupied the southern portion of the country. The simultaneous invasion of French North Africa, Operation Torch, by combined Anglo-American forces allowed many Frenchmen to make another choice over their allegiances in the war. While the Anglo-French occupation of North Africa was resisted by the French Imperial troops stationed there initially, French forces eventually came around and joined the Allied cause, helped by the obvious change in circumstances of Pétain's government in France, now effectively a prisoner of the Germans. Despite the limited support that de Gaulle's Free French forces had enjoyed since 1940, the formation of the Committee of National Liberation in June 1943 gave France a government-in-exile, free from foreign direction.

Resistance

While the Vichy regime commanded considerable support, for a variety of reasons, not all Frenchmen were happy with the situation, especially those in the north, under German occupation after the surrender. Indeed, resistance movements sprang up all over occupied France and all over occupied Europe in general. Resistance fighters came from all walks of life: sometimes they were ex-soldiers, many were civilians, and many were women.

The Allies attempted to support the burgeoning resistance movement in occupied Europe. Organizations such as the British Special Operations Executive (SOE) and later the American Office of Strategic Services (OSS) were established to provide material support, such as weapons and explosives, which were parachuted in. They also supplied agents who could help coordinate resistance activities and provide skilled wireless operators to maintain contacts with London.

The life of resistance fighters was fraught with danger, especially in the early years, with many being betrayed to the Germans and either imprisoned or shot out of hand. Although the true number of those killed will probably never be known for certain, it is estimated that in the region of 150,000 Frenchmen and women were killed during the German occupation and many more in other countries.

One of the most successful and audacious acts of resistance involved the assassination of the Governor of the Czech portion of Czechoslovakia, Reinhard Heydrich. This act would demonstrate the full potential of resistance as well as all the dangers. Heydrich, then serving as the Deputy Protector of Bohemia-Moravia, and also Himmler's deputy as leader of the Gestapo security apparatus, was killed by British-trained and equipped Czech patriots, parachuted into their homeland with the specific aim of killing him. However, the operation did not go according to plan. The SOE men initially tried to shoot Heydrich, but the Sten gun jammed at the vital moment and another man instead threw a hand-grenade. This grenade failed to kill Heydrich on the spot, but he later succumbed to blood poisoning – the result of the horsehair stuffing of his car seats entering his system after the bomb thrown by the would-be assassin exploded.

The German response to the attack was swift and brutal. The two principal assassins, Jan Kubis and Josef Bagcik, were hunted down and eventually trapped in a church in Prague, where, surrounded by German troops and police, they killed themselves rather than surrender. Their fate, at least, was quick. The German reprisals were less so. In response, an SS police unit surrounded and destroyed the Czech village of Liddice. The village was burnt to the ground; all the male inhabitants were shot with the women and children being sent to Ravensbruck concentration camp. Nine children were spared as they were considered to be racially suitable for adoption.

This massacre was followed by a general clampdown on resistance activity. In total probably 5,000 people were killed as direct retribution for the assassination of Heydrich – a terrible figure and one that would cause subsequent missions to be reconsidered in light of the probable response of the German occupiers.

The Pacific

The Pacific War was a clash of cultures and races – not only between East and West, but also between the Japanese and other Asian peoples. It brought death to millions, and hardship and misery to hundreds of millions of people across east and south-east Asia. Yet the civilian population of the USA remained largely untouched by the war.

Japan

In Japan, by the time of Pearl Harbor, an authoritarian government was already exercising tight control over the economy. Soon, as shipping was diverted to military purposes, supplies of food and other goods became restricted. Except for the ineffectual Doolittle raid in April 1942, Japan was free from enemy attack until June 1944, and even these attacks did little damage until

1945. Nonetheless, as the Allied blockade took effect, life became increasingly hard. Black market prices for all manner of goods soared. In 1943 about 11,000 Tokyo shops closed their doors for lack of merchandise or staff. In September 1943 unmarried women under 25 were conscripted to a labor volunteer corps and by the following year 14 million women were wage earners.

By the last year of the war, most Japanese civilians were hungry, eating anything that would grow – thistle, mugwort, and chickweed – or anything that could be caught, such as dogs and cats. Working hours became longer and workers became listless through malnutrition and illness. Japanese society was being strangled. Youths were indoctrinated to serve the Empire and the nation, and young boys expected to die for their country. The age for military conscription was lowered to 18, but eventually boys were permitted to volunteer at 15.

Dissent was suppressed. The military police – the Kempeitai – who kept law and order in the military, turned their attention to civilians. The special higher police – the Tokku, equivalent to the German Gestapo – arrested critics of government policy. The editor of a respected magazine was arrested by a Tokku inspector who told him that he knew the editor was not a communist, 'But if you intend to be stubborn … we'll just set you up as a communist. We can kill communists.'

Japanese cities, with thousands of closely built houses of wood and paper, were particularly vulnerable to incendiary attacks. When the US Twentieth Air Force turned to low-level incendiary attacks in March 1945, the result was devastating. By the end of July nearly 500,000 Japanese had been killed, some 2 million buildings had been destroyed, and 9–13 million people were homeless, living in shanties.

Imperial General Headquarters initiated plans to defend the homeland. In June 1945 the People's Volunteer Combat Corps was formed for men between 15 and 60, and women between 17 and 40. Most were armed with only spears and staves. Government propagandists advocated 'The Glorious Death of One Hundred Million' to defend the nation. By the time of the surrender in September 1945, Japanese society was on it knees, its people mentally and physically exhausted.

One constant feature was the authority and position of Emperor Hirohito, who was seen as the symbol of Japanese nationalism. The standard view is that Hirohito was a constitutional monarch with no control over the direction of his government. Nonetheless, as a nationalist he supported prosecution of the war once the decision had been made.

Korea

Although the Japanese populace suffered severely and its economy was shattered, Japan survived by ruthlessly exploiting its colonies – Manchukuo, Korea, and Taiwan – and the conquered lands of China and south-east Asia. Korea was treated harshly. The Korean language was banned from schools and Koreans were ordered to change their names to Japanese ones. In 1942 Koreans began to be conscripted into the Japanese army and civilian workers were sent overseas. More than 650,000 Koreans worked in Japan, where 60,000 died. Tens of thousands of Korean women were forced to work as 'comfort women' in Japanese army brothels in south-east Asia and the Pacific. Korea was stripped of its rice production and anything else that could be used for war purposes.

China

Life in wartime China was perhaps even harder than in Korea, as the Japanese army made war on the civilian population, conducting 'three all' punishment operations – kill all, burn all, loot all. In 1937 China had an estimated population of 480 million, 85 percent living in rural areas. In response to the Japanese offensives, about 12 million Chinese migrated west, away from the Japanese, suffering much misery on the journey, but millions more remained under Japanese rule, where they either voluntarily collaborated or were compelled to do so. In 1943 a famine in Honan Province, caused by drought and grain requisitions by Nationalist and provincial authorities, took hundreds of thousands of lives. Whether under Japanese or Nationalist rule, Chinese peasants suffered from rice requisitions, conscription, taxes, and corruption. It is not possible to determine how many Chinese died as a result of the war. Chinese military casualties exceeded 5 million killed and wounded. Perhaps between 10 and 20 million civilians died from starvation and disease. Both Chiang Kai-shek's Nationalists and Mao Tse-tung's Communists bided their time, waiting until the end of the war before they turned on each other.

India

India, the 'jewel in the crown' of the British Empire, played a crucial role in the Pacific War. In 1941 it had a population of 318 million, and although it was underdeveloped and its people were poor, the country was so large that it still had the capacity to provide great quantities of manufactured goods and raw materials. The outbreak of the Pacific War accelerated the wartime mobilization, and the economy was directed primarily toward supporting the British–Indian operations in Burma.

The Bengal famine, in which probably more than 3 million perished, was caused by the failure of the harvest but was exacerbated by the war. It was no longer possible to import rice from Burma, transportation was disrupted by the needs of the war effort, and the Allies gave a low priority to shipping that might have brought food from overseas.

The Viceroy ruled India on behalf of the British government, although Indians held many senior administrative positions. The war brought increased agitation for independence. Some members of the Indian National Congress party saw the war as an

Initially the Japanese were not interested in the Indonesian independence movement, but only in exploiting the oil fields in Sumatra and Borneo, and obtaining other resources such as tin, rubber, coffee, and rice. With the Dutch removed from administration, however, the Japanese had to use Indonesian administrators, and enlisted the support of nationalist and Islamic leaders. Here Emperor Hirohito (left) meets the Indonesian nationalist leader, Sukarno (centre). (Corbis)

opportunity to put pressure on Britain; others supported the war effort but with an eye to future independence. The Indian leader Mohandas Gandhi led a campaign of nonviolent civil disobedience. Congress was banned, its leaders were imprisoned, and Gandhi was interned. The government had to deploy troops to put down sporadic insurrections. Despite this disruption, through the provision of troops and munitions India made a huge contribution to the conduct of the war. Nonetheless, it became clear that the British Raj would not be able to continue much beyond the end of the war.

After the fall of Singapore in February 1942, Japan encouraged the formation of the Indian National Army from among Indian army prisoners captured in Malaya and Singapore. Initially, 20,000 of the 60,000 prisoners volunteered, although the force was later reduced in size. In June 1943 the Indian revolutionary Subhas Chandra Bose, who had spent the early war years in Germany, took command and directed his force to assist the Japanese in their attack on India in 1944. Large numbers deserted to the British or surrendered during 1944 and 1945. The Indian National Army was never a credible fighting force, but its existence partly encouraged the Japanese to invade India in 1944.

Australia and New Zealand

Australia and New Zealand had been at war since September 1939. Both countries sent forces to fight in the Middle East, while at home they began gearing their economies to support the war effort. The outbreak of the Pacific War completely changed the complexion of these measures. With a population of only 7 million, Australia now found itself isolated from British support and faced with the possibility of Japanese invasion. In January 1942 Japanese forces landed in Australian mandate territory in New Guinea and the next month Japanese aircraft bombed the northern city of Darwin. Sporadic air raids continued until late 1943. Japanese submarines attacked coastal shipping.

Australia relied on Britain and the USA for the supply of sophisticated military equipment such as aircraft, but tried to become self-sufficient, and eventually constructed certain types of aircraft. With one in seven Australians in the armed forces, the supply of labor was a major problem, resulting in the conscription of labor, the employment of women and even the use of Italian prisoners of war. Australia provided food and other supplies to its own armed forces, to the American forces in the South-West Pacific Area, and to Britain. With stringent rationing and restrictions on travel, life was hard for Australian civilians.

Australia became a vast military base. Australian servicemen trained in northern areas before deploying for action, and casualties returned to Australian hospitals. Allied aircraft conducted operational raids from northern Australian airfields throughout the war, while Allied surface ships and submarines were based at Australian ports. The arrival of thousands of American servicemen in 1942 had a noticeable effect on both the military situation and Australian political and social life. The Prime Minister, John Curtin, looked to General MacArthur for advice on the strategic conduct of the war. Indeed, MacArthur and the Australian government joined forces to oppose the Allied policy of dealing with Hitler first. American requirements dictated the construction of airfields, roads, and other facilities around the country.

New Zealand too received an influx of American servicemen, although in smaller numbers and for a shorter period. It was further from the action and did not receive attacks on its territory. Otherwise, the war had similar effects to Australia, with rationing, labor shortages, and hardship.

The curtain falls

The world at war

At the end of 1943 the world was poised on the brink of the final act of the Second World War. In 1944 the war was effectively decided beyond any doubt. The three Allied powers, Britain, the USA, and the Soviet Union, would now combine effectively for the first time, bringing their resources to bear against Nazi Germany. The final victory, as well as being a triumph for the alliance against Germany, also marked, dramatically, the end of European global hegemony. It was the USA and the Soviet Union that would be the dominant forces in the world hereafter.

Between 1939 and 1943 the Second World War had grown from a comparatively localized conflagration centered, as so many wars had previously been, on western Europe, to encompass virtually the whole globe. Only the continent of the Americas escaped the ravages of war, although the localized effects of the 'Battle of the River Plate' and Japanese 'fire-balloons' on the west coast of the USA served to remind Americans of what the wider world was experiencing.

The war that had begun in Europe had spread to the Far East. Japanese aggression swiftly deposed the colonial regimes of the British (in Malaya, Singapore, and Burma), the French (Indo-China), and the Dutch (Dutch East Indies). However, Japanese aggression had also brought the USA into the war, and the entrance of the United States tipped the balance decisively in favor of the Allies. The vast economic potential of the USA, once harnessed effectively, out-produced the Axis decisively, although numbers of weapons alone are not the most significant determinant.

By early 1943 the war economy of the USA was beginning to influence the fortunes of all the Allied forces. In January, British Prime Minister Winston Churchill and US President Franklin Roosevelt met for a major summit at Casablanca, North Africa. Following their deliberations they issued a joint ultimatum to Germany, demanding that she surrender 'unconditionally.' This was a major development; it effectively ruled out a negotiated peace in the future. Adolf Hitler and many leading Nazis continued to believe that some form of *rapprochement* was still possible with the two western allies because of the inherent tensions present in their alliance with the Soviet Union. However, despite these German hopes of a separate peace, which prompted Heinrich Himmler, the head of the SS and Gestapo, to attempt negotiations with the British and Americans in the last weeks of the war, the unlikely alliance of East and West, capitalist democracies and communist dictatorship, held firm until the defeat of Germany.

The 'unconditional surrender' ultimatum nevertheless galvanized the German populace. Whatever they may have felt about the rights and wrongs of the war, and irrespective of the common cause that the average German might or might not have felt with the Nazi Party, after the Casablanca ultimatum it was obvious that there was no way out for Germany. Unconditional surrender obliged Germany to fight on until she was defeated, totally.

The Germans also fought on for the same reasons that had prompted the outbreak initially. Put simply, a state that had been built on ideas of racial superiority was unlikely to seek to negotiate a peace, even if one had been on offer. And, as the Allies frequently pointed out, such an option did not exist. The extent to which all Germans were avid believers in all aspects of Nazi ideology has always been an area of considerable debate. Certainly, however, even those who opposed the Nazi regime had little option but to either keep quiet or face arrest and death, so strong was the security apparatus of Nazi Germany.

The brutal fashion with which Nazi Germany had waged the war also ensured that her opponents' determination to see the conflict through to a decisive conclusion was total. Nazi Germany's commitment to the ideas of racial supremacy made their dogged resistance all the more determined, as did their increasingly firm belief in ultimate victory. Arthur Harris, the man in charge of Bomber Command, once said of Hitler's Germany that 'they have sown the wind and, now, they shall reap the whirlwind.' In 1944 and 1945, Hitler's Germany was to reap the whirlwind in no uncertain fashion.

The price of admiralty

The outcome of the Second World War in Europe had depended on two things: the

This chart shows the principal causes of damage to Allied merchant shipping. Contrary to the prewar belief of both the German and British naval leaders, the surface ship played only a small role in inflicting damage against Allied merchant ships; the submarine inflicted by far the greatest damage.

fate of the Soviet Union and control of the Atlantic. But in many respects the Soviet Union's fate also rested on the sea. Without control of the Atlantic and Arctic oceans, there would have been no lend-lease supplies to Stalin's beleaguered state in 1941 and 1942, and no eventual second front in western Europe. The fact that Nazi Germany was unable to achieve control of the waters around Great Britain meant that a second front was always a possibility. The Kriegsmarine's inability to deny the Atlantic to the Allies made it a certainty.

Germany was eventually reduced by the Allies from all sides, and in the air, on land, and at sea. The hard-won Allied stranglehold in the Mediterranean permitted victory in North Africa, and successful landings in Italy and eventually southern France. The inability of Germany to fend off the maritime power of its adversaries from the coast of northwest Europe meant that the superior resources of the Allies could be applied where wars are ultimately won, on land.

Allied victory at sea came at a heavy price. The Royal Navy alone had suffered 50,860 killed, 14,685 wounded, and 7,401 taken prisoner, a casualty rate of almost a tenth of its wartime strength of 800,000 personnel. The Allied maritime air forces together had lost 1,515 aircraft and 8,874 of their crews killed, with another

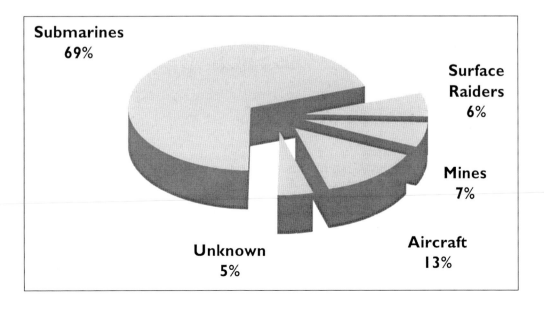

Submarines 69%

Surface Raiders 6%

Mines 7%

Aircraft 13%

Unknown 5%

2,601 wounded. In all, 2,714 British merchant ships had been sunk and 30,248 British merchant sailors had lost their lives in the effort to keep the sea-lanes open.

Many other nations had also suffered. For example, in 1940 the Norwegian merchant fleet was, at 4.8 million tons, the fourth largest in the world and included a fifth of the global tanker fleet. About 85 percent of the fleet, some 1,000 ships, managed to escape German control and served with the Allies. By the spring of 1942 over 40 percent of Great Britain's oil and petrol was being moved by Norwegian tankers. However, more than 500 Norwegian vessels and 3,000 seamen were lost.

Similarly, at the time of the German invasion of Denmark, 230 of its merchant ships with their 6,000 crew were outside home waters and the majority would serve with the Allied merchant navies. By 1945, 60 percent of this fleet had been lost along with some 1,500 Danish seamen. Nearly half of the Dutch fleet of 640 ships was also lost to Axis action, along with some 3,000 Dutch seamen. In all, some 5,100 ships totaling over 22 million tons were lost. The price of admiralty was indeed high.

The price of failure was higher, however, and not just in strategic terms. The German navy lost over 48,904 killed and more than 100,256 missing. The navy was destroyed. Of more than 1,160 U-boats, 784 were lost or surrendered to the Allies. A total of 27,491 German submariners lost their lives, which, along with another 5,000 taken prisoner, represents a casualty rate of 85 percent. This sacrifice resulted in the sinking of 2,828 merchant ships or 14,687,231 tons of merchant shipping, and 158 British or British Commonwealth and 29 United States warships, by far the largest share of the damage wrought by the Kriegsmarine. By the end of the war, 3 million tons of German shipping had been sunk by the Allies, whilst the Germans had managed to build 337,841 tons, which were supplemented by the shipping they were able to seize in captured ports. About 3,000 German merchant seamen also lost their lives. The navy of Germany's ally, Italy, also suffered heavily: some 15,000 men were killed out of a strength of 33,859, whilst over 800,000 tons of merchant shipping were sunk.

But it was not just manpower that had to be mobilized and sacrificed. In the long run,

This chart shows the principal causes of damage to German submarines. The greatest threat to the submarine proved to be the aircraft.

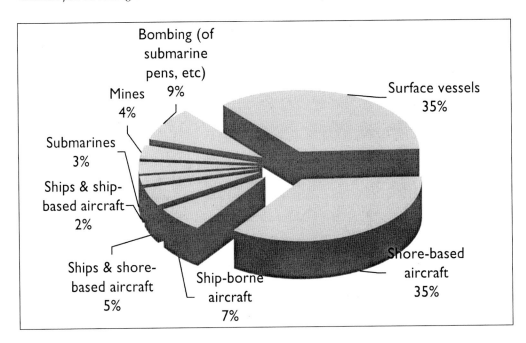

the Allies were better able to mobilize their scientists, engineers, and economies. This had been a war of production and technology. The conflict proved the danger of the submarine, but it also confirmed the importance of maritime air power in all its guises, whether land-based or operating from carriers. Those who did not heed this lesson were at an enormous disadvantage, as Forbes found off Norway in the spring of 1940, and Cunningham discovered a year later in the desperate battles around Crete. Imagine the difference a completed *Graf Zeppelin*'s air group of Me-109 fighters and Ju-87 dive-bombers would have made to the outcome of the *Bismarck*'s ill-fated foray. However, whilst the battleship had undoubtedly been eclipsed, the Royal Navy's superiority in this category had certainly prevented the Kriegsmarine's heavy units running amok in the Atlantic. Naval warfare was proved once again to be not only decisive but also complex.

There was also another technical development that, whilst it did not have an effect on the outcome of the war in Europe, would have a profound effect on the world and, so it appeared at the time, on the immediate future of maritime power. With considerable irony, across the other side of the globe, maritime power made possible, through the amphibious conquest of the Pacific island of Tinian, the construction of an airbase from which Boeing B-29 Superfortresses carrying atomic bombs could reach Japan. With the dropping of atomic bombs on Hiroshima and Nagasaki in August 1945, it seemed that the whole future of traditional maritime power, which had made such a decisive contribution to Allied victory in the Second World War, was threatened.

The end of empire

The Mediterranean theater varied in importance as the Second World War progressed. Before the entry of Italy in June 1940 it was inactive; from that time onward,

until the German attack on the Soviet Union in June 1941, it was the main operational area and the only one where there was fighting on land. It assumed increasing significance, especially after the Anglo-American landings in French north west Africa in November 1942, until August 1943 when plans for the cross-channel invasion of Europe were approved. However, after Operation Overlord was mounted in June 1944, the Mediterranean became a secondary theater.

In achieving the final defeat of Nazi Germany the campaigns in the Mediterranean had a subordinate role. The number of troops involved was a minuscule proportion of the armies raised by the Axis and Allied nations. At El Alamein, for example, about 12 Axis divisions faced 13 British divisions and in Italy the Allied armies at their maximum strength reached some 20 divisions to face up to 25 German divisions. By comparison, at the height of the war in Europe in 1944 some 300 Axis divisions fought 300 Russian and 70 British and American divisions. The casualties suffered were still significant, though correspondingly lower than other regions of the war, and are notoriously inaccurate, but it is estimated that Allied losses were 180,000 British, 136,000 Americans, 65,000 New Zealanders (including many captured in Greece and Crete), 45,000 French, 22,000 Southern Africans, 21,000 Australians, 12,000 Poles, 2,000 Brazilians, and about 100,000 Greeks, while Axis losses were 768,000 Germans and 623,000 Italians, many of whom were captured in east Africa, the Western Desert and Tunisia.

Allied victory in the naval war fought in the Mediterranean between June 1940 and September 1943 was hard won. The Italian Navy certainly did not win the war, and ended it by surrendering its ships to the Allies at Malta as part of the armistice. However, contrary to common belief, the Italian Navy was far from inept. Italian sailors succeeded in maintaining the supply routes to Africa and the Balkans, and sank more British ships than they lost. The Italians lost 1,278 merchant ships totaling

2,272,607 tons and 339 naval ships totaling 314,298 tons, including 11 cruisers, 34 destroyers and 65 submarines. In comparison the British lost 238 naval ships totaling 411,935 tons, including a battleship, two aircraft-carriers, 13 cruisers, one monitor, 56 destroyers and 41 submarines.

Although the fighting in the Mediterranean theater did not materially contribute to the defeat of the Axis armies, it was the decisive training ground for British and American forces. It allowed expertise to be developed in infantry tactics, air- and ground-operations support, combined arms and amphibious operations, as well as allowing the new allies time to work out unity-of-command issues before the Allied armies undertook the massive challenge of launching a cross-channel invasion of Europe. The powerful military organization of the Grand Alliance that proved so effective in operations against the Germans in Europe was forged in the Mediterranean.

Decolonization

There is no obvious reason why a war between European powers should be fought in Africa and the Middle East, but the Second World War spread to this area simply because the British and the Italians were already there. The British had established an imperial presence some 60 years earlier and the Italians had belatedly attempted to find their own place in the sun by establishing a colony in Africa. The French too had an empire, based on their control of Algeria and the Levant, so that the entire southern shore of the Mediterranean Sea from the Atlantic Ocean to the Red Sea was under European dominion. Germany became involved only to save its Italian ally and, as a result, in this arena the European nations fought an essentially European war.

But the campaigns in the Mediterranean and Middle East were fought against a background of conflict between colonial ruler and subject, between imperial power and nationalist aspirations, and between Arab and Jew. While the war years themselves saw a remarkable resurgence of confidence in the imperial structure and the strength of colonial ties, the Second World War acted as a trigger for the forces of anti-imperialism that exploded with ferocity in the decades after the war and led to the rapid unwinding of the colonial system. Although only a relatively small part of Africa had been directly touched by the fighting, the economic and social impact of the Second World War dramatically affected the African continent. There had been just three truly independent countries in Africa before the war but with the dissolution of the European empires a wave of decolonization spread rapidly across the continent and within just 30 years of the end of the war all of Africa consisted of independent sovereign states. In the Middle East the internal politics and society of the colonized areas were affected equally dramatically by the war but with even more profound consequences.

The Italian Empire

Italy had borne the main cost of the war in the Mediterranean but had, in the year before the war ended, already begun the move toward a new status as a modern, liberal society with functioning democratic institutions, a new role in Europe and a modernized economy. Relief from the financial burden of the empire, which had always been a drain on the country's slender resources, boosted the domestic economy, but the disposition of Italy's colonies was a question that had to be considered before the peace treaty officially ending the war with Italy was signed in February 1947. Italy renounced all claims to its possessions but the treaty was vague, stating only that these territories should "remain in their present state until their future is decided." The US, Britain, France and the Soviet Union took over responsibility for the colonies and established the Four Power Inquiry Commission, but failed to reach agreement on their future and so, in September 1948, referred the matter to the General Assembly of the United Nations.

In Libya British and French authorities had taken over the civil administration when the fighting had finished. This situation continued in the immediate postwar period as British, French and Italian administrators established a civil framework and trained local officials, but there was a general international commitment to finding an acceptable system of independent government. In 1949 a UN resolution approved a federal system of government with a monarch, which became effective on 24 December 1951 when King Idris I proclaimed the independence of the United Kingdom of Libya as a sovereign state.

The decolonization of the fascist empire took place when the colonial powers were still strong, in contrast to the liberation of most other European colonies two decades later. The latter were liberated as single units while the liberation of Italian East Africa, which the fascists had ruled as a single entity, was, on the contrary, effected piecemeal, and resulted in the fragmentation of the territory once more into three political entities: Ethiopia, Eritrea and Somalia. Each emerged to independence separately, and at a different time, which militated against the maintenance of regional unity that the Italians had established.

During the war in Ethiopia, British military officials left responsibility for internal affairs in the hands of Emperor Haile Selassie, and an interim Anglo-Ethiopian arrangement in January 1942 confirmed Ethiopia's status as a sovereign state. About the same time, a US economic mission arrived, thereby laying the groundwork for an alliance that in time would significantly affect the country's direction. After the post-war relationship with Britain wound down in 1952, in keeping with a 1950 UN resolution, the emperor asked the US for military assistance and economic support, increasing his dependence on Washington. Despite his many years as emperor and his international stature, however, there was almost no significant section of the Ethiopian population on which Haile Selassie could rely to support him in his efforts at economic, social and political reform. A failed coup d'etat in 1960 heralded a period of frequently violent

agitation to confront land reform, corruption and famine that culminated in a military coup in 1974, in which the ageing emperor was arrested and imprisoned.

Eritrea was placed under separate British military administration in 1941, but the first settlement providing an autonomous Eritrean Assembly and Constitution did not occur until September 1952. The UN resolved that Eritrea should be linked to Ethiopia through a loose federal structure under the sovereignty of the Ethiopian crown but with a form and organization of internal self-government. Almost from the start of the federation, however, the emperor's representative undercut the territory's separate status under the federal system. In November 1962 the Eritrean Assembly voted unanimously, amidst allegations of bribery, to change Eritrea's status to that of a province of Ethiopia, but the extinction of the federation consolidated internal and external opposition to union. Beginning in 1961 the opposition turned to armed struggle and by 1966 challenged imperial forces throughout Eritrea, intensifying the internecine guerrilla war.

The British military government in Italian Somaliland departed on 1 April 1950 when the country became a UN trust territory under Italian administration and was renamed Somalia. Independence was granted on 1 July 1960 when Somalia merged with the former British protectorate of Somaliland to form the Somali Democratic Republic. However, no clear legal border was agreed with Ethiopia and the twin evils of war and famine that grew out of the negligent and corrupt Italian East Africa soon began to flourish. A coup d'etat in 1969 augured the creation of a socialist state under a Supreme Revolutionary Council and following a severe drought in 1974 Somalia began its descent into anarchy.

The French Empire
North west Africa
After the fall of the Algerian Vichy regime, Muslim opinions hardened against deep-rooted French colonial attitudes and an increasing number of nationalists called for

armed revolution. Tensions between the Muslim and Colon communities exploded on 8 May 1945, V-E Day, during demonstrations calling for Algerian liberation, in which 103 Europeans were killed. Postwar elections were blatantly rigged and Colon extremists took every opportunity to persuade the French Government of the need for draconian measures against the emergent independence movement.

On 1 November 1954 the National Liberation Army (ALN), the military arm of the National Liberation Front (FLN), began the Algerian War of Independence with a number of guerrilla attacks. In response, the French Government declared that the Algerian *départements* were part of the French Republic and that there could be no conceivable secession, and sent 400,000 troops to put down the uprising. The populist guerrilla war paralyzed Algeria and the brutal methods used by the French forces, including torture, turned world opinion against France. The French Government was caught between a colonial policy based on racism and exploitation, which elicited invidious comparisons with totalitarian regimes and Nazism, and its place as a standard-bearer of democracy.

Recurrent cabinet crises focused attention on the inherent instability of the Fourth Republic and the feeling was widespread that another debacle like that of Indochina in 1954 was in the offing. Many saw de Gaulle, who had not held office since 1946, as the only public figure capable of rallying the nation and preserving French Algeria, and in 1958 French Army commanders staged a coup d'état.

De Gaulle became premier with the support of the political extreme right and was given carte blanche to deal with Algeria. The French Army won military control in 1958–59 but de Gaulle announced a referendum for Algerian self-determination. The Colons and units of the French army saw this as a betrayal and staged unsuccessful insurrections in January 1960 and April 1961, but the "generals' putsch" marked the turning point in the official attitude toward

the Algerian war. A ceasefire was announced in March 1962 and despite a ruthless terrorist campaign by Colon vigilantes a referendum was held in July.

Nearly eight years of revolution and 42,000 recorded terrorist incidents had cost the lives of up to a million people from war-related causes, but the Democratic and Popular Republic of Algeria was formally proclaimed at the opening session of the National Assembly on 25 September 1962. Within a year 1.4 million refugees, including almost the entire Jewish community and some pro-French Muslims, had joined the exodus to France. Fewer than 30,000 Europeans chose to remain in Algeria.

Following the Axis surrender in 1943, control of Tunisia was handed over to the Free French and the reigning *bey* was arrested as a German collaborator, which triggered nationalist unrest. Violent resistance to French rule erupted in 1954 and France promised the protectorate full internal autonomy under a Tunisian government. In March 1956, the French recognized Tunisia as a sovereign state, ruled as a constitutional monarchy under the *bey*, but the following year Tunisia was proclaimed a republic and many French residents fled. Relations with France deteriorated still further in 1957 when Tunisian and French troops clashed along the Algerian border and Tunisia demanded the French evacuate a naval base at Bizerte, which Tunisian troops held under siege in July 1961. After UN intervention France finally withdrew from Tunisia in October 1963.

In Morocco King Mohammed V first demanded independence in January 1944 after the defeat of the Vichy regime, and revived resistance to foreign occupation in 1947. His exile in 1953 sparked a revolution, but without the violence that occurred in Algeria or even Tunisia, and in 1956 France recognized the independence of the Kingdom of Morocco.

Syria and Lebanon

The promise made by the British and the Free French during the capture of Syria and

Lebanon in 1941 to honor their independence precluded any return to French rule, either directly or by mandate. In 1943 new independent governments were elected and in 1944 the Soviet Union and the US granted Syria and Lebanon unconditional recognition as sovereign states; British recognition followed a year later. Anglo-US pressure forced the French to concede real powers to the indigenous governments but France attempted to secure special cultural, economic and strategic privileges in Syria before agreeing to withdraw. Syrian opposition culminated in May 1945 when demonstrations occurred in Damascus and Aleppo and, for the third time in 20 years, the French bombed and machine-gunned the ancient capital. De Gaulle ordered a ceasefire, but only after Churchill threatened to send British troops to Damascus to intervene. The French acceded to a UN resolution in February 1946 calling for a withdrawal and by 15 April all French troops were off Syrian soil. Even de Gaulle was forced to accept that defeat in 1940 had cost France its position in the Levant. When the British left Syria in 1946 the country became a republic but political instability followed with one military coup after another.

For a while after 1943, independent Lebanon was a model ecumenical society. Its strategic location and relatively stable government made it a major trade and financial center. But an unbalanced power-sharing arrangement and the rise of the Arab–Israeli conflict, which Lebanon was gradually drawn into, were fatal flaws that marred the country's chance for lasting peace.

The British Empire
Iraq and Iran
With the end of the war the rationale for the occupation of Iraq and Iran had ended. Britain evacuated Iran in keeping with the tripartite treaty of alliance signed in January 1942, under which Britain and the Soviet Union agreed to respect Iran's independence and territorial integrity, and to withdraw their troops from Iran within six months of the end of hostilities. Soviet troops, however, remained in Iran to pressure the government for oil concessions by supporting autonomous Azarbaijan and Kurdish Republics, and were evacuated reluctantly only after intense US, British and UN pressure. In 1947 Iran and the United States signed an agreement providing military aid to support the Shah and his pro-western government while in Iraq the British maintained their influence through the new young King Faisal II as various pro-Western pacts were signed.

Both countries continued their tortuous path to full independence but the bitterness that had been engendered between the military occupiers, colonial rulers, pro-British politicians, the monarchy and Islamic nationalists continued in the postwar world. The bitter opposition to union with the West, exemplified in a series of uprisings and attempted coups d'etat that included the 1941 Rashid Ali movement, came to a climax in Baghdad in 1958 when the Hashimite monarchy was overthrown in a military coup and Iraq was proclaimed a republic, all of which in turn led to the ongoing troublesome relationship with the United States.

Egypt and Sudan
Unfettered control had enabled Britain to turn Egypt into a massive military depot, from which the war in the Mediterranean was won, but the social and political consequences were, therefore, far more profound. Relations between the British and Egyptians had always been strained but under the pressure of wartime conditions, and with an enlarged military population, anti-British sentiment became more volatile. When, in February 1942, the pro-British government resigned following popular demonstrations in favor of Rommel, King Farouk refused to comply with a directive from the British ambassador, Sir Miles Lampson, to abdicate or appoint a pro-British government led by Mustafa al-Nahhas, head of the Wafd, an upper-class nationalist movement. Almost immediately British armored cars and infantry surrounded the Abdin Palace and King Farouk was

browbeaten into yielding to the British demand. In turn the King was obliged to keep the pro-British Nahhas government in office until nearly the end of the war.

King Farouk resented continued British dominance but some of the extremist nationalist officers in the Egyptian Army, such as Gamal Abd el-Nasser and Anwar Sadat, were in touch with the Germans, without understanding that Axis occupation would be far more oppressive than the British. The officers were arrested and by its show of power Britain secured its base for the decisive campaigns during 1942. However, the underlying effect was to humiliate the royal house, on which the British had long relied for access to the political process, while the imperial domination exacerbated Egyptian antagonism towards the British, exhausting the last vestiges of their support. This episode left a bitter legacy that contributed to the animosity during the Suez crisis, just over a decade later.

As the war moved away from Egypt the domestic situation diminished in importance to the British and to the overall war effort, and the rise of Egyptian nationalism became more serious. With the threat to the Suez Canal removed the Wafd called for the immediate evacuation of British troops from Egypt, but the British were slow to respond and Egyptian resentment exploded in anti-British riots and strikes. Under pressure from the Wafd and the highly organized Muslim Brotherhood, which had grown in power and influence during the war years, British troops were evacuated from Alexandria in 1947 and the headquarters of the Middle East command was transferred to Cyprus.

The Wafd blocked British attempts to renegotiate the Anglo-Egyptian Alliance and when Nahhas became prime minister in 1952 he repealed the 1936 treaty that had given Britain the right to control the Suez Canal. His dismissal by King Farouk ignited anti-British riots that were put down by the army, which in turn compelled a group of army officers, led by Nasser, to stage a *coup d'etat*. King Farouk was forced to abdicate, all political parties were banned, the Constitution was nullified and in 1953 the Egyptian Arab Republic was declared. The following year the British finally left Egypt.

Britain retained control of the Sudan, despite growing demands by the Egyptians for British withdrawal, and in 1953 the two governments agreed to allow a three-year transitional period leading to total Sudanese independence. The first Sudanese elections were held late in 1953 and the first all-Sudanese government took office in 1954, when the new Republic of the Sudan was born.

Palestine

In May 1939 Britain adopted a pro-Arab stance to secure its position in Palestine and the Middle East and consolidated its hold in 1941 by removing French imperial interests and thwarting German attempts to exert control, all of which saved the British Empire in the Middle East during the war – but not beyond. The British also worked with the Jewish Agency, a Jewish quasi-government that contributed much materiel to the British war effort. Although the Zionists favored the establishment of a Jewish national home in Palestine, they refrained from harassing the British so long as the war lasted, but they in turn resorted to violence when the war ended.

Hitler's barbarous treatment of the Jews engendered a powerful Jewish nationalism and a passionate desire within the Jewish community for the immediate creation of a Jewish state that could accommodate the survivors and ensure that there was a haven for all Jews for all time. The British Government controlled Palestine under a UN mandate, but, fearful of fermenting Arab unrest, had refused to amend the limit set in 1939 of 75,000 Jewish immigrants over five years, despite US pressure to admit 100,000 survivors of the Holocaust. Haganah, the semi-official Zionist militia, sided with radical Jewish terrorists such as the Irgun and the Stern gang against the British authorities and began a guerrilla campaign in October 1945. By spring 1946, with 80,000 British troops deployed in Palestine, the territory trembled on the edge of insurrection that threatened to develop into open war. The British Government attempted to keep Palestine peaceful, and British, but the blowing up of the King David Hotel in Jerusalem in July 1946, in which 91 people were killed, particularly shocked the conscience of the civilized world. Unable to find a political solution and confronted by implacable Arab opposition to a Jewish state of any kind in Palestine, the British Government, suffering war-weariness and under domestic pressure to bring the troops home, decided in February 1947 to refer the Palestine problem to the UN and pulled out. The Jews then took up arms against the Arabs, who came up against them jointly if not in a unified front, and evicted half of the Palestinian population through violence and fear. On 14 May 1948 the state of Israel was proclaimed and a new chapter in Middle-Eastern history was opened.

Ultimate consequences

The First World War caused the collapse of Turkish Ottoman rule. Instead of satisfying the ambition of an Arabia for the Arabs, however, the French and British victors selected the choicest regions and simply replaced the rule of one empire with the rule of another. The Second World War was also a European war that was fought out on the tableau of Middle-Eastern national aspirations, but victory left a political vacuum. Early defeat of the French eliminated it as a first-ranked power and the internecine struggles to hold on to its colonial vestiges left such a bad taste that its empire was lost. The British had fought a bitter struggle to the very end and lacked the heart to continue fighting for something to which they themselves felt they no longer had the right.

Moreover, the global political situation had changed. In the Atlantic Charter, announced in August 1941, Britain and the US had asserted that one of the principles for which they would fight fascist despotism was "the right of all peoples to choose the form of government under which they will live." This noble declaration gave a legitimacy to the forces of anti-imperialism but the major

victors, the US and Soviet Union, were themselves implacably opposed to European colonialism.

The establishment of the UN, in part to ensure a more equitable world order, also gave an impetus to the process of decolonization. In the Mediterranean and the Middle East, therefore, new opportunities were created for Arabs that coincided with the swelling nationalist and revolutionary currents in the Arab world. But the Second World War introduced a new check on Arab ambitions in the form of Zionism and the creation of the State of Israel. By galvanizing and brutalizing the Zionist movement it is ironic that in their own perverted way Hitler and the Nazis probably did more for Zionism than any Jewish leader.

The Mediterranean and the Middle-East region nevertheless remains what it has been for centuries – one of the world's most convenient arteries for travel and commerce – and in the twentieth century it became one of the world's primary sources of oil wealth. For these reasons the rest of the world maintains its interests there, and, although the interests have taken on a new guise, the region remains as unsettled as ever.

How the war transformed the Asia-Pacific

The Pacific War saw the deployment of huge forces across a vast geographic area, but it was still a relatively small war by comparison with the European theater – especially with respect to the numbers of soldiers mobilized for land operations. From a population of 194 million, the Soviet Union raised as many as 30 million troops, of whom more than 8 million were killed or died. Germany raised almost 18 million and more than 3 million died. British forces numbered almost 5.9 million with deaths exceeding 300,000 – mostly in Europe.

The eminent military historian John Keegan noted that 'although the Japanese had mobilised 6 million men, five-sixths of those deployed outside the home islands had been stationed in China; the number committed to the fighting in the islands had perhaps not exceeded that which America had sent.' Of the 29 US army and Marine divisions in the Pacific, only six army and four Marine divisions 'were involved in regular periods of prolonged combat.' By comparison, in the European theater in mid-1944, '300 German and satellite divisions confronted 300 Russian and seventy British and American divisions.' The Japanese army still suffered heavily, incurring 1.4 million deaths. But this heavy loss of life was caused by the weight of firepower delivered by the Americans and the willingness of the Japanese to fight to the death, rather than by large-scale land battles.

Significantly, the Japanese navy also lost heavily – 400,000 deaths. The US navy lost 36,900 killed, mostly in the Pacific. These figures underline the maritime nature of the war. Japan began the war with a well-developed capacity for amphibious operations supported by carrier-based aircraft. As the war progressed, the US navy developed the concepts for carrier and amphibious operations to a new level. The US navy's carrier task forces became the most powerful elements of its fleet and this concept has continued through to the present time. In the South west Pacific Area, MacArthur used newly built jungle airstrips in the same way that Nimitz used his carriers, to provide air support for amphibious operations deep into enemy territory. The American naval operations were sustained by a huge fleet of supply ships – the fleet train. The naval war also showed the value of a competent and aggressively handled submarine force.

Allied naval and land-based air forces played a key role. For example, one assessment of the 2,728 Japanese ships sunk during the war reveals that 1,314 were sunk by Allied submarines, 123 by surface craft, 1,232 by direct or indirect air attack, and 46 by a combination of air and sea attack. Aircraft provided an invaluable means of transportation and resupply in a theater where land transport was extremely difficult

and often impossible. Chinese and American forces in China were supplied by aircraft flying 'the hump' from India. Transport aircraft moved troops in both the Burma and New Guinea campaigns. Troops were sustained by air resupply, often by parachute when landing fields were unavailable. Towards the end of the war, American strategic bombers alone brought Japan close to surrender, validating a concept that had produced less clear-cut results in Europe.

The atomic bomb attacks on Hiroshima and Nagasaki transformed warfare. As the American strategist Bernard Brodie wrote in 1946, 'Thus far the chief purpose of our military establishment has been to win wars. From now on its chief purpose must be to avert them. It can have almost no other purpose.' He was only partly right. Countries now tried to limit wars so that they would not escalate to the nuclear threshold.

Some of the skills learned in the Pacific War were employed in the limited wars of the following decades. For example, revolutionary forces in China, Malaya, Vietnam, and the Philippines exploited their guerrilla warfare expertise. The security forces deployed by the British Commonwealth in Malaya in the 1950s had learned their jungle warfare skills against the Japanese in Burma and New Guinea. The Allies had also learned how to provide logistic support in this difficult environment and to counteract the debilitating effects of tropical disease.

Although in 1945 the Allies deployed armies with up to a dozen divisions in Burma and the Philippines, they did not conduct the large-scale mechanized and armored operations that characterized the campaigns in Russia and north west Europe and set the benchmark for the growth of mobile warfare in the following decades. Not much was modern about the grinding land battles of the Pacific War. But the use of carriers, amphibious operations, and air power in the Pacific set the stage for the further development of modern war. More generally, the war demonstrated the importance of cooperation between land, naval, and air forces.

Rebuilding Japan

At the end of the war, the immediate problem was to decide what to do with Japan, which could never again be allowed to conduct a war of aggression. Japan was a shattered society, but such societies can breed revolution and resentment of neighbors that can lead to future war. By the end of 1945, 13 million Japanese were unemployed. In the winter of 1945–46, the population was close to starvation. One survivor recalled, 'Every last one of us was involved in the black market.' A magistrate who nobly refused to become involved in the black market reputedly died of malnutrition.

General MacArthur, Supreme Commander for the Allied Powers, established his headquarters in Tokyo and presided over an occupation force composed of mostly American troops with a small British Commonwealth force commanded by an Australian general. MacArthur set about establishing a Japanese government on largely Western democratic lines, and a new constitution came into effect in May 1947. Among its provisions were the renunciation of war forever as a sovereign right and the prohibition against maintaining military forces.

Determined to bring those responsible for the war to account, in 1946 the Allies established the International Tribunal for the Far East to try Japanese leaders with 'crimes against peace.' The charges included conspiracy to wage war and the waging of aggressive war, as well as conventional war crimes and 'crimes against humanity.' Some Japanese leaders, such as Prince Konoye, committed suicide before they could be arraigned. The Emperor, whom many thought should have been tried, was exempted from prosecution and from appearing as a witness, allegedly 'in the best interests of all the Allied powers.' The president of the court was an Australian judge, Sir William Webb. Two defendants died in custody and one was found mentally unfit to stand trial. All the others were found guilty of at least one charge. Seven, including Tojo, were hanged in 1948 and the remainder imprisoned.

Across south east Asia, the Allies also conducted about 2,000 trials of those charged with murder, maltreatment of prisoners and

Japanese servicemen arriving at Otake, Japan, from Sumatra after the war. Millions of soldiers and sailors had to be repatriated from overseas in Allied ships and demobilized. (Australian War Memorial)

civilians, and 'crimes against humanity.' About 3,000 of 5,700 defendants were found guilty and imprisoned; 920 were executed. In the Philippines, General Yamashita was charged with permitting atrocities against civilians during the defense of Manila. He claimed that he had no idea that the atrocities had occurred, but he was found guilty and hanged. General Homma was found guilty for permitting the Bataan Death March, despite claiming he had not heard of it, and was executed by firing squad.

The Allied occupation of Japan has been described as 'wise and magnanimous.' By September 1951, when the peace treaty was finally signed at San Francisco, the Japanese people hardly noticed the transition from the occupation administration to independence. At the same time, to help alleviate the fears of Australia and New Zealand about a possible resurgence of Japan as a military power, the USA signed a security treaty with those countries – the ANZUS Treaty. A year later the USA and Japan signed a security treaty, which continues to the present day. Sheltering behind the treaty, Japan grew into an economic powerhouse that contributed to the remarkable economic development of its former colonies and foes – China, Taiwan, South Korea, Hong Kong, and Singapore.

Reshaping the Asia-Pacific region

Although the Allied (mainly American) occupation of Japan enabled that country to be rebuilt as a democratic and eventually prosperous nation, elsewhere across the region the end of the war brought further turmoil and upheaval.

The most far-reaching was the civil war in China between Chiang Kai-shek's Nationalists and Mao Tse-tung's Communists. The Nationalists had liberated much of southern China from the Japanese and were armed with US Lend-Lease equipment. In the north, the Communists built up their army with captured Japanese weapons and with the assistance of the Soviet forces that flooded into Manchuria in August 1945. The war continued until 1949. On 1 October 1949 the Communist People's Republic of China was proclaimed at Peking, and by December the surviving Nationalist forces had withdrawn to Taiwan.

The Soviet invasion of northern Korea in August 1945 resulted in the division of Korea along the 38th parallel, and the establishment in the north of the Communist regime under Kim Il-sung. The Republic of Korea was formed in the south under Syngman Rhee. In 1950 North Korean forces attacked the South, initiating the Korean War. The 1953 armistice halted hostilities along the line of the original division, but Korea still remains divided (see Osprey Essential Histories, *The Korean War*, by Carter Malkasian).

In south east Asia the revolutionary forces that had been formed during the Pacific War seized the opportunity to take over from their colonial masters. In Vietnam, for example, the communist nationalist leader Ho Chi Minh formed an independent government in August 1945. French troops reoccupied the country and were soon in battle with the Viet Minh. After their defeat at Dien Bien Phu in 1954 the French withdrew, leaving the country divided between the communist North and the Western-oriented South. The stage was set for the disastrous war involving the USA in the 1960s and 1970s that led to the unification of the country under communist rule.

In Indonesia, Sukarno proclaimed the formation of an independent republic. When British troops arrived, they were confronted by Indonesian forces. Dutch troops replaced the British, and for three years they struggled to regain control of the islands. In December 1949 the Netherlands formally surrendered sovereignty over Indonesia.

Unlike the French in Indo-China and the Dutch in Indonesia, the USA had no desire to retain the Philippines, which formally became a republic in July 1946. One of the wartime guerrilla groups fighting the Japanese – the Hukbalahap, or Huks – was led by the communists, although it drew support from a wider group of peasant unions. Believing that they had been shut out of the new government, the Huks mounted a rebellion that continued until the mid-1950s.

The British government saw the trend of events and quickly gave Burma its independence. The new Burmese government soon faced a communist insurrection. Independence for India was not achieved until 1947, which saw the bloody and acrimonious partition of the country into mainly Hindu India and Muslim Pakistan. About half a million Muslims, Hindus, and Sikhs lost their lives during the massive relocation of the population.

Britain promised to grant independence to Malaya, but in 1948 the Malayan Communist Party launched an armed struggle using the Malayan Races Liberation Army (based on the wartime Malayan People's Anti-Japanese Army). Most of the insurgents were ethnic Chinese and hence the Malayan nationalists sided with the government. Malaya became independent in 1957. The Emergency, as it was known, officially ended in 1960, although some terrorist activity continued for many years.

The Pacific War was thus followed by 30 years of lesser (but still very bloody) wars across the Asia-Pacific region. They were driven by two imperatives – communism and decolonization – that came to prominence because of the Pacific War. At the end of that time the region had been transformed from that which existed before the onset of the Pacific War. In 1937 only Japan, China, and Thailand were independent countries and the Chinese Nationalist regime was not in full control of its country. The rest of the area was dominated by Britain, France, the Netherlands, the USA, and Australia. By 1975 China was a powerful united country under communist rule, except for Taiwan, already gaining strength as a separate economic entity. North and South Korea were in existence with the latter also becoming an economic power. Farther south and west, Vietnam, Laos, Cambodia, the Philippines, Brunei, Malaysia, Singapore, Indonesia, Papua New Guinea, Burma, Bangladesh, Sri Lanka, India, and Pakistan had become independent countries.

The Pacific War confirmed the involvement of the USA as a Pacific power. It committed large forces to the Korean and Vietnam Wars, and has continued to base forces in Honshu, Okinawa, South Korea, and Guam. For many years it had air and naval forces in the Philippines. The mighty carrier battle groups of the Third and Seventh Fleets still patrol the waters of the Pacific. The USA's former enemy, Japan, is now one of its principal allies. Its former allies, the Soviet Union (now Russia) and China, have been seen more as adversaries than as friends.

Japan's economic strength has given it friendly access to South Korea, China, south east Asia, and Australia. But South Korea and China, and many people in the other countries, cannot forget Japan's wartime brutality. They are dismayed that some Japanese leaders (admittedly a minority) still refuse to acknowledge that their country fought an aggressive war and that their forces treated innocent civilians in an inhuman manner. The Pacific War might have transformed the region strategically, politically and economically, but its shadow will hang over it for decades to come.

From alliance to Cold War

In 1938, when the British and French Prime Ministers met the German and Italian dictators at Munich to decide Czechoslovakia's fate, the Soviet Union was not invited. In 1945 Stalin hosted the Potsdam Conference of Allied leaders in Berlin, which his troops had captured 12 weeks previously. They had played the decisive role in defeating Germany, and had brought Soviet power into central Europe.

This was accomplished by a regime so oppressive that many of its subjects welcomed the invaders, and its soldiers initially surrendered in unprecedented numbers. Over 600,000 of them served the German army as auxiliaries, over 50,000 joined the turncoat General Vlasov's 'Russian Liberation Army.' Many Ukrainians, Cossacks, Balts, Caucasians, and central Asians joined the Waffen SS, or the various 'Legions' raised by the Germans, or served as guards and executioners in extermination camps.

That this regime survived disasters far exceeding those that brought down Tsarism in 1917 owed much to its ruthlessness, but more to other factors. These included the industrialization Stalin initiated in 1931, the talents of the managers and designers it produced, and, after Stalin's Civil War cronies, Voroshilov, Budenny, and Kulik, proved incompetent, the professionalism of younger generals, mostly in their forties. Other factors included a General Staff that became a very efficient tool for Stalin's direction of the war. Intelligence and counterintelligence significantly out-performed their German counterparts. Like the British, the Soviets succeeded in killing or 'turning' all German spies on their territory; so information reaching the Abwehr or Foreign Armies East was systematically 'doctored,' whereas Soviet agents in Germany provided a steady flow of high-quality information. The Soviets may also have solved the German 'Enigma' cipher

code early in 1943, but even if they did not, the British passed on information from deciphered messages, and so did some of the 'famous five' spies, Philby, Blunt, Cairncross, McLean, and Burgess.

Two external factors that also affected the war in the east were Allied bombing and Allied, especially American, aid. During the Cold War, Soviet writers customarily disparaged the Allied contribution and questioned Allied motivation, citing the delays in mounting the 'Second Front,' and quoting *ad nauseam* Senator, later President, Truman's statement of July 1941 that when the Germans were winning, the USA should help the Russians, and when the Russians were winning, it should help the Germans. Allied bombing, though it began delivering the expected results only in the final year, diverted two-thirds of German fighter aircraft and anti-aircraft guns from supporting

A Ukranian woman welcoming German troops 1941. (AKG Berlin)

the army to defending Germany, and a similar proportion of aircraft production from bombers and ground-attack aircraft to fighters. From mid-1944 attacks on the hydrogenation plants that produced oil from coal, and on transport arteries, severely reduced German mobility, while 438,000 American-supplied vehicles greatly enhanced the Red Army's. Allied supplies of vehicles, machine tools, aircraft, railway equipment, radios, cable, raw materials, textiles, and food enabled Soviet industry to focus on out-producing Germany in tanks, guns, and aircraft.

The most powerful single factor in the victory was Russian patriotism. Stalin quickly sensed its importance, and his speeches became replete with invocations of past Russian victories and victors. Persecution of religion ceased, Tsarist officer ranks and insignia, and the title of 'Guards' were revived, and names of past heroes were used for new medals and as codenames for major offensives. Even where initially welcomed, the Germans outwore their welcome by their brutality, and in any case preference for native over foreign oppressors is implicit in the Russian proverb 'Pust khuzhe da nashe' ('Let it be worse, provided it's ours').

Soviet soldiers undoubtedly fought in expectation of a better postwar world, but Stalin continued to make war on his people long after Germany's defeat. Ex-prisoners of war, troops escaped from behind enemy lines, and civilians from formerly occupied areas underwent lengthy interrogations, often followed by imprisonment, and so did many partisans, simply because they had lived where the Soviet writ temporarily did not run. Several small nations were deported *en masse* to Siberia or central Asia, the Volga Germans in 1941, the Karachais, Crimean Tartars, Chechens, Ingush, Kalmyks, and Meskhetians after reconquest of the Caucasus and Crimea in 1943–44, because some of them collaborated with the invaders. The total deported in 1943–44 was at least 1.5 million. Stalin's refusal to support the Warsaw Rising, and his recognition as government of Poland of a Communist

'national committee' that enjoyed little Polish support was in a sense the first act of the Cold War.

The victories his generals gained made them dispensable. Fearing their popularity, and to emphasize his own role as a military leader, Stalin revived for himself the rank of Generalissimus, extinct since 1800, just before joining the war against Japan, and in his victory speech on 2 September 1945 he presented himself as avenging Russia's defeat by Japan in the war of 1904–05. Until after his death, the retreat to the Volga was depicted as deliberate, luring the enemy on the better to destroy him, like Kutuzov in 1812.

The most successful marshals were posted far from Moscow and each other: Zhukov went to a provincial command, Rokossovsky and Konev to command Soviet forces in Poland and Hungary, and Malinovsky was kept in the Far East until 1951. Stalin did not arrest Zhukov, but had numerous lesser lights arrested and tortured to testify to a nonexistent 'Bonapartist' conspiracy headed by him. Novikov, the air force Commander-in-Chief, was imprisoned on additional trumped-up charges of sabotaging aircraft production; naval Commander-in-Chief Kuznetsov was dismissed and demoted; and three other admirals were imprisoned on charges that included giving maps of Soviet harbors to the British – the maps were Russian copies of British Admiralty charts.

The victors imposed their social order wherever their armies went, but the democracy imposed by the Anglo-Americans proved more acceptable and, ultimately, more durable than the Communism of eastern Europe or of the Soviet Union itself. But that outcome was preceded by four decades of Cold War between the alliance systems created by the two countries elevated to superpower status by the Second World War.

Soviet military capability tended to be as overestimated in that period as it had been underestimated prewar, and anti-Soviet canards were propagated, such as that the western allies demobilized but the Soviet

German Army Cossacks belonging to the largest among several 'Foreign Legions' that the Germans raised from among Soviet prisoners of war. (AKG Berlin)

The division of Germany and the emergence of the Cold War in Europe, 1945–57

Berlin: Divided into four national occupation zones 1945–49; West Berlin became part of the German Federal Republic in 1949, despite being entirely within the Soviet-controlled German Democratic Republic.

SOVIET OCCUPATION ZONE 1945–49

THE NETHERLANDS

BRITISH OCCUPATION ZONE

Berlin

GERMAN DEMOCRATIC REPUBLIC (from 1949)

BELGIUM

Bonn

Rhine

Elbe

Neisse

SILESIA

Oder

AMERICAN OCCUPATION ZONE 1945–49

Saar

Alsace-Lorraine

FRENCH OCCUPATION ZONE

FRANCE

SWITZERLAND   FRENCH ZONE

AMERICAN ZONE

BRITISH ZONE

Prague

CZECHOSLOVAKIA

Vienna

SOVIET ZONE

Danube

NORTHERN EAST PRUSSIA

Kaliningrad (Königsberg)

Gdansk (Danzig)

POMERANIA

SOUTHERN EAST PRUSSIA

Warsaw

POLAND

SOVIET UNION

↑ N

HUNGARY   ROMANIA

German Federal Republic from 1949; joined NATO 1955
Reconstituted Yugoslav state
Reconstituted Polish state
Parts of pre-1939 Germany ceded to Poland
Parts of pre-1939 Germany ceded to Soviet Union
Warsaw Pact zones

0   100 miles
0   200 km

1. Eupen-Malmédy: Annexed by Germany from Belgium in 1940; returned to Belgium in 1945.
2. Luxembourg: Annexed by Germany in 1940; restored as an independent state in 1945.
3. Saar region of Germany: To France 1945–57.
4. Alsace-Lorraine: Annexed by Germany from France in 1940; returned to France in 1945.

YUGOSLAVIA

Union did not, and that its objective was world domination. Ample evidence was available at the time that masses of Soviet troops were heading home in summer 1945 for discharge, in everything from horse-drawn carts to freight trains. With 70,000 destroyed villages and 1,200 towns to rebuild, and collective farms run for the past three years by women, children, the old, and the disabled, the soldiers were needed in civilian life. The Soviet armed forces, numbering 11,365,000 at the war's end, were back by 1948 to their 1939 level of just under 3 million. Only after Stalin's death would his successor, Khrushchev, proclaim war between capitalism and Communism no longer inevitable, but Stalin did not believe it imminent, and probably did not believe it inevitable either. One of his last pronouncements was that a

third world war would, like the first two, more likely be between the capitalist countries than between capitalism and Communism.

As for world domination, Communism claimed to be historically destined for universal adoption, but had no timetable for it; nor did Stalin commit the Soviet Union to fight a war for it. His expansionism was opportunist, aimed at restoring as far as possible the frontiers of the former Empire, establishing subservient states in the east European corridor through which all Russia's invaders except the Mongols had come, and weakening western positions elsewhere if that could be done at low risk.

In Germany he tested Anglo-American resolve in 1948 by blocking access to Berlin, cautiously not proclaiming a ban, but declaring all rail, road, and water access

At the Potsdam International Conference in July 1945, the four victorious major Allied powers – 'the Big Four' – agreed the postwar division of Europe. Here Churchill and American President Truman pose for the press. The conference agreed that Germany should return to its pre-1936 boundaries, and be divided temporarily into four national Allied occupation zones. The quadripartite Allied Control Commission in Berlin administered the country. (IWM BN 8944)

routes simultaneously closed for repairs. The western powers surprised him by mounting an airlift to supply their sectors; it experienced only some 'buzzing' by Soviet aircraft, and the Berlin Air Safety Center continued to operate. Had the Soviet controllers been withdrawn, the airlift could have operated only in daylight, and might have failed, prompting the more confrontational western riposte that some American generals advocated. When Stalin realized it could continue indefinitely, and was bringing the West propaganda advantage, he declared all surface routes repaired and reopened.

Alarm bells rang in the West when Communist victory in China in October 1949 was followed in June 1950 by Communist North Korea's invasion of

the south. The belief that both were implementing a plan devised in Moscow was, however, erroneous. Stalin did not believe a true Communist movement could be built, as was the Chinese one, on peasants rather than on industrial workers, and in 1946 he had advised the Chinese Communists against initiating a civil war.

The North Korean leader, Kim Il-sung, persuaded Stalin and Mao in 1950 that the South Korean masses would rise in his support if his Soviet-equipped army invaded, so both assumed South Korea would fall before the West reacted. When that proved wrong, Stalin confined Soviet participation to some Mig-15 jet fighters and pilots, happily saw China join the war, but sent it a bill for everything he supplied. He took no action even after US aircraft bombed a Soviet airfield near the border, and refrained from further provocative acts up to his death in March 1953.

'The most devastating and costly war'

On 23 May 1945, 15 days after Germany's unconditional surrender, the Allies dissolved Dönitz's residual government. From that point, the German state, in effect, had ceased to exist, and instead the Western Allies and the Soviets established interim military occupation administrations based on the territory they had liberated by the end of the war. This situation lasted until July when, at the Potsdam International Conference, the 'Big Four' – America, Britain, France, and the Soviet Union – confirmed earlier agreements to establish four separate occupation zones within a territorially reduced German state. The conference ceded German territory east of the Oder–Neisse River line, plus southern East Prussia, to the re-established Polish state, and the northern part of East Prussia to the Soviet Union. Elsewhere, Germany returned to its 1936 boundaries, which meant the restoration of an independent Austria and the return of Bohemia-Moravia to a reconstituted Czechoslovakia; in addition, the French temporarily acquired the Saar industrial region.

This quadripartite Allied administrative division of Germany left the Soviets controlling the country's four eastern provinces (*Länder*), the British administering northern Germany, the French southwestern Germany, and the Americans central and southern Germany. In similar fashion, the four victorious powers also divided the German capital, Berlin – now entirely within Soviet-controlled eastern Germany – into four separate sectors, the Soviet zone being in the east of the city. Berlin housed the Allied Control Commission, the supreme executive power in Germany. The Potsdam Conference also guaranteed access routes from the Western Allied occupation zones into West Berlin by air, road, and rail. Last, the Allies also established four similar occupation zones in a reconstituted Austrian state detached from Germany. As these cooperative arrangements unfolded, however, the Soviet Union simultaneously began creating Communist satellite regimes in the territories it had liberated, namely Poland, Czechoslovakia, Hungary, Romania, and Bulgaria.

As the four Allied powers began their administration of Germany, they found the country in a ruinous condition. During the last months of the war, seven million Germans had fled from the east to the Reich's western *Länder* to escape the Soviet advance. In the weeks following the German surrender, a further three million either fled or were expelled from Communist-controlled areas into the western occupation zones. These refugees, together with the two million displaced persons already in the three western occupation zones, created a vast administrative burden for the Western Allies. If this was not bad enough, all four Allied powers had also to deal with some nine million former prisoners and slave-laborers then located within the Reich, who required repatriation back to their original countries.

As 50 percent of German housing had been destroyed by May 1945, the Allies had to improvise vast refugee and internment camps

The vast destruction and dislocation inflicted on the Reich during the last months of the war left the victorious Allies with an immense burden: how to feed the millions of German refugees and displaced persons. Here, British troops supervise the distribution of food to hungry German refugees. (Imperial War Museum BN 2698)

to house these displaced persons, plus five million surrendered service personnel. Any German house lucky enough still to possess an intact roof in June 1945, for example, soon came to house several dozen inhabitants in exceedingly cramped conditions, while many families had to live in the cellars of bombed-out dwellings. Not surprisingly, conditions both in these camps and in German towns were often rudimentary, and for most Germans during late 1945 the best they could hope for was to subsist.

To make matters worse, by May 1945 Germany's industrial centers had been so smashed by protracted Allied strategic bombing that production remained at just 15 percent of prewar levels. The combination of this destruction with the devastated German transport system and the masses of displaced persons meant that in late 1945 the production and distribution of food and goods within Germany proved extremely difficult. The Allies had strictly to ration whatever meager food supplies remained available to prevent major shortages, and so hunger visited many Germans during the second half of 1945. The delivery of food parcels by the International Red Cross saved the lives of many thousands of destitute Germans, yet despite such efforts, the poor living conditions led to the outbreak of several epidemics that cost the lives of several thousand already malnourished individuals.

Not surprisingly, during summer 1945 it was not just the German economy, but that of the whole of Europe, that bore the terrible scars of the previous five years of war. Total industrial production across the continent during 1946, for example, was just one-third of that in 1938, while European food production remained just one half of its prewar levels. The French economy had declined by one half by 1946, compared to 1938, while that of the Soviet Union had slipped by 13 percent. Indeed, it would take much of Europe until the late 1950s to recover from the disruptions caused by the war.

One of the few 'winners' of the war, however, was the United States, whose economy proved capable of taking advantage of the disrupted international trade flows, and thus grew by some 50 percent during 1941–45. This boom enabled the Americans, from late 1947, to pump $13 billion of Marshall Aid into Europe to rebuild the shattered continent, as part of the Truman Doctrine that offered support to democratic peoples around the world.

The Marshall Aid scheme epitomized the extent to which the international politico-economic influence of Britain and France had declined through their prosecution of the Second World War, and how much that of America had grown. Indeed, during the 1950s it was clear that there were now just two superpowers – the Americans and Soviets. Of course, it would take years for the former European colonial powers fully to recognize their own decline – with Britain, for example, only doing so after the humiliation of the abortive 1956 Suez intervention.

Meanwhile, for the German people during 1945–49, their fate lay entirely in the hands of the occupying powers, since their state had effectively ceased to exist. Although at Potsdam the four Allied powers had agreed to execute uniformly the principles that underpinned their occupation – demilitarization, deNazification, deindustrialization, decentralization, and democratization – the implementation of these tenets varied enormously between the zones. These differences increased during 1946–48, as the cooperation evident in late 1945 between East and West degenerated into suspicion.

In the three western-controlled sectors of Germany, the locals generally encountered a severe, but largely reasonable administration. However, some interned German military personnel received fairly harsh treatment, for in the emotive last period of the war not even the Western Allies proved immune from the desire for vengeance on the vanquished Nazi regime. The American Treasury Secretary Hans Morgenthau, for example, suggested deindustrializing Germany completely to prevent it ever again being capable of waging aggressive war, while British Prime Minister Winston Churchill suggested summarily executing 100,000 leading Nazis. In reality, such excesses did not occur in the western occupation zone.

In the Soviet-controlled sector, however, the life of ordinary Germans was extremely harsh. Such severity was not surprising, given the terrible privations that the Soviets had suffered during the war, and the heinous occupation policies that the Germans had implemented within Nazi-occupied Soviet territory. Understandably, the Soviets wished to extract recompense for these losses when they occupied eastern Germany, and so implemented a *de facto* reparations policy by either shipping industrial plants back east, or else systematically exploiting them *in situ* for the benefit of the Soviet state. This policy, which breached several Allied understandings, was one of the principal reasons for the growing division that emerged between the Western Allies and Soviets during 1947. The ruthlessness with which the Soviets exploited their zone in Germany certainly caused many thousands of Germans to succumb to disease brought about by malnutrition and physical hardship.

Another facet of the Allied administration of Germany was deNazification, the process of both 'cleansing' the German people of the 'disease' of Nazism and seeking justice for the terrible crimes committed by the Nazis. The most prominent part of this process was the indicting of German war criminals in the Nuremberg International Tribunal. This court prosecuted 22 senior German political and military leaders on the counts of conspiracy to conduct aggressive war, crimes against peace, war crimes, and crimes against humanity. The third count revolved around the barbarous German war-fighting methods seen especially in the east, while count four related mainly to the genocidal policies of the Holocaust that destroyed

the majority of Europe's Jewish population, some 5.5 million human beings. After an 11-month trial, the court sentenced 12 of the defendants to death, and three to life imprisonment, while also condemning the Gestapo and SS as criminal organizations.

In addition to the high-profile Nuremberg proceedings, during 1945–47 the Western Allies carried out thousands of de-Nazification hearings against lesser figures, including members of the criminal organizations condemned at Nuremberg. At these hearings, convicted individuals received sentences of one or two years in a deNazification camp. In contrast, Soviet courts in this period sentenced, in rather arbitrary fashion, several million German prisoners of war to the standard Stalinist 'tenner' – 10 years' forced labor in the infamous camps of the Gulag Archipelago. Only 60 percent of these German prisoners survived their 'tenner' to return to Germany in the mid-1950s.

The Nuremberg process epitomized the desire evident within the 'Big Four' during 1945–46 to establish effective Allied cooperation that would help produce a new, more stable, international environment. The Allies' creation of the United Nations (UN) in June 1945, with an initial membership of 50 states, encapsulated this desire. Replacing the defunct League of Nations, this organization sought to help states peacefully resolve their differences, thus saving mankind from the 'scourge of war.' In addition, the UN would help promote international economic development and the spread of democratization. Such efforts mirrored those undertaken in the wake of the 'total wars' of 1792–1815 and 1914–18 to create international institutions that would help promote peace and prosperity. While the UN has had its failures, in the decades since 1945 the organization has clearly contributed to ensuring a more stable and prosperous international system.

During 1946–47, however, the effective cooperation evident in late 1945 between the Western Allies and their Soviet partners over both the founding of the UN and the

At the Nuremberg International Tribunal, 22 senior German political and military leaders – including Karl Dönitz, Hermann Göring, Alfred Jodl, and Wilhelm Keitel – were tried for the crimes that the Nazi Third Reich had committed over the previous 12 years. Both Jodl and Keitel were subsequently executed for their complicity in the terrible crimes committed by the Nazi regime. (AKG Berlin)

administration of Germany degenerated into mistrust. This was epitomized by Churchill's March 1946 warning that an 'Iron Curtain' was coming down over Soviet-occupied eastern Europe. As the Soviets tightened their grip on eastern Germany to create a Communist satellite state, the Western Allies increased their cooperation until their three zones coalesced into one entity, termed 'Trizonia.' To help this entity and the other democratic states of western Europe recover their economic vibrancy so that they could resist the threat of Communism, from late 1947 the Americans began to pump Marshall Aid funds into western Europe.

The 1948 Berlin Blockade, during which the Soviets tried to block access to West Berlin, permanently severed any prospects, however remote, of continuing cooperation over Germany. The blockade now pushed the rapidly emerging division of Germany into western and Soviet-controlled zones into a formalized status. During 1949 these

areas became *de facto* independent states – the German Federal and Democratic Republics, respectively – better known as West and East Germany. Each of these states, however, refused to recognize the existence of the other and both aimed for an eventual reunification of Germany – an ambition not achieved until the end of the Cold War in 1989–90.

Subsequently, during the 1950–53 Korean War, western Europe began to rehabilitate West Germany politically and militarily as a bulwark against the military threat offered by the Communist Warsaw Pact. This process culminated in 1955 with the admission of the German Federal Republic into the North Atlantic Treaty Organization (NATO), the anti-Communist European collective security organization formed in April 1949. The Soviets responded in kind by rebuilding East Germany to serve the needs of the Warsaw Pact.

The specter of a Third World War in Europe, therefore, forced both the East and West during 1949–55 to reconstruct their respective parts of the devastated pariah postwar German state. This led directly to the West German 'economic miracle' of the 1960s, a process that – after German reunification in 1990 – helped Germany emerge as the dominant economic force

Many of Europe's most impressive architechtural sites suffered extensive damage during the 1939–45 war, due either to ground fighting or to aerial bombing. This image depicts St Paul's Cathedrral surrounded by fires after a Luftwaffe bombing attack on London During the 'Blitz' of 1940. (Ann Ronan Picture Library)

within early twenty-first-century Europe. Clearly, the consequences of a 'total war' such as that of 1939–45 are both complex and long lasting.

All in all, the Second World War in Europe was the most devastating and costly war ever fought. Some 55 million human beings perished in a conflagration that sucked in no fewer than 56 states, excluding colonial possessions. During the five-year conflict, Germany incurred 2.8 million military and 2 million civilian deaths, including 550,000 by Western Allied strategic bombing. The Soviets suffered the worst, with 6.3 million military and perhaps 17 million civilian deaths. Europe's other populations suffered a further 1.8 million military and 10.5 million civilian deaths, the latter including 5.5 million Jews. The three Western Allied powers incurred 700,000 military deaths in the European theater. Financially, too, the burden of the war was crippling, with all the belligerents spending some £326 billion at 1946 prices – equivalent to £2,608 billion at 1980 prices – in prosecuting the conflict.

Whatever the enormity of the victory achieved in stopping Hitler's heinous Nazi regime, it is clear that the price of this triumph was so high that it would take many of the alleged 'victors' of the war decades to recover from the uniquely appalling experience that was the Second World War.

Further reading

Addison, Paul, *The Road to 1945: British Politics and the Second World War*, London, 1994 (1975)

Allen, L., Burma: *The Longest War 1941–45*, London, 1984

Allen, T.B., and Polmar, N., *Code-Name Downfall: The Secret Plan to Invade Japan and Why Truman Dropped the Bomb*, New York, 1995

Auphan, P., and Mordal, J., *The French Navy in World War II*, Annapolis, MD, 1959

Balkoski, J., *Beyond the Bridgehead*, Harrisburg, PA, 1989

Barker, Elizabeth, *British Policy in Southeast Europe in the Second World War*, London, 1976

Barnett, Correlli (ed.), *Hitler's Generals*, London, 1989

Barnett, C., *Engage the Enemy More Closely: The Royal Navy in the Second World War*, London, 2000

Barnett, Correlli, *The Desert Generals*, London, 1960

Baynes, John, *The Forgotten Victor, General Sir Richard O'Connor*, London, 1989

Behrendt, Hans-Otto, *Rommel's Intelligence in the Desert Campaign 1941–1943*, London, 1985

Bell, Philip, *The Origins of the Second World War*, London, 1986

de Belot, Raymond, *The Struggle for the Mediterranean*, Princeton, 1951

Bennett, Ralph, *Ultra and the Mediterranean Strategy 1941–1945*, London, 1989

Bergot, Erwan, *The Afrika Korps*, London, 1976

Bimberg, Edward L., *Tricolor Over the Sahara: The Desert Battles of the Free French, 1940–1942*, Westport, 2002

Bix, H.P., *Hirohito and the Making of a Modern Japan*, New York, 2000

Blair, C., *Silent Victory: The US Submarine War against Japan*, Philadelphia, 1975

Blaxland, Gregory, *Plain Cook And The Great Showman: First and Eighth Armies in North Africa*, London, 1977

Bond, Brian, *British Military Policy between the Two World Wars*, Oxford, 1980;

Bond, Brian, *France and Belgium, 1939–40*, London, 1975

Blumenson, M., *Breakout and Pursuit*, Washington, DC, 1961

Blumenson, M., *The Duel for France, 1944*, Boston, 1963

Bradford, Ernle, *Siege: Malta 1940–1943*, London, 1985

Bradley, O.N., *A Soldier's Story*, New York, 1951

Bragadin, M.A., *The Italian Navy in World War Two*, Annapolis, MD, 1957

Bragadin, Marc' Antonio, *The Italian Navy in World War II*, Maryland, 1957

Breuer, William B., *Operation Torch: The Allied Gamble to Invade North Africa*, New York, 1985

Buckley, Christopher, *Five Ventures: Iraq-Syria-Persia-Madagascar-Dodecanese*, London, 1977

Bullock, Alan, *Hitler A Study in Tyranny*, London, 1965

Cabinet Office (CAB) an War Office (WO) Papers, The Public Records Office, Kew. Enemy Document Series (EDS) and Field Marshal B.L. Montgomery [BLM] Papers, Department of Documents, Imperial War Museum, London

Callahan, R., *Burma, 1942–1945*, London, 1978

Cameron, Ian, *Red Duster, White Ensign: Story of the Malta Convoys*, Garden City, 1959

Calvocoressi, Peter and Guy Wint, *Total War: Causes and Courses of the Second World War*, London, 1995 (1972)

Carrell, Paul, *Foxes of the Desert*, Atglen, 1994

Carrell, P. (pseud) [Paul Karl Schmidt], *Invasion They're Coming!*, London, 1962

Carver, Michael, *The War in Italy 1939–1945*, London, 2001

Cervi, Mario, *The Hollow Legions*, New York, 1971

Chapman, Guy, *Why France Fell*, London, 1968

Churchill, Winston, *The Second World War*, 6 vols, London, 1948–51

Coffey, Thomas M., *Lion by the Tail*, New York, 1974

Collier, B., *The War in the Far East 1941–1945*, London, 1969

Connell, John, *Auckinleck*, London, 1959

Connell, John, *Wavell: Scholar and Soldier*, New York, 1964

Craven, W., and Cate, J., *The Army Air Forces in World War II*, 7 volumes, Chicago, 1948–58

Cunningham, Admiral Andrew B., *A Sailors' Odyssey*, London, 1951

Daw, G., *Prisoners of the Japanese: POWs of World War II in the Pacific*, New York, 1986

Deighton, Len, *Fighter: The True Story of the Battle of Britain*, London, 1978

Deist, Wilhelm, etal., "The Mediterranean,South-East Europe and North Africa 1939–1941" in *Germany and the Second World War*, Oxford, 1990

D'Este, Carlo, *Bitter Victory: The Battle for Sicily, 1943*, New York, 1988

D'Este, Carlo, *World War II in the Mediterranean, 1942–1945*, Chapel Hill, 1990

D'Este, Carlo, *Fatal Decision: Anzio and the Battle for Rome*, New York, 1991

D'Este, Carlo, *Patton: A Genius for War*, New York, 1995

D'Este, Carlo, *Eisenhower: A Soldier's Story*, New York, 2002

D'Este, Carlo, *Decision in Normandy: The Unwritten Story of Montgomery and the Allied Campaign*, London, 1983

Doubler, M., *Closing with the Enemy: How GIs Fought the War in Europe*, Lawrence, KS, 1994

Dower, J.W., *War without Mercy: Race and Power in the Pacific War*, New York, 1986

Drea, E.J., *MacArthur's ULTRA: Codebreaking and the War Against Japan, 1942–1945*, Lawrence, KS, 1992

Dull, P.S., *A Battle History of the Imperial Japanese Navy, 1941–1945*, Annapolis, 1978

Dulles, Allen, *Secret Surrender*, New York, 1966

Eisenhower, D.D., *Crusade in Europe*, New York, 1948

Ellis, Maj. L.E., *Victory in the West*, 2 vols, London, 1960, 1968

Ellis, J., *Brute Force: Allied Strategy and Tactics in the Second World War*, London, 1990

English, J.A., *The Canadian Army and the Normandy Campaign: A Study in the Failure of High Command*, London, 1991

Feis, H., *The Road to Pearl Harbor: The Coming of the War between the US and Japan*, Princeton, 1963

Foot, M.R.D., *SOE in France*, London, 1966

Foot, M.R.D., *Resistance: European Resistance to Nazism, 1940–1945*, New York, 1977

Frank, R., *Guadalcanal: The Definitive Account of the Landmark Battle*, New York, 1990

Fraser, David, *Knights' Cross*, London, 1993

Fuchida, M., and Masatake, O., *Midway: The Battle that Doomed Japan*, Annapolis, 1955

Galley, H.A., *The War in the Pacific: From Pearl Harbor to Tokyo Bay*, Novata, CA, 1995

Glover, Michael, *Improvised War: The Abyssinian Campaign of 1940–1941*, London, 1987

Gooch, John, *Italy and the Second World War*, London, 2001

Greene, Jack and Alessandro Massignani, *Naval War in the Mediterranean, 1940–1943*, London, 2002

de Guingand, Maj.-Gen. E., *Operation Victory*, London, 1947

Hamilton, N., *Monty*, 3 vols, London, 1982–86

Harrison, G., *Cross Channel Attack*, Washington, DC, 1951

Hart, R.A. *Clash of Arms: How the Allies Won in Normandy*, Boulder, CO, 2001

Hart, R.A., 'Feeding Mars: the role of logistics in the German defeat in Normandy, 1944', *War in History*, vol. 3, no. 4 (Fall 1996), pp. 418–35

Hart, S.A., *Montgomery and "Colossal Cracks": The 21st Army Group in Northwest Europe, 1944–45*, Westport, CT, 2000

Harrison, Frank, *Tobruk: The Great Siege Reassessed*, London, 1999

Hart, S.A., "Montgomery, morale, casualty conservation and 'colossal cracks': 21st Army Group operational technique in north-west Europe 1944–45," in B.H. Reid (ed.), *Fighting Power*, London, 1995

Hastings, M., *Overlord: D-Day and the Battle of Normandy*, London, 1984

Hastings, Max, *Bomber Command*, London, 1979

Haupt, Werner, *The North African Campaign, 1940–1943*, London, 1969

Heckman, Wolf, *Rommel's War in Africa*, New York, 1995

Hellenic Army General Staff, Abridged History of the Greek—Italian and Greek—German War, Athens, 1997

Herrington, John, "Air War against Germany and Italy, 1939–1943" in *Australia in the War of 1939–1945*, Canberra, 1957

Hinsley, F.H. et al, *British Intelligence in the Second World War*, 5 volumes, London, 1981–1990

Hirszowicz, Lukasz, *The Third Reich and the Arab East*, London, 1966

Horne, Alistair, *To Lose a Battle: France 1940*, London, 1999 (1969)

Horne, A. and Montgomery, B., *The Lonely Leader: Monty 1944–1945*, London, 1994

Horner, D.M., *Blamey: The Commander-in-Chief*, Sydney, 1999

Horner, D.M., *High Command: Australia and Allied Strategy 1939–1945*, Sydney, 1982

Hough, R., *The Longest Battle*, London, 1986

Howard, Michael, *The Mediterranean Strategy in the Second World War*, London, 1968

Ienaga, S., *The Pacific War: World War II and the Japanese, 1931–1945*, New York, 1978

Ike, N. (ed.), *Japan's Decision for War: Records of the 1941 Policy Conferences*, Stanford, CA, 1967

Irving, David, *Hitler's War*, London, 1977

Irving, David, *The Trail of the Fox*, London, 1977

Italy, Esercito, Corpo di Stato Maggiore, Ufficio Storico, 27 volumes, Rome, 1946–1988

Italy, Marina Militaire, Ufficio Storico, *La Marina Italiana Nella Seconda Guerra Mondiale*, 22 volumes, Rome, 1952–1978

Jackson, R., *The German Navy in World War II*, London, 1999

Jackson, W.G.E., *The North African Campaign 1940–1943*, London, 1975

James, D.C., *The Years of MacArthur*, Volume II, 1941-1945, Boston, 1975

Keegan, John, *The Second World War*, London, 1989

Keegan, J., *Six Armies in Normandy*, New York, 1982

Kelly, Orr, *Meeting the Fox: The Allied Invasion of Africa, from Operation Torch to Kasserine Pass to Victory in Tunisia*, New York, 2002

Kennedy Shaw, W.B., *Long Range Desert Group*, London, 2000

Kershaw, R.J., *It Never Snows in September: The German View of Market Garden and the Battle of Arnhem, September 1944*, Ramsbury, England, 1990

Kesselring, Albert, *Memoirs of Field Marshal Kesselring*, Novato, 1989

Kieser, Egbert, *Hitler on the Doorstep: Operation Sea Lion*, trans. Helmut Bogler, London, 1997

Kirby, S.W. et al., *The War Against Japan*, 5 volumes, London, 1957–69

Kirby, S.W., *Singapore: The Chain of Disaster*, New York, 1971

Kirk, George, *The Middle East in the War*, London, 1952

Kitchen, Martin, *A World in Flames: A Short History of the Second World War in Europe and Asia 1939–45*, London, 1990

Knox, MacGregor, *Mussolini Unleashed, 1939–1941*, Cambridge, 1982

Latimer, Jon, *Alamein*, London, 2002

Levine, Alan, *The Strategic Bombing of Germany*, New York, 1992

Levine, Alan J., *War against Rommel's Supply Lines, 1942–1943*, Westport, 1999

Lewin, Ronald, *The Chief*, London, 1980

Lind, Lew, *Battle of the Wine Dark Sea: The Aegean Sea Campaign, 1940–1945*, Kenthurst, 1994

Long, G. (ed.), *Australia in the War of 1939–1945*, 22 volumes, Canberra, 1952–77

Long, Gavin, "Greece, Crete, and Syria" in *Australia in the War of 1939–1945*, Canberra, 1953

Love, R.W., *History of the US Navy*, 2 vols, Harrisburg, PA, 1992

MacArthur D., *Reminiscences*, Greenwich, CT, 1965

Macintyre, Donald, *Battle for the Mediterranean*, New York, 1964

Macksey, Kenneth, *Crucible of Power: The Fight for Tunisia 1942–1943*, London, 1969

Maier, Klaus (ed.), *Germany's Initial Conquests in Europe: Germany and the Second World War*, Oxford, 1991

Majdalany, Fred, *Cassino: Portrait of a Battle*, London, 1999

Marwick, Arthur, (ed.), *Total War and Social Change*, London, 1988

Maughan, Barton, "Tobruk and El Alamein" in *Australia in the War of 1939–1945*, Canberra, 1966

Merchantmen at War: The Official Story of the Merchant Navy, 1939–1944

Messenger, Charles, *Tunisian Campaign*, London, 1982

Millet, Alan R., and Williamson Murray (eds.), *Military Effectiveness: The Second World War*, London, 1999

Mitcham, Samuel W. and Friedrich von Stauffenberg, *The Battle of Sicily*, New York, 1991

Mockler, Anthony, *Our Enemies the French*, London, 1976

Mockler, Anthony, *Haile Selassie's War: The Italian—Ethiopian Campaign 1935–1941*, New York, 1984

Montagu, Ewan, *The Man Who Never Was*, Oxford, 2001

Montgomery, B.L., *Normandy to the Baltic*, London, 1947

Moorehead, Alan, *Desert War: The North African Campaign 1940–1943*, London, 2001

Morison, S.E., *United States Naval Operations in World War II*, 15 volumes, Boston, 1947–62

Muggenthaler, A.K., *German Raiders of World War II*, London, 1978

Nimitz, C.W., Adams, H.H., and Potter, E.B., *Triumph in the Atlantic: The Naval Struggle Against the Nazis*, NJ, 1960

Overy, Richard, *Why the Allies Won*, New York, 1996

Pal, Dharm, *Official History of Indian Armed Forces in the Second World War: Campaign in Italy, 1943–45*, Delhi, 1960

Patton, G.S., *War as I Knew It*, Boston, 1947

Pitt, Barrie, *The Crucible of War: Western Desert 1941*, London, 1980

Pitt, Barrie, *The Crucible of War: Year of Alamein 1942*, London, 1982

Playfair, I.S.O. (ed.) et al, *The Official History of the Second World War: The Mediterranean and the Middle East*, 6 volumes, London, 1954–1988

Potter, E.B., *Bull Halsey*, Annapolis, 1985

Potter, E.B., *Nimitz*, Annapolis, 1976

Prange, G.W., *Miracle at Midway*, New York, 1982

Prange, G.W., Goldstein, D.M., and Dilon, K.V., *At Dawn We Slept: The Untold Story of Pearl Harbor*, New York, 1981

Prasad, Bisheshwar, *Official History of Indian Armed Forces in the Second World War: East African Campaign, 1940–41*, Delhi, 1963

Ray, John, *The Battle of Britain: New Perspectives – Behind the Scenes of the Great Air War*, London, 1999

Reynolds, C.G., *War in the Pacific*, New York, 1990

Rohwer, J., *War at Sea 1939–1945*, London, 1996

Rolf, David, *Bloody Road to Tunis: Destruction of the Axis Forces in North Africa, November 1942–May 1943*, Mechanicsburg, 2001

Roskill, S.W., *The Navy at War, 1939–1945*, London, 1960

Roskill, S.W., *The War at Sea, 1939–1945*, Volume 1, London, 1954

Ryan, C., *The Longest Day*, London, 1960

Sadkovich, J.J., *The Italian Navy in World War II*, London, 1994

Sandford, Kenneth, *The Mark of the Lion: Charles Upham*, Auckland, 1963

Schmidt, Heinz Werner, *With Rommel in the Desert*, London, 1997

Schulman, M., *Defeat in the West*, London, 1968

Shores, Christopher, *Dust Clouds in the Middle East*, London, 1996

Shukman, H. (ed.), *Stalin's Generals*, London, 1993

South African War Histories Committee, *The South African Forces in World War II*, 11 volumes, Cape Town, 1952–1982

Slim, W.J., *Defeat into Victory*, London, 1956

Smith, E.D., *Victory of a Sort: The British in Greece, 1941–1946*, London, 1988

Smith, Peter C., *Pedestal: The Convoy that Saved Malta*, Manchester, 1999

Spector, R.H., *Eagle Against the Sun: The American War with Japan*, New York, 1985

Speidel, H., *We Defended Normandy*, London, 1951

Spooner, Tony, *Supreme Gallantry: Malta's Role in the Allied Victory, 1939–1945*, London, 1996

Stacey, Col. C.P., *The Victory Campaign*, Ottawa, 1960

Stewart, Richard A., *Sunrise at Abadan: The British and Soviet Invasion of Iran, 1941*, Westport, 1988

Strawson, John, *Italian Campaign*, London, 1987

Taylor, A.J.P., *The Origins of the Second World War*, Oxford, 1963

Terraine, J., *Business in Great Waters: The U-Boat Wars 1916–1945*, London, 1989

Thompson, R.W., *Montgomery the Field Marshal: A Critical Study*, London, 1969

Thorne, C., *Allies of a Kind: The United States: Britain and the War against Japan, 1941–1945*, New York, 1978

Thorne, C., *The Issue of War: States, Societies and the Far Eastern Conflict of 1941–1945*, London, 1985

Toland, J., *The Rising Sun: The Decline and Fall of the Japanese Empire 1936–1945*, London, 1971

Tuchman, B.W., *Stilwell and the American Experience in China, 1911–1945*, New York, 1970

US Army, *United States Army in World War II: The War in the Pacific*, 11 volumes, Washington, 1948–63

US Army, *United States Army in World War II: The China—Burma—India Theater*, 3 volumes, Washington, 1953–59

Van Creveld, Martin, *Hitler's Strategy: The Balkan Clue*, Cambridge, 1973

Vat, D. van der, *The Atlantic Campaign: The Great Struggle at Sea 1939–1945*, London, 1988

Vat, D. van der, *The Pacific Campaign: The US-Japanese Naval War 1941–1945*, New York, 1991

Vella, Philip, *Malta: Blitzed but not Beaten*, Valletta, 1989

Warner, Geoffrey, *Iraq and Syria, 1941*, London, 1974

Watson, Bruce Allen, *Exit Rommel: The Tunisian Campaign, 1942–1943*, Westport, 1999

Weigley, R.F., *Eisenhower's Lieutenants: The Campaigns of France and Germany 1944–5*, 2 vols, London, 1981

Whitaker, W.D. and Whitaker, S., *The Battle of the River Scheldt*, London, 1985

Willmott, H.P., *Empires in the Balance: Japanese and Allied Pacific Strategies to April 1942*, Annapolis, 1982

Willmott, H.P., *The Barrier and the Javelin: Japanese and Allied Strategies*, February to June 1942, Annapolis, 1983

Willmott, H.P., *The Second World War in the East*, London, 1999

Wilson, Henry Maitland, *Eight Years Overseas, 1939–1947*, London, 1950

Wilson, M., *A Submariners' War: The Indian Ocean, 1939–1945*, Gloucestershire, 2000

Woodburn, K.S., *History of the Second World War: The War Against Japan II*, London, 1958

Woodman, Richard, *Malta Convoys, 1940–1943*, London, 2000

Wynter, H.W., *Special Forces in the Desert War, 1940–1943*, London, 2002

Young, Desmond, *Rommel*, London, 1950

Zweig, Ronald W., *Britain and Palestine during the Second World War*, Suffolk, 1986

Index

References to illustrations are shown in **bold**.